TRUSTS AND RELATED TAX ISSUES IN OFFSHORE FINANCIAL LAW

TRUSTS AND RELATED TAX ISSUES IN OFFSHORE FINANCIAL LAW

ROSE-MARIE BELLE ANTOINE

LLB (UWI); LLM (Cambridge); D Phil (Oxon)
Attorney-at-Law

OXFORD
UNIVERSITY PRESS

OXFORD
UNIVERSITY PRESS

Great Clarendon Street, Oxford OX2 6DP

Oxford University Press is a department of the University of Oxford.
It furthers the University's objective of excellence in research, scholarship,
and education by publishing worldwide in

Oxford New York

Auckland Cape Town Dar es Salaam Hong Kong Karachi
Kuala Lumpur Madrid Melbourne Mexico City Nairobi
New Delhi Shanghai Taipei Toronto

With offices in

Argentina Austria Brazil Chile Czech Republic France Greece
Guatemala Hungary Italy Japan South Korea Poland Portugal
Singapore Switzerland Thailand Turkey Ukraine Vietnam

Oxford is a registered trade mark of Oxford University Press
in the UK and in certain other countries

Published in the United States
by Oxford University Press Inc., New York

British Library Cataloguing in Publication Data

Data available

Library of Congress Cataloging in Publication Data

Data available

ISBN 0–19–925222–X

1 3 5 7 9 10 8 6 4 2

Typeset by RefineCatch Limited, Bungay, Suffolk
Printed in Great Britain
on acid-free paper by
Biddles Ltd., King's Lynn

FOREWORD

Oliver Wendell Holmes, the father of the great judge of the same name, once wrote: 'Put not your trust in money, but put your money in trust.' We can imagine the enthusiasm with which he would have greeted that modern phenomenon, the offshore trust, which is the subject of this excellent new book.

Professor Ross Cranston and I had the pleasure of co-supervising Rose-Marie Antoine's doctoral thesis on offshore financial law, a thesis highly commended by the examiners, part of which later grew into a larger specialist work published under the title Confidentiality in Offshore Financial Law, by Oxford University Press. In that work Dr. Antoine graphically depicted the tension between the desire of offshore jurisdictions to respond to the needs of international business and finance, through strict confidentiality rules, tax advantages, and the like, and the concern of onshore jurisdictions to counter tax evasion and money laundering, and drew attention to the important constitutional issues involved. *Confidentiality in Offshore Financial Law*, a splendid work, is now followed by this second offering from Dr. Antoine's pen, an equally fine text which explores the distinctive characteristics of the offshore trust, an institution combining the traditional trust developed by the English common law with new features designed to protect the trust assets from the claims of creditors, bypass inconvenient rules on succession and counter challenges by onshore jurisdictions.

In this new book Dr. Antoine combines a rigorous analysis of the complex legal issues surrounding the offshore trust with a balanced policy perspective in which she stoutly defends the institution of the offshore trust as a legitimate instrument of estate planning based on freedom of contract and of property while acknowledging that it may be abused and that onshore jurisdictions have legitimate concerns which need to be addressed. The book is wide-ranging, covering matters as diverse as the liability of trustees and the validity of exculpatory clauses, tax implications, the use of human rights law to protect the essential features of the offshore trust, and issues of the conflict of laws, including an examination of the Hague Convention on the Recognition of Trusts. It is at once a challenging work for the scholar and a *vade mecum* for the practitioner, and I have no doubt that it will be welcomed as warmly as its predecessor.

Roy Goode
Oxford
November 2004

PREFACE

The idea or notion of a 'statutory trust' is to some heresy and to others a contradiction in terms. Since the trust is a creation of equity, then statute, by definition, cannot create a trust. Yet, it is precisely what the creators of the offshore trust have dared to do. It is little wonder, therefore, that the offshore trust has been described as a bastard offspring of equity.

This new creation, the offshore trust, is, in many ways, extraordinary. On the one hand, it borrows heavily from the traditional trust, created and fashioned by the principles of equity. Yet, on the other hand, it embodies unique concepts radical to the traditional trust. It has attempted to surmount the forced heirship regime of the civil law. It has created the original entity that is the 'purpose trust'. It has embraced selected principles of company law, married these principles to equity, and created a vehicle for offshore investment. It has attempted to exploit universal principles of tax law which advance tax mitigation. It has promoted the cause of the freedom of disposition of property, even to the extent of prioritizing the interests of named beneficiaries and trust purposes over future, unidentifiable creditors. As the challenge to its existence mounts, its creators constantly seek to reshape it to enable it to adapt to its changing environment. Perhaps the best example of this is the so-called 'VISA' trust, recently created in the British Virgin Islands. All of these innovations and revolutions have been done in the name of commercial pragmatism and viability, to create an efficient mechanism suitable for the modern international business environment.

The fascinating legal framework of the offshore trust and its evolving jurisprudence is the subject of this book. It is a subject with which every trust practitioner and every person associated with the business environment should familiarize themselves. Notwithstanding its obvious usefulness to the practitioner, the very existence of this new trust, the first truly indigenous and carefully planned trust creation of modern times, should be a stimulating topic of inquiry for the academic and the student alike. The book serves also as a companion volume to *Confidentiality in Offshore Law*.

Part I explores the underlying principles of the offshore trust and explains its anatomy and functions. Special trust vehicles are described and examined. Inevitably, one is never far away from either defending or trying to explain the jurisprudential tensions surrounding the offshore trust. This leads to Part II, which focuses on the challenges to the offshore trust, and the common pitfalls encountered by practitioners and others who seek to create such trusts, thereby giving advice as to how they should be avoided. How and why an offshore trust may be deemed a sham is a major subject of inquiry. Great attention is also given to the duties of trustees in managing offshore trusts, potential fraudulent conveyances, the liability of third parties to the trust, and the liability of directors of offshore corporate trustees.

Part III focuses on the offshore tax function. Here, I have chosen to explore, *inter alia*, the responses to the tax function of offshore trusts, the increasingly hostile counter-measures by onshore jurisdictions against offshore trusts, the reaction by offshore jurisdictions, and even the efforts at judicial engineering associated with the offshore tax function. This enables the reader to make a realistic and much needed assessment of how the offshore trust functions in the international tax sphere. Nowhere are the tensions between offshore and onshore jurisdictions more evident than in the tax functions of the offshore trust.

In Part IV, the book seeks to explore the intriguing issues that arise in conflict of laws as they relate to the offshore trust. It is perhaps the first time that this complex and important subject is explored in a major work. This includes new ideas as to how the offshore trust should be approached from a conflict of laws perspective, for example the initial question of the capacity to create an offshore trust. Hence, the ingenuity of the creators of the offshore trust is introduced as they try to create mechanisms through the offshore trust to override conflicts arising from competing legal traditions. Issues of the jurisdiction of the offshore trust, its proper law, and the recognition of the offshore trust in civil law countries invite investigation and exegesis. Perhaps the most fascinating aspect of the efforts of the offshore trust to be accommodated and accepted in the civil law tradition has been its efforts to contend with the principles of forced heirship, an essential initiative if the offshore trust is to be marketed successfully in a global environment.

The book concludes with an examination of two subjects, the capacity to create the offshore trust and the initial transfers of assets, and the non-enforcement of foreign judgments under offshore trust law. These areas of discussion are essential to understanding, and preparing for, the survivability and endurance of the offshore trust.

Offshore law is unquestionably comparative in scope, depth, and character. This alone makes this work comprehensive in the treatment of the subjects and themes selected for analysis. The book examines not only the offshore law current in the several offshore jurisdictions, but also assesses offshore law from an onshore law perspective, including pertinent issues that arise when that onshore law belongs to the civil law tradition.

Rose-Marie Belle Antoine, Saint Lucia
January 2005

ACKNOWLEDGEMENTS

I am deeply indebted to the persons who undertook the challenging task of reading the manuscript (rather larger than first envisioned), making several helpful suggestions and comments which have certainly enhanced this book. These are: my colleague, Ms Tracy Robinson; my brother, Dr Robin M Antoine; and my husband, Dr Kenny D Anthony. Many thanks must also go to the superb editorial and production staff at Oxford University Press for their hard work and patience, in particular to Katarina Wihlborg and Michelle Thompson, as well as to Catherine Minahan, the copy editor.

CONTENTS—SUMMARY

IV THE CONFLICT OF LAWS AND THE OFFSHORE TRUST

CONTENTS

TABLES OF CASES

CAYMAN ISLANDS

HONG KONG

ISLE OF MAN

ITALY

JERSEY

NEVIS

NEW ZEALAND

NORWAY

SINGAPORE

SOUTH AFRICA

SWEDEN

SWITZERLAND

UNITED KINGDOM

UNITED STATES

VANUATU

TABLES OF NATIONAL AND INTERNATIONAL LEGISLATION

United Kingdom Statutory Instruments

UNITED STATES OF AMERICA

PART I

FUNDAMENTALS OF THE OFFSHORE TRUST

1

INTRODUCTION—THE PLACE OF THE OFFSHORE TRUST IN THE OFFSHORE FINANCIAL CENTRE

A. Introduction

The offshore financial centre remains one of the most important and intriguing **1.01** new phenomena in the international financial sector today, accounting for billions of investment dollars worldwide.[1] Of the several innovative financial products that the sector has spawned, perhaps none is more deserving of study than the offshore trust, sometimes called an international trust.[2] This type of trust, a modern creation, serves as an important vehicle for the estate planning,

---

[1] For example, in the Cayman Islands, trust assets in 2002 were more than US $980 billion. See www.trusts-and-trustees.com/trends/td.

[2] Note that a dichotomy between the terms 'offshore trust' and 'international trust' is peculiar to Barbados. There, an international trust is one established under the International Trusts Act 1995, as amended in 1998, where the settlor and beneficiaries are non-resident and, except where the trustee is another offshore entity or charity, the trustee is non-resident. In an offshore trust, the trustee must be an offshore bank and the settlor and beneficiaries non-resident. The assets must consist solely of foreign securities and currencies. Barbados's trust law must also be considered within the context of its double taxation treaty regime, discussed in chapter 16, at paras 16.41–16.48. For our purposes, it is the international trust regime which may be approximated to offshore trust regimes.

asset protection, tax planning, and broader investment objectives of offshore investors.

1.02 Maitland once demonstrated that the trust is one of equity's most ingenious devices.[3] The offshore trust confirms this ingenuity of equity, albeit with the help and intervention of statute. Its elasticity is particularly useful in a commercial context, such as the offshore financial sector. Indeed, some argue that the modern trust is established primarily for business purposes.[4]

1.03 As we saw in a previous book,[5] offshore jurisdictions[6] offer to investors a wide range of creative and often revolutionary financial and investment products, including international business companies, captive insurance, tax planning vehicles, and offshore banks. The offshore trust is but one of these financial products. Since the trust is created by offshore financial centres, it is useful to review the basic features of these centres.

B. Features of Offshore Centres

1.04 An offshore financial centre may itself be defined as

> a regime which has chosen as a main or important path to development, legislative, financial and business infrastructure which is more flexible than orthodox infrastructure and which caters more specifically, and often exclusively, to the needs of non-resident investors . . . this legislative framework includes innovations in trust, banking, fiscal, insurance, financial and company law.[7]

This definition recognizes that many financial centres, including those of metropolitan countries, such as New York and London, do in fact offer special incentives and initiatives to non-residents. However, because of the dominant entrepreneurial thrust of financial centres described as offshore, it makes a

---

[3] FW Maitland, 'The Origin of Uses' 8 Harv L Rev 127, 130 (1894).

[4] See, eg, J Langbein, 'The Secret Life of the Trust: The Trust as an Instrument of Commerce' (1977) 107 Yale LJ 163, 165. The trust has long been recognized as a useful device for gratuitous transfers, particularly between generations. He notes too, that in the US, most of the wealth placed in trusts is 'incident to business deals': ibid, 166.

[5] R-M B Antoine, *Confidentiality in Offshore Financial Law* (Oxford University Press, New York, Oxford, 2002).

[6] The use of the term 'offshore' when used to describe countries or jurisdictions is in no way pejorative and should not be taken to mean that those countries do not have well-established and legitimate legal and economic financial structures in place. It is merely used to describe countries which have recognized financial systems that utilize offshore financial law and are engaged in offshore investment, as described below. Onshore countries are simply those which may be distinguished from offshore countries, although we will see that, increasingly, onshore countries are borrowing legal concepts from offshore jurisdictions.

[7] Antoine, above, n 5, 8.

distinction between these centres and those which are the subject of this book. Yet we should acknowledge that the distinction between offshore and onshore financial centres is becoming blurred with the advent of financial developments in certain states in the US that are emulating the investment functions of offshore financial centres.[8]

For purposes of this book, the definition of offshore financial law in the case of *Re Asia Credicom Ltd*[9] is adopted. In that case, offshore financial law is described as   **1.05**

> legislation, legal practices and law concerned with investment, financial arrangements and entities created by non-residents of a particular jurisdiction but structured within that jurisdiction. Such investments or arrangements are typically focussed on some business advantage, tax avoidance, protection from creditors and judgment debtors or privacy.[10]

The offshore trust operates within such a special legal framework and makes a significant contribution to offshore financial law. Like other offshore entities, it caters essentially to non-resident settlors who wish to avoid the restrictions of domestic law in their own onshore jurisdictions.

Armed with these definitions about the nature of offshore financial centres and offshore financial law, the offshore trust may be described as a trust which caters to non-residents and subsists in offshore financial regimes. It is subject to the special trust laws and policies enacted exclusively for offshore financial entities. McMullin J, in the case of *South Orange Growers Association v Orange Grove Partners*,[11] in analysing the provisions of the International Trusts Act 1984 of the Cook Islands, made this clear when he noted: 'The International Trusts Act applies only in respect of international trusts and not to what may be called onshore trusts which continue to be governed by the domestic legislation of the Cook Islands.'   **1.06**

The above definition is qualified to the extent that it must be acknowledged that offshore trusts, being essentially hybrid in nature, sometimes fall under law and policy which apply to all trusts in the offshore jurisdiction. This includes orthodox or traditional domestic trusts serving residents. Yet even where the trust legislation does not apply exclusively to offshore trusts, it will contain provisions which speak directly, or sometimes exclusively, to non-resident or offshore trusts or trusts established by non-residents. A good example of such   **1.07**

---

[8] See the discussion in chapter 5, 'Questions of Legitimacy and the Offshore Trust', at paras 5.27–5.32.

[9] (Sup Ct, BVI) No 20 of 1999, decided 30 July 1999. Moore's definition is taken from R-M B Antoine, 'Obtaining Mareva Injunctions and Related Orders Against Offshore Assets' [1998] Carib LR 212.

[10] *Asia Credicom*, ibid, 31.

[11] [1997–1998] 1 OFLR 3, 5 (CA), Cook Islands.

a model is found under the Belize Trusts Act 1992, as revised in 2000. While the Act does not expressly confine itself to offshore trusts, provisions such as the following clearly address only offshore trusts and the exclusion of onshore law:

> Where a trust is created under the law of Belize, the court shall not . . . set it aside or recognise the validity of any claim against the trust property pursuant to the law of another jurisdiction or the order of a court of another jurisdiction in respect to—[12]

1.08 To the extent that traditional trusts law, as existing in the particular jurisdiction, is not modified by special offshore trusts provisions, it should, therefore, be regarded as saved.[13] This saving of existing trusts law where special offshore legislative provisions are absent, means that the traditional jurisprudence on trusts will be crucial to the discussion on offshore law. This is aside from its possible influence even where new offshore legislative provisions are in effect.

1.09 The offshore trust, a statutory creation, is a significant departure from the traditional trust which emerged from the equitable principles of the English legal tradition. Yet it borrows heavily from the traditional trust, evolving into what may be described as a hybrid trust. It is, in essence, a dynamic evolution of the trust and orthodox trust law. It embodies significant and often radical concepts, such as the purpose trust and trusts created specifically to avoid forced heirship regimes. Together with the entity of the company, the trust serves as a basic vehicle for offshore investment. Indeed, the way in which these two entities, the trust and the company, intertwine in offshore financial centres, is itself worthy of mention. Perhaps the most vivid demonstration of this is the new legislative provisions for VISTA trusts,[14] which allow traditional obligations of trustees with respect to the use of shares in investment, grounded in equity, to be exercised by directors of underlying companies.[15]

1.10 In the following chapters, we examine the fascinating legal framework of the offshore trust and its corresponding jurisprudence in detail. In this legislative environment we must also consider the important place of treaties and other international law instruments. These instruments impact significantly on offshore trusts. As tax planning is a common motive for the establishment of offshore trusts and other offshore entities, tax issues arise in several areas

---

[12] Section 7(6). Under s 64, trusts with non-resident settlors and beneficiaries are exempt from taxes.

[13] Some legislation makes this patently clear. See, eg, s 3 of the International Trusts Act 1984 of the Cook Islands, which reads: 'The law applicable to trusts in force in the Cook Islands shall apply to international trusts except in so far as they are inconsistent with or have been modified by the provisions of this Act.'

[14] The name coined for trusts established under the Virgin Islands Special Trusts Act 2003 of the British Virgin Islands.

[15] ibid, s 12.

concerning the offshore trust. Accordingly, these are addressed throughout the text, whether directly or indirectly.[16]

C. Offshore Trusts Force a Jurisprudential Review of Trusts

The offshore trust has compelled jurisprudential re-thinking about the nature **1.11** and functions of the traditional trust. It has invited, and sometimes forced, judges and policy-makers to assess the varied functions and characteristics of trusts in modern commercial settings. Admittedly, to some, the offshore trust is a bastard offspring of equity. Whatever the view, it is undeniable that the off-shore trust has been responsible for important new directions in trust law and practice. Contentious new principles in offshore jurisdictions, born out of statute, are now steadily seeping into domestic trust law. This book offers an appraisal of the several controversial questions which arise from the institution of this new type of trust. The book should also serve, therefore, as an instrument for re-assessing the traditional trust, and for tracing and understanding the current evolution of the trust in general.

The offshore trust will be examined both from its statutory origins and com- **1.12** paratively, taking into account presumptions about the trust and other legal principles which impact upon the offshore trust. The fact that the offshore trust is a creation of statute adds to its peculiar existence. Its nature and character continue to challenge onshore courts. Thus, this book is not simply an exposition of offshore legislation but examines how the legislation and juris-prudence offshore interrelate with the law onshore. This enables the practitioner to source solutions to the conflicts which may arise from time to time.

An assumption is made that the reader is familiar with the principles of trust **1.13** law. Consequently, such principles are not repeated here, except if necessary to underline important aspects of offshore trust law. In some circumstances, the offshore trust will have to grapple with orthodox questions of trusts law. For example, in what circumstances will breaches of trust be incurred, or third parties or directors become liable for wrong-doing? While traditional trust prin-ciples are useful starting points for addressing these questions, the originality of the offshore trust brings to bear different and more complex elements in finding responses to these questions.

---

[16] See, eg, chapter 8, 'The Offshore Trust as a Sham' and chapter 10, 'Duties of Trustees in Managing Offshore Trusts'. However, Part III, 'The Offshore Tax Function', addresses such issues more directly.

D. Wider Issues Relating to Offshore Financial Centres

1.14   Offshore trusts have not been insulated from broader questions surrounding offshore financial centres, questions which touch on the potential for unlawful, or, at minimum, unethical or undesirable conduct. These are critical issues for onshore jurisdictions. They are also discussed, particularly in relation to tax planning, asset protection, and confidentiality functions.

1.15   The arrival of offshore financial regimes has introduced duality into domestic legal systems. The offshore sector is designed for non-residents. There is often one set of laws for offshore trusts for the benefit of non-nationals and another for domestic trusts established by residents in the offshore jurisdiction. This has led to complaints about 'ring-fencing'. It has been seized upon by the dominant players in the international commercial landscape, on the ground that the regime is inherently discriminatory.

1.16   Public policy concerns therefore emerge as unavoidable elements in these often contentious debates. The inherent tensions within offshore financial law are strikingly evident when the institution of the offshore trust is examined carefully.

E. Suitability of the Trust to International Commerce

1.17   The trust is a popular and important vehicle of investment in the offshore sector, and its ability to conquer the multi-national borders of the industry is remarkable. It is the inherent flexibility of the trust that makes it such an attractive tool for offshore investors. However, such flexibility is not without limitations or difficulties.

1.18   A notion of dual ownership is fundamental to the underlying character of the trust. In the traditional trust, the legal interest is vested in the trustee, while the beneficial ownership vests with the beneficiaries. It is this duality which makes the trust such an appropriate and flexible tool in the world of offshore finance. This is a world which often relies on the manipulation of the elements of ownership and control for its success. Most significant in offshore trust planning is the fact that with the establishment of a trust, the original owner of the assets, the settlor, although he or she initially determines the pattern of investment for the trust, is no longer considered to be the owner of the assets under trusts law.

1.19   The anxiety to locate or identify the offshore trust in jurisprudential terms, has led some to argue that the modern trust has a contractual basis, as opposed to being grounded in property law.[17] If so, it appears that the offshore trust is particularly well suited to this analysis, being, as it is, a product developed for commercial needs. As creatures of contract, the parties to offshore trusts may have much more freedom and flexibility to agree to do things, or incorporate trust arrangements hitherto unknown to the onshore trust, provided, of course, that they are not illegal. They may, however, run into danger on grounds of public policy.[18]

The inherent flexibility of the trust has meant that it is a useful tool for accommodating the often unique demands of the rapidly-changing and increasingly sophisticated world of finance, particularly offshore finance. Indeed, we can measure the success of the offshore trust as an international tool of commerce by the fact that today, even civil law nations are having to acknowledge the existence of, and in some cases work directly with, the trust.[19]   **1.20**

Offshore trusts will typically be found in those offshore jurisdictions whose legal traditions stem from English law,[20] since the trust itself is a creature of the English Common Law legal tradition.[21] Nonetheless, in the context of transnational offshore business, those jurisdictions which do not incorporate the trust concept into their law, apart from merely interacting with the trust, have gone further and emulated trust jurisdictions. In particular, some offshore jurisdictions which belong to the civil law tradition have found it expedient to incorporate the trust or 'trust-like' concepts, so as to capitalize on this lucrative aspect of offshore business.[22] In addition, generally, civil law jurisdictions are increasingly confronting the trust as a result of transnational business. This phenomenon, though welcome from an offshore commercial point of view, inevitably raises issues of private international law which have to be addressed.   **1.21**

---

[17] See J Langbein, 'The Contractarian Basis of the Law of Trusts' (1995) 105 Yale LJ 625.

[18] For example, they may undermine traditional beneficiary rights. See, eg, paras 7.22–7.58, in relation to acquiring information about the trust.

[19] See chapter 21, 'The Recognition of the Offshore Trust in Civil Law Countries'.

[20] In particular, the ex-colonies of the United Kingdom, eg, Bermuda, Dominica, Grenada, Belize, Saint Lucia, Saint Vincent, Saint Christopher and Nevis, The Bahamas, and remaining UK territories such as the Cayman Islands, Anguilla, The British Virgin Islands (BVI), the Isle of Man, Jersey, and Guernsey. However, some non-common law offshore jurisdictions have embraced the trust concept, or a variant of the trust. See, eg, the foundation in Liechtenstein. Other civil law countries which are offshore jurisdictions are Switzerland and The Netherlands.

[21] The trust is, of course, an equitable concept and not a common law concept. When we refer to the common law trust in this book, we mean belonging to this common law legal tradition and not as distinct from equity.

[22] See, eg, Liechtenstein and Panama.

F. Direction of the Work

1.22   The book does not take the well-known route of a country-by-country description of offshore jurisdictions. Rather, it is concerned with important issues in offshore trust law and, by extension, offshore financial law.[23] As such, it takes a thematic approach—but from a comparative view, describing similarities and differences in legislation and policy in relation to the issues. Whilst the transplantation of the trust to new frontiers is an important theme in our discussions, more emphasis is placed on the offshore trust law in offshore jurisdictions which belong to the common law tradition. This is a justifiable approach since:

(1) as we have noted, the trust is essentially a common law phenomenon. While some civil law jurisdictions, such as Liechtenstein, have incorporated it, or some form of it, its natural home is in common law jurisdictions; and

(2) the majority of the leading offshore jurisdictions are common law jurisdictions, many of them in the Commonwealth Caribbean.

G. Relative Uniformity in Offshore Trusts Law

1.23   There is considerable parity in relation to offshore legislative provisions, but they are not identical. Consequently, the choice of location for the offshore trust may be crucial to its effectiveness. Offshore jurisdictions which have more traditional legal provisions relating to the trust will offer less protection than those which have specifically legislated to deter creditors and others seeking to reach assets. However, more offshore financial centres are moving toward the latter. We should note, however, that offshore jurisdictions tend to borrow from one another, so that there are more similarities than there are differences in relation to offshore trust law. As will be seen, differences in degree and in the interpretation of legislation can be quite important.

1.24   Yet, with few exceptions, policy objectives in offshore jurisdictions are similar. One important difference might be the extent to which the offshore trust is prepared to go to facilitate settlors who are seeking ultimately to avoid creditors, even if those creditors may be in the future. This difference will, of course, be reflected in the relevant legislation.[24]

---

[23] The book is conceptualized as a companion text to R-M B Antoine, *Confidentiality in Offshore Financial Law* (Oxford University Press, Oxford, 2002), which examines another important aspect of offshore financial systems.

[24] Those prepared to do so will enact more liberal laws on fraudulent conveyancing, discussed in chapter 9, 'The Law on Fraudulent Conveyances and the Offshore Trust'.

In addition, some jurisdictions may be more advanced, in general, in the **1.25** codification of their trust laws. In particular, they may have progressed further in enacting statutory provisions which mirror more modern developments in traditional case law on trusts. A good example would be the rules on trustees' duties with regard to investments. These more contemporary provisions are evident, for example, in the dependent English territories.[25]

In a sense, we can argue that there are two modes of offshore trusts law, one **1.26** evident in the remaining English territories, which has a more pronounced common law flavour. On the other hand, there has been a more marked attempt to introduce radical deviations to traditional trusts law.[26]

Nonetheless, although other offshore financial centres may have not have codi- **1.27** fied such jurisprudential developments, we should bear in mind the hybrid nature of offshore trusts law, with its common law overlay. Often this means that, in the absence of statutory provisions to the contrary, such case law will continue to define the interpretation of offshore trusts law.

H. Persuasive Precedents in Similar Offshore Jurisdictions

Because of the shared common law orientation and the similar legislative thrusts **1.28** of offshore trust jurisdictions, the cases originating in one jurisdiction are important indicators of jurisprudential direction in other offshore jurisdictions. At minimum, they will be persuasive precedents. In the case of the Common- wealth Caribbean states which are offshore jurisdictions, the linkages are even more direct. These jurisdictions have all retained the Judicial Committee of the Privy Council, based in the UK, as a final court of appeal. Consequently, juris- prudential practice, if not theory, has determined that precedents from one Commonwealth Caribbean country will be binding in the next.

The Caribbean Court of Justice (CCJ) will soon replace the Privy Council as the **1.29** final court of appeal for some of these countries. The Bahamas, for example, a leading offshore jurisdiction, has stated that it is not yet ready to be part of the CCJ arrangement. This opens the possibility of greater differences in legal thinking between Commonwealth Caribbean offshore jurisdictions—those

---

[25] See, eg, the Trusts (Jersey) Law 1984, the Trusts (Guernsey) Law 1989, and the Trustee (Amendment) Act 2003 of the British Virgin Islands. See also the Trusts Act 1992 (rev'd, 2000) of Belize and the Trustee Act 1986 of The Bahamas. Trustees' duties are discussed in chapter 10, 'Duties of Trustees in Managing Offshore Trusts'.

[26] This is perhaps most evident in the Cook Islands, under the International Trusts Act 1984, and its progeny, such as the International Trusts Act 1997 of Dominica and the International Trusts Act 1994 of Nevis.

which still retain the Privy Council and those which do utilize the CCJ. However, it is at least arguable that the differences may be more illusory than real.

1.30 The point should be made that these offshore courts are themselves steeped in the English common law legal tradition. It is not to be assumed that they are better equipped to deal with radical trusts law than onshore courts, or, indeed, that they are willing to deviate from traditional trust law principles. At least one court was conservative in its approach in this regard.[27] Even if they were to do so, for those courts which still depend on the Privy Council as a final court of appeal, they cannot count on that court upholding their decisions.

1.31 Where there are omissions or uncertainties in offshore legislation, or where such legislation merely codifies traditional trusts law, the interpretation of offshore trust law, even after consideration of its ultimate purposes, may mirror traditional trusts law according to established principles of equity. As such, in many of our discussions, these traditional trust law principles are addressed. All of these phenomena help to impute a certain uniformity to offshore trusts law.

1.32 The institution of the offshore trust is poised on the brink of an explosion in litigation. Questions remain to be answered if the inherent conflict between the rights of those seeking to reach the trust assets, such as creditors, and those of the owners of assets is to be resolved. Challenges will continue to issue against the sometimes complacent assumptions made under the umbrella of relevant offshore legislation. With the increased use of offshore trusts, one should expect the development of relevant jurisprudence on the subject, thereby filling the gaps and clarifying the uncertainties in the present barren legal landscape. Indeed, we are already witnessing this revolution.

---

[27] *South Orange Growers Association v Orange Grove Partners* [1997–98] 1 OFLR 3 (CA, Cook Islands), discussed more fully in chapter 9, paras 9.93 and 9.113–9.114. The court did not accept that the the International Trusts Act 1984 Act aimed to abrogate the rights of onshore creditors in the interest of commercial expediency.

2

ANATOMY AND FUNCTIONS OF THE OFFSHORE TRUST

A. Nature of the Offshore Trust

The Offshore Trust as a Hybrid Trust

While the legal source for the offshore trust is largely statutory, its historical **2.01** inspiration is in equity. Through legislation, the offshore industry has been responsible for the transformation of the adaptable trust into what this writer views as a hybrid creature designed specifically to meet the needs of offshore investment. This has been achieved by combining well-known features of the traditional trust with other, more flexible features.[1] In some cases, it is merely a question of increasing powers already permitted in traditional trusts. For example, as discussed below, the powers given to a settlor, the degree of confidentiality granted to the offshore trust, and the ability of the trust to protect the assets against challengers, all may be exaggerated.

In other instances, entirely new powers, roles, and functions are created for the **2.02** offshore trust, such as special provisions to preclude forced heirship arrangements,[2] or to sustain trusts without identifiable beneficiaries,[3] or instituting protectors as officers of the trust.[4] Thus, some entities, such as the 'reversible trust' and the 'purpose trust', are peculiar to the industry. Yet the transformation

---

[1] See below, paras 2.12–2.67.
[2] See chapter 23.
[3] That is, purpose trusts, discussed in chapter 3.
[4] See chapter 4.

of the institution of the trust, for motives which are often controversial, can sometimes create difficulty for its application to offshore law.

Popular functions of the offshore trust

2.03   Despite popular misconceptions, the modern offshore trust may have little to do with tax avoidance. Indeed, several countries, including the UK and USA, have enacted legislation which undermines the tax advantages of offshore trusts.[5] The prime rationale for the contemporary offshore trust is the protection of assets from potential onshore creditors and other claimants to the settlor's assets. This does not necessarily suggest that the function of asset protection is either non-controversial or legitimate.

2.04   There are several other functions which offshore trusts may serve, even where they are primarily designed for asset protection. Many of these are particularly useful to persons with international estates, or assets or businesses located in several different countries. The offshore trust may be used for one or more purposes. The main uses include:

(1)   as a substitute to wills to avoid probate, and to make succession and the transfer of assets more efficient by minimizing delay, problems of access to assets, and other procedural problems associated with probate;

(2)   as a means to provide for privacy by utilizing the confidentiality laws of offshore jurisdictions, bearing in mind that probate and related procedures are often public processes, but within a modern, well-regulated environment which provides 'cutting-edge' safeguards against money-laundering;

(3)   to strengthen spendthrift provisions in order to prevent the wastage of other challengers to the trust assets. Where this protection involves protection from irresponsible family beneficiaries, the estate is protected for future heirs and the said beneficiaries protected against their own harmful acts;

(4)   as vehicles for global investing and other business;

(5)   to plan more effectively for the potential disability or unavailability of the settlor, called a grantor in the US, as the offshore trust typically provides more flexibility than does an onshore trust;

(6)   to enable self-settling in order to maintain some measure of control without usurping the powers of the trustees;

(7)   to avoid the risks of expropriation and other political risks;

(8)   to alleviate avoidable tax liabilities, including the avoidance of double taxation;

(9)   to give to a settlor the freedom to choose the most appropriate law to govern the trust which will administer his or her assets and, by extension,

---

[5] See Part III, 'The Tax Function of Offshore Trusts'.

the possibility of avoiding uncertainties relating to the proper law and jurisdiction of the trust;

(10) to centralize assets dispersed worldwide under one expedient and effective management structure, for reasons of convenience, cost, and tax efficiency, and to ensure that beneficiaries have knowledge of their entitlements. Note, however, that an offshore trust may be deliberately structured to avoid this very knowledge;[6]

(11) to protect a family estate, or assets generally, from claims either from disinherited family members, or from other potential creditors or challengers, thereby preserving the estate for future generations;

(12) to enable the original owner of the assets to have more freedom to dispose of his or her property by avoiding mandatory succession laws and regimes. Note that in an international estate, a person from a common law legal system may have assets located in a civil law jurisdiction;

(13) generally, to allow for more efficient management of assets through the use of mechanisms more suited to the demands of modern international commerce and which allow a living settlor some 'say' in the direction of investment, including more flexible means of achieving philanthropic objectives through the use of the purpose trust;[7]

(14) to minimize costly probate processes[8] and incompatibilities between different probate procedures in various countries, or different approaches to the distribution of assets after death;[9]

(15) to allow the acquisition of life insurance from foreign carriers under more favourable terms than under domestic, onshore laws, through the use of a non-resident person who is not subject to the law of the onshore jurisdiction, as the trustee of the offshore trust;

(16) to permit the avoidance of rules considered detrimental to commercial expediency, such as the rule against perpetuities, thereby creating a type of 'dynasty trust', the rule against accumulations, the rule in *Saunders v*

---

[6] If settlors wish beneficiaries to be informed, the trust instrument must make proper provision for this, in order to avoid the kind of scenario seen in *Lawrence v Berbier* (2003) 5 ITELR 9, where the assets were locked away for years without beneficiaries and without even the settlor's attorney having proper information on the trust.

[7] Provided, of course, that such 'say' does not override a trustee's ultimate discretion over the trust assets.

[8] Administrative costs may be significant, particularly where the process must be repeated in every country where there is an international estate. There will be duplication of estate taxes, legal and tax advice, appointment of executors, and so on.

[9] Problems of jurisdiction may also occur in relation to probate with questions being raised about a deceased's domicile, residence, etc These will have to be resolved before probate can be completed.

Vautier,[10] and the prudent investor rule in trusts, the last of which is still evident in certain trust jurisdictions, including some states in the US;[11]

(17) conveniently to establish trusts on beneficial terms, for relatives not resident onshore;

(18) to be better placed to hold interests in foreign enterprises.

2.05 The use of a trust environment in which there are highly sophisticated specialist trust professionals, experienced in dealing with offshore trusts and who operate within well-developed and complementary banking and financial facilities,[12] is not to be underestimated as a useful function in itself.

2.06 The functions listed above may be conveniently abridged into main subject areas which will be discussed further in detail in the following chapters. These are:

(1) asset protection, in particular the avoidance of potential creditors;

(2) avoiding mandatory succession, especially forced heirship regimes;

(3) the offshore tax function; and

(4) the conflict of laws in relation to the offshore trust.

2.07 The strict confidentiality which attaches to offshore trusts is also a significant issue in our discussion of the rationales and methods of such trusts. However, it is discussed in this text only briefly, as it is the subject of an entire book, which serves as a companion to this work.[13]

The implications of hybridity for the offshore trust

2.08 In examining the offshore trust, one cannot avoid addressing certain central issues which will be explored in the following chapters either directly, or as related elements in broader discussions. The first question which may be posed is this: Is the offshore trust a legitimate or true offshore trust? It is suggested that the distinct features of hybridity which the offshore trust displays have serious implications. Can, or should, such a hybrid entity be accommodated under the broad and traditional principles of the trust? This line of inquiry is relevant both to the extent that existing legal rules of the onshore trust can be imposed upon this legal mutation and to the extent to which the hybrid trust can be allowed to expand or undermine trust jurisprudence. It questions the ability of both domestic onshore laws and private international law to challenge the legitimacy

---

[10] (1842) 4 Beav 115, 49 ER 284.

[11] The effect of these changes to the rules in question is considered more fully in paras 2.12–2.67 below and in chapter 4.

[12] In existence since the 1920s, in some cases.

[13] R-M B Antoine, *Confidentiality in Offshore Financial Law* (Oxford University Press, Oxford, New York, 2002).

of the offshore trust. It goes to the very *raison d'être* of the offshore trust. The issue assumes particular importance if one considers that the true aims of the offshore trust and those of the onshore trust may be quite different.

Some may come to the conclusion, for example, that the offshore trust is merely   **2.09**
a distortion of the pure trust concept, an imposter, existing simply to obfuscate objectives which are undesirable. Similarly, it can be argued that its very existence is against public policy. On the other hand, there is merit to the argument that the offshore trust serves a legitimate function in a modern international business environment. It may be sufficient for courts and jurists to be concerned not with the question of whether it conforms to the legal form of the English trust as we know it, but with the more fundamental question of the rationale for the offshore trust, a rationale which, in truth, has much in common with the historical functions of the trust.

The second issue is related to the first. Even if one accepts that the offshore trust   **2.10**
is a legitimate (albeit a hybrid) entity, one must still test its validity, either on its own or against the backdrop of traditional principles of the traditional trust. The legal analysis must involve the issues of proving the validity of the transfer of assets into the trust and the trust instrument itself. This is true whether one is attempting to discern if the trust is a fraudulent conveyance, a 'sham', or whether it should be foiled because it violates other legal fundamentals of the trust. These include rules on certainty, equity, and perpetuity.[14] The validity of the trust can also be tested against conflict of laws principles and the extent to which onshore laws are antagonistic to the offshore trust. Addressing this central issue of validity is, therefore, essential before other legal questions are resolved.

Onshore law has not as yet fully assessed the hybrid offshore trust. When one   **2.11**
juxtaposes traditional ideas of law with the innovative and aggressive trust law principles embodied in the offshore legal infrastructure, there are discernible conflicts. These stand to be resolved and have already begun to be tested before the courts.

B. Characteristic Features of the Offshore Trust

Features of hybridity in the offshore trust

A distinct jurisprudence has evolved which stems from the enactment of special   **2.12**
trust legislative provisions to govern the trust in offshore jurisdictions.

---

[14] See, eg, the discussion of the difficulties of the law on charitable objects in the case of *Armenian Patriarch of Jerusalem v Sonsino and Others* (2002) 5 ITELR 125 (HC), one rationale for the establishment of offshore purpose trusts.

Generally, these provisions are designed to encourage investment offshore. They undermine the ability of onshore jurisdictions to challenge the hybrid offshore trust and seek to counter onshore laws antagonistic to offshore investment. These include changes to company law and trust law to make the trust more commercially viable and mobile, laws relating to bankruptcy and the enforcement of creditors' claims which attempt to preserve the integrity of offshore assets, and provisions specifying the governing law of the trust and jurisdiction.

2.13   Although the offshore trust relies heavily on the onshore trust for its essential form, there are several features of the offshore trust which are quite alien to its onshore equivalent. These unique features can be taken as evidence of hybridity.

2.14   The notion of hybridity extends to its functions. Sometimes the offshore trust will perform unique functions, such as to carry out a specified purpose in the absence of identifiable beneficiaries. In other instances, one can argue that although some functions performed by the offshore trust can, in theory, be performed onshore, the repeated use of the offshore vehicle for such functions makes them characteristically 'offshore'. Consider, for example, the use of the offshore trust for creditor protection. Where such functions are carried out by the offshore trust, they may assume added significance. Different considerations with respect to tax, jurisdiction, confidentiality, or even ethical concerns, may be inferred. These considerations again give added force to the argument of hybridity.

Type of trust and method of creation

2.15   The usual form of the offshore trust is an accumulation and discretionary settlement created by a living settlor, an *inter vivos* trust. It is established in the offshore jurisdiction, which typically either has a zero-tax regime, or imposes no tax on trust capital, income, or capital gains, although a nominal registration or licensing fee may be imposed on the trust. The trust instrument will typically contain provisions for apportionment between income and capital, for the holding of trust investments in nominees' names, for acquiring and holding property, for borrowing, and for the remuneration of the trustees.[15] This is not exclusive to offshore trusts. Assets may either be placed in a single trust, or may be divided amongst several offshore trusts.

---

[15] M Grundy, *Grundy's Tax Havens: A World Survey* (Sweet & Maxwell, London 1993). However, the notion of 'hybridity' is not conceptualized.

Offshore law makes special provision for protective or spendthrift trusts.[16] For **2.16** example, under s 12(1) of the Belize Trusts Act 1992, as revised in 2000, the terms of the trust may make the interest of a beneficiary:

(a) subject to termination;

(b) subject to a restriction or alienation of or dealing in that interest; or

(c) subject to diminution or termination in the event of the beneficiary becoming insolvent or any of his property becoming liable to seizure . . . for the benefit of his creditors . . .[17]

The Act further precludes the application of rules which prevent protective **2.17** trusts. It states: 'Any rule of law or public policy which prevents a settlor from establishing a protective or a spendthrift trust of which he is a beneficiary is hereby abolished.'[18]

The purpose trust deserves special mention. It aims to fall under the exception **2.18** to the general trust principle that a trust must be set up for an identifiable beneficiary rather than a specific purpose. The exception under onshore law allows the establishment of a trust for a specific purpose only in very limited circumstances, such as where the purpose is charitable. In contrast, in the offshore context, a trust may be established for a number of purposes, falling under the category of a 'beneficial purpose' or other specified purpose. In addition, the concept of a 'beneficial purpose' is much wider and includes a purpose for commercial advantage.[19]

The offshore trust will generally be established in one of two ways: either with **2.19** the assets remaining in the onshore jurisdiction, or by transferring the assets to the offshore jurisdiction. The second method is seen to be safer, as it employs the use of offshore trustees, mechanisms, and structures, and more deliberate

---

[16] Spendthrift or protective trusts specifically protect against the reach of creditors. The interest of the beneficiary cannot be assigned to him or reached by his creditors. See Hanbury and Martin, *Modern Equity* (15th ed) (Sweet & Maxwell, London, 1997).

[17] See also s 6 of the International Exempt Trust Act 1997 of Dominica; s 31 of the Trusts (Jersey) Law 1984; s 10 of the International Trusts Act 1996 of Saint Vincent; s 39 of the Trustee Act 1998 of The Bahamas; s 19 of the International Trusts Act 2002 of Saint Lucia; s 13F of the International Trusts Act 1984 of the Cook Islands; s 34 of the Trusts Law (2001 Revision) of the Cayman Islands.

[18] Section 12(4).

[19] The function of the purpose trust may be asset protection. For example, the trustee might be a private trust company and the shares of the private trust company are held by a offshore trust company on the trusts of a purpose trust. The purpose might be described as 'to hold the shares of the private trust company'. The settlor demonstrably has no control over the trust assets and the offshore company is not the trustee of the offshore trust, nor does it own the trustee beneficially. See ss 12–16 of the Trusts (Special Provisions) Act 1984 (am'd 1998) of Bermuda; s 84 of the Trustee Amendment Act 2003 of the BVI; s 15 of the Trusts Act 1992 of Belize; s 18 of the Perpetuities Act 1995 of The Bahamas. See chapter 3 for a fuller discussion of the purpose trust.

attempts to avoid the reach of the onshore jurisdiction.[20] In the first method, although the assets remain physically onshore, they are held under a complex structure whereby a domestic entity, such as a family limited liability partnership, or an offshore limited liability company or partnership, holds the assets. The offshore trust is thereby established together with this other entity and interests in the partnership or company are conveyed to the offshore trustee. The hope here is that the offshore trust law will apply to the assets.[21]

Companies existing alongside the trust

2.20　The offshore trust does not usually exist in isolation. It is generally established with another business interest. While this is not unique to offshore trusts, it is far more prevalent in offshore jurisdictions than in onshore jurisdictions, where trusts established for limited family purposes may be more common. Where the trust is to be used for investment or the holding of shares in one or more operating companies, a company or companies will generally be specifically incorporated for such purposes. Such companies will be made resident in the jurisdiction of the trust or some offshore jurisdiction offering typical offshore trust advantages, such as tax benefits, the shielding of assets, and anonymity.[22]

2.21　Foreign securities owned by such companies may be less vulnerable to tax liability in the onshore jurisdiction than would be securities or assets owned by a trust. Companies may also be useful as subordinate investment vehicles in jurisdictions where the trust is not recognized, such as in civil law jurisdictions. They also offer significant advantages, bringing together the assets in a convenient manner and sometimes in one place, with one set of laws, thus enabling them to be more easily managed and controlled. Where there are underlying companies, directors and portfolio managers may play significant roles in managing the assets and ultimately the trust, as allowed under the trust instrument.

2.22　In *Stuart-Hutcheson v Spread Trustee Co Ltd*,[23] Clarke JA described the complex structure of such company—trust arrangements in this way:

> Cedar is, in reality, the creature of the trustee, beneficially owned as to 50% by the No 2 and No 3 Settlements. The actual directors are two companies with the same stable as the trustee. Those two companies are two of the seven companies, the others including the trustee who, according to a search, were the registered shareholders of Cedar, which has at all relevant times been beneficially owned by the No 2 and No 3 Settlements. We may, I think, legitimately infer that the trustee

---

[20]　See discussion in Part IV, 'The Conflict of Laws and the Offshore Trust'.

[21]　However, assets may be physically relocated offshore at a later date. The assets of the offshore trust need not be in either the onshore jurisdiction, or the offshore jurisdiction where the trust is established. For example, they may be in another offshore trust jurisdiction.

[22]　Grundy, above, n 15.

[23]　(2003) 5 ITELR 140, 156 (CA) Jersey.

runs the Board. Further, Cedar is the vehicle by which the trustee holds one of the two principal trusts . . .[24]

Characteristics of persons and offices associated with the offshore trust

The persons, both corporate and personal, directly associated with the trust are the trustee, the settlor, and the beneficiaries. In offshore trusts there may also be a protector and an enforcer. All of these persons may display characteristics unique to the offshore trust. The protector is an intermediary between the settlor and the trustee and exists to enhance the trust's management. The enforcer is appointed to enforce the purpose trust. These individuals are often not found in onshore trusts at all and are discussed separately in following chapters.[25]

2.23

Nature of the beneficiaries

More and more skilful ways of utilizing offshore trusts are being devised. One route is to structure trusts so that interests reserved to onshore beneficiaries would be less and less identifiable, for example, by having very wide classes of beneficiaries. This is in accordance with a tax planning objective. Lord Walker, in an *obiter* observation made in the case of *Rosewood Trust Ltd v Schmidt*,[26] described such arrangements as follows:

2.24

> . . . increasingly stringent anti-avoidance measures encouraged legal advisors to devise forms of settlement under which the true intended beneficiaries were not clearly identifiable in the settlement. Indeed, their interests or expectations were often barely perceptible. Rarely did a beneficiary take an indefeasibly vested interest with an ascertainable market value . . . and once the offshore tax avoidance industry has acquired standard forms its inclination is to use them, subject perhaps to some more or less skilful adaptation, even for clients whose aim is not to avoid UK taxation.

The incidence of the settlor being a beneficiary is also greater in the offshore trust than in the onshore trust.

2.25

In some cases, flexibility in relation to beneficiaries may be abused. An example is what has become know as 'Red Cross trusts', in which a well-known charity, such as the Red Cross, is named as a beneficiary. However, in this arrangement, there is no real intention for that beneficiary actually to benefit from the trust. The practice was remarked upon in *Steele v Paz*.[27]

2.26

---

[24] Note that the offshore trustee will often itself be a company.
[25] For the protector, see chapter 4, 'The Role and Powers of the Offshore Protector'. The enforcer is also discussed in chapter 3, 'Special Trust Vehicles', at paras 3.45–3.60.
[26] (2003) 5 ITELR 715 (PC) 728.
[27] [1993–95] Manx LR 102.

The trustee

2.27   Characteristically, in offshore trust jurisdictions, the obligations of the trustee are undertaken not by individuals but by corporations which make a business of doing so. These may be called trust companies or corporate trustees.[28] A trust company, or corporate trustee, may be formed either specially to act as a trustee of a particular trust, or to provide a trustee and associated services, in particular investment management services, for a number of trusts. The latter is the more popular approach. Trust companies serving several trusts are often owned by banks, law firms, accounting firms, and even professional individuals. The private trust company will confine its trusteeship activities to one family or business group. Where there are several trusts in the family grouping, this enables better administration and control. The offshore trust instrument will usually empower the trustees to accumulate the trust income during the whole of the perpetuity period. Further, trustees are commonly given wide powers of investment, including powers to form companies. The trustees have the usual discretionary powers to distribute capital and/or income to beneficiaries.

Identity of the settlor and nature of the settlor's interest

2.28   The settlor of the offshore trust is distinguished by the degree to which he or she can exert influence over the trust either directly, through an office, or indirectly, and the extent to which he or she can engage in self-settling. The settlor may be amongst the class of discretionary beneficiaries, or may have a life or other interest which will end in certain circumstances, or within a specified time period. He or she may, alternatively, have a reserved interest.[29] In extreme examples, such as in Belize, the settlor may be a trustee, a beneficiary, or a protector.[30] Those offshore jurisdictions which have sought to create special asset protection regimes have, in conjunction with such provisions, incorporated wide settlor powers, together with provisions to restrict creditor access to trust assets.[31]

---

[28] As companies are regarded as persons, they may act as trustees. Trust companies are regulated and will usually require licences. See, eg, the Trusts Companies and Offshore Banking Act 2000 of Anguilla. Some of these regulations speak to anti-money laundering initiatives and mandate trustees to report suspicious conduct, or impose specific duties with respect to the identification of clients. See, eg, the Financial Transactions Reporting Act 2000 of The Bahamas. See further discussion on this point in chapter 7, 'Disclosure and Confidentiality Obligations'.

[29] See s 12(4) of the Belize Trusts Act 1992 (rev'd 2000) and s 12 of the International Exempt Trusts Act 1997 of Dominica.

[30] Under s 9(2) of the Trusts Act 1992 (rev'd 2000). See also s 31(4) of the International Exempt Trusts Act 1997 of Dominica; s 16(3) of the Trusts Ordinance of Anguilla; s 13 of the Trusts Law (2001 Revision) of the Cayman Islands.

[31] Most offshore jurisdictions have asset protection legislation. Exceptions include most of the UK territories, such as the BVI, Jersey, Guernsey, and the Isle of Man. Asset protection is discussed further in chapter 3 and in chapter 9, 'The Law on Fraudulent Conveyances and the Offshore Trust' and chapter 8, 'The Offshore Trust as a Sham'.

Such changes to traditional trust law may be repugnant to many common law onshore jurisdictions. When read with provisions which expressly allow protective or spendthrift trusts, they create a radical change in trust law. This rejects established trust principles which prevent protective trusts where the settlor is also a beneficiary of the trust, that is, self-settled spendthrift trusts. This deliberate policy change is confirmed under offshore trust legislation in some jurisdictions. Typically, the Belize provision abolishes any legal rule or public policy which hinders a settlor from establishing a self-settled, protective trust.[32]   **2.29**

Another peculiarity of the offshore trust is the importance that may be attached to the identity of the settlor. The offshore trust may engage a dummy settlor, sometimes called 'Uncle George'. Typically, Uncle George is neither a national, resident, nor domiciled in the country where the beneficiaries reside. This facilitates freedom from exchange currency controls and any tax liabilities there.[33] The 'Uncle George' persona is also designed to avoid jurisdictional challenges detrimental to asset protection or anti-forced heirship purposes, discussed below. In the offshore financial environment, interests in settlements may be bought and sold in order for beneficiaries to acquire an 'Uncle George'. The use of the 'dummy settlor' was demonstrated in the case of *Schmidt v Rosewood Trust Ltd*.[34] Here, the claimant's father was one of eight Russian businessmen who transferred more than US $ 105 million into two Manx trust settlements through a 'dummy settlor'. The father died intestate and the son was left with the task of trying to unravel the arrangement, which had assets in several countries. To do so, he sought disclosure of the trust accounts and other relevant information. He finally succeeded in contentious litigation which went to the Privy Council and which produced a controversial judgment.   **2.30**

Settlor influence

The settlor may perform a pivotal role in the direction which the offshore trust is to take, whether direct or indirect. A firm relationship between the settlor's wishes and the trustees' functions is allowed under offshore law. This is often achieved through a memorandum or letter of wishes.[35]   **2.31**

The settlor may also indicate his or her wishes through the protector, often through the execution of a letter of wishes to the protector. Further, he or she   **2.32**

---

[32] Section 12(4) of the Belize Trusts Act 1992 (rev'd 2000). See also s 6 of the International Exempt Trusts Act 1997 of Dominica.

[33] Grundy, above, n 15.

[34] [2003] UKPC 26; [2003] 2 WLR 1442 (PC) Isle of Man. The issue of disclosure to beneficiaries is discussed in chapter 7, 'Disclosure and Confidentiality Obligations', at paras 7.22–7.58.

[35] Outlined below, paras 2.64–2.67. Provision may be made for the memorandum of wishes under offshore legislation, but such provisions are not necessary for its utilization.

may be a member of an advisory committee to the trust, or may retain the authority to replace the trustee or protector. Any of these functions may pose a danger to the trust under the 'sham' rule, as discussed below.[36]

Trust not invalidated by enhanced powers or interests of settlors

2.33   Offshore trust legislation in several jurisdictions purports to insulate the offshore asset protection trust from various lines of attack pertaining to settlor influence. For example, in Dominica,[37] the International Exempt Trusts Act 1997 states that:

> An international trust shall not be declared invalid . . . if the settlor . . . retains . . . or acquires . . . power to revoke [or] amend the trust; any benefit, interest or property from the trust; power to remove or appoint a trustee or protector; power to direct a trustee or protector on any matter; or is the beneficiary of the trust solely or together with others.

In addition, the likelihood of such provisions exposing the trust to a successful sham attack is diminished if the challenge comes before offshore courts. This is because the offshore trust will inevitably be governed by the offshore law, and jurisdiction to consider trust questions will typically be granted exclusively to the offshore jurisdiction. Even if the sham challenge reaches the onshore court, that court may honour the chosen offshore law as the governing law. However, these are contentious questions and are addressed more fully in following chapters.[38]

Extended perpetuity and accumulation periods

2.34   The rule against perpetuities is a characteristic of the onshore trust. Under this rule the trust cannot continue in perpetuity unless it is a charitable trust. The rule has constantly been criticized as being a hindrance to investment.[39] In response, the offshore sector, in keeping with its hybrid character, has redesigned this rule to maximize its investment purposes. Thus, many offshore jurisdictions have increased the maximum specified perpetuity period, for example, 120 years in Belize, or have abolished the rule against perpetuities

---

[36] Chapter 8, 'The Offshore Trust as a Sham'.

[37] Under s 46. Or the statute may give the court power to declare the validity of the trust. See, eg, s 56 of the Trusts Act (rev'd) 2002 of Anguilla; s 47 of the International Exempt Trust Ordinance 1994 of Nevis; s 9 of the International Trusts Act 1996 of Saint Vincent; s 13C of the International Trusts Act 1984 of the Cook Islands; s 18 of the International Trusts Act 2002 of Saint Lucia; s 2(4) of the Trustee Act 1990 of the BVI; s 3 of the Trustee Act 1998 of The Bahamas.

[38] See Part IV, 'Conflict of Laws and the Offshore Trust'.

[39] See, eg, D Hayton, 'Time to Overhaul Trust Laws' (1991) 141 NLJ 210, 211; E Cash, 'The Bahamas: An Overview of the Perpetuities Act 1995' [1995] 4 JIntP 104.

altogether.[40] Where there is no perpetuity period, or an extended perpetuity period, this can alleviate considerably the difficulties and risks associated with the diversification of trust assets.

Similarly, traditional trust rules permit income to be accumulated only for a limited period. The United Kingdom, for example, allows a maximum accumulation period of the settlor's life. In contrast, offshore jurisdictions may permit accumulation throughout the perpetuity period, or significantly increase the accumulation period itself.[41]   **2.35**

Currently, the UK is considering an increase in both the perpetuity and accumulation periods. A Consultation Paper[42] published by the Lord Chancellor's Department followed from the recommendations made in the Law Commission's Report entitled *The Rules Against Perpetuities and Excessive Accumulations*.[43] The Consultation Paper proposes that the current perpetuity period be replaced with a standard period of 125 years. To achieve this, the accumulations periods under s 164 of the UK Law of Property Act 1925 would be abolished. The accumulation period for charities is proposed to be restricted to 21 years, and the new accumulation periods extended to settlements and donations made by corporations. This is, perhaps, an example of the impact on onshore jurisdictions of developments in trust law in offshore jurisdictions.   **2.36**

Increased protection against creditors and others threatening the assets

As we shall see in the following chapters,[44] several offshore jurisdictions have introduced legislation which aims to add to the security offered to persons who settle property into trust when faced with creditors. In particular, the law applicable to fraudulent conveyances, as it relates to offshore trusts, has been modified. This change also impacts on onshore bankruptcy law and the ability of onshore doctrines on fraudulent conveyances to impact on offshore trusts and effect resulting judgments.   **2.37**

---

[40] Section 6 of the Belize Trusts Act 1992 (rev'd 2000). See identical provisions under The Bahamas Perpetuities Act 1995 and s 6 of the International Exempt Trusts Act 1997 of Dominica. See also s 9 of the International Trusts Act of Grenada 1996; s 7 of the International Trusts Act 1995 of Barbados; and s 8 of the International Trusts Act of St Vincent.

[41] See, eg, s 43 of the Trusts (Guernsey) Law 1989: '(1) Subject to section 12, the terms of a trust may direct or authorise the accumulation of any period or part of the income of the trust.'

[42] *A Lord Chancellor's Department Consultation Paper: The Rule against Excessive Accumulations —Consultation Paper on the partial implementation of the Law Commission's Report, 'The Rules Against Perpetuities and Excessive Accumulations' by way of a Regulatory Reform Order*, September 2002; www.lcd.gov.uk/consult/rro.exacc.htm.

[43] www.lawcom.gov.uk/library/lc251/lc251ind.htm.

[44] See, in particular, chapters 3 and 9.

2.38   All of these provisions have been enacted with a view to insulating the trust against attacks by onshore jurisdictions. Yet even jurisdictions which have not enacted such creditor-specific legislation can boast of enhanced protection to would-be creditors and others attempting to reach the trust. This is due to the fact that, under offshore law, provisions which offer specific protection against would-be creditors are only part of a general thrust toward increased protection of the assets placed in trust. Whether the assets are being threatened by creditors, onshore tax authorities, mandatory heirs, or others, the offshore trust seeks to provide more insulation to them than its onshore counterpart. Thus, with regard to this aspect of offshore law, the offshore trust regime should be viewed holistically. Provisions such as securing greater confidentiality, precluding the enforcement of onshore judgments, preserving jurisdiction exclusively to offshore courts, prioritizing offshore trust law as the proper law, flight and duress clauses, raising the bar against future creditors and so on, all upgrade the protection offered to the assets placed in the offshore trust and enhance the integrity of the trust. These varied aspects are discussed separately in this book, but are actually several aspects of a dynamic whole.

Statutory provisions aimed at reconciling potential conflicts of law

2.39   Offshore trust law will typically contain provisions designed to rationalize conflict of laws rules on the trust. These conflict of laws provisions attempt directly, or indirectly, to oust the application of onshore laws to the trust. Instead, the offshore trust law should apply.[45] Again, these provisions may be creative and alter more traditional rules where these are disadvantageous to offshore investors, or seek to fill in the gaps where existing rules are vague. They also reach out to investors from civil law jurisdictions where the trust is relatively unknown and attempt to reconcile potential conflicts of laws, such as the lack of recognition of

---

[45] The several provisions and their application are discussed in detail in Part IV, 'Conflict of Laws and the Offshore Trust'. The provisions may oust laws such as forced heirship or onshore laws protecting creditors' rights. See the discussions of these phenomena in chapters 23 and 9 respectively. See, eg, s 29 of the International Exempt Trusts Ordinance 1994 of Nevis; s 28 of the International Trust Act 1997 of Dominica; s 91 of the Trusts Law (2001 Revision) of the Cayman Islands; s 7(2) of the Trusts (Choice of Governing Law) Act 1989 (am'd 1996) of The Bahamas; s 33 of the International Trust Act 1996 of Saint Vincent; s 20 of the International Trusts Act 1996 of Grenada; s 34 of the International Trusts Act 2002 of Saint Lucia. The legislation also attempts to exclude foreign laws which do not recognize the *type* of trust envisaged under offshore law, ie the hybrid features we have been discussing. For example, s 28 of the Dominica Act reads: 'Neither an international trust governed by this Act and any disposition of property . . . shall be declared void, voidable, liable to be set aside or defective in any fashion, . . . by reason that the— (a) laws of any foreign jurisdiction prohibit or do not recognize the concept of a trust . . .; (b) international trust or disposition avoids or defeats rights, claims or interests conferred by the law of a foreign jurisdiction upon any person . . . or (c) laws of Dominica or the provisions of this Act are inconsistent with any foreign law.'

the trust and the capacity to create the trust. Such provisions may address, directly, conflicts which may arise because of mandatory succession regimes in civil law jurisdictions.

Defeating the *Saunders v Vautier* rule

In traditional trusts known to the common law tradition, the beneficiaries of the trust may come together and bring the trust to an end by agreement. The act of termination results in a distribution of the trust property among the beneficiaries. This is the well-known rule established by the case of *Saunders v Vautier*.[46] The autonomy given to the beneficiaries to defeat the trust in this manner will often be unacceptable to offshore trusts and contradict the intent of the *inter vivos* settlors. Consequently, offshore legislation may seek to undermine and even nullify the rule.

2.40

This may be accomplished in three ways. First, the enactment of purpose trusts legislation, which permit trusts which have no identifiable beneficiaries, logically results in the conquest of the rule in *Saunders v Vautier*.[47] Secondly, because of the elevated confidentiality norms and practices which surround the offshore trust, beneficiaries will often have little or no information about the offshore trust. Indeed, they may not even know of its existence. Consequently, they will not be in a position to benefit from the rule. Thirdly, legislation in offshore jurisdictions may aim, specifically, to prohibit the application of the rule in *Saunders v Vautier* either for all trusts, or for selected trusts. For example, in Belize, s 47(1) of the Belize Trusts Act[48] codifies the rule as postulated under the Common Law. However, beneficiaries under a protective or spendthrift trust, which are typical forms of the offshore trust, are expressly prohibited from concluding agreements which allow them to benefit from the rule.[49]

2.41

An example of a more expansive approach to prohibiting the rule in *Saunders v Vautier* is seen in The Bahamas.[50] The legislation states that the beneficiaries interested in the trust property are not entitled 'to terminate or modify the trusts affecting the property, if this would defeat a material purpose of the settlor in creating the trust, unless the settlor is living and also consents'. This material purpose is to be 'ascertained from the trust instrument (directly or by inference)

2.42

---

[46] (1842) 4 Beav 115, 49 ER 284.
[47] See chapter 3.
[48] 2000, revised from the 1992 Act, Chapter 202.
[49] See s 47 (2) of the Belize Trusts Act 1992 (rev'd, 2000)
[50] See s 87 of the Trustee Act 1998 of The Bahamas. See also s 12 of the Virgin Islands Special Trusts Act 2003.

or by collateral evidence'. Yet in other offshore jurisdictions, the rule may merely be codified without any express limitations.[51]

2.43 Where the rule has not been abolished or modified by offshore legislation, or where the legislation merely codifies it, its application is identical to that in traditional trust jurisdictions. Indeed, the rule was considered in *Moss v Integro Trust (BVI) Ltd*[52] and *Bank of Nova Scotia Trust Company (Caribbean) Ltd v Tremblay*.[53] In both instances, the jurisdictions in question, the BVI and Barbados, followed the Common Law position and this was not contested by the courts.

2.44 In *Tremblay*, for example, the application of the rule was thwarted only on the facts, that the interest was not vested solely in the settlor/beneficiary and remoter beneficiaries were involved. The case demonstrates that, without statutory intervention, settlors must take care that the structure of the interests in the trust cannot frustrate any future intentions. The use of certain devices in offshore trusts, such as 'dummy' beneficiaries evident in 'Red Cross trusts',[54] could easily do so. The more certain position is thus obtained under statute, and it is noteworthy that the BVI have now changed their position with respect to trusts of shares within a 20-year period from the establishment of the trust.[55]

2.45 The relevant provision reads:

> (1) Notwithstanding any rule of equity or practice . . . but subject to subsection (2), neither a beneficiary who is solely interested in any designated shares, nor all the beneficiaries who together are the persons interested in any designated shares, shall be entitled, although in existence and ascertained and of full capacity, to call for or direct a transfer of those shares or to terminate or modify the trust relating to them if and so far as that entitlement is, without offending any rule of perpetuity or remoteness, excluded by the trust instrument.
>
> (2) No such exclusion of entitlement shall have effect, or continue to have effect, after the expiration of 20 years from the creation of the trust.

2.46 The statute which contains these new provisions is itself a dynamic and original piece of legislation which aims to achieve the maximum flexibility of commercial viability for corporate trustees, by reducing interference into corporate matters by trustees and making the directors of underlying companies responsible for the business affairs of the trust. It also curtails the equitable

---

[51] For example, in Guernsey, under s 48 of the Trusts (Guernsey) Law 1989.

[52] [1997–1998] 1 OFLR 427 (BVI).

[53] (1998) 1 ITELR 673 (Barbados).

[54] In such trusts, beneficiaries which are charities are often not intended to benefit, a practice which has been often criticized. This was the subject of contention in the case of *Steele v Paz* [1993–95] Manx LR 102, 108; digested in [2000] *Trusts and Trustees* 6. However, the more important point concerned the use of protectors, discussed in chapter 3.

[55] By virtue of s 12 of the Virgin Islands Special Trusts Act 2003.

obligations placed on trustees. Further, it prioritizes the settlor's long-term goals for the trust, enabling shares in underlying companies to be retained as trust assets for as long as the directors think fit. The legislation creates 'VISTA trusts' and applies only to trusts established by shareholders of BVI international business companies and BVI companies.

Trading trusts

Offshore trust legislation does not typically make provision for trading trusts. However, in practice, a number of options are open to trustees and these are commonly employed to limit their personal liabilities with respect to trading. For example, limited recourse clauses or limited liability companies may be utilized.   **2.47**

Flight clauses and duress clauses which shield the offshore trust

One of the attractions of offshore investment is its inherent mobility and flexibility. This is often in response to possible challenges to the trust assets, particularly from onshore jurisdictions. Such flexibility is facilitated by the use of flight clauses (or redomiciliation clauses) and duress clauses, which may be inserted into the trust. These are quite common in offshore trusts. They are devices for securing the assets of the trust from any imminent or perceived threats.   **2.48**

There are various reasons for the relocation of offshore entities. It may be because of a response to political instability, increasingly restrictive laws in the offshore jurisdiction or other adverse event, or merely the advent of more favourable offshore conditions elsewhere. Most common would be the desire to escape the enforcement of an onshore judgment against the trust and its assets, or the reach of onshore trust challenges. In recognition of this, redomiciliation provisions within the offshore legislative framework facilitate movement either to or from other jurisdictions.   **2.49**

Where the trust has underlying companies, we may need to consider the flight clause in the context of these companies too.[56] With regard to companies, redomiciliation provisions or 'flight clauses'[57] enable the incorporation of the company to be automatically transferred to an alternative location. In the case of trusts, flight clauses will often be in the trust instrument. These permit a person who is not subject to the jurisdiction of the offshore country to have power to change the trustees or relocate the trust. Where the trust relocates, new trustees   **2.50**

---

[56] Note also that with trusts, the trustee's residence, and thus the residence of the trust, need not be in the same jurisdiction as the jurisdiction of the governing law of the trust, as the settlor may choose another law to govern the trust.

[57] Also called 'escape' or 'Cuba' clauses.

or directors of underlying companies may be appointed from within the new trust location.

2.51 The redomiciliation of companies or trusts raises a number of complex legal issues. When juxtaposed with confidentiality mechanisms, such flight clauses exacerbate the already high risk of the dissipation of assets and have led to more favourable decisions toward disclosure and restraint orders.[58] Further tensions in offshore law may arise as offshore jurisdictions may discourage outflows while encouraging inflows of such transfers into the jurisdiction. Flight clauses may also raise contentious issues of jurisdiction. In *Private Trust Corporation v Grupo Torras*,[59] the flight clause was combined with a provision which sought to oust the jurisdiction of The Bahamas courts. This was an unusual provision which did not find favour with Gonsalves-Sabola P. The court had no need to consider the effect of such an ouster. However, it is doubtful whether such a provision could survive. In *Grupo Torras*, the risk of removal of the assets, which the flight clause created, was sufficient for the court to issue a *Mareva* injunction.

2.52 Duress clauses, although contentious, are quite common. This is a clause inserted into the trust document which allows a vulnerable aspect of the trust's structure or arrangement to be severed on the happening of a triggering event. The triggering event will be one which it is assumed will have adverse consequences for the trust. A common example of a duress clause is the removal of a settlor as a beneficiary or co-trustee where claims are made against the settlor and an attempt is made to reach the trust assets by treating them as still belonging to the settlor, or, more generally, where the trust is treated as being capable of conferring a benefit on the settlor. Examples of such duress clauses were seen in the cases of *Re Lawrence* and *In re Larry Portnoy*.[60] In both these cases, the presence of the duress clauses served to cast suspicion on the trust and the trusts were treated as fraudulent conveyances.

Changing the proper law of the trust

2.53 Alternatively, or in conjunction with a flight clause or duress clause, will be the use of a clause to change the proper law of the trust as is deemed necessary. The 'flight clause' may also enable the law governing the trust to be changed upon relocation. Such provisions may lead to a conflict of laws. This is particularly so

---

[58] The new jurisdiction may not recognize such 'flight clauses.' Alternatively, where relocation occurs, the status of the entity under conflicting laws in the new jurisdiction may be contentious. Parity of laws on transferability of companies or trusts may not exist.

[59] [1997–98] 1 OFLR 443.

[60] (2002) 5 ITELR 1 and (1996) 201 BR 685, US Bankruptcy Court, NY, T Brozman, Chief Judge, respectively, discussed further in chapter 8, 'The Offshore Trust as a Sham'.

as they can be used for evasion and to abuse creditors' rights by obstructing legal investigations.[61] Such a clause may also be considered a type of duress clause. While it may simply facilitate changing the location of the trust, it is more likely to be used as a further level of protection for a trust faced with some adverse event, particularly where a challenge is to be made before the courts in the jurisdiction whose law is the current proper law of the trust.[62]

The potential abuse of such provisions is the rationale behind the recent **2.54** amendment to the British Virgin Islands legislation. The use of changes of proper law and flight clauses is now restricted in certain circumstances where law enforcement needs are designated as paramount. This is an example of the changing landscape of offshore investment to meet the demands of fighting international crime.[63]

When offshore trusts have been challenged, the use of flight clauses, duress **2.55** clauses and 'change of law clauses', in conjunction with provisions allowing self-settling, have been problematic. Nonetheless, for the majority of offshore trusts which have not been the subject of hostile litigation, they have proven effective.

C. Constituting a Valid Trust

In constructing an offshore trust, even with all of its several hybrid features, the **2.56** settlor will also have to ensure that basic trust law rules about the constitution and formation of *inter vivos* express trusts, which are of general application, are observed.[64] Accordingly, requirements for the valid constitution of the trust include:

(1) that the assets to be held in trust are ascertained and specified;
(2) that the assets to be conveyed to the trust be owned by the settlor;
(3) that the settlor has the capacity to transfer the assets into trust;

---

[61] ibid.

[62] See chapter 20.

[63] Thus, under s 7 of the Trustee (Amendment) Act 2003, which amends s 81 of the parent Act of 1993, a new subs (4) is added. Under this subsection, the events for which such clauses are restricted are: '(a)an order of the court; (b) the institution of criminal proceedings against the settlor, the trustees or any of the beneficiaries; and (c) an investigation in relation to the settlor, the trustees, any of the beneficiaries of the trust or any part of the trust property by the Financial Services Commission pursuant to any enactment.'

[64] See C McKenzie, 'Maintaining the Integrity of Trusts', unpublished mimeo, BVI 2002; and D Brownbill, 'The Proper Constitution of a Trust' in Antoine R-M B (ed), *Legal Issues in Offshore Financial Law* (Caribbean Law Publishing Company, Jamaica, 2004), chapter 12.

(4) that a valid disposition of those assets be made to a trustee;

(5) that the intent to create a trust on the terms set out in the trust deed be expressed and that the terms be sufficiently certain;

(6) that all terms of the trust be lawful under trust.

Title and transfer of trust property

2.57 Before a trust may be validly constituted, title to the assets to be placed into the trust must be completely transferred to the trustee. The usual requirements for a transfer of property under the domestic onshore law will obtain. The settlor must effect a legal transfer of the assets to the trustee, or cause the assets to be so transferred.[65] The settlor must make a Declaration of Trust declaring the trusts on which the property is to be held. There may be different and further rules in relation to different types of property. If the trust property is to consist of company shares, for example, registration of such shares in the name of the trust may be required; or where bearer shares are involved, there may need to be delivery of those shares as well. The trust deed is to be distinguished from any instrument granting title for the trust property and conveying the said property to the trustee.

Clear trust deed in written form

2.58 In offshore trusts, unlike domestic trusts, the trust is often required to be evidenced in writing. Even where the law accepts oral declarations of trust, which is the norm under traditional trusts law,[66] for reasons of clarity and adherence to best offshore trust practices, offshore trusts will rarely be constituted in that manner. Given the deviations from traditional trust law permitted under offshore trust law, a high degree of care should be taken to draft trust instruments which are clear and concise.[67] The settlor need not be named in the trust instrument and, indeed, in the offshore trust is often not named, as the

---

[65] Under English law, where the transfer of assets has not been completed, it may be still possible for the trust to be created. This, however, is a difficult and uncertain route for trusts. See, eg, *Midland Bank Executor and Trustee Company Ltd v Rose* [1948] 2 All ER 971; *Rose v IRC* [1952] 1 All ER 1217 (CA).

[66] As, eg, Art 7, Jersey Trusts Law 1984. Increasingly, as more offshore trusts are being required to be registered for supervisory purposes, the trust will need to be in writing. In Belize, for unit trusts, under s 5 of the Trusts Act 1992 (rev'd 2000).

[67] The language in the trust instrument should be clear enough to demonstrate that the three certainties have been met. These are: (i) that the intention to create the trust is demonstrated; (ii) that the trust property which forms the subject matter of the trust is suitably identified; and (iii) that in trusts other than purpose trusts, the beneficiaries, and the manner in which the property is to be applied, are adequately identified and, in the case of the purpose trust, that an appropriate purpose is identified.

settlor may wish to be distanced from the trust. In such cases, the trust instrument is executed only by trustees.[68]

Additions of property

Where trust property is to be added to the trust, a separate declaration of trust **2.59** must be made with respect to this additional property, by way of an additional trust document, whether a deed or memorandum (a deed of addition). Further conditions may be specified in the trust instrument for the addition of trust property. These must be met before the trust will be validly constituted.[69]

Where there are underlying companies to be structured alongside the offshore **2.60** trust, additional considerations come to the fore. Again, domestic law requirements will obtain, in particular the need for the relevant corporate formalities to be followed for the holding in the company's name of assets previously owned by the settlor, the appropriate issue of shares, and the proper appointment of directors of the companies in question.

Capacity of the settlor

The settlor must have the mental capacity to understand the nature of the **2.61** transaction. The degree of understanding required will vary according to the nature and circumstances of the transaction, and may depend on the size of the gift into trust. Where the trust replaces a will, the settlor must also be able to understand the claims of all potential donees and the extent of the property being disposed of. Capacity is an important issue for offshore trusts, as it impacts on the ability of persons from civil law jurisdictions to establish valid trusts, a desirable investment objective for offshore centres. Thus, apart from merely codifying the usual requirements for capacity, such as mental soundness and the like, offshore jurisdictions have created special provisions which seek to ensure that persons from civil law jurisdictions have capacity.[70]

The aim of the disposition of property is to establish a valid settlement with **2.62** clear terms under which the settlor has made effective current and future gifts, retaining no entitlements of his or her own, but remaining the object of the trustee's dispositive powers. Alternatively, the settlor may retain valuable rights

---

[68] It is a settlement only if both trustee and settlor are parties to the instrument. If the settlor does not sign the trust document, proof that a trust has been declared by the settlor will need to be established from sources outside of the trust instrument.

[69] For example, the trust may be required to 'accept' the additional trust property as part of the trust fund. In the case of trust companies, where this may require a resolution, McKenzie warns that is advisable for the trustees to be parties to the deed of addition, which would be executed after the appropriate trustees' resolution has been entered into. See above, n 64.

[70] See chapter 22.

and entitlements (which will be exposed, at least during his or her lifetime, to claims of spouses and creditors).[71]

2.63 The offshore trust, like any trust, will fail if the trustee is a bare trustee or a mere nominee for the settlor. Consequently, the assets will continue to be treated as belonging to the settlor, thereby frustrating tax planning or asset protection objectives. Under English trusts law a settlor may reserve various powers over the trust fund without bringing the validity of the trust into question. These include powers of appointment, powers of revocation (including powers of appointment and removal of trustees and protectors), and powers to direct investments. However, to avoid the trust being deemed a bare trust or otherwise prejudicing the trust, the settlor may not, with few exceptions, retain the entire beneficial interest in the trust fund and the income.

Letter or memorandum of wishes

2.64 A letter or memorandum of wishes will often accompany the archetypal offshore trust. This is a document which ostensibly serves merely as a guide to the trustees but which does not seek to instruct the trustee, or undermine the trustee's discretion over the trust. For example, in Belize:

> **13** (1) [T]he settlor . . . may give to the trustee a letter of his wishes . . . with regard to the exercise of any functions conferred on the trustee by the terms of that trust.
>
> . . .
>
> (4) Where a letter of wishes or a memorandum of wishes is given to or prepared by the trustee of a trust then—
>
> > (a) the trustee may have regard to that letter or memorandum in exercising any functions conferred upon him by the terms of the trust; but
> > (b) the trustee shall not be bound to have regard to that letter or memorandum and shall not be accountable in any way for his failure to have regard to that letter or memorandum.[72]

2.65 It is apparent from the statutory language used that a trustee has no duty to follow the settlor's wishes as expressed in the letter of wishes. Even if the letter states that the trustee should do so, albeit an inadvisable option, this, of itself, should not be unlawful, or even inappropriate under the sham doctrine or other trust principles. Rather, it is the conduct of the trustee in following the instructions to a letter that will jeopardize the trust.[73]

---

[71] See Brownbill, above, n 64.

[72] The Belize Trusts Act 1992 (rev'd 2000), s 13.

[73] It will, however, provide fodder for inferring a sham, or sham intent. See chapter 8, 'The Offshore Trust as a Sham'.

In reality, the memorandum of wishes is an instrument used to influence, albeit **2.66** indirectly, the direction of the trustee and the trust. Care should be taken to avoid an interpretation that the memorandum of wishes is, in truth, evidence of the settlor's control over the trust, in which case the trust may be deemed a sham trust. The letter of wishes is not conceptualized as a binding trust document. However, because of overreaching with regard to the use of the letter of wishes, wherein it is used effectively to instruct trustees, in recent times it has been judicially scrutinized and treated as a trust document. This trend has been most apparent in sham allegations and with regard to attempts to gain information about the trust.[74]

It is usually the settlor who will issue a letter of wishes to the trustee. However, **2.67** legislation may also provide for the beneficiaries to issue such a document.[75]

---

[74] See chapters 7 and 8 respectively.
[75] See, eg, s 13(2) of the Belize Trusts Act 1992 (rev'd 2000).

3

SPECIAL TRUST VEHICLES

A. Asset Protection Trusts

3.01 While all offshore trusts, and indeed all trusts, seek in some sense to preserve the integrity of assets placed into trust, the term 'asset protection trust' has been coined to describe a particular type of trust found in offshore jurisdictions. Perhaps the true difference between such trusts and other trusts which may perform similar functions, is the enactment of specific legislative provisions which attempt to offer better protection for the trust assets than may be available onshore, or in other Common Law jurisdictions. This includes enhanced protection against creditor judgments and bankruptcy proceedings.[1]

3.02 The 'asset protection trust' is usually distinguished from other offshore trusts which seek to protect the assets from the reach of 'forced heirs' or mandatory heirs, or perform other functions unrelated to avoiding creditor judgments.[2] Although these latter trusts perform an asset protection function (which, incidentally, all trusts do), the philosophical rationale of these trusts is different to those which protect against creditors. Thus, some offshore jurisdictions have enacted special legislation against forced heirs but have declined to enact

---

[1] Even in some other offshore jurisdictions, as not all offshore jurisdictions have specific asset protection legislation against creditors. Note, eg, the BVI. Those that do, depend not only on special provisions against creditors, but also seek to preclude foreign laws which assist creditors. See chapter 9. In addition, foreign creditor judgments will be specifically excluded. See chapter 24.

[2] Trusts which exist primarily to protect against mandatory heirs and utilize specific legislative provisions to do so, are discussed separately in chapter 22.

provisions which aim, specifically, to protect against creditors.[3] Despite this distinction, which is often made by offshore jurisdictions themselves, both types of offshore trusts, in the sense that they attempt to protect the trust and its assets from identifiable persons or events, may be labelled, broadly, 'asset protection trusts'. Nonetheless, where the trust is established specifically to protect against judgment creditors, it is more adequately described by the term 'creditor protection trust'.

3.03 The offshore asset protection trust aims to shelter offshore assets from any threatening source which might procure financial loss. The focus is on preventing onshore creditors and others wishing to obtain the assets from reaching them, by utilizing the dual nature of the trust. Since the person who initiates the trust, the 'settlor,' (or 'grantor' in the USA), can no longer be viewed as having legal ownership of the assets, a challenge to the settlor will not easily reach the assets he or she has settled in the trust. Recall that, in theory, once a trust is validly founded, its assets, in as far as attempts to reach them are concerned, are treated as if they have been given away completely. The offshore legal environment of confidentiality which surrounds the offshore trust enhances this protection.

3.04 The fear of expropriation of assets, usually for political reasons, has historically been a popular rationale for placing assets offshore, in the form of a trust. The contemporary offshore asset protection trust, however, is more popularly used by wealthy professionals[4] seeking a reprieve from expensive tort actions, and to provide cover for inadequate insurance for such actions. It may also be used to 'hide' assets from present or ex-spouses and children who may otherwise be entitled to them. In recent years, such trusts have been increasingly marketed. As one enthusiastic US estate planning practitioner commented:

> As our national litigation epidemic continues to spread . . . people are becoming increasingly concerned about the loss of assets to satisfy claims of unknown future creditors. The asset protection trust is a tool designed . . . to respond to this growing problem.[5]

During the recession of the late 1980s, offshore trusts were also used to prevent assets from depletion in order to protect against over-generous personal guarantees to financial lenders. Fears of exchange rate fluctuations have provided another impetus for the offshore asset protection trust.

3.05 As the function of protecting assets is variable, the legal issues which arise are diverse. The answers to the difficult legal questions posed could be quite different depending on the particular situation. For example, where the offshore trust is

---

[3] Above, n 1.
[4] Mainly from the USA.
[5] R Amari, 'Asset Protection Trusts—Nuclear Bomb Shelter' [1992] Flor BJ 1.

set up to protect assets from expropriation by hostile governments, they would vary from those in a situation where a medical practitioner sets up such a trust to avoid large future payments to potential creditors arising from malpractice suits. Thus, the issue of the legitimacy of the offshore trust is different depending on its aims and purposes.

It is not merely the capacity of the offshore trust for 'jurisdiction hopping' or **3.06** generally frustrating creditors' claims which is the true source of its effectiveness. Rather, it is the juxtaposition of two, often fundamentally opposed systems of trust law, the aim being to bring offshore trusts squarely under the jurisdiction of an innovative and efficient body of hybrid offshore trust law. This is achieved by avoiding adverse judgments and legislation which use the notions of *domicile* and residence as prerequisites for jurisdiction and which are hostile to offshore purposes. This flows logically from the appointment of a trustee who is legally neither a resident nor domiciled in the onshore jurisdiction from which the settlor wishes protection. Such offshore law acts as a foil or legal bar to claims emanating onshore.

The discretionary nature of the typical offshore trust further enhances the pro- **3.07** tection offered under the trust. It does this by helping to insulate the beneficiaries' interests from attachment orders issued by onshore courts for the benefit of creditors and other trust challengers. Since the beneficiaries have no right to the assets, their interests may be attached only where direct distributions are made.[6] The exception in this scenario would be a beneficiary who is also the settlor. In that case, clawback provisions under bankruptcy law or legal rules treating the property as still belonging to the settlor, such as where the transfer is deemed to be fraudulent or a sham, could apply. Modern onshore tax laws hostile to the tax function of offshore trusts, also challenge the inherent logic of the trust, that beneficiaries own trust assets only when distributed to them.[7]

B. The Emergence of the Purpose Trust

The purpose trust—a response to the rule against non-identifiable beneficiaries

One of the most revolutionary innovations of offshore law is the purpose trust. **3.08** This type of trust is a statutory response to the Common Law rule that a trust

---

[6] Where there is a danger of attachment, a trustee would, obviously, not make a distribution except where he or she desires to pay the beneficiaries' debts.

[7] Discussed in chapter 14, 'Overview of Statutory Tax Countermeasures Against Offshore Trusts'. See, eg, s 88 of the Taxation of Chargeable Gains Tax Act 1992 of the UK.

must have identifiable beneficiaries to be considered a valid trust. The Common Law permits only very narrow exceptions to this general rule, such as an exception for charitable trusts. In contrast, purpose trusts permit the creation of trusts for wide and varied purposes, even those unconnected with charity. In the purpose trust, therefore, the trustee will hold the trust property conveyed into the trust for the specified purposes instead of for beneficiaries. Like the traditional trust, the trustee incurs fiduciary obligations as a result of the trust, but these are toward the administration of the trust property, in fulfilment of the stated purpose of the trust. The offshore purpose trust is thus a significant deviation from the Common Law position.

3.09   What, therefore, is the modern rationale and justification for the rule requiring identifiable beneficiaries? This is a question which is being raised under offshore law, albeit implicitly. Indeed, offshore law may be seen to have provided some legitimate answers to this compelling question. The rationale of the Common Law rule against trusts without identifiable beneficiaries can be traced to a fundamental assumption about the nature of a trust, that it is a set of obligations which are enforceable. This is viewed as being achievable only if there are specific and ascertainable persons who can enforce the obligations owed to them under the trust, against the trustee. The enforceability of these obligations is viewed within the context of specific performance, and the Common Law trust must be able to compel the trustee to perform those obligations in favour of identifiable beneficiaries.[8]

3.10   Thus, these ascertainable persons serve as the object of the court's power to enforce the trust, or to decree specific performance in relation to the trustees. The beneficial interest held by the trustees must be held by a person or persons within the life of the trust—the period of perpetuity—and the trust must exist for a specific purpose. A trust set up merely for public or business purposes, for example, would be considered too vague.

Arguments in favour of purpose trusts

3.11   The Common Law rules against the validity of trusts which have no identifiable beneficiaries, but which have instead identifiable purposes for which the trustee must act, have long been viewed as frustrating the broader commercial objectives of trusts. Further, the exception for trusts which are established for charitable purposes in the absence of identifiable beneficiaries has been construed narrowly and would render void many trusts which are of benefit to the public at large. Similarly, exceptions made to the rule in favour of certain

---

[8] See the landmark case of *Morice v Bishop of Durham* (1804) 9 Ves 399.

non-charitable purpose trusts may be viewed as erratic and inconsistent, lacking any clear direction in legal policy.[9]

The exception for charities is itself evidence that the rule no longer means that personal accountability alone is its rationale, or is even necessary. General accountability standards can be achieved in other ways, albeit pointing to a larger role for the court.   **3.12**

It is arguable that the so-called exceptions to the rule requiring identifiable beneficiaries are not exceptions at all, but merely attempts to strain the concept of identifiable beneficiaries within the context of the rule.   **3.13**

Another argument may be raised that the rule which apparently speaks against the absence of identifiable beneficiaries is more accurately concerned with the uncertainty of subject matter. Certainly, trusts for purposes which have been upheld, such as for animals, do not fall squarely under the rule. Animals surely cannot be viewed as the kind of identifiable beneficiaries the courts have in mind!   **3.14**

While the rule requiring identifiable beneficiaries is of ancient vintage and established pedigree, it seems oddly out of sync with more modern commercial law. For example, limited liability companies, anonymity in company affairs, impersonal commercial relationships, and even less personal liabilities, such as third party liabilities, are all common features of the contemporary commercial context. The trust itself has become less personal, with the advent of unit trusts, pension trusts, and a general movement away from domestic, family-type trusts. All of these, perhaps, point to the need for a change of the rule against non-identifiable beneficiaries. In addition, Article 2 of the Convention on the Law Applicable to Trusts and on their Recognition[10] acknowledges purpose trusts as valid trusts.[11] Indeed, the trend appears to be going in the direction of purpose trusts and well-respected traditional trust jurists seem to approve of, or at least accept, them, perhaps recognizing their efficacy in commercial environments. Waters, for example, suggests that purpose trusts will be accepted in Canada and that the beneficiary principle is losing ground in the US.[12] Indeed, two Law Reform Commissions recommended the adoption of non-charitable purpose   **3.15**

---

[9] See below, paras 3.22–3.27.
[10] Hereinafter, 'The Hague Convention on the Recognition of Trusts', The Hague, 1 July 1985; UKTS 14 (1992); Cm 1823; 23 ILM 1388.
[11] Article 2 speaks of trusts 'for a specified purpose'.
[12] D Waters, 'Protectors and Enforcers: Drafting the Trust Instrument' Vol 8(4) 2000 JInTCP 237, 259. Waters also suggests that the purpose trust would be upheld because a Canadian court will give effect to an offshore choice of law as the proper law. Several provinces in Canada have also ratified the Hague Convention on the Recognition of Trusts.

trusts in Canada. Draft model legislation was also prepared for consideration.[13] Hayton, too, opines that such trusts should be recognized.[14]

3.16 Notably, while the purpose trust was initially seen as a radical intervention into trust law, there is evidence that it is influencing traditional trust law regimes, including no less a regime than that of the UK. There are current proposals in the UK for a more liberal approach to what constitutes a charity, an acknowledgement of the restrictiveness of the rule on identifiable beneficiaries.[15]

Administrative unworkability and lack of enforceability

3.17 As we have seen, the rule against non-charitable purpose trusts rests on two interrelated pillars. On the one hand, the fact that there are no identifiable beneficiaries; and on the otherhand, the lack of enforceability because of the absence of such beneficiaries. Nonetheless, it is the lack of enforceability that appears to be the more pressing concern.

3.18 An absence of identifiable beneficiaries may further raise the related principle of a lack of certainty. However, in a broad sense, even this difficulty may be subsumed under the heading of enforceability. Yet the question of enforceability is not one tied to some substantive tenet of equity. Rather, it is a means to an end, to achieve aims which the settlor set out in the trust document. It is suggested, therefore, that the objections raised against purpose trusts are grounded essentially in administrative unworkability. If the legal regime were to find a rational means of solving the enforceability question, the fundamental objections to non-charitable purpose trusts would be removed. This is at the heart of purpose trust legislation in offshore jurisdictions.

3.19 Why, then, has the purpose trust not found life in onshore jurisdictions thus far, if there is no fundamental objection to a trust which exists solely for a purpose? The answer may well have to do with expediency, rather than judicial or legislative hesitancy or grounds of principle. A system which relies on an external, impartial quasi-judicial officer to enforce non-charitable purpose trusts is an ambitious, and perhaps costly, one. In contrast, in offshore jurisdictions, policy rationales propel trust law in a different direction toward commercial viability. The creation of such a system, with the administrative responsibilities and costs which it entails, is thought to be outweighed by the financial advantages brought by increased trust business. Thus, there is a functional response to what

---

[13] *Manitoba Law Reform Commission, Non-Charitable Purpose Trusts*, September 1992, Report No 77 and *Law Reform Commission of British Columbia, Non-Charitable Purpose Trusts*, November 1992, LRC 128, cited in Waters, ibid.

[14] D Hayton (2001) 117 LQR 96.

[15] See the Cabinet Office Report, *Private Action, Public Benefit*, www.cabinet-office.gov.uk/innovation/2002/charity/inded.shtml.

is, in reality, a practical problem, the administrative difficulty in enforcing trusts.

Common Law position recognizing purpose trusts

It has been suggested that the true position under the English Common Law, in contrast to contemporary 'conventional wisdom', is a recognition of the validity of the non-charitable purpose trust.[16] The argument explains away latter-day judicial antagonism towards such trusts by an assertion that the offending judges failed to appreciate or apply the law correctly. This is a contentious thesis which relies on ancient cases for support.

3.20

While the English Common Law is sprinkled with examples of the courts recognizing trusts which could be described as non-charitable trusts,[17] the issue is not clear-cut. In addition, the later cases have swung very much against such trusts, and these later cases must be viewed as proclaiming the more authoritative position under the Common Law. What may be gleaned from the evidence of the early cases, and even a few more contemporary cases, however, is that the English Common Law cannot be said to be inherently opposed, as a matter of policy, to trusts which have been established primarily for non-charitable purposes. Yet it is certainly true that the viability of such trusts, for a variety of reasons, many of them pragmatic rather than philosophical, is problematic.

3.21

Exceptions for non-charitable trusts

Examples of non-charitable trusts which have been declared valid by English courts include trusts for the upkeep of animals,[18] the maintenance of graves,[19] memorial services for the deceased[20] and, in certain situations, to confer benefits on unincorporated associations.[21]

3.22

In these cases, the rule on perpetuities has been maintained and, in some instances, judges have opined that the purpose had something of a charitable quality, being for the public good. So, for example, the upkeep of graves in a churchyard has a public element. In other cases, such as those involving trusts for unincorporated associations, it could be argued that the rule on identifiable beneficiaries was not infringed. Rather, the class of beneficiaries was extended. There is a suggestion, too, that the true rationale is that the trusts in question

3.23

---

[16] P Baxendale-Walker, *Purpose Trusts for Commercial and Private Use* (Butterworths Tolley, London, 1999).
[17] See, eg, paras 3.22–3.27.
[18] *Re Dean* (1889) 41 Ch D 552.
[19] *Re Eighmie* [1935] Ch 524.
[20] *Re Hetherington* [1990] Ch 1.
[21] *Neville Estates Ltd v Madden* [1962] Ch 832.

were not invalid because of uncertainty, since their objects could be identified, albeit with greater difficulty.

3.24   The existence of alternative rationales for the recognition of such non-charitable purpose trusts by the courts, makes it difficult to determine whether the objection of English law is one which goes to the heart of purpose trusts in general, or whether it is because purpose trusts violate some other fundamental principle, such as the rule on perpetuities or uncertainty.

3.25   In *Re Denley*,[22] which concerned a trust to maintain land as a sportsground for employees, the view was expressed by Geff J that the difficulty with previous courts' objections to non-charitable purpose trusts was not so much because of the 'purpose or object *per se*', but because of purposes or objects which were 'abstract or impersonal',[23] so that the rule on beneficiaries had to be limited to situations where the objects and purposes of the trust were concrete and personal. Trusts for purposes could, therefore, stand where their purposes were for beneficiaries, either directly or indirectly. This was a broad interpretation of the beneficiaries rule. To what extent can such an interpretation be stretched? How remote must be the eventual beneficiary to the purpose? We could argue that every purpose is, ultimately, for the benefit of some person. Once we begin to shift the boundaries containing the identifiable beneficiaries principle, the entire structure weakens. That being the case, the beneficiary rule cannot logically stand as a bar against purpose trusts and the real reservations must be in relation to enforceability or uncertainty.

3.26   It is apparent that the non-charitable purpose trusts which have been upheld by the courts are quite different in nature to the modern-day commercial purpose trusts seeking to be recognized in offshore jurisdictions. Nonetheless, the trust, in general, has evolved from being an essentially domestic concern to being an efficient business vehicle and this, of itself, is no reason to invalidate purpose trusts. In fact, it provides a reason for the law to keep abreast with such developments.

3.27   The issue of the validity of non-charitable purpose trusts is still, therefore, quite uncertain and they cannot be said to be outlawed as a matter of policy. Offshore jurisdictions have sought to capitalize on this irresolution and ambivalence within the Common Law, attempting to give direction to some of the difficult areas involving non-charitable purpose trusts, with a view to elevating trust vehicles as viable commercial entities.

---

[22] [1969] 1 Ch 373.
[23] ibid, 380.

Focus of offshore purpose trusts

Offshore legislation focuses on two main aspects of purpose trusts. On the one **3.28** hand, it prioritizes purposes which are certain and precise, so as to avoid questions of uncertainty of objects. Under this heading, we may place resolutions to the problem of perpetuity. Undoubtedly, purposes are as capable of being identified as precise and certain as are beneficiaries. The other arm of the legislation gives life to mechanisms which can serve to counter issues of enforceability raised in relation to such purpose trusts. A correlative concern is that such trusts are managed and regulated efficiently within the legal system, so that the aspect of enforceability is adequately maintained. At the same time, many legislatures have sought to expand the restrictive law relating to the recognition of charitable trusts.

The statutory regime established for purpose trusts is, by and large, untested. **3.29** However, the fact that the Hague Convention on the Recognition of Trusts recognizes purpose trusts, is an important indicator of the credibility of such trusts in contemporary contexts. Further, the increasing acceptance of purpose trusts in onshore common law jurisdictions suggests that offshore purpose trusts are likely to be accepted as well.[24]

C. Description of Key Provisions on Offshore Purpose Trusts

Express recognition of non-charitable purpose trusts

The majority of offshore legislatures have enacted provisions which expressly **3.30** recognize and give validity to non-charitable purpose trusts (called purpose trusts), thus seeking to avoid prejudicial and ambivalent Common Law rules relating to such trusts.

In Bermuda, for example, purpose trusts are given validity under s 12 of the **3.31** Trusts (Special Provisions) Amendment Act 1998,[25] where their purposes are

---

[24] See above, paras 3.15–3.16.

[25] See also s 12 of the International Trusts (Amendment) Act 1999 of the Cook Islands; s 4 of the Labuan offshore trusts Act 1996; and the International Trusts Law 1992 of Cyprus, which has similar provisions to the Cook Islands. In Jersey, under Article 19A of the Trusts (Amendment) (Jersey) Law 1996, non-charitable purpose trusts are valid if an enforcer is appointed and, under s 10, similar to other jurisdictions, if their purposes are certain, moral, and not against public policy. For other similar legislation, see the International Trusts Act 1995 of Barbados; s 21 of the International Trusts Act 2002 of Saint Lucia; the International Trusts Act 1996 of Saint Vincent; and the International Trusts Act 1996 of Grenada. An asset protection purpose is common, and a common route for this will be to structure the purpose trust to hold the shares of a private trust company.

lawful, sufficiently certain to allow the trust to be carried out[26] and not contrary to public policy.[27]

3.32 The provisions of the Cayman legislation, the Special Trusts (Alternative Regime) Law 1997 ('STAR'), now incorporated into the Trusts Law (2001 Revision), are more far-reaching than other purpose trust legislation. STAR legislation is not confined to purpose trusts and charitable trusts but caters to trusts for beneficiaries or persons as well. The regime caters exclusively to 'special trusts' as defined by the STAR Act under s 2(1). This merely means trusts subject to STAR which are created under a written instrument and contain an express declaration that STAR is to be applied. Where the declaration is absent and the power or trust is created by written instrument in exercise of a special power within the meaning of STAR, subject to a contrary intention, STAR will be deemed to apply.[28]

3.33 The expression 'trust' in the Act includes 'a trust of a power', both administrative and dispositive power, and a 'trust of property'. This logically means that STAR applies to all fiduciaries. As noted, both persons or purposes may be objects of a special trust, and may be non-charitable provided that they are lawful and not contrary to public policy.[29]

3.34 Section 15 of the Belize Trusts Act 1992,[30] whilst more detailed than its Bermudan counterpart, is to similar effect. Purpose trusts are valid where:

(1) they are specific, reasonable, and capable of fulfilment;

(2) they are not immoral, unlawful, or contrary to public policy;

(3) the terms of the trust are not so uncertain that its performance is rendered impossible; and

(4) the terms of the trust provide for the appointment of a protector who is capable of enforcing the trust and for the appointment of a successor to any protector.

3.35 In contrast to the above provisions, s 10 of the STAR regime of the Cayman Islands provides that a special trust is not void because of uncertainty as to its objects or mode of execution. This is because the terms of the special trust may

---

[26] For example, where a trust is 'for good works', as in *Re How* [1930] 1 Ch 66, this may be too uncertain.

[27] The trust may also be varied by application to the Supreme Court by an appointed person, settlor, or trustee, under s 12 of the Act. Purpose trusts created before the amended Act under the 1989 version of the statute are deemed to satisfy the criteria laid down in the amended s 12 and are, therefore, valid.

[28] Section 3(2).

[29] Section 6(3).

[30] As revised 2000.

give the relevant person, such as the trustee or enforcer, a wide power to resolve any uncertainty as to objects or mode of execution. Presumably, such a power does not exclude the inherent supervisory jurisdiction of the court to question the exercise of the power in all circumstances, although it is likely that the court will view the enforcer's jurisdiction as a mandatory first step. The Act speaks directly to the court's intervention where the power has not been resolved pursuant to the terms of the trust, but this is only one example of an inquiry into the exercise of a power or purported power.

In addition, the court may intervene to resolve an uncertainty as to objects where the uncertainty has not been resolved by the appropriate person. Section 10(4) lays down the route to resolving that uncertainty as: **3.36**

(1) reforming the trust;
(2) settling a plan for the administration of the trust; and
(3) in any other way that the court deems appropriate.

Where the court is unable to resolve uncertainty surrounding the objects of the trust, even by looking at the general intent of the trust and admissible evidence as a matter of probability, the court may declare the trust void.[31] **3.37**

In the Isle of Man, the criteria established for the creation of a purpose trust under the Purpose Trusts Act 1996 are that the purposes be certain, reasonable, and possible, and not be unlawful, contrary to public policy, or immoral.[32] The purpose is to be established by a will capable of probate in the island, or by deed. **3.38**

In a Bahamas case, *Re Krishna Books Publishing Trust Sutton v Fedorowsky*,[33] the court, in determining the validity of a trust, applied a liberal approach to the requirement that a purpose trust be certain. According to the court, clauses establishing the trust should be construed with a presumption in favour of the validity of a clause. The clause in question created a trust for a broad, as opposed to an identifiable, class of beneficiaries, or a charitable purpose trust, and was held to be valid under the Trustee Act 1998 of The Bahamas. **3.39**

---

[31] Section 10(4), STAR Law. The court may also reform the trust *cy-près* under s 11 where its execution becomes impossible, impracticable, unlawful, contrary to public policy, or obsolete. See also s 21 of the International Trusts Act of Saint Lucia 2002.

[32] Section 1. The purpose trust is defined under s 9 of the said Act as one with a purpose that is (a) for the benefit of particular persons whether or not immediately ascertainable; or (b) for the benefit of some aggregate of persons ascertained by reference to some personal relationship; or (c) for charitable purposes. See also s 21 of the International Trusts Act 2002 of Saint Lucia, where the purpose trust may be established for a purpose which is specific, reasonable, capable of fulfilment, and not unlawful or contrary to public policy.

[33] (2002) 4 ITELR 665 (Sup Ct, The Bahamas).

Common purposes of offshore purpose trusts

3.40 Purpose trusts may be employed for a wide variety of purposes. Some common uses are:

(1) to take the place of a charitable trust established under Common Law (often unpredictable) rules;

(2) to own a private trust company which acts as the trustee of a trust or groups of trusts, usually for family purposes;

(3) to facilitate a corporation of underlying offshore companies to enable specific types of transactions (such as balance-sheet financing through an orphan company);

(4) to own special purpose vehicles;

(5) to hold assets in succession planning arrangements structured for family businesses;

(6) to facilitate the development of special companies or businesses;

(7) to be able to frustrate the rule in *Saunders v Vautier*;[34]

(8) to enable deferred pension and emolument plans and other approved employee schemes.[35]

3.41 The purpose trust will often form part of a complex offshore arrangement which facilitates tax planning, asset protection, or other business purposes aimed at commercial savings. The use of the purpose trust for private trust company arrangements, for example, will usually be structured so that no profit is accumulated by the trust. The orphan special purpose vehicle, which utilizes the purpose trust arrangement, facilitates the settlor or other commercial parties who do not wish to be identified with the trust. Purposes for the holding of land are generally excluded in statutory purpose trusts.[36]

Addressing hybrid features of purpose trusts

Use of Common Law interpretation

3.42 As we have noted, offshore trusts are essentially hybrid trusts which borrow from the Common Law. Offshore purpose trusts are no exception. Thus, it seems likely that the interpretation of familiar terms used to establish such trusts under offshore legislation will be similar to Common Law statutory construction.

---

[34] (1842) 4 Beav 115, 49 ER 282, which allows beneficiaries to come together to defeat a trust.

[35] One example is the Rabbi trust, a US approved entity which permits deferred compensation in an employee pension scheme, thereby resulting in tax savings. Revenue Procedure 92–64, IRB 1992–33, 11 (July 28, 1992) Code Secs, 83, 451, 671 and 677.

[36] See, eg, s 12D of the Trusts (Special Provisions) Amendment Act 1998 of Bermuda; s 16 of the STAR legislation of the Cayman Islands; s 5 of the Purpose Trusts Act 1996 of the Isle of Man.

Questions such as whether the purpose trust is uncertain, against public policy,[37] or immoral, for example, stand to be resolved by examining Common Law interpretations unless expressly excluded. Because of policy differences between onshore and offshore jurisdictions, however, it may be expected that areas of doubt will be resolved in favour of the validity of the purpose trust.

The various laws require that purpose trusts be evidenced in writing.[38]   **3.43**

Proper law of purpose trusts

The creation and validation of the non-charitable trust in offshore jurisdictions   **3.44**
are given life by the characteristic, but perhaps incestuous, proper law provisions found under offshore legislation, which make the offshore law the proper law of the trust.[39] Thus, the question of the purpose trust is left exclusively to the offshore jurisdiction whose laws, in turn, proclaim its validity.

Creation of the institution of the enforcer

An institution, labelled an enforcer, which has as its main function the enforce-   **3.45**
ment of the non-charitable purpose trust, is created in offshore jurisdictions which validate such trusts. The enforcer may be a protector,[40] or a special and separate office created to enforce the trust. In addition, the trust may rely on a separate person, called a 'designated person' (usually a trustee), to assist in the enforcer's functions. A public officer, often the Attorney General, is usually reserved as a 'back up' for the enforcement of the trust, though in some jurisdictions his role may be more proactive.

The enforcer may be viewed as a merger between the beneficiary and the trustee.   **3.46**
In some instances, he or she enforces the trust in similar manner to a trustee, ensuring that the intention of the settlor as outlined in the purpose established is carried out, and is protected by indemnities in so doing. In other circumstances, the enforcer is more like a beneficiary, entitled to rights similar to those of beneficiaries, such as information, and rights against defaulting trustees and third parties where breaches of trust occur.[41]

In Bermuda, the creation of the enforcer is dependent upon an order from the   **3.47**
Supreme Court upon application to it by the settlor, trustee, a person appointed

---

[37] The infamous case of *Re Pinion* [1965] Ch 85, which struck down a trust to establish schools for prostitutes, would apply, for example.

[38] See, eg, s 12A(3) of the Trusts (Special Provisions) Amendment Act 1998 of Bermuda.

[39] See chapter 20 for a discussion of the proper law of the trust.

[40] See chapter 4, 'The Role and Powers of the Offshore Protector', for a description and analysis of the office of the protector in offshore jurisdictions.

[41] See, eg, the enforcer function under s 8 of the Special Trusts (Alternative Regime) Law 1997 of the Cayman Islands.

as enforcer under the trust, or any other person whom the court deems to have sufficient interest in the enforcement of the trust.[42] This means that one of the above must make application to the court for enforcement, for the purpose trust to be valid at all. However, no particular person is burdened exclusively with the duty, so it may not be possible to impose sanctions. Certainly, where a person is appointed as enforcer in the trust instrument, that person has the primary duty to apply. It is presumed that, in practice, one of the list of persons named will make such application.

3.48   Where no application is made to the court by any of the persons listed as having authority to apply for enforcement, the Attorney General has authority to apply to the Supreme Court for enforcement of the trust. This places an administrative burden on the state to ascertain which trusts are deficient in terms of lacking an applicant enforcer.

3.49   In Belize, under s 15 of the Trusts Act 1992, as revised in 2000, the protector of the trust is given power to enforce the trust. This is also the situation in Grenada, Saint Vincent, and Barbados.[43] A protector and his or her successor must be appointed to enforce the trust. However, the Attorney General is given a residual power to appoint a protector where the appointed protector is not able or willing to act, or where no protector has been appointed. Under s 16 of the Trusts Act, the protector in Belize[44] may be either the settlor or a trustee. It does not appear that the Attorney General can intervene otherwise to ensure the enforcement of the trust. Where the enforcer is also the trustee, he or she acts not in his or she capacity as trustee, but only as enforcer. He or she therefore owes a 'fiduciary duty' to the specified purpose of the trust.[45] This should be interpreted broadly. A similar provision is absent from the Bermuda legislation, so that the requisite standard of care is uncertain.[46]

3.50   In the Cayman Islands, the STAR legislation reserves the enforcement of the trust exclusively to a specially appointed enforcer. The appointment must be under the terms of the trust, or by order of the court.[47] Since the right of

---

[42] Section 12A of the Trusts (Special Provisions) Amendment Act 1998 of Bermuda.

[43] International Trusts Act 1996, International Trusts Act 1996, s 13 and International Trusts Act 1995, respectively.

[44] See also s 13 of the Saint Vincent International Trusts Act 1996.

[45] Section 16(5). The Act does not define the requisite interest. Since there are no beneficiaries, this might mean the settlor or persons who are affected indirectly by the purpose.

[46] In Jersey, under s 10 of the Trusts (Amendment) (Jersey) Law 1996, the trust instrument must provide for an enforcer and for his replacement. The trustee cannot be the enforcer.

[47] Section 7 of the STAR Law. Recall that STAR trusts may be established for purposes or beneficiaries, or both (see para 3.33). The special enforcer applies even where the STAR trust has beneficiaries, thereby taking away the right of the beneficiaries to enforce the trust except if the right is expressly conferred upon them by the trust instrument.

beneficiaries to enforce the trust is expressly taken away, the STAR legislation deliberately sets out to override the Common Law presumptions that beneficiaries must be able to enforce the trust for there to be a trust at all. However, the enforcement of the trust by the enforcer may be merely a right and not a duty, as the Law allows standing to enforce the trust as either a right or a duty under s 8(1). The duties relating to enforcement are buttressed by strict penalties and sanctions.

Where an enforcer has a duty to enforce the trust and fails to do so, the court may, on the application of a trustee or other specified enforcer, appoint a substitute enforcer.[48] Where the trust instrument contemplates the appointment of an enforcer but none has been appointed because of impossibility, or because it is difficult to do so without the court's assistance, the court may also intervene upon application by the trustee.[49] Further, where there is no enforcer capable of enforcing the trust due to incapacity or similar defect, the trust has a duty to apply to the court for the appointment of an alternative enforcer. Failure to do so may result in summary conviction and a fine.[50]   **3.51**

There is a fiduciary duty placed upon the Cayman Island enforcer to act reasonably and responsibly in his or her enforcement of the trust.[51] Trustees, co-enforcers authorized to do so under the trust instrument, may sue enforcers who are alleged to fail in this duty.[52] The standard expected of an enforcer is that of a reasonable and responsible enforcer and not an ordinary person.   **3.52**

The enforcement provisions under the STAR legislation are bolstered by special trustee provisions under s 12 to which criminal sanctions apply where there are breaches. Thus, the trustee of a STAR trust must be a trust corporation[53] and is required to keep documentary records of: **3.53**

(1) the terms of the trust;
(2) the identity of the trustee and the enforcers;
(3) settlements of the trust property and the property subject to the special trust at the end of each accounting year;
(4) the identity of the settlor; and
(5) the distributions and applications of the trust property.

---

[48] Section 7.
[49] ibid. Under the BVI Act, the Trustee Ordinance 1990, provision is made for application to the court for directions where there is no designated person.
[50] ibid. A enforcer has capacity to enforce the trust where he or she is of full age and sound mind.
[51] Section 8, STAR Law.
[52] ibid.
[53] That is, a body corporate licensed to conduct business in the Cayman Islands under the Banks and Trust Companies Law 1995.

3.54 It appears that the enforcer may have rights to indemnities which are similar to those given to trustees in the performance of their legitimate trust functions. Such protection is expressly granted under s 8 of the STAR legislation of the Cayman Islands.

3.55 In the Isle of Man, the concept of the 'designated person' is employed in the enforcement of the trust. Under the Purpose Trusts Act 1996, the purpose trust must have at least two trustees, one of whom must be the 'designated person' expected to assist in supervising the enforcer's function. The designated person must be:

(1) an advocate;
(2) a legal practitioner registered in the Isle of Man;
(3) a person qualified under s 14(1) of the Companies Act 1982 (Isle of Man) for appointment as an auditor of a public company;
(4) a member of the Chartered Institute of Management Accounts;
(5) a member of the Institute of Chartered Secretaries and Administrators;
(6) a fellow or associate member of the Institute of Bankers; or
(7) a trust corporation in accordance with the Trustee Act of the Isle of Man.

Criminal sanctions apply for failure to perform the duties laid down under the Act.[54]

3.56 Designated persons are required to keep documents relating to the trust, including documents identifying the settlor, a summary of the purpose or purposes of the trust, the contact information for the enforcer, and documents establishing the financial status of the trust, including distributions made. Such documents are made available to the Attorney General for inspection.[55]

3.57 The actual enforcer must be appointed by the trust deed and is required to be independent of the trustees.[56] The trust instrument must also make provision for the replacement of the enforcer. Where the enforcer is unable or unwilling to act, or has ceased to be independent of the trustees, the trustee has a duty to give written notice of the unsuitability of the enforcer to the Attorney General or other government appointed authority, providing him with a copy of the trust instrument. The Attorney General may then apply to the High Court for a

---

[54] Purpose Trusts Act 1996, s 6. He or she is allowed the defence that he or she took all reasonable steps to comply with the statutory obligations. However, relying on the advice and information of another is not reasonable. Under s 8, directors are made liable for breaches of duty in addition to corporate trustees.

[55] ibid, s 2.

[56] ibid, s 1.

replacement enforcer.[57] The High Court of the Isle of Man is given a wide discretion to assist the enforcer generally in enforcing the trust, or in gaining access to trust documents and related information.[58]

In the Cook Islands, it is not mandatory for the trust instrument to appoint an **3.58** enforcer for the purpose trust, although a person so named has the authority to enforce the trust under s 12 of the International Trusts (Amendment) Act 1999. As in other jurisdictions, the court is given the power to replace enforcers where an enforcer is removed, resigns, is otherwise replaced, or is unfit or unwilling to perform the enforcement function, and if it is not possible to appoint a successor under the terms of the trust instrument. The court's discretion is invoked by an application by the trustees. The court may also make an order empowering the Attorney General to enforce the trust.[59] The arrangements created by statute to enforce the trust where the purpose trust fails or may fail, are similar to those made for cy-près trusts. They are found in several offshore jurisdictions.[60]

In *Re Krishna Books Publishing Trust Sutton v Fedorowsky,*[61] the Supreme Court **3.59** of The Bahamas had no difficulty in appointing new trustees to a purpose trust in a situation where the current trustees faced hostile litigation in a Californian court. The protector had earlier sought to remove the trustees in order to protect the trust, but faced procedural difficulties in doing so. This was an appropriate situation in which the court should intervene.

Rights to information in enforcing the trust

The enforcer of a purpose trust will often have rights to information about the **3.60** administration, terms, and related matters of the trust, similar to rights given to beneficiaries.[62] In Jersey, the right to information includes access to the accounts of the trust.[63] However, following *West Lazard Brothers & Company (Jersey) Ltd,*[64]

---

[57] ibid, s 3. Similarly, in Dominica, under the International Exempt Trusts Act 1997, and in Nevis, under the International Exempt Trusts Act 1994, it is the Minister who is given the power to act on behalf of the trust where the protector or enforcer fails to exercise his or her powers. In Saint Vincent, there is a special office called the Offshore Finance Inspector, which will perform this function.

[58] Purpose Trusts Act 1996, s 3.

[59] See also the International Trusts Law 1992 of Cyprus, which has similar provisions to the Cook Islands. However, there is no provision to allow the court to replace the enforcer.

[60] See, eg, in Saint Vincent, Barbados, Grenada, Saint Lucia, and the Cayman Islands.

[61] (2002) 4 ITELR 665 (Sup Ct, The Bahamas), *per* Hutton AJ.

[62] Section 9, STAR Law. But note the recent modifications concerning the rights of beneficiaries to information about the trust, discussed in chapter 7, 'Disclosure and Confidentiality Obligations' The right of enforcers to information may be expressly withheld under the trust instrument. See similar provisions under s 1 of the Purpose Trusts Act 1996 of the Isle of Man.

[63] Under Article 25 of the Trusts (Amendment) (Jersey) Law 1996.

[64] [1987–88] JLR 414.

provisions on such information rights should be construed broadly to include documents corresponding with the general administration of the trust, but excluding the trustees' reasons for the exercise of their discretion.

Modification of perpetuity and accumulation principles

3.61   In purpose trust legislation, the rules against perpetuities may be modified to complement the commercial objective of such trusts. In Belize, for example, under s 6 of the Trusts Act 1992, the application of the rules against perpetuities and accumulation to offshore trusts, including purpose trusts, is expressly excluded.[65] In the Isle of Man, the purpose trust may be created for a maximum period of eighty years. The trust instrument must also indicate the event which can terminate the trust and make provision for the disposition of the assets upon such termination.[66]

Extension of charitable trusts

3.62   Offshore legislation incorporates the purposes considered by English trusts law as legitimate charitable purposes,[67] but may significantly extend the categories allowed for such purposes. The scope of the various provisions is broad, extending to charitable purposes effected outside of the offshore jurisdictions.[68] The established categories are for the relief of poverty, the advancement of education and religion, and other purposes similarly beneficial to the community. More contentious are purposes for the preservation of the environment and human rights. The last two are also, however, typically included as legitimate in offshore legislation. For example, in Belize, s 14 of the Trusts Act 1992 outlines the purposes which are recognized as charitable. Generally, these purposes are to be for the benefit of the community, which is akin to the 'public benefit' limitation under the Common Law. They are:

(1)   the relief of poverty;
(2)   the advancement of education;
(3)   the advancement of religion;
(4)   the protection of the environment;

---

[65] See also s 12A of the Trusts (Special Provisions) Amendment Act 1998; the STAR Law of the Cayman Islands; s 6(1) of the International Trusts (Amendment) Act 1999 of the Cook Islands; s 7(2) of the Barbados International Trusts Act 1995; s 9(2) of the International Trusts Act 1996 of Grenada; s 84 of the Trustee Ordinance 1990 of the BVI, as amended 2003.

[66] Purpose Trusts Act 1996, s 1.

[67] See, eg, the categories of accepted charitable purposes as outlined in the authoritative decision of *Commissioners for Special Purposes of Income Tax v Pemsel* [1891] AC 531, 583.

[68] See, eg, s 14(3) of the Belize Trusts Act 1992 (rev'd 2000).

(5)   the advancement of human rights and fundamental freedoms; and

(6)   any other purposes which are beneficial to the community.[69]

In the Cook Islands, the list of charitable purposes deemed acceptable includes all purposes substantially for any of the above-named except (4).[70] The use of the word 'substantially' in the provision is a considerable deviation, as it divorces itself from the Common Law principle that a purpose must be exclusively charitable. **3.63**

The provision in the Cook Islands also appears significantly to relax the requirement that the charitable purpose must be entirely for the benefit of the public, or for a sufficient section of the public. This suggestion is derived from a reading of s 12, which provides: '. . . notwithstanding that the object or purpose may not be of a public nature or for the benefit of the public, but may be for the benefit of a section of the public or members of the public'. This may, however, be simply a question of degree, although the standard for sufficiency under the Common Law is hardly consistent.[71] However, there is no doubt that the provision envisions that the public benefits in some consequential way.[72] **3.64**

In the Cayman Islands, the STAR legislation provides for charitable trusts which are lawful and not contrary to public policy.[73] **3.65**

---

[69]   See also s 4 of the Labuan Offshore Trusts Act 1996 for a similar listing, except that the promotion of art and science are included with the category of religion. Generally the provisions in Labuan are very similar to those in Belize.

[70]   Under s 12 of the International Trusts (Amendment) Act 1999. See also the International Trusts Law 1992 of Cyprus, which has a similar provision to the Cook Islands under s 7(1) except that the word 'substantially' is substituted for 'main purpose'. There appears to be no conceptual difference between the two phrases. In Cyprus, s 7(3) defines a purpose trust as one 'with beneficiaries being particular natural or legal persons whether or not immediately ascertainable' and a trust which is not one 'with beneficiaries being an aggregate of particular natural or legal persons ascertainable by reference to some personal attribute or relationship'.

[71]   See *Inland Revenue Commissioners v Baddeley* [1955] AC 572.

[72]   Section 12(1).

[73]   Section 6(3).

4

THE ROLE AND POWERS OF THE OFFSHORE PROTECTOR

A. Introduction—Rise of the Institution of the Protector

Given that the offshore trust caters to persons who are based overseas, with a **4.01** professional trustee based in the offshore jurisdiction who is often unknown to the settlor, an intermediary known as the protector may be installed to oversee the trust. Increasingly, the institution of the protector is becoming a key player in the management of offshore trusts. Its rise and development can be seen as further evidence of the flexibility of the offshore trust as it seeks to meet the demands of international finance. Yet the existence of the protector does present some problems in interpreting and administering the trust, leading sometimes to increased litigation.

B. Description of the Protector

Nature of protector

The protector functions like a liaison officer between the trustees and the **4.02** beneficiaries, which may be especially important since the typical trustee in offshore transactions is a corporation. However, his or her role may go far beyond this simple function. The High Court of Justice of the Isle of Man, in the case of *Steele v Paz*,[1] helpfully explains the office and functions of the protector:

> In order to ensure that the [offshore] trust was subject to the Manx tax regime, it would normally be necessary for the trustees themselves to be resident within the Isle of Man. A disadvantage from the settlor's standpoint might be that he might have no personal knowledge of such trustees. Whilst he might, therefore, wish to exercise some degree of supervision over their activities, he could not safely do so without putting at risk the tax advantages that he might be seeking to achieve. If, however, he were to appoint a person in whom he might have greater personal confidence with power to scrutinise and veto proposed decisions of the trustee, he might be better placed to ensure that his wishes would be given proper consideration without jeopardising his fiscal objectives. Such a person would not be a trustee and would not have any trust property vested in him and need not be a resident of the Isle of Man. On the other hand, he would be independent of the settlor who could not, therefore, be said to have retained any control over the trust funds.

Of course, protectors are widely used also in offshore trusts, and even onshore trusts which have purposes other than tax avoidance.

4.03   The protector may have a more intimate relationship with the beneficiaries than the trustee. Typically, he or she is a close friend or relative of the settlor,[2] although more recently we have seen the rise of professional protectors. Where the protector is a family friend, an additional advantage may be gained from the fact that the protector can import his or her personal knowledge of the family's business affairs to the administration of the trust. This is particularly useful in a typical offshore scenario, where the trustee is a corporate trustee who has no knowledge of the family business and who may not wish to be entirely responsible for the day-to-day management of the family's affairs. In a trust where the main settled assets are the settlor's majority shareholding in the private family company, for example, it would be more common to have this type of protector.

4.04   Where the trustee or the settlor believes that the investment functions are complex, the use of a protector may fulfil another important role. It may help to buffer the effect of recent common law rules which make the duties of the trustee in relation to investment very wide.[3] It is unclear to what extent a trustee may avoid liabilities for violating such duties, even where exculpatory clauses are utilized. However, where the trustee instrument clearly leaves certain investment functions to the protector, the arrangement is more likely to be honoured.

---

[1] [1993–95] Manx LR 102, 108; digested in [2000] *Trusts and Trustees* 6.
[2] *Re Star 1&2 (Revised) Trusts Von Knieriem v Bermuda Trust Co Ltd and Grosvenor Trust Co Ltd* (Sup Ct, Bermuda) Nos 154 and 162 of 1994, decided 13 July, 1994; *Steele v Paz*, n 1 above; *Crocker–Citizens National Bank v Younger* 4 Cal 3d 202 481 2d 222 93 Cal Rptr 214 (1971). But the protector need not be a natural person.
[3] See, eg, *Bartlett v Barclays Bank Trust Co Ltd* [1980] 1 All ER 139, discussed in chapter 10, 'Duties of Trustees in Managing Offshore Trusts'.

The protector is not an institution unique to the offshore trust, although the **4.05** label of 'protector' emerged through the use of offshore trusts and became fashionable through them. The practice of giving power, both dispositive and administrative, to non-beneficiaries has been in existence for some time. As Smith J explained in *Rawson Trust Co Ltd v Perlman and Others*:[4] 'The term protector is not a term of art and is not known as such to our law. The functions and powers which the protectors were given in the . . . [trust] Deed are, however, very familiar.'[5] Today, the use of protectors in onshore trusts is also becoming popular.

Despite the existence of protectors or protector-like offices in onshore jurisdic- **4.06** tions, the office of the protector in the offshore jurisdiction may be distinguished from its onshore counterpart in that its nature and powers will often be broader. Further, offshore law may permit greater direction to be given to the protector by the settlor. These differences will usually arise as a result of specific legislative provisions pertaining to the office of the protector.[6] However, not all offshore jurisdictions have specific legislation defining the office and powers of protectors.[7] It should be underlined that the office of the protector need not be instituted through legislation. Indeed, the use of protectors is common in practice even in offshore jurisdictions without specific protector legislation.[8] Where such legislation is lacking, the traditional rules of equity apply.

Since the protector, unlike the trustee, is not a creature of equity, its existence **4.07** and powers come into being solely on the basis of the written trust instrument or legislation.

---

[4] (Sup Ct, The Bahamas) No 194 of 1989, decided 25 April 1990, *per* Smith J.

[5] ibid, 5.

[6] See, eg, the Trusts Ordinance 1994 (am'd 2000) of Anguilla, s 16; the Trustee Act 1998 of The Bahamas, s 81; the Trusts Act 1992 (rev'd 2000) of Belize, s 16; the International Trusts Act 1995 of Barbados; the Trustee Ordinance 1993, am'd 2003, of the British Virgin Islands, s 86; International Trusts Act 1994 of Nevis, s 9; International Trusts Act 1984 of the Cook Islands, s 20; Trusts Act of St Christopher and Nevis 1996; International Trusts Act 2002 of Saint Lucia, s 23; International Trusts Act 1996 of Saint Vincent, s 16; and International Exempt Trust Act 1997 of Dominica, s 9.

[7] See, eg, the Cayman Islands, Bermuda, Isle of Man, Cyprus, Jersey, Guernsey, and the Turks and Caicos Islands. In the last three jurisdictions, statute provides for a person who will consent to the trustee's decisions, but the role is not defined as a protector. This person is deemed not to be a trustee. See, eg, art 84 of the Trusts (Jersey) Law 1984; s 28 of the Guernsey Trusts Law 1989; and s 23(3) of the Trusts Ordinance 1990 of the Turks and Caicos Islands.

[8] Indeed, the Cayman Islands is considering the introduction of specific statutory provisions on the protector. Alternatively, legislation may simply give authority to any person who assists the trustee. In Jersey, art 20 of the Trusts (Jersey) Law 1984 says that the trust instrument 'may require the consent of some person other than the trustee in relation to the exercise of specific powers'.

Functions, powers, and duties of the protector

4.08   Protectors may have a wide variety of functions and duties. Some may be dispositive, concerning the distribution of the trust assets to the beneficiaries, while others may be administrative, for example relating to investment and other business concerns of the trustee. The distinction between the two types of functions and duties is not always clear, and perhaps not as important as first appears. The protector's powers may extend to those normally left to trustees, or may even include powers not usually given to trustees (such as changing the proper law of the trust). With regard to powers relating to the trustee, the protector's powers may be proactive, aimed at directing the functions of the trustee,[9] or they may merely be reactive, to affirm trustee actions or engage in consultation with the trustee.

4.09   Offshore legislation usually allows the trust instrument to add powers not delineated in the legislation. For example, s 23 of the International Trusts Act 2002 of Saint Lucia states that '[t]he terms of an international trust may provide for the appointment of a protector of the international trust'. The section thereafter provides that a protector shall have specific powers as listed in the section, unless the terms of the trust instrument provide otherwise.[10] It then goes on to list the specific powers. In the rare instance where no power to add is given, the powers of the protector should be confined to those listed.[11]

4.10   Typically, offshore legislation allows protectors to be instituted for any offshore trust, and not merely limited categories of offshore trusts such as purpose trusts.[12]

4.11   Common functions and duties of the protector include:

(1)   to police and supervise the administration of the trust by the trustee. For example, the trustee may be required to obtain consent from the protector before acting. The protector is normally consulted by the trustees about any requests from the beneficiaries for distribution, or concerning major changes to the trusts;

(2)   to act as an intermediary between the trustee and the beneficiaries;

---

[9] See, eg, the International Trusts Act 1984 (am'd) of the Cook Islands, which defines a protector as 'a person who is the holder of a power which, when invoked, is capable of directing a trustee in matters relating to the trust and in respect of which matters the trustee has a discretion . . .'.

[10] Section 23(2). See also s 16 of the Belize Trusts Act 1992 (rev'd 2000); s 23 of the International Trusts Act 2002 of Saint Lucia; s 16 of the International Trusts Act 1996 of Saint Vincent; and s 9 of the International Exempt Trust Act 1997 of Dominica.

[11] As is the case, eg, in Barbados, under s 26(2) of the International Trusts Act 1995.

[12] An exception is Grenada, which permits the office of the protector only for purpose trusts. See s 15 of the International Trusts Act 1996.

(3) to act as a financial adviser or consultant and provide business advice to the trustee;

(4) to protect the trust by having the power to change the *situs* of the trust if some adverse event necessitates it, or to change the proper law of the trust;

(5) to remove and appoint trustees and add or delete beneficiaries; and

(6) to consult with any professional advisers to the trust and trustee, such as, for example, attorneys, accountants, business and investment consultants. Indeed, the trust arrangement may require the protector's consent before the trustee can act on the advice of any of these professionals.[13]

Settlor control through the protector

A protector's most important function might be to give the settlor the opportunity to influence and control the trust, albeit indirectly. This might occur simply by enabling the settlor to communicate his or her wishes through the protector. In some instances, indirect control is achieved by allowing the trust to be affiliated to a company. Since the protector is responsible for decisions relating to that company, the protector may be entrusted with power to remove or appoint trustees. Indeed, the settlor may be a director or other officer of the company. This function, however, on its face, is not one acceptable to the trust arrangements under the sham doctrine and will not, or should not, be made explicit under the trust arrangement.[14]   **4.12**

In offshore trust arrangements, there is a fairly common practice that the settlor may sign a letter or memorandum of wishes, which is a non-binding document laying down guidelines for the trust. This memorandum may point to the desired functions of the protector. The danger here, however, is that the use of the memorandum may be viewed as an indication of the settlor's desire to retain control of the trust and thereby jeopardize the trust.[15] It further increases the likelihood of the memorandum being deemed a trust document, which must, for example, be disclosed.   **4.13**

Proper exercise of protector powers

Protectors are held to basic *ultra vires* principles in relation to the exercise of their powers. There are two main ways in which the exercise of the protector's   **4.14**

---

[13] See, eg, s 86(2)(a) of the Trustee Act 1993 (as am'd 2003), where the protector's powers include the following: '(a) determine the law of which jurisdiction shall be the proper law of the trust; (b) change the forum of administration of the trust; (c) remove trustees; (d) appoint new or additional trustees; (e) exclude any beneficiary as a beneficiary of the trust; (f) include any person as a beneficiary of the trust; and (g) without consent from specified actions of the trustees either conditionally or unconditionally.'

[14] See chapter 8, 'The Offshore Trust As a Sham'.

[15] See chapter 3, paras 2.64–2.67.

powers may be validly questioned but, ultimately, the law is interested merely in giving effect to the intention of the settlor. First, the protector must confine the given power to its lawful purpose and must ensure that he or she has actually been granted the power which is exercised. In effect, this rule merely contains the protector's exercise of the power within the ambit of the powers given to him or her.

4.15 Where the protector exercises a power outside of the purpose for which it was given, this may be regarded as a fraudulent use of the power, a 'fraud on the power'. The term 'fraudulent' here does not connote criminal intent or malicious purposes; it merely means an improper or unlawful usage of the power.

4.16 Secondly, the court may inquire into *how* the protector exercises the legitimate powers conferred by the trust instrument. This is perhaps a more complicated review, as it imports elements associated with the use of fiduciary power. However, as we will see below, it is not certain that the protector is to be viewed automatically as a fiduciary. As with any fiduciary, the standard of care expected of a protector deemed to be a fiduciary includes acting in good faith, with due diligence as would a prudent person, taking only relevant considerations into account, exercising control as would the reasonable person, and so on.[16] In addition, the protector is expected to exercise his or her discretion independently and with properly informed judgement. This is particularly important given the many business and investment functions of offshore trusts. Where the protector is a professional protector, such as an accountant, the duty of care is higher, elevated to that of the reasonable and prudent professional.[17]

4.17 It would be difficult to resist tortious liability where a duty of care is established on the part of the protector toward the beneficiaries, or even to the trustee, where the protector is expected, for example, to advise the trustee on investment matters.

The nature of the protector's powers

4.18 The exact nature of the power given to the protector, and consequently his or her legal position, is still a controversial question. This is particularly the case where the legislation is silent, or where the particular jurisdiction does not have legislative provisions which formally recognize protectors. Given the relatively recent nature of the office, it is also a question which has attracted little jurisprudence thus far.

---

[16] *Whitely v Learoyd* (1886) 33 Ch D 347.

[17] *Bartlett v Barclays Bank Trust Corporation* [1980] 1 Ch D 515; [1980] 1 All ER 139. See the discussion on the duty of trustees in relation to investment in chapter 10, 'Duties of Trustees in Managing Offshore Trusts'.

The related issue to that of the nature of the power, is the extent to which   **4.19**
protectors can be controlled by the courts in the execution of their duties and
powers. If the power is to be construed essentially as a personal one, the court's
interference and supervision will be minimal or even non-existent. On the other
hand, if the protector is, in essence, a fiduciary, as is the trustee, he or she will be
subject to the full inherent supervisory jurisdiction of the courts and all of the
resulting rules, such as the rules requiring 'good faith', honesty, accountability,
reasonableness, objectivity, and so on. Certainly, where the protector is acting as
a quasi-trustee, exercising powers normally given to the trustee, there are compelling reasons for treating him or her, in like manner to a trustee, that is, as a
fiduciary.

Legislation specifying the nature of the power as fiduciary

In some jurisdictions, legislation specifically prescribes that the protector is a   **4.20**
fiduciary. For example, in Belize, under s 16 of the Trusts Act 1992, as revised in
2000, there is a presumption that the protector is a fiduciary either for the
benefit of identifiable beneficiaries, or where he or she performs his or her duties
in relation to a purpose trust.[18] Where, as in the British Virgin Islands, the
legislation does not specifically identify the protector as a fiduciary but establishes an exculpatory clause for the protector where he or she exercises the power
given in a 'bona fide' manner, we may infer that he or she is a fiduciary.[19] In
contrast, in the Cook Islands, there is a presumption that the protector is not a
fiduciary, unless otherwise provided in the trust instrument.[20]

It is arguable that, despite the apparent aims of such legislative provisions, they   **4.21**
are not definitive of the issue of the nature of the protector. Thus, while the case
law and analysis in this section is more directly applicable to those jurisdictions
which do not stipulate the nature of the protector's power, it may also be
relevant to offshore jurisdictions which do. What happens, for example, if
the protector is given extremely wide powers usually reserved to the trustee? Is
he or she still not to be viewed as a fiduciary? Further, the provisions which
deem the protector a fiduciary tend to outline to whom he or she owes duties,
that is, the beneficiaries,[21] or to specify that he or she is not liable for *bona fide*

---

[18] See also the Trusts Ordinance 1994 (am'd 2000) of Anguilla, s 15; the International Trusts
Act 2002 of St Lucia; the International Trusts Act of Dominica; the International Trusts Act 1994
of Nevis; and the International Trusts Act 1996 of St Vincent.

[19] Section 86, Trustee (Amendment) Act 2003.

[20] Section 20. See also The Bahamas Trusts Act, where the protector is exonerated from
liability, which suggests also that the protector is not a fiduciary, although flexibility is left to the
trust instrument.

[21] See, eg, s 16(5) of the Belize Trusts Act 1992 (rev'd 2000): 'subject to the terms of the trust,
in the exercise of his office a protector shall owe a fiduciary duty to beneficiaries of the trust or to
the purpose for which the trust is created'.

actions. This suggests that the question of duties outside of those boundaries, for example to the trustee where the protector advises him or her, or for actions which are not *bona fide*, is still open. We are left, ultimately, with a continued search to define the protector's powers by examining closely the duties he or she has been given and the manner in which he or she performs them.

Exemption for bona fide *exercise of powers*

4.22   Legislative provisions which provide that the protector is to be exempted for *bona fide* exercises of his or her power are also to be scrutinized carefully.[22] The trustee may not be excused where higher duties of care are expected. Further, since legislation inevitably grants the trust instrument autonomy to circum-scribe even such exemptions, the protection may be more illusory than first appears. Where the protector is only liable for actions outside of the *bona fide* exercise of his or her powers, it may be that he or she is to be viewed as a limited or qualified fiduciary and not a fully-fledged one. Thus, the powers of the protector will be circumscribed.

Protector deemed not to be a trustee

4.23   The prescription of the protector's powers as a fiduciary is usually accompanied by a clause that the protector is not to be treated as a trustee or substitute trustee.[23] Even legislation which does not specify that the protector is a fiduciary may specify, nonetheless, that he or she is not a trustee.[24] The legislative intent here appears to be an attempt to preclude the protector from incurring liabilities usually placed on trustees with respect to their wide duties toward the trust and the beneficiaries. Nevertheless, it is unclear whether such provisions can absolve protectors from liability for breach of fiduciary duties when, in fact, they per-form trustee-like duties. In such cases, the inherent jurisdiction of the courts to supervise such legal relationships may not be proscribed. Further, the bringing together of provisions which declare that the protector is a fiduciary with provi-sions that specify that he or she is not a trustee, is not an optimal compromise. At best, the result is confusing; at worst, meaningless.

---

[22] See, eg, s 81(3) of the Trustee Act 1998 of The Bahamas: 'unless otherwise provided in the trust instrument, [the protector] is not liable to the beneficiaries for the bona fide exercise of the power'. See also s 81 of the Trustee (Amendment) Act 2003 of the BVI.

[23] See, eg, s 16 of the Trusts Ordinance 1994 (am'd 2000) of Anguilla; s 16 of the Belize Trusts Act 1992; s 9 of the International Trusts Act 1994 of Nevis; s 23 of the International Trusts Act 2002 of Saint Lucia; s 20(4) of the International Trusts Act of the Cook Islands 1984 (am'd 1999).

[24] See, eg, s 26 of the International Trusts Act 1995 of Barbados; s 86 of the Trustee Ordinance 1993 of the BVI; s 81 of the Trustee Act 1998 of The Bahamas; s 23(4) of the Trustee Ordinance 1990 of the Turks and Caicos Islands.

C. Case Law Approach to the Protector—Fiduciary or Non-Fiduciary

The protector as a fiduciary

Where there are no legislative provisions defining the nature of the protector's **4.24** powers, or where the legislation is unclear or leaves the final determination to the trust deed, the emerging case law must be considered. Several cases seem to suggest that, notwithstanding the absence of legislation, the protector is a fiduciary, a view shared by commentators.[25] For example, in *Steele v Paz*,[26] the court found that the power was 'properly to be categorized as a fiduciary power'. However, we may argue that a better reading of the cases suggests that the response to this question depends very much on the *kind* of power given to the protector by the settlor. Thus, it is suggested here that to consider the protector as a fiduciary is too simplistic a view. Not all protectors are created equal. Indeed, this is part of the difficulty of identifying what he or she is, or whether he or she should be controlled.

Settlors may intend protectors to have either personal or fiduciary powers. **4.25** Indeed, settlors are not usually keen on defining the protector as a fiduciary, with all the resulting obligations that this entails. The former designation will be akin to powers normally reserved to a settlor, while the latter will be powers which seek essentially to oversee the trustee and his or her administration of the trust. We must look carefully to the trust instrument for clues as to the nature of the protector in question. This, indeed, was the approach in *Re Z*,[27] where it was decided that the protector's power was a qualified fiduciary power. Such a power may imply only a duty to act in good faith. The answer, then, turns initially on the interpretation of the trust instrument.

In this vein, using *Steele v Paz* and other like-minded cases as authorities of wide **4.26** application to declare that the protector is always a fiduciary may be misleading. If *Steele v Paz* is contained to its facts, it will be noticed that, on closer examination, the court was very much aware that the power given to the protector, in the absence of statute, was of substantial importance and administrative impact to the trust and was more than a 'mere power'. It was not a personal power

---

[25] See, eg, R C Lawrence, 'The Role of the Protector—An Insulator for Corporate Fiduciaries?' [1993] (2) JInTCP 89. Lawrence, while conceding that there were few authorities on the point, suggests that the position of the protector can be viewed similarly to any trust adviser, which has been determined by the courts to be fiduciary. Hence, he views the protector as a fiduciary.

[26] See n 1 above.

[27] [1997] CILR 242 (Grand Ct).

'conferred on the protector in his own interests, to be exercised, or not, at his whim'.[28] Rather, the power in question was to give or withhold his consent to the exercise of many of the 'most important' powers of the trustee, in particular, its power to nominate additional beneficiaries and its power to appoint income and capital to the beneficiaries. In effect, the court's action confirmed that a fiduciary power must be subjugated to the supervision and intervention of the courts in the interest of beneficiaries, and, more generally, the trust.[29]

Protector as non-fiduciary

4.27   In contrast, in *Rawson Trust Co Ltd v Perlman and Others*,[30] the protectors (there were three in this instance) were found to be non-fiduciary since the type of power given to them was personal in nature, in the sense that it was to further and protect their own interests. The power in question enabled the protectors to give or withhold consent to the trustee of a trust company administered as a trust. The trustee had to obtain the written consent of the protectors in order to exercise its discretion. This power, at first blush, may appear to be administrative in nature. However, in this case, the key distinction from that of *Steele v Paz* was that the protectors were also beneficiaries, a common provision in offshore trusts, and, in fact, one of the protectors was the settlor. In one sense, this clouds the issue since, in making what appeared to be important administrative decisions on trustee matters, the protectors/beneficiaries were also making decisions as to what was in their own best interest.

4.28   A similar situation existed in *Sociedad Franciera Sofimeca v Kleinwort Benson (Jersey) Trustees Ltd*.[31] Indeed, the court found that in this particular trust it had been necessary for the beneficiaries to have protection of their interests and prospective shares, and it appeared that this was the reason for establishing the beneficiaries as protectors. The power given to the protectors was not primarily for the proper administration of the trust. It seems that, prima facie, a power granted to a protector to protect the personal interests of a settlor is a personal power, albeit a risky one with respect to the integrity of the trust.

4.29   The discussion on the nature of the powers of the protector was extended in *Re Star 1&2 (Revised) Trusts Von Knieriem v Bermuda Trust Co Ltd and Grosvenor*

---

[28] See n 1 above.
[29] ibid.
[30] (Sup Ct, The Bahamas), No 194 of 1989, decided 25 April 1990, *per* Smith J. We should recall that The Bahamas legislation, s 81 of the Trustee Act 1998, delineates the functions of the protector but gives autonomy to the trust instrument and allows the trust instrument to prescribe further powers. The protector is deemed not to be liable for the bona fide exercise of his power unless the trust instrument specifies otherwise.
[31] (Royal Ct, Jersey), 13 July 1992.

Trust Co Ltd.[32] In this case, the protector, a friend of the settlor, requested the trustee to confirm that he would vote against a resolution to remove the settlor from the board of directors of the holding company. The trustee refrained from acting on the request, pending more information on the situation. He was consequently removed by the protector acting under a clause in the trust deed that gave power to appoint and remove trustees.[33] The trustee sought the court's determination as to whether the protector's powers of appointment and removal were fiduciary in nature and, if they were fiduciary, whether the protector had properly exercised the powers of appointment and removal.

The trustee argued that the protector's powers were fiduciary and should be exercised in the interests of the beneficiaries and not according to the personal wishes of the settlor. The trustee further contended that he was obliged to act independently and not follow instructions from either the settlor or the protector.   **4.30**

The court held that the protector had validly exercised the power of removal. This power was fiduciary only to the extent that it prevented the protector from benefiting himself, which was not in issue.[34] Further, it imposed a high burden of proof for establishing an improper purpose. A mere possibility of an improper purpose was not sufficient. Consequently, to obey the settlor rather than to act in the interest of the beneficiaries was not enough to prove that the protector acted improperly. The trustee had not been removed improperly in breach of any fiduciary duty.   **4.31**

Problems with Von Knieriem

The *Von Knieriem* decision[35] is unsatisfactory for a number of reasons. There was no question that the protector had the power to appoint and remove trustees. Thus, the object or purpose to which the protector directed his power was lawful and well within the limits of his power. The more important question was the lawful exercise of that power, and it was here that the court's explanation fell short. While it spoke in the language of fiduciary powers on the question of whether the protector had exercised the power for an improper purpose, there was no real discussion as to how the protector should have gone about exercising his discretion. What is more, very little evidence was harnessed to support the conclusion that the protector had acted properly, particularly in the face of the   **4.32**

---

[32] (Sup Ct, Bermuda), Nos 154 and 162 of 1994, decided 13 July 1994, *per* Meerabux J.
[33] The beneficiaries here threatened the trustee with a breach of trust action if it either complied with the protector's request, or relinquished the trust assets.
[34] The court declined to follow earlier decisions such as *Mettoy Pensions Trustees v Evans* [1990] 1 WLR 1587.
[35] See above, n 32.

allegation that he had acted solely for the purpose of satisfying the settlor's wishes. Surely, that could not have been an objective exercise of the protector's discretion.

4.33 Further, while the court found that the appointment of the second trustee was proper, based on rational considerations, including the fact that it was a reputable company, no similar inquiry was apparently made in relation to the trustee's removal in the first instance. Was this act of removal objective, rational, in good faith, and in the best interest of the beneficiaries? These were the questions to which the court should have directed itself, but regrettably did not. Further, if the protector had been found to be acting merely to satisfy the settlor, not only would his action have been a violation of his fiduciary duties, but it would also have been a violation of the fundamental trust rule which prohibits a settlor from retaining control over the trust. The better test of whether a purpose was proper in such a situation would be whether it was an independent exercise of power in the interest of the beneficiaries.

4.34 Clearly, if a protector is granted powers which inevitably impact in some way upon the management of a trust and the beneficiaries' equitable interests, it is more likely that he or she will be viewed as a quasi-trustee, with fiduciary powers answerable to the courts. The same conclusion can be reached where the protector is intimately involved with the affairs of the trust. However, it is difficult to see how he or she can be involved in this way without legitimate powers so to do in the first instance.

Interference by the protector leads to control as a fiduciary?

4.35 Unfortunately, the case of *Re X Charles Richard Blampied and Abacus (CI) Ltd* [36] apparently makes the suggestion, and certainly seems to have been read in this way, that the protector's interference in the trust, by itself, may lead to the court's intervention and its treatment of the protector as a fiduciary. This is as opposed to merely preventing a protector from acting outside of the boundaries of his or her powers. In *Abacus*, the court concluded that the protector came close to 'intermeddling', but its initial acknowledgement that the protector had acted in the best interests of the beneficiary should more correctly be viewed as the basis of the court's intervention. It meant that he was acknowledged as a fiduciary. One commentator on the case suggests that 'a protector who oversteps the mark may be treated like a trustee and be exposed to additional duties and liabilities'.[37] This view is questionable. It is only a fiduciary protector who

---

[36] (Royal Ct, Jersey), 28 January, 1994.
[37] A Dessain, 'The Duties and Liabilities of Protectors' [1999] November, *Trust and Trustees*, 34.

should be so treated in the first instance, where he *exercises* his power improperly. Protectors with personal powers are merely to be contained to their powers.[38]

Rationale for protector influence

One may well ask, why go to such lengths to give powers to protectors which the settlor may quite legitimately reserve to himself or herself, provided that he or she does not retain control over the trust? This is particularly curious where the settlor actually intends the power to be a personal power but, by the very act of giving the protector so much power, renders the protector vulnerable to a finding that his or her powers are, in fact, fiduciary. The answer seems simply to be an attempt to 'err on the side of caution' and not tempt the court into a finding that the trust is actually a sham. But it should be noted that even trusts with powers exercised through a protector may be challenged as shams, particularly where they are exercised for the personal benefit of the settlors.[39] Part of the problem also is that it is becoming increasingly difficult for settlors to reserve wide powers to themselves in offshore trusts. The courts, in particular the onshore courts, have become aggressive in vitiating such powers.   **4.36**

Another note of caution is warranted here with respect to the taxation of off-shore trusts by onshore jurisdictions. If the protector's power is such that the trust is deemed to be managed and controlled by the protector and not the trustee, it is the protector's residence that will determine the trust residence for purposes of taxation. This would jeopardize the trust where the protector is a resident of the onshore jurisdiction.   **4.37**

D. Accountability of the Protector

Effect of protector's power on the rights of beneficiaries

The complaint can be made that the instalment of a protector who is a fiduciary has the effect of taking away the beneficiaries' rights to accountability. Such rights may be regarded as 'core obligations',[40] so that this alleged diminution thereby violates the trust relationship. The obligations to accountability, hitherto vested in the beneficiaries, can perhaps be viewed as now being transferred to the protector; but because of the uncertainty of the protector's position and the intrinsic nature of the rights allocated to beneficiaries, this may not be   **4.38**

---

[38] See above, paras 4.27–4.31.
[39] See the discussion of the sham trust in chapter 8.
[40] The point on the irreducible core of trust obligations is made by D Hayton in 'The Irreducible Core Content of Trusteeship' in AJ Oakley (ed), *Trends in Contemporary Trust Law* (Clarendon Press, Oxford, 1996), chapter 3.

satisfactory. This is particularly so in view of the influential powers given to protectors, often in lieu of the trustee and for which no discernible obligations or responsibilities attach under trusts law, or even in the trust instrument. Where the protector's liabilities are not identifiable and the settlor's powers and the parallel enforceable obligations have been displaced by the protector, what protection remains for the beneficiaries?

4.39 A neat question is whether protectors, even powerful ones, can displace the inherent right of the beneficiaries to accountability, a right which arises in equity. Certainly, it is always open to the courts to act as the guardian of the beneficiaries' rights by exercising their inherent supervisory jurisdiction over the administration of trusts. In fact, this is what they seem to have done in recent cases involving questions on the beneficiaries' rights to information,[41] and in emerging cases where they have allowed the protector to apply to the court to enforce obligations under the trust.[42]

Exempting the protector from liability

4.40 An important question which arises, particularly in view of the wide duties being placed on protectors in offshore trusts, is the extent to which a protector can be exonerated from liability for failures to perform the duties owed under the trust. This question, of course, applies more particularly to the protector who is a fiduciary. Such exemption may be achieved by means of an exculpatory clause either in statute, or in the trust instrument.

4.41 Offshore legislation which provides that the protector is accountable to the beneficiaries only if 'bad faith' is demonstrated is mirrored in offshore trust practice even in the absence of legislation. Usually the trust instrument is drafted accordingly, to shield protectors from wide obligations under the trust. Nevertheless, given the courts' expanded expectations of trustees with regard to their duties under current trusts law and, in particular, the reach of the reasonable standard into the trust relationship,[43] the threshold for liability might be lower than anticipated. As protectors are officers of trusts, courts are likely to import similar standards as are applied to trustees, particularly professional trustees.

4.42 A further difficulty with the need to ensure that protectors are accountable to beneficiaries is that, often, in offshore trusts beneficiaries have no knowledge

---

[41] See chapter 7, 'Disclosure and Confidentiality Obligations', at paras 7.1–7.21. Note that the protector may still be liable for negligence. See below for a discussion of legislative attempts to protect him or her from such liability, at paras 4.40–4.45. The protector may also incur third party liability, as discussed in chapter 11.

[42] See *Von Knieriem*, discussed on this point above, paras 4.29–4.36.

[43] See chapters 10 and 11.

whatsoever as to the affairs of the trust in relation to the protector. Indeed, they may not know of the existence of the offshore trust at all. A more satisfactory solution would be to infer rights to account, and this might well be what recent courts have been doing in treating protectors as fiduciaries and asserting jurisdiction, control, and supervision over them. The alternative would be to ensure, when one is drafting the trust instrument, that the protector is not given powers which are too wide. In this way, the balance of power between the trustee and the beneficiary may be maintained. A similar balance may be achieved between the protector and other players in the trust.

In situations where the protector acts as a fiduciary and monitors the actions or omissions of the trustee on behalf of the beneficiaries, it may not be readily evident that this in any way impairs or interferes with the right of the beneficiaries to seek redress against the trustee for any breaches of the trust. Nor is it clear that it would be desirable to take away this inherent right of trust beneficiaries, although it may well be the intent of the settlor that it is the protector alone who must perform this function. The presumption here must be that such rights of beneficiaries are preserved. This uncertainty leads to another controversial question, that is, the right of beneficiaries to information about the offshore trust to enable them to exercise any entitlement to seek redress.[44]   **4.43**

In practice, exculpatory clauses are more common for trustees than they are for protectors.[45] Further, they are given legislative life in some offshore jurisdictions.[46] Clauses attempting to exonerate the protector's liability may be worded so that a protector who has duties similar to a trustee cannot inherit a trustee's liability. For example, the Trustee Ordinance of the British Virgin Islands reads: 'A person exercising any of the [protector's] powers set forth . . . shall not by virtue only of the exercise of the power be deemed to be a trustee; and unless otherwise provided . . . is not liable to the beneficiaries for the bona fide exercise of the power.'[47]   **4.44**

Even if such an exculpatory clause is created, how wide should it be and could it survive? If, for example, the protector is negligent in fulfilling duties relating to investment, thereby causing considerable loss to the trust assets, should he or she be exculpated from liability? It is suggested that such exceptions should be no wider than they are for trustees. Indeed, these exceptions have been construed quite narrowly in the case of the latter.[48] Generally, the law, as expressed   **4.45**

---

[44] Discussed in chapter 7, at paras 7.22–7.100.
[45] See, eg, in relation to trustee exculpatory clauses, Article 26(9) of the Trusts (Jersey) Law 1984.
[46] See, eg, s 86(3) of the Trustee (Amendment) Act 2003 of the BVI.
[47] ibid.
[48] See the discussion of exculpatory clauses in chapter 10, at paras 10.99–10.123.

in statute, will protect the *bona fide* exercise of duties.[49] However, this will not prevent liability for other conduct, such as gross negligence.

4.46　Lastly, it should be noted that even if the parties have expressly agreed that the protector's powers are not to be made reviewable, or even supervised by the courts, the fiduciary element is not taken away. This view is even shared by those who argue that modern trusts have a contractual basis.[50]

The protector as the settlor's shadow

4.47　In anticipation of the discussion of sham trusts below,[51] it goes without saying that the protector is not expected to be the settlor's shadow and function merely as a facade to enable the settlor to retain control of the trust. This would be an exercise of a power which should be struck down, even if this was the purpose intended by the settlor. Yet the court in *Von Knieriem*[52] did not appear to appreciate this view of what is an appropriate purpose of a protector when it held that the protector's removal of the trustee was not for an improper purpose. This was without proving the need for a valid removal of the trustee (the only apparent reason was that he would not go along with the wishes of the settlor as communicated through the protector).

Respecting the powers of the protector

4.48　The courts have thus far accorded full respect to the powers given to a protector in a trust instrument, and other officers of the trust will be expected to act in accordance with such powers. In *Re Hare Trust, Ukert v Interface Trustees Ltd and Another*,[53] there was an express provision in the deed of a Jersey trust which gave the protector the power to appoint new trustees. The trustees acted in defiance of the provision and, purporting to retire, appointed the defendants (partners in the same trust company) as sole trustee in their place. The substitution was made by deed of appointment without any reference to the protector whatsoever.

4.49　The settlor and the protector were dissatisfied with the performance of the new trustee, and were also frustrated by their inability to arrange a transfer of the trust to another company. This was due to an unresolved question of an indemnity for the current trust company. Consequently, the protector sought, and

---

[49] See, eg, s 86(3) of the Trusts (Amendment) Act 2003 of the BVI.
[50] J Langbein argues that the modern trust has a contractual basis, as opposed to being grounded in property law, in 'The Contractarian Basis of the Law of Trusts' (1995) 105 Yale LJ 625.
[51] See chapter 8, 'The Offshore Trust as a Sham'.
[52] See n 32 above.
[53] (2001) 4 ITELR 268 (Royal Ct, Jersey).

obtained, an order from the Royal Court that the appointment of the new trustee was invalid and the appointment of the substitute trustee was declared void. Interestingly, no argument was raised as to whether the protector was estopped from challenging the substitute on the ground that he had, by his conduct, accepted the transfer before he proceeded to disapprove of his performance.

Locus standi to approach the court

Given the somewhat nebulous nature of the role and powers of the protector, the question arises whether he or she has *locus standi* to approach the court on matters pertaining to the trust, despite the fact that no trust property is vested in him or her and, except where he or she is also a beneficiary, he or she has no right or interest in the trust. The protector can certainly ask the court to intervene in order to ensure that the powers given to him or her specifically are recognized and enforceable. The broader question is this: can the protector enforce the trust itself? Similarly, as he or she, does not expressly act on behalf of the beneficiaries, can the protector enforce powers on their behalf, for example where the trustee fails to carry out his or her obligations towards them? These questions have not been adequately tested. However, in *Re Star 1&2 (Revised) Trusts Von Knieriem v Bermuda Trust Co Ltd and Grosvenor Trust Co Ltd*,[54] the protector successfully applied to the court for an order directing the trustee to transfer the trust assets to another trust company.

4.50

Trustee liability in the face of protector authority

Questions relating to possible wrongdoing on the part of the protector dovetail with the broader issue of the relationship between the trustee and the protector. More particularly, such questions speak to the extent to which the trustee has, or should have, control over such wrongdoing, or may question such wrongdoing. If related duties arise on the part of the trustee, questions of liabilities for omissions to act are pertinent.

4.51

Thus, the fact that a protector may be given wide powers and duties in relation to the trust, in some cases requiring the trustee to obtain consent from the protector, does not necessarily absolve the trustee from liability for breach of trust or other harm which befalls the trust. Even in contexts which give the protector independent discretion to do certain things, the trustee cannot turn a 'blind eye' to the protector's actions or omissions. This, in itself, would constitute a breach of trust on the part of the trustee. This is particularly the case where legislative provisions specifically prohibit the protector from being

4.52

---

[54] (Sup Ct, Bermuda), Nos 154 and 162 of 1994, decided 13 July 1994, *per* Meerabux J.

deemed a trustee, which suggests that the role of the trustee is not to be abdicated.

4.53 Where the trustee obtains consent from the protector for an act, this of itself cannot excuse him or her from liability, since the person actually exercising the discretion here remains the trustee. Responsibility for the decision must, therefore, remain with the trustee, although the protector may be viewed as an accomplice. The situation is slightly more complex where the protector expressly withholds consent for something which the trustee wants to do and the trustee is obliged to go down the route that the protector prescribes. It is suggested that in such a situation the trustee must seek the directions of the court.

Trustee's redress

4.54 Further, we may consider whether the trustee has the authority to act when the protector's actions or omissions are prejudicing the trust, or might do so. Certainly, under the trust instrument, the trustee will not usually have any power to require the protector to do anything. However, the trustee still has the sanction of the court as a safety valve and ultimate authority as to the proper conduct in relation to the trust. In situations of doubt, for example where the trustee is unsure about a direction from the protector in relation to investment decisions, the trustee can apply to the court for directions.[55] Further, to the extent that the protector is unable to perform his fiduciary obligations, he might be viewed by the court as delinquent and in conflict of interest.

4.55 At minimum, the trustee may be in a position to inform the beneficiaries, who may be better placed to make demands on the protector with respect to functions carried out on their behalf.

Drafting the trust instrument to include a protector

4.56 The difficulty in identifying the exact nature and powers of the protector may lead to problems in drafting an appropriate trust instrument. In attempting to draft trust clauses establishing the protector, one must first be certain as to what he or she is intended to be—fiduciary or personal power holder. The draftsman must then make this intention clear in the trust instrument. As seen above, uncertainties on this issue have the potential for generating much litigation.

4.57 However, the terminology used in the trust instrument cannot be the final word on the subject. A power which is inherently fiduciary cannot masquerade as a personal power simply by the insertion of appropriate sounding words in the trust instrument. This would go against all accepted principles on the nature

---

[55] See, eg, *Johnson Matthey Bankers Ltd v Shamji* [1985–1986] JLR 26 (Royal Ct).

and interpretation of powers and, perhaps, of all legal concepts, notwithstanding any claims that a trust may have in contract law. At the very least, it will be against public policy. In hard cases, however, what the settlor states to be his or her intention, as illustrated by the trust instrument, would be good evidence of what kind of power it is. In fact, offshore trust instruments often do state the nature of the power intended.

Although the development of the law is leading to answers in relation to **4.58** protectors who are fiduciaries and who act incorrectly, dishonestly, in bad faith, make omissions, and so on, it may be wise for the trust instrument to set out clearly the extent of the protector's liability or lack thereof. Nonetheless, given the wide powers that may be granted to the protector, care should be taken in including an exculpatory clause in the trust instrument for the protector.

Powers to appoint and remove protectors

A provision to remove and appoint protectors may be found in statute. For **4.59** example, in Belize, the Trusts Act 1992, as revised in 2000, gives authority to the protector to enforce the trust and to the court to appoint a protector where the position of protector becomes vacant.[56] Provisions on liability should, therefore, extend to instructions for the removal of the delinquent protector and the appointment of a new one.

It now appears that, even in the absence of such provisions, the court has the **4.60** authority to appoint a protector where the office becomes vacant. This occurred in *Re A Irrevocable Trust*[57] and was also a feature in the case of *Steele v Paz*.[58] In *Re A Irrevocable Trust*,[59] the court merely appointed a new protector when the office of the protector became vacant. However, when one considers the court's eager assumption of the fiduciary nature of the power held by protectors, the next logical step would appear to be to remove and appoint protectors under the court's broad discretion. It may be a step easily taken by the courts.

E. The Enforcer

The office of the enforcer, of even more recent vintage than the protector, **4.61** is perhaps better explained in our discussion on purpose trusts.[60] Here, we note

---

[56] Section 58.
[57] (2000) 2 ITELR 482 (Cook Islands), an offshoot from the US case of *FTC v Affordable Media (Re Anderson Trust)* (1999) 2 ITELR 73.
[58] See n 1 above.
[59] Above, n 57.
[60] See chapter 3, 'Special Trust Vehicles'.

that the enforcer is of like character to the protector and that similar issues apply. We may, however, outline some of the important differences between the two:

(1)   The enforcer has remained an office peculiar to offshore trusts, unlike the protector which has been transplanted onshore.

(2)   Since the purpose trust has no identifiable beneficiaries, the enforcer's ultimate function is not, as with the protector who is a fiduciary, to act on behalf of the beneficiaries.

(3)   There seems to be a more compelling claim to the enforcer being a fiduciary, as he or she is not burdened by questions of personal power. The enforcer's only purpose is to further the purpose or rationale of the trust itself, and this purpose is inevitably one of a commercial nature, or business purpose.

5

QUESTIONS OF LEGITIMACY AND THE OFFSHORE TRUST

A. Introduction

Despite the utility and versatility of the trust in offshore finance, certain **5.01** problems may occur, particularly in instances in which traditional principles of trusts law are ignored or misunderstood. In other situations, the statutory changes brought to the trust in offshore jurisdictions exacerbate common difficulties faced by trusts. They can also encourage suspicion and challenge by onshore courts, which appear to be uncomfortable with this deviance from traditional trust forms. Often, such courts resort to public policy to question offshore trusts. Indeed, it is at least arguable that the offshore trust has gone beyond the accepted norms of the equitable trust in order to meet market demands, hence the suspicion (and even hostility) sometimes emanating from some onshore courts. In effect, the legitimacy of the offshore trust is questioned, and sometimes doubted.

The legitimacy of the offshore trust can be contemplated on different levels. **5.02** When viewed within the context of its aims, functions, and objectives, the concept of the offshore trust itself may be questionable. Some may argue that the rationale of the offshore trust may be at odds with traditional equitable principles, fuelled, as it is, by individual commercial interests of settlors and the economic motives of offshore jurisdictions. Often, the offshore trust is set up for the benefit of the settlor and merely uses the vehicle of the trust. For some this is a legal contrivance, in substance if not in form. Inevitably, one is drawn to answer the question whether the offshore trust offends the orthodox, technical rules of the traditional trust.

5.03 We can consider the problems that may arise from two main perspectives. First, we may examine the inherent qualities of typical offshore trusts, which may pose challenges under traditional onshore law or policy. Secondly, problems that occur and which have more to do with errors in trust formation, albeit within the context of specialized offshore trusts, may be discussed separately. These include, for example, the situations where the trust is established fraudulently to evade creditors. This is a problem which is not confined to offshore trusts, although the legal environment in which the problem arises will be quite different to that relating to other trusts.

5.04 The change in the priorities of trust formation first calls into question the legitimacy of the offshore trust. Offshore trusts which emphasize confidentiality, for example, may significantly impair attempts by persons onshore to reach the assets of the trust, or to acquire information to make the trustees accountable. This, in turn, encourages policies, laws, and judicial activism onshore, aimed at undermining confidentiality in favour of disclosure. Confidentiality, therefore, as a characteristic feature of the offshore trust, may present a significant challenge to the offshore trust.

5.05 Similarly, offshore trust functions which undermine onshore rights protecting creditors and the inheritance of family members, or which aim to avoid tax liability, are not likely to be seen as serving the public interest, if the public is the onshore public. This assumes added importance where conflicts of laws issues arise. It is better explored in a following chapter which questions whether the offshore trust is valid, or whether it violates public policy.[1] The fact that offshore trusts often seek to achieve what is prohibited onshore, such as the creation of spendthrift trusts for one's own benefit, itself raises questions of policy.

5.06 The exploitation of the duality of the trust form for such functions also challenges the legitimacy of the offshore trust. Two intrinsic characteristics of the offshore trust provide evidence of this exploitation. These are, first, the extent to which self-settling is allowed and, secondly, the extent to which the settlor is allowed to retain control of the trust.

---

[1] See below, chapter 6, 'Acceptance of the Offshore Trust'.

B. Self-settled Protective Trusts and Public Policy

Generally, the most important function of the traditional trust is to provide for beneficiaries, who are usually persons other than the settlor. In contrast, under the offshore trust, often the rationale of the trust is to provide a mechanism to benefit the settlor, whether this benefit is protection from creditors or tax liability.[2] **5.07**

Allowing the settlor to be a beneficiary in a protective or spendthrift trust is repugnant to what may be seen as the hallowed principle that one ought not to control and benefit from property while shielding it from one's creditors, a rule of public policy in the US. The egocentric functions of the offshore trust may, therefore, undermine traditional trust principles and the public interest. The US case of *Texas Commercial Bank v Shurley*[3] illustrates this principle. Here, the court, in repudiating self-settled trusts, declared that it was 'against public policy to permit a man to tie up his own property in such a way that he can still enjoy it but can prevent his creditors from reaching it'.[4] **5.08**

The settlor's control

The *de facto* control by the settlor also brings the offshore trust into controversy. Control by the settlor includes subtle forms of control which the 'sham' rule, discussed below, may not reach. For example, protectors may carry out the instructions of the settlor while maintaining the fiction of trustee control. **5.09**

Offshore trusts, are often, in reality, ways for persons or companies to invest and benefit from that investment by using a vehicle which ostensibly distances them from the exercise. The profits and benefits of offshore trusts are usually intended to go to the original settlor. To obtain these benefits, the settlor must, in some way, retain control over the trust. It is a question which transcends that of *form* and strikes at the very essence of the legitimacy of the offshore trust structure. Except in relation to taxation, the issue has only recently begun to be broached by the courts. Previously, the courts concerned themselves mainly with a supervisory role, examining traditional questions of form, rather than questions of policy. Yet offshore asset protection trusts invite the defeat of deep-seated public policy which challenges their legitimacy. **5.10**

---

[2] Protective trusts which protect against creditors may exist onshore. See, eg, s 33 of the UK Trustee Act 1925. Note, however, in offshore jurisdictions, the juxtaposition with provisions allowing settlors to be beneficiaries.

[3] 118 S Ct 444 1997 (Sup Ct) US; US LEXIS 6924; 139 L Ed 2d 380; 66 USLW 3354 (1997), discussed further in chapter 9.

[4] ibid, 15.

5.11   The validity of the offshore trust further depends on whether the transfer of assets can be seen to have been legally valid or impeachable in the first instance. The question whether assets are safely protected in the offshore entity also hinges on this initial issue. While any trust can be challenged under these principles, the nature of the offshore trust, as described above, is more vulnerable to attack.

5.12   The validity of the transfer of assets in respect of legal form can, therefore, be challenged in a number of ways. The normal constraints of trust law will obtain and may form a basis for challenge in both onshore and offshore courts, although the rules for their determination may be less restrictive under offshore law. Such challenges include, for example, whether there was a true intention to create a trust as opposed to a 'sham' or 'alter ego', and whether the transfer of assets is not an equitable transfer at all but is, in reality, a fraudulent conveyance.

C. Justifying the Use of Offshore Trusts

5.13   Despite the concerns raised in relation to offshore trusts, in particular asset protection trusts, they can be justified on the grounds of public policy or consistency. Such trusts are in line with other types of asset protection mechanisms which are recognized by law. These include limited liability companies and partnerships. Thus, the assumption that such a function is inherently illegitimate, or illegal as a sham or fraud, discussed below,[5] may be doubted. Modern commerce has already accepted the notion that a person may legitimately divest himself or herself of property before entering business. It is expected that the law would reflect changing attitudes about what constitutes appropriate or fraudulent transactions or business arrangements, and not be seen to exist as an abstraction.

5.14   Further, the orthodox trust itself has for centuries catered to the needs of investors and those wishing to protect their property. In fact, this was its original rationale. Indeed, 'trusts have always concerned asset protection'.[6] The use of the trust in modern offshore investment is, therefore, neither an original nor a scandalous function. It is merely an ingenious mutation which elevates the essential protective qualities of the trust.

---

[5] Chapters 8 and 9.
[6] P Willoughby, 'International Trusts Under Fire: The Increasing Scope for Litigation' [1996] PCB 226, 227.

A more benign view suggests that offshore asset protection trusts are simply **5.15**
a precursor of traditional estate planning.[7] Yet the results of offshore trust
planning are effected not after the death of the settlor, as in traditional estate
planning, but immediately. The potential for abuse is thus greater. It is this
potential for abuse which should concern courts and legislators.

Upholding the freedom of disposition principle

More philosophical arguments could also be used to ground the concept of **5.16**
offshore trusts. These are its compatibility with the right to property and the
freedom to contract. They imply a liberty to dispose of one's property, a sacred
right at common law. This principle also grounds the common law rules on
succession. The trust has always been an instrument of creativity and freedom,
'the means by which the English threw off the yoke of primogeniture and
acquired testamentary freedom'.[8] Its creative role in liberalizing international
finance seems appropriate. In addition, other types of *inter vivos* dispositions are
presently allowed in law. These include gifts to children, charitable contribu-
tions, and so on. Thus, the argument that wealth should be preserved for
mandatory heirs or unknown future creditors is not a credible one and may
offend fundamental concepts under the common law.

It seems illogical to suppose that the law, as expressed under notions of freedom **5.17**
of property, intends the owners of assets to enjoy their full benefit and yet so
severely restricts the ability of such persons to carry out transactions disposing of
such property. Indeed, the essence of estate planning is always asset protection in
some form. Even tax avoidance is, in itself, a legitimate trust function![9] If the
ultimate goal of the trust is to secure and protect wealth, how can the offshore
trust be isolated for criticism when viewed against other types of *inter vivos*
dispositions? It does not seem plausible that the law requires a person to put all
of his or her assets at risk. While a balance must be struck between the rights of
owners of property and those of rightful creditors, the analogy with other types
of business arrangements points in favour of the offshore trust.

Commercial rationale does not undermine legitimacy

Similarly, the fact that offshore trust law has created innovative rules and **5.18**
functions to respond to commercial needs, and which challenge orthodox
trust law, is not, of itself, sufficient reason to question the validity of these

---

[7] See, eg, T Bennet, 'Asset Protection and Offshore Creditor Trusts', in *Tolley's International Tax Planning*, (Tolley, Crydon, 1994).
[8] A Duckworth, 'A View of Forced Heirship' [1995] PCB 270, 272.
[9] *In the Matter of Moody Jersey A Settlement* [1990] JLR 264, at 266.

new trust law principles. Rather, developments such as purpose trusts, protectors, enforcers, rules abolishing perpetuity period limitations, accumulations, and so on, may be seen as logical and beneficial developments of trust law in a more sophisticated commercial environment. Law, including trust law, is not static, and commercial law is expected to keep apace of modern business demands.

D. Defending Public Policy Challenges to Offshore Trusts

5.19   Public policy is a wide rubric which can hide a 'multitude of sins'. Indeed, one may argue that public policy is often used by courts when they can find no legal principle, with which to challenge an act, principle, or entity, but wish to do so anyway. Undoubtedly, one reason for which public policy should be invoked is where the fundamental principles of law and practice in the land are offended. Certainly, offshore trusts law has made innovative changes to orthodox trust law principles. The question is whether these are fundamentally offensive to trad-itional trusts law, or other law and practice? Consider, for example, the use of trusts for tax planning or protecting against future creditors, usages employed for centuries. As onshore countries continue the recent trend of themselves creating domestic structures with which to attract tax and estate planners and offer competition to offshore jurisdictions, the public policy argument is being undermined in its logic, thrust, and intention.

5.20   Similarly, in relation to forced heirship, the fact that A, whilst alive, can do various things to disinherit his or her heirs, must surely mean that it cannot be against public policy to do this through a trust. Only if the trust takes effect after death (as opposed to the heirs finding out after the settlor's death), should this perhaps be considered against public policy. Further, anti-forced heirship regimes created in major onshore countries, such as the US, have been recog-nized for a long time. It is inconsistent to refuse them recognition where they originate in offshore jurisdictions.

5.21   In the same vein, the rules against non-identifiable beneficiaries, perpetuities, and accumulations can hardly be said to be rules which go to the fundamental nature of a trust. Rather, they are rules of a practical nature, concerned about seeking more convenient approaches to trust formation. With more modern commercial practices, which are in themselves more expedient ways of doing business, such rules are rendered obsolete and even obstructive.

5.22   While the courts have used the public policy argument in several ways to undermine offshore trust arrangements, for example to enforce onshore tax judgments, the validity of the trust itself, once legitimately established, is not easily questioned on the grounds of public policy. In *In re Abacus CI Ltd (Trustee of the Esteem Settlement) Grupo Torras SA v Al Sabah*,[10] the Jersey Royal Court set a high benchmark for invalidating a trust which had been established before the settlor, a convicted fraudster, had perpetuated his acts of fraud. The creditors sought to discredit the trust by a claim that the settlor's intention had always been to retain control of the trust. Consequently, they argued, the trust had become invalid on the grounds of public policy as it had been used as a vehicle for fraud. The court did not agree, finding that once the trust had been validly established, it would require highly 'exceptional circumstances' before it could become invalid on public policy grounds. An example given was where the trust was set up for charitable purposes and was subsequently used for terrorist purposes.

The various functions and characteristics of offshore trusts and offshore law can, therefore, be seen to be acceptable in modern financial regimes. **5.23**

E. Attacks on Offshore Financial Regimes

In recent times, offshore financial regimes, particularly those in small, develop- **5.24** ing nations, have come under strong attack from international organizations, such as the OECD, and certain developed onshore countries. The main thrust of this attack has been on taxation, in particular claims that offshore states engage in unfair tax competition and 'ring-fencing', that is, offering financial incentives and other benefits only to non-nationals and non-residents and not to nationals in the offshore country. The attack has been clothed with insinu- ations of money-laundering. Often, the approach is not so much to accuse offshore jurisdictions of harbouring and encouraging money laundering, but to suggest that they are vulnerable to money laundering. Indeed, the former would be difficult to prove, given the evidence that the major money laundering activ ities are consistently carried out through the use of onshore financial centres. Nevertheless, the approach succeeded in damaging the reputation of offshore centres and even placing some of them on a 'blacklist'. These claims have been more thoroughly analysed in the companion book to this text, *Confidentiality in Offshore Financial Law*.[11]

Some of the confrontations which are faced by the offshore trust have more to **5.25** do with the fact that the offshore trust is an *inter vivos* trust, rather than with any intrinsic 'wrongness' or inappropriateness of the features of offshore trusts themselves. For example, the concerns about the offshore trust being susceptible

---

[10] (2003) 6 ITELR 368 (Royal Ct, Jersey).
[11] R-M B Antoine, (Oxford University Press, Oxford, NY, 2002).

to abuse through the settlor's control of the trustee and the trust, particularly where a large majority of the settlor's assets are involved, are not likely to be raised with trusts that have dead settlors.

Economic rationale for attacking offshore trusts exposed

5.26   However, we should note that the criticisms and antagonisms from the international arena have been extended to offshore trusts. This is because they are viewed as vehicles of tax avoidance and vessels which succeed in filtering investments and profits from onshore to offshore economies. It is suggested that many of the modern-day challenges which face the offshore trust have less to do with its distinct legal mutations than with its effectiveness in undermining tax revenues and avoiding creditor judgments onshore. This results in considerable financial losses to onshore states and exposes an economic, rather than a jurisprudential, rationale for the offensive against offshore trusts. Proof of the argument comes conveniently from onshore jurisdictions themselves and their recent initiatives toward emulating characteristic offshore principles and forms, for use by wealthy foreigners, in their own jurisdictions.

5.27   We refer here to the recent phenomenon of 'tax haven' initiatives in onshore countries, more specifically in Europe, Canada, and some states in the US. These appear to have developed as a response to the successes of offshore centres and aim at providing competition to these centres. It suffices to say at this juncture that challenges and attacks on offshore financial centres must now be assessed in conjunction with these several initiatives, which have been launched by onshore nations themselves. The *raison d'être* of such initiatives is economic, to offer tax incentives and to encourage foreign investment. These are initiatives which are strangely familiar to offshore policy-makers. Examples include both special trust regimes established onshore for non-resident investors, such as in Delaware and Atlanta, and more general tax incentives designed to welcome wealthy foreign investors and investments, including trusts.[12] Of course, one may take the view that places like New York and London have always been tax havens, as they have historically offered tax incentives and better tax conditions to non-resident individuals.[13]

Offshore type mechanisms created onshore elevate offshore trusts

5.28   These US developments include asset protection trust and tax planning features in six main states: Alaska, Delaware, Montana, Nevada, Rhode Island, and

---

[12] See, eg, the Canadian approach, under its Income Tax Act, discussed more fully in chapter 14.
[13] However, these are not considered as offshore centres under the definition of offshore financial centres in this book. See para 1.04.

Colorado. Offshore type features now also exist to a lesser extent in several other US states, including Idaho, Illinois, Maine, Maryland, Arizona, Missouri, New Jersey, Ohio, South Dakota, Virginia, and Wisconsin. This latter group, for example, instituted 'dynasty trusts' by abolishing the rule against perpetuities and allowing estate taxes to be deferred indefinitely.[14] Familiar asset protection features, against creditors, challenging forced heirship regimes, and so on, are evident.[15] In particular, the rule against self-settled trusts, long considered to be a rule of public policy in the US,[16] and a lethal weapon against offshore trusts, has been expressly overruled in some of these states.[17]

These developments in the US represent a shift in the legal paradigm regarding **5.29** self-settled trusts and other well-established rules of trust law in the US, para-doxically through state legislation. It is a sharp movement away from the trad-itional legal landscape which prohibits self-settled trusts. The underpinnings of this changed paradigm have an entrepreneurial source, that is, the desire to repatriate assets believed to be lost offshore.

The developments invite speculation about the credibility and ethics of the **5.30** claims against offshore financial centres by onshore courts and commentators. At minimum, they diminish considerably onshore public policy arguments against offshore trusts, as the very activities being challenged are occurring in their own countries! Yet while such developments make it more difficult for onshore countries to attack offshore trusts credibly, they also demonstrate the impact that offshore financial law has had, and continues to have, on onshore legal systems, itself a criterion for legitimacy.

Nonetheless, we cannot avoid, in our discussion on the legitimacy of offshore **5.31** trust law, issues which are essentially ethical or moral ones and which concern all trusts and even the function of law in a particular society. These are not ques-tions which can be resolved satisfactorily in this forum. Essentially, they are broad questions of justice that must be answered by an appropriate weighing of competing interests and rights in any society.

---

[14] See, eg, the Banking Law of Colorado, Title 11 (Rev), which provides that non-residents transacting with banks in Colorado incur no state taxes with respect to income from bank deposits, certificates of deposit, purchases of gold, silver, platinum, and other precious metals, foreign currency exchange for US dollars, and other forms of personal, tangible property. See also the Qualified Dispositions in Trusts Act 1996 of Delaware.

[15] See, eg, Title 18 of the General Laws of Rhode Island; the Qualified Dispositions in Trust Act 1999 of Rhode Island; and the Alaskan Trust Act of 1997.

[16] See chapters 8 and 10.

[17] See, eg, the Spendthrift Trust Act 1999 of Nevada; the Qualified Trust Company Act 1999 of Colorado; Delaware Code Amd. tit 12, 3570–73 (2001); Nev Rev Stat–Am 166 040–06 (michie 1993); Colo Rev Stat 38–10–111 (1997).

F. Future Discussions on Validity

5.32   As seen above, the underlying principles of the offshore trust may offend and undermine deep-seated precepts of established trust law, or onshore law in general. The courts have been more willing to consider issues of validity as they relate to the form and structure of the trust. However, judicial thinking has yet fully to confront the legitimacy of the offshore trust in a more substantive sense. This latter, more far-reaching question is considered further in following chapters, as it is, in essence, an issue of the difficulties which arise when two very different legal concepts and systems confront each other.

5.33   The existence of special trust legislation in offshore jurisdictions does not guarantee the legitimacy of the offshore trust. Uncertainties concerning the validity of the trust remain. Such uncertainties extend to conflict of laws issues, such as those pertaining to jurisdiction and choice of law. Nonetheless, significantly, recent trusts cases on the conflict of laws point to more successful outcomes for offshore trusts.[18]

5.34   Offshore judicial decisions have often supported the offshore legislative framework and the legal policy which underpins it. Consequently, the onshore legal system now has to come to terms with the jurisprudence shaping the development of the offshore trust. Thus, the form, functions, and motives of the offshore trust have begun to be measured by onshore courts.

Hurdles to defeating offshore trusts

5.35   While there may be doubts about the legitimacy of the offshore trust, and even the legitimacy of offshore legislation designed to sustain it, the efficacy of the offshore legal regime is on firmer footing. For example, offshore laws on jurisdiction and conflict of laws present formidable legalistic obstacles to trust challengers. Even if these may be successfully resolved, the sheer cost, in particular the use of two sets of attorneys, one in the onshore jurisdiction and the other offshore, is intimidating. Some jurisdictions also require that a security bond be posted before an action against the trust is initiated.[19] Thus, notwithstanding the potential challenges to the offshore trust, much optimism surrounds its continued use for financial purposes. Anecdotal evidence suggests that the sheer

---

[18]   See Part IV for a discussion of such cases.
[19]   See, eg, under the International Trusts Act of Nevis 1994 and the International Trusts Act 2002 of Saint Lucia.

difficulty in mounting a successful challenge is often an effective deterrent to litigation.[20]

Successful development of the offshore trust

Indeed, the offshore trust sector seems to be thriving, at least for the time being.[21] The evolution of the trust into the offshore seems to be due to its capacity to adapt quickly to the changing needs of the particular moment. At first glance, one may see the offshore trust as a creature of its time. However, when viewed from a holistic perspective, it apparently has a durable, if chameleon, life. Since its inception, the offshore trust has served a variety of important business purposes. This demonstrates that the offshore trust is not likely to retreat into the background but is increasingly evolving as a permanent, viable, commercial legal entity.

5.36

A concurrent and consistent body of jurisprudence is emerging to determine the tensions and problems, whether legal, commercial, or ethical, which this new hybrid creature creates. The extent to which the courts have allowed, or are willing to allow, offshore trusts to survive, by measuring their radical new trust laws against orthodox legal principles, invites discussion. It is suggested that a balance must be achieved between clear abuses of this hybrid trust form for unlawful purposes, such as fraud, and the need to elevate the trust to a viable, modern commercial entity. If the hybrid nature and functions of the offshore trust are allowed to flourish, trust jurisprudence, whether onshore or offshore, will surely be transformed.

5.37

---

[20] Largely as a result of the difficulty faced by creditors in litigation. They are usually settled out of court. Similarly, *The Economist* reports, for example, that one US law practice, with 400 APT clients, defended only 24 trust cases, all settled out of court: *The Economist*, 5 October 1991.

[21] It is estimated that there is US $5 trillion in offshore centres and that US $1 trillion of this is in the form of APTs. See J Geer, 'In Foreign Countries We Trust' [1994] 1 *Financial Planning* 6.

6

ACCEPTANCE OF THE OFFSHORE TRUST

A. Introduction

The hybrid character of the offshore trust invites the question whether it is a **6.01** valid or true trust. This is a question which may confront the offshore trust if onshore courts are tempted to assess the offshore trust against orthodox trust principles. These are in reality two, separate questions. Notwithstanding the inherent character of the entity as a trust, could it be challenged on the ground that the particular category of trust or trust function is not acceptable in the onshore country? The second question presents a philosophical challenge. If the offshore entity is not a trust at all, what is it? To some extent, of course, we examine these questions throughout this book, in the discussions of sham trusts, fraudulent conveyances, legitimacy of the offshore trust, and so on. Yet they are also questions which can stand on their own.

B. Category of Trust—Hybrid Functions and Their Validity

For some, the hybrid functions and form of the offshore trust take it outside **6.02** the acceptable parameters of trust law. Onshore courts, for example, may not be willing to accept such functions as acceptable expressions of the trust. Where the offshore trust varies significantly from the strict legal requirements of the onshore trust, onshore courts may contest its validity. Onshore courts may not be impressed with offshore countries' enthusiasm for commercially advantageous purpose trusts that actively seek to encourage a clientele. Recent legislation in

Dominica may have had such challenges in mind when it provided that Dominica law is to be the proper law where the law with which the trust is most closely connected 'does not provide for international trusts or the *category of international trust* involved'.[1]

6.03   One example may be the offshore purpose trust, which might offend the orthodox rule that a trust is to be established for an identifiable beneficiary instead of a specific purpose.[2] 'Purposes' allowed under this offshore concept include those which are entirely self-serving and deviate from traditional exceptions to the rule for charitable purposes.[3] In *Steele v Paz Ltd*,[4] this issue was considered in relation to a trust whose assets were held for the Red Cross in the absence of the usual protector. At first instance, the court held that the trust was void for uncertainty as there was no protector who could confirm the appointment of the beneficiaries. The decision was eventually reversed in favour of the trust on the basis that the trustees had power to appoint a protector who, in turn, could appoint beneficiaries. For the rule on certainty of objects to be satisfied, it may be sufficient that there is a possibility that beneficiaries can be identified. Still, the Hague Convention weakens the challenge to the purpose trust. Its definition of a trust includes one 'for a specified purpose'.[5] This recognizes and validates the purpose trust.

C. A True Trust—Recharacterization

6.04   Offshore jurisdictions have so varied the traditional principles of the trust in relation to legal form, technical rules, objects, and purposes, that in substance the offshore trust may be regarded as a bastardized offspring, challenging the very essence of the trust. Is the hybrid offshore trust so different to the orthodox trust that traditional trust systems will refuse to recognize it as a trust?

6.05   Given its mutant characteristics, an onshore court might deem it to be, in substance, another entity, such as a corporation, a will which is incorrectly executed, a bailment, agency, or nomineeship.[6] If viewed as another entity, the

---

[1] Section 4(1)(c) of the International Exempt Trust Act 1997, emphasis added.

[2] *Maurice v Bishop of Durham* (1804) 9 Ves 399, 405. It may also offend the rule on perpetuities.

[3] See, eg, s 15 of the Belize Act, which is typical. A trust may be created for a purpose which is non-charitable, provided that 'its purpose is specific, reasonable and capable of fulfilment; . . . not immoral, unlawful or contrary to public policy'.

[4] [1993–95] Manx LR 102 (Isle of Man).

[5] Article 2.

[6] This last notion is attributed to P Willoughby, 'International Trusts Under Fire: The Increasing Scope for Litigation' [1996] PCB 226, 227, who supports, in principle, much of the argument in this section. See *In Re Pfrimmers Estate* [1936] 2 DLR 460 (Manitoba).

designated proper law of the trust will be inapplicable and some other conflict of laws rule will apply. Offshore trusts could thus be subjected to the antagonistic laws of the onshore jurisdiction.[7]

The newest creation of the offshore world, the 'international company', reco-   **6.06**
gnizes the limitations of identifying such offshore structures as trusts. This entity was established as a trust substitute because of the potential challenges to the validity of the offshore trust, in particular the spectre of the 'sham'.[8]

D. Public Policy and Validity

Under a conflict of laws approach, the legitimacy of the offshore trust may also   **6.07**
be challenged on public policy grounds, although this is a challenge which courts must approach cautiously.[9] Certainly, the argument of public policy failed when it was raised before a court in a civil law country, in which trust law was not part of the legal system.[10] It would be ironic if such a contention were to succeed more easily in a trust law jurisdiction.

The argument against validity might be that the purposes, functions, and forms   **6.08**
of the offshore trust are alien and repulsive to the orthodox trust. Few persons will question motives such as protection against governmental oppression or a racist regime, both previous rationales for trust formation. However, seeking to undermine what may be viewed as 'rights' of creditors, heirs, or spouses may be unacceptable. Even offshore courts give weight to these when examining the offshore trust.

Recent onshore legislation and case law which challenge offshore trust structures,   **6.09**
by making settlors resident in the jurisdiction liable to taxation for their offshore trusts, also confirm this. The basis of these challenges is to deem such structures as belonging to the onshore jurisdiction for purposes of tax. This suggests that onshore authorities view such trusts as inherently artificial entities with unacceptable motives, which should be challenged in the public interest.[11]

Equally contestable is the argument that the offshore trust does not conform to   **6.10**

---

[7] For example, if deemed to be a corporation, the relevant law might be the place of management and control.

[8] Created under the International Company Act 1997 of Antigua and Barbuda, it attempts to adapt companies for use in ways similar to those of trusts. Specifically, it has enhanced gift-making and succession capabilities. See D Ward and D Brownbill, 'The International Company Act, 1997' [1997] JIntP 15, 18, for further discussion of this entity.

[9] See Part IV for a full discussion of conflict of laws issues.

[10] *Casani v Mattei* (1998–99) 1 ITELR 925, Tribunale of Lucca, Italy.

[11] See chapter 14.

the notion of a true trust because of distortions to fundamental trust principles or the inclusion of hybrid ones. The public's interest in upholding orthodox trust principles may itself be a basis for challenge.

6.11 Paradoxically, the most damning dicta to substantiate this proposition come from an offshore court. This was from the case of *South Orange Grove Growers Association & Others v South Orange Grove Partners*,[12] a decision from the Court of Appeal of the Cook Islands. McMullin J was here analysing the provisions of the International Trusts Act 1984, acknowledged to be one of the most aggressive pieces of offshore trust legislation in the offshore sector, particularly in relation to its anti-creditor provisions. He had little sympathy for its aims or objectives, as stated by counsel. Indeed, he was loath to accept counsel's view of its purpose as 'unashamed soliciting of funds to improve the economic position of the Cook Islands by giving protection against creditors exercising their rights'.[13] The court, obviously believing that such a function would have been scandalous, noted that Parliament should not be presumed to have such inappropriate intentions. Indeed, it cautioned: '. . . we cannot think that Parliament ever intended that by passing the International Trusts Act the Cook Islands should become an Alsatia in the South Pacific from which the commercial comity of nations was completely ousted'.[14] The court consequently granted the injunction sought. *South Orange Grove* turned on the ambiguity of the offshore statute, but the judge seemed more concerned with public policy considerations.

6.12 Further evidence of the possible reluctance by offshore courts steeped in a traditional trust tradition to deviate from established trust principles in the interest of commerce is seen in *Bridge Trust Company v AG*.[15] Here, the validity of a trust set up as a charitable trust was in issue. The Attorney General of the Cayman Islands argued that the offshore trust should be more flexible than the orthodox trust because of the need of the Cayman Islands to offer investors a viable form of investment. He clearly saw this as a legitimate progression in trust jurisprudence. This, according to him, was an aspect of 'Cayman Islands public policy' which was

> relevant to the determination of the issues before the court . . . the Cayman Islands' economy rests on its role . . . as one of the world's most sophisticated and successful offshore financial centres . . . it is home to countless trusts . . . Any judgment of the court which casts doubt . . . on the validity of such trusts or other entities might have very damaging effects on the confidence of those who have

---

[12] [1997–1998] 1 OFLR 3.
[13] ibid, 6.
[14] ibid, 8.
[15] [1996] CILR 52.

hitherto used this jurisdiction for these purposes or who might consider doing so in the future.[16]

However, the court disagreed with the need to be flexible: **6.13**

> I would not have regarded it as being in the best interests of the Cayman Islands as a respectable offshore financial centre to take any radical new approach in relation to the law of charity. Any perceived policy reason that I should do so is in my view misconceived.[17]

Thus, in *Bridge Trust Company v AG*,[18] an important reason identified for   **6.14**
refusing to validate offshore entities which did not closely resemble the orthodox trust was the need for certainty in trust principles throughout the common law world. The deliberate manipulation of the international environment of the trust for self-serving purposes may be repugnant to such an objective.[19]

The cases suggest that, at least in the absence of a clear statute, even offshore   **6.15**
courts might be reluctant to accept a liberal view of the trust. Indeed, the very duality of the offshore legal regime might be a ground for a public policy argument. Consider this: in offshore jurisdictions the hybrid offshore trust legal system is available only to non-residents and exists alongside the domestic legal system with its orthodox trust principles which the offshore trust regime might offend. The same judges who preside over domestic trust cases also hear offshore matters. Even an offshore court might find this incongruous. The *South Orange* case,[20] where the court found its own offshore trust legislation wanting, provides evidence of this.

E. Evolution of the Trust

An alternative view is to treat the offshore trust as an entity in formation,   **6.16**
constantly evolving. Equitable concepts are inherently evolutionary, as evidenced by the *Mareva* injunction. The evolution of the offshore trust must, therefore, be seen against such other trust developments. The trust has made dramatic accommodations in the past. For example, the rule against purpose trusts was changed to facilitate charitable purposes. As Neuhoff put it: 'It is a historical

---

[16] ibid, 60.
[17] ibid, 62, *per* Harre CJ.
[18] See above, n 15.
[19] In *Armenian Patriarch of Jerusalem v Sonsino and Others* (2002) 5 ITELR 125 (HC), a UK court had to consider the recognition of an Indian trust which had trust features unacceptable in the UK on the question of what constitutes an uncharitable purpose.
[20] See above, n 12.

accident that the Court of Chancery hijacked the charitable gift and squeezed it (with some difficulty) into the pre-existing framework of the trust.'[21]

6.17   Some writers take a cynical but accepting view of 'client driven trusts' such as the offshore trust, seeing them as part of the modern legal industry, as is life assurance. In their view, such a trust is 'a product serving a commercial need. To some extent, like all law and legal institutions, it is a conjuring trick.'[22]

6.18   These are important jurisprudential questions about the nature of the trust. When one considers domestic uses of the trust for less than beneficial purposes, can a broad argument against recognition and validity be sustained? A commercial purpose does not necessarily strip a trust of its equitable character.

6.19   Onshore courts could decide to treat the offshore trust question along lines already drawn in relation to taxation of the trust, thereby asserting jurisdiction and control of the trust.[23] Whether onshore courts do this on the grounds of public policy, or on the basis that the offshore trust is inherently a sham structure and not a true trust, the result will be the same. The offshore trust will be stripped of meaning and will be rendered ineffective.

6.20   Yet the evolution of the trust offshore is being paralleled by developments and questions concerning the place and functions of the trust onshore. Increasingly, traditional trust law principles are found wanting. At the same time, the globalization of commerce generally is propelling traditional commercial vehicles, including trusts, toward legal usages and characteristics more accommodating to this new commercial environment. No better demonstration of this can be seen than in the movement, in onshore jurisdictions, in places like Delaware and Atlanta, toward introducing trusts which mimic the fundamental characteristics of offshore trusts. The evidence suggests that offshore trusts and offshore trust legal principles are fast entering the mainstream of trust and commercial law.

---

[21]   K Neuhoff, *Trusts and Foundations in Europe* (Bedford Square Press, London, 1971).

[22]   P Matthews, 'The New Trust: Obligations Without Rights', International Trusts Association Seminar, UK 1996, 35–6. He warns that obligations are attached to such entities. Even purpose trusts which have no beneficiaries must belong to somebody in the end.

[23]   See chapter 4.

PART II

CHALLENGES TO THE OFFSHORE TRUST AND COMMON PITFALLS TO AVOID

7

DISCLOSURE AND CONFIDENTIALITY OBLIGATIONS

A. Introduction

Offshore jurisdictions are well known for the confidentiality they offer to offshore investors. No exception is made for investors who establish offshore trusts, which are thus subjected to these special and far-reaching confidentiality laws typically found in offshore jurisdictions. Since the subject of confidentiality has been treated elsewhere,[1] here we merely summarize the key rules relating to confidentiality as applied to offshore trusts. Note, however, that many of the issues associated with confidentiality and disclosure discussed previously, will be relevant to offshore trusts.[2]   **7.01**

The confidentiality afforded to offshore trusts springs from two sources: **7.02**

(1) specific statutes and/or policy promoting confidentiality; and
(2) the common law.

In the first construct, confidentiality norms originating in a statute and/or public policy are themselves buttressed by common law principles of confidentiality and constitutional values in privacy. With respect to the statutory duty of

---

[1] R-M B Antoine, *Confidentiality in Offshore Financial Law* (Oxford, Oxford University Press, 2002).

[2] ibid. For example, apart from the issues considered in this chapter, rights to privacy and the privilege against self-incrimination should be considered. Similarly, rules of comity and against fishing expeditions will apply in relation to disclosure requests.

confidentiality, we should not expect to find fundamental differences to the duty as it is applied to other offshore entities.

7.03 Apart from these statutory duties of confidentiality, trustees also have a duty under the common law to keep the affairs of the trust confidential. The exception, with regard to beneficiaries and others who seek disclosure of information about the trust, is addressed in Part C of this chapter.

7.04 Confidentiality, while viewed as a positive feature by offshore investors, presents significant challenges to offshore entities because of the law enforcement and tax collection concerns of onshore authorities, and the challenges, by creditors and other individuals to the offshore trust. Consequently, confidentiality must be examined within the context of these several challenges, which are brought about by attempts at disclosure of information, related to the trust. Thus, parallel to our discussion is a consideration of the specific duties toward disclosure and rights to information, and the ways in which they impact on the trust.

B. Trusts and Confidentiality Norms in Offshore Jurisdictions

Legislative provisions on confidentiality and trusts

7.05 The duty of confidentiality in offshore financial affairs has been codified in most offshore jurisdictions.[3] These statutory obligations toward confidentiality may be enforced by either criminal or civil sanctions, or both. The confidentiality obligation is therefore no longer based on common law notions of contract and, in fact, extends to third parties outside of the relationship of banker and client.[4] In the few offshore countries where financial confidentiality as a general principle has not been supported by legislation, such as in the British Virgin Islands and Barbados, it should still be viewed differently from its pedigree. This is because in offshore financial jurisdictions, even where financial confidentiality as a formal legal principle is absent, it assumes a more direct and important policy focus which is clearly lacking elsewhere. We should note too, that offshore jurisdictions without separate, general confidentiality legislation will still mandate duties of confidentiality with respect to certain entities or types of

---

[3] See, eg, the Cayman Islands' Confidential Relationships (Preservation) Law of 1979 (rev'd 1999); the Confidential Relationships Act 1985 of Saint Kitts; the Bank and Financial Institutions Act 1995, Offshore Banking Act 1996, the International Business Companies Act 1996 of Belize; the Banks and Trust Companies' Act 1990 (am'd 1995) of the British Virgin Islands; and the Banks and Trust Companies Regulation Act 2000 of The Bahamas, recently revised from the 1980 statute.

[4] The classic application of confidentiality in financial affairs is to the banker—client relationship, given life in *Tournier v National Provincial Bank* [1924] 1 KB 461.

functions, for example with respect to company or insurance formation and, of course, the trust.[5]

Thus, what may be described as a confidentiality norm in offshore jurisdictions **7.06** goes beyond legal rules, as the very nature of the offshore trust is conducive to confidentiality. For example, offshore trusts are created with a fiduciary, holding assets in his or her own name for a beneficiary. Where trusts are combined with a confidential bank account, or with underlying companies, as is often the case with offshore trusts, this creates a triple level of security for investors.[6] The three-tier structure of the trust, with assets being held by a trustee who is legally distinct from the settlor, on the behalf of beneficiaries, of itself enhances confidentiality. Consequently, when the notion of confidentiality as a legal obligation is referred to in offshore matters, it relates to this extended concept.

The wide ambit of offshore provisions on confidentiality in offshore jurisdictions **7.07** and their application to trusts, is seen, for example, in the provisions of applicable legislation in St Kitts and Nevis, which extend norms of confidentiality to all persons, including lawyers, professionals and officers handling financial affairs, and any person who:

(a) being in possession of confidential information, however obtained—

(i) divulges it to any person not entitled to possession thereof; or

(ii) attempts to divulge it to any person not entitled to possession thereof . . .

Such persons are deemed, in the language of the criminal law, to be 'guilty of an offence'. It is a defence if such a person 'did not know and did not have reasonable grounds to suspect that, in so doing, it would be a breach of an express or implied duty to preserve confidentiality'.[7]

Alternatively, duties of confidentiality specific to offshore trusts are found in **7.08** statutes establishing such trusts. A trustee may be required to keep as confidential the documents and files relating to the creation of the trust, the names of settlors and protectors, and the trust's purposes and financial position.[8]

---

[5] These will take the form of confidentiality provisions in individual legislation. See, eg, in Saint Lucia, s 20 of the International Insurance Act 1999, s 25 of the Registered Agents and Trustee Licensees Act 1999 (but the duty here is not general but is directed at the Director, his agent, or an agent of the Financial Centre Corporation, the regulatory authority), and s 19 of the Banks Act 1999.

[6] See M Langer, *Practical International Tax Planning* (Practising Law Institute, NY, 1988), for discussion of such methods.

[7] See s 4(1) of the Confidential Relationships Act 1995. See also s 15(1)(a) to (f) of the Banks and Trust Companies Regulation Act 2000 of The Bahamas. Exceptions to confidentiality for regulation and supervision by designated authorities are imposed.

[8] See, eg, s 52 of the International Trusts Act 2002 of Saint Lucia.

However, duties of confidentiality in relation to the trust extend outward, to all persons and to all information concerning the offshore trust. Thus:

> [A] trustee, protector or other person shall not disclose to any person not legally entitled thereto, any information or documents respecting an international trust, including without limitation—
>
> > (a) the name of the settlor or any beneficiary;
> > (b) the trustee's deliberations as to the manner in which a power or duty was exercised . . .;
> > (c) the reason for the exercise of the power or discretion or the performance of the duty or any evidence upon which such reason might have been based;
> > (d) any information relating to or forming part of the accounts of an international trust; or
> > (e) any other matter or thing in respect of an international trust.[9]

7.09 The obligations under the various confidentiality statutes with regard to the financial details of offshore trusts were tested in a case from the Cayman Islands, *In re H*.[10] Here, it was held that an US subpoena might not compel disclosure of information on Cayman trust assets in breach of the Cayman Islands' confidentiality legislation.

Avenues for disclosure

7.10 Despite the strong confidentiality ethic in offshore jurisdictions, more and more avenues exist for piercing the confidentiality of the trust and other offshore entities. Many of these are concerned with providing mechanisms for preventing criminal activity and assisting in law enforcement. Others, such as the rights of access to information discussed in the following section,[11] have more pragmatic rationales, for example to allow beneficiaries to enforce the trust or bring the trustees to account.

7.11 These routes to disclosure may be found in statutes as exceptions to

---

[9] Section 53(1). Certain rights are reserved to beneficiaries and protectors. Protectors are given specific rights to information under s 52, while beneficiaries are given rights to information about the trust accounts under s 53(2). See also similar provisions in s 28 of the International Trusts Act 1995 of Barbados, s 64 of the International Trusts Act 1996 of Saint Vincent, s 28 of the Trusts Ordinance of the Turks and Caicos, and s 47 of the International Trusts Act 1996 of Grenada. In fact, prohibitions against the disclosure of information on the Register are not as radical as first appears and are a feature of modern trusts law. See also s 23(1) of the International Trust Act of the Cook Islands 1984: 'Except where the provisions of this Act require, . . . it shall be an offence under this Act for a person to divulge or communicate to any other person information relating to the establishment, constitution, business undertaking or affairs of an international trust.' Under s 23(2), trust proceedings are to be held *in camera*.

[10] [1996] CILR 237 (Grand Ct).

[11] Section C of this chapter.

confidentiality obligations,[12] or in related legislation pertaining to anti-money laundering, or to the reporting of financial transactions.[13] Under anti-money laundering legislation, offshore trustee companies, in common with other financial institutions and providers, will be subject to duties to identify persons associated with the trusts, to keep routine records, and to report suspicious activities. They will also be criminally liable where they facilitate money laundering activities, or under 'tipping off' provisions if they alert persons suspected of money laundering. Other obligations may exist under treaties.[14] For example, offshore trusts are subject to the more recent provisions requiring disclosure under various treaties and international agreements. Chief among these are Mutual Legal Assistance Treaties, Exchange of Information Treaties, and anti-money laundering agreements which are often incorporated into domestic law.[15]

There are also new routes to disclosure, such as judicial initiatives to help **7.12** enforce onshore judgments, or reject jurisdiction and proper law claims which favour offshore law. Statutory exceptions to confidentiality may be made subject to approval by a court.[16]

The common law duty of confidentiality in relation to trusts

The duty of confidentiality which is attached to the offshore trust does not **7.13** spring only from statute. Under the common law, the trust is treated as a private document, for which there is a public interest in maintaining privacy. The trustee is thus required to keep information about the trust confidential and has a wide discretion with respect to confidentiality. Part of the rationale for

---

[12] See, eg, recent changes to International Business Company legislation which abolish bearer shares, Banks and Trusts Companies under the Regulation Act 2000 of The Bahamas. Under the Banks and Trust Companies 2000 Act of The Bahamas, eg, regulatory and supervisory authorities to whom information on all offshore trusts may be given include the Governor of the Central Bank or his agent. This stems from the new and wider powers of inspection and supervision under the Central Bank Act 2000 of The Bahamas. There may also be 'gateway' provisions in several statutes which allow disclosure in well-defined circumstances.

[13] See, eg, Money Laundering Act (Proceeds of Crime) Act 2000 of The Bahamas; the Money Laundering (Prevention and Control) Act 2001 of Dominica; and the Financial Transactions Reporting Act 2000 of The Bahamas, this last making financial information reporting routine.

[14] See, eg, Treaty between Antigua and Barbuda and the United States of America on Mutual Legal Assistance in Criminal Matters 1999 (Antigua and Barbuda), 31 October 1996.

[15] Offshore jurisdictions are increasingly willing to conclude Mutual Legal Assistance Treaties with onshore countries, since these are part of the campaign against international crime. The importance of such treaties has been noted by the courts, eg, in the case of *Bertioli v Malone* [1990–91] CILR 58. Courts have also encouraged international legal assistance generally. For example, they have been interventionist with respect to restraint orders because of this need to assist in the fight against international crime, evident in cases such as *Solvalub Ltd v Match Investments Ltd* [1997–98] 1 OFLR 152 (CA, Jersey) and *Credit Suisse Trust v Cuoghi* [1997] 3 WLR 878.

[16] See, eg, s 15 of the Cayman Islands Act, above, n 3.

these confidentiality obligations is explained by the fiduciary responsibilities of trustees. In effect, the nature and scope of confidentiality are contingent upon the quality of the trust relationship.

Legal professional privilege cannot protect against fraud

7.14   Under the common law, the professional relationship between an attorney and his or her client also gives rise to a well-established privilege that information gleaned as a result of that relationship will be protected as confidential. While legal professional privilege will normally apply to trust transactions, it is inapplicable where fraud is proved. Thus, in *E and B v A*,[17] in an action for discovery of trust documents in order to establish that the trust had been set up fraudulently to avoid the bank creditor, legal privilege could not protect the settlor. The settlor had transferred his property into the trust after defaulting on a guaranteed payment of a US $17 million promissory note. Consequently, the court found that a prima facie case of fraudulent conveyance had been made.

7.15   The court reiterated that, as a general rule, it would be reluctant to interfere with the privilege, but it had a discretion to see whether a *prima facie* case of fraud was made out. The question of fraud went beyond a fraud *simpliciter* and captured any commercial practice or business dealing that could readily be described as dishonest to the point of fraud by a reasonable business person. It should be observed that, in *E and B v A*, the privilege was held to be inapplicable even in the face of strong confidentiality laws in the Cook Islands.

Tax issues and disclosure

7.16   Disclosure imperatives may also emanate from onshore tax legislation which impacts significantly on offshore trusts. Consider, for example, the recent anti-avoidance trust provisions enacted in the United States.[18] The focus of the new legislation is not 'loophole closing' but information about taxable income and on the trust structure itself. The legislation targets offshore trusts created by US citizens or residents, including corporations, or US trusts migrating to low tax or tax-neutral jurisdictions. It also targets US beneficiaries of such trusts and tax-motivated expatriates, all of whom will now be subject to tax. Further, the legislation imposes stricter reporting requirements for such trusts and stiff penalties for non-compliance.[19] A US person who transfers property to a foreign

---

[17]   (2003) 5 ITELR 760 (CA, Cook Islands).

[18]   See the Small Business Job Protection Act 1996. See also s 679 of the Inland Revenue Code. Similar provisions now exist in Canada under the Income Tax (Amendment) Act 1996. See chapter 14 for a fuller discussion of these tax initiatives of onshore countries.

[19]   A penalty of 35% of income, for example.

trust will be treated as the owner of the trust unless the terms of the trust preclude the possibility of a US beneficiary.[20]

Such legislation may reach not just the settlor and beneficiaries resident onshore, but also, indirectly, the trustee. This is because the trustee, although theoretically outside of the reach of the onshore jurisdiction, may have to assist beneficiaries and the settlor caught by the provisions, in surrendering information on the trust.[21]   **7.17**

The erosion of confidentiality also occurs through the utilization of international instruments permitting assistance to onshore countries in tax matters. While international agreements and other instruments have not traditionally encompassed fiscal matters in their scope, they are doing so increasingly, because of the continuing efforts of onshore countries and international organizations such as the OECD, discussed further below, to persuade offshore countries to be more open with regard to fiscal matters.   **7.18**

Another trend relating to the international arena should be noted. This is the development which threatens the well-established rule against the non-enforcement of fiscal law. The surrendering of this rule to a more facilitative stance necessarily impacts on strict confidentiality norms. All of these developments identified in the international law approach to tax and confidentiality are discussed further in Part III of this book.[22]   **7.19**

The OECD and confidentiality obligations of offshore trusts

In the recent OECD initiatives against offshore regimes,[23] the offshore trust was targeted for its capacity to hide the identity of the beneficial owner of assets. The solution posed is the maintenance of records of such beneficial owners and the exchange of relevant information, as requested by onshore countries in the enforcement of their laws and tax policies. Other initiatives include provisions for the routine exchange of information by way of treaties.   **7.20**

Although the offshore trust is vilified by the OECD because it discourages transparency, it is common practice in onshore trust law that the details of   **7.21**

---

[20] Except in limited circumstances, a non-resident settlor can no longer be considered the tax owner of a trust (domestic or foreign). Instead, trust income is to be taxed when distributed to US beneficiaries, rather than attributed to the non-resident settlor, as was previously the case. Previously, the income of grantor trusts created by a non-resident alien, under which income is distributed to a US beneficiary, was not subject to US federal income tax.

[21] See chapter 17, 'Duties of Offshore Trustees in Relation to Tax' for a fuller discussion of such issues.

[22] 'The Offshore Tax Function'. See, in particular, chapters 14 and 16.

[23] See, eg, *Toward Global Tax Competition—Progress in Identifying Harmful Tax Practices* (the OECD Report 2000) (Paris, OECD, 26 June 2000).

beneficial owners are not revealed and other common law duties of confidentiality apply.[24] Indeed, as we have seen, the survivability of the trust concept itself perhaps depends on some feature of secrecy. One wonders whether the requested change in offshore trust law would be transplanted to orthodox trust law onshore and to onshore trust instruments, so as to create a level playing field between onshore and offshore financial systems. If not, the demand for reform is discriminatory and unacceptable. We recall here our earlier discussion of recent initiatives in onshore jurisdictions, for example in Atlanta and Delaware in the US, which mimic offshore trust regimes. This onshore—offshore trust law infrastructure has not been subjected to the international pressures from organizations such as the OECD as have offshore jurisdictions.[25]

C. Rights to Information on the Offshore Trust

Dimensions of disclosure in offshore trusts

7.22 The question whether trustees owe a duty to beneficiaries and, more recently, to protectors to disclose information about the offshore trust is a contentious one. It is a question which is mirrored in the uncertainty surrounding the issue in traditional trust law. Such a duty, matched by a parallel right to information by the beneficiaries or protectors, assumes more complexity in the offshore trust. It is thus unsurprising that several offshore jurisdictions have sought to clarify respective obligations and rights where information to beneficiaries is concerned. It is therefore important to consider to what extent such legislative provisions extend the legal norms identified under traditional trust principles. It is thus necessary at the outset to assess the position under traditional trust law before the full impact of offshore law in this area can be determined.

7.23 Several issues peculiar to offshore trusts arise. Among the most important are the following:

(1) The implications of the general confidentiality norm, often statute based, that exists in offshore jurisdictions and which applies to offshore trusts.[26] This may well be a policy issue.

(2) The very existence of protectors, who often act on the behalf of beneficiaries in overseeing the trust. The question must be asked whether this activity

---

[24] For example, under s 360 of the English Companies Act 1985, 'notice of any trust, express, implied or constructive' is prohibited on the Register.
[25] See chapter 5.
[26] Discussed above, paras 7.06–7.09.

displaces the rights of the beneficiaries to information, particularly where these rights arise from duties to account owed by trustees to beneficiaries.[27]

(3) The offshore trust is, typically, an *inter vivos* trust, with a settlor often having clear views about the management of the trust. In the case of a self-settled trust, the settlor is a primary beneficiary. Could this mean that less priority is to be given to other beneficiaries?

Typically, there is a wide discretion given to the trustee in favour of a widely **7.24** defined class of beneficiaries (usually for tax avoidance purposes). The settlor, whose true identity may sometimes be hidden behind some corporate figure-head, can often influence the exercise of the trustee's discretion.[28] The very structure of the offshore trust, in which there may be no reliable indication of who will eventually benefit from the settlement, is a point of note.

An offshore trust which promotes a strong confidentiality ethic should be **7.25** distinguished from a 'blind trust', or even a secret trust, the latter established to protect the identity of a beneficiary or beneficiaries. The blind trust is a discretionary trust that contains an explicit restriction of the right of a particular beneficiary to inspect the trust accounts. The trust is established by the said beneficiary, who desires no influence in the management and investment of the trust assets. Such a clause is usually inserted to protect a politician against future accusations that he is using his political office to gain financial advantages for himself. The blind trust, while not a creature of the English common law, has been recognized in other countries such as Canada and Australia. While the blind trust and the offshore trust are not the same, their motives with regard to the disclosure of information are similar, and the acceptance of blind trusts in several countries lends credibility to the objectives of the offshore trust in this regard.

Traditional bases for assuming rights to information

The elements characteristic to the offshore situation must be added to the **7.26** factors which have traditionally formed the bedrock of the argument that bene-ficiaries have rights to information about the traditional trust. These latter elements are:

(1) the duty of a trustee, as a fiduciary, to account to the beneficiaries for his or her stewardship of the trust; and

(2) the existence of a beneficiary's proprietary interest in the trust property.

---

[27] See also the discussion of the duties and rights of protectors in chapter 4.
[28] This scenario was recognized in *Schmidt v Rosewood Trust Ltd* (2003) 5 ITELR 715 (PC, Isle of Man) [2003] UKPC 26.

7.27 Where one accepts that the proper basis for a beneficiary to acquire information about the trust is his or her proprietary interest, this poses problems for the beneficiary who is merely the object of a discretionary trust power, where the proprietary interest in the trust property is not identifiable until the trustee exercises his or her discretion in the beneficiary's favour. As the typical offshore trust is a discretionary trust, this basis for assuming a right to information is tenuous. The fact that the settlor may often be the primary beneficiary, as is the case with the offshore trust, only accentuates the difficulty. Indeed, the object of the discretionary power has only a right to be considered and has no right or legitimate expectation to benefit.[29]

7.28 The most persuasive rationale for disclosure of information by trustees to beneficiaries of the trust is the duty to account. This, indeed, has been the most common juridical basis, as revealed by the case law. Yet even if one accepts that the rationale for information giving should be ascribed to the duty to account, there is the difficulty that this may considerably narrow the spectrum of information which a trustee may be obliged to give to the beneficiary, to only that relevant to account keeping. Important decisions, such as decisions on future investments, may thus be excluded. It seems, however, that under this duty, in appropriate circumstances, the right to information may extend to unwritten information and casual notes which are not part of any formal document.[30]

7.29 Hayton argues that the duty to account is part of the irreducible core of obligations under the trust. A clause attempting to keep the existence of the trust secret from the beneficiaries and prohibiting persons from informing the beneficiary that he or she is a beneficiary is, therefore, repugnant to the trust concept.[31] However, as will be seen, the cases do not suggest that this is a unanimous view.

Procedural disclosure

7.30 Beneficiaries may also be entitled to disclosure where they are parties to litigation concerning the trust. This is part of the general practice of discovery, cemented in the procedural rules of the court in proceedings. However, the

---

[29] But see *Scott v National Trust* [1998] 2 All ER 705, where it was held that in certain circumstances such a beneficiary may have a legitimate expectation that the discretion will be exercised to his benefit. One such situation would be where the discretion had been so exercised previously and the discretion holder was contemplating taking it away. At the very least, reasons should be given here.

[30] Such as the memorandum of wishes. See *Re Rabbaiotti 1989 Settlement* [2000] JLR 173 (Royal Ct), considered further below, at paras 7.61–7.63.

[31] D Hayton, 'The Irreducible Core Content of Trusteeship' in AJ Oakley (ed), *Trends in Contemporary Trust Law* (Clarendon Press, Oxford, 1996), chapter 3, affirmed in *Re Murphy's Settlement* [1998] 3 All ER 1.

debate on whether beneficiaries are entitled to information about the trust centres more on the general, equitable rights which may accrue and not on discovery for purposes of litigation or procedural disclosure.

Rules relating to discovery are determined by the particular jurisdiction, but **7.31** documents relevant to a particular issue in proceedings will usually be available, particularly to a beneficiary who alleges fraud or wrongdoing on the part of the trustee. Nonetheless, it is clear that a beneficiary will not be successful in obtaining information if he or she commences proceedings merely to obtain such information in order to determine whether a valid cause of action for trial may exist.[32] This general principle may be circumvented only in exceptional cases.[33] The prohibition is a common law rule, but statute has sometimes intervened to make exceptions for cases of, for example, personal injury litigation.[34]

In addition, *Norwich Pharmacal* orders may be sought in defiance of the rule. **7.32** This allows for third party discovery of innocent parties who have information relating to the matter at hand.

Rationales against disclosure

On the side of the growing number who argue against disclosure of information **7.33** in relation to the traditional trust may be found the following factors:

(1) confidentiality obligations which arise because of the nature of the trust relationship;

(2) the failure of the law to require trustees to provide reasons for the exercise of their discretions, as opposed to merely giving information on accounts or routine management matters;[35]

(3) public interest reasons that centre around a person's freedom not only to dispose of his or her property as he or she wishes, but also to impose certain conditions, or checks and balances, on his or her gift, or on the recipient of the gift. Confidentiality about the trust fulfils this objective; and

(4) the developed jurisdiction of a court to check the unrestrained or inappropriate use of power by a trustee if the occasion warrants it. This, of course, presupposes an action by the beneficiaries. However, the court has

---

[32] See *In re CA Settlement* [2002] JLR 312.

[33] ibid.

[34] See, eg, the Disclosure and Conduct before Action (Jersey) Law 1999. The rule is not generally applicable in the US.

[35] Where the trustee does give reasons, the court is at liberty to examine them, and such reasons must conform to the rule that a trustee must take relevant considerations into account and not take irrelevant ones. See *In re Hastings-Bass* [1970] 2 All ER 193. For a discussion of this rule as it relates to investment, see chapter 10, 'Duties of Trustees in Managing Offshore Trusts' and chapter 17, 'Duties of Offshore Trustees in Relation to Tax'.

authority to examine issues on a case-by-case basis without allowing for an absolute right to information on the part of the beneficiaries. Indeed, it is fundamental to the law of trusts that the court has jurisdiction to supervise and, if appropriate, intervene in the administration of a trust.[36]

7.34 The obstacle surrounding the giving of reasons is one not peculiar to trustees but common to holders of discretionary power, although public law is lessening the scope of this particular restriction in the interests of fairness and good administrative decision-making. Clearly, where the trust instrument provides that the trustee must give reasons, he or she is mandated to do so.

7.35 With regard to confidentiality, the settlor may have deliberately chosen the offshore trust just because of its enhanced protection of confidentiality. He or she may not wish the beneficiaries to know even of the existence of the trust, or of the extent of the settlor's assets, or of the size of any entitlement that may come to them, except at the appropriate appointed time. A parent may want, for example, to instil initiative into an offspring and may not wish him or her to know of a generous legacy until the appropriate time. The use of the institution of a protector to safeguard the interests of the beneficiaries and generally to supervise the trust renders the need for a beneficiary to supervise the trust, if not obsolete, less important. It ensures that supervision can be achieved without sacrificing the confidentiality of the trust to the beneficiaries' demands for information.[37]

7.36 There are other legitimate reasons for investors to desire confidentiality, in addition to reasons of confidentiality connected directly to beneficiaries. One common rationale will be a commercial secret. There is a risk that disclosure of information to the beneficiaries may prejudice these objectives. On the other hand, there are difficulties associated with the approach of secretly 'locking up' assets where beneficiaries have no knowledge of them. These come to the fore particularly when the settlor dies, as is ably demonstrated in the case of *Lawrence v Berbier*.[38]

Statutory provisions on information

7.37 Several offshore jurisdictions have enacted provisions on the disclosure of trust information to beneficiaries. However, these provisions are not consistent with one another. Some provisions seem merely to codify the less contentious aspects

---

[36] See *Schmidt v Rosewood Trust*, above, n 28, 729, discussed in more detail below, paras 7.73–7.87.

[37] The use of a protector creates its own problems, not the least of which is accountability, but the modern view is that protectors are indeed accountable when fulfilling such functions. See the discussion of protectors above, in chapter 4.

[38] (2003) 5 ITELR 9.

of traditional trusts law, such as the right of beneficiaries to see accounts. Others seek to preclude rights to information generally, although a trustee will generally retain a discretion to decide whether to disclose such information. Offshore legislation may provide for an absolute entitlement to information, or the entitlement may be conditional either on the terms of the trust, or on the discretion of the trustee, where he or she considers disclosure to be reasonable.

7.38 Non-discretionary routes to disclosure of information to beneficiaries are found, for example, in Jersey and The Bahamas. In Jersey, the beneficiaries are only absolutely entitled to information on the accounts.[39] In The Bahamas, the provisions are more comprehensive and certain beneficiaries are entitled to more than just information on the accounts. The provisions in The Bahamas are perhaps more comprehensive than elsewhere. First, The Bahamas Act makes a distinction between beneficiaries with vested interests and other beneficiaries, for example those who have contingent interests or who are mere objects of discretionary powers.[40] This is an important distinction which is made under case law but not found in offshore legislation elsewhere. Consequently, in other offshore jurisdictions, it is a matter ripe for judicial litigation.[41] Only the former class of beneficiaries has an entitlement to information under The Bahamas Act.[42]

7.39 The information which is required to be disclosed to beneficiaries entitled to such information under The Bahamas Act is:

(1) the documents relating to the trust instrument and all other documents in which the terms of the trust or any exercise of any trust, power, or discretion are to be found;
(2) all financial statements of the trust; and
(3) all financial statements of companies wholly owned by the trustees as trustees of the trust.[43]

---

[39] Article 25 of the Trusts (Jersey) Law 1984. The Jersey Act stipulates that subject to 'the terms of the trust and subject to any order of the court, a trustee shall not be required to disclose to any person any document which (a) discloses his deliberations as to the manner in which he has exercised a power or discretion or performed a duty . . .; or (b) discloses the reason for any particular exercise of such power or discretion or performance of duty . . .; (c) relates to the exercise or proposed exercise of such power or discretion or the performance or proposed performance of such duty; or (d) relates to or forms part of the accounts of the trust, unless, in a case to which sub-paragraph (d) applies, that person is a beneficiary under the trust not being a charity, or a charity which is referred to by name in the terms of the trust as a beneficiary under the trust [or the enforcer in relation to any non-charitable purposes of the trust].'
[40] Section 83(1) of the Trustee Act 1998 of The Bahamas.
[41] See discussion below, paras 7.56–7.59.
[42] Under s 83(5)(c).
[43] Section 83(6).

The documents mentioned under (3) are noteworthy, since in other jurisdictions, their inclusion in any entitlement to information is unclear and case law has had to determine the matter.[44]

7.40 Trustees are not required to disclose to any beneficiary the settlor's letter of wishes, documents disclosing the deliberations of the trustees on the exercise of their discretion, the trustees' reasons for acting, legal advice, and any documents relating to the exercise or proposed exercise of their discretion.[45]

7.41 While beneficiaries without vested interests have no right to information, the trustee in The Bahamas retains a discretion to disclose information to them, or he or she may be required to do so by order of a court.[46] However, the trustee may disclose information on the trust to beneficiaries without vested interests only in adherence to the conditions laid down under the Act. First, he or she is under no legal obligation to disclose to beneficiaries without vested interests, unless 'a person vested by the trust instrument with power to request or approve disclosure requests or approves such disclosure'.[47] However, he or she has an absolute discretion to disclose to such beneficiaries.[48] Secondly, the trustee is constrained by considerations of the confidentiality of other beneficiaries. Thirdly, he or she may not be required to disclose items enumerated under s 83(8), that is the memorandum of wishes, the trustee's reasons, and so on. Lastly, he or she may not disclose information to beneficiaries without vested interests where the trust instrument prohibits him or her from doing so.[49]

Subject to the terms of the trust

7.42 In other jurisdictions, the entitlement of the beneficiaries to information may be curtailed by the trust instrument.[50] Provisions which give substantial leeway to trustees to withhold information from the beneficiaries under the authority of the trust instrument may be found in Guernsey,[51] Barbados,[52] St Vincent,[53] and St Lucia.[54] In Guernsey, for example, the provision reads:

---

[44] See below, paras 7.88–7.92.
[45] Section 83(8).
[46] See s 83(5) (b) and s 83(10) of the Trustee Act 1998 of The Bahamas.
[47] Section 83(5)(a).
[48] Section 83(5)(b).
[49] Section 83(9).
[50] Recall too, the Jersey provisions, under Article 25 of the Trusts (Jersey) Law 1984, which only grant an absolute entitlement to information on the accounts. For other kinds of information on the trust, the trust instrument may prohibit it.
[51] Section 22 of the Trusts (Guernsey) Law 1989.
[52] Section 28 of the International Trusts Act 1995.
[53] Section 64 of the International Trusts Act 1996.
[54] Section 53(2) of the International Trusts Act 2002.

> Subject to the terms of the trust, a trustee shall, at all reasonable times, at the written request of any beneficiary . . . provide full and accurate information as to the state and amount of trust property.[55]

Discretion to disclose where reasonable

Another legislative construct for the disclosure of information to beneficiaries is to give trustees a discretion to disclose where they believe that it is 'reasonable' to do so. This formula is found in identical provisions in Belize[56] and Grenada.[57]   **7.43**

Relevance of case law and the jurisdiction of the court to order disclosure

With the exception of The Bahamas, Belize, and Grenada, in all of those jurisdictions which have enacted provisions permitting the disclosure of information to beneficiaries, the information required to be released relates only to the accounts and financial statements of the trust. In Jersey, the statutory right of beneficiaries to see information relating to accounts was affirmed in *Bhander v Barclays*[58] and *Re The Den Haag Trust*.[59]   **7.44**

Where the legislation contains a blanket prohibition against all disclosure except information on accounts, as in Saint Lucia[60] and Saint Vincent,[61] there would appear to be no room for case law to manoeuvre. However, where the legislation merely states, as in Jersey,[62] that the trustees have no legal obligation to disclose information *except* for accounts, or where it merely outlines an obligation with respect to accounts,[63] the question of disclosure of other kinds of information on the trust is left open. As such, with respect to requests for information other   **7.45**

---

[55] Section 22(1) of the Trusts (Guernsey) Law 1989.

[56] Section 28(1) of the Trusts Act 1992, as revised 2000. Beneficiaries are entitled to information on the 'state and amount of trust property' and the conduct of trust administration 'so far as is reasonable'.

[57] Section 28 of the International Trusts Act 1996.

[58] [1997–98] 1 OFLR 497.

[59] [1997–98] 1 OFLR 495.

[60] Section 53 of the International Trusts Act 2002 of Saint Lucia provides: '(1) . . . subject to the terms of the instrument creating an international trust . . . a trustee . . . shall not disclose to any person not legally entitled thereto, any information or documents respecting an international trust . . . (2) —Notwithstanding subsection (1) . . . the registered trustee shall, at the written request of a beneficiary named in the international trust, disclose any document . . . relating to or forming part of the accounts of the international trust . . .'

[61] Section 64 of the International Trust Act 1996, which reads: '(1) . . . no trustee . . . shall disclose to any other person . . . information or documents respecting an international trust . . . (2) Notwithstanding subsection (1) but subject to any other more specific terms of the trust instrument, the Registered Trustee shall, at the written request of a beneficiary named in the trust, disclose any document or information . . . forming part of the accounts of the international trust . . .' The section further ties the disclosure to the restrictive provisions of the Confidential Relationships Preservation Act of Saint Vincent, which requires that the beneficiary who receives the information must keep it confidential.

[62] Article 25 of the Trusts (Jersey) Law 1984.

[63] As in Guernsey.

than accounts, the following discussion on the jurisprudence concerning whether, and in what circumstances, trustees should be required to disclose information to beneficiaries, remains pertinent for these jurisdictions.

7.46 With respect to Belize and Grenada, given that disclosure depends on the standard of reasonableness and upon written requests by the beneficiaries, case law will continue to be important in determining when such requests should be legitimately heeded. In The Bahamas, beneficiaries without vested interests may ultimately have to depend on the courts for orders granting them access to documents. Here too, case law will continue to be important.

7.47 It is also notable that legislation may specifically allude to the court's authority to allow the disclosure of information to beneficiaries. This may be a limited authority.[64] However, it should be reiterated that even without such specific references to the courts' power in this regard, the courts may retain jurisdiction to order that information be disclosed.

7.48 The power of the court to order disclosure in the face of statutory provisions which attempt to regulate the disclosure of information was affirmed by the Jersey courts in *In re CA Settlement*.[65] In this case, the statute specifically retained the authority of the court to do so, although only imposing a legal obligation on the trustee to give information on accounts. The court found that its powers were wide and went beyond documents relating only to the accounts.

7.49 Further, although statute may specifically exclude certain documents, such as memoranda of wishes or trustee deliberations, from the obligations of the trustee to disclose information, the court may order their disclosure.[66] In *Re Rabbaiotti 1989 Settlement*,[67] for example, the Royal Court of Jersey made it clear that although the statute allowed a trustee to withhold a letter of wishes from the beneficiaries, the court retained a discretion to permit disclosure as part of its general power to order disclosure under the statute.[68] Indeed, Article 25 of the Trusts (Jersey) Law not only allows the court to order any document

---

[64] See, eg, s 28(3) of the International Trusts Act 1996 of Barbados, which reads: '(3) Notwithstanding any other law but subject to subsection (4), the court may, in any civil or criminal proceedings, allow the disclosure of information or document referred to in subsection (1) on the application of a party to the proceedings in such circumstances as the court thinks fit. (4) . . . in making an order under that subsection the court shall, *inter alia*, have regard to the importance of the information or document to the outcome of the proceedings.' Note also s 83(10) of The Bahamas Trustee Act 1998; Article 25 of the Trusts (Jersey) Law 1984.

[65] [2002] JLR 312, construing Article 25 of the Trusts (Jersey) Law 1984.

[66] See, eg, Article 25(b) and (c) of the Trusts (Jersey) Law 1984, as amended 1996, and s 53(2) of the International Trust Act 2002 of Saint Lucia, s 64 of the International Trust Act 1996 of Saint Vincent, and s 83 of the Trustee Act 1998 of The Bahamas.

[67] [2000] JLR 173.

[68] ibid, at 190.

for disclosure, but further permits that disclosure on the behalf of non-beneficiaries.[69]

Written requests for information—determining the existence of the trust

In most jurisdictions, statute provides for information to the beneficiaries only **7.50** upon written requests to the trustees.[70] Where the duty to disclose is dependent upon a written request, without a collateral duty to inform beneficiaries of the existence of the trust, problems of accountability may arise. The beneficiaries may not even know of the existence of the trust and cannot seek relevant information, although they may be entitled to it under legislation. As such, the duties toward disclosure may be nullified. Only The Bahamas legislation states explicitly that beneficiaries, at least those with vested interests, are entitled to information as to the existence of the trust and its terms.[71] In other jurisdictions, the matter is one which may still remain within the ambit of the court's discretion.

Inconsistent approaches to disclosure under the common law

An examination of the existing case law reveals that there are cases to justify **7.51** both arguments, for and against rights to information about the trust. The historical balance swings, arguably, in favour of a right to information, at minimum in relation to certain documents and in certain defined circumstances. This is now, of course, being threatened by the *Rosewood* case, discussed further below.[72] In addition, there seem to be no clear tests as to when the right applies or when it does not, and the distinctions between the two schools of thought are blurred and unconvincing, to say the least. This paves the way for the offshore trust more easily to define its role in the debate, and it is perhaps no accident that several of the more instructive decisions have come about in relation to the offshore trust. This is possibly because there are more compelling rationales for confidentiality in offshore trusts.

---

[69] See *In Re CA Settlement* above, n 65, construing Article 25 of the Trusts (Jersey) Law 1984, where the person seeking disclosure was the sister of the beneficiary, trying to establish whether there was cause to set aside a will. The application was turned down on other grounds. The court also interpreted Article 47 of the Trusts (Jersey) Law 1984, which lays down general provisions for orders of the court. In Jersey, the statutory provisions do not appear to override general principles of litigation, such as those limiting pre-trial discovery. Such principles prohibit the disclosure of documents sought merely to establish whether an action can be grounded.

[70] See, eg, in Saint Vincent, Guernsey, Belize, Grenada, Barbados, and Saint Lucia.

[71] Section 83(1). The trustee also has a discretion to disclose such information to beneficiaries without vested interests.

[72] *Schmidt v Rosewood Trust Ltd* (2003) 5 ITELR 715 (PC, Isle of Man); [2003] UKPC 26. See paras 7.73–7.87.

What type of information is in issue?

7.52 The best-known case on the right of beneficiaries to information on the trust is perhaps *Re Londonderry*.[73] It establishes that the disclosure of information on the trust may go beyond formal trust documents, such as the trust deed, and extend to other documents. Examples of documents which may be disclosed include:

(1) trust accounts on the status of the trust assets;

(2) deeds of appointment and removal of trustees;

(3) professional advice pertaining to the trust;

(4) details as to trust property and investments, including formal documents of same, such as mortgage deeds and property deeds;

(5) matters concerning the trust capital and assignments to beneficiaries;

(6) information concerning legal matters, such as legal opinions, instructions to counsel, and advice from counsel, which concern the terms of the trust and the extent of the trustees' duties.[74] This, however, may not extend to other legal correspondence, such as that which involves litigation, in particular litigation where the beneficiary is the hostile party.[75]

7.53 The list is not conclusive. However, it is well settled that whatever obligations may arise in relation to the disclosure of trust documents, these cannot extend to all documents which relate in some way, however small, to the trust. In *Re Londonderry*,[76] for example, it was conceded that '[t]he category of trust documents has never been comprehensively defined'. In the final analysis, relevant trust documents for disclosure would be judged on a case-by-case basis, during which the court will determine whether the beneficiaries are entitled to have knowledge of them.

7.54 It seems reasonably clear, however, even where there is found to be a duty to disclose, that such disclosure does not include documents:

(1) concerning meetings held between trustees, or between trustees and protectors, and correspondence between them;[77]

(2) such as the memorandum or letter of wishes;[78]

(3) concerning correspondence between trustees and beneficiaries;[79]

(4) containing the trustee's reasons for dispositive and administrative decisions.

---

[73] [1965] 1 Ch 918, 938.
[74] ibid.
[75] ibid.
[76] ibid.
[77] ibid.
[78] ibid. Cf *Re Rabaiotti 1989 Settlement* [2000] JLR 173.
[79] *Re Londonderry*, above, n 73.

The list should be read with an understanding that courts can hold, and have   **7.55**
held, any of the above documents and related information to be disclosable in a
particular situation. In addition, given the importance attached to memoranda
of wishes in offshore jurisdictions, there may be more compelling reasons to
view them as documents which should be disclosed.[80]

Different types of beneficiaries

The distinction between beneficiaries with vested interests and beneficiaries   **7.56**
who are mere objects of a discretionary power may be important in determining the question of the disclosure of information by trustees to beneficiaries,
although the more recent decisions illustrate that this difference may not be
conclusive.

Previous cases have held that the objects of a discretion are owed a duty by the   **7.57**
trustee to provide trust accounts and investment details about the trust. A
trustee is under no duty to inform the objects of his or her discretion of their
potential entitlement, so that it is difficult for those objects to enforce any
such right to information. This is exacerbated in offshore trust arrangements,
which are inherently confidential structures. English law on the question is
informed by the case of *Murphy v Murphy*,[81] although it can hardly be said to be
authoritative.

Murphy v Murphy[82] was concerned with a beneficiary's right to obtain informa-   **7.58**
tion (as to the identity of the trustees) from the settlor himself. However,
Neuberger J discussed the position of the plaintiff as a discretionary object and
stated:

> The facts that in this case the plaintiff is merely within the class of discretionary
> beneficiaries (as opposed to being someone with a vested beneficial interest in the
> trust property) and that there is no suggestion of wrongdoing on the part of the
> trustees appear to me to go to the question of whether to exercise the discretion [to
> exercise what the judge called the equitable jurisdiction] rather than whether the
> discretion exists at all.[83]

In contrast, it was thought that beneficiaries with a vested interest were entitled   **7.59**

---

[80] Note, eg, that they were held to be disclosable in *Re Rabbaiotti 1989 Settlement* [2000] JLR
173 (Royal Ct), discussed below at paras 7.61, 7.65, and 7.96.
[81] [1999] 1 WLR 282 and followed in *Re Rabbaiotti 1989 Settlement* [2000] JLR 173
(Royal Ct). See also *Spellson v George* (1987) 11 NSWLR 300, a decision from New South
Wales.
[82] Above, n 81.
[83] ibid, 290.

to disclosure.[84] As seen below, recent cases have focused on this distinction in returning to the question whether information should be disclosed, challenging and even rejecting it as a credible or sufficient basis for disclosure.[85]

Recent exceptions to disclosure of information

7.60   Offshore trusts have been instrumental in laying down principles which seem to challenge, or perhaps clarify, this area of trust law, often finding that no rights to information accrue to beneficiaries at all. Some of these recent cases which prohibit disclosure should perhaps be viewed as exceptions to the general rule on disclosure as opposed to rules in themselves.

7.61   Interestingly, whereas the courts in later decisions have refused to order disclosure of documents in cases for which there would previously have been a considerable consensus that disclosure was appropriate, on the other hand they have also been willing to order disclosure for documents which, on the face of it, were not disclosable. *Re Rabaiotti 1989 Settlement*[86] is a good example of this latter phenomenon. Here, it was decided that although there was a strong presumption against the disclosure of a letter of wishes from the settlor to the trustee on the basis that it was a confidential document, in the instant case, a strong argument for discovery had been made. Accordingly, the document should be disclosed. The beneficiary bringing the claim for disclosure was involved in divorce proceedings in England, and the High Court there had ordered him to disclose copies of relevant documents (including the letter of wishes) of the trust settlements in order to make an appropriate financial award for the beneficiary's wife.

7.62   The Royal Court of Jersey, in examining these circumstances, felt that they met the high standard required to make a clear case for disclosure. It found that without disclosure the English court might proceed on an erroneous basis, given that the information before it was essentially different to that in the letter of wishes. It was, therefore, in the beneficiary's best interest that disclosure was ordered.

7.63   The decision fits neatly into the category of cases which allows procedural disclosure as the information was required for assistance in court proceedings. The court's emphasis, however, was on the best interests of the beneficiaries where exceptional cases are presented. The decision is thus of wide application.

---

[84] See *Chaine-Nickson v Bank of Ireland* [1976] IR 393, affirmed in *Schmidt v Rosewood Trust Ltd*, above, n 28.

[85] See paras 7.73–7.87.

[86] [2000] JLR 173 (Royal Ct).

Commercially sensitive documents

One valid exception has been determined to be where the documents in ques-   **7.64**
tion are commercially sensitive and disclosure of them would cause an unjusti-
fied interference in the business concern of which the trustee was a partner.
This was an issue in *Re Ojjeh Trust*,[87] which concerned a request for information in relation to matters of underlying trust companies. Here, Smellie J
confirmed the general rule that beneficiaries are normally entitled to information on the trust, as Cayman law is the same as the English common law on the
matter.[88]

The interest of other beneficiaries

Disclosure may also be refused to a beneficiary who requests it on the basis that,   **7.65**
when balanced against the interests of other beneficiaries, it might be prejudicial
to such other beneficiaries. In *Re Rabaiotti 1989 Settlement*,[89] the court examined such a case but found the interests of the beneficiaries in seeking information to be more important. However, this was not a difficult decision as the
remaining beneficiaries supported full disclosure.[90] The concession to other
beneficiaries appears to arise mainly where the value of such disclosure to the
requesting beneficiaries is minimal, or where the trust itself is threatened. These
were the influential factors in *Re Lemos's Trust Settlement*[91] and in *Re the M and L
Trusts Nearco Trustee Company (Jersey) Ltd v AM and Others*.[92]

In the latter case, one of the beneficiaries challenged the validity of the trust   **7.66**
as a sham, seeking information on the trust assets for the purposes of associated litigation before an Illinois court. The court held that it would not have
been in the interest of the beneficiaries as a class to make such disclosure,
since, if the trust was declared invalid, the other beneficiaries would receive
nothing.

Similarly, in *Re Lemos*, some of the beneficiaries had instituted proceedings in   **7.67**
the Greek courts seeking to set aside a Cayman Island trust. The court found
that documents should not be released for such a purpose, again on the ground
that the abortion of the trust, if the motion was successful, could not be in the
interests of the beneficiaries.

---

[87] [1992–93] CILR 348 (Grand Ct). The substantive issue of disclosure in relation to
information from underlying trust companies is discussed below, paras 7.88–7.92.
[88] ibid, at 362, relying on *O'Rourke v Derbishire* [1920] AC 581.
[89] Above, n 86.
[90] See also the Australian case of *Rouse and Others v IOOF Australia Trustees Ltd* [1999] SASC
181, Supreme Court of Australia.
[91] [1992–93] CILR 26 (Cayman Islands) (CA).
[92] (2003) 5 ITELR 656.

Where information is sought to ground an action

7.68   Offshore courts will uphold the general principle of litigation under the common law which stipulates that a potential plaintiff is not entitled to pre-action discovery of documents to enable him or her to establish whether he or she has a cause of action. This principle was upheld even in the face of statutory provisions which were sufficiently wide to allow such discovery in a hostile trust action. This was in the case of *In re CA Settlement*,[93] which interpreted the Trusts (Jersey) Law 1984.[94]

7.69   The court construed the Act to mean that a third party or stranger to the trust could, in fact, obtain disclosure of information on the trust under Article 25. However, with respect to pre-trial discovery, while the court acknowledged that, theoretically, it had the discretion to order disclosure on behalf of a stranger to the trust under the statute, it found it inappropriate to do so, as the thrust of the provision was toward administrative expediency: '. . . there were no reasons of principle or public policy for placing a potential plaintiff in hostile trust proceedings in a preferable position than in any other type of action'.[95]

7.70   The existence of Article 47, which was clearly intended to give a general power to the court to give directions in administrative proceedings, should not be used as a 'back door' method, allowing pre-trial discovery to a non-beneficiary who wishes to attack a trust.[96] However, this is not an absolute rule. The court may order such discovery in an exceptional case, although Deputy Bailiff Birt found it difficult to envision such circumstances.[97]

7.71   In *Re Lemos*,[98] the rule was also applied, this time in relation to beneficiaries who were seeking information with which to attack the trusts.

7.72   To disclose information on the trust, where such information could be used to invalidate the trust, would not only be to the detriment of the beneficiaries, and thus a violation of the trustee's duty to protect beneficiaries, but also against

---

[93] Above, n 65.

[94] Article 47, which reads: '(2) The court may, if thinks fit: (a) make an order concerning—(i) the execution or the administration of any trust; or . . . (iii) a beneficiary or any person having a connexion with the trust; . . . (3) An application to the court for an order or declaration under paragraph (2) may be made by the Attorney General or by the trustee . . . or, with leave of the court, by any other person.'

[95] [2002] JLR 312, at 319.

[96] ibid.

[97] ibid. The circumstances at hand were the saving of costs, the fact that the documents would be disclosed in the event that the action commenced, and the fact that pre-trial discovery would be more limited than the full discovery required at trial. These were all insufficient to make an exceptional case.

[98] Above, n 91 followed in *Re CA*, above, n 65.

public policy. This was the view of Smellie J, of the Cayman Islands Grand Court, in the case of *In the Matter of H*.[99] Here, the requirement for information on a Cayman Island trust came at a time when the trust was the subject of litigation pending in the Cayman Island courts on the question of invalidity.

The courts' inherent supervisory discretion to order disclosure

The most thought-provoking and perhaps authoritative decision to date on the disclosure of trust information is that of *Schmidt v Rosewood Trust Ltd*,[100] a decision which places the question of disclosure squarely within the court's inherent supervisory discretion. This approach sidelines some of the other issues thought previously to be important, such as differences between beneficiaries with vested interests and those who are objects of a power. The court here was primarily concerned with the question whether a beneficiary who was the object of a discretionary power had a right to disclosure. **7.73**

In *Schmidt v Rosewood Trust Ltd*, a beneficiary made application to the court for access to the documents of a discretionary trust, in order to validate his claim to a share of the trust fund and his allegation that the trustee had been over-charging for his services. He asserted the right to such information on the basis that he was the object of a power. In the final leg of the litigation, the beneficiary appealed to the Privy Council. **7.74**

Giving a comprehensive review of the most important decisions to date,[101] the court affirmed what it considered to be a fundamental principle of a trust, whether a discretionary trust or other form of trust. This is, that 'the trustee is subject to a personal obligation to hold, and to deal with, the trust property for the benefit of some identified, or identifiable, person or group of persons'.[102] All trustees are, therefore, subject to the courts' jurisdiction to supervise the administration of the trust. From this arose the trustees' correlative duty to account. That, in the court's view, formed the basis for the proposition that rights to information could not automatically be excluded from beneficiaries who were mere objects of a discretionary trust. **7.75**

However, although concerned more particularly with beneficiaries who were objects of a discretionary power, the court could find no compelling reason to **7.76**

---

[99] [1996] CILR 237 (Grand Ct).
[100] Above, n 28
[101] Such as *Mettoy Pensions Ltd v Evans* [1991] 2 All ER 513; *McPhail v Poulton* [1971] AC 424; *O'Rourke v Darbishire* [1920] AC 581; *Re Londonderry's Settlement Peat v Walsh* [1965] Ch 918, [1964] 3 All ER 855; *Hartigan Nominees Pty Ltd v Rydge* (1992) 29 NSWLR 405; *Chaine-Nickson v Bank of Ireland* [1976] IR 393; *Spellson v George* (1987) 11 NSWLR 300; *Murphy v Murphy, Re Murphy's Settlement* [1998] 2 OFLR 725, [1998] 3 All ER 1.
[102] At 740, approving *Spellson v George* (1987) 11 NSWLR 300, 315.

make clear distinctions between such objects and beneficiaries with proprietary interests. This was also the finding in *Stuart-Hutcheson v Spread Trustee Company Ltd*,[103] a case emanating from Guernsey.

7.77 In *Stuart-Hutcheson*, the discretionary beneficiary, who had concerns about the management of the trust and the distribution of benefits, applied for delivery of the trust instruments and all other formal trust documentation, including the minutes of companies owed by the trust and related correspondence. The trustee applied to the court for directions as to whether a discretionary beneficiary with no vested interest was entitled to demand information relating to the trust. The Court of Appeal found that all beneficiaries of a trust had a right to information from the trustees as to the assets of the trust and their manner of dealing with them.[104]

7.78 A discretionary beneficiary, at any rate if he or she belongs to a limited class, has the same interest in receiving an account of the unappointed assets as any other kind of beneficiary because he or she is a permissible object of the trustee's discretion.[105]

No beneficiaries have rights to information

7.79 The court's refusal in *Schmidt v Rosewood Trust Ltd* to give credence to the perceived dichotomy between discretionary and other trusts, led to a more general finding that there was no absolute right of *any* beneficiary to information. The court here, while drawing on recent cases, invoked older authority on the issue.

7.80 However, the recent cases also confirm[106] that no beneficiary (and least of all a discretionary object) has any entitlement as of right to disclosure of anything which can plausibly be described as a trust document.[107]

7.81 Yet this is not the end of the matter. The absence of an absolute and general right to information on the part of beneficiaries does not take away the court's inherent jurisdiction to supervise and, if appropriate, intervene in the administration of trusts. According to their Lordships in *Rosewood Trust Ltd*:

> a beneficiary's right to seek disclosure of trust documents, although sometimes not inappropriately described as a proprietary right, is best approached as one

---

[103] (2003) 5 ITELR 140 (CA, Guernsey).

[104] The court found also that Guernsey had received the common law on trusts and disclosure of information, and parts not changed by the Guernsey Trusts Law 1989, which did not codify the entire law of trusts or law of disclosure, were retained.

[105] (2003) 5 ITELR 140, at 152, adopting *Murphy v Murphy*, above, n 101.

[106] As had been stated as long ago 1886 in *Re Cowin, Cowin v Grauett* (1886) 36 Ch D 179.

[107] *Schmidt v Rosewood*, above, n 28, at 742.

aspect of the court's inherent jurisdiction to supervise (and where appropriate intervene) in the administration of trusts. There is therefore in their Lordships' view no reason to draw any bright dividing-line either between transmissible and non-transmissible (that is, discretionary) interests, or between the rights of an object of a discretionary trust and those of the object of a mere power (of a fiduciary character). The differences in this context between trusts and powers are (as Lord Wilberforce demonstrated in *McPhail v Doulton*) a good deal less significant than the similarities. The tide of Commonwealth authority, although not entirely uniform, appears to be flowing in that direction.[108]

What the court must do is to balance, on a case-by-case basis, the competing   **7.82**
interests that arise in determining the question. This is particularly so where there are issues as to personal or commercial confidentiality. In such a case:

> the court may have to balance the competing interests of different beneficiaries, the trustees themselves, and third parties. Disclosure may have to be limited and safeguards may have to be put in place. Evaluation of the claims of a beneficiary (and especially of a discretionary object) may be an important part of the balancing exercise which the court has to perform on the materials placed before it.[109]

Ultimately, this may leave us under the discretion of a court. It may mean that   **7.83**
there will be many more applications for directions in the future. The question of the disclosure of information must be a question of fact. In *Schmidt v Rosewood*, the underlying question of fact as to whether disclosure was warranted in the particular instance was remitted to the High Court to decide. Nonetheless, the court helpfully indicated what it considered might be a weak case: '[In] many cases the court may have no difficulty in concluding that an applicant with no more than a theoretical possibility of benefit ought not to be granted any relief.'[110] In contrast, in the instant matter, there was a strong case for disclosure as it involved a personal representative and a breach of fiduciary duty was alleged. The balance thus remains more heavily weighted in favour of a beneficiary with a proprietary interest, or the likelihood of a proprietary interest.

Offshore policy considerations

The *Schmidt v Rosewood* court was obviously influenced also by the peculiar   **7.84**
nature of the typical offshore trust. Underlying its finding seems to be a concern that should a rule ousting discretionary objects be broadly applied, this would fail to harness offshore trusts as an entire class of trusts which could go unchecked. Policy considerations, therefore, very clearly underline the judgment.

The court analysed the case of *Chaine-Nickson*[111] in a modern context, finding   **7.85**

---

[108] ibid.
[109] ibid.
[110] ibid.
[111] Above, n 101.

that counsel's implication that it was a special and unusual case because of the lack of a beneficiary who had a fixed interest in default of exercise of the trustees' discretion, and who would be in a position to require disclosure of accounts, was no longer valid in the face of contemporary trust structures such as offshore trusts. Indeed,

> offshore settlements do very commonly, for reasons already noted, have no ascertained beneficiaries with fixed interests and real economic stakes in the enforcement of the trustees' fiduciary duties. The appropriate authority was, with respect, too ready to dismiss *Chaine-Nickson* as untypical and unhelpful. The contrary view does indeed lead to remarkable results.[112]

7.86   In the final analysis, a strict rule that a discretionary object could not obtain information would lead to 'remarkable results'.[113]

The settlor's intention

7.87   While the court in *Schmidt v Rosewood* was obviously aware of and influenced by the peculiarities of offshore trusts, surprisingly it made no mention of the typical settlor's intention in such a trust. Indeed, this is an unfortunate oversight, whether with respect to all trusts, or to offshore trusts. In placing all trusts in one category and suggesting that it is for the court to decide when to order disclosure, the settlor's intent should surely be at least a relevant consideration in the exercise. In offshore trusts, where the intent to keep the trust confidential may be overwhelming, the omission with respect to intention is glaring.

Disclosure of information on trust related companies

7.88   Where the offshore trust is structured alongside an underlying company, the question of any right on the part of beneficiaries to inspect documents is even broader. It may extend to a right to inspect the documents relating to the companies alongside the trust. This should be treated as an exception to the general rule under the common law, which normally precludes such disclosure, evidenced in cases such as *Re Ojjeh Trust*[114] and *O'Rourke v Darbishire*.[115] Offshore arrangements appear to meet the requirement that disclosure of such information is merited only in exceptional cases.[116]

---

[112]   ibid, at 739.

[113]   ibid.

[114]   [1992–93] CILR 348 (Grand Ct).

[115]   [1920] AC 581.

[116]   *Re Ojjeh* is not necessarily out of sync with the *Rosewood* and *Stuart-Hutcheson* (see para 7.89 below) line of cases, as it did not completely deny disclosure of information of underlying companies in all circumstances. This supports our earlier contention that such cases on disclosure may be treated as exceptions to a general rule rather than rules in themselves.

In *Stuart-Hutcheson v Spread Trustee Company Ltd*,[117] for example, the trustee **7.89**
held 50% of the shares in an underlying company in Guernsey. The officers of
both the trust and the underlying company came from the trustee company, and
the documents of the underlying company were held by the trustees as trustees
of the trust. The applicant, a discretionary beneficiary of the trust, sought to
inspect the documents, specifically the company accounts and minutes of meetings of the underlying company. Section 22(2) of the Trusts Guernsey Law
1989, provided for the right of beneficiaries to inspect trust documents and also
provided for the authority to exclude such a right. Finding first that the Act did
not apply to the trust in question, as it had been established before the com-
mencement date of the statute, the court had to decide whether the basic
principles of trust law, including the duty of trustees to account to beneficiaries,
had been received in Guernsey and constituted a law in force apart from the
statute law.

The court found that trust law had been received. Accordingly, a beneficiary was **7.90**
entitled to inspect trust documents, as this was considered to be part of the duty
of trustees to account. More importantly, for our present purposes, the right
extended to a right to inspect the documents of the underlying company as
there was no real distinction or separation of the trust and the company in
relation to such documents:

> The question remains whether the minutes of the directors of Cedar are records of
> the actions of the trustees, which they should be required to reveal to the bene-
> ficiaries . . . we must, in my view, look at the substance of the matter, Cedar is, in
> reality, the creature of the trustee, beneficially owned as to 50% by the No 2 and
> No 3 Settlements. The actual directors are two companies with the same stable as
> the trustee. Those two companies are two of the seven companies, the others
> including the trustee who, according to a search, were the registered shareholders
> of Cedar, which has at all relevant times been beneficially owned by the No 2 and
> No 3 Settlements. We may, I think, legitimately infer that the trustee runs the
> Board. Further, Cedar is the vehicle by which the trustee holds one of the two
> principal trusts . . . In those circumstances it seems to me that these minutes, too,
> are liable to be produced.[118]

From this case a narrow principle emerges. A right to inspect company docu- **7.91**
ments, where a trustee has interests in the company, arises where the trustee and
that company are closely connected and the trustee and director relationships
are closely intertwined. In such a case, there is no real separation of identity
between the trustee and the company, at least for purposes of accountability,
and no real distinction between trust and company documents.

---

[117] (2003) 5 ITELR 140 (CA), *per* Clarke JA.
[118] ibid, at 156. This may also have implications for nominee directors.

7.92   In the recent decision of *Schmidt v Rosewood Trust Ltd*,[119] the disclosure of documents relating to the business of a company in which the trustee holds shares or is a partner, was also acknowledged as a special category of case which might militate toward disclosure. Here, neither side made any submissions seeking to distinguish between trust documents and documents relating to the affairs of a company controlled by the trustees.[120] However, the court hinted at the important distinction between such trustee controlled companies and others, finding *obiter* that '[the former] may have represented a realistic decision made by the trustees in the light of how the two settlements were in fact administered'. This was a circumstance which had to be considered carefully to assess the reach of any right to information.

Trustees' duties to disclose attorney correspondence

7.93   A trustee may be required to disclose to beneficiaries correspondence between the trustee and its attorney that concerns the administration of the trust. In the absence of a US appellate decision, Wettick J, in the case of *Fdlansbee v Gerlach*,[121] relied on common law jurisdictions and accepted and applied the principle.

7.94   In *Fdlanshee*, the beneficiaries sued the attorneys for the trust, alleging that one of the attorneys had legally represented another beneficiary whose interests were hostile to theirs, enabling the other beneficiary to file a declaratory judgment action which would prejudice them. It was also alleged that the attorneys induced the bank trustee to claim the status of a shareholder in the litigation. The aggrieved beneficiaries therefore subpoenaed documents consisting of communications between the trustee and the attorney from the bank trust trustee. The bank trustee asserted attorney/client privilege over the documents.

7.95   The court ruled that in most jurisdictions there was a distinction between communications about trust administration and communication about potential liability. The attorney/client privilege is applicable only to communications concerning liability. Thus, the duty placed on trustees to furnish information on the management of the trust includes the opinions of attorneys procured by the trustee to guide the trustee in the administration of the trust. The trustee was, therefore, required to make disclosure.

---

[119] Above, n 28. See also *Re Ojjeh Trust*, above, n 87.
[120] See also *Butt v Kelson* [1952] 1 Ch 197 for an earlier case making this point.
[121] (CCP 06/13/02), digested in [2003] *Trusts and Trustees* 15, *per* Wettick J.

Disclosure of memorandum of wishes

As we noted earlier, the memorandum of wishes is not usually a document **7.96** which the trustee is expected to disclose, even where he or she has a duty to disclose trust documents.[122] We have also noted that offshore legislation often specifically excludes the memorandum of wishes from any stated obligations toward disclosure.[123] Yet in *Re Rabaiotti 1989 Settlement*,[124] the Jersey courts felt that where legislation did not attempt to oust, generally, the jurisdiction of the court to make orders for disclosure, the court could order production of the memorandum of wishes.

However, the memorandum of wishes is not envisaged as a trust document and **7.97** it is meant to be non-binding.[125] The circumstances in which a court could, or should, order such disclosure are, therefore, limited. The most important circumstance will, perhaps, be where the trust is challenged as a sham. In this situation, the memorandum of wishes will be directly relevant to the challenge, as the settlor would, typically, avoid setting out his or her real instructions and intentions toward the trust in the trust document, but would have sought to 'hide' them in the memorandum of wishes. The courts, would, therefore, be disposed to 'look through' the formal trust structure and examine other documents which may be evidence of the alleged sham. The memorandum of wishes may be such a document and may, consequently, be surrendered up for disclosure.[126]

Secrecy clauses

As indicated earlier,[127] confidentiality duties may arise in relation to offshore **7.98** trusts because of the generous attitude of offshore jurisdictions and legislatures toward confidentiality. Apart from these broad duties of confidentiality, a settlor may demand confidentiality of his or her trustee or protector by inserting a confidentiality clause into the trust document. One or more, or even all, trust documents may be required to be treated as secret. However, the latter situation, whereby all trust documents and, by extension, trust arrangements, or even the very existence of the trust, are to be treated as secret, is likely to encourage litigation, with predictable success to the challengers. It is unlikely, for example, that such a trust document could oust the inherent supervisory jurisdiction of

---

[122] See above, paras 7.49 and 7.55.
[123] ibid.
[124] Above, n. 86.
[125] See discussion in paras 2.64–2.67.
[126] See the discussion of sham trusts in chapter 8.
[127] See above, paras 7.05 ff.

the court over trusts. Similarly, it would be very difficult, if not impossible, for such a clause to override the trustee's duty to account, thought to be a fundamental rule of trust law. It appears, however, that the courts are likely to tolerate such secrecy clauses within certain limits.[128]

Partial disclosure

7.99   The court may, in its discretion, order only partial disclosure, that is, allow an applicant to obtain only limited documents. This was the case, for example, in *Lemos v Coutts and Co*,[129] where the beneficiaries applied to the Grand Court of the Cayman Islands for discovery of certain documents which had been referred to in the affidavits of related proceedings. The documents included the deeds of appointment, letters of wishes, formal trust accounts, and records. The trust deed specifically gave the trustee a discretion to deny production of such accounts. The plaintiffs were also seeking an injunction to restrain the assets pending the outcome of the substantive case for, among other things, the trustee's alleged dishonesty and mismanagement.

7.100   The court held that, in the interest of fairness to enable the plaintiffs to dispose of their related case, an order for inspection would be allowed. However, because of the preliminary stage of the related proceedings, the plaintiffs were only allowed to inspect:

(1) the deeds of appointment, since they were entitled to know the identity of the trustees and their history in relation to the trust; and

(2) the letter of wishes.

At that initial stage, it was not necessary, and indeed would be prejudicial, for the beneficiaries to obtain information about the books, records, and various kinds of accounts. Hence, the request for inspection in relation to these items was denied.

---

[128] See, eg, *Rouse and Others v IOOF Australia Trustees Ltd*, above, n 90.
[129] [1992–93] CILR 5.

8

THE OFFSHORE TRUST AS A SHAM

A. The Essence of a Sham Trust

An important question of legitimacy which confronts the offshore trust, perhaps more so than the onshore trust, is the question whether the offshore trust may be deemed a sham. The fundamental principle of the trust is the transfer of legal ownership to the trustee. Thus, where it can be proved that there was a transfer of ownership in *form* only and not in *substance*, and the true intentions of the parties are different to the acts done, the trust can then effectively be challenged as a 'sham'. The effect of a declaration of a sham is that the trust will be void.[1] **8.01**

Sham trusts may be classified as 'formal shams', in which the trust instrument, on its face, reserves so much control to the settler that the trustee is deemed to be a mere nominee, or 'substantive shams'. In the latter, the trust may be correct in form, but in reality there is an agreement, whether implicit or explicit, that the settlor will, in fact, remain in control. The sham doctrine is particularly significant for the offshore trust, as settlors, understandably, will often be fearful about placing their monies abroad, in the hands of little known, foreign, professional trustees. Nevertheless, if real and effective transfer of control is not effected, the trust is vulnerable. **8.02**

Where a settlor seeks refuge in an offshore trust but is reluctant to forfeit control of his or her assets, the issue of ownership is open to speculation. Questions concerning the proper transfer of assets and control into the discretionary **8.03**

---

[1] Cf the discussion of 'partial shams' below, para 8.79. Note that the notion of a sham is not confined to trusts. It may refer to any transaction, document, or relationship.

offshore trust are, therefore, pertinent to its validity and, ultimately, the ability of challengers to the trust to reach its assets.[2]

Definition of a sham and the *Rahman* decision

8.04   The classic definition of a sham was pronounced by Lord Diplock in the case of *Snook v London and West Riding Investments Ltd.*[3] As a legal concept, a sham

> means acts done or documents executed by the parties to the 'sham', which are intended by them to give to third parties or to the court the appearance of creating between the parties legal rights and obligations different from the actual legal rights and obligations (if any) which the parties intend to create.

8.05   The fact that the act or document is uncommercial, or even artificial, does not mean that it is a sham. A distinction is to be drawn between the situation where parties make an agreement which is unfavourable to one of them, or artificial, and a situation where they intend some other agreement to take effect according to its tenor. In the latter situation, the agreement is not to bind their relationship.[4] Indeed, the benchmark for a sham is a high one. In the court's view, as a first principle, there must be a 'good reason not to recognize the validity of a formal legal document freely entered into by a person of sound mind'.[5]

8.06   In *Snook*, Lord Diplock was speaking in the context of structured financial transactions (a refinancing operation). However, the sham doctrine has been successfully transplanted to trusts law.[6] In the trust, the manifestation of the sham will often be in the control that the settlor exercises over the trust, to the detriment of the trustee's exercise of discretion and the integrity of the trust. Further, that should have been the intended result. However, Lord Diplock's clear definition can sometimes falter when applied to trusts. It can appear that the sham is easier to identify than it is to define. The result is a doctrine, when applied to trusts, which at times appears ambivalent.

8.07   The case of *Rahman v Chase Bank Trust Co Ltd*, which came before the Royal Court of Jersey, has often been seized upon as the *locus classicus* on the 'sham' rule with respect to offshore trusts.[7] Yet *Rahman* was more properly concerned

---

[2] The trust is also open to challenge if the settlor retains a life interest or fixed interest in the income of the trust, or the trust is revocable.

[3] [1967] 2 QB 786, 802; [1967] 1 All ER 518, 528.

[4] *In re Abacus CI Ltd (Trustee of the Esteem Settlement) Grupo Torras SA v Al Sabah* (2003) 6 ITELR 368 (Royal Ct Jersey), at 390, relying on *Snook*, above n 3.

[5] *Abacus*, above n 4, 394.

[6] In cases such as *Wily (Trustee of the Bankrupt Estate of Fuller) and another v Fuller and Others* (2001) 3 ITELR 321. See also the reinstatement of the sham principle in *Hitch v Stone (Inspector of Taxes)* [2001] EWCA Civ 63; [2001] STC 214.

[7] [1991] JLR 103.

with the principle of *donner et retenir ne vaut*, applicable in Jersey.[8] The judgment, being, as it was, more immediately concerned with that principle, offers very meagre reasoning on the nature of, and the principles necessary to ground a sham trust. It is particularly defective in its failure to project appropriate tests for the issues of an intention to create a trust and the sufficiency of a unilateral sham.

Rather unhelpfully, the court stated that the trust   **8.08**

> was a sham in the sense that it was made to appear to be what it was not. The *don* was *don* to an agent or nominee. The trustee was never made the master of the assets. KAR intended to and in fact retained the control of the capital and income of the trust fund. KAR's advisors and the trustee lent their services to the attainment of his wishes . . . Accordingly, . . . the settlement and the gifts to the trustee were wholly invalid and of no effect . . . in that firstly, the powers contained in the settlement breached the maxim or rule of law that *donner et retenir ne vaut* and, secondly, the settlement was a sham which KAR did not intend to have legal effect.[9]

It is true that intention and control are portrayed as key ingredients in the sham,[10] but the parameters of that intention are not outlined.

Not surprisingly, therefore, the Royal Court, in the later judgment of *In re*   **8.09** *Abacus (CI) Ltd (Trustee of the Esteem Settlement) Grupo Torras SA v Al Sabah*,[11] which provides a comprehensive analysis of the sham doctrine (and indeed, of the nature and circumstances of typical offshore trusts), discredits *Rahman* as a classic sham case, saying, 'we find it impossible from this slender base to know whether the court in Rahman's case considered that a unilateral sham was sufficient'.[12]

In the US, the parallel idea to the 'sham' is the 'alter ego', where the trust or   **8.10** trustee is viewed as an alter ego of the settlor. It is now also a term in use in other jurisdictions. In *Pack v US*,[13] the concept was applied to allow the enforcement of a tax lien against the property of an offshore trust on the ground that both the trust and the trustee were the 'alter egos' of the taxpayer-settlor. The court viewed the settlor as the true owner of the trust assets as there was no 'legal

---

[8] This describes the situation where a person purports to give away something but retains the power of disposal and is capable of exercising it freely.

[9] [1991] JLR 103, 114.

[10] 'The court is satisfied that Ramel Abdel Rahman intended (a) to retain control of the capital income of the trust fund throughout his lifetime': ibid.

[11] Above, n 4. This was another arm of the complex litigation by Grupo Torras against the settlor Sheik Fahad, who established trusts in several offshore jurisdictions.

[12] See p 398, ibid. The unilateral sham is discussed more fully below at paras 8.35–8.38.

[13] US District Court for Eastern District of California, 77 AFTR 2d Par 96–476. No. CV-F–92–5327 REC.

separateness of the individual and the alter ego' and 'the observance of the fiction of separate existence would . . . promote fraud or injustice'. Several other US cases have held that offshore trusts are 'sham' trusts which lack economic substance and should be disregarded.[14]

Indicators of a sham

8.11   The cases illustrate that, at least in relation to the offshore trust, there are indicators which lead to a finding of a sham. These include, but are not limited to:

(1) the degree and extent of control by the settlor;

(2) evidence of self-settling, whereby the settlor becomes a beneficiary;

(3) the retention of powers by the settlor to revoke and appoint trustees;

(4) the appointment of the settlor as the protector;

(5) the creation of the trust solely for tax purposes and the lack of a genuine 'business' purpose;

(6) the creation of the trust as a means to avoid creditors;

(7) the placement of all, or the major part, of one's assets into the trust; and

(8) the extent and degree of the revocable powers of the settlor.

All of the above factors will be evidence that there was no real intention to create a trust, although on their own they may not be sufficient.

Vulnerability of the offshore trust to a sham claim

8.12   Given the changes that the statutory offshore trust has brought—in particular, the expanded capacity to self-settle, to protect against creditors, and the ability of the settlor to act as an officer of the trust[15]—the offshore trust may be especially vulnerable to charges that it is a sham trust. Increasingly, investment into offshore trusts is being examined within the context of the sham rule. Both offshore and onshore courts accept the rule and have been willing to declare certain offshore trusts to be 'shams' in appropriate cases.

8.13   On the other hand, many offshore jurisdictions recognize the vulnerability of the offshore trust to claims of invalidity, and have sought to insulate it from such attacks by enacting provisions which proclaim its validity where certain powers are reserved to the settler. While such provisions may succeed in prevent-

---

[14] See, eg, *US v Mueller*, US Court of Appeals for Eleventh Circuit, 77 AFTR 2d Par 96–457 No 90–3617; *Zamuda v Commissioner of Inland Revenue* 79 TC 714 (1982), affd 731 F 2d 1417 (9th Cir 1984); *Rendel v Commissioner of Inland Revenue* TC Memo, LEXIS 589; 70 t c m (Cch) 1571; *Sandvall v Commissioner of Inland Revenue* 898 F 2d 455 (5th Cir 1990); *Dahlstrom v Commissioner of Inland Revenue* 765 F 2d 784, 798 (9th Cir 1985). The issue of the effect of tax policy on sham trusts is considered further in chapter 15, at paras 15.29–15.41.

[15] Discussed above, chapter 2.

ing the trust from being declared a sham because of the grant of isolated powers as laid down by statute, they cannot prevent an examination of the intention to create the trust and the abdication of a trustee's control to the settler. Thus, the following discussion of the relevant case law remains pertinent.

Ascertaining control

As we have noted, in a challenge to an offshore trust, the question of who wields **8.14** actual control of the trust will be crucial to determining whether the trust is a sham. Where it appears that the trustee does not, in fact, have the necessary control, creditors and other claimants may have the right to such assets, since they may be viewed as still being vested in the settlor. The offshore trust, by its nature and structure, perhaps too easily lends itself to a finding of a 'sham' on this ground as, typically, settlors are reluctant to relinquish control over assets placed into trusts managed in a foreign country. Further, devices such as the protector, memoranda of wishes, and so on, aid the settlor in retaining control indirectly.

Even where discretionary trust powers are created, ostensibly to be exercised **8.15** by an independent entity, a closer look at the actual operations of such powers is necessary to detect whether true discretion has been granted to the trustee. Consider this possibility: if the trust terms make the trustee's power to distribute assets mandatory, or subject to strict conditions or restrictions, this might force the conclusion that the trustee has no genuine discretion and that the settlor retains real control.[16] This is not to say that a settlor may not maintain some influence over the trust. Rather, any legitimate powers to be reserved to the settlor must be listed in the trust deed and followed strictly.[17]

The settlement in *Rahman*[18] was constituted under Jersey law and gave powers **8.16** directing the trustees to hold the trust fund and income from the trust upon such trusts as the settlor should appoint in his lifetime, with the consent of the trustee. There was a proviso that the settlor could, in any twelve-month period, appoint one-third of the capital of the trust fund without consent. In fact, on at least one occasion, Rahman removed approximately $1m from the trust without even informing the trustee.

The trust provided for the distribution of the trust capital and income, in **8.17** default of such appointment and on the settlor's death. Further, it was the settlor, aided by a consultant friend and not the trustee, who made the investment

---

[16] *Anderson v Patton* [1948] 2 DLR 202.
[17] See *Re WKR Trust (OD Bank (in liquidation) v Estate of Rey (a bankrupt)* (1999) 4 ITELR 487, 512, discussed further below, paras 8.21–8.25.
[18] See above, n 7.

decisions surrounding the trust. The trustee was empowered to pay or apply the capital or income to, or for the benefit of, the settlor. In addition, the trustee was directed to have regard solely to the interests of the settlor in making a determination whether or not to exercise such powers. Further, prior written consent was required of the settlor for several of the administrative powers of the trust. The settlor continued to take all decisions about the management of the trust and merely notified the trustee of his wishes.

8.18 In *Rahman*, it was clear that the trustee did not have independent administration of the trust and he was merely kept informed of decisions about the trust and its assets. The trustee had never taken control of the trust assets and had never acted on his own initiative. Thus, the court concluded correctly that the settlor had retained full control of the assets and had never truly intended to create a trust. In effect, the settlor continued to treat the assets as his own and the trustee as his mere agent or nominee. There had been no valid transfer of rights and duties to the trustee, as required for a trust to be established. Consequently, the court held that the Jersey trust was a 'sham'. In doing so, the court deviated from its earlier decision in *Johnson Matthey Bankers v Shamji*,[19] concerning a trust in which powers of influence had been reserved to the settlor in a similar manner to the *Rahman* trust. These were powers to add to the class of beneficiaries, to change the trustees, and to veto distribution. Yet the court in *Johnson Matthey Bankers* did not treat the trust as a sham.

8.19 In *Private Trust Corporation v Grupo Torras*,[20] the settlor's control was evidenced by several factors. An important fact was that, upon request by the settlor, who was also a beneficiary, the trustee had the sole discretion to apply either principal or net income of the trust fund to him, thereby terminating the trust at the exhaustion of the principal. Here, the court viewed the trustee, a reputable bank, as a 'puppet' of the settlor. The discretion of the trustee was 'subject to the written consent' of the primary beneficiary, the settlor. Further, the trustee was liable to be removed from office by the protector, who, in turn, was appointed by the settlor. These provisions, the court concluded, pointed to a sham.

8.20 According to the court:

> Since Article 1.2 expressly contemplates the termination of the trust upon exhaustion of the principal of the trust fund by such distribution, it is wholly unreal to think that the trustee, relying only on his sole discretion would stand against [the

---

[19] [1985–1986] JLR 26 (Royal Ct).
[20] [1997–98] 1 OFLR 443, CA, The Bahamas. The court proceeded to order a *Mareva* injunction against the offshore trust. See chapter 25.

settlor] who requests distribution to himself of the trust fund. The trustee was amenable to the beneficiary's self-serving proposals for distribution . . .[21]

The terms of the trust, discretionary though it purports to be, reserve to [the settlor] powers of a significant nature.[22]

More subtle pressures exerted on a trustee by the settlor may also be construed as evidence of control leading to a sham. This may be implied particularly when there is other circumstantial evidence of control. The case of *WKR Trust (OD Bank (in liquidation) v Estate of Rey (a bankrupt)*,[23] is instructive on this point. An influential factor in the Swiss court's finding of a sham in this case was a proxy that allowed the representation of the main shareholder at a general meeting of the company in question. In more than one instance, while the trustee signed the proxy, the settlor also signed and added the comment, 'I agree'. The court gave weight to this agreement. A person who adds the comment, ' "I agree," influences the decision-making process'.[24] **8.21**

As in other sham cases, this conclusion seemed to owe as much to the surrounding circumstances of typical offshore trusts, where the settlor is also a beneficiary and where there is a professional trustee, as to the agreement given by the settlor. Other infringements by the settlor attempting directly to control the trust tilted the balance against the settlor. For example, the settlor continued to dispose of the assets as before, and even declared the trust assets as his own when audited. Further, he actively participated in meetings and set the agenda for such meetings. There was, therefore, no 'abandonment' of his proprietary interest in the trust property, and this violated an essential principle of trust law, thus rendering the trust invalid. **8.22**

The declaration of the trust as a sham also accorded with the Swiss concept of 'abuse of law', a broader principle of public policy of Switzerland which looks to the substance, rather than the form, of a transaction or entity. Where the arrangement underpins a purported trust and offends against public policy, its existence will be terminated.[25] **8.23**

Any untoward display of influence by the settlor could, therefore, lead to the assumption that it is the settlor and not the trustee who maintains legal control over the trust. Ironically, it is this very need for trustee power which can lead to another important problem for the offshore trust. This is the question of a **8.24**

---

[21] ibid, 451. Relying on *Re A Company* [1985] BCLC 333 and *TSP Private Bank International SA v Chabra* [1992] 1 WLR 231, that a company should not 'dance to the bidding' of some dominant shareholder.

[22] ibid, 450. See also *Banco Ambrosiano Holdings SA v Calvi* (Sup Ct, The Bahamas) No 237 of 1987, decided 16 September 1987.

[23] Above, n 17.

[24] ibid, 514.

[25] ibid, 519.

breach of fiduciary duty or negligence by the trustee.[26] The dilemma is that few settlors are willing to surrender complete control to professional trustees in offshore jurisdictions. Nevertheless, this is imperative for the trust to survive.

Elements of settlor influence not necessarily sham-like

8.25 Yet we should be wary in concluding that the mere reservation by the settlor of certain powers to himself or herself, or the mere fact that the settlor is a beneficiary, is indicative of a sham. Such features are commonly found in traditional onshore trusts and, indeed, are endorsed by the Convention on the Law Applicable to Trusts and on their Recognition.[27] As we will see below, the finding of a sham requires a higher burden of proof than is established by these elements. In addition, the assumption of control by the settlor does not, in itself, render a trust invalid on grounds of public policy, but merely renders the trustee in breach of trust.[28]

8.26 Consider, in context, for example, cases such as *Private Trust Corporation v Grupo Torras*.[29] This line of cases concerned applications for *Mareva* injunctions and were related to substantive proceedings for fraud. It is evident that the courts were persuaded that justice required that they should be reluctant to refuse *Mareva* injunctions, where such refusals could facilitate international fraud. They considered only *prima facie* evidence of a sham, which was viewed as sufficient in grounding a *Mareva*. In cases where such circumstances are absent, a higher threshold would be necessary to substantiate the sham doctrine. For example, in a more recent case, *In re Abacus (CI) Ltd*,[30] the Jersey Royal Court found nothing untoward about provisions that allowed the settlor to make requests for distributions, regarding them and the need for settlors and trustees to maintain harmonious relationships as quite usual in trust arrangements.

8.27 We must also consider the effect of provisions in some offshore legislation which declare that the retention of certain powers by the settlor 'shall not invalidate the trust'. These provisions immunize certain settlors' powers[31] and challenge

---

[26] An increasingly litigious issue which is discussed in chapter 10, 'Duties of Trustees in Managing Offshore Trusts'. See *Agip (Africa) Ltd v Jackson & Others* [1992] 4 All ER 451; *Royal Brunei Airlines v Tan Kik Ming* [1995] 3 WLR 64.

[27] Hereinafter, 'The Hague Convention on the Recognition of Trusts', The Hague, 1 July 1985; UKTS 14 (1992); Cm 1823; 23 ILM 1388. Under Article 2(c), which reads: 'The reservation by the settlor of certain rights and powers and the fact that the trustee may himself have rights as a beneficiary, are not necessarily inconsistent with the existence of a trust.' See also the discussion below of *In re Abacus* above n 14, at paras 8.26–8.36. Powers to be reserved to the settlor must be clearly set out in the trust instrument.

[28] See *In re Abacus*, above n 4, at 428.

[29] Above, n 20

[30] See above, n 4.

[31] See below, 'Legislative Responses to Sham Attacks, at paras 8.81–8.84.

directly the sham rule as outlined in the *Rahman and Private Trust Corporation* cases, discussed above,[32] with the result that a higher threshold for settlor control will need to be established before a sham will be declared.

The requirement of intention

While the trend in offshore case law appears to be that trusts can effectively be challenged where settlors merely exercise or retain control over the trust, this is only one aspect of the sham rule. The analysis of the sham trust is further assisted by another tenet of the sham doctrine, that of intention. For a sham to be exposed, there must be a common intention to enter into an arrangement which is essentially a disguise or a cloak to hide the real intentions of the settlor. There should have been, in relation to the trust, no true intention to create a trust. This is different to the situation where there is in fact an intention to create a trust but, during the life of the trust, the parties, in particular the trustee, conduct the trust inappropriately, acting as if the trustee has no control over it and abdicating discretion to the settlor. In such a situation there is no sham but merely a breach of trust, and a bare trust may be the result. This is the essential point made in the leading case of *In re Abacus (CI) Ltd.*[33] The emphasis placed on an appropriate intention before a sham is declared, is particularly emphasized in the Australian and English courts.

8.28

In *Sharrment Pty Ltd v Official Trustee in Bankruptcy*,[34] the settlor, Wynard, was engaged in a number of convoluted transactions for tax planning purposes. They concerned several small 'two dollar' companies controlled by him. He then purchased a substantial property. The transactions, in themselves, lacked any true commercial purpose. The court found that Wynard had not regarded the property as an asset of the family trust, but rather as an asset at his personal disposal. It therefore concluded that the companies were all 'alter egos' (or shams) of Wynard and that the transactions were merely artificial devices used to cloak the true intention of Wynard, giving an appearance that a debt was due by Wynard to one of the family trusts.

8.29

A subsequent appeal against the initial finding of a sham was successful. This was because there was a failure to prove another key ingredient of the sham trust, that is, the element of the disguise which the sham seeks to conceal. It was thought essential to sustain a sham argument to prove the existence of the other transaction which the facade disguises. Yet in modern sham trust law,

8.30

---

[32] See paras 8.07–8.17.

[33] Above, n 4.

[34] (1988) 18 FCR 449, relying on the English decision of *Snook v London and West Riding Investments Ltd*, above n 3.

as in *Rahman* and beyond, this latter requirement can only be deemed necessary in the line of sham cases where there is, in fact, intention to conceal something else, as opposed to merely creating a relationship which is a farce.[35] By far the bulk of offshore cases which will be challenged as sham trusts fall into the latter group.

8.31 In *Rahman*,[36] while the court did not elaborate on the elements of the intention to create a sham, it was clear that it formed the opinion that Rahman did not really intend the trust to have legal effect. Accordingly, while in an arrangement in which there is no intention to create a trust it will invariably be shown that the trustee has no real control, the converse is not always true.

8.32 Nevertheless, the cases have not always been consistent in requiring that both these elements, control and intention, be proved before a sham is declared. More recently, the issue of control by the settlor seems to have been the overriding factor, and sufficient in itself to deem a trust a sham. This appeared to the case, for example, in *Private Trust Corporation v Grupo Torras*,[37] where no real discussion of an intention, or lack thereof, was engaged in and the judgment centred around the 'substantial or effective' control which the settlor, who was also a beneficiary, exercised. Indeed, the court was at pains to acknowledge the reputable nature of the trustee in this case.

8.33 In contrast, in *Wily (Trustee of the Bankrupt Estate of Fuller) and another v Fuller and Others*,[38] the Federal Court of Australia insisted on the requirement of the intention to create a sham before it could be declared. This case concerned a blind trust where certain charities were named as beneficiaries. The trustee was a professional trustee based in Jersey. The settlor drew up a memorandum of wishes and continued to exert substantial influence on the management of the trust by giving detailed instructions to the trustee, which the latter accepted. Upon adjudication of the settlor as bankrupt, the trustee in bankruptcy applied to the court for a declaration that the trust assets in question were held on a bare trust for the benefit of the settlor and were part of the estate in bankruptcy.

8.34 The court was at pains to point out that control by the settlor, even a 'remarkable degree of control' as in this case, was not sufficient to declare a trust to be a sham. Rather, what was needed was 'a common intention of the parties to it that the instrument or transaction was a disguise for some other and real transaction or no transaction at all'.[39] It is important here to recognize, as indeed

---

[35] See the discussion of intention below, paras 8.31–8.34.
[36] Discussed above, n 7.
[37] Discussed above, n 20.
[38] Above, n 6.
[39] ibid, 339, relying on *Sharrment*, above n 34.

Sharrment[40] makes clear, that 'control is not necessarily to be equated with ownership, particularly equitable ownership'.[41] However, where there is not the requisite intent, the fact that parties subsequently departed from their original agreement does not necessarily mean that they never intended the agreement as effective and binding.[42]

The question of a unilateral sham for trusts

The question of intention to create a sham where trusts are involved is not, **8.35** however, free from difficulty. What is particularly worrisome is the scope of that intention, specifically, whether it is sufficient for the settlor alone to have an intention to create a sham—a unilateral sham—or whether both the trustee and the settlor must have the intention to create the sham.

This question was not adequately explored in *Rahman*, but another opportunity **8.36** for a response to it arose in the later case of *In re Abacus (CI) Ltd*, albeit in a broader context.[43] A primary difficulty is the fact that trusts, unlike the form of a sham in *Snook*, are not contracts, with parties which need to agree, but more in the nature of gifts. Since it is a unilateral transaction, there is a school of thought that only the settlor's intention should matter.[44] However, despite the cases on offshore trusts which almost seem to bypass intention totally, the weight of the authorities is against this view. The Royal Court of Jersey specifically rejected this approach in *In re Abacus (CI) Ltd*, wedding itself to the traditional rule which requires a 'common intention' in both parties, that is, in the case of trusts, both the settlor and the trustee.

It is suggested that the approach in *In re Abacus* is correct. If we were to **8.37** accept the unilateral sham approach, the law could lead to absurdity: the settlor, unknown to the trustee, intends the trust to be a sham but the trust is duly established; thereafter, the trustee acts as any appropriate trustee should, and exercises independent control over the trust, thereby undermining the settlor's true, but unknown, intent. Such a situation could hardly be labelled a sham.

Nonetheless, while the *Abacus* approach is generally correct, the reality of **8.38** offshore trusts, and perhaps other types of trusts, suggests that certain factors might distort the purity of the reasoning in this approach. Consider, for example, the situation where the trustee may not intend to go along with the

---

[40] Above, n 34.
[41] *Wily v Fuller*, above n 6.
[42] See *Garna and Grain Company Inc v HMF Faure and Fairclough Ltd* [1966] 1 QB 650, 683–84, *per* Diplock LJ.
[43] See above, n 4.
[44] This was counsel for the trustee's argument in *Re Abacus*, ibid.

sham intent (or may not even know of it), but is incapable of exercising his or her discretion independently in order to prevent the sham because of the settlor's actions. This could occur in an offshore trust, for example where the settlor, at the slightest hint that the trustee is exercising his or her discretion independently, against the settlor's wishes, uses power that he or she has to penalize the trustee, or even remove the trustee. The settlor may do so even indirectly, through the protector. In such a situation, unlike our first scenario, the settlor can, and does, prevent the trustee from exercising his or her discretion, regardless of any lack of a common intent on the part of the trustee. As we have seen, offshore trusts commonly reserve such draconian powers to settlors. Should not such a trust be declared a sham too, although the intent here is merely unilateral?

Subjective intent required but recklessness may suffice

8.39 It is well established that the intention required of the trustee and the settlor is based on a subjective standard.[45] Following the expanded concepts of liability expressed in the *Royal Brunei/Walker*[46] line of cases, *In re Abacus (CI) Ltd* further suggests, *per curiam*, that intention may be inferred from recklessness. This is in keeping with the principle that recklessness is to be equated to dishonesty and incurs liability.[47] This, of course, in the case of trusts, will apply more appropriately to the trustee, where the trustee goes along with the settlor's intention to create a sham 'without knowing or caring what it had signed and that both parties intended to give a false impression of the position to third parties or to the court'.[48]

Evidence of the intention

8.40 As reiterated in *Wily*, the onus lies on the person alleging the sham to establish that a trust deed apparently validly entered into was but a facade or disguise.[49] However, extrinsic evidence may also be examined in the 'sham' inquiry, and so the settlor's conduct *after* the execution of the declaration of a trust will be relevant to determine the true nature of the trust document and his or her real intent. Given the fact that the courts can look at conduct *after* the creation of the trust, it would seem that intention can be easily inferred from evidence of

---

[45] See, eg, *In re Abacus*, ibid, 389, 396.
[46] *Royal Brunei Airlines v Tan Kik Ming* [1995] 3 WLR 64, PC (Brunei, Darussalam); *Walker v Stones* [2000] 4 All ER 412 (CA).
[47] See chapter 10.
[48] (2003) 6 ITELR 368, 401.
[49] Above, n 6, 339.

excessive control by the settlor, as was demonstrated in the 'control' cases, discussed above.[50]

The value of extrinsic evidence was again illustrated in the case of *Midland Bank* **8.41** *v Wyatt*.[51] The settlor made a declaration of trust in favour of his wife and children, and then incurred liabilities to the bank. Here, the settlor's conduct after the creation of the trust, specifically his actions and statements to the bank and others inferring that he retained a beneficial interest in the trust property, was crucial to the successful challenge of a 'sham'.

The settlor's statement by way of an affidavit, that his objective was protection **8.42** from long-term commercial interest, gave credence to the 'sham' challenge. The court found that the settlor had no real intention of benefiting his wife and children, and the trust was a mere pretence or sham.

B. Identifying Offshore Trusts as Shams

Self-settling and creditors

If the settlor retains an identifiable interest, challengers to the trust and its assets **8.43** will be on equal footing to the settlor. This situation is different where the settlor is merely included in the class of beneficiaries, which is, fortunately, the popular scenario in offshore trusts. Indeed, the settlor may be the first beneficiary of the trust. As noted in *Re WKR Trust (OD Bank (in liquidation) v Estate of Rey (a bankrupt)*,[52] 'This dual [settlor-beneficiary] role is accepted in trust law.'[53] The crucial distinction here is that control with regard to distributing the income to beneficiaries resides in the trustee and not the settlor. However, while the dual role of settlor/beneficiary is generally accepted in trust law, a court may infer the existence of a sham if other factors dominate, for example excessive settlor control.[54]

In *Private Trust Corp v Grupo Torras SA*, for example, in a trust found to be in **8.44** reality controlled by the settlor/beneficiary, the Court of Appeal of The Bahamas found that the assets were, 'in equity and/or law the assets of the settlor'.[55] The court noted that the trust fund was 'in reality, as distinct from legal theory' the

---

[50] *Private Trust Corporation and Rahman*, above nn 20 and 7 respectively. See also *In re Abacus (CI) Ltd* above n 4, 389: '[T]he court is not restricted to examining the four corners of the document'.

[51] [1995] 1 FLR 696; [1995] 3 FCR 11; [1994] EGCS 113, ChD.

[52] Above, n 17.

[53] ibid, 512.

[54] See *Re WKR Trust*, above n 52.

[55] Above n 20, 452.

settlor's money, placed by him where it was available to himself as an object of the trust 'in the lawful exercise of the trustee's discretion'.[56]

8.45 Again, in *Banco Ambrosiano Holdings SA v Calvi*,[57] the Bahamian Supreme Court held that it could treat trust assets as belonging to the settlor of an offshore trust where 'assets were held in a manner that effectively conceals his true beneficial interest'.[58] The court disapproved of the fact that the defendant had brought into existence 'an elaborate structure of corporations and trusts that effectively concealed his true beneficial interest' in assets and 'made it impracticable' for creditors to 'reap the fruits of any legal proceedings they might take'.[59] A *prima facie* case of a sham trust was sufficient to ground a *Mareva* injunction.

Public policy position in the US against self-settled spendthrift trusts leading to shams

8.46 Offshore trusts may be particularly vulnerable to the sham rule in the US courts. This is demonstrated in a recent line of cases. In each of these cases, the real problem was the issue of control by the settlor, in an arrangement which benefited him. Offshore trusts which are settled purely for the benefit of the settlor and which attempt to preclude creditors from reaching assets, described as self-settled spendthrift trusts, are particularly problematic in the US and have often been struck down on grounds of public policy.

8.47 In *In re Brooks*,[60] for example, the settlor retained control of the assets in a self-settled, spendthrift asset protection trust in Jersey. A Connecticut court declared that such trusts violated Connecticut's public policy. The court found that as self-settled, spendthrift trusts, they could not be recognized to the detriment of creditors of the debtor (the settlor). This led to a declaration that the trust property was actually the property of the estate.

8.48 In *Affordable Media*,[61] the settlor was also the protector in a self-settled trust, which fact rendered the trust even more vulnerable. He was actually jailed for contempt of court for failing to obey an order to repatriate the trust assets when the court ruled that the trust was, in effect, a sham. The case is also important in demonstrating the danger of fraudulent conveyances into trusts as a means to evade creditors.

---

[56] ibid, 450.

[57] (Sup Ct, The Bahamas) No. 237 of 1987, decided 16 September 1987.

[58] ibid, 13.

[59] ibid, 13.

[60] 217 BR 98, 101 (Bankr D Conn 1998); see also *Re Larry Portnoy*, 201 BR 685, 700 (Bankr SDNY 1996).

[61] *Federal Trade Commission v Affordable Media* (1999) 2 ITELR 73; LLC 179 F 3d 1228 (CA-9, 1999) (popularly known as *Re Anderson*).

The sham elements were familiar in the New York case of *In re Larry Portnoy*,[62]   **8.49**
which concerned a creditor's claim. However, it contained an additional element
that aided the court in ignoring the trust. This was the conflict of laws factor.
The court was not persuaded that the trustee had absolute discretion over the
trust income. Rather, it treated the fact that the protector, as settlor and beneficiary, had successfully directed the trustee to pay for a legal analysis of Jersey
law from the trust assets, as evidence that the settlor/beneficiary had substantial
influence and control. Indeed, the trustee's fidelity to the protector was clearly
apparent, to the extent that the trust and other beneficiaries were 'blindly'
footing the costs of the protector's personal litigation.

The trust instrument stated that Jersey law was the governing law, but the   **8.50**
settlor's domicile was New York. The court deemed the law of New York to be
the proper law on grounds of public policy, and the trust was consequently
treated as void. The effect of this was that the trust assets were viewed as
remaining with the settlor. A significant factor in this case was that Jersey law
did not claim exclusive jurisdiction over the trust, unlike the law of other
offshore trust jurisdictions.[63] This left the questions of jurisdiction and proper
law open, important elements to the success of a sham challenge. Onshore
jurisdictions are more likely to find powers allowed under statutory provisions
offshore as evidence of a sham.[64] The court in fact remarked that it did not
know whether the assets were in the US or in Jersey, and this may have been a
significant aspect of the court's assertion of jurisdiction.[65]

The *Portnoy* case thus turned more on the question of the proper law of the trust   **8.51**
than on, whether the trust was a sham, although the court was influenced by the
control which the settlor retained over the trust. At the heart of the judgment
was the court's distaste for a trust arrangement which not only sought to evade
the plaintiff's legitimate creditors, but also violated the fundamental rule of US
law against self-settled spendthrift trusts. This attack on the trust was a vivid
demonstration of a public policy triumph.

Self-settled spendthrift trusts were also examined in the case of *Texas Commercial*   **8.52**
Bank v Shurley.[66] Here, the issue was whether the debtor's interest as the beneficiary of a family trust could be considered the property of the bankruptcy
estate, thereby making it available to creditors. The court found that the debtor
exercised great control over the trust. In the result, the trust property was part of

---

[62] 201 BR 685 (1996).
[63] For example, Cayman Islands law. See the discussion of jurisdiction in chapter 19.
[64] See, eg, *Re A Company SIB Ltd v Vwagh* [1985] BCLC 333.
[65] Above, n 62, 698.
[66] 118 S Ct 444 1997 (Sup Ct) US, US LEXIS 6924, 139 L Ed 2d 380; 66 USLW 3354
(1997). See also *Estate of German v US* 7C Ct 641 (1985).

the bankruptcy estate since the trust could not qualify as a spendthrift or discretionary trust. In the words of the court: 'Protective trust settling is a form of control that unfairly handicaps present and future creditors without restricting a settlor's beneficial use of the assets.'[67]

8.53   In *Shurley*,[68] the court examined receipts to conclude that the debtor was in fact the true owner of the assets of the trust. It was clearly concerned about the stretching of the trust concept to legitimize what it considered inappropriate offshore arrangements. Similar sentiments were expressed by the court in *International Credit Investment Company (Overseas Ltd) v Adham*,[69] which viewed the assets of a BVI trust as 'indirectly controlled' by the settlor in order to benefit himself.

8.54   In contrast to the position taken in some US courts, that self-settled spendthrift trusts are against public policy, there would appear to be no such innate restriction on public policy grounds in English common law courts. Indeed, in *In re Abacus (CI) Ltd*,[70] in a self-settled spendthrift trust which allowed the settlor-beneficiary to make requests for distributions to the trustee, a reputable institution, the trust was not viewed as invalid on grounds of public policy, since the court found that exceptional circumstances were necessary to ground a public policy argument.[71]

8.55   It should be noted that this is not a universal trend. Restriction on grounds of public policy has been expressly overruled in some US states which are encouraging offshore trust-like entities.[72] This undermines considerably the public policy rationale of the principle in a contemporary context.

Tax purposes

8.56   The treatment of trusts established for tax avoidance purposes is discussed in later chapters.[73] Here it suffices to note that trusts which are used solely for the purpose of tax avoidance also face impugnment under the sham rule. This is often combined with other red alert signals, such as self-settling and settlor control.

---

[67] *Re Shurley*, above, n 66. Note that in the USA, under the Restatement (Second) of Torts § 156 (1959), a person may not create a valid spendthrift trust for his or her own benefit.
[68] See above, n 66.
[69] 141 SJLB 56; *The Times*, 10 February 1997.
[70] See above, n 4.
[71] The court did not find that the settlor was in control here.
[72] See chapter 6 for a discussion of these US developments.
[73] See the chapters contained in Part III, 'The Offshore Tax Function'.

Trusts established for non-business purposes

The problem of trusts established purely for tax purposes is part of a wider **8.57**
difficulty that some courts have had in relation to trusts and trust arrangements
which appear to have no real 'business' purpose or substance, thus leading to
inferences of shams. This was the case, for example, in *Rothmore Farms Pty Ltd v
Belgravia Pty Ltd and others*.[74] Under suspicion was part of an elaborate trust
arrangement, a sale of the trust assets by A to an adviser of A's family in
consideration of a parcel of opals. The assets in question were valued at
approximately $600,000, while the opals had a value of between $2,000 and
$10,000.

The Federal Court of Australia found that A had 'no genuine reason' for under- **8.58**
taking the transaction. The disproportion in the consideration offered for the
sale of the assets led to the conclusion that the transaction was undertaken to
'provide a screen' and was not a genuine transaction, thereby rendering it a sham.

Establishing who is a creditor for sham purposes

Trusts set up to deny other persons who claim a stake in the assets may be **8.59**
challenged as shams. Former spouses, for example, who are frustrated in their
attempts at claiming assets in divorce settlements, may have arguable cases.
However, it appears that other groups of would-be claimants are less easily
identifiable as worthy by the courts, and the threshold for proving the case of a
sham may be higher.[75]

This seems to have been the situation in *Hess v Line Trust Corporation*.[76] Here, **8.60**
the husband transferred the majority of assets that could have been claimed by
his wife into trust. The wife, now the ex-wife, challenged the trust, claiming that
it was a sham and could be avoided, as it was established to defraud her, since
the settlor had not kept sufficient assets to meet any prospective or contingent
liability (relating to her). However, the Appeal Court of Gibraltar, which heard
the matter, refused to declare the trust a sham, finding that the plaintiff wife had
to show clearly that this was the case. In other words, she had to establish that
there had been the requisite intention to create a sham to avoid her claims. The
fact that the trust had the *effect* of frustrating the claim was not sufficient.

The court also seemed to have been persuaded by the fact that the plaintiff **8.61**
had not established in law that she was, in fact, a creditor, not having yet

---

[74] (1999) 1 ITELR 159, 200.
[75] The issue of fraudulent conveyances is discussed separately, in chapter 9, 'The Law on
Fraudulent Conveyances and the Offshore Trust'.
[76] (1998–99) 1 ITELR 249 (AC, Gibraltar).

obtained a judgment in her favour. The plaintiff was found to have had no *locus standi* to seek an order that the trust was a sham. It would appear that where the alleged purpose of the trust is to avoid creditors, a judgment in favour of the creditors must be obtained before the sham claim can be brought. This is a surprising and questionable view.

Piercing the corporate veil and look through rules

8.62 The courts may be prepared to 'pierce the corporate veil', or 'look through' the trust, to discover whether the settlor is the true owner of the assets. This becomes another means of invalidating the trust, in effect treating it as a sham. This phenomenon occurs most often in cases where it is suspected that a trust has been established for the sole purpose of tax avoidance, or the avoidance of creditors, as discussed above. It is readily apparent that the idea of 'piercing the corporate veil' is borrowed from company law, and similar principles apply. It is, however, ironic that the trust, which prides itself as being distinct from companies and corporate structures and goes to great lengths to underline this fundamental difference, should now utilize a principle of company law to discover its essential character.

8.63 The threshold for piercing the corporate veil of a trust may be merely *prima facie* evidence that the trust is controlled by the settlor, where the trust arrangement benefits a beneficiary who is also the settlor. These were the circumstances in *Private Trust Corporation v Grupo Torras*.[77] Here, a Bahamas court, *per* Gonsalves-Sabola, confirmed that the principles of *Salomon v Salomon*,[78] which distinguish a company as a separate legal entity from its owners (the share-holders), applied *prima facie* in a situation where the company 'danced to the bidding' of a dominant shareholder. The analogy, said the court, applied squarely to a trust corporate structure, such as the offshore trust:

8.64 The court is not thwarted by the complexity of the legal structures into which a defendant has caused his funds to disappear, so that only he or his agents could disentangle his personal interest, thereby guarding against future judgments.[79] Thus, the Court of Appeal of The Bahamas found that where there is evidence that a settlor, as the primary beneficiary of a trust, treats the trust as an alter ego, the court will lift the corporate veil to determine to what extent the trust assets fall under his or her ownership and control. Yet Gonsalves-Sabola warned that corporate veils could not be pierced easily in The Bahamas, because of the existence of confidentiality provisions.[80]

---

[77] Above, n 20.
[78] [1897] AC 22.
[79] ibid, 45.
[80] See chapter 7, 'Disclosure and Confidentiality Obligations'.

The corporate veil was also pierced in the landmark English case of *Re Tucker, a*   **8.65**
Bankrupt.[81] Here, the issue was whether property placed in offshore trusts in the
Isle of Man and Guernsey formed part of the debtor's estate. Evidence was
examined to determine whether a *prima facie* case had been made out by the
plaintiff, in order to justify service out of the jurisdiction. The property in issue
was acquired by an Isle of Man (offshore) company. This was the subsidiary of
another such company, the shares of which were held by a trust, allegedly
established by the debtor's brother but subsequently found effectively to be
settled by the debtor. In addition, the debtor resided at the property at all times.
These intricate arrangements in relation to the trust, which the court found
were typical of offshore trusts, moved Millet J to remark: 'Now this, of course,
is fairyland.'[82] The court found the trust to be a 'sham' as the debtor was the
de facto owner of the property.

The test in *Private Trust Corporation* may be contrasted with that in *Hess v Line*   **8.66**
Trust Corporation,[83] in which the court refused to look through a registered trust
to find a sham, warning that an 'arguable case' needed first to be established. In
that case, it was not enough that the effect of the trust had been to remove the
assets from the reach of the settlor's ex-wife; intention to do so was necessary.
Note, however, that such a transfer, particularly of all or the majority of assets,
would normally be highly persuasive evidence of a sham.

Should the piercing of the corporate veil concept apply to trusts?

The case of *Re Abacus (CI) Ltd*[84] is significant for its finding on the application   **8.67**
of the 'piercing' or 'lifting of the veil' concept to trusts. It was held that the
concept, one that originates from company law, was not suitable for application
to trusts, and the court therefore treated the veil concept as distinct from the
sham doctrine. The basis for this argument was the settlor-beneficiary's alleged
control of the trust.

The Royal Court noted that the veil concept, as applied to companies, required   **8.68**
control over the company and some illegality or impropriety which resulted in
the company being used as a mask. This was a remedy to defeat the conscious
abuse of a formalistic separation of legal personality. It reasoned that if the
settlor exercised control over the trustee, it would be unlawful and unenforceable in equity as a breach of trust, since the trustee would have abdicated his or
her fiduciary duty. Further, it noted that there was a separation of economic

---

[81] [1988] 2 All ER 339.
[82] ibid, 397.
[83] Above, n 76, 261.
[84] Above, n 4.

interests in a trust, unlike in a company. In a trust, assets are held not for the settlor, but for the beneficiaries; whereas in a company, the economic interest lies with the controlling shareholder. If the court were to 'pierce the veil', it would be giving effect to a deemed appointment, which would be a breach of trust and liable to be set aside by the court. In considering the question whether there was an intention to create a sham, the court rejected the notion of a unilateral sham and the argument that it was sufficient for a sham if the settlor alone lacked the intention to create the trust. Rather, both the settlor and the trustee must lack the intention to create a trust.

8.69   Lastly, the effects of a 'piercing the veil' claim and that of a breach of trust radically differ. In a breach of trust, the decision is rendered void but the assets remain with the beneficiaries; in a 'piercing the veil' claim, the assets are viewed as retained by the settlor. For these reasons, the veil concept could not apply.

8.70   While the Jersey court disapproved of the veil concept and treated it as separate from a sham, it is expressly approved in the US courts. However, it is suggested that the US courts have appeared to assimilate the two concepts. Yet the actual exercise that the US courts employ is a sham exercise, albeit with a less rigorous threshold than elsewhere. Thus, what is being utilized is not an entirely different principle which can obliterate trusteeship by rendering the trust invalid. The difference that should be addressed is not so much the semantics involved, but the different standards used in the US courts, as compared to other common law courts, for deeming trusts shams.

C. Neutral Features Which May Lead to Sham Findings

The protector may be evidence of a sham

8.71   Even where the trust legitimately provides for protectors or a committee of advisers, and the settlor is the chairperson of the committee or its protector, the assets may be compromised under the sham doctrine. For example, the settlor may give advice on investment decisions through this route and thus retain indirect control of the trust. If the protector acts merely as the settlor's shadow, or if it is demonstrated that the trustee is devoid of the freedom to ignore the advice of such a committee or protector, the trust is threatened. Consequently, an examination of the nature and extent of the power given to the protector might be an avenue for discovering whether the settlor retains indirect control of the trust.

8.72   Where a protector who is under the settlor's influence has wide powers that can effectively veto any independent decision of a trustee, the trust can be challenged as a sham. Yet the Supreme Court of Bermuda, in *Re Star 1&2*

(Revised) Trusts von Knieriem v Bermuda Trust Co Ltd and Another,[85] was reluctant to examine this facet of settlor control in offshore trusts. In issue was the extent to which the protector's power placed him in the position of a fiduciary. The court sought to determine whether the protector could exercise his power to remove the trustee according to the personal wishes of the settlor and without regard to the interests of the beneficiaries. The court found that the protector's act of removing the trustee was neither a breach of his fiduciary duty, nor an improper purpose. The implication from this was that there was no sham. A different conclusion would have been reached if the test in *Rahman*[86] had been utilized. It is important for both the trustee and protector to function independently of the settlor if a trust is to avoid the 'sham' label. The tests used to measure this cannot seem to cancel each other out, as appears to be the case with the *von Knieriem* decision.

The provision for the removal of trustees in *von Knieriem* is quite typical in offshore trusts. Where the settlor is also given power to remove the protector, the settlor can indirectly influence the trustee's decisions and/or remove him or her, effectively retaining control of the trust fund. By refusing to require that such powers be exercised for purposes compatible with the true purpose of a trust, that is for the benefit of the beneficiaries, the question of real control is avoided. Here, it seemed that the underlying rationale of the 'sham' rule was 'side-stepped'. Rather, the court appeared to be influenced by the desire to provide incentives and reassurance for offshore investors. The case thus highlights the difficulty of reconciling the conflicting interests between offshore commerce and the need to protect the fundamental principle of true trusteeship. Offshore courts may resolve this in favour of the former in offshore jurisdictions. **8.73**

The *von Knieriem* decision also demonstrates that a challenge to the validity of the offshore trust will not be easy where less than obvious forms of control by the settlor are evident. Such cases avoid a deeper consideration of the 'sham' nature of a trust. Where, as in this case, the protector is merely following the wishes of the settlor, the very trust should arguably be suspect, since he or she is not acting independently (which the court requires) but in the interest of the settlor. However, the practical effect of the *von Knieriem* decision is that it would be almost impossible to prove an improper motive by the protector in such cases. **8.74**

The role of the protector was viewed as more damaging to the offshore trust in the judgment of *Affordable Media*.[87] In this case, not only did the settlor retain **8.75**

---

[85] (Sup Ct, Bermuda) Nos 154 and 162 of 1994, decided 13 July, 1994, *per* Meerabux J.
[86] Above, n 7.
[87] Above, n 61.

control but he was also the protector of the trust and had the power to remove the trustees. These factors clearly validated the court's position that the trust could, in effect, be disregarded and the assets viewed as still belonging solely to the settlor.

Power to appoint and revoke trustees

8.76   The power of the settlor to appoint and revoke trustees is not in itself invalid. However, such a power must be specifically reserved in the trust deed and be followed strictly. Yet this element may be viewed as one indicator of a sham trust, as seen in the *Lawrence* line of cases.[88] These cases emphasize that a lack of a true intention to create a trust could evidence the creation of a sham.

8.77   In *Lawrence*, the court viewed this power to appoint and revoke trustees in conjunction with the ease with which such a power could reinstall the settlor as a beneficiary. It noted:

> The importance of these clauses and provisions, when read together, is that the appellant, as settlor and prospective beneficiary, retained *de facto* control over the trust through his ability to appoint trustees who could in their absolute discretion reinstate the appellant as a beneficiary and assign the entire proceeds to him.[89]

8.78   Where control can be traced to the settlor by virtue of his or her wide powers of removal of trustees, either directly or indirectly through the protector, the trust may be prejudiced. The *von Knieriem*[90] and *Private Trust Corporation*[91] cases, discussed above, are again pertinent here. However, the two cases came to contradictory conclusions. In *von Knieriem*, the wide power retained by the settlor was exercised indirectly through a protector and was permissible. In contrast, in *Private Trust Corporation*, indirect control by the settlor was sufficient to invalidate the trust. Consequently, as yet, it is unclear where the line will be drawn with respect to indirect control by the settlor.

Partial shams

8.79   The sham concept may apply only to particular provisions of a trust deed. If the evidence of sham intent is applicable only to part of the arrangement, the trust itself may still be valid and the offending part will be vitiated.[92] For example, the trust may contain various dispositive powers but the settlor may have intended that, with respect only to distributions to himself or herself, the trustee will have no real discretion and the settlor would receive whatever distributions he or she wishes.

---

[88]   *Re Lawrence* (2002) 5 ITELR 1; see also *Re WKR Trust*, above n 52.
[89]   *Lawrence*, above, n 88.
[90]   Above, n 85.
[91]   Above, n 20. See also paras 8.32, 8.44, and 8.63.
[92]   *Hitch and Others v Stone (Inspect or of Taxes)* (2001) *The Times*, 21 February.

Memorandum of wishes and intent

While the memorandum of wishes is usually regarded as a non-binding document,[93] which is not part of the formal trust instrument, it is becoming increasingly important as evidence of the intent of the settlor for purposes of the sham doctrine. If the trustee appears strictly to follow the 'wishes' of the settlor, as contained in this document, this would be even more damning evidence of a sham. For example, a memorandum or letter of wishes can often be drawn in terms which, effectively, allow the settlor considerable influence over the trust fund, or delineate the settlor's wish to have an interest in the entire income. Such a letter may override the trustee's genuine discretion over capital and income, as outlined in the trust deed. In such an instance, the letter may be treated as the mandatory instructions of the settlor. If the trustee in fact appears to follow the settlor's instructions 'to the letter', the sham doctrine may apply to a challenge to the trust, on the ground that the trust is effectively controlled by a letter of wishes issued by a settlor. This application of the doctrine was accepted in cases such as *Wily v Fuller*.[94]

8.80

D. Protecting Against Sham Attacks

Legislative responses to sham attacks

In response to the attacks on offshore trusts as shams, some offshore legislatures have intervened, attempting to raise the bar for a finding of a sham. For example, the Trusts (Amendment) (Intermediate Effect and Reserved Powers) Law 1998 of the Cayman Islands,[95] seeks to define the boundaries outside of which a trust that contains powers reserved to a settlor may be declared a sham. In addition, the Law makes provision that a trust deed which is not declared to be a will, or a codicil to a will, should be presumed to have effect as a deed.

8.81

Under the Cayman Law, the powers which may be reserved to a settlor under a trust, without the danger of invalidating the trust, are wide. Unsurprisingly,

8.82

---

[93] See, eg, *Bank of Nova Scotia Trust Company (Bahamas) Ltd v De Barletta* (Sup Ct, The Bahamas) No 550 of 1984.

[94] Above, n 6, discussed at paras 8.33–8.34. See also chapter 7, at paras 7.96–7.97 for a discussion of whether the memorandum of wishes is a document which the trustee is legally required to disclose to the beneficiaries and statutory provisions which expressly state that the trustee has no such duty.

[95] See also s 9 of the International Trusts Act 1996 of Saint Vincent; s 46 of the International Exempt Trust Act of Dominica 1997; and the Trusts Act 2000 of Belize.

they mirror some of the problem areas encountered under the sham trust doctrine. These include the:

(1) power to revoke, vary, or amend the trust;
(2) power to appoint income or capital;
(3) power to act as a director of any company where shares are owned by the trust;
(4) power to give trustees binding directions for the investment of trust property;
(5) power to appoint or remove trustees or protectors;
(6) power to change the proper law of the trust; and
(7) power to require the trustee to obtain the consent of the settlor before exercising any power.

8.83   Similarly, in Dominica, an

> international trust shall not be declared invalid . . . if the settlor . . . retains . . . or acquires . . . power to revoke [or] amend the trust; any benefit, interest or property from the trust; power to remove or appoint a trustee or protector; power to direct a trustee or protector on any matter; or is the beneficiary of the trust solely or together with others.[96]

8.84   It remains to be seen to what extent courts outside of the offshore jurisdictions in question will accept these declarations of validity of trusts, which would otherwise be declared as shams. Unquestionably, however, where, as is anticipated, an issue of an alleged sham reaches the offshore court, or an onshore court proceeds to apply the offshore trust law as the appropriate proper law, proving the sham will be a difficult exercise.

Criteria for sustainable offshore trusts

8.85   The challenges brought by the sham doctrine are not fatal to the offshore trusts and such trusts may survive scrutiny. The most elemental criterion to a successful challenge remains the evidence of control by the settlor, or, to put it another way, preventing a trustee from exercising true discretion over the trust.

8.86   Equally, it is unwise for a settlor to settle all of his or her assets in the offshore trust. If this is done, leading to a situation of insolvency, it raises an almost non-rebuttable presumption of a sham and, further, an invitation to conclude a fraudulent conveyance.

---

[96] The International Exempt Trusts Act 1997 of Dominica, s 46. See also s 47 of the International Exempt Trust Ordinance 1994 of Nevis; s 9 of the International Trusts Act 1996 of Saint Vincent; s 13C of the International Trusts Act 1984 of the Cook Islands; s 18 of the International Trusts Act 2002 of Saint Lucia; s 2(4) of the Trustee Act 1990 of the BVI; s 3 of the Trustee Act 1998 of The Bahamas.

It remains a sensible option to place trust assets physically offshore (and not **8.87** structure mere limited interests) to increase the likelihood, in a conflict of laws situation, that the trust will be governed by offshore law and not onshore law. This was an important distinction between the *Brooks*[97] and *Portnoy* cases.[98] In the latter, the assets were located physically offshore, and this allowed a settlement as the creditors could not reach the assets. In contrast, in *Brooks*, the assets were located in the US and were easily accessible.

A recent Jersey case has checked, at least temporarily, what seemed like a tide of **8.88** offshore trusts being deemed shams. In *Re Abacus (CI) Ltd*,[99] the settlor, a convicted fraudster, who had established the trust before the fraud, was a beneficiary of the trust, along with his wife and his son. A claim attacking the trust as a sham was brought in the hope that the assets could be reached by the settlor's creditors. The assets of the trust had been used liberally by the settlor and no request for distribution had ever been refused by the trustee, including requests for payments to enable the settlor to develop personal residential property. The Royal Court of Jersey found nothing surprising about the fact that the settlor's requests had been agreed to, and compared the arrangement to many others where trusts had been legitimately set up for tax and inheritance purposes. What mattered was that the settlor-beneficiary had only an expectation that his requests would be met, and the trustee retained the control over the assets and ultimate discretion to decide. However, the court noted that it was expected that there would be a harmonious relationship between a trustee and beneficiary, so that reasonable requests should not be denied.

The application of the sham doctrine to trusts is still (relatively) in the infant **8.89** stage. While the sham concept itself is an orthodox one of extraordinary tenacity, its transplantation to trusts law is complicated by the revolutionary characteristics of offshore trusts. Nonetheless, the courts have demonstrated an enthusiasm for the sham doctrine and the doctrine will no doubt endure in offshore trust jurisprudence. More contemplative thinking about the sham, however, as reflected in later cases such as *In re Abacus (CI) Ltd and Hess v Line*[100] and so on, will nevertheless ensure that the sham concept is not used merely as a convenient scapegoat with which to desecrate, and even annihilate, the offshore

---

[97] *In re Brooks*, 217 BR 98, 101 (Bankr D Conn 1998); *In re Lawrence*, 227 BR 907, 916 (Bankr SD Fla 1998). These courts followed the reasoning of the court in *In re Portnoy*, 201 BR 685, 700 (Bankr SDNY 1996).
[98] *In re Portnoy*, above, n 97.
[99] See above, n 4.
[100] See above, nn 4 and 76 respectively.

trust as a viable and legitimate trust entity. In particular, given the onshore/offshore trust developments in the US, the view that features of offshore trusts, such as those which allow greater settlor influence and which emphasize creditor protection more aggressively, are inherently lawful should be rejected.

9

THE LAW ON FRAUDULENT
CONVEYANCES AND THE
OFFSHORE TRUST

A. The Relevance of Fraudulent Conveyancing Law to Offshore Trusts

Introduction

For the purposes of creditor protection planning, the validity of the transfer of   **9.01**
assets into an offshore trust, and the trust itself, cannot be divorced from a
consideration of the laws on fraudulent conveyances and, by extension, the law
on bankruptcy. Such laws dictate that owners of assets cannot transfer or conceal
assets, or voluntarily render themselves bankrupt in order to avoid the legitimate
claims of creditors. These laws are equally relevant to assets placed offshore.
Where a court determines that assets have been moved offshore for such reasons,
the transfer will be treated as fraudulent and can be voided or set aside. This
debilitates the trust and allows creditors access to the assets.

Laws on fraudulent conveyances and bankruptcy[1] are particularly applicable to   **9.02**

---

[1] Such actions may also vanquish a bankrupt's claim to a discharge under bankruptcy law. See,
eg, *Re Portnoy*, 211 BR 685 (1996) US Bankruptcy Court, NY; *Re Stephen Jay Lawrence* (2002) 5
ITELR 1 (Court of Appeals for the Eleventh Circuit), USA, discussed below, paras 9.15–9.18.

offshore trusts given that one of the essential purposes of the offshore trust is to protect assets from the reach of onshore challengers to the trust. The issue of fraudulent conveyances must also be discussed from the perspective of offshore legislation designed to modify the traditional rules on fraudulent conveyances. Such offshore legislation aims, inevitably, to offer more protection to settlors, often exploiting what are 'grey areas' in orthodox laws concerning fraudulent conveyances, outlined below.[2] It should be noted that orthodox laws on fraudulent conveyances may also exist in offshore jurisdictions, often alongside these more investor-friendly legislative provisions. The latter will apply only to offshore trusts.

9.03   The challenge to the offshore trust, where the issue of a fraudulent conveyance is raised, brings into focus, perhaps more than any other, the fundamental question of the legitimacy of the offshore trust and the offshore legal system itself. This is because the inquiry (more so than the previous question on the 'sham' trust) goes beyond legal form to inquire into its motive and purpose. As the transfer of assets into the offshore trust is likely to be judged also by the onshore laws of fraudulent conveyances, an examination of the scope and intent of such laws is important.

Description of orthodox fraudulent conveyances laws

9.04   Fraudulent conveyancing law is informed by an archaic but hardly obsolete statute, namely the Statute of Elizabeth 1571 of the UK. This statute evolved into s 172 of the Law of Property Act 1925 of the UK, and s 42 of the Bankruptcy Act 1914 of the UK. In fact, generally, bankruptcy law builds on the principles found in the law on fraudulent conveyances. In the United Kingdom, current provisions in relation to this aspect of fraudulent conveyances are contained in the Insolvency Act 1986, Sch 10.[3] The relevant provisions in the USA are found under The Bankruptcy Code and the Uniform Fraudulent Transfer Act 1984 (UFTA),[4] the latter of which replaced the Uniform Fraudulent Conveyances Act. Laws which protect against fraudulent conveyances purport to void any conveyance of assets made with the purpose of hindering or defrauding creditors and others of their lawful debts. The original statute on fraudulent conveyances in the UK has profound significance to the offshore world, since similar legal rules have been adopted in other Common Law jurisdictions which treat with offshore nations. They were also, of course, received in offshore trust

---

[2] Paras 9.4–9.10.
[3] See ss 339–342, in particular.
[4] 11 USCS § 544 (b) (2004) and 11 USCS § 548 (2004) respectively.

jurisdictions.[5] Because of this reception, together with the modifications to the orthodox laws on fraudulent conveyances made by offshore legislation and the interplay between these two streams of related law, the original law on fraudulent conveyances needs to be carefully understood. English case law interpreting fraudulent conveyancing provisions, both original and current, is, therefore, pertinent to our discussion.

9.05 The original simplicity and restrictiveness of the law on fraudulent conveyances were expanded by subsequent precedent, requiring that 'all statutes made against fraud should be liberally and beneficially expounded to suppress the fraud'.[6] In today's context, this may lay the framework for further expansion of the law to address potential abuses of the offshore trust, hinged on concerns of the public's interest. This presumably requires that the rights of creditors be given priority. Whether owners of assets have equal rights on the grounds of public policy, especially where such persons use offshore trusts, is a question still to be answered.

9.06 The expansion is seen, for example, in the possible inclusion of intent to defraud future creditors, as opposed to existing creditors, discussed below. The interpretation can be understood in the light of wording used in the statute to include 'others', which, under the *ejusdem generis* rule, can include other classes of creditors, such as future creditors.

9.07 As we have seen, the idea of a fraudulent conveyance is not a novel one, neither is the use of the offshore trust as a vehicle for asset protection. Rather, it is the use of the offshore trust for protection against a broad category of creditors which is relatively new. It is this juxtaposition of the notion of hindering such creditors with the protection offered under the dual ownership concept of the trust, supported and expanded by creative, settlor-friendly offshore legislation, that may produce difficulty. This reorientation of the traditional precepts of the law on fraudulent conveyances can create potential conflicts about the validity of the offshore trust. Courts may find that transfers into offshore trusts are tainted with intent to defraud creditors.[7]

---

[5] The Statute of Elizabeth 1571 is also known as the Fraudulent Conveyances Act 1571 or Statute of Frauds, now repealed in the UK, but the essential principles are retained in the Insolvency Act 1986 and similar type legislation in the common law world. In *Conway v Queensway Trustees Ltd* (High Court, Nevis) No 16 of 1999, decided 28 July 1999, Smith J, in a rare assertion of sovereignty, admonished counsel for the plaintiff, who had erroneously pleaded the Fraudulent Conveyances Act 1571 of the UK, reminding him that Saint Christopher and Nevis was an independent nation, so that the statute did not apply in that country any longer.

[6] *Twyne's case* (1601) 3 Co Rep 8; (1602) 76 ER 809.

[7] Such a finding is not limited to offshore trusts. Any trust raises this risk. See, eg, *Ideal Bedding Company v Holland* [1907] 2 Ch 157; *Smith v Dresser* (1866) LR 1 Eq 651.

Presumption of a fraudulent conveyance

9.08 Some factual situations have, by their frequent occurrence in fraudulent convey-ance cases, become identifiable as evidence of fraudulent intent. These have been labelled 'badges of fraud',[8] as they will often lead to an inference of a fraudulent conveyance.[9] They include:

(1) the transfer of assets into trust by an insolvent debtor;

(2) where a trust is created by a settlor for his or her own benefit and with a spendthrift clause;[10]

(3) instances where the donor continues in possession, uses the goods as his or her own, or takes advantage of the item transferred;

(4) gifts made secretly or with undue haste;

(5) a conveyance made absolute in form, but which effectively is a security; and

(6) instances in which the settlor places all or most of his or her assets into the trust. This last is inferred from more recent judgments, discussed below.

9.09 Clearly, the prevalence of self-settled, spendthrift trusts in offshore financial centres presents problems. Similarly, offshore secrecy norms and the offshore trust's claim as an avenue for indirect investment, may lend credence to the 'badge' argument. Indeed, the original justifications for the law on fraudulent conveyances were to prohibit 'actions to abuse [creditors'] confidence' or 'secretly undermining their interests'.[11]

9.10 Under fraudulent conveyance law, or parallel bankruptcy law, where the transfer of assets into a trust renders the settlor insolvent there is a presumption of fraudulent intent.[12] However, in a conveyance made for inadequate consider-ation which does not make the settlor insolvent,[13] fraudulent intent must be proved as a matter of fact.[14]

---

[8] *Twyne's Case*, above, n 6.

[9] *Weatherly v Massay-Ferguson Inc*, 432 SW 2d 18, 245 Ark 317 (1968).

[10] *Re Portnoy*, above, n 1, discussed further below at paras 9.15–9.17; *Bank of Dallas v Republic National Bank of Dallas* 540 SW 2d 499, 501 (Tex, Civ App- Waco 1976, writ ref'd n r e).

[11] D McDowell and J Monroe, *Kerr on the Law of Fraud and Mistake*, 7th edn (Sweet & Maxwell, London, 1952).

[12] The burden of proof is shifted onto the transferor. See *Freeman v Pope* (1870) LR 5 Ch App 538.

[13] See, eg, *Traders Trust Co v Cohen* [1927] 3 WLR 473, 8 CBR 513 (Man KB).

[14] But as high a standard as a criminal intent to defraud is unnecessary. See, eg, *Cadogan v Cadogan* [1977] 1 All ER 200 and *Butterworth, Re, ex p Russel* (1882) 19 Ch 588. For a discussion of the requisite standards of intent under Australian law, see *Official Trustee in Bankruptcy v Alvaro* (1996) 138 ALR 341, Federal Court.

Sham trusts, settlor control, and fraudulent conveyances

Where it is determined that the conveyance was not made in 'good faith' but was merely a 'sham', the real intent being to effect only the appearance of a transfer of property, an inference of a fraudulent conveyance may be made.[15] To avoid an inference of a fraudulent conveyance with respect to a trust, there must have been an intention to create a trust, whereby ownership and control of the assets are transferred to the trustee for a genuine business purpose.[16] Recent developments appear to have accentuated the connections between sham trusts and fraudulent conveyances.

9.11

Parallels can be drawn with such developments in the law and the earlier discussion on 'shams'.[17] If the analogy is brought to its logical conclusion, one may discern that the offshore trust, already vulnerable to 'sham' challenges because of certain features which are facilitative of settlors' influences, is equally precarious because of the 'bad faith'–'sham' principle under the law of fraudulent conveyances.[18]

9.12

In *Aspen Planers Ltd v Delsham Development Ltd*,[19] for example, it was held that a fraudulent conveyance action lay against a company that had conveyed its property to frustrate the financial expectations of one of its main shareholders. Real control continued to vest in the company. The creditors had standing to reach assets of a parent company and the disposition of the company was regarded as a disposition by the settlor. The implications for the interrelated structure of the offshore trust and offshore trust company are obvious. Similarly, the existence of a reversionary interest may have negative implications. In *People's Bank of Charlestown v Colburn*,[20] the settlor established an offshore asset protection trust in Bermuda and retained a reversionary interest. The settlor was the protector and maintained an advisory role over the trust's assets. Subsequently, the settlor filed for bankruptcy but neglected to list his reversionary interest, claiming that it was valued at zero. The court disagreed. His actions were taken as evidence of intent to hinder or delay creditors, and the trust was thereby discredited.

9.13

---

[15] *Banque de Hochelaga v Patvin* [1924] 1 DLR 678, reaffirmed in *Legal Remedies of the Unsecured Creditor after Judgment*, Third Report of the Consumer Protection Project, Vol 11, New Brunswick (1976).

[16] See the discussion of shams in chapter 8, 'The Offshore Trust as a Sham'.

[17] ibid.

[18] Self-settlement may be treated as a fraudulent conveyance irrespective of intent or a requirement for constructive fraud, as reaffirmed in *Texas Commercial Bank v Shurley* 118 S Ct 444 1997 (Sup Ct) US, US LEXIS 6924, 139 L Ed 2d 380; 66 USLW 3354 (1997), 33–34.

[19] (1981) 11 AC WS (2d) 128 (BC Co Ct).

[20] 145 BR 85 (Bankr ED Va 1992).

9.14 Further, offshore trusts which are drafted in a manner that reserves important controlling functions to the settlor are vulnerable to fraudulent claims or similar allegations under bankruptcy laws, even if not *formally* deemed shams. Provisions indicating settlor control lead courts to draw inferences that the conveyance of the assets was fraudulent, with the objective being to hide assets from creditors. They are also susceptible to the 'look through' powers of the courts. The result would be that the assets are treated as belonging to the settlor.[21]

9.15 The issue of continuing settlor control and its impact on a finding of a fraudulent conveyance is a recurring theme in US law and was discussed in a number of leading cases, in particular bankruptcy cases. *Re Larry Portnoy*,[22] for example, concerned a settlor who placed virtually all of his assets into an offshore trust in Jersey, just months before his personal indebtedness to his corporation was called. The court had to decide whether the action was fraudulent as a deliberate scheme to conceal his assets under the Bankruptcy Code.[23] It should be noted too, that under US bankruptcy law, US courts retain wide powers to reach assets which should be made available to creditors. The evidence showed that Portnoy knew of the impending debt two months before he established the trust, so that an inference that the timing was purposeful was drawn. The settlor was the primary beneficiary under the trust, and the court's view was that he had retained considerable *de facto* control and that the trustees' 'fidelity' to him was plainly apparent. For example, the court found it remarkable that the trustees paid, without hesitation, all of Portnoy's legal expenses in defence of the bankruptcy charge. Significantly, Portnoy also had a power to appoint and remove trustees, as did the settlor in another leading case, that of *Re Stephen Jay Lawrence*.[24]

9.16 In *Re Stephen Jay Lawrence*, the settlor not only retained a power to appoint new trustees, but sought to conceal his authority over the trust by the use of duress clauses which disengaged (at least temporarily) his interests in the trust. Lawrence filed for bankruptcy, but the court held that the trust was part of the estate and ordered him to hand over the trust assets. Lawrence contended that he had no power to order the trustees to do so. The court, finding that Lawrence still exercised *de facto* control over the trust, as he had the authority to appoint new

---

[21] But recall that there must also be an intention to create a sham, recently reiterated in *Re Abacus CI Ltd (Trustee of the Esteem Settlement) Grupo Torras SA v Al Sabah* (2003) 6 ITELR 368 (Royal Ct, Jersey).

[22] Above, n 1.

[23] Particularly ss 727(a)(2)(A) and (a)(4). The first provision reads: '(a) The court shall grant a debtor a discharge unless . . . (2) . . . the debtor, with intent to hinder, delay, or defraud a creditor or an officer of the estate charged with custody of property under this title, has transferred, removed, destroyed, mutilated, or concealed, or has permitted to be transferred, removed, destroyed, mutilated, or concealed . . . (A) property of the debtor, within one year before the date of the filing of the petition.' The case also considered issues of jurisdiction and proper law of the trust, with the court finding that it had jurisdiction on the grounds of public policy, despite an exclusive jurisdiction clause given to the Jersey courts.

[24] Above, n 1.

trustees who could, in their discretion, reinstate the settlor as a beneficiary and assign the whole proceeds to him, ordered him to be imprisoned for contempt of court.

The combination of a self-settled trust with settlor influence was a significant injury to Portnoy's defence to the allegation of fraud in *Re Larry Portnoy*. In particular, under New York law, which was held to be the proper law by the court, it was against public policy to allow self-settled trusts to defeat the claims of legitimate creditors.[25] This has often been presented as a US rule, but in the light of recent developments, in which certain US states have enacted legislation which is similar in thrust to offshore trusts, and which explicitly repeals the rules against self-settled spendthrift trusts, the public policy rationale of this rule is now questionable.[26]

9.17

Similar inferences were raised in *Federal Trade Commissioner v Affordable Media*,[27] where the settlors, the Andersons, established an offshore trust in the Cook Islands. The determining indicator of settlor control here was the fact that the Andersons were also the protectors of the trust.[28] Their contention, that they could not order the trustee to repatriate the assets in compliance with the court's order, was rejected, as the court found that the protector's power over an offshore trust was significant given that the protector enjoyed affirmative power, such as the power to appoint new trustees. The Andersons attempted to resign as protectors, and this, in itself, was found to be evidence of control. The Andersons were also held in contempt of court.

9.18

Significantly, in *Re Affordable Media*, the court found it incredible that a 'rational person' could send millions of dollars overseas and retain no control over such assets.[29] Indeed, as seen in *Portnoy*, it is clear that the courts will be more hostile to such trusts where all or a substantial part of the settlor's assets are conveyed into the trust.[30] The scepticism demonstrated in *Re Affordable Media* led easily to an inference of control. This prompts the question whether there are any circumstances in which the US courts will accept that an offshore asset protection trust is a genuine conveyance, with a settlor not in control directly or indirectly.

9.19

---

[25] Citing *Credit Corporation v Chase Manhattan Bank* 100 AD 2d 544, 546; NYS 2d 242 (ed Dept 1984); Restatement (Second) of Trusts §156 (1959). Here, intention to defraud was irrelevant. Cf *Herzog v CIR* 116 F 2d 591 (2d Cir 1941).

[26] See chapter 5 for a discussion of these onshore developments. See, eg, the Spendthrift Trusts Act 1999 of Delaware.

[27] (1999) 2 ITELR 73; 179 F 3d 1228.

[28] They were also former co-trustees.

[29] (1999) 2 ITELR 73, at 90; 179 F 3d 1228, 1241.

[30] *Portnoy*, above, n 1. In fact, in *Portnoy*, the court affirmed the US rule that where a person creates a discretionary trust for his own benefit, his creditors can claim the maximum amount that the trustee under the terms of the trust can pay out to the settlor-beneficiary, even where the trustee is not willing to exercise his discretion in the settlor-beneficiary's favour.

Duress, termination, and flight clauses

9.20   Duress clauses and flight clauses inserted into trust documents have also raised the suspicions of certain courts in determining whether a conveyance is fraudulent. In *Re Stephen Jay Lawrence*,[31] Lawrence, the settlor, established an offshore trust worth over US $7 million, and included a duress clause and a clause terminating his life interest in the event of his bankruptcy. The trust also contained a spendthrift clause. Soon thereafter, the settlor had judgments entered against him in the amount of US $20.4 million dollars. The trust was then amended, declaring Lawrence an 'excluded person'. The trustees also issued a declaration of intent, stating that the 'excluded person' status was irrevocable. When the court held that the trust assets were part of Lawrence's estate, he claimed that he had no power to hand them over as they were entirely within the discretion of the trustees. However, the court viewed such provisions as specifically designed to shield assets from adverse judgments and to prevent permanent revocation of the settlor's powers. The fact that the discretion to determine what was an event of duress was left to the settlor and not to the trustees, was an influential one. The court found, further, that the duress clauses had been created solely to aid the settlor to evade contempt of court while pretending to comply with the court's order to turn over the assets.[32]

9.21   In *Affordable Media*[33] there was also a duress clause in the trust, which provided that in the event of duress the Andersons would be terminated as co-trustees. Once again, it proved detrimental to the sustainability of the trust.

Public policy concerns on duress clauses and control

9.22   It is clear that the US courts, at least, view self-settled spendthrift trusts as violations of public policy. On this ground alone, they should not, in the courts' view, be allowed to stand against legitimate creditors.[34] The addition of duress clauses further exacerbates public policy concerns. In *Lawrence*, for example, the settlor had established a self-settled, spendthrift trust and used a duress clause to

---

[31] Above, n 1.

[32] The court's rather harsh position should be read together with its finding that Lawrence still retained control over the trust through his power to appoint and remove trustees. See above, para 9.16.

[33] Above, n 27.

[34] See *Portnoy*, above, n 1; *Affordable Media*, above, n 27; and *Lawrence*, above n 1. However, Danforth argues that this approach is fundamentally flawed as it is based on a misunderstanding of the relative duties and rights of settlors. Thus, it assumes that the settlor has more control over the assets than he actually has, and erroneously presumes that creditors should take precedence over beneficiaries. Danforth also points out that in the light of several other generous routes to sheltering assets from creditors allowed under US law (such as tenancies by the entirety, homestead rules, and limited partnerships) asset protection trusts should not be criticized as being against public policy. Danforth therefore concludes that asset protection trusts may, and should, be effective in certain circumstances. See R T Danforth, 'Rethinking the Law of Creditors' Rights in Trusts' (2002) 53 Hastings LJ 287, 360–62.

enhance further the trust's ability to secure assets from creditors. The court frowned upon the situation which the settlor had created. It said:

> . . . validation of such a position would contravene public policy, proscribing a debtor from shielding money placed in a trust for his or her own benefit and to the prejudice of legitimate creditors.[35]

Thus, duress clauses do nothing to absolve settlors from implications of control over the trust. If anything, they add weight to likely inferences that the settlor exercises *de facto* control.

In *Lawrence*, the trustees' declaration that the decision to exclude Lawrence as a beneficiary was irrevocable, was not accepted as credible by the court, as the court speculated that the trustees, in their absolute discretion, could revoke their decision. Yet it is difficult to see how such a trustee power is different from any other trustee power, even trustee powers in onshore trusts. The rejection of this argument by the US court is further evidence of the scepticism that the court allowed to inform its decisions concerning offshore trusts.   **9.23**

While the recent cases, particularly from the US, demonstrate a clear hostility against offshore trusts, comfort may be gained from the fact that, in each of the cases, the settlors came to the table without 'clean hands', thus violating a fundamental principle of equity. There was credible evidence that the settlors in question at least suspected that they were about to incur huge debts, and that this was the real reason for the establishment of the trusts. It is not clear under the law on fraudulent conveyances whether debts which are not already in existence can be properly harnessed.[36] As such, the courts employed other routes, such as public policy, to come to what were, perhaps, just decisions, allowing the 'ends to justify the means'.   **9.24**

B. The Problem of Identifying Appropriate Creditors

Common Law unclear

A serious difficulty with the orthodox law on fraudulent conveyances for the purposes of offshore jurisprudence, is that onshore law is itself sometimes unclear as to what constitutes a fraudulent conveyance. This is particularly so with respect to identifying clearly the classes of creditors to which the law applies. Most important are the questions whether the law is applicable to future   **9.25**

---

[35] *Lawrence*, above, n 1, 7. Lawrence argued an 'impossibility' defence to the demand for repatriation of the assets. This was rejected by the courts on the ground that the so-called impossibility was self-created, and therefore he was not able to demonstrate that he had made good faith attempts to repatriate the assets: ibid.

[36] Discussed below, paras 9.42–9.47.

creditors, with which the majority of offshore trusts are concerned, and how the term 'future creditor' is to be interpreted.

9.26 Problems with fraudulent conveyance law, and by extension that of bankruptcy in relation to offshore trusts, hinge on two fundamental and interrelated questions. First, must there be an actual intent to defraud creditors as a result of the transfer and, if so, how is actual intent to be interpreted? Does it, for example, require an identifiable creditor to which intent is directed, or can there be an actual intent in isolation, thereby covering all or any creditors who come along? Secondly, is the law applicable to all creditors, whether existing, subsequent, or future, whom the transfer affects, even if the effect is in the distant future, and regardless of whether there was an intent to defraud such persons?

9.27 When one examines offshore asset protection trusts, particularly creditor protection trusts, it seems clear that their ultimate motive is to restrict or defeat the claims of creditors and others who may wish to control such assets, even if such an event is uncertain and in the distant future. Whether such an intent to defeat can be equated to an intent to defraud is the real issue.

Offshore approach to uncertainty

9.28 The response offshore has been to take the view—which is, in itself, a popular one onshore—that unidentifiable future creditors are not the appropriate subjects of the law on fraudulent conveyances, or, alternatively, that the concept of a 'future creditor' must be interpreted restrictively. With this single stroke investors have been granted more security for their assets. At the same time, offshore law does not reject the notion of a fraudulent conveyance. It concedes that it is unacceptable to remove assets where creditors are existent at the time of the transfer. Such creditors are not, therefore, subjects of contention. The offshore law on fraudulent conveyances is, in effect, a neat compromise, which succeeds in elevating the security of an investor in the interest of commercial efficiency, while attempting to prevent recognized forms of abuse.

9.29 Offshore legislation on fraudulent conveyances has thus deviated substantially from the UK jurisprudence on the subject—what we may call the 'common law approach', albeit validated by statute. Yet it is important to our understanding of asset protection planning to discuss this case law, both to give an appreciation of the important differences created in offshore jurisdictions, often deliberately, in order to address perceived legal gaps, inadequacies, and injustices within the common law approach, and because such case law may still, in some respects, have influence on the interpretation of offshore law.

9.30 For the overseas creditor to pursue a claim of fraudulent conveyance, often he or she must first invoke the traditional law on the subject in the onshore country, and if a judgment is obtained, seek to enforce it in the offshore jurisdiction. This attempt to enforce judgments poses its own problems, which are more fully addressed in a subsequent chapter.[37] Further, not all offshore jurisdictions have legislation which can be labelled 'asset protection legislation' and which emphasizes the protection of debtors over creditors. In these offshore jurisdictions, a finer appreciation of 'domestic' fraudulent conveyances law—law which emulates the common law approach—is necessary.[38]

Addressing future creditors

The focus of the law on fraudulent conveyances has, until now, been on a limited **9.31** class of creditors. A consensus exists between offshore and onshore laws, that present and existing creditors at the time of the transfer of the assets are afforded firm protection under the relevant law. This is despite the practical difficulties involved in reaching such assets placed offshore.[39] In contrast, the ambit of that law in relation to future creditors, that is, identifiable creditors who were not immediately within the contemplation of the settlor at the time of the transfer, has yet to be clearly defined. There is now a possibility that fraudulent conveyance law may extend to future or potential creditors, particularly if public policy demands it.

There is uncertainty with this new approach. How is the term 'future creditors' to **9.32** be interpreted? Are such creditors to be limited to creditors already on the horizon, whom the owner of assets knows about, but who perhaps have not yet sued, or is the term to be given a wide interpretation to include all future creditors? The latter may include creditors of, for example, a medical practitioner, who, fearing potential negligence suits in the unforeseeable future, and bereft of insurance protection, decides to place his or her assets into an offshore trust.[40]

It is possible to discern from extant case law a narrow explanation of the term **9.33** 'future creditor'. Older examples of the law seem to have been primarily concerned with creditors who had not yet had the opportunity to file claims or begin proceedings, but where the set of circumstances leading to such a claim was already in existence at the time of the transfer. Historically, courts have not interpreted statutes to protect unknown future creditors.[41] This leads to an

---

[37] Chapter 24.
[38] See, eg, the law of the Isle of Man, as considered in *Re Heginbotham's Petition* (1999) 2 ITELR 95 (High Ct, Isle of Man).
[39] See, eg, *Duttle v Bandler and Kass* (1992) 82 Cir 5084 (KMW); 1992 US Dist LEXIS 8894.
[40] *See Martin v Martin* [1937] 3 DLR 418 (Ont HC).
[41] *United States v Chapman* 756 F 2d 1237, 1240 (5th Cir 1950). Indeed, US writers appear to concede that unidentifiable, future creditors are not appropriate subjects of the law. See, eg, Lynn M Lo Pucki, 'The Death of Liability', 106 Yale LJ 1, 35 and Danforth, above, n 34, 330. For a future creditor to establish liability, he or she must establish a 'causal link' between the fraudulent disposition and the injury suffered. Danforth, ibid, citing the case of *Oberst v Oberst* 91 BR 97 (Bankr CD Cal 1988). See also J Sullivan III, 'Future Creditors and Fraudulent Transfers: When a Claimant Doesn't Have a Claim, When a Transfer Isn't a Transfer, When Fraud Doesn't Stay Fraudulent, and Other Important Limits to Fraudulent Transfers Law for the Asset Protection Planner' 22 Del J Corp L 955, 971–5, 981–8 (1987). Note that the causal connection test also applies to claims of constructive fraud, Danforth, ibid, 332.

assumption that the law may contemplate subsequent creditors only within the context of the existing creditor. This would require present and existing creditors at the time of the transfer, before the question of 'subsequent creditors' could arise. This inference arises from an analysis of the case law which views the subsequent creditor's right as arising not by statute, but from his or her equitable right to participate equally with prior creditors, based on the principle that all creditors should be treated equally.[42]

9.34 If this is the correct interpretation of previous precedents on subsequent creditors, the question then becomes: Should the status of the subsequent creditor be confined to its original formulation under the law, or should a new meaning, in accordance with changed circumstances, be assigned?

C. Tests to Determine to Which Future Creditors the Law Applies

9.35 A number of tests have been fashioned to determine the question of who is a 'future creditor' for the purpose of liability under the common law. Yet none of these is conclusive. They merely underline the uncertainty of the present law of which offshore legislators have taken advantage. It should be noted, however, that the notion of a 'future creditor' who has *locus standi* has been considerably defined under modern bankruptcy and insolvency law in favour of creditors.

Intent to defraud future creditors

9.36 An intent to defraud is usually a necessary ingredient in the law on fraudulent conveyances, albeit a concept which has not been easy to define where certain categories of creditors, such as future creditors, are involved.[43]

9.37 In more recent interpretations of the law on fraudulent conveyances, liability in relation to a future creditor is made contingent on the existence of actual intent to defraud. This was seen in *Eurovest Ltd v Segall.*[44] However, if the settlor intends to defeat future creditors and in fact defeats an existing creditor, it is no defence to a claim of fraudulent conveyance that there was no intent to defeat that existing creditor.[45]

---

[42] See *Jenkyn v Vaughan* (1856) 3 Drew 413, 425.

[43] Such an intent may be unnecessary under bankruptcy laws where the settlor is rendered insolvent by the transfer, or where other elements lead to an obvious inference of fraudulent intent by an objective observer, ie, constructive fraud. Under New York law, eg, self-settled, spendthrift trusts are against public policy and may render the question of intent irrelevant. See *Credit Corporation v Chase Manhattan Bank* 100 AD 2d 544, 546; NYS 2d 242 (ed Dept 1984); Restatement (Second) of Trusts §156 (1959).

[44] 528 S 2d 482 (1988) 483–4. The notion of actual intent may be narrowly construed. See *Hurlbert v Shackleton* 560 S 2d 1276 (Ct App Fla, First District).

[45] See *Petrone v Jones* (1995) 33 CBR (3d) 17 (Ontario Court of Justice).

The requirement that there be intent to commit a fraudulent conveyance is **9.38** sometimes construed liberally. In *Katzschke v Walter*,[46] the plaintiffs brought an action against the bankrupt, his wife, and a friend, alleging that transactions involving the transfer of real estate and chattels between the bankrupt, his wife, and the friend constituted fraudulent conveyances and should be voided. The court emphasized that a plaintiff did not have to show that creditors were defrauded, only that there was an intent to defraud creditors.[47] This would mean that a conveyance into an offshore trust could be fraudulent, even if the settlor never had creditors in the future, once he had the intention to defraud them if they ever came into being! This interpretation is not, however, validated by the following cases which suggest that the creditor must be identifiable for the requisite intent to qualify for fraudulent conveyances purposes.

In addition, *Re Trustee of Pehrsson (a bankrupt)*[48] provides an alternative, and **9.39** better, interpretation to that of *Katzschke*. It establishes that for the purposes of fraudulent conveyances law (in this case, the Fraudulent Conveyances Act 1571 of Gibraltar), the intention to convey is relevant, but it is not the donor's state of mind when he or she forms an intention to convey that is important but the intention when the conveyance is actually made.[49] The mere intention to convey is, therefore, not sufficient.

In *Pehrsson*, it was claimed by the bankrupt that he had gifted shares now being **9.40** claimed as part of the estate, to a female partner at a time when he was solvent. If this were the case, it would not have constituted a fraudulent conveyance. However, while the court did not challenge outright his intention to transfer the shares, the intended gift was viewed as incomplete and could not be a fraudulent conveyance. This was so because, although the registration of the shares was not necessary to demonstrate the intention to grant the gift,[50] the nominee shareholders had not as yet executed transfers to his partner, nor delivered their shares into her possession. The donor could, therefore, countermand the gift if he so desired.

The intent must be conscious. Thus, if a settlor did not realize that he was **9.41** insolvent, he may be held as lacking the intention to make a fraudulent conveyance. In *Re Malisic*[51] the bankrupt was laid off, and received a severance payment. Assuming that he would also receive unemployment insurance benefits, he used the severance payment to pay off loans to friends. He later

---

[46] (1995) 32 CBR (3d) 153 (Sup Ct, British Columbia).
[47] ibid, 155.
[48] (1999) 2 ITELR 230 (PC, Gibraltar).
[49] ibid.
[50] Relying on *Re Rose (deceased) Rose v Inland Revenue Commission* [1952] 1 All ER 1217.
[51] (1995) 117 DLR 4th (Ontario High Court). The law in question was the Bankruptcy and Insolvency Act, RSC 1985, c B-3, s 95(2), Canada.

discovered that he was ineligible for unemployment benefits and he declared personal bankruptcy. An action that the payments made to his friends were fraudulent preferences failed, as the beneficiary was found to have lacked the necessary intention.

Rejecting future unidentifiable creditors

Requirement that creditors, claims, and debts be existing and identified

9.42   A corollary of the analysis above, that there must be an actual intent to defraud, is the argument that the future creditor must be specifically identified, as opposed to existing in the abstract, for a claim of fraudulent conveyance to succeed. A dichotomy between subsequent creditors, who are protected under the law, and mere future potential creditors, who are not, is discernible. It would seem that the latter are not always identifiable, since no evidence would exist that the settlor intended to commit malpractice in relation to them. Instead, they may be ignored by the law as too vague a class to be adequately addressed without the necessary proof of actual intent. This interpretation would favour the offshore trust.[52] For example, in *Roland v US* the court stated that a 'subsequent creditor could reach a grantor's interest in property conveyed to others if that transfer was made with intent to defraud that *particular* creditor'.[53] Such cases outline the assumption by the courts that intent needs to be specifically directed for it to ground an action in fraudulent conveyance. Unidentifiable potential creditors may not be contemplated by the law.

Interpretation of the common law from an offshore court

9.43   In *Re Heginbotham's Petition*,[54] a case from the Isle of Man, the High Court of Justice clarified the question relating to future creditors whose debts were not known or ascertainable at the date of the transfer of assets into the trust. Such future creditors, the court found, were not within the scope of the law on fraudulent conveyances. The case concerned a petition under the Fraudulent Assignments Act 1736 of the Isle of Man to enforce a judgment against two Isle of Man companies on the basis that fraudulent transfers had been effected. The petitioner had entered into an agreement to sell his business to the company in question. The agreement was never carried out, and in a subsequent suit damages were awarded to the petitioner. While the suit was proceeding, the defendant transferred shares out of the relevant company to another company, thus preventing the petitioner from being able to enforce the judgment obtained.

---

[52] See also *Speer v Stewart*, 3 Wash 2d 334, 100 P2d 404 (1940).

[53] 838 F2d 1400 (5th Cir 1988), 1402 (emphasis added). See also *Hurlbert* above, n 44, 1279–80.

[54] Above, n 38.

The petitioner thereafter claimed that the transfer of the shares was a fraudulent conveyance.

The court found that a transfer in such circumstances could not be set aside unless the transferor was in a state of insolvency at the time of the transfer, that is, that he was not in a position to pay his known and ascertainable debts, including those falling due on a future date. Even if there had been knowledge of the counterclaim, there was no existing or present debt. The requisite intent to defraud creditors must be applied only to present debts, not to contingent or future debts 'which may never materialize'.[55] The court was also influenced by the fact that there was arguably a viable business motive to the transfer of shares, although losses were incurred. In addition, the transactions did not appear to be shams.

9.44

The judgment therefore affirms the viability of asset protection arrangements and interprets the issue of 'future creditors' restrictively, in favour of settlors. However, it also points to the danger of settlors placing all of their assets into trust, a point underscored in the *Affordable Media* line of cases.[56] It is apposite to draw attention to the judgment's usefulness and interest for another reason. This is that the Isle of Man is one of the few offshore jurisdictions not to have enacted specific asset protection legislation incorporating anti-fraudulent conveyancing provisions. The judgment represents, therefore, a useful interpretation of the problem from a common law perspective, from a court willing to address the issue in a new and dynamic environment. It also gives a long-awaited interpretation of the relevant law in the Isle of Man. It is an interpretation which appears to be more generous (and certainly clearer) to settlors than that employed by the UK courts.

9.45

The Canadian case of *Stone v Stone*[57] goes further, and establishes that an existing claim of action may be required at the time of the transfer of assets before a claim of fraudulent conveyance can be sustained. This also lends credence to the argument that, for future creditors to be covered, they must be existing and identifiable. In this case, the plaintiff's husband transferred the family home into trust for the benefit of his children, thereby not complying with the requirements of the Family Law Act 1990 of Ontario, which created a mandatory share in a family estate for a spouse. The plaintiff argued that the transfer was made with intent to defeat her entitlement and was therefore void under s 2 of the Fraudulent Conveyances Act 1990 of Ontario. In issue was whether the Family Law Act established a claim on behalf of the plaintiff.

9.46

---

[55] ibid, 112.
[56] See above, paras 9.15–9.18.
[57] Above, n 21.

9.47   The court found that in order to qualify as a 'creditor or other' under s 3 of the Fraudulent Conveyances Act 1990, the claimant had to have an existing claim against the other party at the time of the impugned conveyance. The plaintiff in the instant case did have such a claim under the Family Law Act, as she had a right to make a claim to prevent dissipation of the assets by her husband.

Not existing creditors where property cannot be reached

9.48   Where the court, in assessing a fraudulent conveyance claim, is not satisfied that the assets in question can be reached by the alleged creditor, the claim may not be entertained. This was the situation in *Hess v Line Trust Corporation*.[58] In this case, the plaintiff, the wife of the settlor of an asset protection trust established in Gibraltar, was denied relief because she was held to have no *locus standi*. This was because only property which could be reached by execution at the time of the alleged fraudulent conveyance was subject to the relevant statute, the Fraudulent Conveyances Act 1571 of Gibraltar. The settlor, who owned 100% of the issued share capital of a Swiss company valued at US $200 million, transferred 92% of the shares of the company to a Gibraltar trust company. A trust was then established with the trust corporation, the defendant, as the trustee. The plaintiff's contention was that the transfer of the shares into the trust was void as it was done to defraud her from an appropriate divorce settlement. The plaintiff had as yet no judgment in the onshore courts for marital claims. The court found that the plaintiff was not in a position to levy execution in Gibraltar against the shares in Switzerland. Indeed, the action by the plaintiff was viewed as premature since she would first have had to have obtained a judgment.

9.49   The judgment goes even further than those cases which emphasize that there must be an existing claim of debts,[59] and serves to insulate offshore trusts further.

The offshore trust as an insurance

9.50   An interesting comparison may be made with the way case law seems to make a distinction between protecting one's assets from the contingencies of a hazardous business and placing assets into trust as a type of insurance against future claims. The rejection of fraud and future creditors in the abstract has been justified by the insurance principle, that is, that such a conveyance merely amounts to efficient financial planning. This was the justification for the upholding of the transfer in *Klein v Klein*.[60] The settlor, a policeman, was concerned that he might 'be sued for . . . some act in connection with his duties

---

[58] (1998–1999) 1 ITELR 249 (CA Gibraltar).
[59] Discussed above, paras 9.42–9.49.
[60] 122 NY S 2d 546 (1952).

in the enforcement of the law ... at some future time'. Consequently, he transferred his property to his wife. In a fraudulent conveyance suit, the court found no element of fraud, stating:

> There has been found no authority that an action such as this must fail for the reason that the grantor, who was without creditors, feared for future dangers, real or imaginative. Surely his hands were as clean as anyone whoever came into equity. What he did amounted to no more than insurance against a possible disaster.[61]

The parallels between the 'insurance' line of cases and the situation of the **9.51** typical present-day settlor of the creditor protection trust are apparent. In fact, the offshore sector markets creditor protection trusts as a type of insurance. Indeed, often, with professionals who fear tortious liability cases, it is precisely because they are unable to obtain insurance coverage that they elect to set up offshore trusts. The offshore trust itself can therefore be viewed as a type of *alternative insurance*. Yet there is a danger that when the various motives behind the offshore trust are considered, the insurance principle might be too wide and all-encompassing for deciding the validity of such transfers of assets.

Transfers for the benefit of the family

Future creditors may also be excluded under the established defence to a fraudu- **9.52** lent conveyance challenge on the grounds of family interest, as outlined in *Tiedmann v Tiedmann*.[62] Here, because of concerns that he might be sued, the settlor transferred the family home into the name of his spouse. In a subsequent suit, the court did not accept that this was a fraud, holding that the 'plaintiff's motive was a good one, the establishment of a home for his family'. Canadian case law has agreed with this interpretation, viewing as an exception to fraudu-lent conveyancing the situation where a debtor enriches the assets of his wife.[63] In this regard, consider *Baby v Ross*,[64] where it was noted that:

> There is no law which compels him [the husband] to work for his creditors if he chooses to live in idleness ... The arrangement [that he should work for his wife alone, she receiving the whole of the proceeds and he getting nothing but his board] ... was neither unreasonable nor illegal and I am unable to compre-hend on what principle it can be said to be ... in order to defeat or defraud creditors.

---

[61] ibid, at 548. See also *Pagano v Pagano* 139 NYA 2d 219 (1955), which involved the transfer of title to family property to the only member of the family who was not involved in the family business, and whom subsequent claims by creditors would not have affected.

[62] 115 NSC 462 1921.

[63] *Shephard v Shephard* [1925] 2 DLR 897, 900 (Ont SCAD).

[64] (1892) 14 OPR 440, 446.

This view appears to have found favour with those practising in the field of asset protection trusts.[65]

9.53   The family defence does, however, seem wide and is vulnerable to a floodgates argument. Believing that even a public policy argument could embrace so broad a justification for creditor protection trusts is difficult. Surely, even where a settlor is blatantly attempting to defraud a present and existing creditor, he is indirectly seeking also to protect his family assets. It is noteworthy that the cases immediately above are not recent, and may not survive in a modern context. Often, under modern legal policy, the law, in balancing creditors' rights and those of a settlor and his family, has decided in favour of the former.[66]

9.54   In addition, such cases are largely founded on anachronistic notions of gender, that is, the patronizing dependence of a wife on a husband and the man's duty to provide for his wife and family. It is doubtful whether a modern interpretation of law, in particular fraudulent conveyance law, will grant such a sacrosanct privilege to the female spouse.[67]

Exceptional situations where future, unidentifiable creditors are addressed

Hazardous business test

9.55   Certain situations may permit fraudulent conveyances law to encompass future, unidentifiable creditors. For example, case law reveals a 'hazardous business test'. This suggests that where a settlor places his or her assets into a trust specifically to protect against the contingencies of a hazardous business, the court may regard this as a fraudulent transfer.[68]

9.56   The rule protects creditors in two situations. On the one hand, the settlor may deliberately intend to owe subsequent debts, as a result of an intention of 'incurring liability', where he or she does not intend to honour these. On the other hand, he or she may simply enter a hazardous endeavour. Here, he or she may not intend specifically to incur debts which he or she will not honour because of the transfer of his or her debts. Yet there is compelling evidence that such debts will probably be incurred because of the nature of the business. In *Re Butterworth*[69] the court said:

---

[65] See, eg, Barry Engel, 'When is a Subsequent Creditor Not a Subsequent Creditor?' [1994] 3 JIntP 105, 114.

[66] See, eg, the Insolvency Act 1986, UK.

[67] See *Wagner v Wagner Estate* [1991] 85 DLR 699: 'Women now have a valued position in the workplace; and legislation promotes the financial independence of spouses from each other.'

[68] *Hemphil Co v Davis Knit Co* 114 Pa Superior Ct 95, (1972). See also, the case of *Watson v Harris* 435 SW2d 667, 38 ALR 3d 582 (1968), Mo.

[69] *Re Butterworth, ex parte Russel* (1882) 19 Ch D 588, relying on *Mackay v Douglas* (1872) LR 14 Eq 106.

[A] man is not entitled to go into a hazardous business and immediately before doing so settle all his property voluntarily, the object being this: If I succeed in business, I make a fortune for myself. If I fail, I leave my creditors unpaid. They will bear the loss.

The difficulty with the 'hazardous business test' is that it begs the question: What is a 'hazardous business' in the contemporary world of finance? Such a description is seldom static. Just recently, most persons would not have viewed doctors and attorneys as practitioners in a 'hazardous business'. However, with the great increase in litigation against such professionals, they may well fall into such a category. Does the fact that a settlor may be aware that there is some risk that *some* time in the future he or she might be facing a malpractice suit because of alleged negligence, mean that he or she is in a hazardous business? **9.57**

The case law does appear to embrace some notion that there must be a real risk of liability and not a remote possibility. If this is the correct interpretation, offshore trusts must be judged on a case-by-case basis, taking into account factual circumstances surrounding the particular trust. **9.58**

Another point of note is that the question mark surrounding a hazardous business sits awkwardly with modern views of limited liability companies where, arguably, it is that very motive, to secure against risk, that is sustained. **9.59**

Foreseeability of future creditors

A foreseeability test may also bring the future creditor within the context of fraudulent conveyances law. Distinctions between 'probable' and 'possible' future creditors,[70] and the requirement for specificity, pose an interesting question. This is whether such reasoning sits comfortably with the 'neighbour principle' to which it seems to have an affinity? Here, the question would not be whether such future creditors could be identifiable in the present, but whether there are, at present, foreseeable circumstances (such as potential negligence) which would affect such persons, thereby placing a duty on the settlor to contemplate them? The lack of actual intent to commit the offending act (be it a negligent act, and so on) may be an unnecessarily high standard upon which to base an absence of intent to defraud creditors. It might lead to an inference that only those transactions where there was a deliberate intent to incur liability, for example, where a person transfers assets and then proceeds to incur debts at the gambling table, would suffice. In the majority of cases, persons who do incur debts in the future, be it from negligence or otherwise, do not *intend* to incur such debts or commit negligent acts. Even the person who ventures into a risky business does not *intend* to become bankrupt. Thus the **9.60**

---

[70] As made in *Hurlbert*, above, n 44.

likelihood of such debts or negligence occurring in the future might be a more appropriate test for the question of liability, and not the intent to create such debts or actions. Liability could be measured not on intent to do harm, but on reasonable forseeability of such harm where it provides the impetus for the creation of the trust.

9.61 Reasonable forseeability also seems an appropriate compromise for resolving the public policy conflicts here. Herein lies the difficulty: on the one hand, investors require some form of insurance for professional risks; on the other, there are creditors who may be bereft of a remedy if assets are protected in the trust. If a too liberal approach is taken, there would be no suitable yardstick with which to measure offshore trusts, which surely have the potential to cause much harm. This is despite the fact that few offshore investors could be proven to have embarked on the creation of the offshore trust with the intention of defrauding creditors. In contrast, too strict an interpretation would challenge all creditor protection trusts.

9.62 A forseeability test is slowly emerging in the literature. In *Leopald v Tuttle*, it was noted that the term 'future creditor' could be construed to include a creditor whose claim is 'reasonably foreseen as arising in the immediate future'. Further, a 'future creditor does not exist unless a conveying party can reasonably foresee the costs of a claim or judgment incurring at the time of the conveyance'.[71]

9.63 The forseeability test seems particularly appropriate if one considers that the bulk of creditor protection trusts is initiated to avoid future actions arising in tort, such as professional negligence in medicine or legal practice, from whence the test originates. Should the law allow potential tortfeasors to put themselves deliberately in a position to frustrate the consequences of a duty of care?

9.64 Still, it is difficult to draw a demarcation line for forseeability. Should the settlor reasonably foresee potential creditors if he or she is in a particularly risky business, such as heart surgery? If so, is there a likely number of potential victims who can be identified, and for which he or she must make provision?

9.65 Further, it is not apparent that a true distinction exists between the 'hazardous business' test and that based on the 'insurance principle'. At best, the adherence to both tests by the courts highlights the remarkable contradictions and inconsistencies in the relevant case law. At worst, the judicial approval granted to the insurance principle represents an exercise in excessive literalism designed primarily to disguise transfers which fit quite properly into the fraudulent conveyance mould.

---

[71] 549 A 2d 151 (Pa Super 1988), at 154. See also the American case of *First National Bank In Kearney v Bunn* 241 NW 2d 127 (1976).

Transfer of assets and bankruptcy or insolvency law

As we have noted, the principles of the law on fraudulent conveyances have   **9.66**
often been incorporated into bankruptcy law, with or without modifications.
Consequently, in addition to the law on fraudulent conveyances, the validity of
the transfer of assets to an offshore trust must be examined in the light of
bankruptcy law. Similar considerations to those discussed in relation to fraudulent conveyance law will apply.[72] Transfers made gratuitously or at an under-
value will be set aside if the settlor is adjudged bankrupt within the specified
period of the transfer.[73]

The most important issue regarding bankruptcy law is whether the settlor was   **9.67**
solvent at the time of the transfer. For example, in many jurisdictions, the owner
of assets is prevented from rendering himself a bankrupt by transferring all of his
assets to another. Both contingent creditors and future creditors may be protected under bankruptcy legislation.[74] In the USA, the transfer may be set aside
within one year of filing of the petition in bankruptcy if the transfer was made at
a time when the debtor was insolvent, or was rendered insolvent as a result of
the transfer. Future creditors are specifically protected.[75] In the UK, it is possible
that claims not actually contemplated at the time of transfer can escape the
seemingly rigid limitation period and be within the scope of the Act. For
example, the phrase 'contingent and prospective' liabilities under s 341(3) of the
Insolvency Act 1986 may be interpreted broadly, to include future creditors and
to cover liabilities under torts not yet committed, or contracts or agreements not
yet in effect.[76] As intention may be irrelevant here, an objective test will be used
to determine 'prospective liabilities'. This presents danger to an offshore settlor:
it makes it easier for a judge faced with existing creditors and extrinsic evidence,
such as the settlor's conduct after the creation of the instrument, to decide the
prospective issue.[77]

For example, in *Midland Bank plc v Wyatt* and *Cohen v Saggar*,[78] a gift of   **9.68**

---

[72] See, in particular, ss 339–342 of the Insolvency Act 1986 of the UK.

[73] See, eg, *Re Butterworth*, above, n 14, where the settlor created a trust for his wife and children, and a month later purchased a grocery business, using most of his assets. As such, he was rendered insolvent from the transfer. In a later suit by his creditors the settlement was voided under s 91 of the Bankruptcy Act. See also *Midland Bank plc v Wyatt* [1995] 1 FLR 696; [1995] 3 FCR 11; [1994] EGCS 113, Ch D, discussed below at paras 9.68–9.70.

[74] See *Official Receiver v Saebar* [1972] ALR 612 on this point.

[75] Section 548 of the Federal Bankruptcy Code. See also ss 4 and 5 of the Uniform Fraudulent Transfer Act 1984.

[76] See *Midland Bank*, above, n 73.

[77] The settlor will also have to be mindful of s 357 of the Act, which makes a settlement within five years before the settlor's bankruptcy a crime unless the settlor can prove that he did not have any intention to defraud, or to conceal the state of his affairs.

[78] Above, n 73 and [1992] BCC 307 respectively.

property made by the settlor to his children by way of trust instrument was challenged under s 423 of the Insolvency Act 1986 as a 'sham'. A principal issue was whether the said section applied only where the settlor was about to enter a high risk (hazardous) business. The English court chose not to stress the idea of a hazardous business. It interpreted the statute liberally, holding that the real question is whether the transaction was entered into for the purpose of putting assets beyond the reach of a person who might at some time make a claim against the settlor. In the instant case, the transfer was unsuccessful.

9.69   *Midland* therefore undermines the significance of the 'hazardous test' and, by implication, demolishes the notion behind the insurance principle. These tests were not found to be appropriate yardsticks by which to measure the viability of a transfer. Further, the settlor's clearly stated objective of protecting his family from long-term commercial risk—in effect, his insurance policy—was not considered to be a powerful reason to validate the trust.

9.70   The decision has important implications for the offshore world, as it seems to sever the links to legality previously relied on, namely, the family ideal, the insurance principle, and the lack of a specific intention to defraud. What is more damaging to offshore settlors is that the trust might be successfully challenged even if it were not the settlor's sole intention to 'insure' assets. There need only be a dominant intention to do so.[79] Yet the decision must be read in the light of its proper context, insolvency.

9.71   If the settlor remains on intimate terms with the trust, the validity of the transfer of assets is questionable and the law may treat this as an act of bankruptcy, albeit voluntary bankruptcy. This is a potential threat to offshore trusts which, as discussed earlier, typically involve settlor beneficiaries.

9.72   Nevertheless, bankruptcy law may offer wider protection to the offshore trust than does the relevant law on fraudulent conveyances. First, despite the expansion of the case law, there has been an attempt to lay down clear limitation periods. Secondly, bankruptcy legislation has the possibility of restricting the purview of creditors and claimants to those who were known and identifiable at the time of the transfer or, at minimum, during the relevant limitation period. In effect, the settlor would have had to be given notice of the pending claims, or to have been able to heed such claims, before the transfer could be voided.[80]

---

[79] See, in particular, *Cohen v Sagger*, ibid.

[80] For example, under the UK Insolvency Act 1986, if the settlor was solvent at the time of transfer, the transfer could be invalidated only if he or she became bankrupt within two years.

Invalidation on grounds of public policy if trust used for fraud

The timing of the establishment of the trust vis-à-vis the alleged fraudulent **9.73**
conveyance should also be considered where the trust is validity established but
is thereafter used for alleged fraudulent dispositions. The question whether
such a trust should be voided on grounds of public policy was considered in
the provocative case of *In re Abacus CI Ltd.*[81] The claim in this case related to
complex, international proceedings involving the settlor, Sheik Fahad, who had
defrauded Grupo Torras of huge amounts of money using a variety of trusts
worldwide. Although several of the trusts worldwide had been emptied pursuant to various judgments against the settlor, the judgment debt was still not
satisfied. The Jersey trust in question had been established before the actual
perpetration of the fraud, but had allegedly been used thereafter to deposit
monies obtained through the fraud. The claimants argued that the trust should
be voided on grounds of public policy, as it had been used as a vehicle for
fraud.

The Jersey court rejected this view, finding that a high threshold was required **9.74**
before public policy could be used to invalidate a trust validly established in the
first instance. An example might be a trust established for charity but which was
subsequently used for terrorist purposes. It found, further, that the mere fact
that a trust is set up with an intent to defeat creditors' claims did not make the
trust invalid. Rather, it was the fact of making dispositions into the trust with
such an intention that invalidated it. The court was of the opinion that 'it will
be highly exceptional that a trust which is initially valid on public policy
grounds will subsequently become invalid'.[82]

Are tax authorities legitimate creditors?

Another important difference between onshore jurisdictions and offshore juris- **9.75**
dictions, even offshore jurisdictions which do not have specific asset protection
legislation, would be the extent to which the tax collector will be considered to
be a legitimate creditor. This would be an additional question to consider, even
if we were successfully to resolve the initial questions of who is a future creditor
and to what extent future creditors can be addressed under the law on fraudulent conveyances. Public policy concerns in offshore jurisdictions would likely
be different to those in onshore countries given the thrust of offshore legal
regimes and their aversion to being used as international 'fiscal policemen'. It is
by no means certain that answers to fraudulent conveyance questions will be in

---

[81] Above, n 21.
[82] ibid, 428, *per* Birt DB, Jurats P de Veulle and R M Bullen. This echoes *Pehrsson*, above, n 48.

favour of such creditors. In this narrow area, at least, offshore jurisdictions, either those with, or those without special asset protection regimes, may be considered to be in tandem with each other.

9.76 In this context, we would need to consider the established rule that foreign fiscal law will not be enforced. For example, in *Re Tucker*[83] the creditor was the UK Inland Revenue and the court viewed the action as an indirect attempt to enforce a foreign fiscal law.[84] The issue is to be treated as inconclusive in some jurisdictions, even some offshore jurisdictions, because of the new developments which challenge the established rule.[85] In the final analysis, it may be best resolved under bilateral treaties on mutual legal assistance.

D. Offshore Legislation on Fraudulent Conveyancing and Related Jurisprudence

Introduction

9.77 From an examination of the literature on the origins of the law of fraudulent conveyances, it seems apparent that the law did not originally contemplate jurisdiction over all classes of creditors, be they existing or future.[86] The rationale for this perspective of the law may quite simply be that the commercial framework of the time did not require such forward-looking and aggressive planning against future claimants. The public policy context has now changed. Neither the common law, nor onshore statutory law has moved adequately to accommodate these changes, and there are still question marks about the proper scope of such laws.

9.78 Given that the law did not originally contemplate such devices as the modern offshore trust, the next question must be, *can* the present law contemplate it? If it can, is it reasonable to attempt to regulate all future creditors given the changed financial landscape, for example, on grounds of public policy? Neither of the present extreme options seems satisfactory, to allow all future creditors to be defeated, or to enable all future claims to be honoured. Still, it is certain that the law on fraudulent conveyances cannot profess to cover all voluntary conveyances. The term 'future creditor' is clearly to be given a narrower interpretation than a

---

[83] [1987–88] JLR 473. The rule is discussed in detail in the section on the non-enforcement of foreign fiscal law, in chapter 16, 'Bilateral Routes to the Tax Function and the Question of Sovereignty', at paras 16.1–16.32.

[84] But see recent trends against the section on non-enforcement, discussed in chapter 16, ibid, and *Le Marquand and Backhurst v Chiltmead Ltd* [1987–88] JLR 86.

[85] For example, in the Isle of Man.

[86] See, eg, *Boid v Dean* 48 NJ Eq 193, 21 A 618 (1891): 'the absence of all authority on the question of whether a transfer is voidable when made in anticipation of liability for torts thereafter to be committed may well be accounted for by the rarity of the occurrence'.

superficial reading might suggest. Yet the precise boundaries of the concept, and consequent liability, are still to be delineated.

The solution in such hard cases might be to examine the circumstances of the **9.79** transfer and judge each case on its merits. It is in this light that the offshore trust must be judged. A professional in the UK who sets up an offshore trust might be in an entirely different position to one in the US, since the UK does not have a history of professional liability cases awarding high damages.

Other alternatives might be simple compromises. These might include a limita- **9.80** tion period, as presently obtains under offshore legislation or bankruptcy law, or allowing only a specified percentage of assets to be placed in trust, leaving the settlor able to settle his or her debts.[87]

There is thus a lacuna in onshore law and legal policy which many offshore **9.81** legislatures have attempted to fill and fashion according to their own needs, seeking to curtail this potentially disastrous avenue for destroying the offshore trust. Typically, offshore jurisdictions have enacted legislation that seeks to narrow the protection offered to creditors and claimants against assets held in a trust. This makes it more difficult, often prohibitively so, for such persons to reach these assets.

Still, there is recognition by the offshore legislative community that sound **9.82** judicial principles, public policy, ethics, and the comity of nations cannot always be sacrificed to commercialism. The need to exercise caution and responsibility is therefore acknowledged. At minimum, offshore law recognizes the possibility of fraud or other abuse. Nevertheless, offshore legislation in the area of trusts is characterized by much innovation and creativity. Such law can, and does, respond readily to contemporary financial and business demands.

Thus, the relevant offshore legislation reveals a marked attempt to swing the **9.83** balance in favour of the settlor by redefining and undermining onshore legal principles on fraudulent conveyances which may challenge the trust. Whether this is sustainable remains to be tested in the courts. The survivability of these provisions when challenged under conflict of laws rules is discussed in following chapters.[88] Here, it suffices to examine the content and aims of such legislation.

It should be reiterated that some offshore jurisdictions, for example the British **9.84** Virgin Islands, Jersey, and the Isle of Man, have not enacted such aggressive

---

[87] *Freeman v Pope* (1870) LR 5 Ch 538.
[88] See Part 1V.

anti-creditor legislation, perhaps fearful of possible abuses.[89] The more traditional common law principles will, therefore, apply. The important policy differences between offshore and onshore jurisdictions in providing protection for investors should be considered, however, and these appeared to be paramount in the generous interpretation given in favour of debtors in the case of *Re Heginbotham*.[90] They are also evident in other legislative provisions which enhance the protections offered against creditors, such as the non-enforcement of foreign judgments and exclusive jurisdiction clauses.

Offshore law limited to existing creditors

9.85   Overall, although offshore legislation recognizes the notion of a fraudulent conveyance, it seeks to limit protection only to present and existing creditors, or to a narrower category of creditors than may obtain onshore. Typical provisions on fraudulent conveyances within offshore legislation may be summarized thus:

(1)   the reversal of the burden of proof for fraud by placing it on the creditor;
(2)   the upgrading of the standard of intent necessary to establish fraud, making it difficult for creditors to establish such standard;
(3)   the imposition of a limitation period, thereby cutting off the potential for future creditors to sue;
(4)   supportive provisions on jurisdiction over the trust to ensure that favourable asset protection provisions are utilized, instead of onshore principles, which make it difficult for creditors even to identify assets;
(5)   supportive secrecy provisions in relation to the trust;
(6)   provisions supporting the validity of the trust in the face of claims by onshore creditors offshore;
(7)   provisions establishing that forced heirship claims cannot give rise to a fraudulent conveyance claim;[91] and
(8)   provisions that preclude the enforcement of creditor judgments.

Trust remains valid despite creditors' claims

9.86   Offshore legislation will typically contain provisions which proclaim the validity of the offshore trust in a number of situations which will normally jeopardize the trust under the traditional law on fraudulent conveyances. Alternatively, offshore legislation might contain an all-inclusive clause proclaiming the validity of the offshore trust and excluding foreign laws which challenge it. For

---

[89] For example, the BVI has been reluctant to introduce asset protection legislation. See R Peters, 'The New Trust Law' *Offshore Trust Yearbook* (International Money Marketing, London, 1993), 159.

[90] Above, n 38, discussed above, at paras 9.43–9.45.

[91] See, eg, the Trusts (Choice of Governing Law Amendment) Act 1996 of The Bahamas.

example, in Belize, under the Trusts Act 1992, as revised in 2000, there is strong anti-creditor language. The Act provides that where a trust is created in Belize:

> [T]he court shall not vary it or set it aside or recognise the validity of any claim against the trust property pursuant to the law of another jurisdiction . . . in respect of . . . (b) succession rights . . . (c) the claims on creditors in an insolvency.[92]

In addition, s 12 of the Act allows the trust to terminate, restrict, or reduce the interests of a beneficiary who becomes insolvent, or whose property becomes subject to seizure by creditors. This permits the trust to amputate any successful claims which may be made on such a beneficiary, thereby further protecting the trust assets. **9.87**

Another variation is to provide that the settlement into trust is not to be presumed to be fraudulent merely because it took place when proceedings in respect of a creditor's cause of action had already begun. This approach is seen under s 13B(5)(d) of the International Trusts Act 1984 of the Cook Islands, litigated in *E and B v A*.[93] The provision imposes a high threshold for fraudulent conveyancing claims. However, the court, perhaps in its zeal to ensure that legitimate creditors were not disadvantaged, interpreted the legislation to mean that the fact that creditor proceedings had commenced was a relevant consideration to be taken into account in deciding whether a *prima facie* case of fraudulent conveyancing was established. The existence of creditor proceedings would, therefore, be a strong element in displacing the evidential burden, and would likely lead to a finding of a fraudulent conveyance. **9.88**

A provision which attempts to bar fraudulent conveyance claims completely is found in Nevis. The provision was examined in the case of *Conway v Queensway Trustees Ltd*.[94] The court here seemed to accept wholeheartedly the complete bar imposed by the relevant legislation, the International Exempt Trusts Ordinance 1994. The provision, s 24, which allows a claimant successfully to establish **9.89**

---

[92] Part 1, s 7(6). See also provisions in the jurisdictions listed below, n 95.

[93] (2003) 5 ITELR 760 (CA Cook Islands).

[94] (High Court, Nevis) No 16 of 1999, decided 28 July 1999, discussed further below, at paras 9.99–9.114. The provision reads: '(1)Where it is proven . . . that a trust settled . . . of property disposed to a trust (a) was so settled . . . with principal intent to defraud that creditor of the settlor; and (b) did at the time such settlement . . . took place render the settlor insolvent . . ., then such settlement . . . or disposition . . . shall not be void or voidable and the international trust shall be liable to satisfy the creditor's claim and such liability shall only be to the extent of such of the interest that the settlor had in the property prior to settlement . . . (3) A trust settled . . . shall not be fraudulent as against a creditor of a settlor (a) if settled . . . or the disposition takes place after the expiration of two years from the date that such creditor's cause of action accrued . . . (5) A settlor shall not have imputed to him an intent to defraud . . . solely by reason that the settlor— (a) has settled . . . property to such trust within two years from the date of that creditor's cause of action . . . (b) has retained, possesses or acquires any of the powers or benefits referred to in paragraphs (a) to (f) of s 47; (c) is a beneficiary.'

fraud, was construed strictly and as subservient to other provisions deeming international trusts incapable of being declared void or voidable.

Forseeability, proof, and intent provisions

9.90   In keeping with the thrust toward existing as opposed to future creditors, offshore legislation often contains provisions requiring proof that the settlor had intent to commit fraud, or should have foreseen the fraud. These may work alongside provisions which raise the standard for the burden of proof. For example, in Dominica, offshore asset protection trust legislation makes liability for fraudulent conveyances dependent on the high standard of proof 'beyond reasonable doubt'. Further, the settlor must have had a 'principal intent to defraud'.[95]

9.91   In Bermuda, the protection of offshore trust assets is found in several statutes.[96] Under the Conveyances (Amendment) Act 1994, the relevant test to ascertain a fraudulent conveyance is whether a 'dominant intention' to defraud is present. The Act refers to future creditors by providing that unless the creditor was owed an obligation at the date of the disposition, he must prove that the transferor should have 'reasonably foreseen' at that time that he would become a creditor. The Act therefore goes some way towards recognizing the kind of forseeability test suggested earlier in this chapter, and is potentially a useful tool for claimants.

9.92   Under the Fraudulent Dispositions Law 1989 of the Cayman Islands, the terms 'intent to defraud', 'creditor', and 'disposition' are redefined.[97] For dispositions to be deemed fraudulent, the settlor must have had an 'intent to defraud',[98] with 'intent' being defined as 'an intention to defeat wilfully an obligation owed to a creditor'. The burden of proof for establishing such intent is placed on the creditor.[99]

---

[95]   Under the International Exempt Trusts Act 1997, s 23. This is, of course, the standard reserved for criminal trials. It is higher than in onshore jurisdictions which use a civil standard. See also the International Trust Act 1995 of Barbados, and s 24 of the International Trust Ordinance 1994 of Nevis. Section 24(6) of the latter Act was amended in 2000 to provide that where the trust is liable to satisfy a creditor's claim, the creditor's right to recovery is limited to the property at the time of the establishment of the trust. See also s 45 of the International Trusts Act 1996 of Saint Vincent; s 13B of the International Trusts Act 1984 of the Cook Islands; and Part XII of the International Trusts Act 2002 of Saint Lucia.

[96]   Sections 45(1), and 47(1) of the Banking Act 1989; s 37 of the Conveyances (Amendment) Act 1994; s 41 of the Matrimonial Causes Act 1974; and s 21 of the Succession Act 1974.

[97]   As amended 1996. See also s 4 of the Fraudulent Dispositions Act 1991 of The Bahamas.

[98]   Fraudulent Dispositions Act 1989 of the Cayman Islands, s 4(1).

[99]   ibid, s 2.

Limitation periods

Limitation periods for pursuing onshore creditor judgments offshore have been inserted further to obstruct predatory creditors.[100] Such time limits may be on uncertain ground since the case of *South Orange Growers Association v Orange Grove Partners*.[101] Here, the Cook Islands court found that the statutory time limit was ambiguous and did not eliminate the right to sue.[102] It interpreted the time limit generously to run from the date of the onshore judgment and not from the date that the cause of action arose. The result was that the proceedings were in time.

9.93

Satisfying legitimate creditors' claims where fraud does not void the trust

In certain offshore jurisdictions, the applicable statutory provisions may allow the survivability of the offshore trust even in the face of a fraudulent transfer. The approach here is that the trust will not be rendered void or voidable, but the creditor's debts will be satisfied through the use of the trust fund while still keeping the trust intact.

9.94

The case of *E and B v A*[103] provided an opportunity to test such a provision in the Cook Islands, under s 13B(5)(d) of the International Trusts Act 1984.[104] The settlor in this case defaulted on a guaranteed payment of an US $17 million promissory note to the A bank. He attempted to avoid the debt by establishing a Cook Islands trust registered in the Cook Islands. Thereafter, a US court entered judgment against E and B. The substance of the action concerned an attempt by the bank to prove that the trust had been settled with intent to defraud it as creditor under the Act, by an application for discovery of documents. E and B claimed that the documents were protected by legal privilege. After an order from the High Court ordering production of the documents, E and B appealed.

9.95

The Court of Appeal, in examining the basis for the production of documents under the Act, confirmed that while the Act established a high threshold for a claim of fraudulent conveyancing, it was not intended to 'give succour to cheats

9.96

---

[100] See, eg, s 37 of the Conveyancing Amendment Act 1994 of Bermuda, which establishes a time limit of six years; s 4(3) of the Cayman Islands Fraudulent Dispositions Law 1989, of six years; and s 23(3) of the International Exempt Trusts Act 1997 of Dominica, with a limit of two years.

[101] [1997–98] 1 OFLR 3.

[102] ibid, 6; s 13B(8) of the International Trusts Act 1984 of the Cook Islands.

[103] (2003) 5 ITELR 760 (CA, Cook Islands).

[104] See also s 49 of the Nevis International Exempt Trusts Ordinance 1994; s 50 of the International Trusts Act 1996 of Saint Vincent; s 52 of the International Trusts Act 2002 of Saint Lucia.

and fraudsters by totally excluding the legitimate claims of overseas creditors'.[105] Rather, the Act attempted to achieve a 'balancing action, preserving the integrity of the trust while granting access to the assets fraudulently disposed'.[106]

9.97 Thus, in these jurisdictions, in a successful fraudulent conveyance action, legislation allows the satisfaction of legitimate creditors' claims whilst still maintaining the life of the trust. In *E and B v A*,[107] the court pointed out the possibility under s 13B of the International Trusts Act 1984 of the Cook Islands of allowing sufficient trust funds to be used to settle a fraudulent conveyance claim without rendering the trust void or voidable.[108]

Judicial pronouncements on the validity of offshore provisions on fraudulent conveyances

9.98 Relatively few opportunities to interpret offshore provisions on fraudulent conveyancing have presented themselves before the courts. Not surprisingly, the cases considered by offshore courts have tended to be supportive of the offshore trust when interpreting the proactive offshore provisions on fraudulent conveyances. The remarks of the court in *Moss and Pearce v Integro Trust*,[109] although *obiter*, are helpful. Moore J said:

> I doubt whether . . . it can be successfully argued that the defendant is liable to anyone who at some time in the future when his identity becomes known, may make a claim against any of the funds currently held by it on trust.[110]

Again, in *Private Trust Corporation v Torras* it was said:[111]

> Nothing in law or equity places any duty on the trustee . . . to protect the interests of future judgment creditors of a beneficiary.[112]

---

[105] *E and B v A*, above, n 103, 763, quoting *South Orange Grover Owners Association v Orange Grove Partners*, above, n 101. See below, paras 9.113–9.114, for further discussion of the *South Orange* case.

[106] ibid.

[107] Above, n 103. Section 13B states: 'Where it is proven beyond reasonable . . . that an international trust settled or established . . . (a) was so settled . . . with principal intent to defraud that creditor . . .; and (b) did at the time such settlement, establishment or disposition took place render the settlor insolvent or with out property by which that creditor's claim (if successful) could have been satisfied, then such settlement, establishment or dispositions shall not be void or voidable and the international trust shall be liable to satisfy the creditor's claim out of the property which, but for the settlement establishment or disposition, would have been available to satisfy the creditor's claim and such liability shall only be to the extent of the interest that the settlor had in the property prior to settlement, establishment or disposition and any accumulation to the property (if any) subsequent thereto.'

[108] See also *South Orange Growers*, above, n 101, 19.

[109] (High Ct, British Virgin Islands), No 261 of 1996, decided 21 February 1997, *per* Moore J.

[110] ibid, 12.

[111] [1997–98] 1 OFLR 443.

[112] ibid, 451.

Another rare opportunity to interpret offshore statutory provisions on fraudulent conveyances came in the case of *Conway v Queensway Trustees Ltd*,[113] which concerned an application for an injunction to prevent the defendant settlor from alienating or otherwise divesting himself of the funds of a trust established in Nevis. The plaintiff also sought a declaration that the trust had been established with intent to hinder or defraud the settlor's creditors and was void under the Fraudulent Conveyances Act 1571 of the UK, a claim which proved to be detrimental to the plaintiff's case.[114] The defendants contended that there was no cause of action sought against them, and that the action was, in any event, barred by the Nevis International Exempt Trusts Ordinance 1994 and by the fact that it was an action which sought the enforcement of a penal judgment of a foreign jurisdiction.

9.99

The defendants' first contention was given short shrift by the court, which reasoned that although the defendant trustees had not been specifically named in the claim as the holders of the property in question, they could be made a party to the action under the court's rules, which would view the trustees as a reasonable and necessary party in the matter.[115] The final contention by the defendants was not actually addressed by the court, and it was contention number two which captured the court's attention.

9.100

Examining carefully the provisions of the International Exempt Trusts Ordinance 1994, Smith J found a number of provisions which precluded a court's finding that an international trust is void or voidable. Section 3 of the Ordinance declares generally that international trusts are valid and enforceable notwithstanding their invalidity under the law of the settlor's domicile or residence. In addition, s 29 provides that dispositions of property into trust cannot be declared void, voidable, or be set aside, and added that the capacity of a settlor to make the disposition is not to be questioned. Section 46 provides that an international trust shall not be void or voidable in the event of the settlor's bankruptcy or insolvency, or by virtue of creditors' suits. Lastly, s 47 of the Ordinance mandates that an international trust cannot be declared invalid because the settlor retains powers to revoke or amend the trust, to remove or appoint trustees or protectors, or is a beneficiary.

9.101

In addition to the broad provisions giving validity to international trusts and precluding declarations that the trust was void or voidable, s 28 prohibits the

9.102

---

[113] Above, n 5.

[114] Claims for vesting orders in respect of the funds, disclosure, and damages were also made.

[115] *Conway*, above, n 5, 7. But the court went on to find that an order of damages against the defendants was not available to the plaintiff as he had not pleaded that the defendants were guilty of any action which could have made them liable to the plaintiff: ibid, 10.

enforcement or recognition of foreign judgments against settlors. Moreover, the Ordinance, under s 49, specifically outlaws the application of the Fraudulent Conveyances Act 1571 of the UK to international trusts established in Nevis, a provision which Smith J found intriguing, as the Act is not applicable in Nevis in any event.[116]

9.103 Setting off the above provisions is s 24, which purports to give a creditor relief where he or she can prove beyond a reasonable doubt that the trust was established with the principal intent to defraud him or her. This would entitle the creditor to an injunction and an order for disclosure. The court seemed to suggest that these could be available only if there could be an order that the trust be set aside, and that such an order was precluded under the Ordinance. Section 24's protection is augmented by s 83 of the Conveyancing and Law of Property Act of Nevis, which contains provisions prohibiting fraudulent conveyances and which, in the words of the court, provides that every conveyance of property made with intent to defraud creditors 'shall be voidable at the instance of every person thereby prejudiced'.[117] Fraudulent conveyancing law is, then, part of the law of Nevis.

9.104 Nonetheless, the court's decision appeared to be based on a view that the application of the general law of fraudulent conveyances to international trusts was absolutely erased by the provisions of the International Exempt Trusts Ordinance 1994.[118] In addition, there were some procedural obstacles to be crossed before a s 24 application could be entertained. The applicant had to deposit a bond of $25,000 with the Ministry of Finance before bringing the action and, further, had to satisfy the court, by affidavit, that the action had been commenced two years before the date of the settlement and that the applicant had no interest in the property before it was settled.[119] The court did not specify whether these procedural conditions had been met, but it concluded that the plaintiff's action must fail.

Criticism of the Conway *case*

9.105 The difficulty with the decision is that it fails to recognize adequately the windows of opportunity left open under the statute to legitimate creditors who wish to pursue fraudulent conveyance claims against a settlor. While the statute clearly intended to ensure that such a fraudulent conveyance claim could not

---

[116] What applied was s 83 of the Conveyancing and Law of Property Act 1994 of Nevis.

[117] *Conway*, above, n 5, 4.

[118] '[I]t would not be open to this court to embark on any trial the purpose of which would be to declare the Cardinal Trust void or voidable': ibid, 11.

[119] Established under s 44 of the Nevis International Exempt Trusts Ordinance 1994 (NIETO).

easily destroy an international trust, it implicitly recognized that some claims could survive by including the s 24 provision. Yet Smith J did not illustrate what might be a good s 24 claim, preferring to emphasize the provisions of the Ordinance as solely in the interests of settlors:

> There may be very good reasons for the safeguards for trusts and similar fund arrangements built into the NIETO. Trusts that are registered under NIETO are insulated against all but the most serious and valid attacks against them so that they may be conducted without too much bother from overly ambitious or malicious detractions.[120]

The question of what is a serious or valid attack is left open. However, it is at least arguable that the procedural conditions aside, a person with a valid foreign judgment could use such a judgment as evidence 'beyond reasonable doubt' that a conveyance has been fraudulently effected.

By juxtaposing all of the provisions under the Ordinance which grant validity to an international trust, Smith J gave greater force to the protective provisions against fraudulent conveyances than perhaps the legislators intended. Section 29, for example, is primarily concerned with validating the trust against attacks relating to recognition, capacity, and forced heirship issues, mainly by civil law settlors.[121] Section 47's focus is on validating the trust where the settlor reserves to himself or herself powers of control and benefit more generous than those in typical domestic trusts, which may be challenged under the sham doctrine.[122] Neither is particularly useful for examining the circumstances in which fraudulent conveyance or creditor claims can be sustained in relation to trusts established for asset protection. Indeed, s 24 makes it clear that, in the context of fraudulent conveyances, a claim for relief need not bring the validity of the trust itself into question, as legitimate claims may be satisfied without disturbing the trust. **9.106**

At most, the Ordinance contemplates that a creditor may be forced, because of the non-enforcement provision under s 28, to bring his or her action directly before the local courts within the time-lines drawn under the Ordinance. However, having done so, the creditor should stand a good chance of obtaining relief once the assets were disposed into trusts fraudulently. **9.107**

The relevant provisions of the Nevis Ordinance (and, by extension, similar legislation), in particular, ss 24 and 27, need to be better reconciled. It is clear that foreign judgments on fraudulent conveyances, where the circumstances are such that a Nevis court could find no legitimate claim of fraudulent conveyances where such judgments violate other procedural limits of the Nevis Ordinance, **9.108**

---

[120] *Conway*, above, n 5, 13.
[121] See chapters 21, 22, and 23.
[122] See chapter 8.

cannot be entertained. However, where the substance or effect of the foreign judgment will not violate the provisions of the Nevis Ordinance, it should be recognized and enforced in accordance with the Ordinance's provisions for satisfying creditors' claims. Section 28 clearly makes the non-enforcement of such judgments conditional upon their inconsistency with the provisions of the Ordinance.[123] Thus, where the Nevis Ordinance can accept the creditors' claim as legitimate and is able to satisfy the claim without invalidating the trust, there would appear to be no bar to enforcing such judgments.

9.109   In this vein, we might perhaps draw a distinction between a foreign judgment which seeks to invalidate an offshore trust and a judgment whose impact is merely to trace the assets of a legitimate creditor's claim. In the first construct, the judgment is clearly unenforceable; in the second, it is enforceable.

9.110   Indeed, it is at least arguable that a judgment which merely proclaims that A owes a debt to B, is in no way directly concerned with the trust. It is not, therefore, a trust question. Since the offshore provision and similar provisions elsewhere are concerned with judgments which go 'against' offshore trusts and 'officers' associated with offshore trusts, they may contemplate only judgments pronouncing on trust law questions. It might be different, for example, if the Ordinance provided that *any* judgment which 'impacts' on the offshore trust or against any 'person' (instead of the settlor, protector, and so on) is not enforceable.

9.111   There is yet another possible argument to be made. In the context of fraudulent conveyances, how is s 27, which precludes preliminary questions of law concerning whether the settlor actually owned the property, to be reconciled with provisions which exclude foreign laws and foreign judgments?[124] If there is a legitimate fraudulent conveyance claim by virtue of a debt owed by the settlor to the creditor before the creation of the trust, is the settler to be viewed as the 'owner' of the property? Certainly, in *Re Portnoy*,[125] the preliminary question of whether the settlor had violated bankruptcy laws was treated as one for determination by the US courts. Here, the Nevis Ordinance concedes not only

---

[123] It reads: 'Notwithstanding the provisions of any treaty . . . [or] law . . . to the contrary, no proceedings for or . . . judgement obtained in a jurisdiction other than St Christopher and Nevis against—(a) an international trust; (b) a settlor of an international trust; (c) a trustee of an international trust; . . . (g) property of an international trust . . . shall be entertained by any Court in St Christopher and Nevis if—(i) that judgement is based upon the application of any law inconsistent with the provisions of this Ordinance . . .'

[124] See chapter 23 for a discussion of such preliminary questions. Section 27 reads: '(1) Nothing in this Ordinance shall validate any disposition of property which is neither owned by the settlor nor the subject of a power in that behalf vested in the settlor. (2) This Ordinance shall not affect the recognition of any foreign laws in determining whether the settlor is the owner of such property or the holder of such power referred to in subsection (1) of this section.'

[125] See above, n 21. This case is also discussed in chapter 20, 'The Proper Law of the Offshore Trust'.

that its provisions do not encompass property not owned by the settlor, but also that the foreign law should decide the issue.

In sum, the reader is left unconvinced that the anti-fraudulent conveyancing provisions of the statute are as inviolable as Smith J in *Conway* suggested. **9.112**

In contrast, as we have seen, offshore courts in the Cook Islands are less willing **9.113**
to accept that legislation similar to the Nevis Ordinance aims solely to protect
settlors above all else. In the case of *South Orange Growers Association*, previously
mentioned,[126] the Court of Appeal of the Cook Islands had to interpret the
fraudulent conveyances provisions under the International Trusts Act 1984 in
order to decide whether a *Mareva* injunction could be granted in view of the
time restrictions laid down under the Act. Counsel argued that the *Mareva*
injunction should not be granted and that the purpose of the Act was to facilitate asset protection trusts and not creditors. He further stated that the purpose
of the legislation was 'the unashamed soliciting of funds to improve the economic position of the Cook Islands'.[127] In granting the *Mareva* injunction to
secure a creditor judgment from California, the court rejected this view of the
legislation. It warned, in words echoed in *E and B v A*, above:[128]

> We think that the better view is that Parliament, in attempting to balance the
> interests of settlors, trustees and creditors, has prescribed certain specific limitation
> periods; that the right to sue on either a cause of action or a judgment is abridged
> but not eliminated, and that a common sense interpretation should allow for
> intention to be given to those two concepts. It should not be lightly assumed that
> Parliament intended to defeat the claims of creditors by allowing international
> trusts to be used to perpetuate a fraud against a creditor.[129]

Consequently, the Act was interpreted in favour of the judgment creditor. The **9.114**
actual interpretation of the time limit is not controversial. However, the underlying disapproval of the court of offshore legislation, even its own, which could
purport to be so radical in its abrogation of the rights of creditors, is noteworthy.

E. Liability of Professionals

Legal professional privilege will not shield a fraudulent conveyance

As we saw in our discussion of confidentiality,[130] a person who sets up a trust in **9.115**
circumstances where fraud is involved, cannot rely on legal professional privilege

---

[126] Above, n 101. See also the discussion above, para 9.92.
[127] ibid, 8.
[128] See above, n 103.
[129] *South Orange Growers Association*, above, n 101, 8.
[130] See chapter 7, 'Disclosure and Confidentiality Obligations'.

to protect him or her. The principle extends to situations where the trust is established in circumstances where it may be deemed a fraudulent conveyance. Thus, the general privilege afforded to communications between an attorney and his or her client will not extend to communications concerning fraudulent conveyances into trust. This is merely part of the broader exception that the privilege does not protect the client's attempts to facilitate crime or fraud.[131] Once a prima facie case of a fraudulent conveyance is made, a court has the discretion to disallow the privilege. The court would use the standard of the reasonable business person to ascertain whether a prima facie case of fraud or dishonesty had been made.

9.116   The issue was discussed in the case of *E and B v A*.[132] Here, the appellants, after guaranteeing payment of US $ 17 million to the respondent bank, transferred their property into a trust registered under the International Trusts Act 1984 of the Cook Islands. Judgment was obtained for the bank in the USA, and the bank thereafter brought proceedings under s 13B(1) of the Act, to set the disposition aside on the ground that the creditor had proved 'beyond reasonable doubt' that the trust had been established to defraud the creditor. In the pursuance of its claim, the bank sought discovery of, *inter alia*, the legal advice that the appellants had received as to the reasons for the formation of the trust. The appellants argued that the information was privileged. However, the Court of Appeal upheld the lower court's judgment that such information was not protected as part of legal professional privilege, as it fell under the fraud exception.

9.117   Where the exception for fraud is to apply, the standard of proof required to displace the privilege is the establishment of a strong prima facie case of fraud, which had been met in the instant case. The court also took the opportunity to reiterate, *per incuriam*, that the statute in question was not to be interpreted to give 'succour to cheats and fraudsters by totally excluding the legitimate claims of overseas creditors'.[133] However, the onus of proof of the settlor's intent to defraud lies on the creditor.

Professional negligence in fraud cases

9.118   Where attorneys set up creditor protection trusts in circumstances where settlors clearly have existing or potential creditors, or advise others to do so, they may open themselves to liability on the grounds of professional misconduct, negligence, or even to liability under money laundering statutes. Similarly, a person who acts as trustee for such a trust may incur liability. The advent of the

---

[131] See, eg, *Williams v Quebarada Railway Land and Copper Company* [1895] 2 Ch 751.
[132] Above, n 103.
[133] ibid.

offshore trust, with its thinly veiled demarcation line between efficient asset planning and fraud, means that the trustee and the attorney have an even greater responsibility to exercise due care in conducting the affairs of such trusts. Such cases are no longer legal oddities. There is emerging case law on professional negligence and breach of fiduciary duty. More specifically, the settlor's attorney or other fiduciary may be liable for assisting in the fraudulent conveyance. Such professionals will be held to modern standards of negligence and honesty, based on reasonableness and forseeability.[134] This is considered more fully in a following chapter.[135]

It is thus important that a trustee who suspects fraud does something to address his or her suspicion, as he or she is in danger of being viewed as a constructive trustee, or held liable for knowing receipt. One safe solution is to apply to the court for directions as to how to deal with the assets.[136]   **9.119**

Conclusion

It is apparent that the traditional laws on fraudulent conveyances are not meeting current needs, whether from the point of view of potential settlors/investors, or from the point of view of creditors. The former must resort to an intricate submission of jurisdiction to offshore law to glean some form of protection, while the latter are not adequately supported due to the uncertainty of the law. Reform of fraudulent conveyances law in general, and in particular of provisions relevant to transfers of assets into offshore trusts, is urgently needed. This is what offshore law achieves indirectly.   **9.120**

In reforming the law, the conflicts between creditors and commercial interests must be addressed. A policy which is in tandem with other business arrangements that limit liability, demands some balance in the law. It may, therefore, be inconsistent to place too wide a restriction on offshore asset protection trusts. To attempt to protect too broad a class of future creditors could have a debilitating spillover effect on all trust arrangements. For onshore law to condemn certain   **9.121**

---

[134] See, eg, *Springfield Acres Ltd v Abacus (Hong Kong) Ltd* [1994] 3 NZLR 503. The court found that a transfer by a company director in favour of persons associated with him which denuded the company of its assets, could indicate a fraudulent design where the fiduciary had 'wilfully shut his eyes to the obvious and had not made the inquiries expected of an honest and reasonable man'. Accordingly, he could be sued for breach of constructive trust. See also *Adams v The Queen* [1995] 1 WLR 52 (PC); *Kuwait Asia Bank EC v National Mutual Life Nominee Ltd* [1990] 3 All ER 404; and *Resolution Trust Corporation v Heiserman et al*, Civil Action No 93-B-944, US District Court (Colorado) 151 FRD 367, 1993 US Dist LEXIS 13198, 14 September 1993. These cases also apply in the context of money laundering.

[135] Chapter 11, 'Liability of Third Parties to the Trust'.

[136] *Finers, a Firm v Miro* [1991] 1 All ER 182.

offshore trusts, deeming them 'fraudulent' and assigning to them illegal and even criminal intent, may not be appropriate.[137]

9.122   Notably, eminent legal practitioners and jurists have begun to clamour for change in onshore legislation to accommodate asset protection trusts. This is to bring them more in line with their more modern and adventurous offshore counterparts. Hayton, lamenting the declining role of the UK in leading the world in the law of the trust, its original creation, says:

> [T]o protect professional persons, who, fearful of negligence claims exceeding their insurance cover, create asset protection trusts, legislation, perhaps on the basis of the Cayman Islands Fraudulent Disposition Law 1989, is necessary.[138]

---

[137] *Report on Fraudulent Conveyances and Preference*, Law Reform Commission of British Columbia, 1988, 93. See too *Agip (Africa) Ltd v Jackson* [1992] 4 All ER 451; *Royal Brunei Airlines v Tan* [1995] 3 WLR 64.

[138] D Hayton, 'Time to Overhaul Trust Laws' (1991) 141 NLJ 210, 211. See also criticisms of the rule on perpetuities.

10

DUTIES OF TRUSTEES IN MANAGING OFFSHORE TRUSTS

A. General Duties under the Common Law

Introduction

As with any onshore trust, the trustee in an offshore trust must adhere faithfully **10.01** to the terms of the trust, exercising his or her discretionary powers contained within the trust instrument, in order to fulfil his or her primary obligation of undivided loyalty to the beneficiaries. Doing otherwise will render the trustee liable for breaches of trust. The trustee must uphold the fundamental principles of the trust and avoid breaches of trust. This will involve a consideration of the collateral duty to exercise reasonable care in managing the trust.

The general duties of trustees may be described as follows: **10.02**

(1) a duty to act unanimously;
(2) a duty to account and to give information;
(3) a duty to convert and apportion;
(4) a duty to invest;
(5) a duty not to profit from the trust;
(6) a duty to distribute.[1]

---

[1] For a description of these general duties, particularly with regard to their application in the

10.03 Of more interest to this book is the nature of the evolving duties of modern-day trustees, in particular offshore trustees, when applied in the commercial context. The nature of the duties to uphold fundamental principles of the trust and not to commit breaches of trust, can be seen to have deviated considerably from those same duties as applied to trustees dealing merely with family estate matters in a domestic setting.

10.04 A trustee is liable for breaches of trust both in the situation where he or she does something which is unauthorized under the trust instrument and where he or she does something which is, in fact, authorized but performs the authorized act improperly, in breach of the duty of care imposed upon him or her.

Application of common law duties of trustees to offshore law

10.05 The general duties of trustees, as outlined above, are essentially the same under offshore law. Although the duties and liabilities of trustees may be prescribed by offshore legislation, often the exercise is merely a codification of the equitable principles found under the Common Law legal tradition.[2] As a result, the following discussion relies heavily on traditional trusts law jurisprudence on this issue. We should note too that, as this is an evolving jurisprudence, case law will often have progressed in advance of the relevant legislation as originally contemplated. As the Common Law is the origin of such legislation, it is expected that such case law will continue to be relevant in interpreting legislative provisions. One important deviation is the extent to which provision is made for trustees administering trusts structured alongside companies, a typical phenomenon in offshore investment.[3] In the ensuing discussion, the relatively few instances where offshore legislation has deviated significantly from traditional trusts law rules are highlighted.

Duty to exercise care in managing the financial affairs of the trust

10.06 Today, the boundaries of the duty to exercise reasonable care in relation to the trust are expanding, placing more and more burdens on the trustee, and in particular on the offshore trustee. Increasingly, the courts are not content with demanding from the trustee that he or she merely follows the written terms of

Commonwealth Caribbean, see G Kodilyne and T Carmichael, *Commonwealth Caribbean Trusts Law*, 2nd edn, Cavendish Publishing Ltd, (London 2002), chapter 11.

[2] See, eg, in Belize under Part VII of the Trusts Act 1992 (rev'd 2000), Parts II and III of the Trustee Act 1998 of The Bahamas, Articles 17–25 of the Trusts (Jersey) Law 1984, ss 27–31 of the International Trusts Act 2002 of Saint Lucia, Part III of the Trusts (Special Provisions) Act 1989 of Bermuda, Part IIIA of the International Trusts Act 1984 of the Cook Islands, Part 4 of the International Exempt Trusts Ordinance 1994 of Nevis, Part III of the International Trusts Act 1996 of Saint Vincent, and Part IV of the Trusts Act (2001 Revision) of the Cayman Islands.

[3] See below, paras 10.123–10.129.

the trust closely and faithfully. Rather, the modern-day trustee, involved in trusts which are structured for commercial purposes, must now be a 'savvy' person of business and must take care to exercise his or her discretion in a manner which will not prejudice the financial success of the trust. This means that the trustee cannot be negligent in performing the business functions of the trust, and he or she will be judged according to the objective standard.[4]

Ordinary person standard versus professional trustee standard

In managing a trust, an unpaid trustee, such as one would find in the typical domestic trust, is required to exercise only such level of care and diligence as is reasonably expected from the ordinary prudent person in managing his or her own affairs. However, where the trustee is a professional trustee, as is typically the case with offshore trusts, that trustee will be held to a higher standard of care, a standard of diligence that is consistent with a high level of skill and knowledge. Since the landmark case of *Bartlett v Barclays Bank Trust Co Ltd*,[5] which outlined this higher duty, several cases have attempted to define the level of care and knowledge expected of the professional trustee.[6] **10.07**

In *Bartlett*, a trust had been established in 1920 which had as its major asset a controlling shareholding in a family trading company. In 1970, the new management of the company and its board of directors took a decision to invest in two property development schemes. One of the schemes was a financial failure, which caused the value of the trust assets to be reduced considerably. **10.08**

It emerged that the bank, which was the trustee and major shareholder, had received annual reports from the company but had made no enquiries about the directors' proposals and had not attempted to intervene in any way in the affairs of the trust. The beneficiaries sued the trust company and were awarded restitution of the loss to the trust assets. **10.09**

By remaining a passive onlooker to the actions of the board of directors when it could have prevented the loss had it intervened, the bank trustee incurred liability for breach of trust. It had a duty to oversee the financial affairs of the trust. A bank holds itself as having special care and skill in financial and investment matters, and the bank trustee should have exercised that care in the instant case. **10.10**

Again, in *Midland Bank Trustee (Jersey) Ltd & Others v Federated Pension* **10.11**

---

[4] It is now fairly common for statute to prescribe the powers of investment. Many of the offshore statutes, above, n 2, are based on the UK Trustee Act 2000, ss 36–38.

[5] [1980] 1 All ER 139.

[6] This higher standard is also enshrined under The Bahamas legislation, s 5(4) of the Trustee Act 1998.

Services Ltd,[7] the trustee delayed in transferring the trust fund to a new fund manager for investment on the Stock Exchange after discovering that the trust fund was not invested as profitably as it could have been. The trustee's delay was due to an error about the nature of its authority, and caused considerable loss to the trust assets. In finding the trustee liable, the court relied on the *Bartlett* principle that a trust corporation which carries on a specialized business has a higher duty of care than the ordinary, unpaid trustee.

10.12   The professional corporate trustee advertises itself as having this special, superior expertise, and it is appropriate that it should be judged accordingly. As noted in *Bartlett*, such a professional trustee has specialist staff and ready access to financial information and professional advice, dealing with trust problems every day.[8] The trustee in that case, which held itself out as an expert in the management of trust funds, was held liable for gross negligence, having violated its duty of care, a duty which was higher than that of an ordinary, unpaid trustee. Gross negligence means simply a 'serious or flagrant degree of negligence, a marked departure from the standard to be expected in the circumstances, beyond mere ordinary negligence'.[9] Gross negligence 'involves no question of intentional or reckless fault'.[10]

10.13   The reasoning in the *Bartlett* line of cases leads to a conclusion that there will be differences even in relation to professional trustees. Ultimately, the court must examine closely the advertisements and other documents outlining the special skills the trustee professes to have, in order to determine its liability. So, for instance, the solicitor-trustee will be in a different position to the corporate trustee which specializes in investment.[11]

Proactive duties regarding advice and information

10.14   From the *Bartlett* case is also derived the principle that trustees have positive duties placed upon them, such as to keep themselves informed about matters relating to the trust assets, to conduct regular reviews of the investment strategy with a view to updating the trust portfolio,[12] to give advice and information on such matters, and generally to act to safeguard the trust assets when they are in danger. In order to demonstrate care, trustees must actively perform these duties.

10.15   While it appears that in *Bartlett* the trustee did have sufficient information at its disposal, a trustee which does not has a duty to seek such information. As

---

[7] [1995] JLR 352.
[8] See above, n 5, 152.
[9] *Midland Bank*, above, n 7, 357.
[10] ibid.
[11] Discussed further below, see paras 10.35–10.36.
[12] See *Nestlé v National Westminster Bank* [1993] 1 WLR 1260.

discussed below, these duties are magnified where the trustee is overseeing assets structured within a company, as is often the case with offshore trustees.[13] However, the trustee's primary duty in acquiring such information remains his or her duty to make prudent investments and protect the assets.

Dishonesty in breaches of trust—honesty no defence

As discussed more fully in the following chapter,[14] the test for dishonesty has now been exported to trusteeship generally, and the concept of dishonesty is today an expansive one. In the performance of his or her duties, the modern trustee will be adjudged according to the combination test for dishonesty as laid down in the case of *Royal Brunei Airlines v Tan Kik Ming*.[15] This test is a combination of subjective elements and the objective standard of reasonableness. Reasonableness here means according to the standard of the reasonable trustee, or the reasonable professional trustee. The dishonesty of a trustee must be assessed by considering whether the belief that a deliberate breach of the trust was to the benefit of the beneficiaries was a belief so unreasonable that no trustee in the class of trustees being considered could have held it.[16]

10.16

More recently, courts have reintroduced an element of subjectivity into the equation. The 'Robin Hood' standard, whereby a person does an act of which he or she knows reasonable persons will disapprove and believe to be dishonest, according to objective standards, but which he or she personally believes is right, is rejected as failing the test of honesty. However, a trustee will not be adjudged as dishonest where he or she does not know that the act in question is dishonest, even if reasonable trustees would not have acted in this way. Thus, for dishonesty to occur, the trustee must know that the thing is dishonest, as adjudged by the standards of honest and reasonable trustees.[17]

10.17

In *Walker and Others v Stones and Another*[18] and *Publishers Representatives Ltd and Lee Sku Kee v UBS (Cayman Islands) Ltd*,[19] the *Royal Brunei*[20] test was acclaimed as the appropriate one for all cases of dishonesty in civil law matters. Dishonesty in this context also includes reckless indifference and recklessness.[21] Dishonesty is a necessary ingredient in claims of fraudulent breaches of trust.[22]

10.18

---

[13] See below, paras 10.123–10.129.
[14] See chapter 11, 'Liability of Third Parties to the Trust'.
[15] [1995] 3 WLR 64, (PC), Brunei, Darussalam.
[16] *Walker v Stones* [2000] 4 All ER 412 (CA).
[17] See *Twinsectra Ltd v Yardley and Others* [2002] 2 All ER 377, 383; *Walker v Stones*, above, n 16.
[18] Above, n 16, 444.
[19] [2000] CILR 473.
[20] From the case of *Royal Brunei Airlines v Tan Kik Ming*, above, n 15.
[21] ibid.
[22] See *Woodland Ferrari v UCL Group Retirement Benefits Scheme* [2002] 3 All ER 670.

10.19   Where trustees act in the honest belief that their actions are in the best interest of the trust, this will not prevent liability, as honesty and sincerity are not the same as prudence and reasonableness, which are what is required.[23] This is particularly the case with professional trustees since, by accepting the position of trustee, they hold themselves out as having the necessary level of expertise. The approach is consistent with the standard of reasonableness in which motive, intention, or even recklessness, is not required.[24] Nonetheless, a mere error of judgement is not sufficient to establish liability for negligence or lack of care.

B. Exploring the Duty to Invest

The standard for investment

10.20   One of the most important aspects of the duties of the modern trustee in administering the trust with care is the duty to invest. This is by no means a new duty, but previously the expectations under the duty were quite conservative. Courts have now gone further than the test laid down in the earlier authority of *Learoyd v Whiteley*,[25] that the relevant standard for a trustee's discretion to invest is that of the 'ordinary prudent man of business who is minded to make an investment for the benefit of other people for whom he felt morally bound to provide'.[26]

10.21   The judicial burden imposed on fiduciaries in relation to investment appears to have increased from the previous obligation merely to consider whether to exercise a fiduciary power, to a positive duty to invest, and to invest reasonably.[27]

Preserving the real value of assets

10.22   In the earlier cases shaped by *Learoyd v Whiteley*, the emphasis was on the duty of trustees to preserve the capital sum of the trust. Today, however, consonant with the challenges of inflation and the more flexible and sophisticated financial

---

[23] See *Cowan v Scargill* [1985] Ch 270.

[24] See *Midland Bank*, above, n 7.

[25] (1887) 12 AC 727 (HL).

[26] *Learoyd v Whiteley* (1886) 33 Ch D 347, 355 (CA), affirmed by the House of Lords, ibid.

[27] Note that the prudent investor rule is now statutorily enshrined in many jurisdictions, eg in England, Canada, the US, including offshore jurisdictions. See, eg, the provisions listed above, n 2. The formulation in Guernsey is somewhat different. Section 19(b) of the Trusts (Guernsey) Law 1989 reads: 'A trustee shall, subject to the terms of the trust and to the provisions of this Law—preserve and enhance, as far as is reasonable, the value of the trust property.' Cf the Virgin Islands Special Trusts Act 2003, which embodies provisions which radically change the equitable rules with regard to trustees holding controlling shares in underlying companies. Discussed below, paras 10.123–10.129, especially at para 10.124.

environment in which trustees operate, the courts have imposed higher duties of investment and financial management on trustees.

Where, for example, trustees merely preserve the capital funds of trusts in situations where they could have made substantial profits for their beneficiaries if they had invested prudently, and the trust fund is now worth less in real terms because of inflation, those trustees will have failed in their duties to exercise due care. In *Re Mulligan (Deceased)*,[28] for example, the value of the trust fund had been eroded so much that, whereas the original sum could have purchased fourteen properties in 1949, the remainder would not have been able to purchase a single such property. This diminution was as a result of inflation and could have been avoided if the trustee had invested in shares rather than simply placing the monies on fixed deposits. The trustees had, therefore, breached their duty of care in not so investing.

10.23

The important difference between the individual investor and the trustee, as outlined in *Learoyd v Whiteley*[29] and elaborated upon in *Re Mulligan*, is to be noted:[30] 'Protection of personal assets is different to the protection of a fund which belongs to beneficiaries.' Investment in this context usually means protecting the value of a trust fund from the corrosive effects of inflation and not so much increasing its value with a view to profit, as an individual investor might seek to do with money of his or her own.

10.24

It is not the case, however, that the trustee is viewed as automatically breaching his or her duty where he or she fails to preserve the real value of the assets. Rather, the correct interpretation of the case law is that the trustee must invest reasonably with a view to preserving value. The courts give leeway, however, to the unpredictabilities of the financial market.

10.25

Failing to diversify the investment portfolio

Each case concerning an allegation of breach of duties related to investment must be judged on its facts. However, where a trustee has absolutely failed to diversify the investment portfolio because of a desire only to maintain capital, the courts appear to be willing to intervene and find a breach of trust. Where the trustee has not remained passive but has diversified, albeit not being as successful with the mix of investments as he or she could have been, the courts are reluctant to interfere, presumably because it is much more difficult to determine a quantifiable loss, or even negligence on the trustee's part.

10.26

---

[28] [1998] 1 NZLR 481 (HC).
[29] Above, n 26, 355.
[30] See above, n 28, 500.

10.27   This was a distinguishing factor between the two important decisions of *Nestlé*[31] and *Mulligan*.[32] In *Nestlé*, the trustees had, in fact, partly diversified the portfolio, and the question was whether the degree of diversification was sufficient in an investment portfolio which already had a satisfactory start by the settlor. In *Mulligan*, the trustees had retained only fixed interest securities and failed to invest in shares, despite recognizing that this was detrimental to the capital fund. Their failure was compounded by their subjugation of the interests of the remaindermen to that of the life tenant, who was also a co-trustee acting in self-interest.

10.28   In fact, in *Nestlé*, Dillon LJ remarked, *obiter*, that the claim of quantifiable loss would have been 'relatively easy to prove' if the annuity fund in that case had been invested solely in fixed interest securities.[33] Indeed, failing in the duty to diversify under the modern portfolio theory might well be considered to be reckless, a category of dishonest conduct which attracts immediate liability.[34]

10.29   The cases may be interpreted to mean that the duty to diversify is stronger where there are competing interests between life tenants and other beneficiaries, as was the case in *Re Mulligan* and *Nestlé*. This, however, may not always be the case with the offshore trust, which may be intended to be more advantageous to beneficiaries (including the settlor) entitled to immediate distributions or other benefits. The settlor may expressly absolve the trustee from the duty to diversify, retaining that discretion for himself or herself.

10.30   In considering whether to diversify, the trustee will need to take into account the returns to be gained from income and capital appreciation, balancing these against the need to preserve capital and to maintain liquidity and regular income in relation to individual beneficiaries.

Caution versus risk-taking

10.31   A modern trustee cannot be overly cautious with the management of the trust fund to the disadvantage of the beneficiaries. This does not mean that the trustee can be speculative and take undue risks. Rather, the trustee is expected to take prudent risks only and err on the side of caution.[35]

10.32   Indeed, it is clear that, despite the need for a trustee to be proactive and alert to the financial environment, the courts continue to place a greater store on the

---

[31]   Above, n 12.
[32]   Above, n 28.
[33]   Above, n 12, 1270.
[34]   See *Armitage v Nurse* [1968] Ch 241 (CA), for a discussion of reckless conduct.
[35]   Note Lord Nicholls' observation in *Royal Brunei Airlines v Tan Kik Ming*, above, n 15, that 'all investments require risk'.

trustee choosing safety over speculation. The prudent investor trustee is still to be viewed essentially as one who will emphasize the preservation of capital over the taking of risks with investments. Thus, the standard of prudence is not a demanding one. In offshore trusts, structured with companies for business purposes, this may be seen to be undesirable. The fact that the trustee's engagement is to 'be judged not so much by success [in investment strategy] as by absence of proven default' may prove to be a limiting factor in the offshore investment portfolio.[36]

In this vein, trustees are not liable for mere errors of judgement, taking into account the unpredictable nature of the financial market. It is sufficient that a trustee acts reasonably, prudently, and with good faith.[37]   **10.33**

Changing standards of prudence

What constitutes prudence in terms of investment duties must evolve with changing economic and financial times and circumstances. Therefore, what the prudent trustee would have been expected to do fifty years ago in relation to the investment portfolio, and generally in managing the trust assets, may not necessarily be appropriate today.[38] Older cases are relevant, therefore, only to the extent that they outline the principle of reasonableness in investment decisions and not for detailing what those investment decisions should be. In addition, the performance of a trustee is not to be judged with hindsight. If, in the 1940s, few investors would have been invested in equities, for example, it is immaterial that in 2003, with hindsight, we could see that in the 1940s those investors would have been better off had they so invested.[39]   **10.34**

Specialist trustees

While all professional trustees are expected to adhere to higher standards than ordinary trustees, there are different expectations in relation to different kinds of professional trustees. Some professional trustees may in fact be investment advisers or strategists. Just as the law now accepts that a trustee's role has evolved from capital preservation to a proactive duty to invest and manage finances   **10.35**

---

[36] 'The virtue of safety will in practice put a premium on inactivity', *per* Leggatt, LJ in *Nestlé*, above, n 12, 1284. Indeed, the limiting nature of this principle to maximizing profits, or conversely managing investments for more personal objectives, is the main reason for the changes to the BVI legislation, enacting the Virgin Islands Special Trusts Act 2003, discussed below, paras 10.123–10.124.

[37] *Bartlett v Barclays Bank Trust Company Ltd*, above, n 5, 150: no businessman, however prudent, 'can expect to be immune' from mere errors of judgement. See also the earlier authority of *Re Chapman* [1896] 2 Ch 763, 778.

[38] *Nestlé*, above, n 12, *per* Dillon LJ, 1268.

[39] In earlier times, a reluctance to invest in shares and merely to preserve capital with a conservative income was the reasonable standard.

because of the new financial environment, the law today also recognizes that there are more specialized types of professional trustees. The roles and responsibilities of these different trustees will be appropriately defined. The specialist investment trustee, for example, may be held to an even higher duty of skill and care in relation to investment, and an expectation of success may be reasonable in such a situation, barring the uncertainties of the market.[40]

10.36   Solicitors, accountants, and other professionals appointed as trustees may have special duties in relation to matters within their area of expertise. A tax attorney who gives erroneous tax advice, for example, may fall into such a category if he or she fails to meet the objective standard expected of tax attorneys. However, in *Bogg v Raper*,[41] the solicitor trustees were held to no higher duty of care in relation to investments than would have been any other non-legal trustees, as this was outside of their range of expertise.

C. Special Considerations for Trustees

Performance indexes and the current portfolio theory

10.37   It is not appropriate to judge the trustee's investment performance merely by looking at indexes such as national equity indexes, which give indications of what are actually the *best* performing investment ratings in the country and not what an ordinary prudent investor could achieve.[42] The average performance of ordinary shares is the preferred standard.[43]

10.38   Similarly, the trustee will be adjudged according to the current portfolio theory, whereby the level of risk accruing to the entire portfolio is emphasized rather than the risk accruing to single and separate investments viewed in isolation. In *Corso, Gonzales and Others v The Chase Manhattan Corporation Ltd*,[44] the placing of trust assets into a partnership which eventually resulted in loss, was only one step in a complex structure of investments.[45] Taken as a whole, it could not be

---

[40] The principle is codified, eg, under s 5(4) of the Trustee Act 1998 of The Bahamas: 'Notwithstanding the reference in subsection (1)(a) to the skill of an ordinary person, trustees who have special skills or expertise, or are named or appointed as trustees in reliance upon their representation that they have special skills or expertise, have a duty to the beneficiaries to use such special skills or expertise.' These considerations should apply, eg, where the trustee holds itself out as being a tax planning specialist.

[41] (1998–99) 1 ITELR 267 (CA).

[42] In *Nestlé*, above, n 12, 1287, the Barclays de Zoete Wedd (BZW) Equity Index was rejected as a definite standard on this ground. But note that such indexes can be used as a guide, as in *Re Mulligan*, above, n 28.

[43] *Nestlé*, ibid.

[44] (Sup Ct, The Bahamas) No 1261 of 1992, decided 8 August 1994.

[45] Approving *Nestlé*, above, n 12, especially at 1280.

said that the trustee had managed the trust without the care expected. The standard expected of the prudent trustee in managing the trust's financial affairs was outlined as that relative to the current portfolio theory. In addition, it is usually not prudent behaviour for a trustee continually to be changing investments.

Quantifying the loss

Modern courts appear to be well able and willing to assess in quantifiable terms the financial loss suffered by a beneficiary where the trustee acts negligently or inappropriately with regard to the management of the trust's assets. Such identifiable losses may be attributed to the trustee, and the trustee may be required to compensate the beneficiary or beneficiaries.[46]   **10.39**

In *Re Mulligan*,[47] for example, using the New Zealand shares index less a discount for lower risk investment as a guide, evidence was adduced that had the trustee invested prudently in shares and invested 40% of the estate, the capital fund would have been worth more than $200,000, from an original sum of $108,000. It had actually been reduced considerably from its original amount at the time of the proceedings. Damages were assessed accordingly, under the principle of restitution. Mrs Mulligan, a beneficiary and co-trustee, was held liable for the breach of trust together with the trust company. Mrs Mulligan's personal estate had been unjustly enriched by her unlawful profits from the trust investments.   **10.40**

Tangible loss caused by breach required

It seems, however, that where the plaintiff is alleging breaches of duties with regard to investment, such a plaintiff must establish that those breaches have actually caused a tangible loss before compensation can be granted. Damages for a mere breach of duty without such loss will not be awarded. There must be a causal connection between the breach and the loss to the trust estate.[48]   **10.41**

This is the interpretation to be given to *Nestlé*,[49] where, although it was accepted that the bank trustee had breached its duties by failing to review the investment portfolio regularly and by misunderstanding the scope of its duty to invest, the plaintiff did not prove that she had suffered loss as a result of the breach. Here, the original testator had set up a very good investment portfolio in the first   **10.42**

---

[46] See, eg, *Midland Bank*, above, n 7.

[47] See above, n 28, especially 508–509.

[48] See also *Target Holdings Ltd v Redferns* [1996] AC 421; [1995] 3 All ER 785 (HL). But this equitable principle is not identical to the common law principle on causation. For example, the test of remoteness of damage does not apply. Once the loss is caused but for the breach, the trustee must restore the trust to its original position.

[49] *Nestlé*, above, n 12, *per* Leggatt LJ, at 1283.

instance. Consequently, although the trustee erroneously believed that it did not have the power to diversify and go beyond the companies in that portfolio, according to the reasonable standard, the trust assets did not suffer considerably as a result.

10.43 The plaintiff is thus unable to claim for a mere loss of a chance. The onus lies on a plaintiff to prove loss, and in *Nestlé* the problem was compounded by the fact that the plaintiff had not adduced financial material to enable the court to assess the strength of, or value of the chance which she claimed to have lost: 'Loss cannot be presumed if none would necessarily have resulted. Until it was proved that there was a loss, no attempt could be made to assess the amount of it.'[50]

10.44 *Nestlé* should not, therefore, be interpreted as a reluctance on the part of the courts to intervene by assessing damages. Rather, the apparent conservatism had more to do with the reasonable performance of the trust fund in the first instance, albeit through the settlor's efforts rather than those of the trustee. The fact that the trustee had done nothing to achieve the modest success was subservient to the larger question of whether the trust fund had underperformed to the beneficiary's disadvantage.

10.45 Nonetheless, the case is unsatisfactory in the sense that it leaves one with a feeling that justice was not done and that the trustee, which had failed spectacularly,[51] attracted no punishment whatsoever. The scenario hardly seems to fit the descriptions attributed to a trustee's duty of care.

Failure to take legal or professional financial advice and acquire relevant information

10.46 The courts do not take kindly to trustees who fail to take legal advice about the administration of the trust, including advice on tax liabilities,[52] thereby going on to commit serious errors. This was the case in *Nestlé*,[53] where the bank, which was the trustee, did not understand the investment clause inserted into the trust and failed to take legal advice as to its scope and authority.[54] As a result, the trustee did not fulfil its duty to review the investments regularly and make further investments. It was argued that had this been done, the trust fund, which was originally worth £269,203, would have been worth more than £1 million.

---

[50] ibid.
[51] The court said here that the trustee had demonstrated 'symptoms of incompetence or idleness': ibid, 1276.
[52] See *Roome v Edwards* [1981] 1 All ER 736 (HL).
[53] See above, n 12.
[54] It was unaware of a legal decision which held that the words 'or other company' was not limited to its particular context.

The trustee in *Midland Bank*[55] also failed in its duty to take legal advice, believing erroneously that it needed a customer agreement to transfer trust funds to another fund manager, and consequently placing the trust money in a deposit account instead, causing huge losses to the trust fund. **10.47**

The words of Staughton LJ are well worth quoting: **10.48**

> Trustees are not allowed to make mistakes in law; they should take legal advice and if they are still left in doubt they can apply to the court for a ruling.[56]

However, that narrow application of the rule was refuted in *Bogg v Raper*[57] by Millett LJ, in reference to the interpretation of a standard exculpatory clause which prevented a professional person appointed as a trustee from incurring liability for acts or defaults in the exercise of his professional duties. The case suggests that there is an appropriate distinction to be made between professional trustees and professionals who are trustees. In cases where it is inappropriate to excuse a professional trustee, there is still room for exoneration of a professional serving as a trustee where he acts outside of his professional expertise. **10.49**

Advice on investment

To meet the standard of reasonableness, therefore, a trustee who is not an investment strategist and who has the opportunity, is expected to take professional financial advice about the trust. Should he or she fail to do so, incurring losses to the trust, he or she may incur liabilities.[58] Offshore trustees are well advised to seek professional advice about foreign markets and other such variables before embarking on an investment strategy. More important, the offshore trustee should not simply rely on the 'advice' of a settlor who may be behind the scenes (a not uncommon problem with offshore trusts), particularly if that settlor is not an investment specialist. Indeed, this would violate the fundamental rule that the trustee is the holder of discretionary power which it must exercise independently and genuinely.[59] The trustee should seek independent advice and take steps to insulate himself or herself against potential claims of negligence in the future. On the other hand, he or she cannot simply reject the advice either, unless it is reasonable and prudent to do so.[60] **10.50**

Relying on wrong information

In contrast to its duty to seek appropriate advice, the trustee must not abdicate its fiduciary duty to inform itself of matters relevant to its decision-making **10.51**

---

[55] See above, n 7.
[56] In *Nestlé*, above, n 12, 1275.
[57] See above, n 41, 279.
[58] See, eg, *Cowan v Scargill* [1985] Ch 270.
[59] See *Mulligan* above, n 28, and *Turner v Turner* [1894] Ch 100.
[60] *Cowan v Scargill*, above, n 58.

power by inappropriately relying on inaccurate information, or taking irrelevant considerations into account.[61]

10.52   The rule has special significance to complicated trust structures, such as the typical offshore trust, where intermediaries or protectors may be instituted to provide information to the trustee. This was the case, for example, in *Abacus Trust Co (Isle of Man) v Barr*,[62] where an intermediary was employed to relay instructions from the settlor to the trustee. The intermediary relayed incorrect instructions to the effect that 60%, instead of 40%, of the trust fund was to be appointed to the settlor's sons. Lightman J found that the trustee had breached its fiduciary duty to acquire relevant information, in this case, to ascertain the true wishes of the settlor. The trustee here had not even bothered obtaining written instructions from the settlor. It had 'failed to take adequate measures to ensure that it received a correct, rather than a garbled version of the settlor's wishes'.[63]

Purpose of the trust and relevant considerations

10.53   As with an onshore trust, the purpose of the offshore trust is a relevant factor which the trustee must take into account when considering an appropriate investment strategy. As offshore trusts may have more varied purposes than traditional onshore trusts, this may be an important point of deviation. Indeed, this requirement may be expressly provided for under legislation.[64]

10.54   Further, as part of their duties to act reasonably and with care, trustees have clear obligations to take relevant considerations into account and not irrelevant ones. Such considerations should be in accordance with the purpose of the trust.

Tax purposes and considerations relevant to tax

10.55   A trustee may have special responsibilities where taxation is concerned, particularly where tax planning is a significant rationale for the trust. The trustee will be required to take this tax objective into consideration when making investment decisions, and to avoid incurring additional tax liabilities where possible.[65] This issue is addressed in more detail in a following chapter and involves consideration of the rule against the non-enforcement of fiscal law, the *Hastings-Bass*[66] rule, and rules relating to the variation of trusts.[67]

---

[61] See *Edge v Pensions Ombudsman* [2000] Ch 602, 627–8; [1999] 4 All ER 546, 567.
[62] (2003) 5 ITELR 602.
[63] ibid, 614.
[64] See, eg, s 55A(4) of the Trustee Amendment Act 1999 of Bermuda: 'In so investing . . . trust property, a trustee shall act as a prudent investor would, by considering the purposes, terms, distribution requirements and other circumstances of the trust . . .'
[65] This is enshrined under s 5(d) of the Trustee Act 1998 of The Bahamas.
[66] From the case *In re Hastings-Bass* [1975] Ch 25, 41.
[67] See chapter 17, 'Duties of Offshore Trustees in Relation to Tax'.

From the point of view of potential breaches of trust, the interests of the **10.56**
beneficiaries will be at the centre of the relevant discussions. This is so whether
the trustee pays foreign taxes in violation of the rule against the non-enforcement
of foreign revenue law, whether he or she refuses to pay such taxes, thereby
exposing the beneficiaries to tax liabilities and penalties under onshore statutes,
or whether he or she fails to avoid tax liabilities which he or she could have
avoided, thereby incurring increased costs for the trust.

Even where tax planning is not the ultimate rationale for the trust, the likely tax **10.57**
implications of a transaction are relevant considerations which any trustee must
take into account.[68]

Of course, this is only one factor in the management of the trust, and the trustee **10.58**
does not have to make the choice to invest in a tax efficient manner unless it is
the route that the prudent investor would take in the circumstances.[69] However,
it is an important factor for offshore trusts which often have, at least as an
underlying motive, a tax planning rationale. It gives greater flexibility to the
investment decisions which a trustee can make without breaching the essential
duties of the particular trust when considered along with its purpose.[70]

Staughton LJ in *Nestlé* was very clear that 'A beneficiary who has been left a life **10.59**
interest in a trust fund has an arguable case for saying that he should not be
compelled to bear tax on the income if he is not lawfully obliged to do so'.[71]
Indeed, a trustee was 'bound' to take such a tax consideration into account
when carving out an investment strategy.

Where an offshore trust has tax planning as its primary objective, distributions **10.60**
to the beneficiaries might be considered to be secondary. It is particularly in this
context that the trustee should consider tax matters which may impact on the
trust as relevant considerations.[72] At the very least, the trustee should not make
investments which incur onerous tax liabilities even if, for example, they result
in more revenues for some beneficiaries in the long run. It is also an important
factor when deciding what weight is to be placed on income generation or
capital formation.[73]

---

[68] This underscores the argument that tax planning is a legitimate function of the trust.

[69] In *Nestlé*, above, n 12, such a factor would only have justified a modest degree of preference
for income over capital growth.

[70] But this duty may not extend to a settlor. See *Prestwich v Royal Bank of Canada Trust Co
(Jersey) Ltd* (1998–99) 1 ITELR 671.

[71] Above, n 12, 1279.

[72] See *Abacus Trust Co (Isle of Man) Ltd v NSPCC* [2001] WTLR 953, 964–5. See the further
discussion on this point, including the *Hastings-Bass* rule, in chapter 17, 'Duties of Offshore
Trustees in Relation to Tax', paras 17.10–17.22.

[73] Discussed below, paras 10.63–10.76.

10.61   Moreover, it is foreseeable that the courts will go further and link investment successes with tax planning successes. It seems odd that the tax purpose should not be considered when assessing the trustee's performance in relation to investment success, discussed earlier. Where an offshore trustee holds itself out as being in a position to enhance tax benefits or tax planning, its investment strategy should be held to account.

10.62   The likely incidence of tax liabilities accruing because of investment decisions about the trust is accepted as a relevant consideration.

D. Finding the Equitable Balance

Trustee to balance interests of beneficiaries

10.63   A trustee is under an obligation to maintain an equitable balance when making financial and investment decisions for the trust fund.[74] This is no less the case, in offshore trusts, even in the face of offshore trusts which seek to prioritize the settlor as a primary beneficiary. This generally means that the trustee must fairly and impartially balance the interests of each beneficiary, weighing carefully the effects of decisions on current income generation for certain beneficiaries and capital preservation for the benefit of other beneficiaries (the remaindermen) in the long term. As we have seen, other factors may weigh in the balance, such as, for example, avoiding tax liabilities.

10.64   In *Nestlé*,[75] the remaining beneficiaries challenged the decision of the trustee which had subjugated the interests of beneficiaries entitled to the capital in residue to a beneficiary entitled only to income under a life interest.

10.65   The failure of the trustee to maintain an equitable balance between beneficiaries was even more pronounced in the case of *Re Mulligan (Deceased)*.[76] Here, the life tenant was the widow of the settlor and was also a co-trustee. Despite repeated advice from the trustee about the desirability of investing some of the trust monies placed on fixed deposit into shares to counter the effects of inflation, she adamantly refused to do so. Over the long period of her life tenancy (more than forty years) the trust fund reduced considerably in value, causing huge capital losses to the remaining beneficiaries.

10.66   Both Mrs Mulligan, the life tenant and co-trustee, and the trust company, which acted as trustee, were found to have breached the trust in their failure to

---

[74] See *In Re Pauling's Settlement Trusts (No 2)* [1963] Ch 576, 586.
[75] Above, n 12.
[76] Above, n 28.

have regard for the interests of other beneficiaries and by not treating the interests of the capital and income beneficiaries evenhandedly.

Determining capital and income and trust accounting principles—who gets what

The concepts of income and capital may be defined under trust law differently **10.67** from the way that they are commonly interpreted by accountants and finance specialists. They need to be distinguished carefully to determine whether it is the income or capital beneficiary who is entitled.

As is commonly quoted, in trust law 'capital is to income as land is to the **10.68** harvest therefrom'.[77] Income yields plus capital growth are combined, and the trustee has a discretion to decide whether to distribute part of the enhanced capital to income beneficiaries. However, the income yield must be paid out to the income beneficiaries. In The Bahamas, the rules on equitable apportionment have been modified under legislation and trustees are given the discretion to apportion capital to income or income to capital, where they deem it necessary to maintain an equitable balance between the beneficiaries.[78]

Where companies are involved, the intention of the company will need to be **10.69** identified in order to ascertain whether distributions are meant to be capital or income.[79] The same rule applies to unit trusts.[80] However, capital profits dividends have been held to be income by the courts despite the contrary description by the company, based on common law principles that a company cannot make payments to its shareholders as capital except as authorized reduction of capital.[81] Similarly, stock purchased as a capital investment and reinvested in the purchase of real estate was viewed as capital in *Re Maclaren's Settlement*

---

[77] *Cowan v Scargill*, above, n 58, 287. See also *Wong v Morgan Trust Company of The Bahamas Ltd* (2002) 4 ITELR 541, 544 (SC, The Bahamas), *per* Hayton AJ. Note that a trustee has no 'absolute discretion' to characterize receipts of the trust as income or capital.

[78] Section 89 of the Trustee Act 1998 reads: '(1) The rules of equitable apportionment known as the Rule in Howe v. Earl of Dartmouth, the Rule in Re Earl of Chesterfield's Trust and the Rule in Allhusen v. Whittel are abolished in all their branches. (2) Whenever trustees in their discretion determine that property held by them for successive interests is not (when considered as a whole) so invested as to maintain a fair balance between beneficiaries interested in current income and other beneficiaries or that a particular receipt disturbs that balance, the trustees shall apportion capital receipts to income of the trust property or estate so far (if at all) as they in their discretion consider necessary in order to restore such balance.'

[79] See the landmark case of *Bouch v Sproule* (1885) 29 Ch D 635, 653, on the question of whether bonuses were intended as income or capital.

[80] See *Re Whitehead Will Trusts* [1959] Ch 579.

[81] See *Re Doughty* [1947] 1 All ER 207, applying *Hill v Permanent Trustee Co of New South Wales Ltd (PC)* [1930] AC 720. Some countries have intervened via statute to reform the rule, eg, in New Zealand under s 64(b) of the Trustee Act 1956, as amended 1986, which gives the court a discretion to decide whether to treat such payments as capital or income. The section was considered in *Manukau City Council v Lawson* [2001] 1 NZLR 599. Such treatment is also possible in the US.

Trusts.[82] More curiously, shares distributed in a demerger continue to be viewed as income.[83]

10.70   In *Wong v Morgan Trust Company of The Bahamas Ltd*,[84] investment from profits accruing to an investment company created to hold trust investments were not deemed to be income payable to an income beneficiary. The court agreed with the trustee's action in ignoring company practice which treated profits and gains on sales of investments as income, in favour of treating them as capital. This accords with the legislative authority under the Trustee Act 1998 of The Bahamas, although the legislation was not addressed directly.[85]

10.71   Thus, the duty to act evenhandedly may override even orthodox corporate accountancy principles which place a premium on income generation and other similar neutral factors. In *Wong v Morgan Trust Company of The Bahamas Ltd*,[86] Hayton AJ rejected counsel for the life tenant's argument that there was no such thing as 'trust accounting principles', emphasizing the special consideration of the equitable balance which a trustee must take into account when making investment decisions.

10.72   The normal expenses involved in administering the trust, including the costs of appointing new trustees, investment advice, and legal advice, will generally come out of the capital.[87]

Relevant considerations in the equitable balance

10.73   In exercising his or her discretion fairly and impartially between the beneficiaries, the trustee must take all considerations relevant to the purpose of the trust into account and ignore irrelevant ones. Once he or she does this, a decision which results in the interests of one beneficiary being prioritized over those of another cannot be legitimately questioned.[88]

10.74   The factors identified as legitimate in weighing the balance include the following.

(1)   The financial circumstances of individual beneficiaries. For example, if the life tenant is living in penury and the remainderman is already wealthy, it might be reasonable to place more emphasis on income generation.

---

[82] [1951] 2 All ER 414.

[83] *Re Kleinworts Settlements* [1951] Ch 860. Exceptions are made for indirect mergers. See *Sinclair v Lee* [1993] Ch 497.

[84] Above, n 77.

[85] Here, the trustee treated investments of the company as if they were trustee investments.

[86] Above, n 77, 546.

[87] *Carver v Duncan* [1985] 2 All ER 645 (HL).

[88] See *Edge v Pensions Ombudsman* [2000] Ch 602, 627, for the general principle on relevant considerations.

(2) The relationship of the individual beneficiaries to the settlor. For example, if the remaindermen are distant relatives and the life tenant is the widow or widower of the settlor and the primary object of the trust, all things being equal, it may be reasonable for the trustee to incline more toward income generation. This should have been accepted as an influential factor in *Re Mulligan*,[89] but it was overshadowed by the life tenant's wealth (she was the widow of the settlor) and her self-interest.

Courts are in fact slow to draw inferences that the settlor really intended to benefit one type of beneficiary over another. In *Wong v Morgan Trust Company of The Bahamas Ltd*,[90] for example, the trust deed made explicit provision for the life tenant (the settlor's son) to have an annual income of $800,000 from an initial capital of $1 of million, and made provision for shortfalls to be made up out of the capital fund. The court recognized that a sum of $1 million would not normally yield an annual income of $800,000 so that some type of preferential treatment was intended. Notwithstanding, Hayton AJ found that this was not sufficient to disturb the equitable balance principle in general. The life tenant, the income beneficiary, had suggested that since his allocated income sum of $800,000 per annum would diminish in value, and the settlor had authorized the trustee to use capital to ensure that his income was at least that amount, income should have been extended to cover all profits or gains on investments. This would have kept the capital fund at around its original value but substantially increased the life tenant's income to approximately $3,600,000. In the court's view, such an assessment would have been 'odd' and 'unfair'.[91] The provision was to be construed narrowly, confined only to the stipulated amount of annual income. Other investment decisions were to be made equitably.

(3) Efficient tax planning strategy and tax exemptions, whether such factors arise from the settlor's original intentions or from a beneficiary's desire to keep his or her share free from tax liabilities.[92]

(4) The ultimate purpose of the trust. This may be closely aligned with (3), tax planning rationales, or it may be that the trust was set up primarily to make provision for a spouse.

(5) Some consistency in the investment portfolio.

(6) The fact that considerable distributions have already been made to an income beneficiary.

---

[89] Above, n 28.
[90] Above, n 77.
[91] ibid.
[92] See above, paras 10.55–10.62.

The above are, in fact, also factors evident in the trustee's general duty of care in relation to investment.[93]

10.75 A further point to be noted is that where the trustee has a power or duty to pay taxes, this might displace the duty to maintain an equitable balance. For example, if paying taxes on the behalf of beneficiary A results in the income of beneficiary B being reduced, it might appear that the equitable balance is disturbed. However, in an alternative light, such conduct may be viewed as acting fairly and equitably in a situation where beneficiary A's share is seriously threatened if the taxes go unpaid.[94]

10.76 The requirement to maintain an equitable balance while pursuing reasonable investment policies can, however, be displaced where there is a dispositive power exercisable for the benefit of the beneficiaries. This would allow a trustee legitimately to administer the trust in a way that favours certain beneficiaries over others.[95] This allows greater freedom to the offshore trustee.

Timing of distributions

10.77 Balancing the interests of beneficiaries speaks not only to the type of investments and distributions to be made, but also to the timing of distributions made to beneficiaries. The courts have, therefore, inquired whether a trustee can pay one beneficiary's share in the estate before another, which may have the effect at a later time of making the trust balance inadequate to meet the intended distribution to the remaining beneficiaries. The situation may arise, for example, where beneficiary A attains a vested interest in possession before the other beneficiaries. The general rule is that provided that the trustee, at the time of the payment to beneficiary A, holds assets in trust which are sufficient to meet the entitlements of the remaining beneficiaries, such initial payments may be made.

10.78 This is consistent with the rule that a trustee's actions may be judged only according to the facts and circumstances existing at the time of exercising his or her discretion and not with hindsight.[96] The trustee, cannot be held liable for an eventual, unseen loss if he or she acted with due care, paying attention to relevant considerations when he or she answered a beneficiary's legitimate demand to call for his or her rightful share.[97]

---

[93] See *Cowan v Scargill*, above, n 58.

[94] See, eg, *Scottish National Orchestra Society Ltd v Thomson's Executor* 1969 SLT 325. The issue of the payment of taxes is discussed more fully in chapter 17, 'Duties of Offshore Trustees in Relation to Tax'.

[95] As in *Edge v Pensions Ombudsman* [1998] Ch 512.

[96] *Nestlé*, above, n 12, and see para 10.34; *Re Hurst*, (1892) 67 LT 96. What is pertinent are the facts and circumstances known to the trustee which he or she ought to have known about as a reasonable trustee in his or her position.

[97] *Re Hall* [1903] 2 Ch 226; *Re Hurst*, above, n 96.

Despite the above factors which may be discerned from the case law, the **10.79** balancing exercise between the interests of income and capital beneficiaries is not a mechanical one and the trustee actually has a wide discretion to make reasonable decisions.

Where the trust deed avoids a discretion to choose between beneficiaries equitably

The principle that a trustee must maintain an equitable balance between the **10.80** income and capital beneficiaries is generally treated as a fundamental rule of trust law. However, the duty to act fairly and equitably may be overridden by terms in a trust deed which give an entitlement to the trustee to prefer the interests of one set of beneficiaries over another. This was indicated in the New Zealand case of *Manukau City Council v Lawson*,[98] concerning a trust in which the trustee distributed as income dividends which the affiliated trust company had defined as capital. The court examined the other cases where the trustee had a requirement to act impartially,[99] finding them unhelpful, as in those cases the trustee had the discretionary power to choose between two different beneficiaries. In contrast, in the instant case, under the trust deed, the trustees were entitled to prefer the interests of the income beneficiaries over the capital beneficiaries. Thus, they did not have to act impartially in making their decisions, although they could not take irrelevant considerations into account.

In *Wong*,[100] Hayton AJ also conceded that the trust deed could clearly indicate **10.81** that one class of beneficiaries could be preferred to another. Recall, however, that he warned that the courts would be slow to draw conclusions about such a preference and went on to find that the trustee had a duty to act fairly. Thus, the trustee should allocate profits from the sale of investments as capital instead of income in order to maintain a balance between income and capital beneficiaries, despite the direction from the settlor that the income beneficiary be granted a certain minimum amount of income.

E. Abdication and Delegation of Discretion

Trustees are given wide discretion to make decisions about investment, consider- **10.82** ing fairly the interests of all beneficiaries. They may not surrender their discretion even to a dominant co-trustee, or to the wishes of a belligerent or self-centred beneficiary. The rule is of particular significance to offshore trustees,

---

[98] [2001] 1 NZLR 599.
[99] Such as *Edge v Pensions Ombudsman* [2000] Ch 602; *Re Zimpel Deceased* [1963] WAR 171.
[100] See above, n 77, 545–6.

who are often faced with beneficiaries who are also settlors and who may, directly or indirectly, wish to promote their own interests above all others.

10.83　No less applicable are situations where trustees remain passive in arrangements where there are *de facto* advisers of the settlor, particularly where underlying companies are involved. Such a situation arose in the case of *Bahamas International Trust Company Ltd and Others v Wyckoff*.[101] Here, the trustee company, on the advice of the defendant, who was the settlor's attorney, incorporated several underlying companies to hold the trust assets. The defendant continued to be influential in making the investment decisions of the company, including an investment into a company later accused of fraud. The plaintiff claimed that the defendant was an agent or fiduciary of the companies and had been in breach of his fiduciary duty to the companies. However, Georges CJ reminded the court that the trustee had duties in relation to the trust, including a duty not to delegate the trustee functions:

> . . . the pleadings appear to disclose that BITCO, though trustee of the assets of the second to fifth plaintiffs [the relevant companies], relied entirely on the advice of the first defendant, taking no care to check independently the financial strength of Drysdale . . . a trustee cannot fail to carry out the very obligations resting upon it as trustee on the plea that it relied on the expertise of some other person. The trustee's duty to make careful and prudent investment can hardly be delegated to a financial advisor.[102]

10.84　Similarly, in *Re Mulligan*,[103] there was evidence that the trustees were intimidated by the life tenant who was a co-trustee, and it was this fear factor which caused them to refrain from investing in shares and retaining fixed deposits in order to secure a favourable income for the life tenant. This was not the decision of reasonable, independent investor trustees, particularly trustees who were aware of the damaging effects of inflation on capital and the conflict of interest of the co-trustee/life tenant. The better course would have been to apply to the courts for directions.

10.85　Each trustee has a separate responsibility to the trust, and due diligence is required from each and every trustee. Such a duty or power cannot be delegated unless express provision is made for this by statute, or in the trust deed. Such a power is provided for in The Bahamas legislation, for example, but only where it is expressly authorized in the trust instrument.[104]

---

[101] (Sup Ct, The Bahamas) No 466 of 1987, decided 3 May 1988.
[102] ibid, 7.
[103] See above, n 28.
[104] Under s 31(1) of the Trustee Act 1998. See also s 34 of the International Trusts Act 1996 of Grenada, Article 21 of the Trusts (Jersey) Law 1984, s 29 of the Trusts (Guernsey) Law 1989, para 17 of the First Schedule to the Trusts (Special Provisions) Act 1989 (am'd 1999) of Bermuda. Under such legislation, the trustee retains a duty to exercise the standard of care of a reasonable

Even if authority to delegate is granted, this could not be interpreted to include **10.86** a *de facto* delegation of the type that occurred in *Re Mulligan*.[105] Rather, such delegative powers contemplate a situation whereby a trustee can delegate the investment management function to an investment specialist who is in a better position than the trustee to invest reasonably.

More expansive powers of delegation

Delegation for investment purposes was considered in the Hong Kong case of **10.87** *HSBC (Hong Kong) Ltd v Secretary for Justice and Others*.[106] Here, the court approached the function of delegation more expansively, not limiting it to the authority to delegate as expressed in the trust deed. Rather, it was viewed as a legitimate evolution of trustee functions in a contemporary commercial context. This wider principle fits neatly into the context of the offshore trust.

Where trustees have the express authority to delegate the functions of investment **10.88** management, it brings with it a duty to exercise reasonable care in choosing an appropriate investment manager. Even after delegation, trustees have duties to oversee the activities of the delegate, at minimum, to ensure that fraud is not being engaged in.

Joint liability for breaches of trust

The liability for losses to the trust where trustees have breached their duties **10.89** under the trust is joint and each trustee shares in it. Each trustee must, therefore, rectify any loss unless it can be established that special circumstances exist whereby a trustee or trustees can be indemnified for the loss. For example, if one trustee is the legal adviser to the trust company, it may be that he or she alone is responsible for negligent legal advice. Thus, the liability for loss in the situation in *Re Mulligan*,[107] in which certain trustees deferred to the wishes of a co-trustee, remained with all of the trustees. Mrs Mulligan herself, as a co-trustee, had a duty to exercise independent judgement and have regard to the interests of the residuary beneficiaries, and not to act purely in her own interest.[108]

---

and prudent man of business in the selection of the delegate. The power is now provided for under the Trustee Act 2000 of the UK and the Financial Services Act 1986 of the UK, so that there is a discernible trend toward delegation. In the Cook Islands, provision is also made for a 'custodian trustee' to hold the property, invests its funds, and dispose of the assets as the managing trustee in writing directs. However, the managing trustee retains managerial functions and responsibilities: s 19F of the International Trusts Act 1984.

[105] See above, n 28.
[106] [2001] 1 HKC 447.
[107] Above, n 28.
[108] Here, there was also evidence that Mrs Mulligan was not so much fearful that shares were unwise investments. Indeed, she had bought shares for her own estate. Her interest was only to

10.90 Where one trustee is a professional trustee and the co-trustee is an individual acting in a personal capacity, it is even more difficult for the professional trustee to benefit from any waiver of liability. Indeed, the professional trustee will be held to higher duties of care and independent decision making.

F. Responsible Business Transactions

Duties not to purchase or sell investments without authority

10.91 A trustee may neither purchase nor retain unauthorized investments,[109] nor sell investments without the authority to do so.[110] In offshore trusts, the problem that arises is that the settlor may wish to be the person responsible for all investment decisions. Such control over the affairs of the trust may endanger the trust under the sham doctrine.[111]

Setting off losses

10.92 While the traditional rule has been that where the trustee commits distinct and separate breaches of trust, he or she cannot use the gain from one to set off the loss from another unless both stem from the same transaction, the courts have been reluctant to follow this harsh rule in modern-day commercial contexts.[112] This was seen in *Bartlett*,[113] where part of the profit made in the Guildford development scheme was used to finance the Old Bailey project which had suffered huge losses. This worked well, and the court viewed it as a legitimate salvage act. The more lenient application of the rule is indeed consistent with the modern approach, which views investment performance as a composite whole,[114] and more in keeping with investment practices.

Duty of a trustee where money laundering or other misfeasance is suspected

10.93 In view of the several and important legislative provisions on money laundering in offshore jurisdictions, and the fact that trustees, as financial service providers,

---

maintain her own generous income from fixed deposits. She went so far as to deny the trustees access to the other beneficiaries, ensuring that the other beneficiaries had no information on the accounts and affairs of the trust.

[109] See *Knott v Cottee* (1852) 16 Beav 77; *Fry v Fry* (1859) 27 Beav 144.
[110] *Re Massingberd's Settlement* (1890) 63 LT 296.
[111] See chapter 8.
[112] However, the traditional rule that is codified in offshore jurisdictions has not caught up with this progression. See, eg, s 50(2) of the Trusts Act 1992 (rev'd 2000) of Belize, s 34(2) of the Trusts (Guernsey) Law 1989, s 14(2) of the International Exempt Trusts Ordinance 1994 of Nevis, and s 22(2) of the International Trusts Act 1996 of Saint Vincent, which prohibit set offs.
[113] See above, n 5.
[114] See above, paras 10.37–10.38.

fall directly within the ambit of such legislation, the duties of trustees in relation to money laundering matters must be considered. Briefly, such provisions render persons involved in money laundering activities criminally liable. Involvement refers not only to the activities of those persons who directly engage in money laundering, but also to those who assist or facilitate them, and designated persons and financial institutions who fail to report suspicious activities as directed by the legislation. Liability may also accrue where designated persons and financial institutions alert suspected money launderers to investigations, or fail to put in place appropriate screening procedures for their clients.

The standard required of trustees when faced with obligations under money laundering and related legislation was explored in *C v M*[115] by the Supreme Court of The Bahamas. The trust deed required the trustee to make payments to two discretionary beneficiaries, one of whom, the defendant, had been the subject of investigation and intervention by the US Federal Trade Commission (FTC). However, the claims against the defendant were unsubstantiated and no legal action had been taken against it. Further, in the approximately six years since the intervention, there had been no evidence that any claims from customers were pending against the defendant. Indeed, the court considered the earlier intervention to have been spurious. The trustee sought approval from the court to pay out the remaining funds to the defendant, wishing to avoid an allegation of dishonest assistance in a breach of constructive trust. The trustee had already done an electronic search in the US to satisfy himself that no legal claims had been brought against the defendant. **10.94**

The matter was considered within the context of money laundering legislation in The Bahamas, the Financial Transactions Reporting Act 2000 and the Proceeds of Crime Act 2000. Under s 14 of the first statute, a financial institution (which includes a trustee) has a duty to report any transactions where it suspects that the proceeds of criminal conduct are involved. Similar duties arose under s 42(1) of the Proceeds of Crime Act 2000. The court found that there was a duty to report only where there were reasonable grounds for such suspicion.[116] **10.95**

Thus, where there is an objective basis for the suspicion, the obligations under **10.96**

---

[115] (2002) 4 ITELR 548. Note that in some jurisdictions, tax offences are caught under anti-money laundering legislation. See the discussion in chapter 16. See also *R v Allen* [2001] UKHL 46, in which 'shadow directors' of Jersey offshore companies were convicted of money laundering offences for evading UK income taxes. Money laundering legislation in offshore jurisdictions is discussed comprehensively in the companion text, R-M B Antoine, *Confidentiality in Offshore Financial Law* (Oxford University Press, Oxford, 2002), chapter 6.

[116] Although the Proceeds of Crime Act 2000 spoke also of a person 'suspecting', as opposed to reasonably suspecting, this was to capture the situation where there were reasonable grounds for suspicion but a person was obtuse and his suspicion was not aroused. In such a situation, he could not avoid liability. But note that a subjective suspicion may not be sufficient. See *Gibbs v John Mitchell Rea* [1997–98] 1 OFLR 719 (PC, Cayman Islands).

the Act and the potential liabilities for dishonest assistance will not displace the duties of the trustee. The trustee has an obligation to carry out his or her contractual or equitable duties unless he or she has 'positive evidence of misfeasance or breach of trust' on the part of the settlor-beneficiary.[117] Positive evidence here should be based on the standard of foreseeable suspicion. It should also be noted that under the Act, suspicion is placed directly on financial institutions and not on third parties.

10.97 Further, in such circumstances, it is not appropriate for a trustee to seek to surrender his or her discretion to the court. Indeed, seeking directions from the court could, in itself, be viewed as an indication that the trustee had reasonable suspicion that the trust fund represented the proceeds of crime or breach of trust. This is not the first time that a court has refused to intervene when a financial institution has been unsure of its next step, when faced with a situation in which it could violate money laundering legislation.[118] The reluctance of the court in this line of cases is at odds with its increasingly interventionist stance in other areas (such as regards rights to information).

10.98 In matters relating to money laundering, it would appear that trustees are very much on their own. They will have to decide, in difficult cases, which is the lesser of two evils—breach of money laundering obligations, or breach of trust. It is suggested that, in real terms, a trustee should give more weight to money laundering and related legislation, if only because of the criminal penalties involved. Further, offshore jurisdictions are anxious to demonstrate that they are cooperating in the fight against such international crime and are unlikely to be lenient in such matters.

G. Avoiding Liability

Exculpatory clauses

10.99 The trust deed may contain a clause which seeks to exempt the trustee from certain liabilities which will usually accrue for errors, omissions, or other wrong-doing. Consistent with the courts' jealous guard of their inherent supervisory jurisdiction over trusts, they have ordained that such clauses are to be construed narrowly. In this regard, the courts seem to lean toward a literal approach.[119]

---

[117] *C v M*, above, n 115, *per* Hayton AJ, 553.

[118] See *Governor & Company of the Bank of Scotland v A Ltd and Others* (2001) 3 ITELR 503.

[119] See *Armitage v Nurse* [1998] Ch 241; [1997] 3 WLR 1046. So that, eg, exclusion of liability for 'errors and omissions' does not exclude liability for positive breaches of trust: *Rae v Meek* (1889) 14 AC 558. The narrow construction extends to a trust instrument where there are two exculpatory clauses, one excluding all trustees from liability and another which expressly

Notwithstanding, such an approach may still leave much room for a trustee to escape liability. For example, in *Bogg v Raper*,[120] the court purported to approve the narrow, literal approach. Yet it interpreted a clause which exempted liability for 'omissions made in good faith' to encompass non-negligent, as well as negligent, omissions.[121] The explanation may lie in both the legislature's and the courts' reluctance to undermine exculpatory clauses which seek to exempt trustees from liability due to mere negligence, an issue discussed in the following section.

Of interest here is the provision in the Cook Islands, which attempts to prevent **10.100** the court adopting such a literal construction, requiring it to give a 'liberal interpretation' of exculpatory clauses.[122] The provision is indicative of the dilemma that many offshore trusts face. Although professional trustees may be necessary for the sustainability of offshore trusts, it is not necessarily envisaged that they should play significant roles in trusts with underlying companies and other broad business functions. As such, they should not be liable for business errors. It is doubtful, however, whether such a provision can interfere with the courts' chosen mode of interpretation. Presumably, a court can claim to be giving a fair and liberal interpretation and still conclude that such a clause is to be interpreted narrowly!

While it is incontestable that exculpatory clauses are to be construed strictly **10.101** and narrowly,[123] there is debate as to the permissible scope of such clauses in terms of subject matter, even where there is intention to exclude. The burden of establishing that an exculpatory clause applies to a trustee's situation falls on the trustee.[124] Further, such clauses do not affect the court's wide power to relieve a trustee for breach of trust, unless expressly curtailed.[125]

---

does not apply to paid trustees. In such a case, paid trustees could not rely on the general exculpatory clause. See *Wight and Another v Olswang and Another* [1998] TLR 564 (CA).

[120] Above, n 41, 283. The court was approving the literal approach laid down in *Rae v Meek*, above, n 119.

[121] Cf *Re Williams Trust* (2000) 2 ITELR 313 (CA), Minnesota.

[122] Section 19E of the International Trusts Act 1984 of the Cook Islands reads: 'Where any provision of a trust instrument limits the liability of a trustee, or provides relief or indemnity for a trustee, such provision shall be valid and effective according to its terms, and every such provision shall be given a fair, large and liberal interpretation so as to give full effect to its tenor, notwithstanding any rule of law or equity to the contrary.'

[123] *Walker v Stones*, above, n 16; *Bogg v Raper*, above, n 41.

[124] *Midland Bank*, above, n 7, *per* Le Quesne JA.

[125] Indeed, in several offshore jurisdictions which have codified traditional trusts law on breaches of trust, this is made patently clear. See above, n 2. For example, see s 50 of the Trusts (Guernsey) Law 1989, which reads: 'The court may relieve a trustee wholly or partly for a breach of trust . . . where it appears to the court that the trustee (a) has acted honestly and reasonably; and (b) ought fairly to be excused—. . . (ii) for the breach of trust; (iii) for omitting to obtain the directions of the court in the matter in which the breach arose.' See also s 31 of the International Trusts Act 2002 of Saint Lucia.

Exemption from gross negligence—wide exculpatory clauses

10.102 In the Jersey case of *Midland Bank Trust Company (Jersey) Ltd Establishment Committee and Day v Federated Pension Services*,[126] Le Quesne JA was of the view that exculpatory clauses could be wide enough to exclude liability even for gross negligence, if the relevant clause was expressed clearly enough. He formed this opinion based on a review of Commonwealth law on the subject.[127] The case was to be heard on appeal to the Privy Council but was settled, depriving us of the opportunity of a final, authoritative view. The difficulty with this finding is that the cases under review were cases involving clauses which did not actually attempt to exclude gross negligence, so that no strong views were expressed in relation to the subject. Further, where the settlor is a sophisticated, aware business person, the view that the exculpatory clause should be upheld is reinforced, since the arrangement will be viewed as akin to a contract between equals.[128]

10.103 The *Midland Bank* judgment foresaw the ruling in *Armitage v Nurse*.[129] The clause in *Armitage* read:

> No trustee shall be liable for any loss or damage which may happen to Paula's fund or any part thereof or the income thereof at any time or from any cause whatsoever *unless such loss or damage shall be caused by his own actual fraud* . . .[130]

The clause was interpreted to exclude liability for breach of trust in the absence of a dishonest intention.

10.104 In contrast, in *Lutea Trustees Ltd v Orbis Trustees Guernsey Ltd*,[131] the court restricted a wide exculpatory clause which purported to encompass negligence generally, including neglect on the part of the trustee. The court found that such a clause did not protect against gross negligence or *culpa lata*, deliberate or reckless acts.

10.105 The view that exculpatory clauses that attempt to exclude liability for gross negligence can, or should, survive judicial scrutiny, should perhaps be approached with caution. Given the lengths to which modern courts have gone to wrest contractual freedom from those who establish trusts in favour of imposing more and more responsibility on trustees, it seems inconsistent to

---

[126] Above, n 7, *per* Le Quesne JA.
[127] ibid, 375. Note that in Jersey, liability for gross negligence is specifically preserved by the relevant statute which permits exemptions, the Trusts (Jersey) Law 1984 (am'd 1989).
[128] See *Roywest Trust Corp (Bahamas) Ltd v Savannah NV and Others* (Sup Ct, The Bahamas), decided 22 July 1987.
[129] [1998] Ch 241. Leave to appeal to the House of Lords was refused.
[130] ibid, 250, *per* Millett LJ.
[131] [1998–99] 2 OFLR 227.

allow settlors to, in effect, give a trustee licence to act carelessly toward, or mismanage the trust.[132]

The concern which may be raised in relation to unpaid trustees, that they may be frightened away from accepting trust offices if liability for gross negligence cannot be exempted,[133] can hardly be said to be applicable to professional persons acting as trustees. This is even more the case in the offshore trust sector, where the professional trustee may also be a specialist trust manager, actively encouraging trust business.

10.106

Very wide exemption clauses make nonsense of the fundamental rule binding trustees to carry out the duties imposed under the trust honestly and in good faith. They may also violate the principle that there are certain fundamental duties (irreducible core duties) which must be left to a trustee to perform if a trust is to subsist.[134]

10.107

Intriguingly, however, some courts have found that the duty to exercise care and diligence does not fall within the irreducible core content of the trust context. Hence, they have held that all that is required is that the trustee acts honestly, in good faith, and reasonably. Clauses attempting to exempt liabilities where trustees act negligently, imprudently, or even contrary to the skills which they proclaimed that they had, do not violate public policy and are allowed.[135]

10.108

Public policy and breaching fundamental principles of the trust

We should also consider whether exculpatory clauses which attempt to exempt liability for gross negligence are void for reasons of public policy. This question was answered in the negative in *Midland Bank*.[136] The decision is curious, particularly because legislation in Jersey had, in fact, specifically provided that liability for gross negligence could not be so excluded.[137] Indeed, this was an amended provision which sought to clarify the law on the point. It seems puzzling that the public policy argument is not strong, at least in such a jurisdiction, where foreign trust investment is actively encouraged and statute has provided that gross negligence attracts liability. The logic in *Midland Bank* on

10.109

---

[132] Certainly, the commissioning, by the UK Law Commission, of a Consultation Paper on the question of whether exemptions from liability for negligence by professional trustees should be allowed, is evidence that the question is not yet settled.

[133] This was the view of Sargent LJ in *In re City Equitable Fire Insurance Co Ltd* [1925] Ch 407, 528.

[134] The notion of an irreducible core of duties is attributed to David Hayton in 'The Irreducible Core Content of Trusteeship', in AJ Oakley (ed), *Trends in Contemporary Trust Law* (Oxford University Press, Oxford, 1996), chapter 3.

[135] *Armitage*, above, n 129, *per* Millett LJ; *Midland Bank*, above, n 7, which distinguished gross negligence from ordinary negligence.

[136] See above, n 7.

[137] See s 5 of the Trusts (Jersey) Law 1984 (am'd 1989).

this point seems circular, that if Parliament had intended such a public policy rationale, it would have expressed it as such in the statute. The court's approach was also influenced by its timidity about being the first to establish such a precedent had it taken the plunge.[138]

10.110 Thus, the wide exculpatory clause seeking to exclude liability for gross negligence was found not to be repugnant to the fundamental principles of, or nature of the trust.[139] Significantly, Le Quesne JA pointed out that such exemption clauses are commonly included in the trust deeds of occupational pension schemes.[140]

10.111 In the US, however, wide exculpatory clauses have been held to be contrary to public policy, and thereby deemed void. In the landmark case of *Browning v Fidelity Trust Co*,[141] the court explained that the law drew a line beyond which the parties cannot agree to relieve a trustee from liability for breach of trust. Acts of gross negligence and acts done in bad faith were recognized as going beyond the acceptable point.

Exculpatory clauses and fraud or dishonesty

10.112 Exculpatory clauses cannot survive, however, in cases of fraud, or where a trustee is found to be acting dishonestly.[142] The standard for dishonesty here is the objective standard. The question of excusing liability must now be viewed within the context of the tests laid down for dishonesty in the cases of *Royal Brunei v Tan Kik Ming*[143] and *Walker v Stones*.[144]

10.113 In *Walker* the question was whether dishonesty includes conduct in which the trustee commits the breach of trust deliberately but with an honest belief that he or she is acting in the best interest of the beneficiaries. Applying the objective standard, the court held that this did amount to dishonesty,[145] in contrast to the court in the earlier case of *Armitage*,[146] where, although the exculpatory clause was similar to that in *Walker*,[147] such conduct was not found to be dishonest. The rule in *Walker*, therefore, is that an exception clause which excludes liability for anything other than dishonesty or fraud, does not protect against a deliberate breach of trust which is committed in the honest or general belief that it is in the beneficiaries' best interest, if the breach was such that no reasonable trustee

---

[138] Except for the earlier case of *West v Lazard Brothers and Co Jersey Ltd* [1993] JLR 321, with which the court disagreed.

[139] See *Midland Bank* above, n 7, 390.

[140] ibid, 391.

[141] 250 F 321 (3rd Cir 1918).

[142] See *Walker v Stones*, above, n 16, 445–6.

[143] See above, n 15.

[144] See above, n 16.

[145] See the discussion of the 'Robin Hood' scenario in chapter 11.

[146] See above, n 129.

[147] The trustee was exempted if he acted in good faith and not dishonestly.

in the particular circumstances would have committed it. In this context, dishonesty must be taken to include reckless indifference and recklessness.[148] The court will, therefore, retain its inherent supervisory jurisdiction to look behind such wide clauses.

The practical effect of the *Walker* principle in expanding liability under the   **10.114** heading of dishonesty based on an assessment of reasonable conduct is to undermine considerably the instances where a trustee may be exempted for negligence, even gross negligence. Types of conduct which were previously viewed as 'mere' negligence, now run the risk of being deemed dishonest under the objective standard.

Settlor's understanding of the exculpatory clause

Where there are exemption clauses inserted into the trust instrument, the court   **10.115** must be satisfied that the settlor understood the full impact of the clause. It is not necessary for the trustee to have advised the settlor to consult an independent lawyer before inserting the clause, although it is advisable for him or her to do so.[149] The fact that the settlor is an astute 'man of business' may be enough to convince the court of his or her ability to understand such a clause. The solicitor trustee breaches no duty in drafting the exemption clause himself or herself, as this in no way undermines the general duty of a trustee to ensure that the terms and effect of an exemption clause are fully explained to the settlor. In *Bogg v Raper*,[150] a wide exemption clause was upheld to protect the solicitor trustees who had drafted the clause, even in the face of apparent gross negligence. It was alleged that the solicitor trustees had failed to supervise the business of the companies in which the trust assets were invested. The value of the shares fell from £8 million to being almost worthless within two years.[151]

The court will view as relevant the fact that the settlor is an attorney-at-law, as   **10.116** was the case in *Corso, Gonzales and Others v Chase Manhattan Corporation Ltd*,[152] where the settlor was described by the court as a 'successful Venezuelan lawyer'.[153] In fact, the settlor here caused a clause to be inserted into the trust deed which enabled him to continue to give directions for the investment of

---

[148] *Armitage*, above, n 129 and *Walker*, above, n 16.
[149] *Bogg v Raper* above, n 41.
[150] ibid.
[151] Such a clause was fundamentally different from a trustee changing clause and did not conflict with the rule that, in the absence of clear words, a trustee may not profit from the trust. The clause did not confer a profit; it merely protected from loss: ibid, 285.
[152] Above, n 44.
[153] ibid, 14.

the assets, including the need for the trustee to consult with the settlor before making investments.[154]

Exemption from liability by the courts

10.117   It follows from our discussion above that, apart from exemptions as expressed in a trust instrument or statute, the court reserves a discretion to exempt or excuse a trustee from liability where his or her breach of trust was in circumstances where he or she acted both honestly and reasonably.[155] The onus lies on the trustee to prove that he or she acted reasonably or honestly, and this is a question of fact. It may be expected that the discretion will be exercised rarely and, given the modern trend, even more so where professional trustees such as offshore trustees are involved.

10.118   In the final analysis, therefore, exemption clauses will be construed by the courts taking into account modern principles of trust law and will not be taken at face value. This makes them unreliable instruments of protection for offshore trusts, which are not really intended to carry full responsibilities for management and investment decisions in the quite sophisticated financial structures created under offshore law and practice.

10.119   Judicial preference appears to be for modest exculpatory clauses. Certainly, the trend in relation to statute is toward restricting the ability of trustees, in particular professional trustees, to be exempt from liability. The exception would be where the trustee is being asked to act in the role of a company director. This is as true for offshore jurisdictions as it is for onshore jurisdictions.[156]

Statutory prescriptions—duties and exemptions

10.120   Increasingly, in offshore jurisdictions, the scope of trustee investment powers is being prescribed by statute. As we saw earlier, legislation may also describe the extent of liability which is to be vested in a trustee with investment powers. Such statutes therefore clarify the current uncertainties in the law and are to be welcomed. In Jersey, for example, s 5 of the Trusts (Jersey) Law 1984, as amended

---

[154] The relevant clause read: '. . . the trustee shall invest the trust assets in such a manner as the settlor shall direct in writing. The trustee shall have no liability for any loss occurring by reason of any action or non-action resulting from the exercise or non-exercise of such power of direction' (ibid, 4). Arguably, such a directing clause will run the trust into trouble under the sham doctrine (see chapter 8).

[155] See *Walker* and *Royal Brunei*, discussed earlier, nn 16 and 15 respectively; and *Re Parson's Settlement* [1917] 1 Ch 541. Recall that reckless or wilful blindness is not honest. Indeed, legislation in many offshore jurisdictions expressly retains this. See above, n 2.

[156] The Law Commission Consultation Paper on *Trustee Exempt Clauses* proposed that trustees should not be able to rely on exemption clauses. See The Bahamas and BVI legislation below, paras 10.123–10.129.

in 1989, provides: 'Nothing in the terms of a trust shall relieve, release or exonerate a trustee from liability for breach of trust arising from his own fraud, wilful misconduct or gross negligence.'[157]

The question remains whether such statutes can override clearly expressed intentions in a trust deed, which are contrary to the statutory provisions. Where legislation is silent on the point, the statutory provisions may restrict the freedom of the parties to the trust to contract, and the trust deed will be read in accordance with the statutory provisions. This was the interpretation given to the relevant Jersey statute in *Midland Bank*.[158] Section 26(9) of the Trusts (Jersey) Law 1984, as amended in 1989, gave a power to exclude liability 'subject to the terms of the trust', but the statutory area of liability given under the Act could not be restricted. Therefore, the trust deed could validly reduce the scope of the statutory exemption from liability but could not extend it.[159] **10.121**

Where, as is the case in Bermuda, the statute clearly bows to the choice of those creating the trust, as expressed in the trust deed, the trust deed's provisions may survive. For example, s 55A(1) of the Trustee (Amendment) Act 1999 of Bermuda provides that the trustees' power of investment shall be 'subject to any enlargement or restriction of powers as set out in the instrument creating the trust'. The unusual provision in the Cook Islands, which goes further and attempts to direct the way such provisions may be interpreted by the court, has already been commented upon.[160] **10.122**

Duties of offshore trustees with respect to underlying companies

As part of an efficient offshore financial structure, offshore trustees often have controlling interests in companies. When this occurs, special responsibilities and liabilities fall on the trustees. Under traditional trusts law, trustees cannot be passive and leave the management of the company entirely in the hands of another without a care as to the impact on the trust assets.[161] Indeed, this may be viewed as part of the responsibility of the trustees not to delegate their discretion. **10.123**

---

[157] See also the Bermuda legislation, the Trustee (Amendment) Act 1999. See too less far-reaching provisions, such as in Saint Vincent, under s 22(6) of the International Trusts Act 1996: 'Nothing in the terms of a trust shall relieve a trustee of liability for a breach of trust arising from his own fraud, self-dealing or wilful misconduct.' See also s 14(6) of the International Exempt Trusts Act 1997 of Dominica, which does not include 'selfdealing'. See further, the provisions exonerating a trustee where he or she acts in a managerial capacity in relation to underlying companies below, at paras 10.123–10.129.

[158] See above, n 7, 387.

[159] ibid.

[160] See above, para 10.100.

[161] See *Re Lucking's Will Trusts* [1967] 3 All ER 726.

10.124   The requisite duties and liabilities may be prescribed by legislation. Of special note must be the recent legislation of the British Virgin Islands, the Virgin Islands Special Trusts Act 2003, creating 'VISTA Trusts'. The legislation will enable shareholders of companies incorporated in the British Virgin Islands to establish trusts which allow trustees to be disengaged from management duties. Instead, managerial duties will rest with the directors of the company. The provisions also aim to avoid what are viewed as limiting principles of equity, which may force a trustee to take investment decisions that may go against the intentions of the settlor in establishing the trust. For example, the trustee may wish to wind up the company where this appears to be an advisable option under the prudent investor rule, but the settlor may have personal reasons for prolonging the life of the company. The trustee is given exemption from liability where he or she invests outside of these equitable principles.[162]

10.125   The Bahamas has also enacted provisions which regulate offshore trustees overseeing underlying companies. For example, provision is made for trustees' dealings where securities of a company are subject to a trust. The trustee may take part in a number of company activities, including sales, acquisitions, and mergers. He or she is not responsible for losses where he or she acts in good faith in relation to the company matters associated with the trust.[163] Further, where the director of an underlying company is the trustee or its employee, the trustee incurs no liability for management, administration, or investment decisions where he or she acts 'pursuant to instructions received from the Settlor or the Protector'.[164] The trustee is also under no duty actively to take part in the management of the affairs of underlying companies, or 'to interfere in the management, administration operations or activities of any special entity'.[165]

---

[162] See, eg, s 6 of the Act, labelled 'Restrictions on trustee's powers': '(2) Voting or other powers . . . shall not be exercised by the trustee so as to interfere in the management or conduct of any business of the company, and in particular, the trustee (a) shall leave the conduct of every such business, and all decisions as to the payment or non-payment of dividends, to the directors of the company.' The liability of directors of trust companies is discussed in chapter 12. Note that these new legislative provisions make British Virgin Islands trustees similar to Delaware trustees, who are not liable for decisions made by delegated investment advisers. See also s 5(3), which provides that: 'the trustee shall not be accountable for losses arising directly or indirectly from holding, rather than disposing of, designated shares, including, in particular, losses arising from any of the factors specified in subsection (4). (4) The factors referred to in subsection (3) are (a) the absence, or inadequacy, of financial return from any designated shares; . . . (c) speculative or imprudent activities of the company . . . (e) liquidation or receivership of the company; . . . (g) the loss of opportunity to make gains from reinvestment of the proceeds of designated shares . . .'

[163] See s 10 of the Trustee Act 1998 of The Bahamas.

[164] Paragraph 8(c) of the First Schedule to the Trustee Act 1998 of The Bahamas.

[165] Paragraph 8(c) of the First Schedule to the Trustee Act 1998 of The Bahamas. Paragraph 7 of the said Schedule to the Act authorizes trustees, director officers, or employees of corporate trustees to act as directors of underlying companies of the trust. Similar provisions are found under ss 7 and 8 of The Trusts (Special Provisions) Act 1989 of Bermuda. See chapter 12, 'Liability of Directors of Offshore Corporate Trustees' for further discussion of this subject.

Duty to acquire information

Perhaps the most important responsibility of such a trustee is the duty to acquire adequate information about the management and performance of the company so that he or she is in a position to utilize his or her controlling shareholding if necessary. In *Bartlett v Barclays Bank Trust Co Ltd*,[166] the court found that the amount and type of information which the trustee must have at his or her disposal must be far greater than that to which an ordinary shareholder is entitled. The later case of *Walker v Stone*[167] confirms this duty. If the trustee receives information that the company's affairs are not being conducted as they should, he or she must take appropriate action.

10.126

A trustee has a variety of methods open to him or her in obtaining information about the company. One way is for the trustee or his or her nominee to sit on the board of directors.[168] *Bartlett*[169] also suggests that creative routes should be sought by the trustee with a controlling interest in an affiliated company, to acquire such information if it is not readily available. Other ways include gaining receipt of copies of the agenda, minutes of board meetings, and monthly or quarterly management accounts where it is a trading concern. In *Bartlett*, it was not sufficient that the bank trustee attended general meetings and received the annual balance sheet and profit loss account, detailed annual financial statements, and the chairman's report and statement. It needed more regular information to meet the adequate information benchmark.[170]

10.127

Yet in the offshore trust regime as defined by statute and practice, it will be more difficult for a trustee to meet the high standards laid down in *Bartlett* and *Re Lucking's Will Trust*.[171] The requirements for company meetings in offshore jurisdictions are, by design, very flexible, attempting to accommodate directors who are not physically in the offshore jurisdiction and who may not even be present together in one place. Offshore trustees need, therefore, to find even more creative ways of remaining 'in the know' about the management of companies to which they are affiliated. Settlors may be the directors of such companies and they may not wish the trustee to be too involved. There is thus a need for balance here. Alternatively, offshore legislation will need to override the effects of *Bartlett* by granting statutory exemptions to such trustees.

10.128

---

[166] [1980] Ch 515, 533–4, affirming *Re Lucking's Will Trust*, above, n 161. In *Bartlett*, the trustee owned a controlling interest in the company which made speculative and disastrous investments with the trust assets.

[167] See above, n 16, 422.

[168] As in *Re Lucking's Will Trusts*, above, n 161.

[169] See above, n 166.

[170] ibid, 533–4.

[171] See above, n 161.

10.129 Consequently, in The Bahamas, the trustee is not bound to the principles laid down in *Bartlett*.[172] Thus, trustees:

> (a) shall be under no duty to keep themselves informed concerning the business or affairs of any special entity the shares of which or some of the shares of which form a part of the Trust Fund or concerning the management or administration thereof by its directors officers agents employees or any of them . . .[173]

Indemnity for costs

10.130 Before proceeding to litigate, the trustee should consider whether he or she would be indemnified for costs in relation to trial. As the offshore trust is becoming increasingly litigious, this is an important question for the trustee, and is worth considering even before the trust deed is drawn up. There is no right to such an indemnity and the answer will depend very much on the nature of the action.

10.131 Trustees, for example, do not have a duty to defend actions challenging the validity of the trust. Their duty is to remain neutral in the face of rival claimants. Accordingly, the trustee is not generally entitled to an indemnity in such circumstances.

10.132 This point was considered in *Alsopp Wilkinson (A Firm) v Neary*,[174] which involved a challenge to the validity of a Jersey trust on the ground that the trust had been established unlawfully in order to defeat creditors. Lightman J reviewed the general principles on obtaining an indemnity for costs. Trustees are entitled to an indemnity against all costs, expenses, and liabilities properly incurred in administering the trust. They also have a duty to represent the trust in a third party dispute, as part of their general duty to protect the beneficiaries. However, in beneficiary disputes, trustees are 'well advised' to seek court authorization before they sue, as a beneficiary dispute is regarded as hostile litigation in which costs follow the event and do not come out of the trust estate. Where there are rival beneficiaries, including implied beneficiaries such as creditors or a trustee in bankruptcy, the trustee must remain neutral and not prefer one beneficiary over another. Nonetheless, the court retains an exceptional discretion in hostile litigation to award an indemnity to a trustee.[175]

10.133 Where the matter is one of general importance to the general administration of the trust, it appears that the courts will be willing to indemnify for costs. In

---

[172] See above, n 166.
[173] Paragraph 8 (1) of the First Schedule to the Trustee Act 1998 of The Bahamas. Recall that in the BVI, trustees are prohibited from getting involved in the affairs of underlying companies altogether; see above, n 162.
[174] [1996] 1 WLR 1220.
[175] ibid, 1224, *per* Lightman J.

Stuart-Hutcheson v Spread Trustee Co Ltd (No 2),[176] the beneficiaries under a trust were involved in substantive litigation on the question of access to information on the trust. They applied to the court for costs relating to the matter to be paid from the trust property on an indemnity basis.[177] The court agreed, reasoning that the substantive matter had not been an ordinary dispute between rival litigants. Rather, the issue for trial was one concerning a previously unresolved point of Guernsey law, and hence important. Further, an application by the trustee would have been justified.

In *Bridge Trust Co Ltd v AG for the Cayman Islands,*[178] the exceptional circum-
stance which persuaded the court to award the trustee an indemnity for costs was the decision of the Attorney General not to appear to defend the interests of charity in a trust purported to be an exclusively charitable trust. The decision was based on foreign policy grounds as the matter concerned issues of concern to the Norwegian Government. This was hostile litigation as the Privy Council had found that the foundation in question was not an exclusively charitable trust. The question then remained as to who was the legitimate owner of the assets, whether the settlor, as alleged by the Inland Revenue of Norway, or the administrator who had acted for the settlor. The court did not depart from the general rule that, in the context of hostile litigation, exceptional circumstances were required before an indemnity would be granted. However, the fact that the charity was not to be afforded protection by the Crown was an exceptional circumstance, which was a factor that militated toward a duty on the part of the trustees to act and on the part of the court to ensure that justice was done. Accordingly, an indemnity was appropriate.

10.134

---

[176] (2003) 5 ITELR 617 (CA, Guernsey), Judgment for Costs.
[177] Under s 65(4) of the Trusts (Guernsey) Law 1989.
[178] (2002) 4 ITELR 369 (PC, Cayman Islands).

11

LIABILITY OF THIRD PARTIES
TO THE TRUST

A. Development of Third Party Liability in Modern Commerce

Introduction

Apart from the liability placed on trustees, liabilities may arise elsewhere where **11.01** breaches of trust occur, as is the case with strangers or third parties to the trust. Third parties may, of course, also incur liability for negligence in relation to their dealings with the trust and those associated with the trust. Recently, there have been important developments of the law concerning the liability of third parties to the trust, in particular with respect to their input where breaches of trusts are involved. Arguably, these developments have been as responses to the increasing commercialization of the trust, with the offshore trust falling squarely within this context.

Trusts, and in particular offshore trusts, have become complex corporate entities **11.02** often comprising layers of investment, with several persons being involved in the dealings of associated commercial transactions. Consequently, this area of law is of increasing importance to trusts involved in investment and business, such as offshore trusts. In many instances, the trustee directly responsible for an inappropriate transaction or action (typically a company) may be insolvent and the plaintiff is left without a remedy. Aggrieved plaintiffs must, therefore, turn to those other persons who were concerned with, or associated with, the transaction but who are not parties to it, seeking to impose on them liabilities arising out of obligations which are deemed fiduciary, or to hold them personally liable for assisting in breaches of trust. Often, such persons are bankers, legal or other advisers, or directors of the company.[1] The liabilities thus imposed arise in equity.

11.03 The person involved in the transaction may be one who simply receives trust property associated with a breach of trust, or fraud. In such a case, the category of strangers or third parties who may incur liability is very broad. This class of persons may be compared to a class of receivers, in the sense that a receiver need not have been directly involved in any breach to incur liability.

Equitable basis

11.04 The rationale for this liability which strangers or third parties to the trust incur appears to be the participation of the third party (either actively or passively) in actions or omissions which negatively impact on the beneficiaries' rights under the trust and which is deemed to be unconscionable in equity. Such persons are held accountable because of their indirect or direct facilitation of the breach.

11.05 The courts have identified three main heads of liability which attach to third parties or strangers to the trust. These are:

(1) liability for 'knowing assistance';
(2) liability for 'knowing receipt' and;
(3) 'liability de son tort'.

The rules concerning the requirements to ground these breaches continue to be in a state of evolution. Of the three, the first two, knowing assistance and knowing receipt, are more prevalent, and indeed should be regarded as more important than 'liability de son tort'.

11.06 However, although the principle of liability is itself well established, the courts are still seeking to clarify the full measure of these third party liabilities. Indeed, in *Royal Brunei v Tan*,[2] the court noted that '[t]he proper role of equity in commercial transactions is a topical question'.

---

[1] It seems that a previous trustee, who hands over the trust assets to a new trustee whom he or she knows or suspects is fraudulent, may be liable as a third party where the new trustee subsequently breaches the trust. This is the implication in *Publishers Representatives Ltd and Lee Sku Kee v UBS (Cayman Islands) Ltd* [2000] CILR 473, although the court there did not settle definitely the question whether the first trustee was to be treated as the relevant trustee, or as a mere accessory.

[2] *Royal Brunei Airlines v Tan Kik Ming* [1995] 3 WLR 64 (PC, Brunei, Darussalam), 66; [1995] 3 All ER 97, 99. As late as 1994, Henry J commented that the law as to knowing receipt and knowing assistance 'cannot be regarded as settled': *Springfield v Abacus (Hong Kong) Ltd* [1994] 3 NZLR 502, 510.

The new emphases placed on the remedies associated with knowing assistance   **11.07**
and knowing receipt make them primary and prominent remedies for persons
who suffer loss under the associated breaches of trust or fiduciary duties.

Rationale for liability—doctrine of constructive trust or general equitable principles?

The liabilities placed on third parties to the trust are often attributed to the   **11.08**
doctrine of constructive trust. This emerged in the familiar case of *Barnes v Addy*,[3]
where it was held that a third party who participates in, or is involved in another's
breach of trust or breach of fiduciary duty is liable if the third party knowingly
receives trust property in breach of the trust (knowing receipt cases), or where the
third party knowingly assists in the misapplication of the trust property (knowing
assistance cases), thereby causing a breach of the trust or fiduciary duty.[4]

The essence of the constructive trust is that the offending person is deemed to   **11.09**
hold the assets for the benefit of the beneficiaries and must therefore turn them
over to them. In *Hussey v Palmer*,[5] it was noted that the principle of unjust
enrichment was central to the constructive trust. This was the basis for the law's
insistence that property, thus obtained unjustly, be returned.

The doctrine of the constructive trust, and its underlying notions of unjust   **11.10**
enrichment and restitution, does not fit neatly into all of the situations in which
modern courts will award remedies for inappropriate conduct by third parties
in relation to trust property. At the heart of those situations is the principle of
good conscience, the foundation on which all equitable jurisdiction has been
constructed. This emphasis is seen more clearly in those cases in which
'unconscionable' behaviour is evident.[6]

In knowing assistance cases, it is the actual participation in the breach of trust   **11.11**
which makes the third party liable. Here, no property is placed in the hands of
the offender. Thus, whilst the language of 'constructive trust' has continually
been used to describe or define liability in knowing assistance claims, it is more
appropriately categorized under more general principles of equity, in particular,
the equitable liability to account for participating in wrongdoing. The more
recent decisions, discussed below, which emphasize this participation, help to
make the distinction clearer.[7]

---

[3] (1874) LR 9 Ch App 244.
[4] See also *Gold v Rosenberg* (1995) 86 OAC 116 (CA, Ontario).
[5] [1972] 3 All ER 70 (CA).
[6] See below, para 11.33.
[7] See the *Royal Brunei* line of cases below, paras 11.17–11.26, and the modern emphasis on dishonesty.

11.12 Knowing assistance cases are described as falling under the category of 'accessory liability', while knowing receipt cases are best described as belonging to the category of 'receipt liability'. The latter may be accepted as belonging to the constructive trust doctrine as there is control and/or ownership of the assets and it is restitution based.[8]

Distinction between knowing assistance and knowing receipt

11.13 It was previously accepted that there was a clear distinction between the tests for establishing the cases of knowing assistance and knowing receipt. In more recent times, however, doubt has been cast on what was thought to be a well-established distinction, suggesting that the tests may be the same, or similar.

11.14 However, as yet it is difficult to make a definitive pronouncement on the point since, while the grounds for establishing knowing assistance appear to be certain, those for knowing receipt are not, as is demonstrated when we explore the cases below. It may well be that when the courts come to a consensus about the elements that constitute knowing receipt, the clear distinction between the two heads of liability may be reinstated.[9]

Levels of knowledge—the Baden *test*

11.15 The question of knowledge, as the terminology in knowing assistance and knowing receipt heads of liability suggests, is still important to assessing liability, though less so in knowing assistance cases, now more appropriately described as 'dishonest assistance' cases. The benchmark for the different levels of knowledge is the earlier case of *Baden v Société Générale pour Favoriser le Développement du Commerce et de l'Industrie en France SA*.[10] *Baden* put forward five different levels of knowledge:

(1) actual knowledge;
(2) wilfully shutting one's eyes to the obvious;
(3) wilfully and recklessly failing to make such inquiries as an honest and reasonable man would make;
(4) knowledge of circumstances which would indicate the facts to an honest and reasonable man; and

---

[8] The liability for dishonest assistance should not properly be viewed as arising in tort. See *Crédit Lyonnais Bank Nederland v Export Credits Guarantee Department* [1998] 1 Lloyd's Rep 19, 36.

[9] *Springfield Acres Ltd (In Liquidation) v Abacus (Hong Kong)* [1994] 3 NZLR 502 (High Ct, New Zealand), for example, accepts the distinction between knowing assistance and knowing receipt.

[10] [1992] 4 All ER 161, 235; [1993] 509, 575–6.

(5) knowledge of circumstances which will put an honest and reasonable man
on inquiry.

The first three categories have generally been accepted as actual knowledge **11.16**
or its equivalent, and the latter two as constructive knowledge. This is by no
means conclusive, however. Indeed, in *Agip (Africa) Ltd v Jackson*,[11] Millett J
warned against a too ready assumption that categories (4) and (5) constituted
constructive knowledge.

The *Baden* categorization of knowledge is not without difficulty and courts have **11.17**
experienced problems in applying it, both in knowing assistance and knowing
receipt cases. It was the view of Nourse LJ in *Bank of Credit and Commerce
International (Overseas) Ltd (in liquidation) and another v Akindele*,[12] that the
levels of knowledge itemized in *Baden* were formulated with knowing assistance
in mind and may not be as useful in knowing receipt cases. However, even in
knowing assistance cases today, the *Baden* test is seldom used since the landmark
decision of *Royal Brunei v Tan*,[13] which also found it unhelpful.

Nonetheless, the element of knowledge itself continues to appear in the case law **11.18**
either with other tests (such as dishonesty), or on its own. It appears even in
those cases where the courts go to great lengths to decipher the test only to
equate it to something else.[14] While Lord Nicholls in *Royal Brunei* found that
the *Baden* categorization was best forgotten,[15] it is clear that his own test of
dishonesty relies essentially on the state of knowledge which can be attributed to
a third party. Perhaps the true interpretation of his dicta is that knowledge alone
is not sufficient to ground liability. It must amount to something else—
dishonesty.[16] The *Baden* expression of knowledge may not be entirely helpful,
but knowledge itself is not to be discounted. None of the other tests suggests
that a defendant who had no idea, or who could not reasonably be expected to
have any idea, of the wrongdoing could be liable.

---

[11] [1992] 4 All ER 385, 404.
[12] [2000] 4 All ER 221 (CA).
[13] Above, n 2.
[14] Such as unconscionable conduct, as in *Akindele*, above, n 12, 235, *per* Nourse LJ: 'All that is
necessary is that the recipient's state of knowledge should be such as to make it unconscionable for
him to retain the benefit of the receipt.'
[15] [1995] 3 All ER 97, 109; [1995] 2 AC 378, 392; [1995] 3 WLR 64, 76.
[16] What Lord Nicholls actually said was: ' "Knowingly" is better avoided as a *defining ingredient* of the principle, and in the context of this principle the *Baden* scale of knowledge is best
forgotten': ibid, emphasis added. Discussed further below, at paras 11.21–11.26.

B. Knowing Assistance or Dishonest Assistance

11.19   The first requirement in locating liability for knowing or dishonest assistance, is the actual breach of trust or fiduciary duty, which is the prerequisite for the defendant's assistance. It is not necessary for the defendant to have received any trust property, or to have benefited personally from the breach of trust. Similarly, the trustee who commits the breach need not have acted dishonestly. An innocent breach will suffice.[17]

11.20   As far as the third party is concerned, however, it is now established that the element of knowledge is not sufficient in knowing assistance cases and that dishonesty must be present. Put another way, the test for knowledge has been redefined and the level of knowledge required amounts to dishonesty. The head of liability is, therefore, now more legitimately to be called 'dishonest assistance'. However, while dishonesty is the key ingredient in dishonest assistance cases, as noted earlier, knowledge, and the degree of knowledge which can be attributed to a third party, remains pivotal to the assessment of liability in both dishonest assistance and knowing receipt cases.

The *Royal Brunei* test for dishonesty

11.21   The test for dishonesty put forward in *Royal Brunei*[18] is a composite of both subjective and objective elements. It is an objective standard in so far that a comparative assessment is undertaken to determine the reasonableness of the act. The assistor's action, although it may be done in a genuine or 'honest belief', must be measured against another person in his or her position (for example, the reasonable solicitor), to ascertain whether the impeached act is reasonable or unreasonable. The assistor is not to be judged according to his or her own moral standard, as a person may genuinely believe that what he or she is doing is morally justified but it may still be wrong or unlawful—the 'Robin Hood' scenario.

11.22   A later case, *Armitage v Nurse*,[19] appeared to deviate substantially from the influential decision of *Royal Brunei* on the concept of dishonesty. In *Armitage* it was stated that trustees could deliberately commit a breach of trust, but their conduct would not be fraudulent if 'they did so in good faith and in the honest belief that they are acting in the interest of the beneficiaries'.[20] This seemed to

---

[17] On this latter point, the Canadian courts have deviated. See *Air Canada v M & L Travel Ltd Martin and Valliant* [1993] 3 SCR 787, approved in *Gold v Rosenberg et al* (1995) 86 OAC 116.
[18] Above, n 2.
[19] [1997] 2 All ER 705 (CA).
[20] ibid, 710, *per* Millett J.

imply that the test was solely a subjective one. The trustee in this scenario, even if misguided, is genuine in his desire to act for the benefit of the beneficiaries. Consequently, he cannot be liable. Nonetheless, the court in *Walker and Others v Stones and Another*[21] felt that the two cases of *Armitage* and *Royal Brunei* could be satisfactorily reconciled. The reconciliatory approach in *Walker* was followed closely in *Publishers Representatives Ltd and Lee Sku Kee v UBS (Cayman Islands) Ltd.*[22] Sir Christopher Slade in *Walker* did not believe that the court in *Armitage* was attempting to distinguish *Royal Brunei*, or create a different test for dishonesty.[23] Rather, he believed that Millett J was directing his mind to 'judicious breaches of trust' and did not intend his dictum to apply in a case where a solicitor-trustee's perception of the interests of the beneficiaries was so unreasonable that no reasonable solicitor-trustee could have held such a belief.[24]

Thus, the purely subjective standard was rightly rejected in cases such as **11.23** *Twinsectra Ltd v Yardley and Others*[25] and *Walker and Others v Stones and Another.*[26] In *Walker*, Sir Christopher Slade explained the test this way: 'A person may in some cases act dishonestly . . . even though he genuinely believes that his action is morally justified.' A classic example, suggests the judge, is that of a penniless thief who picks the pocket of a millionaire.

Going further, as explained by Lord Hutton in *Twinsectra*,[27] *Royal Brunei* is not **11.24** to be taken to mean that a third party can be held liable even though he does not realize that what that party has done is dishonest by the ordinary standards of honest people. Rather, the third party must himself or herself appreciate that what has been done is dishonest by the standards of honest and reasonable men. Indeed, Lord Nicholls in *Royal Brunei* must have meant this when he suggested that, in most cases, an honest person would have little difficulty in knowing whether his participation in a proposed transaction would offend the normally accepted standards of honest conduct.[28] Thus, in *Twinsectra*, it was accepted that there was an element of subjectivity in the equation. The majority in that case rejected Lord Millett's interpretation of *Royal Brunei* on the ground that it

---

[21] [2000] 4 All ER 412 (CA), 444.
[22] [2000] CILR 473.
[23] *Walker*, above, n 21, 445.
[24] ibid.
[25] [2002] 2 All ER 377, 383.
[26] Above, n 21, 444.
[27] Above, n 25, 384–5, Lord Millett dissenting. However, the majority view of Lords Hutton, Steyn, and Hoffman have been followed in later cases. See, eg, *Manolakaki v Constantinides* [2004] 1 All ER 47; *Papamichael v National Westminster Bank plc* [2003] EWHC 164 (Comm); and *Re Bank of Credit and Commerce International SA (in liquidation) (No 15); Morris and Others v Bank of India* [2004] 2 BCLC 279.
[28] *Royal Brunei Tan Kik Ming* [1995] 3 All ER 97, 107; [1995] 3 WLR 64, 73–4.

came too close to a purely subjective standard for dishonesty. Lord Hutton thus reintroduced the element of subjectivity into the equation.

11.25 The *Royal Brunei* test considers specific subjective elements such as, for example, the level of intelligence and experience of the third party who makes the decision to 'assist'. Note that in *Walker*, Sir Christopher Slade limited his discussion to the case of the solicitor-trustee, but conceded that the test of dishonesty may vary from case to case, depending on, among other things, the role and calling of the trustee.[29]

11.26 Lord Nicholls in *Royal Brunei* acknowledges that it is difficult to pinpoint what is dishonest in dishonest assistance cases. The baseline may be simply what is deemed to be 'commercially unacceptable conduct', as explained in *Cowan de Groot Properties Ltd v Eagle Trust plc*.[30] At the end of the day, the defendant's state of knowledge is still an important factor in assessing his or her honesty, as well as his or her personal attributes, which demonstrate how he or she is able to assess that knowledge. A genuinely foolish person will therefore not be in the same position as a genius even though they both had the same information, and the answers as to their respective levels of honesty may be different.

No requirement for dishonesty on the part of the trustee

11.27 While the accessory must have acted dishonestly, it is not essential for the trustee or fiduciary who commits the breach to have acted dishonestly. This speaks plainly to situations such as, for example, where sophisticated third party advisers take advantage of innocent trustees, encouraging them unknowingly to commit breaches of trust. In fact, this situation mounts a stronger claim to liability on the part of the third party.

11.28 In coming to its decision, the Privy Council in *Royal Brunei* rejected the confines of the earlier line of authority flowing from *Barnes v Addy*,[31] which had hitherto linked third party liability to a dishonest and fraudulent design on the part of the trustee. In their Lordships' view, the approach following *Barnes v Addy* (that case had in fact concerned fraud on the part of the trustee) had been inimical to the analysis of the underlying concept.[32] It was therefore necessary to examine why a third party who had received no trust property was liable at all. This line of questioning led the Privy Council to hold that the basis for such liability was, in fact, dishonesty on the part of the third party, and not necessarily

---

[29] Above, n 21.
[30] [1992] 4 All ER 700, 761.
[31] See above, n 3.
[32] Above, n 2, [1995] 3 WLR 64, 70.

on the part of the trustee. As discussed above, the court went on to find a suitable test for such dishonesty.

Negligence

While *Royal Brunei* has often been interpreted to mean that negligence can   **11.29**
never be taken as a ground of liability in third party cases, a closer look at the judgment reveals that the possibility of negligence is not ignored. Lord Nicholls did not rule out the heading of negligence entirely. Rather, he found that negligence will ground liability only in an exceptional case.

He makes a distinction between those situations where the third party is an   **11.30**
adviser or fiduciary in relation to the trustee, such as is often the case with consultants, bankers, agents and so on, and where the third party is not in such a position.[33] A person in the role of an adviser or fiduciary owes the trustee a duty to exercise reasonable skill and care and is, therefore, accountable to the trustee. The presumption here is that we are speaking of an honest trustee, as different considerations apply in relation to the dishonest trustee.[34] The rights flowing from such a duty of care form part of the trust property. In such situations, the beneficiaries may enforce such rights if the trustees are unable or unwilling to do so. The logical implication here is that the enforcement of any such right must be confined only to breaches of trust which arise as a direct result of those fiduciary obligations or duties to take care, and will be exceptional cases.

Then there are third parties who are neither advisers nor fiduciaries owing duties   **11.31**
of care. Such third parties may not have the obligations accruing to fiduciaries imposed on them without good reasons.

In the case of third parties who act for or deal with dishonest trustees, however,   **11.32**
Royal Brunei and its progeny now make it clear that mere negligence on the part of the third party is not sufficient to ground liability and cannot be equated to dishonesty. There is no duty placed on a third party to 'check that a trustee is not misbehaving'. All that is required is that the third party acts honestly. As all investment involves some level of risk and mere imprudence is not dishonesty, as 'a general proposition . . . beneficiaries cannot reasonably expect that all the world dealing with their trustees should owe them a duty to take care lest the trustees are behaving dishonestly'.[35]

However, not all courts have been comfortable with the view that negligence is   **11.33**

---

[33] ibid, 75.
[34] Recall that under the *Royal Brunei* principle, an honest trustee who commits a breach of trust or fiduciary power can now bring into effect liability on the part of the third party.
[35] *Royal Brunei*, above, n 2, [1995] 3 WLR 64, 76.

generally an inappropriate ground for liability in relation to strangers to the trust. For example, the New Zealand courts, partly because of the difficulty of fitting into the *Baden* knowledge scale alluded to earlier, have not ruled out negligence but have sometimes preferred to use other terminology, such as 'unconscionable behaviour'.[36] Consider that *Royal Brunei* was a decision from the Judicial Committee of the Privy Council but has been influential even outside of New Zealand.

Reckless indifference

11.34 Reckless indifference to or disregard of another's rights or interests may constitute dishonesty for the purposes of the dishonest assistance test. This was confirmed in *Royal Brunei*[37] and approved in *Walker*.[38] While mere carelessness or imprudence is not dishonesty, 'imprudence may be carried recklessly to lengths which call into question the honesty of the person making the decision'.[39] The honest person, therefore, must use the information or knowledge available to him or her, and use it wisely. He or she cannot simply ignore it, or pretend that he or she is unaware of it. In some cases, and particularly where he or she is in doubt, he or she may need to seek advice.

Royal Brunei the standard for all cases of dishonesty in civil cases?

11.35 Aside from the distinctions in the elements which ground the heads of liability of dishonest assistance and knowing receipt, it appears that the *Royal Brunei* test, of a combined subjective and objective standard, has emerged as the applicable test for all civil law cases where dishonesty is in issue, and is not confined to dishonest assistance cases. This was the approach taken in *Walker and Others v Stones and Another*[40] and in *Publishers*.[41]

11.36 Consider *Publishers*[42] and *Walker*.[43] In both cases, the defendants were trustees and not third parties. In issue was whether the defendants, as solicitors acting as trustees, had committed breaches of trust which were dishonest. In both cases, the courts adopted the test for honesty in *Royal Brunei*,[44] finding that in the case of a solicitor-trustee, the question was not whether he had genuinely believed

---

[36] See, eg, *Powell v Thompson* [1991] 1 NZLR 597, 615.

[37] Above, n 2.

[38] See above, n 21, 448. See also *Twinsectra*, above, n 25, although the defendant in that case was not found to be dishonest, and *Armitage*, above, n 19.

[39] *Royal Brunei*, above, n 2, [1995] 3 All ER 97, 106–107. See also, *Publishers*, above, n 22, *per* Sanderson J, 481.

[40] Above, n 21.

[41] See above, n 22.

[42] ibid.

[43] See above, n 21.

[44] See above, n 2.

that he was acting honestly. Instead, the objective test was to be employed, that is, whether his so-called 'honest belief', though actually held, was so unreasonable that no reasonable solicitor-trustee could have thought that what he did or agreed to do was for the benefit of the beneficiaries. Thus, although the test in *Royal Brunei* arose in a case of accessory liability, it is now to be expanded to other avenues of liability. Unlike in criminal cases, it is now impossible to eliminate reference to objective standards in civil cases.[45]

C. Knowing Receipt

Introduction

Traditionally, in knowing receipt cases, what is required to establish liability is **11.37** that the third party received trust property as a result of a breach of another's fiduciary duty, or in breach of the trust, and the third party had knowledge that the property so received was as a result of that breach. Identifying these elements allows the plaintiff to trace his or her assets. In *El Anjou v Dollar Land Holdings plc*,[46] Lord Hoffmann helpfully summarized the three distinct elements that a plaintiff must establish, placing them within the context of tracing. These are:

(1) disposal of his or her assets in breach of a fiduciary duty;
(2) beneficial receipt by the defendant of assets which are traceable as representing the assets of the plaintiff; and
(3) knowledge on the part of the defendant that the assets he or she received are traceable to a breach of fiduciary duty.

Yet in more recent times, locating the touchstone of liability in knowing receipt **11.38** cases has been difficult for the courts. It is clear that the receiver need not have been directly involved in the actual breach and that knowledge is required. However, there are areas of contention, particularly with regard to the appropriate level of knowledge necessary to ground a knowing receipt claim, and whether dishonesty is an ingredient in that requisite knowledge. Where knowledge is found to be the appropriate test, there is a broader category of knowledge which is applicable than in dishonest assistance cases (for example, all five levels of *Baden* may be applicable). At the very least, it is incontestable that a third party who is wilfully blind, or who recklessly disregards an obvious

---

[45] *Walker*, n 21 above, 444.
[46] [1994] 2 All ER 685,700. Followed in *Caltong (Australia) Pty Ltd (formerly Tong Tien See Holding (Australia) Pty Ltd) and Another v Tong Tien See Construction Pty Ltd (in liquidation) and Another* (2002) 5 ITELR 187 (CA, Singapore).

inference that the property received is in breach of trust, is liable.[47] Thus, the state of the law on knowing receipt remains unsettled.

Threshold of liability

11.39   Despite the difficulty of concluding a final test for knowing receipt, at minimum there seems to be some consensus that liability for knowing receipt requires a lower threshold than liability for knowing or dishonest assistance. It is perhaps appropriate that persons who receive property are placed under higher duties of accountability than those who act in situations of doubtful responsibility. At any rate, as explained above, the question may now be academic, at least where fraud for unlawful activity is involved, or perhaps even for tax transactions. This is because, in the bulk of cases, it takes the third party into the realm of the criminal law.

Actual knowledge or constructive knowledge

11.40   The earlier and more consistent school of thought on what constitutes knowledge for the purpose of knowing receipt is that both actual knowledge and constructive knowledge can ground the head of liability.

11.41   In *Bank of Credit and Commerce International (Overseas) Ltd (in liquidation) and another v Akindele*,[48] Nourse LJ deviated from earlier Court of Appeal decisions which found that either actual or constructive knowledge was sufficient to ground liability for knowing receipt, choosing to follow first instance judges, in particular Megarry VC in the case of *Montague's Settlement Trusts, Re Duke of Manchester v National Westminster Bank Ltd (1985)*.[49] In *Montague*, Megarry VC laid down a test based only on actual knowledge, finding that constructive knowledge was not sufficient to ground liability.

11.42   The proposition put forward by Megarry VC in *Montague* was based on his distinction between the rules for a purchaser without notice, leading to a doctrine of tracing, and the person who receives property under a constructive trust. Only in the latter context does a person have imposed upon him or her the personal obligations and burdens of trusteeship. For such obligations to be imposed by equity there needs to be a higher threshold to establish liability, and the receiver's conscience must be taken into account. His or her conscience must have been sufficiently affected to justify the imposition of the constructive trust. This is because these personal obligations go beyond mere property rights

---

[47]   See, eg, *Hampshire Cosmetic and MutschMann* [1999] CILR 21 (Grand Ct, CI) 31, following *Eagle Trust plc v SBC Securities Ltd* [1992] 4 All ER 488 (ChD).
[48]   Above, n 12.
[49]   [1992] 4 All ER 308.

as in the case of the purchaser without notice. As such, the two doctrines, the equitable doctrine of tracing and the imposition of a constructive trust, are governed by different rules and must be kept distinct.[50]

In *Hampshire Cosmetic v Mutschmann*,[51] the Grand Court of the Cayman Islands discussed the well-known case of *Agip (Africa) Ltd v Jackson*,[52] which had found that constructive knowledge was pertinent. This was in a situation where clandestine circumstances suggested impropriety, and professional persons involved in the offshore sector ought to have been aware of the risk of laundering money on the behalf of fraudsters.

11.43

Smellie J in *Hampshire* was undecided as to whether the *Agip* approach was appropriate. In any case, the circumstances did not suggest constructive knowledge of the head of liability involved. Interestingly, he found that circumstances suggesting mere impropriety could not impute constructive notice of fraud. Specifically, the defendant had had constructive knowledge that there was impropriety, but she had believed that the impropriety was tax avoidance. She could not, therefore, be held to have had constructive knowledge of fraud. Nevertheless, the wilful blindness of the defendant to the breach of trust was sufficient to raise liability.

11.44

Judges subsequent to *Montague* had been reluctant to adopt Megarry VC's dicta wholesale,[53] but appeared willing to apply it to commercial transaction cases, on the reasoning that 'if we were to extend the doctrine of constructive notice to commercial transactions, we should be doing infinite mischief and paralysing the trade of the country'.[54] This appears to be good news for offshore trusts, which are essentially commercial entities. However, while the courts appear to be reluctant readily to import liability for knowing receipt in commercial cases, they are also mindful that persons should not be allowed to escape liability for wrongdoing on the excuse of the 'exigencies of commercial life'.[55] In relation to third parties, there is, therefore, a balance to be struck between commercial expediency and the extended reach of equity in order to effect culpability.

11.45

Further, some cases suggest that knowledge, in the sense of the *Baden* test, is not to be used as a reliable test in knowing receipt cases at all. This was the view of

11.46

---

[50] *Montague*, above, n 49, 329–30.
[51] [1999] CILR 21.
[52] [1990] Ch 265; [1992] 4 All ER 385; on appeal [1991] Ch 547; [1992] 4 All ER 45.
[53] See, eg, *Eagle Trust plc v SBC Securities Ltd*, above, n 47, 506. See also *Cowan Groot Properties Ltd v Eagle Trust plc*, above, n 30.
[54] *Bank of Credit and Commerce International (Overseas) Ltd (in liquidation) and another v Akindele*, above, n 12, 234, quoting *Manchester Trust v Furness* [1895] 2 QB 539, 545.
[55] *Akindele*, ibid.

Nourse LJ in *Akindele*, who rejected the *Baden* categorization of knowledge[56] as unhelpful and too difficult. He preferred a 'single test of knowledge for knowing receipt. The recipient's state of knowledge must be such as to make it unconscionable for him to retain the benefit of the receipt.'[57] In his view, 'unconscionable conduct' was the hallmark for identifying liability in knowing receipt cases. Whether knowledge was actual or constructive was not the point.[58] In so doing, Nourse LJ disowned his own previous dicta in the case of *Houghton and Others v Fayers and Day*,[59] where he had found that constructive knowledge was sufficient to establish knowing receipt.[60] Note that the Judicial Committee of the Privy Council in *Royal Brunei v Tan*[61] had discussed the suggestion that the test for liability be that of unconscionable conduct and had found it wanting and vague.[62] It was acceptable only where it could be equated to dishonesty, in which case, 'dishonest conduct', was thought to be the better term.[63]

Dishonesty not the test for knowing receipt

11.47   Since the *Royal Brunei* decision, the debate on the appropriate test for assessing knowing receipt cases has become more complicated. What the *Royal Brunei* line of cases should *not* be taken to mean is that the test for both dishonest assistance and knowing receipt is now to be equated to dishonesty. Although some courts have strayed, the weight of opinion is in favour of the view that dishonesty is not required for knowing receipt cases, whereas it is for dishonest assistance cases. This is what Rix J of the Court of Appeal, in the case of *Dubai Aluminium Company Ltd v Salaam and Others*,[64] failed to appreciate in his obiter statement:

> In the light of *Tan*, the question arises whether the mental element of 'knowing' is to have the same content in knowing receipt as in what should now be called 'dishonest assistance' . . . in case he[65] was wrong to say . . . that constructive

---

[56] Above, n 10.

[57] *Akindele*, above, n 12, 235.

[58] ibid.

[59] (2000) 2 ITELR 512.

[60] He noted that previous decisions had not considered the question in depth. *Akindele*, n 12 above, 231.

[61] Above, n 2.

[62] Further, it was not a term in 'everyday use by non-lawyers': [1995] 3 WLR 64, 76.

[63] The English courts appear to take a different stance to those of other parts of the Commonwealth, such as in New Zealand and Canada, on the question of the appropriate test for knowing receipt cases. There, the preponderance of authority is in favour of the view that constructive knowledge is enough. See, eg, *Westpac Banking Corporation v Savin* [1985] 2 NZLR 41. There, the head of liability seems squarely rooted in the doctrine of unjust enrichment and restitution, which leads to an acceptance of constructive notice. See also *Alers-Hankey v Solomon et al* [2002] BCCA 227 (CA, British Columbia).

[64] [2003] 2 All ER 451.

[65] Meaning the judge in *Cowan de Groot Properties Ltd v Eagle Trust plc*, above, n 30, whose judgment was approved in *Royal Brunei v Tan*, above, n 2.

knowledge would not suffice to render a defendant liable in knowing receipt. It seems to me that in the circumstances, the test in knowing receipt and dishonest assistance is likely to be the same.

Rather, the claim of knowing receipt remains essentially grounded in know- **11.48**
ledge, whether actual or constructive, or knowledge linked to 'unconscionable' conduct and without the need for proof of dishonesty. However, given that the *Royal Brunei* test of objectivity is now to be the universal standard for all civil law suits invoking dishonesty, where a person is alleged knowingly and dishonestly to have received, his or her dishonesty must be measured against the *Royal Brunei* test. Dishonesty, therefore, being a higher threshold, is a sufficient but not a necessary element in knowing receipt cases. Knowing receipt should remain within the categories of restitution and unjust enrichment.

The dishonesty test for knowing receipt claims was specifically rejected in **11.49**
Akindele[66] and in *Twinsectra Ltd v Yardley*,[67] where Lord Millett disagreed with *Twinsectra's* earlier Court of Appeal judgment which had applied the dishonesty test,[68] upholding instead a test of constructive knowledge as sufficient for knowing receipt cases. In Canada too, the clear distinction between dishonest assistance and knowing receipt survives in cases such as *Alers-Hankey v Solomon et al*,[69] *Citadel General Insurance Company v Lloyds Bank*,[70] *Canada, Lac Minerals Ltd v International Corona Resources Ltd*,[71] *Air Canada v British Columbia*,[72] and *Air Canada v M & L Travel Ltd, Martin and Valliant*.[73]

In *Alers-Hankey*, the Court of Appeal of British Columbia explained the different **11.50**
rationales of the two offences:

> The rationale and remedy for knowing receipt are restitutionary. The knowing recipient must . . . return his benefit and restore to the plaintiff on the grounds of unjust enrichment . . . the doctrine of knowing assistance does not depend on the defendant being enriched. Rather, that rationale is fault-based and equity intervenes to protect the plaintiff's proprietary interest where the defendant actually knew that he was an accessory to reprehensible conduct by the trustee.[74]

This points in favour of an argument for constructive notice. It should be pointed out, however, that by speaking of 'unconscionable' conduct within the

---

[66] Above, n 12.
[67] Above, n 25, 383.
[68] [1999] Lloyd's Rep 438 (reversed on appeal).
[69] Above, n 63.
[70] [1999] 3 SCR 805.
[71] [1989] 2 SCR 574, 669.
[72] [1989] 1 SCR 1161, 1202–03.
[73] [1993] 3 SCR 787, 809–11; 108 DLR (4th) 592, 606–08.
[74] See above, n 63, 239, para 20, quoting from PM Perell in his article 'Intermeddlers or Strangers to the Breach of Trust or Fiduciary Duty' (1998) 21 Adv Q 94, 113.

context of knowledge, one draws remarkably close to what the layperson might describe as dishonest behaviour.

Receipt for personal benefit

11.51 For knowing receipt to be established, it is not required that the receiver receives the property for his or her own benefit, or retains possession of the property. It is enough that he or she acts as the owner of the property and exercises control over it at the time of the receipt.[75] This is to be distinguished from the situation where the receiver is a mere agent. In *Springfield Acres Ltd (In Liquidation) v Abacus (Hong Kong)*,[76] Abacus received funds from a company engaged in an attempt to avoid creditors reaching certain assets. Abacus, which was the trustee of a trust in which the beneficiaries had an interest in the avoidance of the creditors, then transferred the funds to another company. The argument that the defendant was merely an agent in such a situation, since it was not the owner of the funds, was rejected. Since Abacus had had control over the funds, there had been a breach of a constructive trust, and the trustee was liable under the knowing receipt head.

D. Special Parties and Strangers Who Assist or Receive

Vicarious liability for partners to strangers who dishonestly assist or knowingly receive

11.52 A question which arises is the extent to which partners to persons involved in dishonest assistance or knowing receipt may be held liable in equity. Given the multi-tiered structure of the typical offshore trust, with the common usage of partnerships and other corporate entities, this is an important question in offshore trust law. This issue was recently considered in the cases of *Dubai Aluminium Company Ltd v Salaam and Others*[77] and *Walker*.[78] It is necessary to make a distinction between persons who are partners to trustees and those who are partners to mere third parties. In the aforementioned cases, the distinction was between trustee-solicitors and solicitors who were not acting as trustees.

11.53 The case of *Dubai Aluminium Company Ltd v Salaam and Others*[79] establishes that vicarious liability for a partner's wrongful acts would be imposed only

---

[75] *Springfield Acres Ltd (In Liquidation) v Abacus (Hong Kong)* [1994] 3 NZLR 502 (High Ct, New Zealand).

[76] ibid.

[77] Above, n 64.

[78] Above, n 21.

[79] Above, n 64.

where all the acts or omissions which were necessary to make the partner personally liable had taken place in the course of the firm's business, or the course of his or her employment. A determination on this question depends on the closeness of the connection between the duties, which, in broad terms, the partner or employee was authorized to perform, and his or her wrongdoing.

Here, the acts of assistance in question, the drafting by a partner of bogus **11.54** consultancy agreements, which led to the claimant becoming a victim of fraud, were so closely connected with the acts that he was authorized to do, that they could fairly be regarded as part of the ordinary course of the firm's business. As these acts were in themselves sufficient to establish equitable liability on the part of the partner, they could ground vicarious liability on the part of the firm.

The approach followed in *Walker v Stones and Another*[80] distinguished *Dubai* **11.55** from cases where the wrongdoing partner is also the trustee. The court here found that breaches of trust committed by a trustee-partner fell outside of the ordinary business of a partnership and were therefore incapable of giving rise to vicarious liability. While the court here was interpreting a local statute,[81] the rationale for the principle appears to be broad-based, that is, that individual trusteeships which a partner might undertake are not undertaken in the ordinary course of the firm's business.[82]

This is a viable proposition except, of course, in those situations where the **11.56** partners of the trustee-partner had authorized him to so act on their behalf in respect of the alleged breaches of trust. In the latter case, the trustee-partner could not be said to be acting independently, and the other partners should be held vicariously liable if they meet the test laid down by *Dubai*.

Liability as an agent—ministerial receipt

Where the third party is a mere agent and receives property in his ministerial **11.57** capacity, liabilities arising out of associated breaches of trust will not normally be imposed on him. The rationale here is that the third party is not in control of the acts or omissions associated with the breach and should not be penalized for it. He is merely following his principal's instructions as to how to deal with the property so received. However, the rules on ministerial receipt should now be read together with new developments in knowing receipt, bearing in mind that the latter are in a state of flux.

The protection granted to such agents does not extend to third-party agents **11.58**

---

[80] Above, n 21.
[81] The Partnership Act 1890, ss 10 and 13.
[82] See above, n 21, 452–4.

who have dishonestly assisted in the breach of trust or fiduciary duty. Further, the protection does not cover trustees de son tort,[83] or situations where the third party agent has received the property for his or her own benefit.[84]

11.59 In *Toukhmanian v Ansbacher (Bahamas) Ltd*,[85] the Supreme Court of The Bahamas held that such an agent would also be immune where he or she honestly believes that the property is not trust property, even in the face of suspicious circumstances which could have put him or her on notice of the breach. This, however, is a very generous interpretation of the protection offered to such an agent, given the move in the English courts to extend third-party liability to situations where the third party is reckless or indifferent. The decision should also be considered in the light of the liberal meaning given to dishonesty in *Royal Brunei*.[86] The result is that such a third party is protected only when placed on notice, if a reasonable third party would have not heeded the suspicious circumstances. He or she will not be protected if he or she turns a 'blind eye' to the obvious and recklessly disregards the evidence before him or her.

Liability as a trustee de son tort

11.60 Where a stranger to the trust performs the functions of the trustee and controls and administers the trust property, that person will be liable as a trustee de son tort in the same way as would a trustee if, in so doing, he or she commits a breach of trust. The trustee de son tort is not an agent acting on the behalf of the trustee. Rather, he or she is one who holds himself or herself out as a substitute trustee, having control over the property. The fundamental requirement here is that the substitute has taken control of the property and is not acting merely as an agent. Note that the trustee de son tort is not personally liable simply for the assumption of duties of a trustee, but only if he or she commits a breach of trust while acting as a trustee.[87]

Identifiable parties

11.61 In relation to companies accused of dishonest assistance or knowing receipt, it is not necessary to identify the particular individuals who were dishonest or acted unlawfully. The relevant test is whether the 'directing mind and will of the

---

[83] See below, para 11.60.

[84] The distinction between mere agents and third parties who accrue liability was explained in *Barnes v Addy*, above n 3.

[85] (Sup Ct, The Bahamas) No 561 of 1997, decided 8 August 1997.

[86] Above, n 2.

[87] *Air Canada v M & L Travel Ltd* [1993] 3 SCR 787, 808–09. See also *Merrit v Klijn and Others Bar C Ranch and Cattle Co Ltd v Merrit* (2003) 5 ITELR 461 (Court of Queen's Bench, Alberta, Calgary).

company' had the requisite knowledge or was dishonest.[88] This does not obstruct the more general rule that where the natural persons who control or manage the company have knowledge of the wrongful act, that knowledge is deemed to be knowledge on the part of the company for purposes of liability.[89]

Accessory liability of directors of trustee companies

The directors of a trustee company may be liable for accessory or third-party liability where there is a breach of trust. For this liability to arise, the requirement of dishonesty must be met under the *Royal Brunei v Tan Kik Ming* test.[90]   **11.62**

E. Other Avenues for Liability

Liability in equity does not preclude liability in tort

The case of *Publishers Representatives Ltd and Lee Sku Kee v UBS (Cayman Islands) Ltd*[91] is authority for the proposition that an independent action in tort for negligence can be pursued together with an equitable claim for breach of trust, as opposed to merely claiming a negligent breach of trust. The court found that there was no authority that precluded the bringing together of these two independent causes of action in a single case.   **11.63**

The principle cannot be expressed broadly, however, and should be confined to negligence by trustees. It will not apply, for example, in knowing receipt and dishonest assistance claims which are brought contemporaneously with claims of negligence. This is because, unlike in the case of a trustee, it is established that third parties are not liable for mere negligence.[92]   **11.64**

Indeed, the *Publishers* case is itself unclear, as the true identity of the defendant, whether trustee or accessory, was not established by the court. The defendant himself argued that he was no longer the trustee and could not therefore be liable for the breach. While the court discussed the principles of accessory liability, it made no certain finding on the point. In addition, part of the alleged dishonesty or negligence was the actual transfer of trusteeship (to another who had been known to be fraudulent), which confuses the issue.   **11.65**

---

[88] *Publishers*, above, n 22, 485.
[89] See, eg, *Belmont Finance Corporation v Williams Furniture Ltd (No 2)* [1980] 1 All ER 393.
[90] [1995] 2 AC 378. See the discussion of the liability of directors generally in chapter 12, 'Liability of Directors of Offshore Corporate Trustees'. See also *Cross v Benitrust* (1998–99) 1 ITELR 341 (CA), J M Collins, QC.
[91] Above, n 22
[92] See above, the *Royal Brunei* line of cases, paras 11.21–11.36.

Effect of anti-money laundering laws on knowing receipt and dishonest assistance

11.66   It is important to note the extent to which the recent anti-money laundering statutes, prevalent in offshore jurisdictions and elsewhere, have made the knowing receipt and dishonest assistance heads of liability, if not obsolete, certainly less attractive where money laundering offences are concerned. Anti-money laundering and proceeds of crime laws make offences such as receiving property obtained under unlawful means, or facilitating money laundering, much easier to prosecute, using standards of criminal liability as clearly defined in the relevant statute. This is in contrast to the elusive standards of liability in civil law matters.[93] Third party liabilities associated with transactions relating to the trust and trustees themselves, may be brought under such legislation.[94]

Failure to advise on offshore options

11.67   Much of our discussion has been with respect to third-party liabilities where they have, in some way, facilitated breaches of trust. There is, however, another interesting possibility which arises. Can a third party incur liability in relation to the trust, or more appropriately, the parties to the trust, even before it is established? The answer to this question is 'Yes' and, unsurprisingly, the question of negligent advice will be raised.

11.68   The boundaries of negligent advice are unlimited. Certainly, where a professional gives negligent advice with respect to the elements necessary for the creation of the trust, he or she may be liable. More omissions would be where the professional gives erroneous advice to a 'would-be' settlor where fraudulent conveyances or a sham arise. The professional may be just as liable in negligence and, in the case of the former, may himself or herself be liable for fraud.

11.69   One may go further and impute liability to the professional where he or she fails altogether to advise X of the possibility of establishing an offshore trust which may offer significant advantages to him. This duty will be most evident in relation to tax planning and tax mitigation opportunities. Possibly, it may extend beyond this to situations where X should properly be advised that a trust is the best vehicle for his other financial activities, for example, his asset protection objectives.

---

[93] See R-M B Antoine, *Confidentiality in Offshore Financial Law* (Oxford University Press, Oxford, 2002), for an analysis of anti-money laundering laws in offshore jurisdictions.

[94] See the case of *C v M* (2002) 4 ITELR 548 (Sup Ct, The Bahamas), in relation to the duties of a trustee and possible dishonest assistance liability, discussed more fully in chapter 10, paras 10.94–10.98.

An excellent opportunity to test this thesis arose in the case of *Slattery v Moore*   **11.70**
Stephens (a firm).[95] In this potentially explosive case, a tax adviser failed to advise
a non-domiciled resident of the UK that he could gain considerable tax advantages by placing his salary in an offshore trust in the Channel Islands, instead of
a UK bank. The taxpayer in this instance was an Irish and Canadian national
who was resident but, more important, not 'ordinarily resident' in the UK.
Accordingly, he would have been able to take advantage of the tax rule that his
income from abroad was taxable only if remitted to the UK.[96]

The court found the tax adviser to be negligent, in not advising what was, in the   **11.71**
eyes of the court, the obvious option to mitigate the taxpayer's tax liabilities by
utilizing an offshore entity. The taxpayer was also found to have contributed to
the negligence. It is apparent that, despite the facts, in which the offshore entity
here was an offshore bank, the principle for other offshore entities, including
trusts, remains the same.

---

[95] [2003] STC 1379; [2003] EWHC 1869.
[96] Under the Income and Corporation Taxes Act 1988, Cases II and III, Sch E.

12

LIABILITY OF DIRECTORS OF OFFSHORE CORPORATE TRUSTEES

A. Whether Directors are Liable for Breach of Trust

As we have noted, offshore trusts are often structured to include underlying **12.01** asset holding companies. The trust fund may be held by a company created specifically to act as the trustee. It is common for companies to be incorporated by trustees with the shares of such companies being held by the trustee company.[1] By way of example, in The Bahamas case of *Corso Gonzalez v The Chase Manahattan Corporation Ltd*,[2] the settlor, by letter, authorized the trustee to invest some of the trust assets in the purchase of 49% of the interest of the limited partner in a limited partnership. The letter further authorized the trustee to take steps to complete the investment. The trust also owned a holding company. The authorizing letter was expressed in the following terms:

> Arrange for the incorporation of one or more corporations and in whatever jurisdictions required and advisable, the shares of which are to be owned by this trust and I would wish your nominees to act as Directors or Officers.[3]

---

[1] Also known as a 'corporate trustee' or a 'trust company'.
[2] (Sup Ct, The Bahamas) No 1261 of 1992, decided 8 August 1994.
[3] ibid, 7.

12.02   Underlying companies are obviously important vehicles for investment. However, the trust corporate mechanism is often used to cloak a trust relationship with the protection of the corporate veil and the fundamental concept of limited liability which a company offers. It capitalizes on the law's recognition of the company as a separate and independent legal personality, under which the company itself is generally responsible for its wrongful acts and not its directors or shareholders.[4] The concept of the limited liability of companies in itself, perhaps, has often given reason for pause. Nonetheless, it continues to be upheld by the courts.

12.03   These offshore captive companies may actually have no substance. In *Bahamas International Trust Co Ltd v Wyckoff*,[5] Georges CJ described such companies as having 'no really independent existence. They have been created for the purpose of affording tax shelter and will be manipulated for that purpose.' He was referring to an arrangement whereby the trustee, a large international trust company in The Bahamas, had incorporated several companies in the British Virgin Islands but resident in The Bahamas. The directors and officers of the plaintiff companies were employees of the trustee company. All of the shares of the companies involved were owned by the trustee company as trustee for the trusts.

12.04   Trustee companies, or corporate trustees, are also useful for avoiding the inconvenience of repeated deeds of appointment and removal where trustees are changed. Further, they provide stability and simplify the process of registering and holding the assets of the trust.

12.05   The question arises whether directors of trustee companies can be held liable for breaches of trust committed by their trustee companies. The practical importance of wanting to impose liability on the directors instead of relying on the liability of the trustee company is that, often, the trustee company may have no funds (particularly in the case where the trustee company is administering only one trust). In contrast, the directors, the parent company, which may be perhaps even a bank which established the trustee company, might be wealthy.

12.06   Several questions may be raised with respect to the personal liability of these directors:

(1)   Whether directors are directly and personally liable for the breach of trust?
(2)   Whether the director may occur direct liability in tort?
(3)   Whether indirect liability for breach of duty, or in tort, may apply—often called 'dog leg claims'?

---

[4]   *Saloman v Saloman and Company Ltd* [1897] AC 22.
[5]   (Sup Ct, The Bahamas) No 466 of 1987, decided 31 May 1988, 7, *per* Georges CJ.

(4) Whether the director may be liable as an accessory to the breach of trust?[6]

In most offshore jurisdictions, the question of any liabilities accruing to directors **12.07** of trust companies is resolved by case law. The few existing provisions tend to be in accord with the evolving jurisprudence on the issue. An examination of this jurisprudence is, therefore, useful both for offshore jurisdictions which have legislated on the issue and for those which have not. The relevant statutory provisions are discussed below.[7]

B. Direct Liability for Breach of Trust

The question whether a director of a trustee company is directly and personally **12.08** liable for breaches of trust, is contingent upon an existing fiduciary duty owed by the director to the beneficiaries of the trust.

The issue is a provocative one mainly because it involves the application of **12.09** company law theory to a trust arrangement. Such a route does not satisfactorily resolve the issue, given the different philosophies underlying trust law and company law on the matters of applicable liabilities and fiduciary duties. More-over, much of company law is statutory. The rationale for the limited liability company is the maxim of profit through risk taking, the spirit of capitalist enterprise. In contrast, the trustee's function is a conservative one, limited to preserving the trust fund. In addition, the levels of decision-making are different. The company is envisioned as a composite structure and its decision-making methods reflect this, with power located at two levels, in the shareholders and in the directors. In contrast, the trust is seen essentially as a uniform decision-making structure, with power being located at one level only, through the trustee. Hence the need for more stringent rules of accountability to be located in the trustee.

It is not suggested that the corporate form, in itself, is inappropriate for the **12.10** trust. Rather, the rules on accountability perhaps do not reflect the realities of the obligations owed under the trust. Moreover, the trust arrangement which utilizes corporate trappings through a trustee corporation, often with nominee directors, might appear to be identical in real terms to a pure trust structure without directors. This might raise a presumption that liability should be inferred.

---

[6] The issue of third party liability generally is addressed in chapter 11.
[7] See paras 12.56–12.63. Cf the British Virgin Islands legislation, the Virgin Islands Special Trusts Act 2003, also discussed below, paras 12.60–12.61.

12.11   Based on common law principles, the question of liability was answered in the negative in the case of *Cross v Benitrust*,[8] which concerned an allegation by the plaintiff beneficiary that the directors of the trustee company had lost the trust funds of a Guernsey offshore trust through an imprudent investment.

12.12   The plaintiff contended that the directors owed him a fiduciary duty and should be held liable for the alleged breach of trust. The Guernsey Court of Appeal disagreed, finding that a director of a trust company owes a fiduciary duty only to the company itself and not to strangers of the trust company, such as the beneficiaries of the trust which the trustee company manages. The principle, as applied to trust companies, does not deviate from the general principle of company law on the fiduciary duties owed by directors.

12.13   Notwithstanding the finding that a fiduciary duty was absent, the Court did not rule out the possibility of such a fiduciary duty being implied in certain circumstances. It found that while such a relationship might arise by implication of law, the facts of the instant case did not raise it.[9] However, the court did not outline what those circumstances might be.

12.14   An earlier Australian case, *Hurley and Another v BGH Nominees Party Ltd*,[10] had also addressed directly the question of directors' liabilities as applied to trustee companies. The court found no authority establishing such liability and remained with the status quo. However, it conceded that such a duty might be identified in future decisions.

12.15   In *HR and Others v JAPT and Others*,[11] an employer company incorporated a corporate trustee to act as the trustee of a pension scheme established for the employees. The trustee company had no assets other than those held on the trusts of the scheme. The director of the corporate trustee had also been a director of the employer. The corporate trustee then lent a substantial sum from the pension scheme monies to the employer, which eventually resulted in a huge loss to the trust fund.

12.16   The court considered whether the director should be held personally liable for the loss caused to the beneficiaries. Four possible grounds of liability were assessed by Lindsay J:

(1)   direct fiduciary duty;
(2)   direct tortious duty;

---

[8]   (1998–99) 1 ITELR 341 (CA, Guernsey), relying on the well-known case of *Bath v Standard Co Ltd* [1911] 1 Ch 618 (CA).
[9]   *Cross*, n 8 above.
[10]   (1982) 31 SASR 250 (SC), *per* Walters J.
[11]   [1997] PLR 99; [1998–99] 2 OFLR 252.

(3) accessory liability;

(4) indirect fiduciary and indirect tortious duty.[12]

On the question of direct fiduciary duty, the court affirmed that it was a **12.17**
well-established principle that directors of a trustee company generally owe a
fiduciary duty only to the company and not to the beneficiaries. This court,
however, unlike that in *Cross v Benitrust*,[13] gave an indication of the accepted
deviations from the general principles. An exception was identified for the
situation where a director purported to act as a trustee rather than as a director.
In such a case, a director may owe a fiduciary duty to the beneficiaries, as well as
to the strangers dealing with the company. Notwithstanding, this was not the
situation in the instant case.

The rationale in this line of cases is the enduring principle of company law that **12.18**
a company is to be regarded as a separate entity and thereby exempted
from personal liability. Nonetheless, the question arises as to the accuracy of this
principle as applied to nominee directors of offshore trust companies where, in
practice, directors do not exercise independent power as the principles of
company law assume.

Despite the allusion made by the court in *Cross v Benitrust*,[14] to a fiduciary duty **12.19**
arising by implication, it would appear that the courts will be reluctant to imply
such a duty where provision is made for the liability of directors under statute.
Such provision is made, for example, in Guernsey,[15] and the Court of Appeal in
Cross v Benitrust had this to say:

> Specific legislation having been passed to govern the matter in question, it would
> not be appropriate for the court to search around to find some equitable or other
> principle by which to seek to replace or supplement such perfectly adequate
> legislation.[16]

C. Methods to Sidestep Limited Liability—Piercing the Corporate Veil

The protective corporate veil of a company may be pierced in certain specific **12.20**
situations. The limited liability protection granted to directors of a trustee

---

[12] The various heads of liability are considered in turn under the respective headings in this
chapter.
[13] Above, n 8.
[14] ibid.
[15] Under s 70 of the Trusts (Amendment) Act 1990.
[16] See above, n 8, 356. The legislation in this case imputed liability, see below, paras 12.62–
12.63.

company will then be dissolved. However, lifting the corporate veil is not an easy option. Further, it is sometimes difficult to predict in what circumstances the courts will consider it appropriate to recognize a company as having a separate legal personality and when it will ignore it, or declare the company a sham. Where the company is treated as a sham, the result will be that the director is treated as the 'alter ego' of the trustee, thereby incurring liability for the breach of trust.[17]

12.21 The threshold for piercing the corporate veil is high, and special circumstances indicating that the company is a 'mere facade concealing the true facts'[18] are required before an action will be successful.[19]

12.22 While the main allegation is that the company is a sham, facade, or concealment without real substance, other situations sometimes overlapping with the sham accusation may be identified as sufficient to allow the court to lift the corporate veil. They include instances where:

(1) the company has been incorporated specifically to evade obligations owed, or for some other improper purpose;

(2) the relationship between a parent company and a subsidiary reveals that the subsidiary is not independent from the parent, when the subsidiary may be ignored;

(3) the relationship between two companies is such that one company may be viewed as merely being an agent of another, when the agent may be ignored; and

(4) the company has shadow directors, that is, persons who actually direct the company and whose instructions the named directors follow.

12.23 Other situations where the corporate veil may be lifted are more uncertain. They include:

(5) where the company is involved in some wrongdoing; and

(6) where it is necessary in the interests of justice.

Wrongdoing and in the interest of justice

12.24 The last two categories were expressly rejected as too wide in *Trustor AB v Smallbone and Another No 2*.[20] The court here preferred to follow the principle

---

[17] Theoretically, if the beneficiary succeeds in piercing the corporate veil, we are no longer speaking of directors' liability since the director is now being treated as if he or she were the trustee.

[18] *Woolfson v Stratchlyde Regional Council* [1978] 1 AC 59, 67 (HL).

[19] ibid, 65.

[20] [2001] 3 All ER 987.

in *Woolfson*,[21] that the special circumstances of a mere facade must exist. *Trustor* is also estranged from the proposition that the involvement of the company in wrongdoing is sufficient to lift the corporate veil. Merritt VC had this to say:

> Companies are often involved in improprieties . . . But it would make undue roads into the principle of *Saloman's Case* if an impropriety not linked to the use of the company structure to avoid or conceal liability for that impropriety was enough.[22]

The two categories listed in (5) and (6) above were, however, upheld in *Jones v Lipman*[23] and in *Re a Company*.[24] It should be noted, though, that a close examination of the latter case suggests that here there was also evidence of a sham and that the principle relating to injustice did not stand alone.   **12.25**

In *Re a Company*,[25] the court's frustration at the defendant's attempt to hide the assets was evident in its finding that the corporate veil could be lifted. It observed that: **12.26**

> the defendant had created a network of English and foreign companies and trusts . . . and, when the insolvency of the plaintiff was imminent and after the alleged fraud had been committed, he had used this network to dispose of his assets. In these circumstances the court would pierce the corporate veil in order to achieve justice.[26]

It should be noted, however, that cases that might demand such justice are likely to be cases of 'judgment-proofing', where defendants attempt to evade creditors. Indeed, it may appear that this is a particularly important aspect of the courts' jurisdiction when considering offshore trusts. Thus, the equitable principle that the court could pierce the corporate veil where necessary to achieve justice would more likely apply in cases where the trustee company itself has been established to avoid creditors. Yet even here, the rationale comes closer to a sham or concealment.   **12.27**

The better view with respect to whether the corporate veil can be lifted on the ground that it is in the interest of justice to do so, is that this might be a subcategory of another important heading, such as where the company exists as a concealment. Indeed, in *Bonotto v Boccaletti*,[27] although the court purported to rely on *Re a Company*,[28] in finding that it could lift the corporate veil as was   **12.28**

---

[21] Above, n 18, as applied in *Adams v Cape Industries plc* [1991] 1 All ER 929, 1024 and *Gencor ACP Ltd v Dalby* [2000] 2 BCLC 734.
[22] Above, n 20, 995.
[23] [1962] WLR 832.
[24] [1985] BCLC 333.
[25] ibid.
[26] ibid, 337–8.
[27] (2002) 4 ITELR 357.
[28] Above, n 24.

necessary in the interest of justice, it also described the company as a sham and was heavily influenced by the fact that the defendant had sought to 'judgment-proof' himself through the company.

12.29 In the *Bonotto* case, the defendant trustee used trust funds at his disposal to set up companies, with himself as the director and through which he swindled the monies. The companies were, in fact, used for several and significant personal financial transactions and profits. The defendant was the principal shareholder and continued to transfer his monies even when he understood that his breach of trust had been exposed. In lifting the corporate veil, the court affirmed that it had the power to do so when the device of incorporation is used for some improper purpose and where necessary in the interests of justice to do so.[29] However, in its finding it further identified as a significant factor the fact that the company was 'imprinted with the hallmarks of judgment-proofing'.[30] It noted too that, in reality, the defendant was the 'owner of . . . a company which "danced to his bidding". The corporate structure put in place [was] a mere sham.'[31]

Inappropriateness of company structure for trusts—inherently sham structures

12.30 Is there room for viewing the establishment of corporate trustees, particularly those with limited or no resources, as inappropriate, given the nature of the expectations and realities under a trust? Trustee corporations are often constructed deliberately to avoid liabilities in the future. The question is whether the practice goes so far as to allow the courts to view it as evading obligations owed, thus enabling the corporate veil to be lifted. Certainly, the concept of limited liability in itself, an accepted commercial principle, may not be sufficient. However, such trustee companies may often contain nominee directors and may exercise very little, if any, real discretion. Real power may be located in a parent company, or in a person who serves as the true trustee, or, worse (for the sham argument), the settlor. In effect, such companies often have shadow directors.

12.31 Further, do corporate trustees strain important principles of trustee accountability and, if so, should they be challenged on the ground of public policy? Alternatively, can they be placed under equitable principles which entitle the courts to ignore the company structure in the interest of justice or fairness? Challenges hinging on such questions have already begun to come before the courts, and it would appear that the issue is one ripe for judicial development.

---

[29] Above, n 27, 364–5.
[30] ibid, 367.
[31] ibid, 363–4.

The dissenting judgment of Fletcher-Moulton LJ in the case of *Bath*,[32] seemed   **12.32**
to go in this direction:

> But if such [trust] principles are wholly inapplicable to the individuals who, in
> the case of a trustee company, are the persons really administering the trust, that is,
> the directors, and if they can use the powers which are thus in their hands to their
> own personal advantage without incurring any liability to the *cestuis que* trust, the
> whole security of the position is gone.[33]

Fletcher-Moulton LJ also found that with respect to knowledge and intention,
the company was 'an abstraction'. In his view, directors are both the 'brains and
hands' of the company and they cannot shelter themselves under the plea that
the knowledge of the trustee is not their knowledge.[34]

Yet the courts have been reluctant to paint trustee companies with such a wide   **12.33**
brush, preferring instead to find directors' liability under more pliable principles
in tort and indirect breaches of duty. Even more difficult, perhaps, is to obtain
evidence of the requisite connections with the trust.

It is suggested that only in an extreme case of 'judgment-proofing', or where the   **12.34**
company is used as a personal financial ploy, both of which occurred in
Bonotto,[35] would the court be willing to lift the corporate veil. Other suitable
cases might be where the trust company is set up to avoid existing creditors, but
such a case may be more conveniently fought under a fraudulent conveyancing
label rather than disturbing the company tag of all corporate trustees.

The high threshold for declaring a trust company a sham was seen in *HR and*   **12.35**
Others v JAPT and Others,[36] where Lindsay J saw no reason to pierce the corporate veil. This was despite the fact that the employer company had, in effect,
treated the trustee company as if it were its own plaything, using its funds to
purchase personal property and to gain considerable profit for itself, with no
regard to the interests of the beneficiaries. Lindsay J emphasized that one could
not say that the trustee company's corporate form was a sham as it had not been
used for any 'concealment'.

D. Negligence of Directors

Directors of a trustee company may also be liable for negligence in relation to   **12.36**
the management of the trust. Liability for negligence must be assessed under the

---

[32] Above, n 8.
[33] ibid, 637.
[34] ibid.
[35] Above, n 27.
[36] Above, n 11.

orthodox principles of tort as applied to a company. As the normal relationship between a director and his or her company is one similar to that of an agent and his or her principal, a director cannot be liable for negligence unless there exists a 'special relationship' between the director and the tortfeasor (the company), and the director assumes personal responsibility for the acts or omissions giving rise to the tort.

12.37 The issue, as it relates generally to directors, was considered in *Williams v Natural Life Health Foods*,[37] which addressed the question of the negligence of a director of a franchising company: 'A director of a contracting company may only be held liable where it is established by evidence that he assumed personal responsibility and that there was the necessary reliance.'[38]

12.38 The Court of Appeal in *Cross v Benitrust*[39] thought that the *Williams* principle could apply widely to directors of all companies, and relied on it to assess the liability of the directors of an offshore trustee company.

12.39 In *Cross*, the fact that the director had signed the cheque authorizing the bank to transfer the funds, which act led to the alleged loss, was not sufficient evidence of an assumption of personal responsibility by the director. Rather, it was merely the act of an agent for the company. There was no relationship giving rise to the personal duty of care required in negligence on the part of the director.

12.40 In *HR and Others v JAPT*,[40] the court agreed that in certain circumstances a duty of care may be imposed on a director where he or she takes it upon himself or herself, to act for the trustee. The court alluded to *Henderson and Merritt Syndicates Ltd*[41] and *White v Jones*,[42] and approved *Williams*.[43] Liability in tort, therefore, could be imposed only in special circumstances and not for actions which the director is expected to take. The type of conduct necessary for grounding tortious liability was not established the instant case.

E. Third Party Liability of Corporate Trustees

12.41 The directors of a trustee company may become liable as accessories or third parties to a breach of trust in certain circumstances. This encompasses liability

---

[37] [1998] 2 All ER 577, 582, *per* Lord Steyn.
[38] ibid.
[39] Above, n 8, 353.
[40] Above, n 11.
[41] [1995] 2 AC 145.
[42] [1995] 2 AC 207.
[43] Above, n 37.

for dishonest assistance, knowing receipt, and, generally, circumstances which give rise to a constructive trust.

The standards to be met for successful claims of third party liability were fully discussed in the preceding chapter, and are merely summarized here with the use of relevant cases. **12.42**

In *HR and Others v JAPT*,[44] for example, there was enough evidence that the director had dishonestly assisted in the breach of trust and engaged in 'commercially unacceptable conduct' in accordance with the tests laid down in *Royal Brunei v Tan*,[45] to ground an action in accessory or third party liability. The requirement of dishonesty, according to the reasonable standard as laid down in *Royal Brunei v Tan*, the modern test, had been met. The court found that there was an arguable case for imposing a constructive trust. **12.43**

As a general rule, where fraud or wrongdoing exists in relation to the trust, directors are vulnerable to the imposition of a constructive trust by the court.[46] For example, in *Springfield Acres Ltd (In Liquidation) v Abacus (Hong Kong) Ltd*,[47] assets of a company were transferred to a Hong Kong company owned by a firm of Hong Kong accountants after first being incorporated as a British Virgin Islands (BVI) company. This was in order to evade the claim of a judgment creditor. A partner in the accountancy firm served as a director in the Hong Kong company, and he had assisted in setting up the BVI company and enabling the Hong Kong company to be used as the corporate trustee. The two companies were acting as trustees of the trusts in question. The court found that the director had shut his eyes to the obvious and had not made the inquiries that an honest and reasonable man in his position should. A constructive trust could, therefore, be imposed over the funds, allowing the assets to be reached.[48] **12.44**

Money laundering legislation increases the risk of third party liability. Professional advisers may, however, be protected by applying to the court for directions if they suspect criminal activity.[49] Nonetheless, the decision of *Governor & Co of the Bank of Scotland v A Ltd*[50] exposes the vulnerability of such third parties to an action for 'tipping off', when applying to a court for directions without taking care that suspected parties are not alerted. **12.45**

---

[44] Above, n 11.
[45] *Royal Brunei Airlines v Tan Kik Ming* [1995] 3 WLR 64 (PC, Brunei, Darussalam).
[46] See, eg, *Agip (Africa) Ltd v Jackson and Others* [1990] Ch 265.
[47] [1994] 3 NZLR 503.
[48] See also *Agip (Africa) Ltd v Jackson*, above, n 46.
[49] *Finers v Miro* [1991] 1 All ER 182.
[50] (2001) 3 ITELR 503, CA.

F. Indirect Fiduciary and Tortious Duty—Dog Leg Claims

12.46   The two headings, 'indirect fiduciary duty' and 'indirect tortious duty', may be considered together since they originate from the same principle. As we have seen, generally, the director of a trustee company owes a duty of care and a fiduciary duty only to the company. This means that only the company can sue the director for wrongdoing. This premise must be juxtaposed with the principle that the director is also a professional adviser to the trust who owes a duty of care to the trustee. Thus, on the authority of *Royal Brunei v Tan*,[51] the rights flowing from these duties should now be viewed as a 'traceable asset', as part of the trust property. Such rights can, therefore, be enforced by beneficiaries if the trustee company is unwilling or unable to do so, with the trustee company itself being joined as a co-defendant. This has become known as a 'dog leg claim'.

12.47   In *Royal Brunei v Tan*,[52] the court, in examining the duties of care owed by professional advisers and others providing services to the trust, explained that these extended to duties owed to trustees to exercise reasonable skill and care. It was those rights to which the trustees were entitled and which formed part of the trust property. As directors are also included in the category of professional advisers to the trust, they therefore fall under the obligations owed, opening themselves up to liability.

12.48   In *HR and Others v JAPT*,[53] it was confirmed that this type of claim is available only where the cause of action is seeking to reach a trust asset and where the trustee company had no other business other than as trustee of the trust in question, there being no other creditors. This was indeed the situation in the *JAPT* case, as the trustee company had been established specifically to deal with the pension fund. Liability could, therefore, be established on this ground.

G. Duties of Nominee and Non-executive Directors

12.49   The prevalence of nominee directors in offshore trust structures makes it imperative that the extent of their duties to the trust is considered. Directors, even if described as nominee directors, continue to owe fiduciary duties to their companies. Indeed, courts have become stricter in relation to all classes of directors. Nominee directors cannot, therefore, hide behind their nomineeship and be passive onlookers.

---

[51] Above, n 45, 75.
[52] ibid.
[53] Above, n 11.

The landmark case of *Daniels v Anderson*,[54] from New South Wales, underlined **12.50** the modern standards expected of non-executive directors. The principle is applicable to nominee directors as a whole. Such directors have general duties to be familiar with the company's business and to ensure that the board is in a position to manage the company properly. There is, therefore, an element of personal responsibility, even if only to see that others do what they are supposed to do.

It follows that the situations in which a nominee director can be held liable **12.51** for indirect breaches of trust and care are increasing, as are the categories of negligence directly attributed to him or her.

In situations where a director is nominated by his or her employer, he or she **12.52** continues to owe fiduciary duties to the company. Thus the director, and not the employer, remains responsible for any breaches of duty. In *Kuwait Asia Bank v National Mutual Life Nominees Ltd*,[55] a foreign bank, the principal shareholder of a New Zealand company, nominated two of its employees to the company. The company was managed on a daily basis by executive directors. The plaintiff was the trustee for the depositors. After the company went into liquidation, the plaintiff brought an action against the bank, alleging (among other things) that it was vicariously liable for the acts and omissions of the nominee directors, its employees.

The Privy Council held that a person who controlled the appointment of a **12.53** director owed no duty to a company's creditors to ensure that the director acted diligently and competently. Upon appointment, nominee directors became the agents of the company. They owed duties of care solely to the company and, as directors, were bound to ignore the wishes of their employer. This was viewed as an aspect of the fundamental principle of the separate personality of a company. Accordingly, the employer bank was not liable.[56]

De facto directors may also have liabilities imposed upon them. In a rare judg- **12.54** ment from Vanuatu, *Barret v McCormack*,[57] partners in an accounting firm were contracted to incorporate a company by a previously unknown investor. The company was operated by the staff of the accounting firm and was set up as a subsidiary of an overseas company of the investor. The company was used for a fraudulent scheme whereby purchasers, and the accounting firm, were conned

---

[54] (1995) 16 ACSR 607 (CA). See also *Kuwait Asia Bank EC v National Mutual Life Nominee Ltd* [1990] 3 All ER 404; *Adams v The Queen* [1995] 1 WLR 53 (PC).

[55] [1991] 1 AC 187 (PC).

[56] *Per curiam*: 'A director does not by reason only of his position as director owe any duty to creditors or to trustees for creditors of the company, although a creditor may by agreement or representation assume a special duty to such creditors or trustees': ibid, 217.

[57] (2002) 4 ITELR 1 (CA).

into believing that it was selling shares in real estate. One purchaser sued, alleging that the purchase money was subject to a trust and that the firm had knowingly assisted in a breach of trust. The court agreed, finding that even in the absence of a fiduciary relationship (here there was a contractual relationship), a constructive trust could emerge on the basis that the property had been obtained by fraud. The property was, therefore, traceable.

12.55 The partners of the accounting firm were acting as de facto directors of the company and owed a duty to the company to ensure that its funds were not being misapplied. By leaving the management of the company to the investor, they had assisted in the breach of trust. Further, the circumstances were such that an honest accountant should have known that fraud was taking place. Instead, they had deliberately closed their eyes to the obvious. Accordingly, they were liable.

H. Modern Statutory Position

12.56 The common law position on the liability of directors of trust companies, where a breach of trust has been committed by a trustee company, has been changed by statute in certain offshore jurisdictions. In Guernsey, for example, s 70 of the Trusts (Amendment) (Guernsey) Law 1990 provides that:

> (1) Where a breach of trust is committed by a corporate trustee which:
>
> (a) is a trustee of a Guernsey trust;
> (b) is resident in Guernsey; or
> (c) is carrying on business in Guernsey or from an address in Guernsey
>
> —every person who, at the time of the breach, was a director of the trustee shall, subject to subsection (2), be deemed to be a guarantor of the trustee in respect of any damages and costs awarded by the court against the trustee in respect of the breach.

12.57 The court retains the authority to relieve a director from personal liability in the interest of fairness, where he or she was unaware of the breach being contemplated or committed, provided that he or she was not reckless or negligent, or if he or she objected and exercised his or her voting rights to try to prevent the breach.[58]

12.58 It should be noted that the provision speaks to the directors of Guernsey trustee corporations as well as to non-Guernsey trustees, provided that the latter are

---

[58] Trusts (Amendment) (Guernsey) Law 1990, s 70(2). See also a similar provision under s 52 of the Trusts (Jersey) Law 1984.

trustees of Guernsey trusts. In the latter instance, the question of the proper law of the trust may first need to be resolved.[59]

Such statutory provisions reflect a modern position which recognises the inter-relationship between directors of trustee corporations and the trust. It recognizes too, the continuing obligations owed by a trustee and the realities of the trust company structure. The modern statutory position in this area moves the law forward significantly.

12.59

Special BVI provisions

Of special note are the provisions in the BVI under the Virgin Islands Special Trusts Act 2003. The legislation challenges the emerging case law on the duties of directors and, indeed, the usual way of structuring offshore trusts. First, s 13 of the Act precludes trustees of designated shares from becoming or acting as directors. These provisions are complementary to other provisions which curtail the influence of trustees on the management and administration of offshore trusts structured with underlying companies. The intention here is to maximize the flexibility of such trust arrangements by avoiding what are perceived to be restrictive principles of equity in relation to breaches of trust and to ensure fairness in the law. This issue was fully aired in a preceding chapter.[60]

12.60

Of interest too is s 7 of the Act, which lays down the general provisions for directors. The intention here, in keeping with offshore objectives toward commercial flexibility, is to soften the effects of jurisprudence which places harsh liabilities on directors. Note, in particular, s 7(4), which reads:

12.61

> No person becoming or remaining a director of the company . . . shall, in the capacity of director, owe fiduciary or other obligations under the trust, or have any fiduciary or other obligations to the trustee, but nothing in this subsection shall affect any duty which that person owes, as director, to the company.

Timing of a statutory action for directors' liability

Statutory provisions on directors' liabilities may require a condition precedent that there is a breach of trust. However, in *Cross v Benitrust*,[61] the Court of

12.62

---

[59] See *Segal v Edwards and Hartley* (2000) 2 ITELR 575, an interim motion, where the High Court of the Isle of Man held that the plaintiffs had an arguable case against the directors of the trust, as guarantors in breaches of trust, under s 70 of the Trusts (Guernsey) Law 1989. The trust was established in Guernsey and its proper law was Guernsey law. The original Guernsey trustees were replaced by Isle of Man trustees with Isle of Man directors, but the proper law of the settlement remained the law of Guernsey. The case suggests that the reach of the Guernsey law is long enough to embrace Isle of Man directors once the proper law is Guernsey law.

[60] See chapter 10.

[61] See above, n 8.

Appeal of Guernsey purposively construed the Guernsey provisions to mean that the statutory requirement of a breach of trust did not preclude a plaintiff from proceeding against the directors before the breach of trust had been proved and damages awarded. Rather, a plaintiff may proceed on a claim of directors' liability, but the claim must be restricted to a claim for a determination of an issue as to the breach of trust.

12.63 On the authority of *Cross v Benitrust*, a plaintiff may also seek a declaration that there is a liability under the guarantee given effect to under the statute, contingent only upon the giving of judgment for damages or costs. The plaintiff cannot go as far as making a claim under the statutory guarantee, or a claim for damages as if those constituted a present liability, until the alleged breach of trust has been proved, as the statutory guarantee does not crystallize until the point of proof.

Statutory liabilities restrict judicial creativity

12.64 It appears that a further effect of such statutory provisions is to curtail the possibility of other avenues of liability being developed by the courts in their application of equity.[62]

---

[62] ibid, 356.

PART III

THE OFFSHORE TAX FUNCTION

13

RESPONSES TO THE TAX FUNCTION OF OFFSHORE TRUSTS

A. Introduction

In establishing and administering an offshore trust, the impact of taxation upon the trust, and those associated with the trust, must be considered. From the point of view of the offshore jurisdiction, few or no tax liabilities will accrue, although offshore entities may be required to be licensed or registered which will subject the offshore trust to a licensing fee. This, of course, will be a nominal fee, given that the thrust of the offshore financial centres is to encourage investment.   **13.01**

Of more significance will be legislative and judicial responses to the offshore tax function which may originate onshore. Often, these responses will result in increased tax liabilities for offshore trust investors. In the main, these can be placed into four categories: **13.02**

(1) the emergence of aggressive anti-tax avoidance initiatives and policies, including statutory tax countermeasures from onshore jurisdictions. These subject the offshore trust or the individuals associated with the trust, such as the trustee, the beneficiaries, and even the settlor, to tax liabilities and harsh penalties. Such countermeasures are often deliberately targeted at offshore investment, including trusts, in order to reduce or curtail tax planning through such vehicles;

(2)   the hardening of judicial attitudes and policies in relation to tax avoidance. This results in a much harsher stance being taken against tax planning in general, and tax planning through the use of offshore financial centres in particular. Such judicial attitudes and postures complement statutory countermeasures which speak to motive and substance;

(3)   the increasing trend of deeming the offshore trust a sham or alter-ego structure. This declaration renders the settlor subject to tax, as the trust is treated, in effect, as null and void. This phenomenon is also addressed in the discussion of the sham rule,[1] but, in truth, it is part of a policy of tax countermeasures by onshore countries;

(4)   tax demands made on either the settlor/grantor, or the beneficiary, or the trustee, which may be honoured through distributions from the tax fund. This question must be considered in conjunction with the principles of trust law, in particular the duty of the trustee to the beneficiaries. It may also involve consideration of a trustee's duties in relation to investment, which in turn will include a duty not to incur unreasonably tax liabilities for the trust and its beneficiaries. Such tax demands may also involve a consideration of the rule against the non-enforcement of fiscal law, which creates a challenge for those wishing to honour tax obligations imposed under 'foreign' onshore tax laws.

13.03   The tax implications for offshore trusts must also be assessed by considering the above phenomena in the light of other principles of law. First to be considered are rules which dictate the manner and degree of assistance which one state will give to another in relation to tax matters. For example, the attitude of offshore countries in relation to international legal assistance sought by onshore countries where tax matters are concerned, will impact on the potential tax liabilities of offshore investors. This may involve formal mechanisms of assistance, such as mutual legal assistance treaties. Similarly, the extent to which the offshore country will follow established rules on the non-enforcement of foreign fiscal law will greatly impact on the ability of the onshore country to enforce tax liabilities imposed on offshore investors resident or domiciled in that onshore country.

13.04   Just as important will be the forms and scope of international legal cooperation with respect to tax matters. In addition, the attitudes toward confidentiality, as it pertains to affairs of the trust, will influence the ability of onshore countries to enforce and even identify tax liabilities.[2]

---

[1]   See chapter 8, 'The Offshore Trust as a Sham'.
[2]   This important issue is explored in R-M B Antoine, *Confidentiality in Offshore Financial Law* (Oxford University Press, Oxford, 2002).

The above considerations may further be seen as part of two broader questions: **13.05**

(1) that of the appropriate jurisdiction to tax where international or transnational investment is concerned; and

(2) that of a level playing field in international taxation, where the smaller jurisdictions are not forced, because of a lack of economic clout, to undermine their tax competitiveness by methods which larger countries themselves do not adhere to.

Undoubtedly, the tax function of offshore entities, including trusts, is a controversial one. This is an issue which involves questions of economics, international law, international trade, private international law, international politics, sovereignty, and even ideological considerations. Onshore jurisdictions perceive that they retain the right to tax persons originating from their shores. This is not an abstract right, as considerable tax revenues are lost from the utilization of offshore structures for tax planning. Onshore jurisdictions challenge the reality of offshore investment and continue, indirectly, to view such investment as still 'belonging' to the onshore country. Conversely, offshore jurisdictions treat such investment as inherently transnational and respect the choice of the settlor to declare its ownership. Offshore jurisdictions further maintain their sovereign right to enact competitive tax laws and distance themselves from any fiscal impropriety that a settlor may engage in, believing that to be the responsibility of onshore states. Further, offshore jurisdictions, quite appropriately, do not equate competitive tax laws with invitations to tax abuses or illegalities. This is particularly the case as competitive tax laws, especially for non-nationals, can now be viewed as a universal phenomenon.[3] To justify their arguments, offshore jurisdictions can further point to the lawful tax planning and tax mitigation, as opposed to the tax evasion, functions to which offshore entities can be put. **13.06**

Consequently, the jurisdictional deadlock which emerges has paved the way for aggressive and continuous unilateral initiatives by onshore states, intent on eroding the offshore tax function. **13.07**

Yet offshore jurisdictions believe that they have considerable ammunition on their side, because of the fact that their policies are based on well-established rules on the acceptance of tax avoidance and the rule on the non-enforcement of fiscal law. These broad tax planning justifications can be considered alongside the historically entrenched tax planning functions of trusts,[4] making the case for the legitimacy of offshore trusts even stronger. However, this perhaps idealistic **13.08**

---

[3] See below, paras 13.17–13.21.

[4] See, eg, G A Wheatcroft, 'The Attitude of the Legislature and the Courts to Tax Avoidance' [1955] MLR 209. Tax planning has been accepted as a legislative function of trusts since the fifteenth century.

position of legal correctness is severely undermined by international political pressures. These force reorientations of legal policy that impact negatively on offshore trusts. Such provisions are supplemented by courts, which appear eager to support legislation and policy initiatives against previously accepted tax planning objectives. Nonetheless, the essential validity of the tax planning function in offshore regimes should not be lost. It is epitomized in the sentiments expressed by the Jersey courts in the case of *Re Moody Jersey A Settlement*,[5] that offshore trusts could legitimately be established to perform tax planning functions for onshore investors.

13.09   Also important is the aspect of the offshore tax function which goes beyond mere tax avoidance and embraces tax-saving opportunities. These are created, for example, by genuine international transactions not available in onshore countries.[6] A further example would be the high interest rates available offshore, which originate from delayed taxation rather than tax avoidance.

13.10   Whilst this book is not a tax planning book, and indeed it would be impossible to discuss the tax measures of each onshore jurisdiction in which citizens do business with offshore nations, the key elements that have emerged in these related issues will be identified and discussed. This is particularly from the point of view of the jurisdictions which are leading the way in this anti-avoidance process, namely, the US, Canada, and the UK. The anti-tax avoidance policies and measures being carried out in these countries are, in fact, being emulated worldwide, by onshore countries concerned about the loss of tax revenue.

13.11   The analysis here should not, however, be taken as a substitute for obtaining tax advice from tax specialists in the relevant onshore country, as is indeed the current practice. This is given the fast-changing nature of tax countermeasures and the continuous creation of new tax planning opportunities.

B. Harmful Tax Competition versus a Level Playing Field for Tax

13.12   The debate surrounding the right of states to tax income with respect to business and investment with multinational and transnational dimensions is not a new one. However, the activities of the Organisation for Economic Cooperation and Development (OECD) and its charge of unfair tax competition levelled at offshore countries, particularly those which are small, developing nations, have

---

[5] [1990] JLR 264, 266 (Royal Ct, Jersey).

[6] Chown and Edwardes-Kerr, eg, describe the phenomenon of international markets in deposits and bonds, and the flow of funds from investors who are themselves virtually free of taxes on the receipt of their interest. See J Chown and M Edwardes-Kerr, 'Tax Havens and Offshore Investment Centres' [1974] *The Banker Annual Review*, 479.

refuelled the debate.[7] This time, the discussion assumes new dimensions. Of particular note is the concern of offshore states that the international perspective on the right to tax must assume the character of a fairminded approach and create a level playing field for all states in the milieu.

Initiatives such as those from the OECD can considerably diminish the economic and legal objectives of offshore trust regimes. They will also obstruct the adherence to the established principles of tax law, the legality of tax avoidance, and the non-enforcement of tax law. As such, offshore financial centres, in particular small, developing offshore financial centres, insist that they should not be expected, in effect, to dismantle considerable portions of their financial regimes, at great cost, without onshore countries and more influential offshore financial centres being asked to do the same. This, it is hoped, will help to neutralize any tax competition advantages that onshore nations and financial centres may gain from the emasculation of offshore centres.   **13.13**

Those attacking the offshore tax function insist that offshore financial centres should introduce transparency in tax structures, facilitate requests for information on tax matters, abolish 'ringfencing' whereby only non-resident investors are granted tax incentives, and generally assist onshore countries in their tax enforcement initiatives.   **13.14**

The notion of a level playing field speaks directly to the issue of restrictive tax rules which have been demanded of offshore jurisdictions. These should apply to all countries and not just small, developing ones. It should also address the concerns about the economic and developmental issues which are involved in international taxation. For most offshore countries, a tax regime which encourages or permits wealthy foreigners to invest, is pivotal to the sustainability of their offshore financial centres.   **13.15**

Onshore countries are, of course, at liberty to offer tax incentives of their own to promote tax competition. Instead, they have, until recently, introduced rules designed to limit the flexibility and tax mobility of investment, for example, the worldwide taxation of income. The head of the Swiss Bankers' Association, URS Roth, has condemned onshore jurisdictions in the European Union for   **13.16**

---

[7] OECD consultations began in a democratic way in January 2001, with the *High Level Consultations on OECD Harmful Tax Competition Initiative*, Barbados, 7–9 January 2001. This was as a result of accusations by offshore countries that the OECD had introduced and threatened to introduce negative measures and blacklisting without first seeking cooperation or consultation with offshore countries. The consultations and the entire debate about 'harmful tax competition' followed from the publication of OECD Reports: *Harmful Tax Competition—An Emerging Global Issue* (OECD, Paris, 1998) and *Toward Global Tax Cooperation—Progress in Identifying Harmful Tax Practices* (OECD, Paris, 2000). More recently, there appears to be a less antagonistic approach by the OECD to offshore jurisdictions.

being 'hell bent on smashing the fiscal sovereignty of an independent low tax state or simply seeking a scapegoat on which to hang the blame for its own internal failures'. He added: 'If a country is experiencing massive tax evasion, is this not a symptom that something has gone wrong in the relationship between that state and its citizens,' adding that there was 'a lot of hypocrisy and discrimination' on the issue.[8] Indeed, the EU countries are now moving toward a lower common tax rate in order to make themselves more competitive.

Onshore—offshore companies and trusts

13.17 We should consider the question of the level playing field more carefully, within the context of recent attempts by onshore countries to make themselves more fiscally competitive to non-residents. For the moment, use may be made of the deliberately misleading term 'onshore/offshore financial centres' to describe the recent phenomenon where onshore countries, in particular states in the US, have sought to emulate offshore countries and offshore entities. For example, they have introduced trusts which mimic offshore trusts in substance and form. These are onshore tax havens which allow and encourage trusts to be used as tax avoidance vehicles. The Banking Law of Colorado,[9] for example, provides that non-residents transacting with banks in Colorado incur no state taxes with respect to income from bank deposits, certificates of deposit, purchases of gold, silver, platinum, and other precious metals, foreign currency exchange for US dollars, and other forms of personal, tangible property.

13.18 While these infant havens pose competition to offshore financial centres, they provide legitimacy to offshore legal and financial concepts and make it more challenging for onshore countries to rule against offshore entities on grounds of public policy, invalidity, or even conflict of laws.

13.19 The existence of special taxing regimes in Europe is also noteworthy. These regimes have been established to attract the headquarter companies of multinationals to their jurisdictions. The main incentive is a very low rate of taxation for these transplanted companies, but there are other comparative advantages. The EU Competition Commission dubbed these mechanisms harmful competition and, more specifically, harmful tax measures. Eleven of these schemes were investigated by the EU Competition Commission in 2001,[10] while four

---

[8] www.trusts-andtrustees.com/trusts/td.

[9] Title 11 (Rev). See also the Qualified Dispositions in Trusts Act 1996 of Delaware.

[10] Including France's Régime des Centrales de Tréoreriel, Ireland's Tax Exemption on Foreign Income, Spain's Special Fiscal Regime, for Bizkaia Co-ordinating Centres, Luxembourg's Coordinating Centre Regime, and Germany's Special Fiscal Regime for Control and Coordinating Centres of Foreign Companies.

were required to halt operations immediately.[11] Yet such schemes continue to flourish in onshore countries. For some, this is blatant evidence of a lack of a level playing field in matters of taxation and the absurdity of the charge of 'unfair tax competition' levelled at offshore financial centres. For example, it was announced recently that the French Government intends to 'woo' foreign executives to France through special tax incentives.[12]

We should also consider the corporate tax exemption for UK resident companies **13.20** with substantial shareholdings in other companies, including foreign companies, established under the Finance Act 2002.[13] This Act inserts a new s 192A into the Taxation of Chargeable Gains Act 1992. The Act is aimed at making the UK an attractive location for investment and is particularly targeted at multinational companies. UK resident companies which qualify are exempted from capital gains tax, where such companies dispose of substantial shareholdings.

Special tax treatment for immigrants is also available in Canada. A non-resident **13.21** who immigrates to Canada will not be taxed for a period of up to five years with respect to non-resident trusts established before immigration and established with the settlor's non-Canadian assets.[14]

C. Impact of Anti-money Laundering Laws on Tax Offences

Developments which impact significantly on the offshore tax function are not **13.22** limited to new and more far-reaching tax legislation. An important development is the expanded thrust of anti money laundering laws. There has been a fundamental paradigm shift in the concept of what constitutes a money laundering offence, deviating significantly from its origin in drug-related offences to what is now labelled 'all crimes' money laundering legislation. Such new legislation embodies not just 'new-wave' crimes such as terrorism, but also tax evasion and related offences. The international pressures on offshore financial centres have resulted in some being forced to take that route, achieving legislative parity with important onshore jurisdictions such as the UK.

From a conceptual point of view, deeming tax offenders 'money launderers' seems **13.23** intellectually suspect, given the acceptable prerequisites of money laundering

---

[11] The four were Belgium's Fiscal Regime of Coordinating Centres, Greece's Fiscal Regime for Offices of Foreign Companies, Italy's Tax Incentives Linked to the Trieste Financial Services and Insurance Centre, and Sweden's Foreign Insurance Companies Tax Regime.

[12] Announcement by Prime Minister Raffarin, reported in AMS Group Newsletter, www.iofc.net/amsgroup/news, 8 March 2004.

[13] Finance Act 2002, s 44 (Sch 8).

[14] Income Tax Act, RSC 1985 (as amended 2002) C1 (5th Supp) Div B, Subdivisions K and I, discussed in the following chapter, paras 14.61–14.70.

that monies should originate from a criminal source and appear to increase at the end of the money laundering cycle. In contrast, in tax evasion, monies are made to appear reduced.[15] Nonetheless, the convenience of this legal advice and the moral objectives of the legal policy are unquestionable. Further, the awkwardness of the combination has not prevented a drive toward the new policy. It is likely that money laundering laws will indeed reduce the incidence of tax evasion, or at any rate filter out the genuine miscreants.[16]

13.24 The effect of this new legislative thrust is not simply on the substantial crime of money laundering. It also means that, because of the harsh criminal penalties, both for money launderers and for those who assist or facilitate them, the very exercise of tax planning becomes a risky business for professional tax advisers. This would clearly impact negatively on the willingness of such professionals to offer advice, resulting in less business for offshore financial centres. As onshore countries continue to widen the net for what constitutes a criminal tax offence, the problem is magnified. Prosecution is enhanced by the use of mutual legal assistance treaties, enabling offshore financial centres to give information on tax offenders and to apply the often draconian investigative and search and seizure powers under these international instruments.

D. Legitimacy of the Tax Function and Jurisdiction to Tax

13.25 The contrasting approaches between onshore and offshore jurisdictions to the offshore tax function may also be explained by the conceptual uncertainties surrounding the question of which state has the right to assert jurisdiction to tax. This lacuna in international law also helps to explain the reluctance of offshore countries to cooperate in mutual assistance efforts in tax offences, and to preclude the application of the international rule on the non-enforcement of the fiscal law of other states. Understandably, offshore jurisdictions and developing nations lend their voices to support the contention that the jurisdiction to tax should be granted in favour of the place where business is located.

13.26 On the one hand, onshore nations perceive that offshore investment does not truly belong to the offshore country and hence should not be taxed by it. On the other hand, offshore jurisdictions could legitimately argue that onshore nations have no basis upon which to assert jurisdiction to tax entities which are located within their borders.

---

[15] We could argue, however, that the unlawful source is the tax evasion itself, but this is a circular argument.

[16] There are also, however, serious concerns about the effectiveness and costs of such extensive anti-money laundering legislation.

There is a third possibility. It is that offshore entities and investment should be   **13.27**
considered truly transnational. If this is the case, the question of the jurisdiction
to tax will need to be resolved by a careful balancing of the factors that can
legitimately define ownership and control. It is question which will involve
considerations of international law and public international law. This is an issue
which is not confined to offshore trusts or offshore entities. At present, there are
no clear principles in law for the taxation of international or transnational
entities or investments. Indeed, it is one area to which the OECD and
like-minded bodies can contribute meaningfully.

Such a debate will have to acknowledge that, with respect to offshore investment,   **13.28**
there are several grey areas, as offshore finance is a complex phenomenon which
embraces varied forms of investment, even through the vehicle of the trust.
Some investments, for example, will be more truly international than others.

The meanings of terms granting jurisdiction, such as 'management and control'   **13.29**
and 'residence', will be essential in resolving the debate. Certainly, the issue of
physical residence may be easily answered in favour of offshore jurisdictions, if
this is predicated simply on the location of assets and the registration of the
offshore company. However, other pertinent questions are not answered so
quickly, nor do they easily suggest a favourable outcome for offshore jurisdictions. Consider that neither real business nor control and management of the
offshore financial centre may be located truly in the offshore jurisdiction. This is
notwithstanding mechanisms which may be utilized to indicate otherwise. A
truly transnational approach to taxation will involve consideration of the extent
to which transnational entities, such as offshore entities, will be granted the
flexibility to choose their legal residence.[17] This will have to be assessed in the
light of principles of private international law, particularly for taxation and
company issues, which challenge such a choice if an entity goes forum shopping
and merely chooses a home jurisdiction to avoid legal obligations in the original
jurisdiction. The entity is not treated as one which was established to engage
genuinely in international business or competition.

However, principles of private international law are not fully developed in   **13.30**
relation to trusts. It is, therefore, unclear to what extent principles applicable
generally in tax or company matters can be applied to trusts. Where trusts have
been established for purely tax purposes, there would appear to be no reason,
however, to ignore such conflict of laws rules on taxation. The result for
companies, for example, would be that they are not treated as having separate

---

[17] Generally, private international law accepts that if a corporation comes validly into existence
by the law of one country, its legal personality is recognized by other countries. AV Dicey, *The
Law of the Constitution*, 10th edn (Macmillan and Co, London, 1960).

legal personalities but are viewed as branches of onshore companies. Such entities would be easily claimed as onshore companies by onshore countries and jurisdiction for tax purposes asserted over them.[18]

13.31   The lack of coherent international law principles for complex forms of transnational business[19] has encouraged a pragmatic and cavalier approach to jurisdiction to tax, whereby countries simply assert jurisdiction over persons and entities where they feel able to enforce or impose the obligations. In the case of trusts, such enforcement may be more complicated than with companies or individuals. As legal ownership of the trust assets vests in the trustees, jurisdiction should appropriately be asserted over them. However, as we have learnt, offshore trustees typically reside in offshore jurisdictions and are, consequently, outside of the jurisdiction of onshore countries. More creative methods have had to be sought, therefore, for ensuring that any assertions of jurisdiction are effective. These are discussed, from a legislative perspective, in the following chapter.

13.32   The practical difficulties associated with the enforcement of onshore tax obligations, as well as the underlying philosophy of onshore jurisdictions that offshore trust assets rightfully belong to the onshore state, have also resulted in more imaginative juridical approaches. Thus, settlors, for tax purposes, may be deemed, in effect, the continued owners of trust property under the sham or alter-ego doctrines.[20] Even more dramatic is the approach of the US courts.[21] Here, settlors of offshore trusts may be treated as the owners of the trust assets and ordered to repatriate those assets. If they claim that it is impossible for them to do so (on the basis that the assets now belong to the trustee), they may be cited for contempt of court and imprisoned.

E. Continued Opportunities in Offshore Tax Planning

13.33   Undoubtedly, tax planning in a modern context requires a more complicated manipulation of the legal environment, particularly when directed offshore. While the uses of offshore trusts to obtain tax advantages may now be prejudiced

---

[18] This may be a matter of public policy. See, eg, *Comptroller & Auditor General v Davidson* [1996] 2 NZLR 278.

[19] See, eg, R L Palmer, 'Toward a Unilateral Coherence in Determining Jurisdiction to Tax Income' (1989) 30 Harv Int LJ 1, who argues that there is a compelling need for a unified income tax jurisdiction theory. See also Sol Picciotto, *International Business Taxation—A Study of the Internationalization of Business Regulation* (Weidenfeld & Nicolson, London, 1992).

[20] See chapter 15, paras 15.29–15.41.

[21] As seen in the line of cases of *Re Anderson, Federal Trade Commission v Affordable Media* (1999) 2 ITELR 73; LLC 179 F 3d 1228 (CA-9, 1999) and *Re Stephen Jay Lawrence* (2002) 5 ITELR 1.

with respect to direct transactions between onshore and offshore jurisdictions, there may still be considerable advantages indirectly. Nonetheless, while specific advice on opportunities for tax planning through the use of trusts by onshore residents is beyond the scope of this book, given the evolutionary and varied nature of the special tax environments, it should be noted that opportunities still do exist. Indeed, the very nature of tax planning is one that responds creatively to its legislative environment.

For example, apart from double taxation mechanisms, discussed below,[22] tax **13.34** advantages may be gained for persons not domiciled in the onshore jurisdiction, although resident there. A good example of this scenario was demonstrated in the case of *Slattery v Moore Stephens (a firm)*,[23] albeit an opportunity lost for the taxpayer in this instance. The taxpayer was an Irish and Canadian national who took up a position at the London branch of his New York bank. Under the relevant legislation, the Income and Corporation Taxes Act 1988,[24] he was considered resident, but not 'ordinarily resident'. Accordingly, he was liable to pay income tax only on income derived from work carried out in the UK, or, on a remittance basis, on income from work carried out abroad which was remitted into the UK.[25] Although the taxpayer hired a tax professional, an accountant, for advice on tax mitigation, he was not advised that he had the option of forwarding his salary to an offshore bank (such as the Channel Islands in this case) and avoid paying UK taxes. Indeed, it was the usual practice for the employer bank. Accordingly, his total salary was remitted to the employer bank. The taxpayer successfully sued the accountant for negligence, as the English court found that any reasonably competent tax adviser would have given the appropriate advice.

The court's finding acknowledges, indirectly, the availability of tax mitigation **13.35** through the use of offshore structures, even in the present antagonistic climate with respect to offshore centres. Indeed, the court considered the offshore option to be an obvious one and was clearly surprised that it had not been taken, even to the extent of finding that the taxpayer himself contributed to the negligence, since he should have been able to question the obviously inaccurate advice.

It is believed, too, that considerable opportunities remain with respect to **13.36** trusts established for employment enterprises. The Rabbi Trust, a deferred

---

[22] See chapter 16, 'Bilateral Routes to the Tax Function and the Question of Sovereignty', at paras 16.41–16.48.
[23] [2003] STC 1379.
[24] Cases II and III of Sch E.
[25] Under the Act, all income paid abroad but then brought into the UK is deemed remitted income, even if immediately transferred out of the country.

compensation arrangement for grantor trusts, which has been approved by the US authorities, can, for instance, offer considerable advantages with respect to executive compensation packages.[26]

13.37   It is also apparent that anti-tax avoidance measures tend to focus on the ownership of offshore property, such as shares, income, and interests in a trust. The issue of rights accruing under contractual arrangements is seldom addressed directly. This leads to opportunities whereby offshore structures can be engineered so that the onshore investor may gain advantages through suitable contractual arrangements. The most commonly named contractual structure for this purpose is the use of insurance. For purposes of tax planning, it may be more advantageous for a settlor or grantor to consider the utilization of an offshore insurance company by the trust. It is suggested, for example, that the use of an irrevocable offshore trust in conjunction with a life insurance policy which can take advantage of the foreign non-grantor trust rules, may be an effective tax planning tool for US citizens and residents. In this arrangement, the offshore trust itself purchases the insurance policy. After the death of the settler and his spouse, US beneficiaries may be added and will be subject to taxation. However, appreciations in the value of the trust should be excluded from the settlor's estate and therefore escape taxation.[27]

13.38   Onshore citizens who are not resident in the onshore jurisdiction may also obtain advantages through offshore trusts. While US citizens are taxed on their worldwide personal income, the focus of such tax planning would be the avoidance of probate in the US, thus deriving tax savings. Other reasons advanced include the reduction of opportunities for persons wishing to file claims against the estate expediently and confidentially.

13.39   In addition, Palmer has argued that the decision in *MacNiven (Inspector of Taxes) v Westmoreland Investments Ltd*[28] creates significant tax planning or tax mitigation opportunities. In *MacNiven*, it was held by the House of Lords that the term 'payment' under s 338 of the Income and Corporation Taxes Act 1988 (UK) had only a juristic meaning and no broad commercial meaning. Their Lordships rejected the Revenue's argument that interest paid by a company to a pension scheme did not count as payments and was, therefore, unavailable for set-off against the company's profits. In Palmer's view, allows several transactions

---

[26] Revenue Procedure 92–64, IRB 1992–33, 11, 28 July 1992.
[27] See R Duke, 'Tax Compliance and Reporting for Offshore Trusts and Uses of Foreign Life Insurance' in *International Estate Planning, Asset Protection Strategies: Planning with Domestic and Offshore Entities* (American Bar Association, USA, 2002).
[28] [2001] 1 All ER 865. See M Palmer, 'MacNiven (Inspector of Taxes) v Westmoreland Investments Ltd: An Unexpected Boon for UK Taxpayers?' [2002] JTCP 1, discussed further at paras 15.11–15.20.

which could be viewed as incorporating concepts which have only juristic meaning and no broad commercial meanings. One such example is the reduction of net value of UK property held by offshore trustees.[29] Palmer advises that an offshore trustee holding UK property worth £1,000,000, where the 10-year anniversary of inheritance tax is looming, should borrow cash equivalent to the market value of the property on a short term basis, charging the borrowing against the property and thereby reducing its value over the 10-year anniversary date for inheritance tax purposes. The result should be significant tax savings.

F. Tax and Human Rights—Protecting Offshore Trusts?

The initiatives against offshore and foreign trusts may sometimes raise human rights issues. Human rights protections have the ability to sustain the integrity of the trust and, by extension, protect it from incurring liabilities, including tax liabilities. Accordingly, they may present, albeit indirectly, tax planning opportunities for offshore investors. However, the few cases involving human rights arguments which have emerged have not always been encouraging. Nonetheless, this is a developing jurisprudence which should be noted. In the UK and its territories, in particular, the enactment of the Human Rights Act 1998 (which incorporated the European Convention on Human Rights) has brought a fresh enthusiasm for human rights litigation. Such litigation with respect to offshore issues is also becoming more popular before offshore courts.[30]

13.40

It is expected that the bulk of cases harnessing human rights arguments would concern issues of self-incrimination, confidentiality, and privacy.[31] However,

13.41

---

[29] Palmer, ibid, 11.8

[30] See, eg, *Attorney General v Financial Clearing Corporation* (CA, The Bahamas) No 70 of 2001, decided 8 October 2002, where Osadebay JA found that the privilege against self-incrimination applied with respect to information on offshore investors. This had been threatened because of new anti-money laundering and general regulatory provisions which saw the institution of a special supervisory authority, the Financial Investigatory Unit (FIU). The FIU had draconian powers to acquire information on offshore investment, to investigate suspicious activities, and to freeze assets. It was argued by the respondent that these were powers akin to a judicial authority and thereby violated the constitutional principle of the separation of powers, and that judicial powers were reserved to the judiciary and could not be exercised by the Executive. However, the majority found that the FIU's powers were to be exercised only for evidential purposes. They were, in effect, temporary powers, and the FIU's orders could be discharged only by a judge of the court. The separation of powers principle was, therefore, not violated.

[31] As demonstrated by *Financial Clearing Corporation*, above, n 30. The constitutional challenge on the ground of privacy failed in this case. See also, on questions of privacy, *Pindling v Douglas* (Sup Ct, The Bahamas) No 318 of 1994, decided 18 May 1994, and *Bethel v Douglas* [1995] WLR 974 (PC, The Bahamas). On the privilege against self-incrimination, see *Arawak Trust Company v Holden* (CA, BVI) No 2 of 1994, decided 19 September 1994.

offshore trusts can conjure up their fair share of constitutional challenges apart from such questions. For example, an issue of discrimination could arise where the treatment of offshore and non-resident trusts is different to that for onshore or domestic trusts. In view of well-established principles of non-discrimination in tax policy, and despite such different treatment meted out to non-resident (offshore) trusts, as discussed in the following chapter, it is surprising that a concerted constitutional challenge has not, as yet, ensued.

13.42   Of note also would be the application of human rights penalties and powers issued under taxing statutes. In addition to assessing the nature of the power exercised and its suitability to human rights protection, the need to ensure that proportionality requirements are met is also important. This is with respect both to penalties and search and seizure provisions.[32] Penalties and powers are also required to be issued or carried out by appropriate judicial bodies, to avoid violations of separation of powers principles.[33]

13.43   The recent appeal of human rights approaches to litigation in tax matters is clearly evident in cases such as *R v Allen*.[34] This concerned the application of the protection under Article 6 of the European Convention on Human Rights, specifically, whether the privilege against self-incrimination was protected. In many jurisdictions, such as in the UK, Europe, and offshore trust jurisdictions, the privilege is viewed as an aspect of the fundamental right to a fair trial. In Europe, it is protected by Article 6 of the European Convention. Consequently, as the right to a fair trial is a fundamental one, common to all democratic states, the privilege assumes the non-derogable character of the parent right, a fair trial. Thus, the right may be protected even in the face of conflicting public interests. This is a more far-reaching approach than that under the common law with its veil of parliamentary sovereignty, as the UK courts discovered in the case of *Saunders v UK*.[35] Here, the European Court of Human Rights, in rejecting the dicta of earlier English courts, declared that the public interest argument could not be used to justify deviations from what it saw as 'basic principles of fair

---

[32] Proportionality is a constitutional principle which requires that where human rights abrogations are unavoidable, the least evasive route to abrogating the rights in question is to be taken. There is a well-established jurisprudence on the issue, particularly in Europe. See, eg, in the context of excessive searches for tax information, cases such as *Mailhe v France* (1993) 16 EHRR 332. See also *Funke v France* [1993] 1 CMLR 897, discussed further below, at para 13.46, which addresses, it directly. Issues of proportionality are aired fully in the companion text, R-M B Antoine, *Confidentiality in Offshore Financial Law* (Oxford University Press, Oxford, 2002).

[33] This was, in fact, an important issue in the Bahamian case of *Financial Clearing Corporation*, above, n 30. Here, the administrative supervisory authority established to oversee offshore transactions had wide powers which were challenged as being judicial in nature. The majority disagreed, however.

[34] [2002] 1 AC 530.

[35] (1996) 23 EHRR 313.

procedure'. The public interest raised here involved the need to fight complex corporate fraud and crime.

In *Allen*, the taxpayer had been compelled by the Revenue to disclose certain **13.44** documents. However, he had submitted inaccurate information, and the court used this fact to sidestep the issue of whether compelled disclosure would abrogate the right claimed. Nonetheless, Lord Hutton did not rule out the possibility of a human rights violation. He conceded that, had correct information been produced, at least a strong argument would have arisen.[36]

The privilege against self-incrimination is well protected under the European **13.45** Convention.[37] There are clear dicta that violations of the privilege may abrogate the right to a fair trial. Indeed, the privilege may extend even to civil trials, where penalties are akin to criminal penalties. As discussed below, this is an especially important point for tax matters where, even in civil matters, powers and penalties are draconian.[38] Under the European Convention, the privilege is also violated if information is compelled, in contrast to the now, perhaps discredited, US position that compulsory disclosure does not amount to a testimonial.[39]

In *Funke v France*,[40] for instance, Funke had been compelled to produce financial **13.46** documents and information relating to an alleged customs violation. The Government contended that he had not been asked to provide evidence of a confession, or to confess, merely to give particulars of evidence found by them. The court, however, rejected this as an illogical argument, holding that once evidence could be incriminating, the privilege applied.

Treating civil tax matters as criminal offences under human rights law

The question of what constitutes a criminal offence, thereby invoking the pro- **13.47** tective provisions of Article 6 of the European Convention and similar human rights instruments, is particularly important to tax matters. This question arises because of the traditionally severe penalties attached to what are classified as 'civil' issues in tax matters. It is expected that such human rights challenges will

---

[36] *Allen*, above, n 34, 542–3, distinguishing the present case from *Saunders v United Kingdom* (1996) 23 EHRR 313. See also *R v Dimsey* [2001] UKHL 46, a case with similar facts which resulted in a similar decision.

[37] Note that the UK is a newcomer to the Convention on the Protection of Human Rights and Fundamental Freedoms (ETS 5–1950) European Conventions and Agreements, vol 1 (Strasbourg: Council of Europe, 1971), 21 (the European Convention).

[38] Paras 13.46–13.52.

[39] Held in cases such as *Fischer v United States* 425 US 391, 408 (1976): The privilege against self-incrimination can be asserted only if the witness is 'compelled to make a testimonial communication that is incriminating'.

[40] Above, n 32.

become more frequent, particularly in the UK, Europe, and offshore jurisdictions themselves. UK citizens, for example, are now increasingly seduced by the malleability of human rights instruments, often interpreted in their favour. The jurisprudence of the European Court of Human Rights provides further precedents for interpreting constitutions and other human rights instruments which have similar provisions. This includes the constitutions of Commonwealth Caribbean offshore jurisdictions, which also state that the privilege applies to 'criminal offences'.[41]

13.48 *King v Walden (Inspector of Taxes)*[42] provides a further example of the use of human rights jurisprudence in tax matters. The taxpayer in this case, who had made use of offshore investments, was penalized under the Taxes Management Act 1970,[43] for wilful default and neglect with respect to his tax returns. He was further made liable to interest on the fines incurred. Among the several points of appeal was the contention that the authorities violated his right to a fair trial,[44] in particular the presumption of innocence, by binding themselves to earlier determinations on his tax liabilities. Here, the appellant was unable to challenge the earlier findings of wilful default or neglect. Thus, the case regarding penalties was virtually decided against him in advance of the decision to impose penalties or the appeal. This, it was argued, made it an irrebuttable presumption against him contrary to Article 6(2) of the European Convention.

13.49 Before proceeding to the substantive issue of the alleged violation of Article 6(2), the court had to determine whether the appeal, a tax matter which was classified as 'civil' under the Taxes Management Act 1970, fell under the protection of Article 6(2). The Article reads:

> Everyone charged with a criminal offence shall be presumed innocent until proven guilty according to law.

The question was, therefore, whether the nature of the penalties imposed brought the matter within the terms of the Convention.

13.50 Relying on strong authorities from the European Court of Human Rights, the English court was persuaded by the argument that it was the nature and substance of a matter, and the nature and severity of the penalties attached to it, that determined whether that matter was to be treated as a criminal offence. In the particular case, the proceeding could be ascribed the character and meaning of a criminal offence. This was because the penalties were severe, punitive, and

---

[41] Note that this issue is discussed in more detail in Antoine, above, n 32, chapter 8. See also below, para 13.55.

[42] [2001] STC 822.

[43] Under ss 46(2), 95, and 101.

[44] Under Art 6(2) of the European Convention.

intended to deter, rather than being compensatory, thereby embodying the essence of a criminal penalty. These factors together were sufficient to categorize the matter as a 'criminal charge' within the meaning of Article 6. The court relied heavily on the case of *Georgiou and anor (trading as Marios Chippery) v UK*,[45] which concerned a penalty assessment in respect of value added tax which was classified as civil but was deemed to be criminal because of the harsh, punitive penalties which had been imposed. In the earlier case of *Bendenoun v France*,[46] the European Court of Human Rights had also noted that the domestic classification of the matter as 'civil' did not prevent its treatment as criminal under the European Convention. In *Bendenoun v France*,[47] the Court held that increases imposed on taxpayers as penalties for tax fraud, which were over and above additional tax demands, were 'criminal in nature'. Further, under the authority of *Gerogiou*, proceedings could be classified as criminal even if they originated from mere tribunal procedures.

In sum, European Court jurisprudence has identified three criteria to be taken into account when determining whether an individual has been charged with a criminal offence for the purposes of Article 6 of the European Convention. These are:

(1) the classification of the offence under national law;
(2) the nature of the offence; and
(3) the nature and severity of the penalty that the person concerned risks incurring.[48]

13.51

In *King*, additional elements helped further to define this basic test and helped to persuade the court of the criminal nature of the offence. First, the amount of the fine was not related to any administrative matter or related cost; secondly, the amount of the fine depended on the culpability of the taxpayer, and a taxpayer was fined more severely the more culpable he was. The court noted here that mitigation was essentially a criminal, rather than a civil, concept.[49]

Moreover, states parties to the European Convention do not have a margin of appreciation to decide what should be treated as civil, or criminal. Rather, the concept of a 'criminal offence' is autonomous, and the same conduct that would be deemed criminal in one state party would be deemed criminal in another.[50]

13.52

---

[45] [2001] STC 80, ECtHR.
[46] (1994) 18 EHRR 54, 74–6.
[47] ibid.
[48] See also *AP MP and TP v Switzerland* (1997) 26 EHRR 541, 558–9.
[49] *King*, above, n 42.
[50] ibid.

Transferring the burden of proof

13.53   Notwithstanding the applicability of the Convention, the court in *King*[51] found against the taxpayer on the substantive point. It held that his entitlement to a presumption of innocence, protected under Article 6, had not been breached. While the right to be presumed innocent is a fundamental requirement, it does not prohibit transfers of the burdens of proof to the citizen to establish a defence. This is provided that the overall burden of proof remains on the prosecution. Further, it does not prohibit presumptions of law or fact, provided that these are within reasonable limits. The court relied on the case of *Salabiaku v France*,[52] where it was said:

> Presumptions of fact or of law operate in every legal system. Clearly, the Convention does not prohibit such presumptions in principle. It does, however, require the contracting states to remain within certain limits in this respect ... Article 6(2) ... requires states to remain within certain limits which take into account the importance of what is at stake and maintain the rights of the defence.

Accordingly, in the *King* case, there was no violation of Article 6 of the Convention.

Human rights litigation in offshore jurisdictions

13.54   Constitutional rights which may accrue to offshore investors may also originate from offshore jurisdictions themselves. In tax matters, these will be most useful in attempting to protect information about investments. As such, rights to privacy and the privilege against self-incrimination will be paramount. The privilege against self-incrimination is viewed as a more fundamental right than privacy, as the latter must be balanced against national interests. Privacy rights with respect to financial information require an elastic approach to the parent protections. In contrast, the privilege against self-incrimination is seen as non-derogable, as it is an intrinsic aspect of the fundamental right to a fair trial.

13.55   The privilege against self-incrimination in offshore jurisdictions with written constitutions is limited to criminal proceedings, although the observances of the European Court of Human Rights with regard to the treatment of civil penalties which are akin to criminal penalties are pertinent here once more. Recent authority from The Bahamas, in the case of *Financial Clearing Corporation*,[53] suggests that this more flexible approach may be taken. In this case, a minority judgment of the Court of Appeal found that draconian powers given to a

---

[51] ibid.
[52] (1988) 13 EHRR 379, 388.
[53] Above, n 30.

supervisory offshore authority to compel information and engage in searches and seizures, violated the privilege. Even in offshore jurisdictions which are still UK dependent territories, such as the BVI and the Cayman Islands, the privilege has been upheld in financial affairs.[54] With the incorporation of the European Convention in the UK, and its consequent extension to such territories, the protection of human rights is enhanced.

Similarly, the right to privacy with respect to financial affairs has been fiercely protected under the European Convention, with even considerations of proportionality being brought into the equation. In contrast, it is less well protected in those jurisdictions where privacy is not an explicit right under the constitution. Further, rights to privacy are subject to derogation, as is reasonably necessary in a democratic society. Accordingly, they are more easily surrendered than the privilege. In the necessary balancing exercise, the needs of law enforcement may hold sway.[55]

13.56

Human rights protection under treaties

Offshore jurisdictions often enshrine the available constitutional protections in international instruments, such as mutual legal assistance treaties and incorporating legislation.[56] This reduces the reach of onshore authorities and helps to insulate trusts which perform tax functions. In *Re Canton of Berne*,[57] the Grand Court of the Cayman Islands upheld the privilege against self-incrimination in the face of a request from the Swiss authorities for information on offshore investment.

13.57

G. Onshore Professionals Have a Duty to Advise on Offshore Opportunities

In passing, it should be emphasized that *Slattery*[58] imposes a duty on onshore professionals to advise clients of the offshore tax planning option, where appropriate. Ths is a gratuitous horizon for offshore entities, including trusts.

13.58

---

[54] See, eg, *Arawak Trust Company v Holden* (CA, BVI) No 2 of 1994, decided 19 September 1994, and *Re Canton of Berne* [1996] CILR 179.

[55] An in-depth discussion of constitutional issues as they related to the offshore sector generally, both from the perspectives of offshore and onshore jurisdictions, is given in chapters 8 and 9 of the companion book, Antoine, above, n 32.

[56] See, eg, the Mutual Assistance in Criminal Matters Act 1996 of Saint Lucia, s 18; Treaty Between Antigua and Barbuda and the USA on Mutual Legal Assistance on Criminal Matters 1996, entered into force 18 January 1999, Art 3(1); Treaty on Mutual Assistance in Criminal Matters Between The Bahamas and the USA (Nassau, 12 June, entered into force 18 July 1990), Art 3.

[57] [1996] CILR 179.

[58] See above, n 23.

14

OVERVIEW OF STATUTORY TAX COUNTERMEASURES AGAINST OFFSHORE TRUSTS

A. Introduction

Development of countermeasures

The development of countermeasures to tax planning or avoidance has occurred **14.01** both by legislative and judicial engineering, with the latter perhaps seeking to reflect the policies of the former. This is an evolutionary, fast-changing process, and very much a reactive one. Countermeasures are usually created as loopholes in tax regulations become apparent. As such, an overview of statutory provisions cannot effectively substitute for current tax advice in any particular onshore jurisdiction.

As with general anti-tax avoidance legislation, the trend in major onshore coun- **14.02** tries in relation to trusts has been to counter their use for tax avoidance tech- niques. For foreign or offshore trusts, the method has been to extend more jurisdiction and control over them, by deeming several typical features of such trusts to be evidence of domestic involvement and character, or by automatically applying special rules of taxation to foreign or offshore trusts. This makes it difficult for trusts established offshore or abroad to be viewed as non-resident trusts which can escape tax liability. Expanded tax liability has been as a result both of increased jurisdiction to tax entities and individuals previously non- taxable, and financial transactions hitherto non-taxable. Indeed, the traditional concept of the residence of the trust, in a sense, is irrelevant for the taxation of trusts. For example, trusts may be liable to taxation where income arises from onshore sources, regardless of residence.[1]

14.03   It will be observed that the rules on residence have been creatively expanded and interpreted in order to capture more offshore trusts established outside of the onshore jurisdiction. The traditional rule of taxation, based upon the principle of territoriality, that is, taxing income only where it originates from a source within that country, is increasingly being eroded in favour of a principle of taxation on the worldwide income of residents, citizens, or domiciled individuals. This occurs, for example, in the US, UK, Canada, and France. The latter principle can significantly undermine the capacity of a person to avoid tax liability from his or her country of residence or citizenship.

Emigration provisions on taxation

14.04   Tax countermeasures do not merely target persons who are resident in onshore jurisdictions. Of significance to offshore investment are the attempts to reach beyond traditional parameters confined to territorial jurisdiction. These include tax provisions and initiatives specifically aimed at citizens and residents who choose to emigrate to low or no tax jurisdictions in order to avoid onerous tax liabilities arising out of their place of residence. These tax initiatives have been designed to bring such persons into the zone of tax liability. The special taxes levied on expatriate residents and trusts may be imposed at the point of departure as an automatic exit tax, or for a designated time-period after emigration. This concept of extended non-resident tax liability is found in several countries.[2]

Tax planning and the trust

14.05   In equity, the essence of the trust is the separation of the original owner of the assets, vesting them in another to hold for the benefit of a third party. In theory, as the owner of the assets is no longer the settlor, the assets of the trust can no longer be viewed as his or hers and he or she should not be liable to tax for them. Tax planning through trusts, therefore, seeks to exploit this distinction between legal and equitable ownership. What tax countermeasures do, however, is to challenge the notion that the assets have actually been separated from the settlor,

---

[1] See eg, § 679 of the Inland Revenue Code of the US, and ss 23, 96, and 102 of the Income Tax Assessment Act 1936 of Australia.
[2] See eg, under the Illegal Immigration Reform and Responsibility Act 1996 of the US. Germany was one of the first to introduce this type of tax, under the Foreign Tax Law (*Aussensteuergesetz*) 1972, ss 2–5.

by going beyond the form and structure of the three-tiered trust to ascertain true ownership. While equity has grown up allowing a fair measure of leeway on this question of ownership, for example by allowing the settlor to be a beneficiary, and offshore laws have gone even further, tax countermeasures go in the opposite direction. Simply put, any hint that the settlor still benefits from the trust will be treated as evidence of ownership. Indeed, there is an underlying presumption that a foreign trust with onshore beneficiaries or an onshore settlor does not transfer ownership. The question of ownership is approached largely through the issues of control and financial advantage.

This policy can be seen to be very detrimental to the offshore trust where the settlor is, typically, a beneficiary who seeks to continue to have some kind of influence on the management of the assets. **14.06**

From a strict legal position, while the offshore trust is not declared null and void, and a trust is treated as if in existence, for purposes of tax the effect is the same as if no foreign trust exists. **14.07**

As the trust is not a legal person, it is usually the individuals involved in the trust, the trustee or beneficiaries, who must bear the brunt of income tax. It should be noted, however, that offshore trusts, such as purpose trusts, may have no identifiable beneficiaries, and anti-tax avoidance measures must take this into account. Since tax countermeasures will not be entirely successful if they place reliance on the income of the beneficiaries alone, settlors are targeted. This was of one of the reasons for the recent change to the Canadian tax laws on trusts.[3] In addition, onshore taxation policy may impose tax liabilities on trust beneficiaries, even in the absence of distributions made to them.[4] **14.08**

As statutory anti-tax avoidance measures target the more typical offshore trust structure, where the settlor is resident or domiciled in an onshore country, the trustee is resident offshore, and the beneficiaries are also in the onshore country, or possibly in another jurisdiction, this is our focus also. However, the ability of settlors and beneficiaries who do not fall into this construct, to continue to take advantage of offshore trusts, is apparent. **14.09**

Presumption that tax avoidance motive unlawful

Modern onshore legislative provisions seeking to undermine tax planning may embody a 'substance over form' approach by emphasizing and outlawing **14.10**

---

[3] See below, paras 14.62–14.67.
[4] See eg, s 86, First Schedule, para 6, of the Taxation of Chargeable Gains Act 1992 of the UK. A beneficiary incurs liability when the trust realizes a capital gain, even if not paid out to that beneficiary. The beneficiary has a statutory right to be reimbursed by the trustee, a right which may not be enforceable, as discussed in chapter 17.

transactions which have tax planning purposes. Consequently, taxpayers who carry out transactions, or establish trusts, with a view to avoiding or evading taxes, immediately run foul of the law.[5] These legislative presumptions encapsulate the modification to the rule on tax avoidance, discussed below.[6]

Civil law assumptions about the trust in tax matters

14.11   Where the trust is established by a settlor from a civil law country, or where the beneficiaries reside or are domiciled in a civil law country, the issue of taxation may fall to be considered by conflict of laws principles. This was the case in *Norway v Olsen*.[7] Here, the trust was established by a settlor who was of Norwegian origin but not resident in Norway, for beneficiaries who were Norway residents. As the trust of the Common Law tradition is not an institution available in Norway, the court had to find a mechanism with which to treat with the trust. It did so by applying rules of private international law.[8] The relevant law, the Corporation Taxes Act 1992, §§ 7-1 to 7-3, imputed tax liability to those who owned or controlled the trust. The court viewed the Norwegian private law concept of ownership as the 'starting point' in determining tax liabilities.

14.12   The issue before the court was whether Norwegian taxpayers had interests which resembled ownership rights. While under the traditional English trusts law the trustee was to be regarded as the owner of the assets, this was not the appropriate approach here. The main objective of the trust was to benefit the beneficiaries, in respect both of current profits and of the estate on liquidation. The court also rejected the fiction of an ownerless trust.

14.13   Although the beneficiaries had received no entitlements under the trust and had no right to distribution, they were regarded as the taxpayers who owned or controlled the trust for purposes of taxation. There was an assumption made that the duty of the trustees to maintain the trust estate and to administer the profits to the benefit of the beneficiaries would result in equal treatment of the different classes of the family beneficiaries. The common interest of the beneficiaries was a decisive factor in the administration of the trust and, in reality, the trustees were not completely free to manage the trusts, without respect to either the interests or the wishes of the beneficiaries.

---

[5] See, eg, Income Tax Assessment Act 1936 of Australia; Income Tax Act 1994 of New Zealand; and the legislation of the UK, US, and Canada, discussed below, paras 14.21–14.79.

[6] Chapter 15.

[7] (2003) 5 ITELR 77.

[8] However, the court rejected the argument that the trust should be treated as an entity akin to the more familiar concept of a 'foundation'. See the discussion below in chapter 21, 'The Recognition of the Offshore Trust in Civil Law Countries', particular, paras 21.8–21.13.

The economic reality of the trust thus demonstrated that the beneficiaries were **14.14** de facto owners of it. The legislation addressed trusts which were under the control of Norwegian taxpayers. Accordingly, in cases in which the beneficiaries directly or indirectly derived benefits from estates in low tax jurisdictions, the beneficiaries fell appropriately within the legislation's jurisdiction and were liable to tax.[9]

Justice Utgard's dissent emphasized the norms applicable to trust ownership, **14.15** noting that: 'A trust is a legal person without parallels in our law.' There are entities under Norwegian law where nobody owns the estate, such as the foundation. As the beneficiaries had no rights to receive distributions and there could be no assumption that the trust would be liquidated under accepted principles of statutory construction and private law, the trust could not be regarded as 'directly or indirectly owned' by the beneficiary Norwegian taxpayers.[10]

It is suggested that the principle in *Norway v Olsen* is not wide enough to force **14.16** the conclusion that, in civil law countries, trust structures will generally be disregarded in such a way as to deem all beneficiaries the owners of trusts. Rather, the decision is to be restricted to the particular facts of the case, where the beneficiaries, because of the peculiar trust arrangement, were viewed as the persons exercising real influence and control over the trust. The court's result was, therefore, similar to the line of cases which disregard trusts as alter-egos or shams, where the trustees do not retain the control and discretion required of their office.[11]

In contrast, in the Swedish case of *Re an Isle of Man Trust*,[12] the trust was viewed **14.17** as a type of foundation, the Swedish legal entity found to be closest in nature to the trust.[13] The Tax Panel had considerable difficulty in ascertaining the legal ownership of the trust property, given its unfamiliarity with the unique concept of the trust. It did, however, find that the beneficiaries were not the legal owners, but could not agree that the trustees were the owners under Swedish law. Whilst it accepted that the trust under the common law is not a legal person, it found it 'convenient to consider that the assets of the trust belong to the trust',[14] hence the analogy to the civilian foundation.[15] Under s 8 of the National Wealth Tax

---

[9] *Norway v Olsen*, above, n 7, 112–13, Justice Utgard, dissenting.

[10] Under § 7-3.

[11] See discussion of sham trusts in chapter 8, 'The Offshore Trust as a Sham'.

[12] (1998–99) 1 ITELR 103, (Tax Panel, Stockholm, Sweden).

[13] The Tax Panel pointed out that the Sweden had not ratified the Convention on the Law Applicable to Trusts and on their Recognition, (The Hague, 1 July 1985; UKTS 14 (1992); Cm 1823; 23 ILM 1388) and therefore had no legal obligations to recognize the trust.

[14] Above, n 12, 113.

[15] Relying on Hassler, *Om Stiftelser,* Stockholm 1952, at pp 20ff, the Supreme Administrative Court RA, 1997, ref 31.

Act of Sweden, the beneficial owner of an asset of the foundation is deemed to be the owner, but this depended on an interpretation that the beneficiary had a 'right to the income'.[16] This excluded the trust beneficiaries in the instant case. There was nobody under the trust at the present time who could be subject to wealth tax, as no one had a right to the income.

14.18　However, s 31 of the Municipal Income Tax Act made persons who received income from employment, including periodic allowances, subject to income tax. The trust beneficiaries qualified under this provision and could, therefore, be subject to income tax. It should be noted, however, that, unlike the beneficiaries in *Norway*, the beneficiaries here became liable to the income tax only when and if they actually received income distributions from the trust. This demonstrates the importance attached to the interpretation given to the trust in civil law countries.

14.19　The Tax Panel accepted that the trust was foreign and not Swedish, as it had been created by a settlor who was not resident in Sweden at the time, although of Swedish origin. Consequently, there was no liability to Swedish wealth or income taxes. Since neither the settlor nor the beneficiaries had a right to the income of the trust and could not be viewed, as owners of the trust, they too could not be subjected to wealth taxes.

Deemed residence and treaty advantages

14.20　The mechanism of treating ostensibly foreign trusts which have resident settlors or beneficiaries as resident in the onshore country, has the effect, for tax purposes, of allowing such trusts to be resident for tax treaty purposes also. Where double tax treaties exist with offshore countries, this may offer tax planning opportunities.[17]

B. The United Kingdom[18]

14.21　Tax avoidance rules in the UK have been engineered so as to override, in certain circumstances, the fundamental principle of trust law which views the settlor as separate and apart from the trust. Consequently, for income tax purposes,

---

[16] Under s 5 of the said Act.

[17] This might be the case with Canada, for example. See chapter 16, paras 16.1–16.37, which discuss tax treaties.

[18] While there are three separate tax statutes for the UK, England and Wales, Scotland, and Northern Ireland, the substance of the laws are the same for the taxation of trusts. Here we examine the statutes for England and Wales.

persons domiciled or resident in the UK who establish trusts outside of the UK, may be liable to income tax where they establish trusts in situations which are viewed as abusive. In effect, the trust is treated as void, with the income of the trust being deemed the income of the settlor, thereby causing the settlor to incur tax liability.[19] The provisions referred to are not confined to trusts but refer to all transfers of assets abroad for the purpose of avoiding UK tax.

As UK residents and citizens, with few exceptions, are taxed on their worldwide income, a UK resident or domiciled beneficiary will also be liable to tax on income earned from a foreign trust such as an offshore trust, except in certain strict circumstances. **14.22**

Trustees who are domiciled or resident in the UK may also be subject to tax. **14.23** However, it is not expected that the trustee, in an offshore trust, will be either domiciled or resident in the UK.

Where settlor retains an interest or is deemed to derive income from the trust

Part XV of the Income and Corporation Taxes Act 1988, imposes an income tax **14.24** on a UK settlor who has retained an interest in the trust as if, in fact, the property had remained the settlor's.[20] An interest is retained by a settlor where the trust property is 'payable to or applicable for the benefit of the settlor or his spouse in any circumstances whatsoever'. The Act contains a number of exceptions to the strict rule, such as where the trust property reverts to the settlor through the bankruptcy of the beneficiary, or upon the death of a beneficiary who is a child of the settlor and is 25 years old or less.[21]

Payments made to a settlor's unmarried minors during the settlor's or his **14.25** spouse's lifetime may also be treated as income accruing to the settlor and taxed accordingly, even where the settlor or his spouse retains no direct benefit in the interest. A similar provision found in South Africa was litigated in the case of *South African Revenue Service v Woulidge*.[22] Here, the settlor sold shares to the trusts established for his minor children by granting a loan to each one, which

---

[19] The main provisions are found under the Income and Corporation Taxes Act 1988, Part XV, Chapters 1A and 1B, ss 660A–682A, and the Income and Corporation Taxes Act 1988, ss 739–746.

[20] Where this occurs, the trustee is not liable to the tax except for certain prescribed taxes such as in relation to interest. The settlor has a corresponding right to recover the tax payment from the trustees.

[21] Income and Corporation Taxes Act 1988, ss 660A(3). Other examples include where both of the parties to a marriage settlement die, or one or more children of the marriage die, and where there is a charge or assignment on the property by the beneficiary.

[22] [2002] SAR 68 (CA).

financed the sale. He declined to charge interest on the loans and thereby minimized his tax liabilities.[23]

14.26   The question of taxable income deemed to have been received by the parent had to be calculated by the court. The Court of Appeal rejected the application of the *in duplum* rule, a rule of public policy that the interest owed on a loan may not exceed the amount of the original loan. The rule was found not to serve public policy considerations where there was no commercial arm's length transaction. As such, the amount of interest on which the settlor should be taxed could not be limited by the application of the rule. Capital sums from the trust or a company connected with the trust, and paid to the settlor or his spouse, are also treated as the settlor's income for income tax purposes.

Special anti-avoidance provisions for non-resident trusts

14.27   Special anti-avoidance provisions have been formulated with a view to countering tax avoidance abroad and are, therefore, particularly significant for offshore trusts. Unlike the more general provisions on the taxation of trusts, a motive to avoid taxation by the transfer of assets abroad is required for liability to arise under these provisions. The provisions have a punitive focus and are wide-reaching. Thus, s 739 of the Income and Corporation Taxes Act 1988 of the UK states:

> . . . this section shall have effect for the purpose of preventing the avoiding by individuals ordinarily resident in the United Kingdom of liability to income tax by means of transfers of assets by virtue or in consequence of which, either alone or in conjunction with associated operations, income becomes payable to persons [including trusts] resident or domiciled outside the United Kingdom.

Despite the wording of the preamble, as made clear by the additional s 739(1A)(b), the charge applies widely to the avoidance of a liability to any tax and is not limited to income tax.

14.28   The transfer must result in the individual, or his or her spouse, having a 'power to enjoy' any income of a non-resident or non-domiciled person (including a trust), or receiving or being entitled to any capital sum in any way connected to the transfer, or any associated operation, for the individual to be made liable to tax.[24] The power to enjoy is not limited to beneficial enjoyment or entitlement but may include the situation where the individual has the power to control, either directly or indirectly, the application of the resulting income.[25] This cannot include a beneficiary who merely has power to appoint trustees, since

---

[23] Note that the Court of Appeal also found that it was not a sham as it was a valid sale transaction with only the forbearance of the interest being gratuitous.

[24] See s 739(2) and (3).

[25] This was the finding in *Inland Revenue Commissioners v Schroeder* [1983] SC 480.

such a beneficiary is not able to control the application of income in a discretionary trust as this power is reserved to the trustee.

Section 739 refers to transferors of the property. Other persons who benefit **14.29** from the transfer of assets abroad, such as the beneficiaries, are caught under s 740 of the Income and Corporation Taxes Act 1988. This latter section makes individuals who are ordinarily resident in the UK and who receive a benefit from a s 739 transfer abroad, but who, not being transferors, are not themselves taxable under s 739, liable to taxation. The benefit does not have to be in the form of income.[26]

Defences and exemptions

Liability to taxation under ss 739 and 740 of the Income and Corporation Taxes **14.30** Act 1988 is excepted where the individual can prove that:

(1) tax avoidance was not the purpose, or one of the purposes, of the transfer of assets or its associated operations; or

(2) the transfer and its associated operations were bona fide commercial transactions and were not carried out for the purpose of tax avoidance.[27]

Taxing capital gains from offshore trusts

Special anti-avoidance rules preclude offshore trusts from benefiting from the **14.31** usual provisions applicable to domestic trusts, whereby non-resident trustees of such domestic trusts can realize income free of UK capital gains tax when they are not carrying on a business in the UK. Further, beneficiaries of offshore trusts are not entitled to exemptions from capital gains tax arising from deemed disposals of interests in the trust.

Residence, which is the prerequisite for the taxation of trusts in the UK, is **14.32** defined differently for capital gains tax purposes than for income tax purposes. A trust is non-resident for capital gains tax purposes where the general administration of the trust is ordinarily carried on outside of the UK and all or the majority of the trustees are either non-resident or not ordinarily resident, criteria easily met by most offshore trusts. To counter this, where the trustee is a professional trustee, the trust is non-resident where the whole of the trust property is, or derives from, property provided by a person neither resident, nor ordinarily resident, nor domiciled in the UK at the time. Where neither the

---

[26] It appears that a non-domiciled UK individual who is ordinarily resident in the UK will not be charged. See *Tax Bulletin*, April 1999, Issue 40, 651.

[27] What is a bona fide commercial purpose is a question of law and may not include merely making investments.

trustees nor the settlor are domiciled or ordinarily resident in the UK, the trust is regarded as an 'offshore trust'.[28]

Events triggering tax liability

14.33   Offshore trusts become liable to UK capital gains taxation upon the occurrence of certain events. These triggering events are:

(1)   where assets are transferred into the trust;

(2)   when the offshore trust realizes a gain;

(3)   when capital payments are made to UK resident beneficiaries;

(4)   when the UK trust emigrates; and

(5)   where the settlor makes a disposal of an interest in the trust in circumstances where the trustees, had they been resident in the UK, would have been chargeable to capital gains tax.[29]

14.34   Despite the fact that the trustees are non-resident, where a settlor or an associated person who is domiciled, resident, or ordinarily resident in the UK retains an interest in the offshore trust, a tax charge may be made, as any capital gain is attributed to the settlor. Certain preconditions must be met. The trust must be a qualifying trust[30] and resident offshore for the entire year. There must also have been, during the year, a disposal of trust property originating from the settlor, in respect of which the trustees would have been liable to capital gains tax had they been resident in the UK. Lastly, the settlor must be alive at the end of the tax year.

14.35   A settlor's interest may be exempted for the purpose of assessing liability in certain circumstances, such as, where the interest arises in defined bankruptcy situations, or on the death of a person under the age of 25 who was beneficially entitled to the property.

Protected trusts

14.36   Protected trusts are not caught by the charging provisions. These are trusts where the beneficiaries are confined to the following persons:

(1)   minor children of the settlor and his or her spouse;

(2)   unborn children of the settlor, or of the current or future spouses of the settlor;

---

[28] Note that the term 'offshore trust' is here used to mean only those foreign trusts which escape liability for purposes of tax onshore under the residence requirements.

[29] The Taxation of Chargeable Gains Act 1992, s 86.

[30] Qualifying trusts are those prescribed by legislation, eg, under s 86 initially and under s 132 of the Finance Act 1998, which extended the definition under s 86. In effect, all offshore trusts except protected trusts, described in the following section, are qualifying trusts.

(3) future spouses of any children or future children of a settlor, or of a spouse or future spouse of a settlor;

(4) a future spouse of a settlor; and

(5) persons who are not 'defined persons'[31] under the Act.

Capital payments and additional charges to beneficiaries

In the case of capital payments made to UK domiciled and resident beneficiaries, it is not necessary for the settlor to be domiciled or resident in the UK for capital gains tax to become payable by such beneficiaries. However, the resident beneficiary must be domiciled in the UK for the charge to apply.[32]   **14.37**

A supplementary charge, referred to as a 'parking charge', is imposed on beneficiaries in order to avoid deferrals of tax that may arise where a capital payment is matched with a trust gain. Without the supplementary charge, beneficiaries can defer making the capital payments where the trust gain arises more than one year previously. The supplementary charge also captures transfers of property from one trust to another.   **14.38**

Emigration of the trust

The emigration of a domestic UK trust can occur where non-resident trustees are appointed to the trust, and these non-resident trustees form a majority of the trustees, or where the UK resident trustees themselves emigrate from the UK. Upon emigration, the trustees are deemed to have disposed of and immediately reacquired the trust property for its market value immediately before the trust emigrates, thus incurring a charge to capital gains tax. The tax is, in effect, an automatic exit or departure tax.   **14.39**

Disposing of interests in an offshore trust

In contrast to domestic trusts, where an interest in an offshore trust is disposed of, it is not exempted from capital gains tax. The gain is calculated by taking into account the market value of the actual disposal proceeds.   **14.40**

Inheritance tax

Offshore trusts are also liable to inheritance taxes in similar fashion to onshore trusts. The tax applies upon transfers of property made upon death and to non-exempted lifetime gifts made within seven years of death. For UK domiciled settlors, the tax applies to property wherever it is situated; whereas for non-UK   **14.41**

---

[31] 'Defined persons' include the settlor, spouse, children of the settlor or his spouse and their spouses, any company controlled by any of the above, and any company associated with one so controlled. See Sch 5 of the Taxation of Chargeable Gains Act 1992.

[32] The Taxation of Chargeable Gains Act 1992, s 87.

domiciled settlors, only assets situated in the UK are caught. Consequently, the creation of an offshore trust does not avoid inheritance taxes where the settlor is domiciled in the UK.

14.42   Certain categories of property are excluded from inheritance taxes. The three main categories are UK government tax exempt securities held by non-domiciled or non-resident UK persons, trust property situated outside of the UK where the trust was created by a non-domiciled UK person, and property situated outside of the UK to which a non-UK domiciled person is entitled. Recent changes made to the rules on inheritance tax made under the Finance Act 2002[33] also exempt certain 'small estates'.

14.43   When a person domiciled in the UK, where certain conditions are fulfilled, dies leaving an estate which has gross assets and specified transfers that do not exceed £263,000, that estate qualifies as an excepted estate and is exempt from inheritance tax. Certain conditions must be met with regard to the assets, for example, the assets must be held in a single trust.[34]

Judicial interpretation of single trust

14.44   The Court of Appeal has now ruled, in the case of *Rysaffe Trustee Co (Cayman Islands) v Inland Revenue Commissioners*,[35] that where the settlor establishes discretionary trusts by separate trust instruments, they should be treated as separate trusts and not as a single settlement. In *Rysaffe*, two brothers executed five trust deeds in respect of nominal sums of £10 each. Thereafter, shares held in private companies were added to the trusts, comprising 6,900 shares in each trust. The Revenue treated the trusts as a single settlement in its interpretation of s 64 of the Inheritance Act 1984, which provided for a charge to tax on 'property comprised in a settlement', at the 10-year anniversary of the settlement.

14.45   The Special Commissioners agreed, relying on s 43(2) of the Act, which defined 'settlement' as 'any disposition or dispositions of property', and s 272, which provided that a 'disposition' included a disposition effected by 'associated operations'. It was found that the establishment of the five trusts and the subsequent transfers of the shares were 'associated operations' within the meaning of s 261(1), resulting in a single settlement. The High Court reversed the decision.

14.46   On appeal to the Court of Appeal, the Revenue's appeal was dismissed. Each of

---

[33]   See also the Inheritance Tax (Delivery of Accounts) (Excepted Capital Estates) Regulations 2002 (SI 2002 No 1733).

[34]   If the deceased is not domiciled in the UK and dies outside of the UK, with assets in the UK, the estate is exempt only if there is a gross value of £100,000 or less and those assets are made up of cash and securities only.

[35]   (2003) 5 ITELR 706 (CA).

the trusts was to be viewed as a 'settlement' for the purposes of the Act, since each satisfied the definition of 'settlement' under s 43(2)(b), namely, a disposition of property whereby the property was for the time being held by trustees on trust. There were five settlements and not one single trust. The 'property comprised in a settlement' was, therefore, 6,900 shares in the company, and not that number multiplied by five, that is, 34,500 shares. There was no need to ask additional questions, such as whether the dispositions were by 'associated operations', as the statutory description of 'disposition' was not intended for cases where there was no dispute that there was a disposition of property falling within s 43(2), such as in the instant case. Rather, it was intended for cases where there was a dispute as to whether there was a relevant disposition at all. The case thus gives some legitimacy to a common tax planning method which may be utilized through offshore trusts.

Meaning of 'property' includes trust powers and rights

The meaning of the term 'property' must be viewed as expansive since the decision of *Melville and Others v Inland Revenue Commissioners*.[36] Here, the settlor was a potential beneficiary and the trust instrument conferred on him a power to direct the trustees to exercise any one or more of their discretionary powers of appointment, including the transfer of all or part of the trust fund to the settlor/beneficiary. The settlor transferred securities to the trustees to be held by the trusts. The transfers were chargeable transfers within s 2(1) of the Inheritance Act 1984. Under s 5(9) of the Act, a person's 'estate' was the aggregate of all of the property to which he was beneficially entitled. Section 272 further provided that, except where the context otherwise required, 'property' included rights and interests of any description. In issue was whether the settlor's power of appointment was 'property' to which he was beneficially entitled under the Act. 14.47

The Court of Appeal of the UK found that the concept of property could include rights which were exercisable over the trust property. Consequently, this type of property formed part of the estate of the person who owned the power to exercise the right and was taxable for purposes of inheritance tax. 14.48

The powers of revocation or appointment under a trust would fall easily into the *Melville* classification of 'property'. The question that would remain is the method of assessment of the value of such property. Given the nature of a power of revocation over a trust, it would appear to be akin to the entire amount of the trust property. 14.49

The rule in *Melville* extends the taxing power to persons not previously caught, 14.50

---

[36] (2002) 4 ITELR 231.

those who have not retained a tangible interest in the property. For a non-UK domiciled person who retains rights exercisable over trust property in an offshore trust, for example, that property could be deemed to be property situated in the UK.

C. Anti-avoidance Measures from the US

14.51   The principle of taxation on a worldwide income basis is perhaps the first defining characteristic of the tax treatment of trusts in the US. This principle of taxation is applied to citizens and to resident aliens of the US. The source of the income is irrelevant for the purpose of taxation, except in strictly defined circumstances.[37] Income from a foreign trust, otherwise referred to as an international or offshore trust, can, therefore, easily be captured under this general rule.[38]

14.52   Apart from the principle of worldwide taxation, special rules of taxation apply to foreign trusts. These rules impact directly on offshore trusts. The special regime for foreign trusts was given impetus by the Small Business Job Protection Act 1996, which provided a new definition of a 'foreign trust' and established an objective two-step test for determining whether a trust is domestic or foreign.[39] Ultimately, the question of control over the trust is crucial to determining whether a trust is domestic or foreign, and whether it is liable to US tax. Under section 7701 (a) 30 IRC,[40] a trust is foreign if:

(1)   a US court is unable to exercise primary supervision over its administration; and
(2)   no US person has authority to control the substantial decisions of the trust.

Jurisdiction over the trust's administration

14.53   The first leg of the test, that of supervision over the administration of the trust, is easily satisfied where the governing law of the trust is stated in the trust instrument to be that of the US. Where the foreign or offshore law is named as the proper law, this will favour offshore trusts attempting to avoid US jurisdiction. It should be noted, however, that a declaration that the governing law is to be

---

[37]   See, eg, under 26 USC, Title 26, The Inland Revenue Code (IRC) 911, where a designated amount of foreign earned income is exempt.

[38]   One interpretation of such trusts is any fiduciary arrangement which holds and conserves assets for others where there is no commercial purpose. See Treasury Regulations § 3017701–4.

[39]   Note also the Economic Growth and Tax Relief Reconciliation Act 2001. This legislation began a phase-out of the Federal estate tax in 2002, with a one-year repeal in 2010. As a result, many states will lose some or all of their estate tax revenues because the Act reduces (in 2003 and 2004) and then effectively repeals most state 'sponge' or 'pickup' taxes after 2004.

[40]   The relevant regulations for this section are found under Treasury Regulations §3017701–7.

other than that of the US, or that another court is to have exclusive jurisdiction, will not by itself be sufficient to exclude a US court assuming jurisdiction over the trust for the purpose of exercising supervision over its administration, or indeed for any other purpose. In *Re Portnoy*,[41] for example, the trust instrument explicitly stated that only the courts of the offshore jurisdiction, in this case the Jersey courts, had jurisdiction over the trust. Despite this, on the grounds of public policy, which precluded, in the view of the US court, recognition of self-settled, spendthrift trusts which sought to evade creditors, the US court asserted jurisdiction over the trust.

In addition, the question of primary supervision over the administration of the trust is to be viewed independently from that of other issues of jurisdiction over the trust. It is possible, for example, for a court of another jurisdiction to have jurisdiction over the trustees, beneficiaries, or trust property, while the US court has authority to exercise primary supervision over the administration of the trust. Under the Treasury Regulations,[42] 'administration of the trust' is interpreted to include the carrying out of duties imposed by the terms of the trust instrument and applicable law, filing tax returns, managing and investing the assets of the trust, determining the amount and timing of distributions, and defending the trusts from suits brought by creditors. **14.54**

A flee or flight clause, which attempts to preclude jurisdiction over the trust by providing that the trust will migrate from the US to another jurisdiction if an attempt is made to assert jurisdiction over it, will be good evidence that the US does not have primary supervision over the administration of the trust, but this is not conclusive. In fact, we have seen elsewhere that such flight clauses have been taken as evidence of a deliberate manipulation of the trust, and may, on grounds of public policy, provide encouragement for a court to assume jurisdiction over a trust.[43] **14.55**

Where the trust instrument is silent as to the place of administration of the trust, there is a presumption that it can be administered in the US and the trust may be deemed a domestic trust. **14.56**

Control over the trust

With respect to offshore trusts, perhaps the more important aspect of the test as to whether a trust is foreign or domestic is that of control over substantial decisions of the trust. The test goes further than mere formal power, such as the **14.57**

---

[41] 201 BR 685 (1996).
[42] Above, n 40.
[43] See, eg, the discussion in chapter 8.

power to vote, and is not limited to examining the question of control with reference to the settlor (called a grantor in the US), or the trustee, but speaks broadly to US fiduciaries. The power to veto decisions will be definitive. Ministerial decisions, which are in the nature of delegated decisions, such as keeping accounts or bookkeeping, are not substantial decisions. Examples of substantial decisions include, but are not limited to:

(1) determining the amount and timing of distributions;

(2) adding or removing beneficiaries, or trustees, or protectors;

(3) whether or when to terminate the trust;

(4) legal actions relating to the trust; and

(5) investment decisions, even where there are investment advisers if the US person is in a position to veto the investment adviser's decisions.

Types of foreign trusts

Foreign grantor trusts

14.58   Foreign trusts are further classified into foreign grantor trusts and foreign non-grantor trusts. Foreign grantor trusts are those in which powers or interests are reserved to US persons, enabling such persons to be treated as the owners or beneficiaries of the trust or trust assets for income tax purposes. The typical *inter vivos* offshore trust is a foreign grantor trust, whereby the trust is established by a US person and there are US beneficiaries. This type of trust is particularly vulnerable to US taxation, since the trust, which is supposed to be an independent legal entity that separates the trust property from the settlor, is prejudiced by its continued links with the settlor. Thus, the trust is effectively ignored for income tax purposes. Consequently, the property which was transferred into the trust is viewed as still belonging to the grantor, and income and losses derived from the trust will be treated as the grantor's and liable to taxation.

14.59   Sections 671–678 of the Internal Revenue Code of the US contain the rules of taxation for grantor trusts. Under §679, the rules are specified as applicable to foreign trusts which have one or more US beneficiaries. Under §679, a US person who transfers property to a foreign trust either directly or indirectly, is treated as the owner of the portion of the trust attributable to that property for that taxable year. The tax liability also applies where there is no US beneficiary at the point of creation of the trust, but a US beneficiary is acquired afterward. A five-year rule exception is in operation, whereby a US beneficiary who did not become a US person until more than five years after the transfer of property to the foreign trusts does not cause the trust to be treated as a US grantor trust.[44]

---

[44] IRC §679(c)(3).

Further, the transfers of appreciated property by US persons are treated as sales of that property for the property's fair market value.[45]

Incomplete transfers

Offshore trusts may also fall under Treasury Regulations sections 25.2511–2(c), **14.60** which lay down rules concerning the taxation of incomplete gifts. A transfer of assets into a foreign trust will be treated as an incomplete gift where the grantor reserves to himself or herself unlimited powers to name new beneficiaries, or to change the interests assigned to beneficiaries. The property therefore continues to vest in the purported settlor. The transfer is also considered incomplete under §2036 of the Inland Revenue Code, with the result being that the property is included in the estate of a deceased settler and made liable to taxation.[46]

Foreign non-grantor trusts

A foreign non-grantor trust is one in which powers or benefits which can be **14.61** viewed as belonging to US persons, thereby subjecting them to US tax liabilities, are absent. For example, a revocable trust established by a US citizen or resident, in which there are no US beneficiaries, may be a foreign non-grantor trust. The transfer of property into such a trust will be treated as a completed gift. The event of the death of a grantor of a foreign grantor trust can also change the characterization of that trust to one of a foreign non-grantor trust. Where US persons can receive distributions only after one taxable year of the grantor or his or her spouse, this may qualify the trust as a foreign non-grantor trust.[47] Tax may be deferred during the period where there are no US beneficiaries.[48]

D. Canada

As in the US and the UK, tax law in Canada seeks to ignore and look through **14.62** the establishment of a foreign trust where the trust is effectively controlled by, or retains substantial connections with, Canadian citizens or residents. In so doing, the trust property is treated as belonging to the Canadian person and renders that person liable to tax.[49] Further, the Canadian tax regime for trusts contains provisions which allow certain transactions, changes, or entities to be ignored

---

[45] IRC §684(a); Reg 1.68401(a)(1).

[46] A completed gift in trust is one in which the settlor completely abandons control of the property. For example, a transfer to a minor child which can be utilized in the year of the transfer by the child or its beneficiaries may be a complete gift.

[47] This may be achieved through an offshore irrevocable life insurance trust, for example.

[48] However, US source income of a foreign non-grantor trust is subject to US taxation.

[49] Under the Income Tax Act, RSC 1985 (as amended 2002) C1 (5th Supp) Div B, Subdivisions K and I.

for the purpose of taxation by emphasizing their substance. So, for example, with respect to property which is transferred by a Canadian resident to a trust on the condition that it may revert to the settlor, any income or gain from that property will be attributed to the settlor.[50]

Income tax in Canada

14.63   Canadian citizens and residents are taxable on their worldwide income, irrespective of its source.[51] The trust is deemed an 'individual' for income tax purposes, and is also taxed on its undistributed worldwide income.[52] Ownership and control are once again instrumental to the taxation of the trust. The trust is defined with reference to its trustees, executors, heirs, administrators, and/or legal representatives having ownership or control of the trust property. If persons who have ownership and control of the trust are residents of Canada, they incur liability to tax. Consequently, for offshore trusts, even where trustees reside offshore but significant control is located in persons in Canada, this may lead to liability to Canadian taxation. Significantly for offshore trusts, *inter vivos* trusts in Canada are taxed at the maximum individual rate of income tax.

14.64   Under s 104(4) of the Income Tax Act, upon the establishment of a trust, the settlor is treated as having made a disposition of the property at its fair market value and the trust is deemed to have acquired the property at this value. After this initial disposition, there will be a deemed disposition of the property every 21 years.[53]

14.65   Beneficiaries of the trust are taxed on the income from the trust which is payable to them, and this amount may be deducted from the taxable amount of the trust.[54] Deductions from the taxable income are also made for the normal expenses of maintenance, and for upkeep of the trust and trust property.

New tax rules for trusts

14.66   The older tax legislation allowed considerable tax advantages, particularly in view of the fact that the residence of beneficiaries was important in assessing tax

---

[50]   ibid s 75(2).

[51]   Either for income earned in Canada covered under Part 1 of the Income Tax Act 1985, above, n 48, or under Part XIII in respect of withholding tax on amounts paid or credited to them.

[52]   Previous rules taxed only income earned in Canada and passive investment income from non-Canadian sources.

[53]   There is no inheritance tax regime.

[54]   There is an exception under s 104(7) of the Income Tax Act 1985 (am'd 2002), with respect to designated beneficiaries under s 210 of the said Act. The portion of the taxable income attributed to the designated beneficiary is subject to income tax. A designated beneficiary is defined as a non-resident person, a non-resident owned investment corporation, specified tax-exempt entities, and certain partnerships and trusts. The list is not exhaustive.

liability. The new amendments to the Income Tax Act aimed to correct this perceived loophole, and generally to make it easier to deem a foreign trust resident in Canada. Thus, a non-resident trust will be deemed to be resident for income tax purposes where a person resident in Canada contributes assets, or loans property, to the trust, regardless of when the contribution was made or, as before, benefits from the trust.

For purposes of determining residence, the person must have been resident in Canada for at least five years. The notion of residence is broad and may include persons, born or resident in Canada, who emigrate for work purposes but who maintain a home in Canada. In addition, the favourable treatment for immigrants is retained, so that a non-resident settlor who immigrates to Canada will not be taxed for a period of up to five years with respect to non-resident trusts established before immigration and with the settlor's non-Canadian assets. Contributors and resident beneficiaries of foreign trusts deemed to be resident, are made jointly and severally liable for the tax liabilities of the trust. However, the liability for tax and reporting requirements lie primarily with trustees.[55]   **14.67**

Capital gains tax in Canada

Capital gains and distributions of the trust are also taxable in Canada. However, where withholding tax is involved, there is a presumption that distributions from a trust are income payments unless proved otherwise. Non-resident beneficiaries may still derive advantages in relation to tax deferrals.[56]   **14.68**

Flow through effect

Income from prescribed sources, such as capital gains, may retain its character for the purpose of determining the tax liability of a beneficiary who receives it. Outside of this prescription, sources of income are taxed as ordinary income from property when distributed to the beneficiaries.   **14.69**

Under s 108(5) of the Income Tax Act, amounts payable to beneficiaries which have not been specified for 'flow throughs' shall be deemed to be income from an interest in the trust and not from any other source, and are taxable for the relevant tax year.   **14.70**

---

[55] There are 'exempt foreign trusts' which are excluded from liability. These include non-resident trusts: (a) for beneficiaries with mental or physical disabilities; (b) established as a result of a marriage breakdown; (c) created for charitable purposes; and (d) established for specified employee benefit schemes.
[56] See, eg, s 107(2) and (5) of the Income Tax Act 1985.

Tax liabilities upon emigration

14.71 Where individuals, including trusts, emigrate from Canada, they are deemed to have disposed of all of their property and a deemed disposition tax becomes due. Property that will continue to be taxed in Canada is exempted from this general rule. In contrast, immigrants to Canada may derive considerable tax savings, as there is a five-year 'grace' period before tax becomes due.

E. Statutory Disclosure Initiatives Relating to Tax and Trusts

Reporting requirements

14.72 A common feature of statutory anti-tax avoidance measures onshore is the requirement to make routine reports about foreign or offshore activities. These enable the tax authorities to identify more accurately the tax assessments due, in situations where they will not normally be able so to do. These reporting requirements apply equally to foreign trusts. The success of such measures is contingent on the attitudes toward bilateral assistance in relation to tax, discussed in a following chapter.[57]

14.73 Reporting requirements also reduce considerably the protection accorded to offshore trusts under laws of confidentiality or privacy. In this vein, we should consider also new developments toward international agreements between onshore and offshore countries, which enable offshore countries to give tax information to onshore countries.[58]

Reporting requirements in the US

14.74 In the US, reporting provisions for foreign trusts and foreign gifts originated in the Small Business Job Protection Act of 1996. This Act expanded information reporting requirements for foreign trusts under §6048 of the Internal Revenue Code. Significantly, the Act introduced new reporting requirements for US beneficiaries of foreign trusts. The civil penalties attached for failure to file information with respect to foreign trusts were considerably upgraded and civil penalties created for failure to report certain transfers to foreign entities.[59]

---

[57] See chapter 16.

[58] Discussed below, 16.39–16.63. See, eg, the Exchange of Information on Taxes Agreement between the Cayman Islands and the US signed by the UK on behalf of the Cayman Islands on 27 November 2001 in Washington DC. The Agreement is due to come into effect in 2005. See more discussion on confidentiality as it relates to tax matters in the chapter 7, 'Disclosure and Confidentiality Obligations', paras 7.18–7.21.

[59] See §§ 6048(c), 6677, and 1494(c), Title 26 USC, Subtitle F, Chapter 61 of IRC.

US persons who receive gifts in excess of $10,000 are also required to file **14.75** information returns under a new section of the Code.[60]

Under §6048(a), a US person must report any gratuitous transfer to a foreign **14.76** trust, except as otherwise provided under Section III E.[61] Non-gratuitous transfers generally are not reportable under §6048(a). However, any transfer in exchange for an obligation that is treated as a qualified obligation[62] must also be reported under §6048(a). Where a reportable transfer occurs by reason of death, the executor of the trust is responsible for reporting the transfer.[63]

Accordingly, the 'responsible parties' are required to file information returns **14.77** with the Treasury Department, for example, when a foreign trust is initially established by a US grantor, where there are beneficiaries,[64] when transfers of property are made to a foreign trust,[65] and when US persons receive distributions from a foreign trust. The person deemed to be the owner of a foreign grantor trust is also required to make annual reports about the activities of the trust and such other information as the Secretary of the Treasury may prescribe.

Reporting requirements in Canada

In Canada, the tax reporting requirements for non-resident trusts are contained **14.78** in s 233 of the Income Tax Act 1985 (as amended in 2002).[66] Canadian residents must file annual information returns if they own foreign property:

(1) where a transfer or loan is made to a non-resident trust; and
(2) where a distribution is received from a non-resident trust, or where a beneficiary owes a debt to a non-resident trust.

The provision applies to any non-resident trust:

---

[60] See IRC §6039F(a).

[61] A gratuitous transfer is any transfer other than (a) a transfer for fair market value, or (b) a corporate or partnership distribution. In relation to a trust, this is irrespective of whether the transfer is a gift for gift tax purposes. See Chapter 12 of Subtitle B of the Inland Revenue Code. A gratuitous transfer to a foreign trust must be reported on Form 3520. The term 'executor' is defined under § 2203 of the Code.

[62] As defined in section III C 2.

[63] Prior to the Small Business Job Protection Act of 1996, a US person who transferred property to a foreign trust was required to report the transfer on Form 3520, 'Creation of or Transfers to Certain Foreign Trusts', within 90 days of the transfer. In addition, US owners of foreign trusts were required to file annually Form 3520-A, 'Annual Return of Foreign Trust with US Beneficiaries'. No reporting was required of US beneficiaries of foreign trusts, or of US persons who received gifts from foreign persons.

[64] There are certain exemptions, such as for the establishment of charitable trusts and pension trusts.

[65] §6048(c)(1) IRC.

[66] Subdivision K.

(1) which has a specified beneficiary resident in Canada, is a corporation or trust with which a person resident in Canada does not deal at arm's length, or which is a controlled foreign affiliate of a person resident in Canada; or

(2) where the terms of the trust permit persons to be added as beneficiaries who may be resident in Canada at the time of being added; or

(3) in which the terms of the trust allow property to be distributed to another trust that, immediately after the receipt of the distribution, can reasonably be expected to be a specified foreign trust.[67]

14.79 Trusts which are exempt from the reporting requirements in Canada include those governed by foreign retirement accounts, a non-resident trust which is providing primarily for superannuation, pension retirement or employee benefits for non-resident beneficiaries, and certain classes of trusts governed by mutual funds.

Reporting requirements in the UK

14.80 Reporting requirements for offshore trusts are also in effect in the UK. Reporting is due upon the creation of an offshore trust, or upon the transfer of property to an offshore trust. In addition, a settlor of an offshore trust who becomes domiciled or ordinarily resident in the UK must report information about the trust within twelve months of the event. Emigrating UK resident trusts also have reporting obligations.[68]

---

[67] See s 233, ibid.
[68] See, eg, s 87 of the Taxation of Chargeable Gains Act 1992.

15

JUDICIAL ENGINEERING OF THE TAX FUNCTION OF OFFSHORE TRUSTS

A. Introduction

It is perhaps no accident that onshore courts, in a legislative environment **15.01** which is increasingly hostile in its approach to tax planning, would appear to mirror this stance in their judicial decisions. Accordingly, in recent years we have witnessed judicial developments which have undermined tax planning in favour of tax collection. This judicial engineering has encompassed even well entrenched rules of the common law, such as the rule on the legality of tax avoidance, as opposed to tax evasion. It extends also to broad concepts able to override trusts which facilitate tax planning, such as the sham doctrine or 'piercing the veil' concept. Offshore courts have, of course, often maintained their independence from such judicial activism, but have not been averse to enhancing their own creative resources. From a bilateral perspective, judicial engineering has meant, further, a reorientation of the rule against non-enforcement of fiscal law. This, however, is considered separately in the following chapter.[1]

Generally, legislation enacted to counter tax measures has been interpreted **15.02** liberally, in favour of Revenue authorities. However, the trend toward judicial engineering in favour of tax responsibility is not uniform. Some courts have questioned their role in this enforcement exercise, or acted in favour of, or sought to maintain, the status quo. These developments are considered in this chapter.

---

[1] Chapter 16, paras 16.1–16.32.

B. Interpreting Tax Avoidance

Tax avoidance lawful according to traditional rules

15.03   The well-known rule on tax avoidance must be assessed when addressing the tax implications for offshore trusts. Stated briefly, the rule may be described as one which affords flexibility to taxpayers to arrange their affairs in such a way as to reduce their tax liabilities to the greatest degree allowed under the stated law. The rule is recognized in both Commonwealth and North American legal systems, and is acknowledged in other legal systems. The authoritative dictum in the *Westminster*[2] case is well known:

> Every man is entitled, if he can, to order his affairs so that the tax attaching under the appropriate Acts is less than it otherwise would be.

15.04   Simply put, taxpayers may take advantage of loopholes in tax legislation, and it is the form and letter of the law, and not motive or substance, which is to be emphasized. A clear distinction between tax avoidance or tax mitigation, a lawful activity, and tax evasion, where both the spirit and letter of the law are violated, is thereby created. As such, the policy objectives of offshore trusts to profit from the legal principle permitting tax avoidance, are unimpeachable in law. Indeed, the principle can be viewed as the foundation or juristic basis for every tax planning initiative, whether onshore or offshore. The compatibility of this generous legal thrust to the underlying philosophy of offshore tax regimes is evident. Yet the distinction between tax evasion and tax avoidance is not always so nicely observed.

15.05   The jurisprudential rationale of the rule is located in the need for certainty in the law, in particular, where the citizen's liberty or interest is involved. The onus is placed on the legislature to ensure that the intent of the statute is clear and certain. It is evident, therefore, that taxpayers have no positive duties voluntarily to assist the state in its objective of harnessing tax revenues.

Challenges to the *Westminster* rule

15.06   There is little doubt that the rule authorizing tax avoidance has been challenged considerably in recent times. It has been clouded by new approaches to statutory interpretation which emphasize intent and substance over form, and by considerations of public policy which disapprove of attempts to undermine tax law and tax policy. Offshore entities, such as offshore trusts, are particularly vulnerable to judicial activism where tax planning is at issue. Indeed, it is safe to

---

[2] *Inland Revenue Commissioner v Duke of Westminster* [1936] AC 1.

suggest that, even in the absence of legislative directives, the very establishment of an offshore trust raises a presumption that there is no true business purpose and that the motive of the transaction is purely tax avoidance.

Consequently, the well-established judicial rule that a taxpayer may take steps to place himself or herself outside of tax liability situations is now questionable. Recent attacks have undermined the *Westminster* rule, albeit not fatally. Nonetheless, with the dramatic increases in legislative anti-avoidance tax measures that attempt to close tax loopholes, even if the rule remains sacrosanct, it is accorded very little room in which to manoeuvre. **15.07**

Ramsay *and its progeny*

The *Ramsay*[3] line of cases ably demonstrates the deviations from the traditional rule on tax avoidance. In *Ramsay*, taxpayers sought, unsuccessfully, to obtain capital gains relief under a scheme which involved highly structured transactions. The scheme, which was viewed as artificial, involved several steps carried out in quick succession and which resulted in a capital loss 'on paper'. While none of the steps was a 'sham', or without substance, the position of the taxpayer at the end of the scheme remained the same as at the start. Consequently, the House of Lords held that such an artificial scheme, carried out only for the purpose of tax avoidance, should be viewed not as a series of short steps, but as a whole. The scheme as a whole was, therefore, self-cancelling, a fiscal nullity. Consequently, the taxpayer was to be treated as if there had been no such transaction.[4] **15.08**

The test is now applied in common law jurisdictions and elsewhere,[5] and several cases can be found which have followed the *Ramsay* approach of 'substance over form', giving to tax statutes a purposive interpretation. For example, in *IRS v McGuckian*,[6] the *Ramsay* principle was upheld in an offshore tax planning arrangement which involved several intricate steps. As the purpose of the arrangement was to secure a tax advantage, the court held that it could disregard those steps, unearthing the substance of the transaction. As such, the dicta in *Ramsay* can be considered a new principle of general application. This new principle is in accord with the US approach and that of civil law jurisdictions which embrace the concept of 'abuse of rights'. It is also a principle which **15.09**

---

[3] *Ramsay Ltd v Inland Revenue Commissioners* [1982] AC 300.
[4] Cf *Fitzwilliam (Countess) v IRC* [1993] 3 All ER 184. Here, the courts appeared to backtrack temporarily. The court held that where the transactions in themselves were not shams, the tax motive was irrelevant.
[5] See, eg, *Re Pong Ten Un (deceased)* (1998–99) 1 ITELR 79 (HC, Hong Kong), involving an offshore trust and confirming that the *Ramsay* principle against tax avoidance applies to Hong Kong.
[6] [1997] STC 908, HL.

appears to fall squarely within the public policy context. When combined with concerns about offshore trusts, the public policy underpinnings of the *Ramsay* principle are magnified.

Substance over form embodied in legislation

15.10   Further, the substance over form approach has now been codified in many onshore jurisdictions.[7] Consequently, legislation now provides that trusts carried out for purposes of tax avoidance violate the terms of tax statutes. Accordingly, the transactors are liable to taxation in the same manner as if no such transaction had taken place. In the case of the settlor of an offshore trust, the settlor will be liable to tax as if the property had remained invested in him or her. Such counter-tax avoidance measures were discussed in the previous chapter. Ultimately, even where offshore trusts are not caught by anti-avoidance statutory rules, they are likely to be addressed by the courts under the 'substance over form' doctrine found in modern tax jurisprudence.

MacNiven—backlash to counter avoidance

15.11   The enthusiastic embrace by the courts of the substance over form approach does not mean that they will be excessively xenophobic about tax planning. Opportunities remain for interpretations of tax statutes which will be generous to taxpayers. For example, one view is that the recent judicial challenges to the *Westminster* rule have suffered a major setback following decisions such as *MacNiven (Inspector of Taxes) v Westmoreland Investments Ltd*.[8] Nonetheless, given the continuing judgments against tax avoidance, these cases, while evidence of a backlash by some courts, do less to stem the tide against tax avoidance and tax planning and more to demonstrate the tensions which exist between tax policy and judicial responsibility.

15.12   *MacNiven* modifies the well-known *Ramsay* rule against tax avoidance. It goes beyond the composite step analysis and creates a dichotomy between terms describing transactions which have commercial meanings and those which have only juristic meanings. In *MacNiven*, a complex commercial scheme was instituted solely for tax avoidance purposes. However, the scheme involved genuine loans and interest payments. A pension scheme made loans to a company, which it used to pay arrears of interest due under earlier loans, then accounting to the Revenue for tax which was then reclaimed by the pension scheme. Because of the transactions, the pension scheme was successful in finding a purchaser for the shares and loan debts of the company. Consequently, when the company's

---

[7] See chapter 14.
[8] [2001] 1 All ER 865. See M Palmer, 'MacNiven (Inspector of Taxes) v Westmoreland Investments Ltd: An Unexpected Boon for UK Taxpayers?' [2002] JTCP 1.

shares were bought, the pension scheme was able to realize a substantial sum for assets which would otherwise have been worthless.

The Revenue argued that in the absence of a commercial purpose, since the scheme was for tax avoidance purposes, the interest paid by the company to the pension scheme did not count as payments of interest within the meaning of s 338 of the Income and Corporation Taxes Act 1988. The company was therefore assessed to corporation taxes for six accounting periods between 1987 and 1992, on the basis that the payments of interest made by the company to the trustees, were not available for set-off against the company's profits. **15.13**

However, the House of Lords disagreed, finding that the term 'payment' under the Act had only a juristic or legal meaning and no broader commercial meaning. The meaning was simply the discharging of a debt, which the company had done by transferring money to the pension scheme. Accordingly, interest had been paid. To hold otherwise would have been contrary to Parliament's intention. *MacNiven v Westmoreland* does not disagree with *Ramsay's* broad principle that a purposive approach to tax legislation should be taken. However, it creates a dichotomy between words and statutory terms which have broad commercial meanings and those which have mere juristic and legal meanings. It is only in the former category that the *Ramsay* principle can be satisfactorily applied. Nonetheless, it appears that *MacNiven* broadens *Ramsay*, in the sense that it applies the principle of purposive interpretation to transactions which do not have composite steps. **15.14**

Another small example is the restrictive interpretation given to the constitution of an 'arrangement' for tax avoidance purposes in the case of *Commissioner of Inland Revenue v Bank of New Zealand Investments Ltd*.[9] Here, the Court of Appeal of New Zealand had to consider the tax liability of an investment structure which involved offshore investments. **15.15**

The Court relied on the interpretation of similar provisions in Australia, such as in *Davis v Federal Commissioners of Taxation*.[10] In the scheme, the Bank of New Zealand (BNZ), using borrowed money, funded its subsidiary, the Bank of New Zealand Investments (BNZI), to enable it to subscribe for redeemable preference shares in companies provided by Capital Markets Ltd (CML). Dividends were earned by the investments. CML then used the proceeds in what was described as complex offshore transactions, which placed the funds in offshore interest-bearing deposits. The dividends on the shares were at rates negotiated between BNZ for BNZI and CML, on the basis that no allowance was required **15.16**

---

[9] [2002] 1 NZLR 450.
[10] (1989) 86 ALR 195, which interpreted s 260 of the Income Tax Assessment Act 1936 of Australia.

for New Zealand tax on downstream income and that the dividends paid would be exempt income as inter-company dividends in the hands of BNZI.

15.17 It was determined by the Inland Revenue that the entire transaction was caught by the anti-avoidance provisions of s 99 of the Income Tax Act 1976 of New Zealand. The High Court disagreed and, on further appeal, the Court of Appeal confirmed the High Court's finding that the transaction was not an 'arrangement' within the meaning of the Act. Rather, such an arrangement for tax avoidance purposes did not exist in a vacuum but required a consensus, a 'meeting of minds' between parties, involving an expectation on the part of each that the other would act in a particular way, having more than merely an incidental purpose or effect of tax avoidance. On the present facts, there was no such 'meeting of minds' as to what steps or activities CML would undertake downstream. It would have been otherwise had CML been BNZI's agent. CML acted in furtherance of its own business, and BNZI had no knowledge of CML's plans.

15.18 However, the Court warned that while knowledge of the tax avoidance purpose is required, a 'commercially realistic approach' should be adopted when assessing the extent of the meeting of minds. In general, a court is unlikely to find persuasive the stance of a taxpayer who professes to have no knowledge of the mechanism by which the tax benefit was to be delivered, and he or she would be regarded as having authorized or accepted the mechanism.[11] In contrast, where, as here, the taxpayer, on reasonable grounds, believes that the tax-saving mechanism used by the other party is legitimate, the requisite consensus will ordinarily be absent. There was thus a natural divide between the upstream and downstream transactions, with the upstream transaction being a standard commercial investment, which would have entitled BNZ to a deduction for interest under the Act.[12]

15.19 It would be inequitable for a taxpayer who entered into an apparently unobjectionable transaction to be deprived of his or her rights thereunder merely because, unknown to the taxpayer, the other party met its obligations under the transaction in a legally objectionable way. The consensus or meeting of minds necessary to constitute an 'arrangement' had to encompass, explicitly or implicitly, the dimension which actually amounted to tax avoidance.

15.20 Cases such as *Rysaffe Trustee Company (Cayman Islands) v Inland Revenue Commissioner*,[13] further reaffirm the longevity and endurance of the tax avoidance

---

[11] Above, n 9, 466.
[12] It was a 'far cry from the self-cancelling and circular schemes that have come before the New Zealand and Australian courts under the general anti-avoidance provisions': ibid, 467.
[13] (2003) 5 ITELR 706 (CA).

rule, despite its recent challenges. In this case, the taxpayer's tax mitigation method, which was to create five separate trusts with shares of £6,900 each, was upheld. The Revenue could not treat the various settlements as one single settlement worth the sum of £6,900 multiplied by five, thereby imputing a greater tax liability to the taxpayer under the terms of the Act.[14] Such decisions grant efficacy to offshore tax-planning routes.

Sustaining foreign tax avoidance and tax minimization arrangements

Judicial boldness with respect to tax matters is not limited to onshore courts. **15.21** Offshore courts have also been spirited when addressing the question of the tax-planning function. Their lack of temerity has been manifested in initiatives actively to assist investors who use trusts to avoid tax in onshore countries. Given the jurisprudential approval of the rule permitting tax avoidance and tax mitigation, it is understandable that the courts have held that there is no obstacle to them upholding offshore arrangements which seek to minimize or avoid taxes. Authority for this also comes from onshore jurisprudence and is tangential to the rule on the non-enforcement of fiscal law. Indeed, in *Re Osias 1980 Settlements*,[15] this was noted as a well-established function of the courts.

The express approval of the courts has come about most often in situations **15.22** where they have been asked to vary trusts for tax reasons. In *Re N*,[16] for example, the Jersey Royal Court, when asked to vary a trust in order to enable the trust to avoid a capital gains tax which otherwise would have arisen onshore, approved the variation. Similarly, in *In the Re Richard Colin Douglas 1990 Settlement*,[17] Deputy Bailiff Birt gave a strong positive response to the question whether the court could give its approval to a requested variation designed to avoid foreign taxes. The court in *In Re Douglas* relied on Lord Denning's dicta in *In Re Weston's Settlements*,[18] to the effect that:

> It [the court] can give its consent to the scheme to avoid death duties or other taxes. Nearly every variation that has come before the court has tax avoidance as its principal object: and no one has ever suggested that this is undesirable or contrary to public policy.[19]

---

[14] The Inheritance Act 1984, ss 43(2) and 64 of the UK.

[15] [1987–88] JLR 389 (Royal Ct), *per* Tomes DB, relying on *Re Whitehead's Will Trust* [1971] 1 WLR 833, 839.

[16] [1999] JLR 86.

[17] [2000] JLR 73 (Royal Ct); (2000) 2 ITELR 682 (Royal Ct).

[18] [1969] 1 Ch 223, 245.

[19] See also Pennycuick VC's dicta in *In Re Whitehead's Will Trust*, above, n 15, affirming the same principle.

This arrangement was to be viewed as a benefit to the persons concerned, the beneficiaries.[20]

15.23   The judgment in *Re Douglas* takes a much bolder step than the earlier case of *Re Osias 1980 Settlements*,[21] where the Jersey Royal Court was ambivalent on the question of whether, and in what circumstances, it could approve an arrangement which would assist in the avoidance of tax. In doing so, it stressed the difference between tax avoidance and tax minimization or tax mitigation. This is, perhaps, a theoretical distinction, but in tax minimization, a taxpayer pays some taxes, although reduced, whereas in tax avoidance, none is being paid. The difference, therefore, is really the degree to which the taxpayer is able to thwart potential tax liabilities and responsibilities.

15.24   In *Re Osias 1980 Settlements*, the trustee sought the court's approval to vary the trusts of two settlements governed by Jersey law, so as to allow them to be constituted under Florida law and the funds in Jersey transferred to trustees resident in the US. The settlors had made the settlements in order to avoid the US estate taxes upon their death and were non-resident in the US at the time. Two companies were incorporated in Jersey which held the trust assets. The settlor assigned her interest to beneficiaries who were US residents. It was thereafter discovered that the beneficiaries would incur punitive tax liabilities in the form of income tax on income earned by the companies, despite the fact that the settlement made no provision for them to receive distributions from those companies. The variation of the trust would avoid such onerous tax liabilities and subject the trust to ordinary taxes accruing to a domestic trust. The court found that it had authority to vary the trust under s 43 of the Trusts (Jersey) Law 1984, on the basis that it would be in the beneficiaries' interest. The discretion was exercisable even where the scheme would result in the minimization of foreign taxes.

15.25   The court in *Re Osias 1980 Settlements* relied on the well-established English rule that a court will assist even where tax avoidance is involved:

> . . . one of the purposes of this appointment [of a foreign trustee] is unquestionably to escape the burden of certain UK fiscal liabilities. It has, however, long been established that there is no reason why the court should not lend its assistance in connection with a particular transaction and in so far as the appointment of new trustees are concerned, it is, I think, an absolutely irrelevant consideration. Those possessing the power are clearly entitled to exercise it as they think best in the interest of the trust estate.[22]

---

[20] Notably, the court ignored the line of UK cases which challenged the rule on the legality of tax avoidance, such as *IRC v MacGuckian* [1997] 3 All ER 817.

[21] Above, n 15.

[22] Quoting from *Re Whitehead's Will Trusts*, above, n 15, 837, *per* Pennycuick VC.

Deputy Bailiff Jones noted:

15.26

> we can, in a proper case, give our consent to avoid tax . . . we were assured that in this case there was no question of avoiding US taxation, the object being to minimise the penal provisions of US tax law. The court was asked to approve a variation which would result in the 'proper' taxes being paid . . . The court must stress that this case is not an appropriate occasion for considering whether the court would give its consent to an arrangement where the avoidance of US tax liability is involved . . .[23]

In contrast, in *Re Douglas*, Deputy Bailiff Birt found no reason 'to adopt a different approach in Jersey to that of the English court'. Consequently, where the principal object of a variation of trust was the avoidance, deferral, or minimization of tax, this was a legitimate object, provided that it was to the benefit of the persons concerned.[24]

15.27

The view that tax mitigation and tax avoidance continue to be legitimate activities has also, of course, been expressed in recent cases from onshore jurisdictions. In *Damberg v Damberg*,[25] for example, an Australian court refused to condemn an intricate scheme to avoid German capital taxes, viewing it as a lawful trust function.

15.28

C. Tax and Sham Trusts

Apart from specific statutory provisions which enable onshore taxing authorities to 'look through' or ignore trusts in certain prescribed instances, the courts have interpreted trusts to achieve the same result. This is under the sham trust or 'alter ego' doctrine.[26] Where a trust exhibits 'sham like' features, the court will 'pierce its corporate veil' or 'look through' the trust, deeming the assets placed into the purported trust the settlor's. Certain features of the offshore trust may precipitate a sham inquiry, such as the retention, by the settlor, of control over the trusts assets. Indeed, onshore jurisdictions are already beginning to legislate against the effects of such provisions. However, where tax is in issue, the sham doctrine goes further, and the very purpose of the trust may discredit it. The increasing number of cases being deemed the 'alter egos' of settlors, or shams, is evidence that the courts are eager to apply the sham rule to offshore trusts, in harmony with legislative policy in onshore states.

15.29

---

[23] *Re Osias 1980 Settlements*, above, n 15, 412. Note that non-enforcement and anti-avoidance positions may be modified by treaty.

[24] *Re Douglas*, above, n 17, 78.

[25] [2001] NSWCA 87.

[26] See the general discussion of the sham doctrine in chapter 8, 'The Offshore Trust as a Sham'.

Tax purpose may infer a sham

15.30   Using the alter ego or sham doctrine, the use of trusts for tax purposes has been challenged effectively, particularly in the US courts. The vehicle for this challenge is the more general approach to trusts which are established for purposes other than bona fide business purposes or true economic purposes. Such trusts create suspicion, and may be treated as shams and disregarded for tax purposes. Since tax planning or tax avoidance is not viewed as a bona fide business or economic purpose, trusts that are established solely for tax avoidance purposes are in danger of being deemed shams.[27] It seems, therefore, that the sham doctrine, under tax law, goes further than the doctrine under trusts law. In the latter, while intent is important, the conduct of the settlor and the trustee after the creation of the trust is determinative.[28] In contrast, under tax law, intent or purpose appears to bear more weight.

15.31   The sham doctrine depends upon certain factors, elaborated upon in *Castro v Commissioner of Inland Revenue*.[29] In determining whether a trust has no economic purpose, or lacks economic substance, the court will consider:

(1)   whether the grantor's relationship to the property purportedly transferred into trust differed materially before and after the trust's formation;
(2)   whether the trust has a bona fide independent trustee;
(3)   whether an economic interest in the trust passed to the beneficiaries of the trust other than the grantor, if he or she is a beneficiary; and
(4)   whether the grantor honoured restrictions imposed by the trust or the law of trusts, for example, whether the trustee had a fiduciary relationship to the trust and the beneficiaries.[30]

15.32   The effect of the above principles is that trusts which make provision for self-settling and settlor control, invite inquiry into the validity of the trust for tax purposes. For example, in *Castro*, the settlor, or grantor, had established two trusts and transferred all of his assets into them. He also made an arrangement to provide lifetime services to the original trust, transferring remuneration earned from such services to the trust. In consideration, the grantor received all 100 units of beneficial interest in the trust. The original trust then established a second trust. The grantor and other relatives were the trustees of both trusts, and the grantor was also a beneficiary. On filing their income tax returns, the trustees claimed income by the trusts which was disallowed by the Inland

---

[27] For further discussion on onshore legislative measures to counter the use of offshore trusts for tax planning by disregarding them in this way, see chapter 14.
[28] See chapter 8.
[29] (2001) 4 ITELR 45 (US Tax Ct).
[30] ibid, 56–7.

Revenue Service (IRS). The IRS also increased the income of the trustees. On appeal, the court found sufficient evidence to disregard the trusts for tax purposes as trusts without economic substance.

Interestingly, the court also found it inherently implausible that the settlor would grant exclusive use of his lifetime services to the trust for no remuneration and make an anticipatory transfer of all future earnings to the trust, as well as transfer practically all of the assets to the trusts for nothing in return, while retaining no control over them.[31] This decision is good evidence of the ingrained judicial hostility of US courts to offshore structures. **15.33**

In *Lund v Commissioner of Inland Revenue*,[32] the question of self-settling was examined by the US courts in the context of a tax avoidance arrangement. Swift J, of the US Tax Court, relied on the test outlined in *Castro* to establish whether a trust was to be disregarded as lacking economic substance for income tax purposes. This was to be decided on the totality of the facts.[33] They concerned a US taxpayer who was the owner of a company valued at US $2 million. He claimed to have transferred the beneficial interest to an offshore trust in the West Indies. However, there was no evidence of any consideration for the transfer, and the company continued to do business just as before the claimed transfer. Further evidence of a sham was the fact that the taxpayer borrowed large sums of money for the company without obtaining the trustee's approval and continued to manage the business. This implied direct control, contrary to the trust deed. **15.34**

The US Inland Revenue Service decided to ignore the transactions made by the settlor in relation to the trust and assess him for tax income from the company. The court held that the trust lacked economic substance. Thus, for tax purposes, the Commissioner could 'look through' the trust and examine the substance and not merely the form of the transactions. This was clearly the right decision. Here, there was no evidence of any real interest but, instead, token payments. **15.35**

The courts in such situations are, of course, aided by the fairly recent initiatives questioning well-established rules on the legitimacy of tax avoidance measures, particularly, it seems, when applied to offshore structures.[34] Trusts and other transactions established or performed for purely tax purposes, are roundly attacked. As we have seen, in the case of trusts, they may simply be ignored, **15.36**

---

[31] ibid, 58–9.
[32] (2001) 3 ITELR 343.
[33] ibid, 349. See also *Markosian v Commissioner of Internal Revenue* 73 TC 1235, 1243.
[34] See above, paras 15.03–15.28.

'looked through', or declared as shams. The effect in all three instances is essentially the same, that is, the trust becomes irrelevant.[35]

Tax purpose in itself not sufficient for sham

15.37   Despite cases which illustrate the difficulties faced by trusts established for tax purposes, particularly in the US, it is important to reiterate that the mere fact that a trust is established to minimize tax liability does not of itself make it an invalid or sham trust. Indeed, historically, the use of trusts for tax-planning purposes has been well established and is not reserved to offshore trusts. Further, as we have seen, a number of cases, both offshore and onshore, demonstrate that the courts will be willing to vary trusts to enable their tax-planning objectives.[36]

15.38   The South African courts have recently confirmed that where a transaction is a real one, the fact that it achieves a desirable tax-planning result, even if that result was intended, does not make the trust a sham. In the case of *South African Revenue Service v Woulidge*,[37] two trusts were established by the respondent for his minor children. The respondent consequently sold shares to the trusts, using loans which he granted to the trusts to finance the sale. He did not charge interest on the loan as he was entitled to do.

15.39   After a few years, upon a restructuring of the group of companies, each trust sold half of its shareholding and paid the loans with the income from the proceeds of the sale. Under the relevant fiscal legislation,[38] any income of a minor is deemed to be the income of the parent if accrued by the minor as a result of a settlement, donation, or other disposition made by the parent. However, the Court of Appeal found that the sale of the shares in this case had not been gratuitous. The purchase price had in fact been paid for the shares, and only the forsaken interest was gratuitous because of the actual refusal to claim interest on the loan. This was despite the delay in the payment. Consequently, only the forsaken interest could be deemed to be income for tax purposes. The transaction was a valid one and the transaction was not a sham.

15.40   In *Re Moody Jersey A Settlement*,[39] the trust was established solely as a means of tax avoidance. Due to an error in which the settlor's wife was included as a beneficiary, the trust did not achieve its intended purpose. The court allowed

---

[35] See *Ramsay Ltd v Inland Revenue Commissioners*, above, n 3.
[36] See chapter 17 and cases such as *Re N*, above, n 16, and *Re Weston's Settlements*, above, n 18, 243.
[37] [2002] 1 SA 68 (CA).
[38] The Income Tax Act No 58 of 1962, s 7(3).
[39] [1990] JLR 264.

the survival of the trust by rectification, allowing the wife to be removed as a beneficiary. It was unconcerned with the tax motive of the trust.

Applicability of the corporate veil concept

The notion that a trust has a corporate veil which can be pierced for tax pur-   **15.41**
poses should now also be reassessed in the light of the decision in *Re Abacus (Cayman Islands) Ltd (Trustee of the Esteem Settlement) Grupo Torras SA v Al Sabah*,[40] which held that this was a corporate concept which was unsuitable for trusts. The case, apart from dismissing the concept of the corporate veil for trusts, establishes a higher threshold for the finding of a sham than is evident in several other offshore cases on shams. For a sham allegation to be proved, both the trustee and the settlor must have lacked the intention to create the trust. That lack of intent should be discernible from the conduct of both the settlor and the trustee when the affairs of the trust are examined.

---

[40] (2003) 6 ITELR 368 (Royal Ct, Jersey). See a full discussion of this objection in chapter 8, 'The Offshore Trust as a Sham', at paras 8.66–8.69.

16

BILATERAL ROUTES TO THE TAX FUNCTION AND THE QUESTION OF SOVEREIGNTY

A. The Non-Enforcement of Foreign Fiscal Law—Sustaining the Tax Function of Offshore Trusts

Introduction—offshore states follow rule on non-enforcement of revenue laws

The legitimacy and efficacy of tax planning through the use of trusts should also be considered from an international law perspective, specifically, the rule against the enforcement of foreign revenue laws. Briefly put, the rule says that a state will not enforce or assist in the enforcement of the revenue laws of another state. The rule, which is well known and recognized internationally, was stated in the landmark case of *Government of India v Taylor*.[1] The rule is 'deeply embedded not only in the common law but also in the law of civil law countries'.[2]   **16.01**

Even without the particular context of offshore business, the law has always recognized that the fiscal and penal matters of one state should be outside the realm of another with respect to the enforcement of foreign judgments. Traditionally, this rule has been followed rigorously in offshore states. In theory, therefore, the several changes to tax law effected onshore which place liabilities   **16.02**

---

[1] [1955] 1 AC 491.
[2] Lord Goff, in *Re State of Norway's Application* [1990] 1 AC 723, 808–809. See also, in France, *Bemberg v Fisc de la Province de Buenos Aires*, 24 February 1949, Tribunal de loi Seine, Semaine Juridique, 1949 II, 4816.

for taxation on trustees, settlors, and beneficiaries of offshore trusts, should be of little concern to the trust located offshore. Such laws are not expected to be enforced, and laws are effective only if enforceable. The status of the rule on non-enforcement is, however, far more convoluted. In more recent times, the rule has been somewhat circumscribed. Offshore jurisdictions themselves have voluntarily bypassed the rule and expressed a willingness to assist onshore tax authorities, particularly in matters where criminal liabilities are involved.

16.03   Further, the rule on the non-enforcement of foreign fiscal law complements the principle of the legality of tax avoidance, discussed earlier.[3] The rule presupposes that offshore states have no legal obligation to assist onshore countries in regulating and enforcing the several counter-tax measures and expanded tax initiatives taken by onshore states. These are measures which undermine attempts by onshore investors to minimize their tax burdens through the establishment of offshore trusts.

16.04   The rule should also be considered within the context of treaty arrangements, either in relation to double taxation treaties, or in the facilitation of exchange of information agreements which modify it.[4] Often these agreements have arisen in response to pressures from the OECD. It is also significant to assess the extent to which confidentiality will be preserved in relation to tax information involving the trust, as it involves legal obligations in relation to the question of assistance in criminal matters.[5]

16.05   Situations in which offshore trusts are caught between the duties to pay onshore taxes either directly, or on the behalf of the settlor or the beneficiaries, may also impact on the rule on non-enforcement. Where the trustee, as is usually the case, does not fall under the jurisdiction of the onshore state, the rule introduces further complications to the trustee's obligations with respect to these taxes. This dilemma is considered in the following chapter. It is noted here, however, that in some cases, offshore courts themselves have undermined the rule by varying trusts, or otherwise allowing trustees to make payments to settle the tax debts of onshore settlors or beneficiaries.

---

[3] Chapter 15, at paras 15.3–15.28.

[4] See the discussion in chapter 7, and paras 16.39–16.62. The most recent agreement is between Switzerland and the other OECD countries, for Switzerland to exchange information on Swiss holding companies. The agreement is soon to come into effect. See 'Switzerland Reaches Agreement with OECD Over Tax Questions' *Tax News.com*, 30 January 2004, www.iofc.net/amsgroup.

[5] See chapter 7. Requests for information on offshore trusts are often pursued as part of the tax proceedings onshore.

Differentiating the rule from other provisions on non-enforcement

The adherence to the rule against the non-enforcement of foreign fiscal law **16.06** should also be considered alongside specific legislative provisions in offshore law which seek to preclude the enforcement of judgments obtained onshore.[6] Taken together, they represent a concerted attempt by offshore states to oust the application and effect of foreign law which can jeopardize the trust. However, since the rule of non-enforcement is wide, and extends to assistance by the offshore state, its application is considered separately here. Its breadth, for example, will encompass requests for assistance in relation to tax information, situations which will not be covered by offshore provisions which preclude the enforcement of foreign judgments.

Rationales for offshore states' adherence to the rule

The contrasting ideological positions on taxation, evident between onshore and **16.07** offshore countries, support the adherence to the rule on non-enforcement in offshore jurisdictions. Further, most offshore countries hold firmly to the principles of international tax competition and the sovereignty of states to enact laws in their own interest. Several offshore countries do not operate under direct taxation regimes and are 'tax free' jurisdictions. Examples are The Bahamas and the Cayman Islands, in which neither citizens, nor residents, nor offshore companies are taxed. In contrast, many onshore countries are high tax regimes. For offshore jurisdictions, the adherence to the rule is also a matter of public policy, and any assistance in matters involving revenue law may be viewed as being at the expense of offshore investment.

These different attitudes to taxation impact directly on requests to enforce **16.08** onshore tax laws from onshore countries to offshore jurisdictions. Such offshore jurisdictions should not be expected to support fiscal regimes with philosophies which they do not share. Consequently, the element of reciprocity, often viewed as essential for international legal assistance and cooperation, will be absent.

There is also a credible argument that the task of law enforcement, in relation to **16.09** tax matters, should be purely a local concern. As such, failures to 'police' tax laws should not be allowed to undermine the sovereign right of offshore nations to enact their own tax laws. Such offshore laws support a financial sector which, by welcoming non-residents, is able to generate much needed investment. The rationale for this offshore policy toward the non-enforcement of foreign fiscal laws is strengthened by the recognition that onshore nations also have tax laws which grant tax incentives to non-residents. These onshore tax incentives have

---

[6] Discussed in chapter 24.

not engendered the hostility that has been directed at offshore states. Indeed, it is arguable that the larger financial centres of the developed nations are the ones that benefit the most from the interest of savings of investors from developing countries.

Rationales of the rule on non-enforcement of foreign fiscal law

16.10   The success of onshore counter-tax measures often lies with the ability of onshore nations to reach offshore assets, so that the application of the rule on the non-enforcement of foreign fiscal law is significant. At this juncture, the rule appears to be applied inconsistently, with considerations of public policy likely to colour the outcome in any given case. It is thus pertinent to examine the rationales of the rule.

16.11   The rule is considered to be based on the argument that an enforcement of a tax claim is an extension of the sovereign power which imposed the taxes, and is therefore an assertion of sovereign authority by one state within the authority of another.[7] Another rationale is that the public order laws of one state may not accord with the policy of another, as it involves solely the internal arrangements of that state. The rule is therefore necessary to avoid another state passing judgment on such laws. As stated in a US case: 'It may commit the domestic state to a position which would seriously embarrass its neighbour . . . no court ought to undertake an inquiry which it cannot prosecute without determining whether those laws are consonant with its own notions of what is proper.'[8] Thus, the matter is one outside of the competency of courts and should be entrusted to other authorities.

16.12   For this reason, in *QRS 1 Aps v Frandsen*,[9] the court was of the view that

> The rule with regard to revenue laws may in the future may be modified by international convention . . . in order to prevent fraudulent practices which damage all states and benefit no state. But, at present, the international law with regard to the non-enforcement of revenue and penal laws is absolute.[10]

16.13   Yet this view is not consonant with other recent cases. In those cases, the courts, with a view to relaxing the rule, displayed generous judicial creativity on the grounds of public policy and the comity of nations.

16.14   The fact that the question of the jurisdiction to tax offshore investment and cross-border investment generally is still a controversial one, makes the rule

---

[7] *Government of India v Taylor*, above, n 1, 511–12, *per* Lord Keith.
[8] *Moore v Mitchell* (1929) 30 F 2d 600, 604, *per* Judge Learned Hand.
[9] [1999] 3 All ER 289, 297 (CA), *per* Simon-Brown LJ.
[10] ibid, quoting from *Williams and Humbert Ltd v W & H Trade Marks (Jersey) Ltd* [1986] AC 368, 428.

against enforcement of foreign revenue laws one of even greater policy significance. Due partly to the fairly recent initiatives to tax onshore residents and citizens on their worldwide income, offshore jurisdictions are faced with requests to assist in proceedings relating to trusts which were previously not taxable. The threat which this poses to the offshore tax function of trusts and offshore investment as a whole, initially incites a 'knee jerk' reaction of self-preservation by construing the rule strictly. Thus, trends toward the relaxation of the rule are less evident in offshore jurisdictions. This, however, is tempered by the international pressures aimed at offshore jurisdictions to surrender the considerable tax investment monopolies that they enjoy to onshore interests in retaining potentially taxable income.

The principle of non-enforcement remains, however, a valid one in both the **16.15** domestic and international arenas. Indeed, it was retained under the Brussels Convention on Jurisdiction and Enforcement in Civil and Commercial Matters,[11] so that revenue matters are expressly excluded from the Convention's jurisdiction. A similar exclusion is made under the more recent Brussels Regulation 2000.[12]

Application of the rule against the non-enforcement of fiscal law

The rule against the non-enforcement of fiscal law has been applied in several **16.16** trust cases from offshore jurisdictions and has gained added importance as a rule of public policy. The sovereignty underpinnings of the rule have also been noted. For example, in *Re Lambert and Pinto*,[13] the Supreme Court of The Bahamas considered that the rule of non-enforcement was a 'principle of international acceptance' in the interest of 'public policy'.[14] The Court pointed out that foreign laws may require the offshore jurisdiction to assist in the administration of justice, and to that extent infringed the sovereignty of the offshore jurisdiction.[15] They also violated the principle that a foreign state should not seek to expand its territorial jurisdiction to tax its residents and citizens where the relevant assets are located offshore.[16]

---

[11] EEC Convention on Jurisdiction and Enforcement of Judgments in Civil and Commercial Matters (The Brussels Convention on Civil Jurisdiction and Enforcement of Judgments 1968) (Brussels, 27 September 1968, EC 46 (1978); Cmnd 7395; [1978] OJ L304/1, 8 ILM 229), hereinafter the Brussels Convention on Jurisdiction and Enforcement.

[12] Council Regulation (EC) No 44/2001 of 22 December on Jurisdiction and the Recognition and Enforcement of Judgments in Civil and Commercial Matters (OJ 2001 L12).

[13] *In the Matter of the Criminal Proceedings Before the US District Court Concerning Lambert and Pinto* (Sup Ct, The Bahamas) No 962 of 1986, decided 30 September 1986.

[14] ibid, 16, borrowing the words of Lord Somervell in *Government of India v Taylor*, above, n 1.

[15] *Re the Matter of H* [1996] CILR 237, 243 (Grand Ct, Cayman Islands).

[16] As occurs in the US, for example. See chapter 13.

16.17 The scope of the rule against non-enforcement is wide. In *Stutts v Premier Benefit Capital Trust*,[17] for example, the receiver of the respondent trust applied for recognition in the Cayman Islands. The receiver had been appointed in the United States while the trust was registered in the Cayman Islands, but conducted its business primarily in Florida. The complaint against the trust was that it had made sales of unregistered securities and had engaged in a scheme to defraud investors. In denying the applicant the relief sought, the court followed the rule closely, noting that it applied both to criminal and civil suits.[18]

16.18 Further, the rule is broad enough to encompass both the direct and indirect enforcement of foreign revenue law. The latter often involves requests by onshore states for assistance in procuring related trust documents. The broad application of the rule was affirmed in *Re Lambert and Pinto*.[19] The court held that the rule applies equally to attempts at indirect enforcement, in this case, a request for information to assist in the collection of taxes.[20]

Modern interpretations of the rule on non-enforcement of foreign tax law

16.19 Notwithstanding the historical resilience of the rule, a recent judicial trend indicates that it is not inviolate. A relaxation of the rule may be identified, particularly with respect to requests for information on offshore entities, such as trusts. This is evidenced from both offshore and onshore courts.

16.20 In *Re State of Norway's Application (No 2)*,[21] for example, an English court held that a request for information relating to tax proceedings did not violate the principle against the non-enforcement of revenue law. The request was with respect to a tax claim by the Government of Norway. The rationale given was that the proceedings were for *access* to documents and not for *payment* of foreign taxes. Further, the request did not even breach the aspect of the rule which precludes the indirect enforcement of foreign revenue laws. Such a request would constitute indirect enforcement only where the foreign state sought a remedy designed to give its laws extraterritorial effect, or where a private party raised a defence based on the foreign law in order to assert the rights of the foreign state.

16.21 This important shift in the law was affirmed in the Jersey case of *R v Charlton*

---

[17] [1992–1993] CILR 605. See also *Clapham v Mesurier* [1990–1991] JLR 5, where the Jersey court found it had no power to enforce in Jersey a claim by the Inland Revenue for taxes in respect of United Kingdom legislation, even if such constituted an indirect claim.

[18] Relying on *Wisconsin v Pelican Ins Co* [1893] AC 157.

[19] Above, n 13. But see *Clapham v Mesurier*, above, n 17.

[20] *Re Lambert and Pinto*, above, n 13.

[21] [1990] AC 723.

et al.[22] Application was made under the Evidence (Proceedings in Other Jurisdictions) (Jersey) Order 1983 for assistance in obtaining confidential information in Jersey for use as evidence in a tax evasion case in England. The Jersey court distinguished between requests from foreign states for documents in relation to tax cases and a request for assistance in relation to proceedings for payment of taxes. It held that the former did not constitute the enforcement of foreign fiscal law, thereby following *Re State of Norway*. It also departed from its own precedent in *Re Tucker*,[23] where the rule against the enforcement of foreign revenue law had been upheld in similar circumstances. The court in *Tucker* viewed the undermining of the rule as being contrary to the public policy of Jersey.

Other offshore courts have followed the trend. In *Re The Petition of McLean*,[24]   **16.22**
a Manx court expressly relied on *Re State of Norway* in finding that information sought for the enforcement of a foreign tax debt was neither a direct nor an indirect enforcement of that debt. Further, it was not an exercise of extraterritorial sovereign authority.

It is evident, therefore, that even offshore courts have relaxed the rule, and have   **16.23**
accepted that a distinction can be drawn between requests for documents and proceedings for payment or enforcement of taxes. This new, generous attitude of offshore courts may be more apparent in criminal proceedings when requests for disclosure of confidential information are made. In such cases, the needs of law enforcement are prioritized. The more narrow interpretation of the rule, as evident from the *Norway* line of cases, is not, however, constant. Contrasting decisions, such as *Lambert and Pinto*,[25] remain. In that case, the Bahamian Supreme Court frowned upon a broad interpretation of the rule and considered that it applied to all requests connected with tax proceedings, including requests for documents. Such requests were viewed as *indirect enforcements* of revenue law and were not permissible.[26]

Given the policy of offshore jurisdictions to protect offshore investment, the   **16.24**
approval of *Re State of Norway* by offshore courts is surprising. In *Charlton*,[27] the rule was bypassed notwithstanding that the English statute considered in *Re State of Norway* applied only to civil and commercial proceedings, while the Jersey law applied exclusively to criminal matters. The Jersey court did not apply the traditional rule as a general principle and distinguished its case from

---

[22] [1993] JLR 360.

[23] [1987–88] JLR 473 (Royal Ct), interpreting the UK Evidence (Proceedings in Other Jurisdictions) Act 1975.

[24] [1997–98] 1 OFLR 818, 826.

[25] Above, n 13.

[26] ibid.

[27] Above, n 22.

Re Tucker.[28] It was, however, careful to pay homage to the rule against non-enforcement of revenue laws as expressed in *Re Tucker.*[29] In distinguishing, it found that *Re Tucker* was not, substantively, an application under the Evidence (Proceedings in Other Jurisdictions) (Jersey) Order 1983, and that the evidence sought was in relation to *civil* and not serious criminal proceedings.

Private parties versus state parties

16.25   The courts appear to be less strict with the rule against the non-enforcement of foreign revenue law where personal creditors and not fiscal authorities are involved. The Royal Court of Jersey in the case of *Le Marquand and Backhurst v Chilmead Ltd (in Liquidation)*[30] refused to apply the rule on this ground, in a situation where there was an Inland Revenue creditor as well as personal creditors.[31] In *Re Tucker,*[32] where there was another creditor apart from the Inland Revenue authority, the Manx courts ignored the rule and granted an application by the trustee in bankruptcy for disclosure of documents and to enable examination of relevant persons.[33]

Comity and public policy deviations from the rule

16.26   Courts may rationalize their refusal to apply the rule on grounds of public policy or concerns about comity. For instance, public policy considerations may subsist in foreign policy, whereby states strive to maintain harmony in their foreign relations. Thus, some courts have held that they will not support transactions such as fraudulent tax evasion schemes which are knowingly designed to violate the revenue law of a friendly state.[34] In *Controller and A-G v Davison* and *Peat Marwick v Davison,*[35] for example, the courts held that the rule could not stand in situations where, if applied, the court would be knowingly assisting in the obstruction or violation of a friendly state's revenue laws. This would be against public policy.[36]

16.27   In *Re Tucker a Bankrupt,*[37] an Isle of Man court also granted assistance to a foreign court where there was a clear case of criminal activity. Again, in

---

[28] Above, n 23.

[29] *Charlton*, above, n 22. *Tucker* was still 'good law'.

[30] [1987–88] JLR 86.

[31] ibid. The court found that the liquidator was not acting as the Inland Revenue's agent.

[32] [1987–88] Manx LR 220.

[33] At the later stage of the enforcement of the claim, the court refused the application, upholding the rule on the basis that the only creditor at that stage was the Inland Revenue.

[34] *Re Emery's Investment Trusts* [1959] Ch 410.

[35] [1996] 2 NZLR 278 and [1996] 2 NZLR 319 respectively.

[36] Laws on fraudulent conveyances could conceivably be undermined also.

[37] [1987–88] Manx LR 8. Note also *Bullen and Garner v UK* 533 So 2d (Fla Appl 4 Dist 1989).

Le Marquand,[38] the Royal Court of Jersey was cognisant of a need to express comity with foreign courts making bona fide applications. In theory, one should not expect many offshore courts to follow such dicta. However, the comity rationale remains a viable exception to the general rule. For onshore courts, it appears that comity will be a useful, and even popular, avenue for addressing concerns about offshore investment. It may be utilized even to assume jurisdiction over offshore matters.[39]

In *Re the Settlements Between X and Blanpied and Abacus,*[40] a Jersey court decided **16.28** that it should assist in an US tax case by ordering the disclosure of information on trust assets because there was a legal duty in the other jurisdiction to make tax returns.

The increasing international legal assistance to onshore countries on tax matters, **16.29** through the use of treaties and other international instruments, also requires a more relaxed attitude to the rule on the non-enforcement of fiscal law.[41] Such international cooperation is indicative of a sympathetic approach to comity, which has, as its *raison d'être*, respect of the laws of foreign states.

Reaffirmation of the rule on the non-enforcement of foreign fiscal law

The 'whittling away' of the rule in certain situations, and particularly, it appears, **16.30** where sympathetic policy concerns are involved, should not be misinterpreted to mean an abolition of the rule. This is made clear in a more recent English decision, that of *QRS 1, Aps and Others v Frandsen.*[42] Here, a liquidator sought to enforce claims against a UK resident in relation to Danish companies, the assets of which had been 'stripped' and converted into shares. The substantive action was for restitution to the value of the assets of the companies which had been thus disposed of. The liquidation followed allegations of tax fraud by the Danish tax authorities. The UK Court of Appeal refused to assist, on the ground that it would violate the rule of non-enforcement of foreign revenue laws. The Court also confirmed that the well-known rule had not been changed by either the EU Convention, or the Brussels Convention.[43]

Although the Danish tax authorities funded the action brought by the **16.31**

---

[38] See above, n 30.
[39] This was the approach in *Peat Marwick*, above, n 35. The court disagreed that the Cook Islands claim of sovereign immunity in alleged tax fraud should prevail over public policy concerns, thereby precluding jurisdiction.
[40] (Royal Ct, Jersey), 28 January 1994. Noted in [1996] PCB 306.
[41] See below, paras 16.39–16.62, for more discussion of such treaties.
[42] Above, n 9, *per* Simon-Brown LJ.
[43] The Court considered the effect of the Brussels Convention on Jurisdiction and Enforcement, above, n 11, which in fact, excludes revenue matters from its purview under Article 1.

companies, the companies contended that the claim was, in form and substance, a private law claim which was enforceable under Article 1 of the Brussels Convention as a civil and commercial matter and was not, therefore, a 'revenue' matter. However, the Court found that the matter was prohibited as it was the indirect enforcement of revenue laws.

16.32   Interpreting the Brussels Convention, the Court held that any claim involving the direct or indirect enforcement of the revenue laws of another country could only properly be brought in the tax authorities' own courts. Indirect enforcement occurred where the foreign state (or its nominee) in form sought a remedy not based on a rule of its revenue law, but which in substance was designed to give it extraterritorial effect. In this case, the sole object of the suit in question was to collect tax for a foreign revenue authority. The rule as it relates to indirect enforcement is to be applied narrowly.[44] The decision echoes the sentiments expressed in *Re Lambert and Pinto*.[45]

Public policy arguments upholding the rule

16.33   Public policy arguments may also be utilized by offshore courts to uphold the rule, rather than to undermine it. Indeed, it is well established that courts could refuse to recognize a foreign judgment if is contrary to public policy.[46] To the extent that the foreign fiscal law would undermine the legislation and purposes of the offshore jurisdiction, its courts may refuse to enforce ensuing foreign judgments and laws. Laws which are likely to be so undermined include innovative offshore trust laws granting capacity, protecting against forced heirship, and so on, all laws seeking to reinforce the viability of the offshore industry. Thus far, similar arguments have been used by offshore courts in finding that disclosure requests which violate offshore confidentiality laws should be denied.[47] It is indisputable that offshore laws serve important public interests. In *Douglas v Pindling*,[48] these public interests, which could ground public policy decisions, were acknowledged by the Privy Council.

Upholding tax-planning functions

16.34   The line of cases from offshore courts which reiterate that those courts have the jurisdiction to vary trusts in order to give effect to the tax mitigation initiatives of onshore investors, also lends support, albeit indirectly, to their continued

---

[44] *Frandsen*, above, n 9, 296.
[45] Above, n 13.
[46] *Vervacke v Smith* [1983] 1 AC 145.
[47] See chapter 7.
[48] [1996] 3 WLR 242.

adherence to the rule against non-enforcement.[49] In these cases, tax evasion was not in issue. Offshore jurisdictions are clear that the existence of any anti-avoidance policies of onshore states imputes no illegality to their established jurisdiction to uphold tax-planning functions. Indeed, such onshore policies are irrelevant to this jurisdiction, generally recognized as a legitimate one. This confidence is increased because of the many onshore trusts which perform the same tax functions.[50]

Tax avoidance not an unlawful purpose that can invalidate trusts

The line of cases which has challenged the traditional rule on the non-enforcement of foreign fiscal law carries with it an underlying suggestion that tax avoidance is itself an unlawful purpose. However, this suggestion was rejected in the case of *Damberg v Damberg*.[51] In a convoluted scheme to avoid German capital gains taxes, the settlor transferred land in Germany to his children. He then used the land as security to purchase farming properties in Australia. A family squabble then ensued over the rights to the various properties and monies owed by the settlor to his children. At first instance, the Family Court held that, although the settlor had intended to transfer the lands on trust, the resulting trust was to be ignored and the transfer treated as an outright gift, as his purpose in doing so was to avoid German tax.

16.35

The Supreme Court disagreed, finding that it had been proven that the father had a definite intention to retain the equitable interest in the property. As such, a resulting trust ensued. The settlor could be barred from relying on the resulting trust only if it had been established for an 'unlawful' or illegal purpose.[52] Avoiding taxes could not, however, be viewed as such an unlawful purpose. Indeed, even if it were established that the settlor had violated German tax law, this could not be relied upon to defeat the trust, as it would constitute an enforcement of foreign revenue law, which was not to be permitted.[53]

16.36

The Court also accepted that the rule on non-enforcement did not depend on whether the foreign state itself was actually suing for a tax debt. The 'form of the action or the nature of the plaintiff' was not to be emphasized.[54]

16.37

---

[49] Cases such as *Re N* [1999] JLR 86 and *Re Osias 1980 Settlement* [1987–88] JLR 389 (Royal Ct). These cases were discussed in more detail in chapter 15, paras 15.21–15.28.

[50] See, eg, *Re Weston's Settlements* [1969] 1 Ch 223, relied upon in the Jersey case of *Re Richard Colin Douglas 1990 Settlement* [2000] JLR 73 (Royal Ct).

[51] [2001] NSWCA 87 (Sup Ct).

[52] Applying *Nelson v Nelson* (1995) 184 CLR 538.

[53] Upholding *Government of India v Taylor*, above, n 1.

[54] Relying on *Buchanan Ltd v McVey* [1955] AC 516 (Sup Ct, Eire) 527, *per* Moore J. See also *Rossino v Manufacturer's Life Insurance Company* [1963] 2 QB 352; *Rothwells Ltd (in liquidation) v Connell* (1993) 119 ALR 538.

Money laundering legislation and the rule on non-enforcement

16.38   The rule may also be upheld by the reservation against disclosure in tax matters which may be expressed in money laundering statutes. Note, for example, s 34(1)(d) of the Proceeds of Crime Act 2000 of St Kitts & Nevis, where the Comptroller of Inland Revenue may make objections to such disclosures on several grounds, including in the public interest.

B.   International Assistance, Treaty Arrangements, and their Impact on the Taxation of Offshore Trusts

Introduction—increased routes to international legal assistance

16.39   Trends toward assistance in fiscal matters are not confined to international agreements and case law. There is increasing assistance on tax matters by off-shore states, enabled by initiatives of the Parliaments of the respective offshore jurisdictions. This is largely a response to loud calls by onshore states for such cooperation. Such responses have been manifested in new legislation and treaty formation which allow such assistance. Assistance may be rendered under general mutual legal assistance treaties, or under specific tax information agreements. Alternatively, ordinary legislation may provide routes for international assistance on specific matters

16.40   The various types of international arrangements and instruments impact directly on the tax function of offshore trusts. On the one hand, double taxation treaties may offer significant tax-saving advantages to offshore investors who qualify for them. On the other hand, international instruments will often mean the undermining of the tax function of offshore trusts, whether through features which require in-depth information on tax planning entities and arrangements, or through treatment of tax offences as criminal or money laundering offences under legal assistance treaties.

Double taxation treaties

16.41   Few offshore jurisdictions operate within the context of investment incentives through the use of double taxation treaties. This is so for two main reasons:

(1)   Because of the fear of treaty-shopping, major onshore jurisdictions, such as the US, have refused to negotiate, and even revoked, such treaties with offshore jurisdictions. Investors who treaty-shop deliberately target lower tax jurisdictions in which to structure investments.

(2)   Double taxation treaties will encompass provisions which mandate the exchange of tax information between treaty partners. Offshore jurisdictions

have been anxious to avoid such provisions because of their adherence to confidentiality norms and their emphasis on the rule on the non-enforcement of foreign fiscal law.

In addition, certain offshore jurisdictions, such as The Bahamas and the Cayman Islands, are unable to conclude double taxation treaties since they are totally tax free regimes. Hence, the element of reciprocity, necessary for concluding such treaties, is absent. **16.42**

Double taxation treaties allow countries to surrender their right to tax to another state, in certain previously agreed situations and for designated activities. They are particularly useful for manipulating the ways in which dividends, interest, and royalties extracted from third countries are taxed. Where a double taxation treaty route to offshore investment is in place, the offshore trust, as an investment and income-earning vehicle, will be encompassed in its scope. **16.43**

Despite the untypical appearance of double taxation treaties in the offshore financial regime, it is worth considering the benefits to those investors who can take advantage of them. Barbados, for example, has pursued rigorously an extensive double taxation treaty network, which intertwines with its offshore sector (also called international financial services).[55] Saint Lucia, a newcomer to the offshore sector, also seems poised to take advantage of any benefits that may accrue from such a programme. **16.44**

Double taxation networks, such as exist in Barbados, may also be utilized through indirect routes, whereby an entity which is in jurisdiction A, which does not have a treaty with country B, is able to derive benefits through its transactions with country C, which does have a treaty with country B. This is labelled 'inversion', and has been strenuously objected to by many onshore countries, including the US, in its treaty relations with Barbados. For example, a US corporation could form a foreign 'shell' company in a low tax country such as Bermuda, which does not have a tax treaty with the US. The corporation exchanges shares of the US-based corporation for shares of the Bermuda parent. Thereafter, the inverted US companies in Bermuda use a third country, Barbados, to channel money to the parent company. Since Barbados has a tax treaty with the US, tax advantages may be gained since the entity is treated as a resident under the Barbados treaty. In effect, Barbados serves as a conduit for such a company.[56] **16.45**

---

[55] Including Canada, Chile, China, Norway, Sweden, Switzerland, the UK, Cuba, Malta. Another notable double taxation treaty partner in the offshore sector is The Netherlands. However, it is not a trust jurisdiction.

[56] Indeed, such an unintended result of the treaty is a major reason for the US's reluctance to continue its treaty with Barbados in the original form. The obstacles in treaty negotiation between

16.46   The Barbados tax treaty network has been particularly useful for corporate structures. Certain international operations, such as trading, financing, offshore banking, manufacturing, e-commerce, and licensing, have been popular under the treaty.

16.47   While the US remains an unreliable tax treaty partner,[57] Barbados has concluded double taxation treaties with major onshore countries.[58] By far the most successful treaty partner, however, has been Canada. Persons wishing to invest in Barbados under its international financial services regime, for example by establishing an international business company, can obtain significant tax savings by utilizing the double tax treaty with Canada. Similarly, if a trust established by a Canadian settlor can be deemed to be a resident of Barbados under Article 4, subsection 1V(I) of the Canada–Barbados International Tax Convention 1980, considerable tax advantages may be gained.

Residence

16.48   The concept of residence will be crucial in determining the applicability of double tax treaties to any trust, and the benefits to be derived thereunder. The concept of residence is by no means uniform. While such treaties will usually attempt to define the concept, the exercise is a difficult one. Various countries define the term 'residence' differently, and it may also be defined in dissimilar ways under the different models of double taxation treaties which are available. For example, in Canada, residence is determined by the residence of the trustee who manages or controls the trust assets.[59]

Barbados and the US relate to the fact that the US, controversially, designated Barbados a 'tax haven'. Barbados wants few changes to the treaty. In contrast, the US wants fundamental changes to avoid the use of the treaty by unintended beneficiaries. The US negotiators were reported as saying: 'The current income tax treaty significantly reduces dividend, interest and royalty withholding tax rates, even though Barbados is essentially a tax haven, and US tax treaties do not normally give such generous benefits to residents of tax havens. Congress, however, has generally denied the new 15% dividend tax rate to corporations that are resident in Barbados under the treaty.' *The Barbados Advocate*, 29 October, 2003.

[57]   Note that in the 1980s, the US revoked several of its treaties with Caribbean offshore nations. It continues to be watchful of treaty abuses.

[58]   Note that Barbados recently announced plans to reform its tax system, reducing its domestic corporation tax rates from 37.5% to 25%. The long-term plan is a common rate for all corporations. The move was partly to allow it to keep and expand international business and allay some of the concerns of its tax treaty partners.

[59]   See the Interpretation Bulletin IT–447, *Residence of a Trust or Estate*, 30 May 1980, Government of Canada. The rule applies even where there are multiple trustees. If there is one dominant trustee with respect to management and control, his or her residence will define residence for tax purposes. Alternatively, if trustees reside in different jurisdictions and trust decisions require a majority decision, the place where decisions are taken, such as the meeting place of the trustees, and the residence of the majority of the trustees, will be taken into account. See, eg, the landmark case of *Thibodeau Family Trust v The Queen* 78 Dominican Tax Cases 6376 (FCTD).

Tax information agreements and commitments to tax assistance

Largely as a result of pressures from international organizations and onshore **16.49** countries, some offshore countries have indicated that they will be more willing to assist onshore states in their law enforcement efforts with respect to matters of taxation. Thus far, these have been, largely, tentative moves by offshore states, characterized more by declarations of intent than by actual legislation and treaty changes.

Further, since the OECD High Level Consultations,[60] offshore states have made **16.50** substantial headway in defending their positions on the legality and validity of their tax polices to the world community. This, coupled with the lack of evidence that onshore states are willing to make the same legislative and policy changes expected of offshore states, has placed the anticipated new directions on tax cooperation in abeyance. Consequently, the status of the commitments, as expressed in several letters of commitment signed by offshore countries,[61] is currently in doubt, as these were conditional on the emergence of a 'level playing field', in tax matters. This 'level playing field', which envisages equal and fair rules relating to tax for both onshore and offshore countries, has not been forthcoming.

However, some states are fairly advanced in the process of cooperation in tax **16.51** matters. Bermuda, for example, has entered into an agreement with the USA which is far more generous than those entered into by some of its offshore neighbours.[62] The agreement not only provides for assistance in tax matters, but dispenses with the requirement for the requesting state to indicate that it has reasonable grounds for believing, or does in fact believe, that the taxpayer has done something which constitutes tax fraud or tax evasion.[63] It is sufficient to initiate assistance if the requesting state indicates that the information sought is relevant to the determination of the liability of the taxpayer. Such a wide authority defeats the established principle against fishing expeditions, that at least a prima facie case of wrongdoing must be made out.[64]

---

[60] High Level Consultations on the OECD Harmful Tax Initiative, OECD/Commonwealth Secretariat, Barbados, January 2001.

[61] But note the Exchange of Information on Taxes Agreement between the Cayman Islands and the US signed by the UK on behalf of the Cayman Islands on 27 November 2001, which was due to enter into force on 1 January 2004, but has been delayed to 2005. The Bahamas also signed a Tax Information Exchange Agreement with the US in 2002, which came into effect in January 2004 with respect to criminal tax matters. See also the Exchange of Tax Information Agreement signed by Antigua and Barbuda in 2002 to assist the US with tax matters.

[62] See the USA/Bermuda Tax Convention Amendment Act 1999, Bermuda. See, especially, s 4. It amends the USA/Bermuda Tax Convention 1996.

[63] This had been contentious under the previous Act of 1986.

[64] See, eg, *Re Ansbacher (Cayman Islands) Ltd* [2001] CILR 16; *First American Corporation v Zayed* [2000] CILR 57.

16.52 The movement toward increased cooperation in tax matters is, of course, a significant paradigm shift for offshore states. Nonetheless, the recent thrusts toward more transparency, and the advanced policy commitments given by offshore countries promising to facilitate information requests on tax matters, should be placed into context. They should not be interpreted as *carte blanche* licences for automatic disclosure. Rather, confidentiality remains a defining ethic in offshore jurisdictions. It is to be expected, therefore, that such assistance is to be carried out prudently, taking into account the appropriate rules for disclosure and the rights and interests of persons to be affected. Consequently, disclosure routes will exist only in narrow and controlled circumstances. For example, established rules on fishing expeditions generally remain. These require that sufficient reasons are given before confidentiality is waived. This continued emphasis was noted in *Re Ansbacher*,[65] a case from the Cayman Islands. The Grand Court noted that 'no change in this policy had been effected by the publication of a policy commitment to the Organization for Economic Cooperation and Development on tax enforcement'.[66]

Mutual Legal Assistance Treaties and tax matters

16.53 Mutual Legal Assistance Treaties (MLATs) may have a significant impact on trusts associated with criminal activity, but may not be used as avenues for routine information-gathering on fiscal matters unless express provision has been made for fiscal information. Given the subject-matter of MLATs, which is confined to criminal matters, only information related to criminal tax offences fall under such treaties. There is still, however, a reluctance on the part of offshore trust countries to include fiscal offences under MLATs. This clearly accords with their commitment to the rule against the non-enforcement of foreign fiscal laws. In this respect, what may be viewed as a lack of cooperation is, in fact, unimpeachable. Offshore jurisdictions have no legal or moral obligation to assist onshore states in tax matters. Offshore jurisdictions recognized that their very assistance to onshore states, while helping to increase the revenue coffers of onshore states, undermines their own economic and national interests. This fact ensures that, on this question, the battlelines continue to be drawn between offshore and onshore states. It is a question not only of sovereignty, but of public policy and even economic survival.

16.54 The result is perhaps a compromise position, one that is careful to preserve as much autonomy to offshore countries as is possible in such a hostile political

---

[65] Above, n 64. Thus, there must be, at minimum, a prima facie case of wrongdoing before requests for disclosure may be entertained.

[66] The court was referring to the Cayman Islands' letter of commitment on assistance in tax matters. See above, n 61.

environment. One sees this careful balancing approach in the new treaties that have been signed. For example, in the USA/Antigua MLAT,[67] while criminal mattes are addressed, information with respect to requests for confidential information held by the Government is restricted. Here, the requested state, Antigua and Barbuda, retains a discretion to deny such requests either entirely, or in part.[68] Assistance for routine civil and administrative matters is clearly not envisaged. This includes the 'regulation, imposition, calculation and collection of such income taxes.'[69] The threshold for a criminal offence encompassed under the Treaty appears to be high. It addresses only those criminal tax offences in the US which include 'a voluntary and international violation of a known legal duty' involving wilful conduct, excluding negligence or carelessness. To meet this standard, the prosecutor must show that the defendant 'took affirmative action on the likely effect which was to mislead or conceal'. This would involve, for example, 'keeping a double set of books, making false entries or alterations to financial records, concealing assets or covering up sources of income'.[70]

More important, the sovereignty of Antigua is respected in the Treaty with the adherence to the dual criminality rule.[71] This means that the criminal conduct in the USA which would form the basis of a request would 'in all likelihood also be criminalized under the law in Antigua and Barbuda'.[72]   **16.55**

Ordinary legislation in conjunction with international assistance

MLATs may work in conjunction with money laundering statutes, some of which have now encompassed tax fraud as part of money laundering.[73] It is clear that these more recent developments are as a result of international lobbying, particularly from the OECD. In addition, 'gateway' provisions in offshore legislation may provide avenues for disclosure in specified matters, upon request by onshore states.[74]   **16.56**

---

[67] Given effect by the Mutual Legal Assistance (Antigua & Barbuda and USA) Ratification Act 2000.

[68] ibid, Art 9.

[69] See *Exchange of Diplomatic Notes—Memorandum*, from J Hyde, US Ambassador to the OECS, Bridgetown, 31 October 1996.

[70] ibid.

[71] ibid. This is a rule which requires that the offence for which assistance is requested is also an offence in the requested country. Offshore financial centres have tended to adhere to this rule.

[72] *Exchange of Diplomatic Notes*, above, n 69.

[73] See chapter 7. The subject of MLATs is discussed in detail in the companion book, R-M B Antoine, *Confidentiality in Offshore Financial Law* (OUP, Oxford, 2002).

[74] See, eg, s 70 of the Insurance Act 1994 of the BVI.

Treaty requirements for disclosure related to taxation of trusts

16.57   In considering the implications of taxation on offshore trusts, we also need to consider the impact of disclosure requirements and requests, which often serve as prerequisites for tax assessments. Such requirements often come about through arrangements for international legal assistance allowing disclosure, exchange of information treaties, and double tax treaties. Money laundering provisions, if tax is provided for as a predicate offence, may also require disclosure.

16.58   As we saw in the chapter on confidentiality,[75] trusts have their own particular rules on confidentiality, and these impact on the extent to which information is given for tax and other purposes.

16.59   The general rule remains that offshore countries are unenthusiastic about concluding international legal assistance agreements which include tax matters in their purview. This is in contrast to their proven willingness to engage in mutual legal assistance efforts with respect to international crime, such as money laundering. Offshore countries will continue to rely on legal principles which support the stances taken on assistance in tax matters. In the current international environment, negotiating satisfactory resolutions requires a balance to be struck between conflicting priorities in relation to the national interests of offshore states and the law enforcement needs of onshore states. International agreements often reflect compromises over key aspects of public policy.[76]

16.60   More recent treaties, such as in Antigua and Barbuda, may also contemplate tax offences, but in a restricted manner.[77] In addition, some of the emerging

---

[75] Chapter 7.

[76] See, eg, the 1990 Mutual Legal Assistance Treaty between the US and the Cayman Islands, Art 19(3), which expressly excluded fiscal and related offences unless such offences were related to narcotics, fraud, promotion of tax shelters, or designated offences connected to illegally obtained income. The more recent letter of commitment given by the Cayman Islands to assist in tax matters does, however, reflect a change in policy. The law does not extend to tax offences except where these arise out of unlawful activities already covered by the Treaty, such as securities fraud and wilfully making dishonest tax returns: Art 19(3)(d) and (e). Under the Protocol to this Treaty its terms were extended to the other United Kingdom dependencies in the Caribbean by way of an *Exchange of Notes* in 1990 and 1991. Extensions to Anguilla, the British Virgin Islands, and the Turks and Caicos were effected on 9 November 1990, and to Montserrat on 26 April 1991. Similar provisions exist in other offshore countries, such as the Turks and Caicos. See the relevant Article 3. Other legislation also exclude tax matters. See, eg, the Financial Services (International Cooperation) Act 2000, BVI, and The Bahamas Criminal Justice (Cooperation) Act 2000, which expressly exclude tax matters.

[77] See, eg, the Mutual Legal Assistance (Antigua & Barbuda and USA) Ratification Act 2000.

offshore countries, such as St Lucia, which have not yet adjusted their MLATs, are expected to do so.[78]

Offshore courts continue to be vigilant regarding requests for information, to   **16.61**
ensure that they are not disguises for what are, in substance, tax matters. A Cayman Islands court emphasized this approach in the case of *Attorney General of the Cayman Islands v McCorkle*,[79] thus underlining the general principle against the non-enforcement of fiscal law.

Where requests for information are concerned, procedural restrictions, such as   **16.62**
dual criminality requirements and other incompatibilities in law, may also be applicable. These may prevent the offshore state from rendering assistance in tax matters, even if it overcomes its natural opposition to such cooperation. Dual criminality restrictions will apply, for example, if the tax offence which is the substance of the request from the onshore state does not exist in the offshore country, or if it is substantially different to a collateral offence in the offshore country. Given the tangible differences in the tax laws of offshore and onshore countries, in particular with regard to those offshore countries which have no system of direct taxation, this may be a significant hurdle.

---

[78] See also the Treaty on Mutual Assistance in Criminal Matters, US–Switzerland, May 1973 (entered into force 1977), 27 UST 2019, TIAS No 8302.

[79] (1998–99) 1 ITELR 3. However, the disclosure request succeeded on other grounds.

17

DUTIES OF OFFSHORE TRUSTEES IN RELATION TO TAX

A. Introduction

Offshore trusts are not only faced with challenges from the courts and onshore legislatures on the question of taxation. Also to be considered are other questions relating to taxation which fall to be resolved by the offshore trustee. First, the trustee must be mindful of conduct which will generate greater tax liabilities for the trust and those involved with the trust, such as the beneficiaries and even the settlor. Secondly, trustees must determine whether, and in what circumstances, they should pay taxes demanded by foreign revenue authorities. These questions also form part of our discussion of the general nature and duties of trustees, with particular regard to investment duties and managing the estate.[1] **17.01**

B. Duty not to Incur Further Tax Liabilities

It is quite clear that, in making investment and general management decisions about the trust, the trustee is under a duty to ensure that, where avoidable, further tax liabilities (either to the trust, or to the beneficiaries) are not incurred. This is irrespective of the trustee's duty to pay the legitimate taxes of the estate. **17.02**

---

[1] See chapter 10.

Settlors may also incur severe tax penalties and liabilities, but it is less certain whether the trustee's duty extends to protecting the settlor.[2]

17.03 Where the trustee's functions include investment decisions, the duty to prevent avoidable tax liabilities should be balanced against his or her duty to invest reasonably.[3] However, it is arguable that should the two duties conflict in a trust set up primarily for tax avoidance or tax-planning purposes, the duty to avoid additional tax liabilities may assume greater importance. The rule may extend even to tax liabilities which the trustee must fulfil personally, particularly where the trustee has authority to indemnify himself or herself through the trust fund.

Failure to ascertain potential tax liabilities

17.04 In the face of increasing efforts to impose tax liabilities on offshore trusts, the duty to avoid incurring tax liabilities is a difficult one. The trustee is obliged to take professional advice to ascertain the correct status of the law and the tax implications of any decisions relative to the trust. It seems, however, that even where the trustee does so, the liability for a breach of duty may not be negated. This, however, is a harsh position in the increasingly complex world of offshore tax planning.

17.05 In *Re Green GLG*[4] and in *Roome v Edwards*,[5] for example, the courts appeared to have little sympathy for professional trustees who failed to take appropriate steps to be aware of potential tax liabilities even to themselves. In both these cases, the UK trustees, who were affiliated to Cayman Island trustees, had not been aware that the trust arrangements would result in tax liabilities to themselves under the UK Taxation of Chargeable Gains Act 1992, and had failed to take adequate legal advice about the matter. This was not viewed as reasonable conduct. In the case of *Green*, the court's position was particularly onerous for the trustee, as he had actually sought legal advice, but the advice was erroneous.

17.06 In *Roome*, the court noted that trustees had 'only themselves to blame if they accept the obligations of trustees' without ensuring that they had adequate protection from fiscal liabilities.[6] There is, therefore, an implied duty to take reasonable care to secure information and act in accordance with the law.

---

[2] See the discussion below, *Prestwich v Royal Bank of Canada Trust Co (Jersey) Ltd* and related cases, paras 17.25–17.28.

[3] See chapter 10.

[4] [2002] JLR 571 (Royal Ct, Jersey); (2003) 5 ITELR 591 (Royal Ct, Jersey).

[5] [1981] 1 All ER 736 (HL).

[6] ibid, 744, *per* Lord Roskill.

Tax considerations are legitimate considerations

As part of their duties to act reasonably and with care, trustees are required to **17.07**
take relevant considerations into account and ignore irrelevant ones. The duty
to assess potential tax liabilities may be expressed as part of the general duty of a
trustee to take relevant considerations into account and not to take irrelevant
ones. The likely incidence of tax liabilities accruing because of investment
decisions about the trust is accepted as a relevant consideration. Where tax
planning is a primary objective of the trust, such potential liabilities loom even
larger, as very relevant considerations.[7] The courts have thus accepted that tax
planning is not only a legitimate rationale for trusts, but that it is a legitimate
consideration for a trustee when mapping out an investment strategy or making
financial decisions about the trust.[8]

The relevance of tax considerations has been attributed to the beneficiary's **17.08**
general interest in keeping his or her share free from tax liabilities.[9] Such a
rationale is also enveloped in the case of *Abacus Trust Company (Isle of Man) Ltd
v NSPCC*,[10] where it was declared: 'Trustees . . . are bound to have regard to the
fiscal consequences of their actions.'

An offshore trust, for example, may have tax planning as its primary objective, **17.09**
and distributions to the beneficiaries might be its secondary objective. At the
very least, the trustee should not make investments which incur onerous tax
liabilities even if, for example, they result in more revenues for some beneficiaries in the long run. This is also an important factor when deciding what weight
is to be placed on income generation or capital formation.[11]

Rule in Hastings-Bass *and tax*

Where trustees take action within their discretion which results in unintended **17.10**
tax consequences for the beneficiary, the rule in *Hastings-Bass*[12] may apply. This
is in circumstances where they would not have taken such action had they been
aware of, or taken into account, relevant considerations, or not taken into

---

[7] Moreover, the tax purpose should be considered when assessing the trustee's performance in
relation to investment success, discussed earlier. Where an offshore trustee holds itself out as being
in a position to enhance tax benefits or tax planning, its her investment strategy should be held to
account. See chapter 10, 'Duties of Trustees in Managing Offshore Trusts'.

[8] *Moody Jersey A Settlement, In the Matter of* [1990] JLR 264 (Royal Ct). See also *Nestlé v
National Westminster Bank* [1993] 1 WLR 1260.

[9] Staughton LJ, in *Nestlé v National Westminster Bank*, above, n 8, 1263, said: 'A beneficiary
who has been left a life interest in a trust fund has an arguable case for saying that he should not be
compelled to bear tax on the income if he is not lawfully obliged to do so.'

[10] [2001] WILR 953, 964–5.

[11] Discussed above, paras 10.64–10.76.

[12] From the case *Re Hastings-Bass* [1975] Ch 25, 41.

account irrelevant considerations.[13] In tax matters, the rule has been applied, particularly in situations where the trustee failed to understand the full effects of tax legislation on the proposed action, even if it had sought legal advice on taxation generally and not been correctly advised. The *Hasting-Bass* rule has often provided a convenient safety valve for offshore trustees unexpectedly caught by onshore tax liabilities.

17.11   The usual effect of the *Hastings-Bass* rule has been to void the act or transaction. The rule was applied in several offshore cases.[14] It has not been modified by offshore statutes and appears, in offshore jurisdictions, to be identical to the rule as interpreted onshore. In *Re Green GLG*,[15] for example, the court found that it applied in Jersey, and saw no reason for the Jersey courts to deviate from the *Hastings-Bass* principle as applied by the English courts.

17.12   In *Re Green GLG*, the trustee had failed to appreciate that a transfer of the trust assets would accrue a tax liability under the relevant tax legislation in the UK.[16] The transaction was viewed as a capital appointment to the beneficiary which was equivalent to a transfer of value. The trustee had sought legal advice on the matter but had been wrongly advised. The court, following the *Hastings-Bass* rule, found that the tax liability was a relevant consideration which the trustee should have considered. He would clearly not have entered into the transaction had he been aware of the tax liability. Accordingly, the transaction was void as the relevant considerations had not been taken into account. This provided an opportunity for the trustee to redirect his investment strategy without apparent penalties.

17.13   Similarly, in *Abacus Trust Co (Isle of Man) Ltd v NSPCC*,[17] the trustee, in using a 'flip-flop' scheme to avoid taxes, made an appointment to the NSPCC following erroneous advice from the English solicitor (and ignoring proper advice from leading counsel) at the wrong time. The scheme therefore failed and a charge to capital gains tax arose. The trustee successfully sought a declaration that the deed of appointment was void under the rule in *Hastings-Bass*. The court found that if the effect of an intended appointment is likely to expose the fund or its beneficiaries to a significant charge to tax, that is something which the trustees have an obligation to consider when deciding whether it is proper to proceed with the appointment. Once relevance is established, 'a failure to take those matters into account must vitiate the exercise of the power'.[18] Accordingly, the deed was voided, which redounded to the benefit of the beneficiaries.

---

[13] The trustee must have acted in good faith.
[14] Such as *Re Green GLG*, above, n 4; *Green v Cobham* [2002] STC 820 (Ch), (2002) 4 ITELR 784; and *Abacus Trust Co (Isle of Man) Ltd v NSPCC*, above, n 10.
[15] See above, n 4.
[16] The Taxation of Chargeable Gains Act 1992 and the Finance Act 2000, both of the UK.
[17] Above, n 10, 964–5.
[18] ibid.

This is a generous result for a trustee who, in effect, makes an error. It is perhaps **17.14** why Patten J was prophetic when, in choosing to follow English law as espoused in *Green v Cobham*,[19] he said, 'the time may come when the limits of the *Hasting-Bass* principle fall to be determined by some higher court'.[20]

Given the fast-changing nature of anti-tax avoidance measures that creates **17.15** uncertainty in the law, the rule is a useful one for offshore tax planners. However, two significant developments to the rule should be noted. First, Lord Walker has questioned whether it is going too far to apply the rule based merely on the actual or potential adverse tax consequences of the exercise of the fiduciary power.[21] The wide application of the rule views as sufficient, a mistake as to the consequences of the fact.

In *Gibbon v Mitchell*,[22] this wide jurisdiction to set aside for mistake was limited **17.16** to cases where there is a mistake of law or fact as to the effect of the transaction, as opposed merely to the consequences, or advantages, to be gained by entering into it. For example, if a trustee believes that by selling shares worth *x* dollars a tax saving will be gained, and this is not the case, this is an error of law. If, however, the shares reduce in value just before the transaction, thereby cancelling out the tax saving, there is no mistake of law, merely an adverse consequence.

The concern for offshore trusts is that the ease with which trustees have been **17.17** able to reverse their adverse tax-planning decisions is now being questioned. The rule also seems strangely 'out of sync' with other trust law principles which encroach more and more on the trustee's margin of error. In the future, courts may well find that a situation such as occurred in *Re Green GLG* is not an error of law or fact that is sufficient to bring the rule into operation.

Effect of the rule

Just as important is Lightman J's redefinition, in the case of *Abacus Trust Co* **17.18** *(Isle of Man) v Barr*,[23] of the *effect* of the rule where it does apply. In this case, the court had to consider the application of the rule where the trustee had been erroneously instructed by an intermediary set up under the trust, and

---

[19] [2002] STC 820.
[20] *Abacus*, above, n 10, 964–5.
[21] Lord Walker, 'The Limits of the Principle in *Hastings-Bass*' [2002] PCB 226.
[22] [1990] 3 All ER 338.
[23] (2003) 5 ITELR 602. There need not be a fundamental mistake for the rule to apply. All that is required is that the trustee would not have acted as he or she did but for the relevant consideration or mistake. See ibid, 611. But the court also reiterated that 'equity does not afford a trustee or a beneficiary a free pass to rescind a decision which subsequently proves unpalatable or unfortunate and substitute another. Relief is only available if the necessary conditions for its grant are satisfied': ibid, 608.

consequently made an error as to the settlor's wishes. As a result, instead of making an appointment of 40% of the funds for the exclusive benefit of the settlor's sons, as the settlor had intended, the trustee incorrectly appointed 60%.

17.19   Finding that the trustee had breached its duty to ascertain the true wishes of the settlor, by inappropriately relying on the information of the intermediary, the court went on to hold that the trustee's decision was voidable, instead of being void. This was on the basis that, if trustees have exercised their discretion and, in doing so, failed to take into account a relevant consideration, or in the process took an irrelevant consideration into account, they have, nevertheless, actually made a decision. Consequently, in the event that such a decision is challenged successfully under the rule in *Hastings-Bass*, in accordance with the ordinary principle of equity that a decision in breach of a fiduciary duty is voidable and not void, the decision must be held to be voidable.

17.20   This is to be contrasted, for example, with the case where the trustee acts without the relevant discretion or power conferred by the trust instrument. In the latter situation, the act would be void. The finding in *Abacus v Barr* is, of course, in contradiction, to the decisions of several courts coming before it.[24] In Lightman J's view, this was merely because those previous courts had not fully considered the issue, if at all.

17.21   The result of this reasoning is that, in relation to a decision found to be voidable, the court has a discretion whether or not to nullify the act or transaction.[25] As with the ordinary principles of equity, the court will examine the fairness and justice of the circumstances of the case, together with the conduct of the parties involved, in coming to its decision whether to void the act or transaction in question. In this context, the cautionary note sounded by Lord Walker on the inappropriateness of the rule as applied to certain tax transactions gone awry, might attract greater reflection.[26]

17.22   In *Re Green GLG*, the Royal Court of Jersey also noted that where the rule in *Hastings-Bass* could apply as a matter of policy, the voiding of an action or transaction was the preferred approach to settling such matters, as opposed to an action for negligence between the trustees, beneficiaries, and legal advisers.[27]

---

[24] See, eg, *Re Green GLG*, above, n 4 and *Green v Cobham*, above, n 9.

[25] In *Abacus v Barr*, above, n 23, the court did not decide on the final question of whether the appointment should have been avoided. Instead, it urged the parties to settle the matter.

[26] By Lord Walker, above, n 21. The court in *Abacus v Barr* also noted, *per curiam*, the public/ private law dichotomy on the question of the concepts of void and voidable. Unlike in public law, in private law there were clear classifications of void and voidable: ibid, 615.

[27] [2002] JLR 571, 581–2.

Tax liabilities on the settlor are relevant

It appears that tax liabilities are relevant considerations for the trustee whether **17.23** they fall on beneficiaries, trust assets generally, the settlor, or, even indirectly, on the trustee. However, the courts appear to be undecided on the question whether this extends to a duty on the trustee to ensure that settlors do not incur further tax liabilities and, if they do, to reimburse them. The related question—whether trustees have a duty generally to pay taxes on the behalf of a settlor—is considered below.[28] The latter two scenarios were seen in *Re Green GLG*,[29] where the settlor had a statutory right to reclaim from the trustee the capital gains tax which arose as a result of the trustee's transaction and which he, the settlor, had paid. The trustee had failed to understand the full effects of relevant tax legislation on a transaction concerning a transfer of trust assets (there was a capital appointment to the beneficiary which was equivalent to a transfer of value). The tax liability was a relevant consideration which the trustee should have considered, and it was clear that he would not have taken the action had he been fully aware of it.[30]

The court described the anti-avoidance initiative and the corresponding statutory **17.24** right of a UK settlor to reclaim from the trustees capital gains tax which he had paid, noting that there was 'clearly an issue as to whether any such right of indemnity could be enforceable in Jersey'.[31] To require the trustee to consider the tax liability of a settlor is a very wide principle when one takes into account that the rationale for the relevant considerations rule is, ultimately, the interest of the beneficiaries.

In the earlier decision of *Prestwich v Royal Bank of Canada Trust Company* **17.25** *(Jersey) Ltd*,[32] the High Court in the UK ruled that there was no duty of care owed by a trustee to a settlor to ensure that the settlor was not made subject to a tax liability. In this case, the settlor became liable for capital gains tax when trustee A made a loan to the trustee of another trust established by the settlor. Under the Taxation of Chargeable Gains Act 1992 of the UK,[33] capital gains of qualifying settlements are chargeable to the settlor of a settlement subject to a right of reimbursement from the trustees. The effect of the loan to the second trust was to 'taint' the trust, making it a 'qualifying settlement' under the Act.

---

[28] Paras 17.60–17.70.

[29] Above, n 4.

[30] Here, the trustee had actually sought legal advice on the effects of the legislation, the UK Finance Act 2000 and the UK Taxation of Chargeable Gains Act 1992, but the advice was incorrect.

[31] [2002] JLR 571, 575.

[32] (1998–99) 1 ITELR 671.

[33] Sch 5, para 6(2).

The trustee resisted the claim for reimbursement, and the settlor failed in his claim that the trustee's action in incurring the tax liability was negligent.

17.26 The uncertainty as to whether there is a duty placed on a trustee to avoid incurring further tax liability in relation to the trust can perhaps be resolved by returning to first principles. Duties owed by trustees under a trust are owed to beneficiaries, not to the settlor. Accordingly, the beneficiaries have a right to enforce a duty of care placed on a trustee in relation to tax liabilities, but a settlor does not (except to the extent expressed in the trust instrument).

17.27 Thus, the question whether the settlor may claim reimbursement from the trustee where legislation has imposed a tax liability on him, in situations where such a tax liability will generally fall on the trustee as the 'owner' of the trust, is an entirely distinct one from a similar question on the liabilities placed on beneficiaries. Certainly, ordinary trust principles do not assist, as they are concerned with the interests of the beneficiaries.

17.28 The real problem, however, is the question of jurisdiction over the trustee and the ability to enforce any reimbursement upon him.[34] This, in fact, was an important issue in *Prestwich*,[35] and the court there thought it appropriate to allow service outside of the jurisdiction for such a purpose. But the court can go no further in enforcing any debt or repayment statutorily owed by the trustee. Indeed, it is precisely because onshore authorities are unable to secure tax payments from foreign trustees that statutes have been enacted transferring liability onto a settlor. A practical solution needs to be sought, such as a written agreement beforehand that the trustee must honour tax claims paid by the settlor on behalf of the trust.

C. Duty of the Trustee to Pay Taxes

17.29 In the offshore construct, the trustee will not be expected to be within the jurisdiction of the onshore courts. Recognizing this, some legislatures have taken the extra step of making the resident beneficiaries and the settlor liable for any defaults of trustees in paying taxes, or in adhering to reporting requirements. Thus, in modern onshore fiscal regimes which are concerned about tax avoidance, taxes may be levied on offshore trusts and reporting requirements placed upon them, despite the unlikelihood of the anti-tax avoidance requirements being fulfilled by the trustee himself or herself. The trustee must, therefore, consider this extra burden being placed on the beneficiaries and, perhaps,

---

[34] Discussed below, paras 17.62–17.70.
[35] Above, n 32.

the settlor, when making a decision as to whether or not to pay taxes, or to reimburse the beneficiaries or the settlor who paid the taxes owed.

Questions of jurisdiction and the enforcement of revenue laws also come into play here. In the offshore trust structure, the trustee may be called upon by an onshore authority to pay taxes in a situation where the onshore jurisdiction has no jurisdiction over the trustee and no means of enforcing any revenue laws or judgments. Trustees may, of course, also be called upon to honour other debts compiled by settlors and beneficiaries, such as creditors' debts. Similar principles will apply. When juxtaposed with the general rule against the enforcement of revenue laws, discussed above,[36] the question assumes more complex dimensions. The trustee may be exposed to liability for a breach of trust where he or she pays taxes in such a situation, as this may be viewed as a tax liability which he or she does not have to meet. The trustee's decision to pay may, therefore, be treated as an abuse of his or her discretion and may constitute a breach of trust. This is particularly relevant in view of the increasing tax liabilities being placed on settlors by onshore authorities. **17.30**

Paradoxically, given the joint and several tax liabilities placed on the beneficiaries of a non-resident trust, the trustee may also be in breach of trust where he or she refuses to pay foreign taxes and the beneficiaries become liable for his or her default, including severe and costly penalties for non-compliance. These are not easy questions to resolve. However, at the heart of the issue lies the trustee's essential duties toward the beneficiaries. **17.31**

Where the trust deed expressly provides for payment of taxes

Where the trust deed makes an express provision for the payment of taxes, there is a presumption that such taxes must be paid. The nature of any expressed power to pay taxes must be carefully scrutinized as it may be a general power, or one which is confined to payments solely in the interests of the beneficiaries. The latter power may exclude, for example, payments which are for the trustee's benefit or the settlor's benefit. **17.32**

Even where the power is to be used in fulfilment of the interests of the beneficiaries, the trustee would still need to consider carefully the exercise of his or her discretion where conflicting beneficiaries' interests arise. **17.33**

Non-enforcement rule overrides specific tax clause

While the trust deed places an obligation on trustees to pay taxes, the issue becomes more complex where the taxes are foreign taxes. In such situations, the **17.34**

---

[36] See paras 16.1–16.37.

competing rule against the enforcement of foreign fiscal law, in conjunction with the fact that the foreign tax authority may have no authority over the trustee, may override the presumption to pay taxes. The nature of an express power to pay taxes was discussed in the Barbadian case of *Bank of Nova Scotia v Tremblay.*[37] The relevant clauses in the four trust deeds in issue were broad and allowed the trustee to pay taxes anywhere in the world. The trust deed also allowed the trustee company to be exempted from liability to the beneficiary where any loss or damage was incurred to the trust fund as a result of the trustee's bona fide exercise of the power conferred.[38]

17.35   The court in this case relied on the general principle of the non-enforcement of foreign revenue laws, finding that this effectively curtailed the application of the wide enabling clause, as it would be difficult to envisage circumstances where payment of taxes by a trustee which he was not obliged to pay, could be a bona fide exercise of the power conferred. The court did not rule out the possibility of such a clause being permitted to survive in such circumstances.[39] However, it would require a 'compelling reason' for this to happen.[40] Unfortunately, the court did not specify what such a compelling reason could be.

17.36   In contrast, in *Re X's Settlement,*[41] in a trust which contained a power to pay foreign taxes, the Jersey court permitted the payment, since it was in the interests of the beneficiaries to do so. If the taxes were not paid, the executor of the trust, who was a US citizen, could have been subject to civil and criminal proceedings under US tax law. The interests of beneficiaries would appear to be a sufficient or 'compelling reason', as described in *Tremblay*.

Where payment of taxes is unexpressed

17.37   If the trust instrument contains no expressed power to pay taxes, the matter is one for the discretion of the trustee. A number of circumstances can occur which will impact on that decision. However, the intention of the settlor and the best interest of the beneficiaries are factors which must be prioritized.

---

[37] (1998–99) 1 ITELR 673.

[38] Under Clause 8.

[39] Further, the court did not rule out the application of the power to pay tax on behalf of persons other than beneficiaries. In this case, the beneficiaries were actually trying to terminate the trust under the rule in *Saunders v Vautier* (1842) 4 Beav 115, 49 ER 284, but were unsuccessful in doing so.

[40] See also *Re Fudger* (1984) 18 ETR 12, 21 (Ontario High Court of Justice): 'To pay foreign taxes simply because a foreign beneficiary under a foreign will might otherwise be exposed to the payment of taxes imposed in the foreign jurisdiction would be an indirect method of enforcing the revenue laws of the foreign jurisdiction.' See, too, *USA v Harden* [1963] SCR 266.

[41] [1994] BOCM 600.

Acting fairly toward the beneficiary

As a first principle, where the trustee is not under the jurisdiction of the foreign **17.38** court demanding the tax and the tax law is not enforceable, the tax should be paid if the beneficiary will be prejudiced. For example, where onshore anti-avoidance measures place the burden on the beneficiary to make up for any non-payments of taxes by the trustee, it seems that the trustee should pay. This is despite the fact that legislative measures may exist which allow the beneficiary to recoup from the trustee.

This general principle was demonstrated in the thinly-worded judgment in **17.39** *Re Marc Bolan Charitable Trust.*[42] Here, a demand was made for the payment of UK taxes on behalf of beneficiaries residing in the UK. These UK beneficiaries were in the majority. The offshore trustee was not under the jurisdiction of the UK court and the claim for payment was unenforceable against him. The trustee, who was resident in Jersey, sought permission from the court to enter into a compromise agreement with the UK tax authorities, in order to pay a discounted settlement amount to satisfy the claim. There was no express power in the trust deed to enter into any such compromise, but the court accepted that it could be viewed as an exercise of the equitable power to apply part of the trust fund for the benefit of the beneficiaries.

The court concluded that trustees could make a payment to satisfy a tax claim **17.40** on the basis that it was in the best interests of the beneficiaries. However, the court did suggest that acts such as those before it were best directed through the court, to avoid future actions for breach of trust. In finding that the proposed payment would be in the best interests of the beneficiaries, and therefore acceptable, the court appeared to be significantly influenced by the fact that without the compromise payment, the beneficiaries would have been left with a considerably reduced trust fund from which to receive distributions. This was because the trustee would have been subject to even greater financial liabilities upon future visits to the UK. Yet the court was quite unmoved by the fact that its action would also protect the trustee. Indeed, this was viewed as merely incidental to the court's true task of protecting the beneficiaries.

The principle here, therefore, appears to be a very narrow one. It is unclear **17.41** whether a court would hold that taxes should be paid if a beneficiary will not be financially affected by the lack of a payment. For example, where the payment will only satisfy the trustee's liabilities, and there is no other justifiable reason in favour of the beneficiaries, such a payment may not be construed as being in the best interests of the beneficiaries.

---

[42] [1981] JJ 117 (Royal Ct, Jersey).

17.42   Further, the trustee may be required to obtain permission from the court before agreeing to settle a tax debt which is unenforceable by the foreign jurisdiction. Such permission will normally be forthcoming only where it is in the interest of the beneficiaries.[43]

17.43   A further consideration would be the intention of the settlor. If the refusal to pay foreign taxes would result in unfairness toward the beneficiary or certain beneficiaries, and a payment would not be contrary to the intention of the settlor, the trustee should pay taxes.

Conflicting interests of beneficiaries

17.44   The trustee may have to face a dilemma between taxes calling to be paid with respect to certain beneficiaries in one jurisdiction and objections to such payment by beneficiaries in another jurisdiction. Often, a settlor's intention may not be clear in such a circumstance, particularly with regard to the fast-changing nature of tax liabilities onshore. This is a more difficult case than the first scenario that had beneficiaries located in one jurisdiction. Not surprisingly, the cases are conflicting.

17.45   In *Re Fudger*,[44] for example, the Canadian trustees were faced with a demand for UK capital estate taxes on a testatrix's estate because of her English domicile. The tax claimed was in excess of the value of one of the properties of the estate, located in Scotland. The Scottish beneficiary, a charity, stood to lose the legacy and argued that it had been the express intent of the testatrix to benefit the charity. The court found that there was an intention to deal with the properties separately and that the assets were to be disposed of separately. Thus, the conclusion was that there was no intention to pay taxes imposed by a foreign statute. The court relied further on the rule against the non-enforcement of revenue laws to support its judgment.

17.46   The *Fudger* decision relies clearly on the general principle that the settlor's intention is to be paramount, and may be distinguished from other cases which appear to rule generally in favour of the payment of foreign taxes in similar situations. Such a case was that of *In Re Hollins*.[45] Here, the testatrix was domiciled in England and left property to persons in different jurisdictions. The English authorities were prepared to enforce taxes on the estate to set off taxes demanded for a foreign legatee over which they had no jurisdiction. The court had no difficulty with the imposition of taxes in such a situation, finding that

---

[43]   *Re Sidney Walmesley (deceased)* [1983] JJ 35.
[44]   Above, n 40.
[45]   79 Misc 200; 139 NYS 713 (Surr Ct NY Co 1913).

the trustees could be compelled to pay taxes where the intention of the testator to benefit the beneficiaries would otherwise be frustrated.

We may also consider the case of *Re Barna Estate*,[46] which concerned a will. **17.47**
Here, the settlor was domiciled in France, but the property and the executor were in Canada. There was a French will and a Canadian will. The latter will created a number of trusts and was formally executed in Canada. Under the French law, where a settlor was domiciled in France, the beneficiaries of a will who were not relatives were liable to a 40% tax on the value of the deceased's worldwide estate. The court sought to determine whether taxes were payable only in relation to property passing under the Canadian will, or under both the French and Canadian wills.

Upon examination of the wording of the Canadian will, the court found that **17.48**
evidence that the defendant intended Canadian law to be the proper law rebutted the presumption that the proper law was to be that of the place of domicile. Evidence of this intention came from the defendant's description of the will as her 'Canadian will', and the fact that it applied only to 'all my property, both real and personal situate elsewhere than in France or Monaco'. The court further noted that the executor was Canadian, that specific reference was made to the laws of British Columbia and to the Income Tax Act of Canada, and that the description of the power of the execution matched that of Canadian executors and not that of French executors. Since the court found that Canadian law was applicable, as the settlor had written the will with reference to that law, it was not hampered by the rule against non-enforcement. The dominant consideration in the case at bar was what the settlor had intended.

This is a useful case for trusts where the proper law is in doubt. The court **17.49**
should infer that payment of foreign duties out of the domestic estate is to be made only where the testator's words are clear and broad enough to do so. This was not the situation in *Re Barna Estate*. Instead, it was clear that the deceased intended to dispose of the various properties separately. Accordingly, only domestic taxes were due, and Canadian law and estate practices were to apply. Consequently, the French taxes were not to be paid.

In the same vein, where a trustee acts in the best interest of the trust by paying **17.50**
taxes, even where he or she may not be forced to do so by a foreign authority, a beneficiary may not easily prevent the trustee from doing so.[47]

---

[46] (1990) 24 ACWS (3d) 114 (Sup Ct, Br Columbia).
[47] ibid. See also *Scottish National Orchestra Society Ltd v Thomson's Executor* 1969 SLT 325, where the Scottish court, in similar circumstances to *In Re Hollins*, above, n 45, again found that the fact that the executor was outside of the jurisdiction of the authorities demanding the tax, was not sufficient to prevent the payment of taxes where a beneficiary's interest was at stake.

17.51　In summary, the trustee must balance the interests of the beneficiaries fairly and equitably, keeping in mind the settlor's intention, a duty which is not unfamiliar to trustees. Further, in the light of developments toward relaxing the rule on the non-enforcement of revenue laws,[48] this, of itself, is not an insurmountable hurdle to a trustee's decision whether to pay taxes in relation to modern-day trust investment. The cases suggest that two competing streams of law are at play. On the one hand, the fundamental duties of a trustee toward the beneficiaries, having regard to a settlor's intention, and on the other, the rule against non-enforcement of fiscal law. It would appear that priority is to be given to the former.

The trustee's self-interest in paying taxes

17.52　A payment of taxes by the trustee may also be in the best interest of the trustee. If taxes are incurred in performing the usual administrative functions of the trust, it is well established that the trustee is entitled to be indemnified for the legitimate costs to himself or herself.[49] It is less well settled whether a trustee can be indemnified from the trust fund for tax payments which arise outside of the trustee's normal administrative functions, particularly where these are not enforceable in the trustee's jurisdiction, but which the trustee is, theoretically, compelled to pay.

17.53　In *Re Reid,*[50] the English trustee administered an estate with assets in England and Canada. Because of tax demands on the English estate, he faced the possibility of a judgment for debts in relation to the English estate and the risk of being wound up. Since the assets of the English estate could not meet the taxes, the trustee had to pay the duty himself. He then sought reimbursement out of the Canadian estate. In ensuing litigation, the beneficiary failed to prevent the payment of taxes out of the foreign estate. The court's reasoning was that the claim was not an enforcement of a tax claim but was merely an effort to effect payment of duties pursuant to English legislation. The indemnity was lawful in such circumstances.

17.54　A contrasting result was obtained in *Stringham v Dubois,*[51] where *Re Reid* was expressly rejected by the Court of Appeal of Alberta, finding that an US trustee could not be allowed to sell Canadian property in order to satisfy demands for US taxes with respect to an estate of an US person. The court was undisturbed by the fact that the trustee would have been liable for the estate tax.

---

[48]　See paras 16.1–16.32.

[49]　See, eg, *Re Grimthorpe* [1985] 1 All ER 765. The issue of indemnities is discussed generally in chapter 10.

[50]　(1970) 17 DLR (3d) 199 (Sup Ct, Br Columbia).

[51]　[1993] 3 WWR 273.

Notably, in *Re Lord Cable (deceased) Garratt and Waters*,[52] the English court **17.55** agreed with the plaintiff beneficiaries that, as a general principle, it could not enforce the foreign revenue laws of another jurisdiction. This was in a case where the settlor had been domiciled in India, and an attempt was being made by the Indian trustees to remit monies from the UK to satisfy estate and death taxes in India. The settlor was domiciled in India and the trust was governed by Indian law. The plaintiffs sought an injunction to restrain the remittance. However, the injunction was refused, mainly on the court's recognition of the harsh consequences that it would have had for the trustees if they failed to pay the taxes. Moreover, the court saw a distinction between its intervention to require trustees to comply with foreign fiscal legislation and its refusal to act to prevent trustees of a foreign trust from complying with fiscal legislation of the county of the proper law, which under such foreign law they are entitled, and indeed obliged, to obey. The latter situation applied in the instant case.

Questioning extraterritorial application of tax to foreign trustees

The question of an arising liability for tax on a foreign trustee is, of course, entirely **17.56** different to the issues of jurisdiction over that trustee and the enforcement of the liability.

In an intriguing case, *Re Clore (deceased) No 3, Inland Revenue Commissioners v* **17.57** *Stupe Trustees (Jersey) Ltd and Others*,[53] the vexing issue of jurisdiction over the tax obligations of foreign trustees was raised. The settlor, who was domiciled in the UK, had established a Jersey trust which was managed by several foreign trustees from various parts of the world. The proper law of the trust was stated as the law of Jersey, and this was not disputed by the court.

Because the settlor, who was deceased, had retained a life interest in the trust, a **17.58** charge to capital gains tax arose which became payable by the trustees under the Finance Act 1975 of the UK. The Revenue sought an account of the property, as provided for under Sch 4, para 2(1)(b) of the Finance Act 1975. The Jersey trustee, who had previously resigned as trustee, resisted the demand for the accounts on the ground that it offended the territoriality principle. This, he argued, was sufficient to exclude the trustee from the provisions of the Act, on the grounds that Parliament would not legislate in respect of extraterritorial matters and that the courts of one country would not enforce the revenue laws of another country.

---

[52] [1976] 3 All ER 417; [1977] 1 WLR 7.
[53] [1985] 2 All ER 819; [1985] 1 WLR 1290; [1985] STC 394.

17.59 Curiously, the extraterritorial argument was not made with respect to the actual tax liabilities placed on foreign trustees, but rather on the related claim for accounts. This deprives us of an opportunity to learn how the courts would have addressed the requirement in its more fundamental application. Not surprisingly, the court made short shrift of the trustee's claim, finding that once he had conceded that he was liable to the tax, as indeed he had, he could not then argue that the accompanying section on accounts did not apply to him. However, the court did note the distinction between the liability for the tax and the means to enforce the tax.

Payment in the interest of the settlor

17.60 In the more complex environment of countermeasures to offshore trust tax planning, an offshore trustee may be called upon to make payments in order to set off taxes paid by the settlor to onshore revenue authorities. This arises in situations where the settlor is subject to 'look through' or transparency legislative provisions in the onshore jurisdiction. Such provisions treat the settlor as the continuing owner of the trust property, by effectively ignoring the trust. An increasing number of onshore jurisdictions, including the UK and the US, have these rules.[54] Beneficiaries may well object to such reimbursements and proceed to instigate litigation.

17.61 The question whether a trustee may pay taxes on the behalf of a settlor (or reimburse the settlor for a tax payment) is more difficult than the one concerning the statutory right of a beneficiary to be reimbursed from the trust, discussed earlier,[55] since the trustee owes no fiduciary duty to the settlor. As this is a fairly recent phenomenon, there are no clear rules as to whether this is a legitimate payment by the trustee, and the few cases are contradictory. Further, the trust instrument may be unhelpful as it will not usually contain an express power to make such payments, a defect which should, perhaps, be remedied in offshore trusts.

Jurisdiction over tax payments

17.62 Some onshore legislatures, recognizing the problem, have added a statutory right for a settlor to claim reimbursement from the trustee. Nonetheless, as the offshore trustee is outside of the jurisdiction of the onshore courts, this right may not be enforceable against the trustee.

17.63 While the taxation of settlors and beneficiaries of offshore trusts may be viewed as an assertion of jurisdiction over the trust, this jurisdiction must be interpreted

---

[54] See chapter 14, 'Overview of Statutory Tax Countermeasures Against Offshore Trusts'.
[55] Paras 17.34–17.51.

as a narrow one for the purposes of taxation of residents. Such jurisdiction cannot extend to matters surrounding the administration of the trust. The payment of taxes by trustees falls within the administration of the trust and is, therefore, outside of the jurisdiction of the onshore jurisdiction. The question should properly be determined by a court in the jurisdiction of the proper law of the trust, which, if the offshore trust goes according to its game plan, would be an offshore court.

How, then, would a demand for the reimbursement of tax payments by a settlor **17.64** be viewed? If the trust is a revocable trust, there would seem to be no practical reason for a trustee's refusal to reimburse, as this may have a direct effect on the interests of the beneficiaries.

The cases thus far have not satisfactorily answered this vexing question. For **17.65** example, In *Re Colin Douglas 1990 Settlement*,[56] the Royal Court of Jersey had to decide whether to vary a Jersey trust in order to avoid capital gains tax being levied against the settlor. The court noted that para 6(1) of Sch 5 to the Taxation of Chargeable Gains Act 1992 of the UK, conferred upon the settlor a statutory right of reimbursement from the trustees after he had paid the capital gains tax. However, the court remarked, *obiter*, that it was an 'open question' as to whether the Royal Court would enforce such a statutory right of reimbursement. Nonetheless, the court's reminder of its duties under the Trust (Jersey) Law 1984, is an indication of how it might decide when faced directly with the question. It observed that under article 43(2) of the said Act, it could approve a variation of the trust only if it was in the interests of the beneficiaries. Here, the variation would have resulted in an avoidance of capital gains tax by the settlor, to be reimbursed out of the trust fund, to the detriment of the beneficiaries.

Another case which considered this question was that of *Prestwich v Royal Bank* **17.66** *of Canada Trust Company (Jersey) Ltd.*[57] The plaintiff, who was the settlor of the trusts in question, obtained a victory on a procedural point, as the court accepted jurisdiction to allow him to serve the defendant outside of the jurisdiction, seeking to recover the sum which he, the settlor, had paid to satisfy capital gains tax levied on him. However, the court found no duty placed on the trustee to avoid incurring tax liabilities on the behalf of a settlor.

Yet in *Re T Settlement*,[58] the Royal Court of Jersey found a way around this **17.67** dilemma on moral grounds. This was a judgment tinged with sympathy for an elderly female settlor who had been, somewhat harshly, caught by the retroactive

---

[56] (2000) 2 ITELR 682; [2000] JLR 73 (Royal Ct).
[57] Above, n 32.
[58] [2002] JLR 204 (Royal Ct).

application of the Finance Act 1998 of the UK. The settlor had established the Jersey trust in 1969 while living in Jersey. The trust fund comprised all of the shares in her investment company. She, along with her children, remoter issue, and their spouses, was an original beneficiary. In 1980 the settlor relocated to the UK, and was thereby excluded from the settlement to avoid income tax liability. Instead, a modest sub-settlement was created for her. Subsequently, the Finance Act 1998 made the settlor, as an English resident, potentially liable for any capital gains realized as a result of sales of the investments in the trust. This was an enormous sum, which the settlor, on her reduced income, would not have been able to pay. The trustee, with the agreement of the beneficiaries, the settlor's children, therefore sought to vary the trust to allow the settlor's tax liabilities to be paid from the trust fund.[59] The application was on the grounds that it would be for the 'moral benefit', and generally in the beneficiaries' interests, to vary the trust for this purpose.

17.68 The court accepted the submission, reaffirming the principle that the benefit required for beneficiaries, in order to vary a trust, did not need to be a 'financial benefit'. It also confirmed that the trust could be varied in order to assist in a scheme to avoid tax. Here, the trust had been established for tax avoidance purposes and the settlor faced a tax liability that had never been anticipated:

> The improvement of the material situation of a beneficiary is not confined to his direct financial advantage . . . It includes the discharge of . . . certain moral or social obligations on the part of the beneficiary, for example, towards dependants.[60]

Thus, the beneficiaries in the instant case would derive a moral benefit from protecting their mother/grandmother, aged 98, who had provided generously for them under the trust. The variation was therefore granted.

17.69 In *Re T Settlement*, the settlor had returned to the UK and was, therefore, within the jurisdiction of the UK courts. She would have been rendered bankrupt by the tax liability. In less harsh circumstances, however, such a moral obligation may not arise.[61] The case does not therefore assist, directly, with the broader question of the enforcement of any judgments obtained in the onshore court. As seen in our discussion of this subject,[62] offshore law is generally hostile to such enforcement.

---

[59] As allowed under article 43 of the Trusts (Jersey) Law 1984.

[60] Above, n 58, 210, relying on *Re Clore's Settlement Trusts* [1966] 1 WLR 955, 958.

[61] In *Federal Trust Company Ltd v Macdonald-Smith* (2002) 4 ITELR 211, the question whether a trustee has a duty to indemnify the settlor or beneficiary where he honours tax liabilities arising in the foreign jurisdiction was again raised, this time in the form of a declaration sought from the Guernsey Royal Court. The court struck down the case, however, on a procedural point, on the basis that this was not the proper route as contemplated under s 62 of the Trusts (Guernsey) Law 1989.

[62] See chapter 24.

Another key issue here, of course, is that the beneficiaries were in agreement that **17.70** the settlor's tax debts were to be paid. Would a court accept that hostile beneficiaries have a similar moral duty? It is suggested that moral obligations could still arise if one returns to the intention of the settlor. If the settlor is unaware of tax liabilities, or the tax liabilities arise after the fact, it is morally wrong to bankrupt the settlor since the trust would not have been created otherwise. This argument is particularly strong where the tax liabilities are created long after the fact. A significant factor would therefore be the impact of the debt or claim on the settlor. Given that the Jersey courts have recently held that trustees may impose benefits on beneficiaries even against their will, this is a plausible argument.[63]

---

[63] *Re Abacus (CI) Ltd (Trustee of the Esteem Settlement) Grupo Torras SA v Al Sabah* (2003) 6 ITELR 368 (Royal Ct, Jersey); [2003] JRC 92. This was one aspect of the complex litigation by Grupo Torras against the settlor, Sheik Fahad, who established trusts in several offshore jurisdictions.

PART IV

THE CONFLICT OF LAWS
AND THE OFFSHORE TRUST

18

TRANSPLANTING THE COMMON LAW TRUST—CONFLICT OF LAWS AND THE ACCEPTANCE OF THE OFFSHORE TRUST

A. Introduction

As we have seen, trust laws in offshore jurisdictions may differ significantly from trust laws in onshore jurisdictions, or from the traditional common law rules on the trust. As offshore laws are tailored specifically to the needs of offshore investors and their assets, it is important that these investors are able to benefit from them. **18.01**

The protection of assets placed in an offshore trust relies on the general principle that the laws and judgments of the settlor's onshore jurisdiction, and those of challengers to the trust, are of no effect in the offshore jurisdiction. Consequently, laws in the offshore jurisdiction, considered to be more advantageous to the trust, apply. The intention is to render the trust fund more secure for the benefit of the individual settlor, or his or her beneficiaries. However, this assumption is too simplistic to address the complexities which the transplantation of the trust offshore brings with it. These include issues relating to choice of law, jurisdiction, recognition, capacity, and the enforcement of foreign judgments. **18.02**

Since the offshore trust is a different creature from its onshore counterpart, orthodox trust law principles may not be compatible with it. As the trust assumes a transnational character offshore, it may also conflict with onshore jurisdictions of a civil law tradition. This is because as the English Common **18.03**

Law legal tradition grounds the institution of the trust. Thus, traditionally, civil law neither recognizes nor understands it fully.

18.04 In the global context of offshore investment, relationships between countries which recognize the trust and those which do not, may be problematic. Offshore trust law must, therefore, reconcile the inevitable conflict of laws that this brings. Consideration must also be given to the degree to which the trust can, or should, accommodate competing civil law concepts such as forced heirship.

18.05 Private international law rules on the trust do not reflect or form part of a '*fully-developed system'.[1] Where they have evolved, rules have developed differently in various countries, although the English Common Law, being the parent of the trust, can be still viewed as the authority on the subject where statute has not intervened.

18.06 As the hybrid offshore trust is a modern phenomenon, it poses a further challenge to the subject of conflict of laws, which has not yet adequately defined rules to address it. Offshore laws deliberately attempt to modify and circumvent existing domestic trust laws and conflict of laws rules, which itself forces a review of conflict of laws and traditional trust law principles. As such, the subject is very much an evolving one. Indeed, the existence of offshore trusts is furthering the development of jurisprudence on private international law rules on the trust.

18.07 Whereas adjudication using orthodox trust principles may fail to address the challenges posed by the offshore trust, a conflict of laws approach might more easily do so. For example, the latter may bring notions of public policy more directly into focus. Similarly, choice of law questions can closely scrutinize issues such as the capacity to create a trust and the trust's validity. The substance of the offshore trust, and not merely its form, may be tested. Yet such challenges, while important indicators of the limits of the offshore trust, do not prejudice its essential viability and legitimacy as a new legal phenomenon.

Methods to avoid onshore law

18.08 The essence of offshore trust planning is the juxtaposition of two conflicting legal systems, with the hope that sustainability for the trust and its assets can be achieved. Planning extends to elements such as jurisdiction, choice of law, capacity, and the enforcement of onshore judgments. It achieves this route to protecting the offshore trust and its assets in two main ways. Both methods

---

[1] Cheshire and North, *Private International Law*, 12th edn, (Butterworths, London, 1992) 879.

present great difficulties to persons attempting to challenge trusts, reach offshore assets, or enforce judgments.

In the first method, the assets may be placed in an offshore jurisdiction and the trust established there with the use of a foreign trustee. This is described as a 'jurisdictional severance approach'. The assets are physically offshore, as is the trust vehicle itself. In effect, the assets have been 'exported'.[2] The method attempts to place the trust in a position that allows it to sever all jurisdictional ties with the onshore state's judicial system. If creditors or others seek to pursue the assets of such a trust, they will be forced to do so in the jurisdiction which is the *situs* of the trust, that is, the offshore jurisdiction. Typically, the laws of that jurisdiction will be favourable to the settlor, and these laws will determine the claimants' rights.

18.09

The second route requires the selection of an offshore jurisdiction with a trust law regime which is advantageous to the settlor, that is, one which is aggressively against claimants and challengers to the trust. A family limited partnership or other onshore entity may be used. Foreign trustees may own the onshore partnership interests. Here, the assets remain in the home country and in strict legal theory are more susceptible to domestic judicial jurisdiction. The success of this arrangement lies in its ability to bring the offshore law to the onshore country enough to defeat, or severely discourage, claimants. Foreign law is therefore 'imported'. Since neither the proper law nor jurisdiction may be based on where the trust assets are, such distinctions may be less important than they first appear.

18.10

Further, using a pre-emptive conflict of laws legislative mechanism, offshore countries have deliberately designed legislation to thwart challengers to the offshore trust, whether these challengers are creditors, heirs, or tax authorities. Such legislation includes attempts to assert exclusive jurisdiction over the trust, to deem offshore law the proper law, to grant capacity to civil law settlors, to oust the application of unfavourable onshore trust law principles, and to avoid the enforcement of unfavourable judgments onshore. Simultaneously, typical offshore legislation will include trust law principles supportive of the validity of the offshore trust, often unknown to the orthodox onshore trust.

18.11

Areas of conflict

Despite the efficiency of offshore jurisdictions in creating legislation to protect the offshore trust and its assets, such legislation may ultimately fail in its objective. Questions of private international law may defeat offshore entities at

18.12

---

[2] A term coined by E Osborne, *Asset Protection, Domestic and International Law Tactics* (Clark, Boardman, Callaghan, NY, 1995).

the outset. Consequently, a prerequisite for the effectiveness of the offshore trust is its ability to be subsumed under the protective jurisdiction of offshore law favourable to its aims and objectives. Applying orthodox trust principles to the complex offshore trust can create unforeseen difficulties. There is a danger that the offshore trust may be forced to surrender to an antagonistic legal regime where conflicts of laws arise.

18.13 Thus, the effectiveness and validity of the offshore trust must be considered against the backdrop of conflict of laws. Indeed, this perspective is crucial to a true understanding of its operation. Conflicts of laws issues permeate almost every facet of the trust, its claim to universality, the reconciling of different jurisdictional approaches to fundamental issues such as tax avoidance and creditor protection, and the application of succession rights like forced heirship. When fundamentally opposed legal philosophies—such as flexibility and commercial viability in the offshore sector and strict regulation in the onshore jurisdictions—are juxtaposed, they widen such conflicts. Increasing litigation between onshore and offshore jurisdictions underscores the need for an appreciation of conflict of laws issues.

18.14 Conflicts of laws in relation to the offshore trust may arise in several ways:

(1) There may be conflict in relation to choice of law, questioning whether the law of the traditional onshore trust law or that of the hybrid offshore trust is applicable as the proper law. It may be determined that onshore law, and not the favourable law of the offshore jurisdiction, governs the trust. As a result, important questions about fundamental aspects of the trust might be determined by onshore trust rules.

(2) The offshore trust may be exposed to onshore legal concepts which undermine it. Under this rubric might be placed, for example, the application of mandatory succession laws.

(3) The question whether an onshore court will have jurisdiction over a trust placed geographically in an offshore state but settled by onshore citizens or residents may have to be determined. The onshore state may unilaterally extend its jurisdiction to tax offshore assets of its citizens or residents and to govern other matters such as creditor protection. On the other hand, the offshore trust law may also aim at extraterritoriality. Both these initiatives require a deliberation of appropriate jurisdiction and choice of law.

(4) The trust may have to be judged against the backdrop of a civil law jurisdiction which does not recognize it and which introduces additional questions as to whether citizens or nationals there have te capacity to create a trust.

(5) The enforcement of onshore judgments in the offshore country may be contentious.

(6) There may be public policy issues or issues relating to the public interest,

which could result in an outcome favourable to the onshore law. In civil law jurisdictions, for example, such a policy might mean that the public interest ('ordre public') in upholding family interests could overturn trust provisions which seek to undermine such interests. Similarly, matters relating to creditors' rights may fall to be resolved on grounds of public policy.

(7) The issue of the validity of the offshore trust, taking into account its radically different substantive rules, may have to be assessed by onshore courts.

B. The Hague Convention on Trusts

The uncertainty of common law rules on trust conflicts has been clarified to **18.15** some extent by the Convention on The Law Applicable to Trusts and On Their Recognition.[3] Even where offshore countries have not ratified the Convention, they have, in their legislation, mirrored important aspects of it.[4] The Hague Convention on Trusts must, then, be viewed as supporting many of the purposes and routes of offshore trust law. To the extent that the Convention is an indication of an international consensus on the appropriate conflict of laws rules for trusts, it is a powerful statement of the legitimacy of the offshore trust.

---

[3] The Hague, 1 July 1985; UKTS 14 (1992); Cm 1823; 23 ILM 1388, Article 7, hereinafter 'The Hague Convention on Trusts'. Incorporated in the UK under the Recognition of Trusts Act 1988. Under the Recognition of Trusts (Overseas Territory) Order 1989, SI 1989 No 673, it has been extended to some British offshore territories, including Bermuda, the Isle of Man, Jersey, and Montserrat, BVI.

[4] See, eg, s 3 of the Trusts Ordinance of the Turks and Caicos on the recognition of trusts, which relates to Article 2 of the Hague Convention on Trusts.

19

JURISDICTION OVER THE OFFSHORE TRUST

A. The Importance of the Jurisdiction Question

Typically, offshore courts are given jurisdiction over offshore trusts in the trust **19.01** instrument. Legislation may alternatively grant jurisdiction to the country of the proper law, or that of the place of administration of the trust. The residence of the trustee and the situation of the trust property may also be bases for jurisdiction. These are all, typically, the offshore country.[1] The trust deed itself will normally contain some form of exclusive jurisdiction and/or conflicts of laws clause which is another basis for jurisdiction.

However, despite these deliberate legislative initiatives of offshore countries to **19.02** oust jurisdiction from onshore countries, jurisdiction is a contentious issue. The question remains whether offshore courts can so easily assume jurisdiction

---

[1] See, eg, s 21 of the International Exempt Trusts Ordinance 1994 of Nevis: 'The court has jurisdiction in respect of any matters concerning an international trust where—(a) the proper law of the trust is the law of Nevis; (b) a trustee of the trust is resident in St Christopher and Nevis; (c) any part of the administration of the trust is carried on in St Christopher and Nevis.' A similar provision is found under s 20 of the International Exempt Act 1997 of Dominica. There may be broader bases for jurisdiction. See, eg, s 35 of the International Trusts Act 1996 of Saint Vincent, which adds 'where . . . (d) the trust is registered under the Act'. The Trusts (Special Provisions) Act 1989, s 8, of Bermuda adds to the Nevis formula, that the court has jurisdiction where it 'thinks it is appropriate'. See also s 4 of the International Trusts Act 1996 of Grenada, which adds 'where any property of the trust is situated in Grenada; but only in respect of the property so situate'. See also s 57 of the Trusts Act 1992 (rev'd 2000) of Belize (which does not have the

unilaterally, grant jurisdiction where no other basis exists for it, or avoid jurisdiction where it should properly be assumed. The precise answer will depend on an examination of the particular rules of the jurisdictions involved. However, it is at least arguable that a jurisdictional challenge based on conflict of laws could nullify offshore legislative initiatives. This is particularly the case as it is the court itself which will determine whether it has jurisdiction. Further, since more than one court may have jurisdiction under conflict of laws principles, legislative provisions which merely proclaim that the offshore financial courts have jurisdiction do not automatically preclude the jurisdiction of other courts.[2]

19.03   Jurisdiction is the initial question on the conflicts of laws issue. Thus, the survivability of the offshore trust may ultimately depend on whether or not an onshore court assumes jurisdiction over proceedings relating to the offshore trust. This is because the onshore court will be free to decide the larger and more controversial question, on identifying the appropriate choice of law, discussed in the following chapter. This makes it essential for us to understand the various bases for jurisdiction which obtain in onshore courts likely to be faced with the jurisdiction issue. The existence of exclusive jurisdiction clauses in offshore trust instruments is not, therefore, determinative of the issue of jurisdiction.

19.04   Further, while any court that assumes jurisdiction over a trust is obliged to apply the proper law which governs that trust,[3] there may be significant procedural and even policy differences between the courts of different jurisdictions. These make it important to resolve the jurisdiction issue satisfactorily.[4]

19.05   It should be noted that the question of the assumption of appropriate jurisdiction,

---

proviso on property). In the BVI, the provisions were similar to those in Bermuda, but s 8 of the Trustee (Amendment) Act 2003 now removes the court's power to assume jurisdiction where it thinks it appropriate, and gives it instead the power to assume jurisdiction where it is the natural forum for litigation, where the parties submit to the jurisdiction of the court, or where the trust instrument contains a provision referring disputes to the jurisdiction to the court. In Saint Lucia, s 35(1) of the International Trusts Act 2002 provides simply that the court has jurisdiction 'in respect of any matter concerning the international trust'. Under s 4 of the Trusts (Guernsey) Law 1989, the Guernsey court has jurisdiction in respect of all Guernsey trusts and, further, over foreign trusts where the trustee is resident in Guernsey, the property is situated or administered in Guernsey, or the trust instrument provides for such jurisdiction. See a similar provision under art 5 of the Trusts (Jersey) Law 1984. Recall that offshore legislation facilitates the choice of the offshore law as the proper law of the trust. See chapter 20.

   [2]   See the discussion of *forum non conveniens* below, paras 19.66–19.76.
   [3]   But note that the ascertainment of that proper law may itself be contentious. See chapter 20.
   [4]   Subject to the EEC Convention on Jurisdiction and Enforcement of Judgments in Civil and Commercial Matters (The Brussels Convention on Civil Jurisdiction and Enforcement of Judgments 1968) (Brussels, 27 September 1968, EC 46 (1978); Cmnd 7395; [1978] OJ L304/1, 8 ILM 229), hereinafter, 'the Brussels Convention', considered below, paras 19.6–19.11. Nationality is now a debatable basis for jurisdiction. Dicey & Morris, *The Conflict of Laws*, 12th edn, (Sweet & Maxwell, London, 1997) 1097.

and indeed the proper law, is distinct from that of the effectiveness of the court's jurisdiction. For example, a court may assume jurisdiction over a trust which has assets in another territory and may be unable to enforce the orders that it makes in relation to those assets. For offshore trusts, this may be a significant advantage. Onshore courts will be reluctant to assume jurisdiction for illusory purposes. Further, the inability to enforce their judgments actually discredits the jurisdiction of the courts, and it may be best to avoid such a situation all together.

B. Traditional Bases for Jurisdiction

Common Law rules and the Brussels Convention

The answer to the question of jurisdiction is not uniform, as rules on jurisdiction vary from country to country. Common Law countries tend to follow the traditional (pre-Brussels Convention) UK rules on jurisdiction. We should recall that most offshore countries will be Common Law jurisdictions. Thus, rules on jurisdiction will generally follow the English common law approach, except where, as above, they have been modified by legislation.[5] However, in England itself the rules have been substantially modified by the Brussels Convention, now further modified by the Brussels Regulation[6] as incorporated into UK law. The common law rules will still apply in England in situations where Article 4 of the Brussels Convention applies. This means that where a defendant is not domiciled in a contracting state, subject to the exclusive jurisdiction rules under Article 16, jurisdiction is to be determined by the law of that state. In addition, where the substance of a claim concerns a matter which lies outside of the scope of the Brussels Convention, the domestic rules (common law rules in this case) on jurisdiction will apply.

19.06

Impact of the Brussels Convention and the Brussels Regulation

The Brussels Convention has now made uniform the rules concerning jurisdiction for European countries, to which it applies. The Brussels Convention is significant not merely because it seeks to harmonize the rules on jurisdiction, but because it applies to many of the countries that will treat with offshore jurisdictions. It may also have particular significance (at least in the future) for

19.07

---

[5] See n 1 above.
[6] Council Regulation (EC) No 44 (2001). The Regulation is not targeted at trusts but may have some impact.

those offshore jurisdictions which are still UK territories.[7] These factors make it important for us to note, briefly, the Convention's rules.

19.08 A primary change under the Brussels Convention is the authority given for the determination of jurisdiction in relation to the domicile of the trust.[8] Where no exclusive jurisdiction is specified, jurisdiction is determined with reference to:

(1) the domicile of the trust (which may be the law of the closest and most real connection);

(2) the defendant's domicile;

(3) the fact that the trust 'ought to be executed' according to the law of the state in question.

19.09 Despite the priority given to the assumption of jurisdiction in relation to the *domicile* of the trust, the Brussels Convention does not contain a uniform test for domicile. Further, the question of the domicile of the trust is to be determined according to the rules of the contracting state. In Common Law countries, this would be the country with which the trust is most closely connected.[9] (A trustee may also be sued in the country of his domicile where that country is a contracting state.[10]) It is conceivable that under this test, where the settlor, assets, and beneficiaries are English, for example, the trust will be deemed to be domiciled in England, even if it is administered in an offshore country. Under such a test, it may be immaterial what the proper law of the trust is, or where the assets are located.

19.10 Consider too the effect of the Convention on trusts originating in any contracting state. Article 5(6) provides:

> A person domiciled in a Contracting State may, in another Contracting State, be sued . . . as settlor, trustee or beneficiary of a trust created by the operation of a statute, or by a written instrument, or created orally and evidenced in writing, in the courts of the Contracting State in which the trust is domiciled.[11]

19.11 However, authority is also granted for choices of exclusive jurisdiction. This is under a provision which allows that a state shall have jurisdiction regardless of

---

[7] As it is incorporated, eg, under the Civil Jurisdiction and Judgments Act 1982, which can be extended to UK territories under s 39.

[8] Article 5(6). That is, the contracting state in which the trust is domiciled.

[9] See *Chellaram and Another v Chellaram and Others No 2* (2002) 4 ITELR 729, which also decided the elements to be considered in ascertaining that 'closest connection'. The trust domicile provisions under Article 5 apply to internal disputes on the trust, such as between beneficiaries and trustees, and not to external disputes with third parties. In such a situation the defendant must also be domiciled in a contracting state.

[10] Article 2.

[11] Neither the Civil Procedure Rules 1998 (CPR), r 6.20(11), of the UK, nor Article 5(6) applies to constructive trusts, only express trusts.

the defendant's domicile in certain situations, such as where the matter concerns rights *in rem* in immoveable property.[12] Thus, the court with the matter before it must give way to the court named as having exclusive jurisdiction.[13]

Domicile and *in personam* jurisdiction

Apart from the Brussels Convention,[14] the question of jurisdiction may depend on nationality or domicile. However, no unified, internationally accepted concept of 'domicile' exists. In companies, domicile may be the place of incorporation or place of control. In view of the latter, this can lead to a finding in favour of the onshore country. Under the common law, the domicile of a trust may be based on the country with which it has its closest and most real connection.[15]   **19.12**

In personam jurisdiction

In some countries, such as the UK and other Common Law countries, a court can assume *in personam* jurisdiction on the basis of physical residence or presence. This may happen even where there is only a fleeting connection between the person and the country.[16] For example, it may exist if a trustee is present only temporarily at the time of service of the proceedings. This has obvious implications for offshore trustees who are non-resident in the onshore country, but who may visit there from time to time. Similarly, the *situs* or presence of the assets in the country where proceedings are initiated may be sufficient to ground jurisdiction.[17]   **19.13**

In *Chellaram v Chellaram*,[18] London solicitors held trust settlements which were drawn up in India for two brothers domiciled in India. The assets of the trust were shares in Bermudian offshore companies. While the administration of the trust had been done in England and the trust settlements were in English form, the trustees had links with both India and England. In an action to remove the trustees, the English court found that it had jurisdiction over a trust governed by   **19.14**

---

[12] Article 6.

[13] Under Article 4 of the Brussels Regulation.

[14] Above, n 4, particularly Article 5. The Lugano Convention is very similar, in particular in relation to its provisions on trusts: Convention on Jurisdiction and the Enforcement of Judgments in Civil and Commercial Matters 1988 (Lugano, 16 September 1988, EC), OJ [1988] L319/9.

[15] As in the UK. Dicey & Morris, above, n 4.

[16] Jurisdiction may also be asserted where a defendant who is outside of the jurisdiction is served, but such service of proceedings must be done with leave of the court. See *Chellaram and Another v Chellaram and Others No 2*, above, n 9. A court also has jurisdiction if the defendant submits to its jurisdiction.

[17] See the Rules of the Supreme Court 1965 (RSC) Ord 11, now replaced by the CPR 1998 and tempered by the provisions of the Brussels Convention. It is a basis for jurisdiction in both common law and continental countries. Dicey & Morris, above, n 4.

[18] [1985] 2 WLR 510. See also Dicey & Morris, above, n 4, 1097.

foreign law where the trustee was subject to the personal jurisdiction of the English court.[19]

19.15 Further litigation by the Chellaram family is even more helpful on the point of jurisdiction over foreign trusts, and also considers the impact of the Brussels Convention. In *Chellaram and Another v Chellaram and Others No 2*,[20] the UK High Court had to consider whether the CPR had changed the rules on jurisdiction in light of the Brussels Convention on Jurisdiction and Enforcement of Judgments in Civil and Commercial Matters 1968 (the Brussels Convention), incorporated under Sch 1 to the Civil Jurisdiction and Judgments Act 1982 of the UK.

19.16 Here there were several trustees, including a Bermuda offshore trust company. The trust deed provided that the proper law of the settlement was Hindu family law, and the forum for the administration of the settlement was to be Bermuda. The court found that the English rules had not been changed by the Civil Jurisdiction and Judgments Act 1982 and that there was still a requirement that a defendant could be served with originating process within the jurisdiction only if he were present in the jurisdiction at the time of service or was domiciled in the jurisdiction. An address in London which was only occasionally used by the trustee could not satisfy the test for residence sufficient to ground jurisdiction.[21]

Domicile

19.17 As previously noted, under Article 5(6) of the Brussels Convention a person domiciled in a contracting state could, in another contracting state, be sued as trustee of a trust created, *inter alia*, by a written instrument, in the courts of the contracting state in which the trust is domiciled. Even where a court has jurisdiction, there is a secondary question whether it will consider it appropriate to exercise its discretion to assume such jurisdiction under the *forum non conveniens* rule, considered below.[22] Today, courts in contracting states must also consider whether they should stay proceedings in favour of the courts in a non-contracting state.[23]

---

[19] Applying *Ewing v Orr Ewing* (1883) 9 App Cas 34, which laid down the equitable basis of such jurisdiction. This was regardless of proper law: '. . . the jurisdiction of the Court of Chancery is *in personam*. It acts upon the person whom it finds within its jurisdiction and compels him to perform the duty which he owes to the plaintiff' (*per* Lord Blackburn, 45–6).
[20] Above, n 9.
[21] A contingent question was whether the trust was governed by English law, and it was not.
[22] Paras 19.66–19.72.
[23] But they do have the authority to do so. *Re Harrods (Buenos Aires) Ltd* [1992] Ch 72.

Matters of substance and a good arguable case

Matters of substance relating to the case may also be relied upon for purposes of **19.18**
jurisdiction. For domicile where there is 'no common ground', the onus is on
the claimant to show a 'good arguable case' to establish that the defendant is
domiciled in a particular territory.[24] The standard of proof for a 'good arguable
case' is more stringent than that of showing merely a serious issue to be tried,
but less stringent than proof on the 'balance of probabilities'.[25] However, in
cases where the Convention does not apply, the claimant must also establish a
'serious issue to be tried on the merits'.[26] In *Canada Trust Company v Stolzenberg
(No 2)*[27] the court also accepted this ground as a basis for domicile.[28]

If the question of jurisdiction depends on questions other than domicile, such as **19.19**
elements linked to the substance of the claim, 'a good arguable case' for each of
those elements must be established.[29]

Sufficient connection

Jurisdiction may also be assumed where there is a sufficient connection with the **19.20**
state concerned. Where proceedings involve transactions prejudicing creditors,
for example, English courts have held that they have jurisdiction where a sufficient connection with England is demonstrated, such as where creditors are in
England, or a bankruptcy petition is being filed.[30] Similarly, in *Australia Securities Commission v Cooke*,[31] a sufficient territorial nexus to ground jurisdiction
was that offers were made in Australia for investment in an offshore trust.

Compliance with orders

An important point for offshore trusts, which was raised in *Chellaram v Chellaram* **19.21**
No 1,[32] was not satisfactorily answered in either of the *Chellaram* cases. This is
the question whether jurisdiction should be assumed in situations where it is
questionable if orders obtained in the court being asked to assume jurisdiction,
could be enforced without a decision from the foreign court. As in *Chellaram*

---

[24] *Chellaram No 2*, above, n 9, 737, and *Canada Trust Company v Stolzenberg (No 2)* [2002]
1 AC 1, 13.
[25] *Chellaram No 2*, above, n 9, 737.
[26] ibid, 762.
[27] Above, n 24.
[28] In contract cases, this often involves matters such as the fact that the contract was breached
in the jurisdiction. See also *Chellaram No 2*, above, n 9, 763, in relation to the Brussels
Convention.
[29] ibid.
[30] *Re Paramount Airways Ltd* [1992] 3 All ER 1 (CA).
[31] [1996] 1101 FCA 1 (Fed Ct, Australia).
[32] Above, n 18.

No 1, it may be uncertain whether foreign law (in that case, Indian law) would recognize such orders and would regard the trustees who obeyed such orders as having discharged their fiduciary obligations under the trust. Scott J rejected these questions outright on the basis that the Indian courts would certainly, on the grounds of comity, afford due respect to the orders of the English courts.

19.22 Yet the same optimism may not be warranted where the foreign court is an offshore court. In considering the comity issue, an offshore court, assessing which court had a greater interest, as expected under the rules of comity, could well come to an opposite conclusion. Given the conflict of laws statutes in offshore trust jurisdictions and the public policy considerations, it may hold that it is not in the interest of the offshore court to give effect to such orders. The legislative policy of offshore states to refuse enforcement of certain onshore judgments should also be considered.[33]

Transnational basis

19.23 The transnational nature of offshore investment may itself be a basis for assuming jurisdiction. Ironically, this point was made by an offshore court in *Stewart v Ask Securities Ltd*.[34] It was an important reason for the Cayman Islands court to assume jurisdiction over the offshore company although concurrent proceedings were being carried on in the onshore jurisdiction. The argument would apply just as easily in an onshore court.

Jurisdiction and proper law

19.24 The issue of jurisdiction could turn on the proper law of the trust, itself a question fraught with difficulty, considered in the following chapter. Thus, in England, where 'trusts ought to be executed according to English law', service out of the jurisdiction may be permitted.[35] However, in *Chellaram No 2*,[36] this factor by itself was not sufficient to permit the inquiring court to assume jurisdiction where several other factors, such as the foreign residence of the trustees, pointed in favour of jurisdiction being vested in the foreign court.

19.25 The proper law rule loses force where the foreign law is substantially the same as the law of the domestic forum, as seen in *Chellaram No 2*.[37] Yet this is unlikely in conflicts involving offshore trusts because of substantive differences to

---

[33] See the discussion on the non-enforcement of these judgments in chapter 24.
[34] [1986–87] CILR 28, 30.
[35] See RSC Ord 11, r1(j), which was enacted in 1983, now replaced by the CPR 1998. But the rule is limited by *forum non conveniens* principles.
[36] Above, n 9.
[37] ibid.

onshore law created by trust legislation and which allow more flexibility in offshore trust regimes.

An examination of offshore legislation on conflict of laws itself lends credence to the principle that the proper law may ground jurisdiction. Often, the proper law, or governing law, of the trust is named as a criterion for assuming jurisdiction.[38] A risk here is that such jurisdiction can be lost where the offshore trust relocates to another country with the use of its 'flight clause'. The move causes a change in the proper law upon which jurisdiction depends. This was noted in *Lemos v Coutts*,[39] where the court feared that the flight clause would 'abort proceedings' in the Cayman Islands. It is, therefore, not a satisfactory basis for jurisdiction, particularly where law enforcement concerns are paramount.

19.26

Assets situated in the jurisdiction

Where assets are situated in the country, this may be sufficient to give jurisdiction to the courts of that country. Under the common law, this is an extraordinary jurisdiction and may come into effect only if the claimant has some demonstrable proprietary right *in rem* in those assets. This may occur, for example, where the assets were removed from the claimant's possession through some fraud or injustice. In such cases, an injunction may be granted against a person in possession or control of the assets.[40]

19.27

This is an important head of jurisdiction for offshore investment where, because of the manipulation of potential conflict of laws elements, there are few connections to the onshore country. The conventional wisdom in offshore planning is that assets should be removed from the offshore country, but this is not always possible. In *Re Larry Portnoy*,[41] a US court seized upon this as a ripe opportunity to assume jurisdiction. This fortuitous assumption of jurisdiction also fell under the more general rule which permits jurisdiction where the matter relates to proprietary rights *in rem*, as these were bankruptcy claims involving alleged fraudulent conveyances that violated creditors' rights.

19.28

Offshore legislation provides for this head of jurisdiction, but it is uncertain whether it is as narrow as under the common law. For example, article 5(3) of the Trusts (Jersey) Law 1984 includes as a head granting jurisdiction, the existence of 'trust assets in Jersey'. This seems to be a much simpler and broader test

19.29

---

[38] See, eg, the Turks and Caicos Islands Ordinance 1990. See n 1 generally. Indeed, the rule is key in the offshore legislative provisions.

[39] [1992–93] CILR 5, 13.

[40] Even innocent parties such as a bank may be cited.

[41] 201 BR 685 (1996).

for assuming jurisdiction on the ground of the *lex situs*, than is allowed under the common law.[42]

New BVI provision

19.30 It should be noted that s 82 of the Trustee Act 1993 of the BVI has recently been upgraded by the Trustee (Amendment) Act 2003. Previously, the legislation provided that the BVI courts had jurisdiction over a trust where the proper law of the trust was that of the BVI, where the trustee was resident or incorporated in the BVI, where the administration of the trust was to be carried out in the BVI, and in respect of trust property situated in the BVI. There was an additional basis for a BVI court to assume jurisdiction under s 82(f) where it thought it appropriate.

19.31 Section 82(f) has now been expanded to allow the BVI courts to assume jurisdiction to resolve trust disputes where they are the natural forum for the litigation, where the parties submit to the courts' jurisdiction, and where the trust instrument contains a provision referring all disputes to the BVI courts.[43]

Service out of the jurisdiction

19.32 A court's discretion to order service out of the jurisdiction is an extraordinary one.[44] As such, it should be approached with caution. Sir Phillip Bailhache, Bailiff of the Royal Court of Jersey, reminds us of this in *Koonmen v Bender and Others*:[45]

> . . . it becomes a very serious question . . . whether this court ought to put a foreigner who owes no allegiance here, to the inconvenience and annoyance of being brought to contest his right in this country . . . I think this court ought to be exceedingly careful before it allows a writ to be served out of the jurisdiction.

19.33 Such dicta may temper the zeal of onshore courts to assume jurisdiction over foreign offshore trustees under common law rules. Settlors go to lengths to ensure that trustees are not domiciled in onshore jurisdictions in order to avoid

---

[42] Similarly, in the BVI, s 82 of the Trustee Act 1993 (am'd 2003), states that jurisdiction may be assumed where there are 'assets situated in the BVI'. However, there is a proviso, that jurisdiction is granted only in relation to property so situated and not over the entire trust.

[43] The new provisions reflected in the Trustee (Amendment) Act 2003 came into force at the end of 2003. I am indebted to Christopher McKenzie of Harney Westwood & Riegels, BVI, and an executive member of the Society of Trust and Estate Practitioners (STEP), for giving me advance notice of these new provisions.

[44] Described as 'exorbitant' by Lord Diplock in *Amin Rasheed Shipping Corporation v Kuwait Insurance Co* [1984] AC 50, 65.

[45] (2002) 5 ITELR 247, 258, quoting Pearson J, in *Société Générale de Paris v Dreyfus Brothers* (1885) 29 ChD 239, 242–3, which was also affirmed in *Amin Rasheed*, above, n 4. See also *Bahamas International Trust Company Ltd and Others v Wyckoff, Kelly and Others* (Sup Ct, The Bahamas) No 466 of 1987, decided 31 May 1988.

assertions of jurisdiction by onshore courts. If the rule is too easily avoided, this would frustrate the rationales of many offshore trusts.

In *Chellaram No 2*,[46] service out of the jurisdiction was considered within its new context under CPR r 6.20, which replaced Ord 11 of the Rules of the Supreme Court, so as to take account of changes in the rules on jurisdiction brought about by the Brussels Regulation.[47] For trusts, r 6.20 applies where there is no *in personam* jurisdiction. Rule 6.20(11) states that a court may assume jurisdiction if the 'claim is made for any remedy which might be obtained in proceedings to execute the trusts of a written instrument where— (a) the trusts ought to be executed according to English law; and (b) the person on whom the claim is to be served is a trustee of the trusts'. **19.34**

The *Chellaram* court found that, in general, under common law rules, service out of the jurisdiction will be allowed where the defendant is a necessary or proper party to the claim (the trustee, for example) and where the trust ought to be executed in the law of the court where jurisdiction is being asserted. However, in *Bahamas International Trust Co Ltd and Others v Wyckoff, Kelley and Others*,[48] a rare case where offshore trustees sought leave to serve defendants in New York, permission to serve outside of the jurisdiction was refused. The court was heavily influenced by the prima facie merits of the case, which were not in the plaintiff's favour. **19.35**

Tax matters and jurisdiction

An important point for offshore trusts which are established for tax planning purposes is that, under common law rules and established rules of private international law, a court will not usually have jurisdiction in proceedings which seek to enforce foreign revenue law, on the ground that such matters are non-enforceable or non-justiciable. The same rule applies to penal and public law. However, the rule, as it applies to revenue matters, should be construed narrowly in a modern context given recent trends to attempt to dilute it. These excluded jurisdictions are discussed more fully in separate chapters.[49] **19.36**

---

[46] Above, n 9.
[47] Above, n 6.
[48] See above, n 45.
[49] See the chapters on taxation in Part III, in particular, chapter 16, paras 16.1–16.32.

C. Exclusive Jurisdiction

Sufficiency of exclusive jurisdiction clauses

19.37 As we have noted, exclusive jurisdiction clauses are typical in offshore trusts. They are also permitted under the Brussels Regulation and the Brussels and Lugano Conventions.[50] Exclusive jurisdiction clauses will usually be followed by common law courts, but their effectiveness is by no means certain. If the clause is invalid under the proper law of the trust, it cannot stand, but this would be rare in offshore trusts as the proper law will likely be the law of the offshore jurisdiction.[51]

19.38 The approach which a court should adopt when confronted with a trust deed that confers exclusive jurisdiction on another court was considered in detail by the Royal Court of Jersey in the case of *EMN Capricorn Trustees Ltd v Compass Trustees Ltd and Another*.[52] The court had before it a clause which purported to give exclusive jurisdiction to the courts of Guernsey in matters relating to a trust which was governed by the law of Guernsey. The Jersey court would have normally had jurisdiction as the trustees were actually resident in Jersey.[53]

Contract analogy found wanting

19.39 The defendants in *Capricorn* applied for a stay of the proceedings, arguing that the exclusive jurisdiction clause should be given effect, in a manner similar to exclusive jurisdiction clauses which apply to contracts. However, the analogy to principles of international law which govern contracts was accepted in principle but with substantial qualification by the court. The reason given was that, with contracts, all parties actually agree to the terms of the contract and are directly involved in future suits. In contrast, with a trust, the persons who establish the trust are not necessarily involved in future litigation. Indeed, the persons to whom the trust is directed, the beneficiaries, may sue, although they may have had no part in any agreements concerning the terms of the trust. The court thus found that the burden on the plaintiff to show why a stay should not be entered was less onerous than in contract cases.

19.40 Nonetheless, the fact that the beneficiaries are not parties to trust arrangements has not hindered courts before. Such courts have sought vigorously to give effect

---

[50] See above, nn 4 and 14, respectively.
[51] See chapter 20, 'The Proper Law of the Offshore Trust'.
[52] (2001) 4 ITELR 34 (Royal Ct, Jersey).
[53] Under art 5(b) of the Trusts (Jersey) Law 1984, jurisdiction is granted where a trustee of a foreign trust is resident in Jersey. The substance of the proceedings was an alleged breach of trust and the trustees were suing the previous trustees.

to the intention of the settlor in other areas of trust law. The question may be asked, why not here?

It is suggested that even if we accept fully the reluctance of certain courts to rely on private international law rules of jurisdiction on contracts for the reasons outlined above, this cannot be justified where the beneficiary is actually the same person as the settlor, and is the sole beneficiary (not unusual in offshore trusts). In such a situation, there are no beneficiaries who were not parties to the original clause. The logic of the proviso relating to contracts is lost and similar principles to contract should apply, that is, relying on the settlor's intention and choice.   **19.41**

Other factors mitigating against choice

Choice of jurisdiction asserted by the parties may also be contested where other variables point elsewhere. For example, a clause in a trust deed may offend some mandatory rule of the forum, or frauds or shams may be apparent.[54] The transnational and hybrid nature of the offshore trust may well give added credibility to such exceptions, at least where a prima facie case of wrongdoing is made out.   **19.42**

Thus, in *Capricorn*,[55] the court rejected the exclusive jurisdiction clause. The court found that it had a discretion whether to grant a stay but that it was not bound to do so. Factors which persuaded the court to decline a stay were that the breach of trust claims arose out of the facts upon which the contract claims were based and that the contractual claims were to be heard by the Jersey courts (there was a consensus on this point). Both parties, therefore, needed to familiarize themselves with the factual background in the case. The court reasoned that the law of Jersey was substantially similar to that of Guernsey so that no injustice would be done. Further, there was no material difference in hearing the matter in Jersey, and there was no difference in convenience and cost between Jersey and Guernsey. Further, if breach of trust claims were heard by the Jersey courts, findings of fact made by the court in the contractual claims case would be binding in relation to the breach of trust claim, but there was no proof that this would be the same in the Guernsey courts (thus, they may not have felt themselves bound by the findings of fact by a Jersey court).   **19.43**

In the final analysis, the court seemed to adopt a compromise position. It appeared to accept the sustainability of exclusive jurisdiction clauses in principle, going so far as to state that such a clause should be accepted on 'its face'.   **19.44**

---

[54] See the discussion at para 19.79 below of *Duttle v Kass* (1992) 82 Cir 5084 (KMW), 5088, Cir 5084 (KMW), United States District Court for the Southern District of New York; 1992 US Dist LEXIS 8894.

[55] See above, n 52.

On the other hand, it suggested that such clauses are not too difficult for courts to ignore.

19.45 Offshore trustees can take comfort from the court's reassurance that justice was its ultimate objective. A just end result, in substance, would not have been altered by the assumption of jurisdiction by a court other than the one of the settlor's choice. We are left to surmise that, were a court to be faced with a case where there was a risk that the outcome would have been different, it would grant a stay, surrendering to the settlor's choice of jurisdiction. Perhaps it is as satisfactory a balance as we are likely to have, considering that courts jealously guard their inherent supervisory jurisdiction over trusts, particularly offshore trusts, which are transnational.[56]

19.46 It is not apparent, therefore, that exclusive jurisdiction selection clauses will of themselves be conclusive of the jurisdiction question, even where an offshore court is determining the issue. The several actions pending before offshore courts seeking enforcement of judgments, demonstrate that such clauses are not foolproof. Cases such as *Capricorn* are serious indictments against settlor autonomy on the jurisdiction question. They offer little encouragement for a legislative policy which is being promulgated by offshore jurisdictions themselves.

Different tests for forum and exclusive jurisdiction clauses

19.47 Despite the reservations made about exclusive jurisdiction clauses, the general rule is still in favour of such clauses and they will be given weight by the courts. For example, the court in *Capricorn*[57] rejected the submission that the test whether to grant a stay in the face of such a clause, was the same as that in a *forum non conveniens* case.[58] In the latter, no exclusive jurisdiction clause is involved. The burdens in the two types of cases are, therefore, different.

19.48 In a *forum non conveniens* case, the burden is placed on a defendant to show that there is another available forum which is more appropriate than the court with the matter before it. In contrast, where there is an exclusive jurisdiction clause, there is a heavy burden on a plaintiff to show why a stay should *not* be granted. There is, therefore, a presumption in favour of the exclusive jurisdiction clause: 'On the face of it he [the plaintiff] should be held to his bargain.'[59] The statement here is, of course, contradictory to the court's earlier statements when it qualified the analogy with contract rules to the effect that the plaintiff may not have been involved in making the bargain. It is more accurate to say that the

---

[56] Recall that the trustees were resident in Jersey, the underlying company was incorporated in Malta, and the documents were in Malta, not in either Jersey or Guernsey.

[57] See above, n 52.

[58] The principle of *forum non conveniens* is discussed below, at paras 19.66–19.72.

[59] *Capricorn*, above, n 52, 40.

settlor's intention should be upheld on the face of it. Indeed, the primary questions in this issue of exclusive jurisdiction clauses are whether the settlor should be allowed the freedom to choose and to have his or her intention honoured.

Cases favouring exclusive jurisdiction

Other cases are more helpful to the objective of exclusive jurisdiction. A good example is *Continental Finance Trading Company SA v Geosurvey Holdings*,[60] a case concerning offshore companies. Here, the Bahamas Supreme Court declined jurisdiction in favour of another offshore jurisdiction, Switzerland, relying on the decision of *Re Jogia, ex parte The Trustee v Pennellier and Co Ltd*.[61] The trust contained a Swiss choice of law clause where exclusive jurisdiction was granted to Switzerland. **19.49**

The court ruled in favour of a presumption to uphold exclusive jurisdiction clauses, agreeing with the defendant's argument that 'there is a prima facie rule that an action brought in this jurisdiction in defiance of an agreement to submit to a foreign jurisdiction will be stayed'.[62] Therefore, whilst the court 'retains jurisdiction to decline to give effect to an agreement as to jurisdiction, this should only be exercised if the plaintiff can establish that there are exceptional circumstances which justify such a course of action'.[63] **19.50**

The position on exclusive jurisdiction clauses is also spelt out strongly in another Jersey case, *Koonmen v Bender and Others*.[64] Here, the Jersey Court of Appeal held that the court is to construe an exclusive jurisdiction clause in a trust deed so as to give effect to the presumed intention of the parties. This approach, in the Court's view, best led to a just result. Nonetheless, the Court reserved a discretion to override a forum which has been agreed to by the parties. This should be done only in exceptional circumstances, particularly where the plaintiff proposes to serve proceedings on a foreigner out of the jurisdiction. **19.51**

In coming to its decision, the Court of Appeal of Jersey took a more favourable approach than its lower court, the Royal Court.[65] There, the Royal Court examined trust clauses which incorporated the phrases **19.52**

---

[60] (Sup Ct, The Bahamas) No 230, decided 13 March 1997.
[61] [1988] 2 All ER 328. Note that the argument here, that those in a trust who construct exclusive jurisdiction clauses may be binding persons outside of the agreement, may also apply to companies, but this has not deterred the courts from upholding such clauses in relation to companies.
[62] *Continental Finance Trading Co*, above, n 60, 42.
[63] ibid.
[64] [2002] JLR N45 (CA), *per* Nutting, Smith, and Rokison JJA. See also the first instance judgment at (2002) 5 ITELR 247 (Royal Ct, Jersey).
[65] Above, n 64.

to the exclusive jurisdiction of which . . . [Clause2] . . . said Island [Anguilla] shall be the forum for the administration thereof [Clause 2] . . . shall thenceforth be the courts of that state or territory [Clause 14].

The case ultimately turned on the principles of statutory interpretation, and the court took a restrictive view of these clauses, holding that they merely proclaimed Anguilla as the jurisdiction of choice and did not confer exclusive jurisdiction on the courts of Anguilla (thereby making a rather spurious distinction between the stated jurisdiction of choice and an exclusive jurisdiction clause). The underlying rationale here was that there was no presumption that exclusivity was what the settlor intended, and indeed, as noted in *Capricorn*,[66] such clauses still come before the courts relatively infrequently. The Royal Court in *Koonmen* then went on to consider the *forum non conveniens* issue, finding in favour of Jersey.

19.53   However, the Royal Court did not explain the difference between an exclusive jurisdiction clause and a clause specifying the jurisdiction of choice. Both appear to point to the jurisdiction of choice of the settlor. Once the court recognizes this intention, it would seem merely to be a question of semantics to differentiate between choice and exclusivity.

19.54   The Royal Court went on to find that the clauses were not clear and rejected the claim to exclusivity, despite counsel's contention that, taken as a whole, the trust deed clearly demonstrated the parties' intent to give exclusive jurisdiction to the courts of Anguilla. Although the court purported to make distinctions between certain types of jurisdiction clauses, it seems that the real issue here was the lack of clarity of the jurisdiction clauses themselves. The case should, therefore, be confined to its facts, a clause which appeared to be badly drafted.[67]

19.55   In contrast, the Court of Appeal's judgment in *Koonmen v Bender*,[68] appropriately gave focus and priority to the parties' intention in drafting the trust instrument. Yet this should not be taken as a licence for the kind of loose drafting found in the *Koonmen* trust instrument.[69] The case serves as a warning to offshore trustees and settlors wishing to include exclusive jurisdiction clauses, to ensure that they are carefully thought out and drafted.

---

[66] Above, n 52.

[67] It should be pointed out that the claim to exclusive jurisdiction was not helped by counsel's arguments, which were not forceful enough on the point. One witness in the action before the Royal Court described the relevant clause as prescribing 'the forum of choice', while counsel for the defendant argued that Anguilla was the jurisdiction with which the action had 'the closest and most natural connection': above, n 64, 260.

[68] Above, n 64.

[69] Described by the Royal Court in *Koonmen* as 'not a model of good drafting', above, n 64, 260. The drafters seem to have employed a 'short cut' and included the controversial clause in the section on 'proper law'.

Indeed, it may be argued that under English law, there is a presumption in **19.56** favour of freedom of choice of law when conflicts of laws rules are being applied. This, in a sense, inheres in the principle of freedom to contract. This certainly was the suggestion of Lord Diplock in the case of *Mackender and Others v Feldia*, although speaking in the context of the proper law:[70]

> The prima facie rule of English conflict of laws—more liberal in this respect than many continental systems, is that the proper law of a contract shall be that system of law which the parties themselves have agreed shall regulate the legally enforceable rights and duties to which their agreement gives rise.

It should be noted that with the courts reserving a discretion to assert jurisdic- **19.57** tion in the face of exclusive jurisdiction clauses, they bring to life the difference between courts having jurisdiction and assuming jurisdiction.[71]

Difference in emphasis between choice of proper law and choice of jurisdiction

It is contended that a choice of jurisdiction to settle questions of conflict should **19.58** be assessed more generously than a choice of proper law. In the latter, the settlor may be accused of 'forum shopping' to get a more favourable 'deal'—a situation which may be frowned upon on the grounds of public policy, although given validity under the Hague Convention on The Law Applicable to Trusts and On Their Recognition.[72] This is not the case with choices of jurisdiction.

In exclusive jurisdiction cases, one would expect few valid objections to the **19.59** expressed choice. One such objection would be that the court of the settlor's choice was deficient in some way, for example through incompetence, delay, or alleged bias. Consider that whatever court assumes jurisdiction, it is obliged to apply the applicable proper law so that the choice of the court should not affect the substance of the matter. In contrast, the argument is not forceful in *forum non conveniens* cases since, in such cases, no clear choice has been expressed by the settlor and trustee in the trust instrument.

Given the fact that a court should reject the exclusive jurisdiction clause only in **19.60** extraordinary circumstances, where it does so, it implies that respect for the courts which should have had jurisdiction exclusively, is not deserving in some way. It therefore makes a negative statement about the courts chosen by the settlor, a statement that any court should be reluctant to make unless clear

---

[70] [1967] 2 QB 590, 602.

[71] In both *Capricorn* and *Koonmen*, above, nn 52 and 64 respectively, the courts would otherwise have had jurisdiction.

[72] Hereinafter, 'The Hague Convention on Trusts', The Hague, 1 July 1985; UKTS 14 (1992); Cm 1823; 23 ILM 1388.

evidence is presented. The court should, on the basis of comity, give way to the court of the settlor's choice unless there are exceptional circumstances indicating otherwise. It seems incongruous that modern courts, particularly under the influence of the Hague Convention on Trusts, can so easily accept choice of proper law but fail to accept choices of jurisdiction, where the latter are less evasive of public policy and other concerns.

Respect for offshore courts

19.61 This argument is supported by the case of *Green v Jernigan*,[73] which also provides evidence that onshore courts will, in appropriate cases, pay respect to exclusive jurisdiction clauses originating offshore. Here, the Supreme Court of British Columbia, Vancouver, considered a claim by the plaintiff, who was the settlor of the trust, that an exclusive jurisdiction clause making Nevis the exclusive forum for matters involving the trust and making Nevis law the proper law, was to be ignored. The court refused to do so, finding that the respective clauses were clear and certain, and that the court would give effect to such clauses unless there was strong cause not to do so. The related action in this case was an alleged breach of trust by the trustees. In coming to its decision, the court relied on *ZI Pompey Industrie v ECU-Line NV*.[74]

19.62 The plaintiff's reasons for wanting to sidestep the exclusive jurisdiction clause were found wanting. The plaintiff argued that the Nevis Bar was very small, and implied that there may have been political interference by the Government. The court found nothing to substantiate the suggestion of potential bias, Groberman J saying: 'I have no evidence before me suggesting that the courts of Nevis are other than independent.'[75] The court alluded to the strict confidentiality laws of Nevis, which may have posed difficulties for the plaintiff's right of discovery. However, it was unsympathetic in this regard, as the plaintiff/settlor was presumed to have had cogent reasons for establishing a 'secretive' offshore trust in the first instance. The offshore confidentiality laws were seen as no bar to the assertion of exclusive jurisdiction under the trust. In sum, there was no real cause for not respecting the exclusive jurisdiction clause: 'Having expressly chosen such a vehicle for their investments, the plaintiffs are stuck with dealing

---

[73] (2003) 6 ITELR 330 (Sup Ct, British Columbia), *per* Groberman J.

[74] [2003] SCJ 23, and the Ontario Superior Court judgment in *Kates v Wayant* [2002] OJ No 503, 27 BLR (3d) 273. Clause 11.01 of the trust instrument read: 'This trust agreement is established under the Laws of the Island of Nevis and shall be construed, interpreted and take effect according to the laws of the Island of Nevis.' Clause 8.01, the jurisdiction clause, read: 'This trust is established under the Laws of the Island of Nevis and the rights of all parties and the construction and effect of each and every provision hereof shall be subject to the exclusive jurisdiction of and construed only according to the Laws of the Island of Nevis which shall be the forum for the administration hereof.'

[75] *Green*, above, n 73, 338.

with those investments under the laws of Nevis and in its courts, even though they may now see those laws as disadvantageous and distasteful.'[76]

Question of appropriate forum relevant only in exceptional cases

If it is accepted that an exclusive jurisdiction clause could stand, unless the court wishes from the outset to exercise its discretion in view of exceptional circumstances, there would seem to be no rational basis for a court even to ask itself what is a more appropriate forum, and the entire question of *forum non conveniens* would be irrelevant. It does not appear that all courts have as yet appreciated this important distinction, and some courts seem to be too eager to enter into inquiries about the more appropriate forum.[77] **19.63**

The correct approach was adopted in the case of *Continental Finance.*[78] Despite the fact that the court here was examining offshore companies and not trusts, it held that the claimant had not displaced its burden to show 'strong cause' why the presumption of jurisdiction in favour of the Swiss courts could not stand. The claimant had to prove, on a 'balance of probabilities', that in all the circumstances it would have been 'unjust' to grant a stay. This is not the identical test for the 'most appropriate forum' since, in the former, a claimant has a higher threshold to displace.[79] **19.64**

US rule on exclusive jurisdiction clauses

As in the UK, Canada, and under the Brussels Convention, in the US, the rule is also that the courts will enforce exclusive jurisdiction clauses, or forum selection clauses. This is a reversal of the previous position, which was that such clauses were unenforceable as against public policy, or unfavourable because they attempted to oust the jurisdiction of the court. The more modern rule is expressed in the landmark case of *The Bremer v Zapata Offshore Co,*[80] a decision of the United States Supreme Court. The court said: **19.65**

> . . . such [exclusive jurisdiction] clauses are prima facie valid and should be enforced unless enforcement is shown by the resisting party to be 'unreasonable' under the circumstances. We believe that this is the correct doctrine to be followed by federal courts.[81]

The court further explained that circumstances in which enforcement might be

---

[76] ibid, 338–9.
[77] As in *Capricorn* above, n 52, and the Royal Court's decision in *Koonmen v Bender*, above, n 64.
[78] Above, n 60.
[79] Relying on *Trendex Trading Corporation and Another v Credit Suisse* [1982] AC 679, *per* Lord Wilberforce, 695.
[80] 407 US 1 (1972).
[81] ibid, 9–10.

unreasonable included fraud, overreaching, or where enforcement contravened a strong public policy of the forum.[82]

D. Rules for Declining Jurisdiction

Forum non conveniens

19.66   Given that both the onshore and offshore courts may have jurisdiction, either court may decline to exercise its jurisdiction because of the *forum non conveniens* principle. This holds that a stay of jurisdiction will be granted where some other available forum has competent jurisdiction and is the appropriate forum for the trial since 'the ends of justice'[83] would be better served.

19.67   In *Gheewala v Compendium Trust Company Ltd*,[84] it was explained that the *forum* principle is applied by adopting a two-stage test. The first leg is a burden placed on a defendant to establish that there is an available forum which is distinctly more appropriate than the forum considering the issue. Secondly, even if the court was persuaded that the other forum was clearly more appropriate for the trial of an action, the court could decline a stay if persuaded by the plaintiff, on whom the burden of proof (now) lay, that 'justice required that a stay should not be granted'.[85]

Determinative factors in forum cases

19.68   As expected, offshore courts guard their jurisdiction over offshore companies and investors jealously, asserting jurisdiction even where there is a discernible connection with the onshore state. In *Barclays Bank v Kenton Capital*,[86] for example, the Grand Court of the Cayman Islands held that the Cayman Islands were the natural and appropriate forum for the hearing of an US securities law suit. This was despite the fact that the trust company solicited investments in the US and had offices there. The deciding factors, in the court's view, were that:

(1)   the contracts between the investors and the company were expressed to be governed by Cayman law;

---

[82] ibid, 15. Note that mere inconvenience was not a sufficient reason to ignore the clause. See also *Manrique v Fabori* 493 So 2d 437 (Fla 1986).

[83] See *Spillada Maritime Corp v Cansoulex Ltd* [1987] AC 460, 46, *per* Lord Goff. The status of the *forum non conveniens* doctrine under the Brussels and Lugano Conventions is controversial. However, in *Re Harrods (Buenos Aires Ltd)* [1992] Ch 72, the Court of Appeal of England applied the doctrine.

[84] [1999] JLR 154.

[85] ibid.

[86] [1994–95] CILR 489.

(2) the company was incorporated in the Cayman Islands; and

(3) the money was held in the Cayman Islands.

Offshore courts have also held that they are the most appropriate forums based on factors such as cost to the parties and the advancement of offshore proceedings.[87] Further significant factors would be that the trust is administered in the offshore country and that the assets are located there. Indeed, factors pointing to the natural forum will always be relevant, in particular, the forum agreed to by the parties and their choice of governing law.[88]   **19.69**

The judgment of the Royal Court of Jersey in *Koonmen v Bender* also outlines several factors which should be heeded when considering the forum question.[89] The sole trustee was an Anguilla trust company, which was a wholly-owned subsidiary of a Jersey trust company. Factors deemed persuasive in determining that the appropriate forum was Jersey, were, first, that the parties resided neither in Jersey nor in Anguilla (the other forum in question), so that neither was more convenient. Most of the evidence was in Jersey, the proper law was not too dissimilar from the law of Anguilla, and the principal professional advisers resided in Jersey. Further, the trust was administered in Jersey,[90] a substantial portion of the assets was held in Jersey (approximately 70%), relevant evidential documents were in Jersey, and six out of the eight defendants were either in Jersey or had submitted to the Jersey courts' jurisdiction. Relevant too was the fact that related proceedings were being coordinated in London and that Jersey was closer to London than Anguilla.   **19.70**

A court will consider the likelihood of delay before the foreign court. This is a factor in the forum test, but potential delay must be very great before a court will base its decision to stay proceedings on this ground.[91] Whether the defendant genuinely desired trial in the foreign country, or was only seeking procedural advantages,[92] will also be considered.   **19.71**

---

[87] See *Touche Ross v Bank Intercontinental* [1987] CILR 269; *In the Matter of Commodore Electronics Ltd* (Sup Ct, The Bahamas) No 473/581, decided 24 June 1997. In *Stewart*, above, n 34, a tracing action, simultaneous proceedings in California were not duplicated and a Cayman company exercised control over the shares.

[88] See the discussion on exclusive jurisdiction clauses, above, paras 19.37–19.64.

[89] Above, n 64. Note that the decision was overturned on appeal (see [2002] JLR N45 (CA)). However, this was on another point, ie, the effect of the exclusive jurisdiction clause. The factors outlined by the court on the *forum non conveniens* issue remain pertinent, therefore.

[90] Note that an element of proof on residence was that the fax cover sheet of the trust gave the address as Jersey.

[91] See *Chellaram v Chellaram*, above, n 18; *Chellaram v Chellaram No 2*, above, n 9, concerning potential delay in India; and *Konamament v Rolls Royce Ind Power (India) Ltd* [2002] 1 All ER 979.

[92] *Capricorn*, above, n 52.

Public policy and forum non conveniens

19.72 Where the proceedings involve questions of interpretation of offshore trust legislation, which in turn might involve questions of public policy, it is likely that the offshore court will hold that it is the more appropriate forum. In *X Trust Co Ltd v A-G*,[93] the Cayman Grand Court refused to stay proceedings in favour of English proceedings inquiring into the validity of a trust set up for charitable purposes in the Cayman Islands. The court considered that it was for the Cayman courts to decide questions of offshore charity law in the light of local policy considerations. The determination of the proper law involved consideration of offshore legislation, which was a question best suited for the local courts.

Extraterritorial jurisdiction inappropriate

19.73 Assumption of jurisdiction may be inappropriate in other circumstances. For example, where the matter is one outside of the territorial jurisdiction of the country, this will also be a significant factor in determining the most appropriate forum. In *In the Matter of Re H*,[94] the Grand Court of the Cayman Islands reminded a US court of this when it considered an application by trust beneficiaries for information on an offshore trust. The application arose from a US grand jury subpoena issued to the trustee of the trust who was the son of the settlor and a US citizen. The assets were situated in the offshore country. The court, in refusing to assist the US court, noted:

> It is a well-established principle that ... a court should not regard as being without territorial limit the matters which it may treat as subject to its own process or the things which it can order a person within its jurisdiction to do elsewhere ... only in exceptional circumstances will the courts seek to exercise extraterritorial jurisdiction so as to exact compliance in another country.[95]

19.74 The court was particularly concerned that the act required would have been in breach of Cayman law. It viewed this as a breach of comity and as a violation of sovereignty. It was considered irrelevant that the person compelled was amenable to American jurisdiction, as the subpoena had effect in the offshore country.

19.75 The point on extraterritoriality has been likened to the expropriation of assets.[96] Thus, even where a trustee is domiciled in an onshore country, jurisdiction might be restrained on the basis of extraterritoriality. Even if jurisdiction is

---

[93] [1995] CILR 41.
[94] [1996] CILR 237 (Grand Court, CI).
[95] ibid, 242, *per* Smellie J. See also *Mackinnon v Donaldson and Jenrette Securities Corporation* [1986] Ch 482; [1986] 1 All ER 653.
[96] See also *Williams and Herbert Ltd v W&H Trade Marks (Jersey Ltd)* [1985] 2 All ER 208.

assumed by the onshore court, it may be reluctant to make certain orders. This includes orders concerning the confiscation or seizure of trust assets which are in the offshore country.

Thus, only in exceptional circumstances will the courts seek to curtail the **19.76** principle against the assertion of extraterritorial jurisdiction. Examples include where it is in the interest of justice to do so and where there is no other avenue available for obtaining evidence which is vital to the outcome of a matter. The principle is one which goes to the heart of the issue of the sovereignty of states.[97]

Lis alibi pendens

The sibling doctrine to *forum non conveniens* is that of *lis alibi pendens*. The **19.77** latter permits a court to stay proceedings where a similar action is pending in a foreign court. The doctrine gives priority to the court before which proceedings were first brought. The dicta in *Contadorra Enterprises v Chile Holdings*[98] are noteworthy, both for the doctrine and for the rule on service out of the jurisdiction. While it is accepted that service out of the jurisdiction may be set aside on grounds of *lis alibi pendens* if the domestic proceedings amount to an abuse of process, it is no abuse if the foreign proceedings referred to are brought solely to secure assets against which to enforce judgment in the domestic court (here the offshore court). In the instant case, mere incorporation was not sufficient to ground such jurisdiction as no economic loss had been suffered. The case concerned a constructive trust arising from a conspiracy to defeat a Cayman Island receivership order by a fraudulent transfer of foreign shares not governed by Cayman Island law.

E. Offshore Factors Important to Jurisdiction

Frauds and shams leading to jurisdiction

An emerging basis for assuming jurisdiction over offshore trusts, particularly by **19.78** US courts, is the *in rem* jurisdiction of the courts in relation to fraud and injustice, utilizing an 'alter-ego' or 'sham' argument. In *International Credit Investment Company (Overseas) Ltd v Adham*,[99] the court found that it could assume jurisdiction over 'shadowy offshore trusts and companies' and 'pierce

---

[97] See *In the Matter of Re H*, above, n 94, 242. This principle is addressed more fully in the companion book, R-M B Antoine, *Confidentiality in Offshore Financial Law* (Oxford University Press, Oxford, 2002), chapter 10.

[98] [1999] CILR 194 (CA), *per* Zacca P, Kerr G, and Collett JJA.

[99] (1997) 141 SJLB 56; see also *Pack v US* 77 AFTR 2d par 96–476. No CV-F-92–5327 REC (California).

the corporate veil' of such entities because they were still 'indirectly controlled' by onshore residents. The court recognized that an earlier generation of judges 'would not have exercised such jurisdiction but felt that such drastic action was now a matter of "necessity" because of international fraud'.[100]

19.79 A Bahamian court came to a similar conclusion in deciding whether to award a worldwide *Mareva* injunction, a decision that depended on the assumption of jurisdiction in the first instance.[101] The prima facie evidence of fraud by a settlor was also the determining factor for the US courts to assume jurisdiction in *Duttle v Kass*.[102] Here, a Liechtenstein trustee refused to submit to the jurisdiction of the New York District Court in relation to a Liechtenstein offshore trust with assets in the US. The court assumed jurisdiction on the ground that it 'would be inequitable to allow a fraudulent settlor . . . to keep the trustee beyond the equitable reach of a court by selecting a trustee who would not appear . . . and refused to submit to jurisdiction'. The court's approach seemed to be heavily influenced by the transnational character of the offshore trust, a character which is deliberately engineered and which is sometimes viewed as exploitative.

Distinction between jurisdiction question for shams and jurisdiction over administration of the trust

19.80 A distinction may be made between jurisdiction in relation to the initial transfer of assets into the trust and jurisdiction over questions concerning the administration of the trust. For example, a 'foreign' onshore court may have no jurisdiction over the trust if breach of trust is alleged,[103] but may have jurisdiction over questions concerning whether the trust is a sham or a fraudulent conveyance. This, at any rate, was the approach taken in the important case of *Re Larry Portnoy*.[104] The trust was established by a US citizen under the law of Jersey, apparently to avoid imminent creditors. There was a clause giving exclusive jurisdiction to the Jersey courts. It was contended on the behalf of the plaintiff that the New York court lacked the jurisdiction to determine whether he had retained control over the trust assets, leading to inferences that the trust was a sham and a fraudulent conveyance under US bankruptcy law. Chief Judge Tina L Brozman vehemently disagreed:

---

[100] Also an important point in *Duttle v Kass*, above, n 54.

[101] See *Private Trust Corporation & Others v Grupo Torras SA & Another* [1997–98] 1 OFLR 443. See also the discussions in chapter 8, 'The Offshore Trust as a Sham', and chapter 24, 'The Non-enforcement of Judgments under Offshore Law'.

[102] Above, n 54.

[103] See *Green v Jernigan*, above, n 73. This may be treated as a preliminary issue.

[104] 201 BR 685 (1996), US Bankruptcy Court, NY, T Brozman, Chief Judge.

Frankly, I do not see how I could lack jurisdiction to determine whether Portnoy retained significant control over the trust assets for purposes of concealment under § 727(a)(2) of the Bankruptcy Code. Although one might question whether I have jurisdiction over the trust itself, that is not terribly relevant, for what is sought is not the enforcement of some right under the trust, but, rather, a determination of whether by concealing his interest in that trust the debtor thereby forfeited his right to a discharge in bankruptcy. Quite plainly, I have jurisdiction to determine whether a voluntary debtor is entitled to the bankruptcy discharge for which he has petitioned regardless of whether or not the property which he is said to have concealed is within my jurisdiction.[105]

While the exclusive jurisdiction clause bound the trustee and the settlor, it could not, in the view of the court, bind creditors. The suggestion here was that even an exclusive choice of law clause importing favourable offshore trust law as the proper law could not bind creditors, albeit that this latter point was framed within the context of public policy.[106]   **19.81**

The court noted that Portnoy had admitted that Jersey did not claim exclusive jurisdiction over the trust. Thus, the decision did not address what is perhaps the more significant question, that is, the possible impact on such assertions of jurisdiction where the laws of the offshore state seek to exclude that jurisdiction. The attempt to vest exclusive jurisdiction in Jersey was located solely in the trust deed, and this was unable to withstand the onshore state's claim to jurisdiction.[107]   **19.82**

Anti-duress clauses, co-trustees, and subsidiaries in relation to jurisdiction

Jurisdiction may be affected by the existence of 'anti-duress' provisions, typical in offshore trusts. These aim at offering additional protection to offshore trust assets by attempting to shield these assets from orders given to onshore co-trustees, beneficiaries, or other persons associated with the trust and/or having control over it and subject to the onshore jurisdiction. Such provisions mandate the foreign offshore trustee to ignore the onshore co-trustee or other party if that person is acting under court compulsion, and/or sever any of their interests in the trust. Since the onshore court has no jurisdiction over foreign trustees, the reach of the assets is, in theory, effectively curtailed by annihilating the power of such co-trustees over the assets. Yet the use of an onshore co-trustee provides a substantial connection to the offshore trust, and this might indirectly give the onshore court jurisdiction over the foreign trustees.   **19.83**

An offshore co-trustee, if a company, may become vulnerable to onshore jurisdiction if, for example, it has a subsidiary in a country with which the onshore   **19.84**

---

[105] ibid, 697.
[106] See the discussion on the proper law dimensions of this case in chapter 20.
[107] Above, n 104.

jurisdiction has a treaty or exchange of information agreement, or is a subsidiary of a corporation based in a jurisdiction with which the onshore country has such a treaty. As exchange of information agreements are becoming increasingly common, even in offshore countries, this is an area which must be considered.

Suits against settlors in offshore jurisdiction

19.85 The claimant may, of course, sue in the offshore courts. Since the settlor may be deemed to have no connection with the trust and the offshore country, such a suit will logically have to be targeted only at beneficiaries and trustees of the trust. An interesting question might be whether offshore legislation retroactively granting capacity to the settlor to transfer the assets into the trust will be sufficient to establish such a connection. Since it is suggested in this book that settlors have the capacity to create trusts independently of such clauses, the short answer here might be 'No'.[108]

Relevant date for jurisdiction

19.86 A further question has arisen. What is the relevant date for determining jurisdiction? Is it the date on which the cause of action arose, or the date of the proceedings? The finding in *Chellaram No 2*[109] was in favour of the latter, which relates to the time when permission is actually sought to serve a summons. The date has become particularly important because of the effect of the Hague Convention on Trusts which enables trusts to be recognized.[110]

---

[108] See chapter 23, 'Capacity to Create the Offshore Trust and Initial Transfers of Assets'.
[109] Above, n 9.
[110] ibid. See also *Canada Trust Company v Stolzenberg No 2*, above, n 27. See discussion of the Hague Convention, above, paras 19.58–19.60.

20

THE PROPER LAW OF THE OFFSHORE TRUST

A. Introduction—Uncertainty of Rules on Proper Law

20.01 The proper law, or governing law of a trust, describes the body of appropriate legal principles and rules of trust law which will apply to the trust in question. The proper law of an offshore trust may be either onshore law, or offshore law. If it is determined that the offshore trust is governed by onshore law, for example, the trust will be deprived of the 'investor friendly' law under the offshore trust law regime. The matter of the proper law of the offshore trust is thus an important one as, ultimately, questions about the validity, and indeed the survival, of the offshore trust will be resolved by a determination of its proper law.

20.02 Yet there is very little case law on the choice of law rules for trusts, and the determination of the proper law of a trust is an underdeveloped subject. Existing rules may also vary depending on whether the trust is testamentary or *inter vivos*. Since the offshore trust is largely *inter vivos*, we are here concerned mainly with the latter. The Convention on The Law Applicable to Trusts and on their

Recognition[1] has now simplified the issue of the proper law, but the paucity and uncertainty of common law rules remain.[2]

20.03 Earlier dicta indicated that the *domicile* of the settlor was instrumental to the choice of law question.[3] The difficulty with the early authorities is that they do not cater for the intricacies of the offshore trust, such as the classic 'Uncle George' persona of the offshore trust.[4]

20.04 In contrast, in *Duke of Marlborough v A-G (No 1)*,[5] the proper law of the trust was held to be the law by reference to which the settlement was made, and which was intended by the parties to govern their rights and liabilities. This suggested that the parties' choice of law was to be given priority.

Where no choice—law most closely connected

20.05 The most consistent and modern view is that the proper law of the trust is the law chosen by the settlor as expressed or implied in the terms of the trust. This rule, granting autonomy to the settlor, is given priority in offshore legislation. It is also the primary rule under the Hague Convention on the Recognition of Trusts. In *Augustus v Permanent Trustee Co (Canberra Ltd)*,[6] for example, the High Court of Australia relied on specific provisions within the trust instrument *implying* proper law to determine the essential validity of the offshore trust. The court used a clause in the trust deed that was interpreted as a reference to the law of New South Wales to find the proper law. This has extensive implications for the offshore trust. For example, forced heirship provisions under civil law might be held to be the proper law governing a settlement where the settlor is domiciled there and assets are identified onshore. This may be so despite onshore laws seeking to override this jurisdiction.

20.06 Where there is no express choice, the emerging proposition is that the trust is governed by the law with which it is 'most closely connected'. This is, in fact, the rule in offshore jurisdictions, and it is the identical approach followed under

---

[1] Hereinafter, 'The Hague Convention on the Recognition of Trusts' (The Hague, 1 July 1985; UKTS 14 (1992); Cm 1823; 23 ILM 1388), Article 7.

[2] Note that the Hague Convention on the Recognition of Trusts was incorporated into English law by the Recognition of Trusts Act 1987. This Act was also extended to UK territories, eg, to the BVI, under the Recognition of Trusts Act 1987 (Overseas Territories) Order 1989 (SI No 673 of 1989).

[3] See, eg, *Iveagh v IRC* [1954] Ch 364 and *Rahman v Chase Bank (CI) Trust Company* [1983] JLR 1.

[4] See chapter 2, para 2.30, for a description of 'Uncle George'.

[5] [1945] Ch 78, 83.

[6] (1971) 124 CLR 245. The settlor and beneficiaries were resident and domiciled in New South Wales, but the trust was executed in Australia. The trustee was a corporation registered in Canberra, which was where the funds were paid by the settlor. Since the proper law determined validity, the validity of the trust, based on the law of New South Wales, was upheld.

the Hague Convention on the Recognition of Trusts.[7] It is also the rule in the United States, where there is a presumption that the settlor intends the proper law to be the trustee's place of business or domicile.[8]

B. Offshore Provisions—Offshore Law Chosen as Proper Law

The pattern for offshore trusts is for the law of the offshore trust jurisdiction to be chosen as the proper law or governing law of the trust. This choice is to be expected, and indeed is recommended, since the offshore trust is seeking to derive the many benefits created for trusts under offshore trust legislation.   **20.07**

Typically, offshore legislation will specify that any conflict that arises in relation to trusts governed by offshore legislation must be determined according to the laws of the offshore jurisdiction, 'without reference to the laws of any other jurisdiction with which the trust is connected'.[9] This exclusive conflict of laws clause purports to extend to all questions relating to the trust, including the capacity of the settlor to create the trust, the validity of the trust, its administration, and the existence and extent of powers conferred or retained.   **20.08**

Two models of offshore provisions on proper law are identified. Both gravitate toward a conclusion that the proper law is to be the offshore law. Both models also uphold the choice of a settlor as to proper law, or the law with which the trust is most closely connected, in accordance with the Hague Convention on the Recognition of Trusts. In the first model, the choice of proper law is given unreservedly to a settlor, without further supporting provisions.[10]   **20.09**

---

[7] Article 7. See too Dicey & Morris, *The Conflict of Laws*, 11th edn (Sweet and Maxwell, London, 1987) 1091; *Iveagh v IRC*, above, n 3, and *Banco v Veira* (1995) 8 ETR (2d) 49 (Ont).

[8] Under the Restatement (Second) of Conflict of Laws 267 Cmt C (1971).

[9] See, eg, s 13 of the Trusts Ordinance 1990, as amended in 1998. See also s 13H of the International Trusts Act 1984 of the Cook Islands; s 7(1) of the Trusts (Choice of Governing Law) 1989, as amended in 1996, of The Bahamas; Part VII, s 90, of the Trusts Law (2001 Revision) of the Cayman Islands.

[10] Not all of these provisions specifically provide that, where there is no choice, the proper law will be the law with which the trust is most closely connected. Those that do include art 4 of the Trusts (Jersey) Law 1984, as amended 1991 (Consolidated), s 10 of the International Trusts Act 1996 of Grenada, and s 8 of the International Trusts Act 1995 of Barbados. See also s 5 of the Trusts (Special Provisions) Act 1989 of Bermuda and s 4(1) of the Trusts Ordinance 1990 of the Turks and Caicos. Other provisions simply underline that the settlor's choice is to be valid. See, eg, s 89(2) of the Trusts Law (2001 Revision) of the Cayman Islands, which provides further that: 'A term of the trust expressly selecting the laws of the Islands are to govern a particular aspect of the trust is valid, effective and conclusive regardless of any other circumstances.' See also ss 4(1) and 6 of the Trusts (Choice of Governing Law) Act 1989, as amended in 1996, of The Bahamas, and s 13G of the International Trusts Act 1984 of the Cook Islands, which are similar to the Cayman Islands provisions.

20.10   In the second, a choice is left to the settlor, but if he or she fails to make that choice, there is a legislative presumption that the proper law is that of the offshore jurisdiction. This model goes even further, as it seeks to ensure that the proper law will be one that can and will recognize and accept the kind of trust that is characterized by the offshore trust. Thus, it aims to fulfil the objectives of the varying conflict of laws provisions to secure the life of the offshore trust. For example, the provision in Belize reads:

> [I]f the law expressed by the terms of the trust or intended by the settlor to be the proper law, or the law with which the trust has its closest connection at the time of its creation, does not provide for trusts or the category of trusts involved, then the proper law of the trust shall be the law of Belize.[11]

20.11   Where legislation provides only that the proper law is that law expressed by the trust to be the proper law,[12] it is not sufficient for the trust instrument simply to leave the choice open to the trustee's selection. Rather, the instrument must state clearly that 'X law' is the proper law.

20.12   There are thus two options open to the settlor of an offshore trust:

(1)   to make a clear and express choice of law as the proper law in the trust instrument; and

(2)   to leave the trust instrument silent on the question of the proper law.

The second option is a risky one, except where offshore legislation provides that such trusts are to be governed by the offshore law.

20.13   However, even where there is an expressed choice of the offshore law as the proper law in the trust instrument, or where the offshore legislation states that offshore law is the proper law, the offshore trust may be challenged on the ground that the law of the offshore country is not the proper law of the settlement. Such a challenge will attempt to oust the trust from the offshore jurisdiction, subjecting it instead to onshore trust law principles.[13]

20.14   Certainly, the unilateral enactment of conflict of law rules to govern the proper law does not guarantee the application of such laws by other countries, in

---

[11] The Trusts Law (rev'd 2000), s 4(1), of Belize. See also s 4 of the Nevis International Exempt Trusts Ordinance 1994; s 4(1) of the International Exempt Trusts Act 1997 of Dominica; s 28 of the International Trust Act 1996 of Saint Vincent. In Saint Lucia, s 32 of the International Trusts Act 2002 simply provides that, in the absence of a choice of law, the proper law shall be 'as in this Act'. This presumes that the proper law is to be the law of Saint Lucia.

[12] See, eg, art 4 of the Trusts (Jersey) Law 1984, as amended in 1991.

[13] The question of *renvoi*, ie, whether choice of law clauses relate to domestic law, as opposed to conflict of law rules, is unclear in the various offshore provisions. However, the application of internal law seems to be the intention. Note that the new BVI legislation has sought to remedy this uncertainty under s 83A of the Trustee (Amendment) Act 2003. It confirms that it is the BVI's conflict of laws rules that will apply.

particular onshore countries. Thus far, onshore countries have not challenged the unilateral approach to determine and to govern the proper law of trusts. Rather, they have sought to delineate the areas to which the proper law applies. For example, some onshore courts have reserved the proper law to matters concerning only the administration of the trust. Onshore courts have yet to extend their reach to questions such as whether it is a true trust at all because of a lack of intention to create a trust. Further, even if unilateral conflict of laws rules are accepted in theory, public policy may prevent their application.

C. Impact of the Hague Convention on the Recognition of Trusts

Several offshore statutes mirror the provisions of the Hague Convention on the Recognition of Trusts, in particular the factors to be taken into account in ascertaining the proper law of the trust.[14] In the English dependent territories, the Convention may be incorporated, as is the case in the UK.[15] As the Hague Convention on the Recognition of Trusts may apply equally to onshore and offshore states, its impact on contracting parties must, therefore, be examined. For example, in the UK, since the advent of the Convention, additional factors must be considered in determining the proper law. We would expect to see close similarities between offshore provisions and provisions and norms in onshore jurisdictions conforming to the Hague Convention on the Recognition of Trusts. **20.15**

To the extent that offshore statutes clarify uncertainties in the common law and conform to international obligations, they can be taken as an authoritative indication of the modern approach. Thus, priority in ascertaining the proper law is to be given to the parties' choice. This choice may be reserved by express provision in the trust instrument.[16] Under the Hague Convention on the Recognition of Trusts, and in contrast to the common law position, the law chosen need not have any connection with the trust, nor the settlor. Offshore law may, therefore, apply to a foreign trust, bringing that trust under the jurisdiction of the more favourable offshore regime. **20.16**

---

[14] Article 7. See, eg, art 4 of the Trusts (Jersey) Law 1984, as amended in 1991 (Consolidated); s 10 of the International Trusts Act 1996 of Grenada; s 8 of the International Trusts Act 1995 of Barbados; s 4 of the Trusts Act 1992, rev'd 2000, of Belize; s 4 of the International Exempt Trust of Dominica 1997; s 80 of the Trustee (Amendment) Act 1993 (am'd 2003), of the BVI; and s 4(1) of the Trusts Ordinance 1990 of the Turks and Caicos.

[15] By virtue of the Recognition of Trusts Act 1987 (Overseas Territories) Order 1989 (SI 1989 No 673). See, eg, the new Trustee (Amendment) Act 2003 of the BVI.

[16] See above, nn 9 and 10.

20.17 The primary test for a trust for which there is no expressed choice of law clause remains the law with which a trust is most closely connected.[17] The test mirrors that under the common law. Whether under the common law or under the Hague Convention on the Recognition of Trusts, the ascertainment of the law with which a trust is most closely connected involves making reference in particular to four main factors:

(1) the place of administration of the trust designated by the settlor;
(2) the *situs* of the assets of the trust;
(3) the place of residence or business of the trustee; and
(4) the objects of the trust and the places where they are to be fulfilled.[18]

D. Peculiarities of Offshore Trusts

20.18 Certain factors, usually referenced as indicating the law with which a trust is most closely connected, could, perhaps, be given less weight in the offshore trust. For example, the assets of the offshore trust are usually intangible movables such as stocks, shares, and bonds. Thus, the concept of the *situs* is, to some extent, fictitious. Placing undue emphasis on the *situs* of the assets may also be inappropriate given the existence of 'flight clauses' in the typical offshore trust.[19]

20.19 Further, the place where the trust deed is executed, or the residence of the trustee, may not sufficiently relate to the substance of the transaction. The transaction may be contrived so as to take advantage of favourable offshore law. An offshore corporate trustee may have more than one place of business. Similarly, management of the trust may ostensibly be carried on in the offshore jurisdiction, but real control may lie onshore. These considerations may lead to public policy questions.

20.20 The plausibility of an argument designating the law of the offshore jurisdiction as the governing law using criterion (4), outlined above,[20] is not immediately obvious when one considers where the trust assets will be invested, and for

---

[17] See Article 7 of the Hague Convention on the Recognition of Trusts.

[18] Under Article 7, ibid. This provision is reproduced in various offshore provisions, eg, s 4(1) of the Turks and Caicos Trusts Ordinance 1990; s 10 of the International Trusts Act 1996 of Grenada; s 28(2) of the International Trusts Act 1996 of Saint Vincent; s 4(2) International Exempt Trust Act 1997 of Dominica; and the International Exempt Trust Ordinance 1994 of Nevis. Other factors which will be given weight include the domicile of the settlor and the place of execution of the trust deed. See *Iveagh v IRC*, above, n 3, and *Re Lord Cable (deceased) Garratt v Waters* [1977] 1 WLR 7.

[19] Note that in a constructive trust, the proper law of a non-contractual claim for unjust enrichment in relation to movables is the law of the place where enrichment occurs. See *Contadorra Enterprises SA v Chile Holdings (Cayman) Ltd* [1999] CILR 194.

[20] That is, 'the objects of the trust and the places where they are to be fulfilled'.

whose benefit.[21] Certain types of offshore trusts may also run foul of this category. For example, the purpose trust, specifically designed for offshore investment, may not sit comfortably here, as its objects may be incompatible with orthodox trust objects and purposes.

Whether emphasis is to be placed on the place of residence of the trustee or the place where property is situated, depends on whether one views the trust as constituting personal obligations of the trustee, or property rights of the beneficiaries. In the first case, the trust should be enforceable in the place of the trustee's residence, and in the second, where the property is located. Some writers suggest that the first is the correct approach.[22] Yet given the peculiar characteristics of the offshore trust, where the trustee is usually a professional corporate trustee under indirect control of a settlor/beneficiary, it is equally appropriate to view the offshore trust as giving rise to property rights to the beneficiaries. This also appears to be the correct legal principle arising from the rule in *Saunders v Vautier*,[23] relied on in the BVI case of *Moss v Pearce Integro Trust (BVI)*.[24] **20.21**

However, the rule may be inappropriate to assess the offshore trust if we consider another factor. In the typical offshore trust, the assets are widely dispersed. Similarly, offshore investments and business of the trust may be truly transnational. It may, therefore, be more suitable to take the trustee's residence as the defining factor. This is the approach suggested by Moshinsky and Goode[25] in relation to securities, which encounter similar problems to the offshore trust. Such an approach will enhance the enforceability of related choses of action. **20.22**

E. Interpretation of Law Most Closely Connected under the Hague Convention on the Recognition of Trusts

In *Armenian Patriarch of Jerusalem v Sonsino and Others*,[26] the High Court of England had the opportunity to identify the elements that grounded the test for **20.23**

---

[21] Often, for the settlor.

[22] See, eg, P Matthews and T Sowden, *The Jersey Law of Trusts* (Key Haven Publications, London, 1993) 44.

[23] (1841) Cr & Ph 240.

[24] [1997–98] 1 OFLR 427, to uphold the right of the beneficiaries to terminate the trust at any time despite a perpetuity period, and their corresponding rights to the trust assets.

[25] M Moshinsky, 'Securities Held Through a Securities Custodian—Conflict of Laws Issues', Paper prepared for a Colloquium at Oxford, May 1998, 7. Moshinsky relies on R Goode, 'The Nature and Transfer of Rights in Dematerialized and Immobilized Securities' [1996] JIBFL 167, who characterizes the custodian of such securities as a trustee and the account holders as beneficiaries.

[26] (2002) 5 ITELR 125 (HC).

the law with which the trust is most closely connected. This case involved a consideration of the Hague Convention on the Recognition of Trusts,[27] as incorporated in the UK under the Recognition of Trusts Act 1987. The court concluded that the test for ascertaining the proper law in this case was the same, whether under the common law or the Hague Convention on the Recognition of Trusts.[28] The court affirmed that where a settlor has made no express choice of law, the trust is to be governed by the law with which it is most closely connected.[29]

20.24 In *Armenian Patriarch*,[30] the trust had been established by a settlor originally domiciled and resident in India, who was involved in litigation in the Indian courts with the plaintiff, the Armenian Patriarch. The litigation was settled by an agreement that was executed in England while the settlor was resident in England. The trust arose out of this settlement and the settlor's obligation to make payments to the Patriarch. Under the trust arrangement, the trustee, an English bank, was to pay the settlor an income for life, and on her death to pay the income to the Armenian Patriarch.[31]

20.25 The court held that in a case concerned with identifying the law with which the trust is most closely connected, the court must have regard particularly to the enumerated items under Article 7 of the Hague Convention on the Recognition of Trusts, that is, the place of administration, and so on.[32] As we have seen, these are also elements enumerated under several offshore statutes.

20.26 Similarly, in *Casani v Mattei*,[33] an Italian court, in applying the terms of the Hague Convention on the Recognition of Trusts, utilized the test of 'the law with which the trust was most closely connected' in order to find the proper law of the trust. It gave weight to the following factors in determining that law:

(1)   the place of administration designated by the settlor;
(2)   the place where the assets were situated; and
(3)   the trustee's place of business.

20.27 All of the above pointed to US law, and the court therefore found in favour of that law as the proper law. Significantly, this finding was reached even though the settlor was domiciled in Italy and the actual succession was governed by

---

[27] Above, n 1.
[28] Above, n 26, 129.
[29] This would be a case falling under Article 7 of the Hague Convention on the Recognition of Trusts.
[30] See above, n 26.
[31] A substantial issue in the case was also whether the objects of the trust, for 'education and advancement in life of Armenian children', were charitable objects.
[32] Above, n 26. See also above, n 18.
[33] (1998–99) 1 ITELR 925 (Tribunale of Lucca, Italy).

Italian law, as the settlor had died in Italy. Further, the trust was one which avoided the forced heirship regime of Italy. This last point was argued by the plaintiff as being against public policy in Italy. The judgment plainly gives credibility to offshore trusts legislation. Such legislation seeks to preclude laws on forced heirship and gives validity to trusts established by persons from civil law jurisdictions in which trust law is absent.[34]

Other factors in determining the law most closely connected

While it is established that the criteria enumerated under Article 7 of the Hague Convention on the Recognition of Trusts are to be used as the first step in identifying the law with the closest connection to the trust, all other surrounding objective circumstances are relevant. In *Armenian Patriarch*, it was noted that direct evidence of the settlor's intention as to the governing law was not, however, admissible.[35]   **20.28**

This last point may be explained by the fact that the settlor has already abdicated his or her right to give effect to his or her choice expressly in the trust instrument. This is if we accept the view that express choice is the best route to determining the proper law. Yet refusing to consider the direct evidence of the settlor's intent is curious if one takes into account the development of the jurisprudence on the proper law of the trust and, perhaps, the realities of how the close connections are identified.[36]   **20.29**

The point on the non-admissibility of direct evidence of the settlor's intention also provokes comment on the deviation from this rule found in some offshore jurisdictions. Some offshore statutes make it abundantly clear that the settlor's intention, although unexpressed in the trust instrument, must be taken into account in ascertaining the proper law.[37] There appears to be no constraint on the method of harnessing that intention.[38] In *Duke of*   **20.30**

---

[34] See chapter 22, 'Rights to Succession, Forced Heirs and the Offshore Trust', and chapter 23, 'Capacity to Create Offshore Trusts and Initial Transfers of Assets'.

[35] *Armenian Patriarch*, above, n 26, 130; see also *Chellaram v Chellaram* [1985] Ch 409, 425, *obiter*.

[36] They tend to relate to what the settlor intended, eg, if he wanted X law to be the governing law. See the discussion at paras 20.32–20.39.

[37] See, eg, s 89 of the Trusts Law (2001 Revision) of the Cayman Islands: '. . . regard is first to be had to the terms of the trust and to any evidence therein as to the intention of the parties'.

[38] Early dicta, as laid down, eg, in *Duke of Marlborough v A-G (No 1)*, above, n 5, determined the proper law by ascertaining 'the law by reference to which the settlement was made and which was *intended* by the parties to govern their rights and liabilities' (emphasis added). Dicey and Morris interpreted this to mean that '[i]n the absence of any express or implied selection of the proper law by the settlor; the system of law with which the trust has its closest and most real connection': Dicey, Morris above, n 7, 1172. The 13th edition continues to use the case of *Duke of Marlborough* as authority for the principle of the law of closest connection: L Collins (ed), *Dicey and Morris on The Conflict of Laws* 13th edn (Sweet and Maxwell, London, 2000) 1089.

Marlborough,[39] the settlor's intention was actually of prime importance in determining the proper law. Including that intention, as ascertained from evidence before the court, should, therefore, be part of the inquiry into close connections.

20.31 Jacob J's dictum in *Armenian Patriarch*[40] means that the court, in the face of a lack of a choice of proper law, is obliged to go directly to consider the law of closest connection, using the test as outlined above, which contains other factors such as the *situs* of the assets and so on. A court could not, therefore, bypass this test and seek to locate the settlor's intention. The court, however, is allowed to garner evidence of the settlor's intent as one factor in the test of closest connection. For example, Jacob J found that the settlor's desire to have English law govern the trust was a persuasive factor in determining the law of the 'closest connection' and, ultimately, the proper law.

20.32 In holding that the proper law of the trust was the law of England and not that of India, the court in *Armenian Patriach*[41] found that the following factors were evidence that the law with which the trust was most closely connected was English law:

(1) the trustee chosen was a professional trustee based in England;
(2) the settlor was resident in England at the time of the establishment of the trust;
(3) the settlor wanted the trust controlled from England, as seen from the evidence;
(4) there was difficulty in extracting money from India; and
(5) the settlor had been trying to get the money out of India.

20.33 The court considered carefully the argument that the law of India governed, because the settlement document was the result of the settlement of Indian probate proceedings and was annexed to the court order. However, this was found not to outweigh the other, more significant connections with England. The fact that the assets came from India was not important.

20.34 Of the court's findings, items (4) and (5) deserve special mention. Both Lawrence Collins J in *Chellaram v Chellaram No 2*[42] and Jacob J in the *Armenian Patriarch* case[43] considered that where a settlor is attempting to get money out of his 'home' country, and it is difficult to do so because of financial restrictions or otherwise, this is a significant indicator that the law in that 'home country'

---

[39] Above, n 5.
[40] See above, n 26
[41] ibid.
[42] (2002) 4 ITELR 729.
[43] Above, n 26, 132.

should not be viewed as the proper law. The argument seems to rely more on the settlor's intention and reasons of the public policy than criteria on close connection. Nevertheless, it is a helpful approach for offshore trusts, many of which are established out of similar circumstances.

The affirmation of the traditional rule paves the way for strong claims to be **20.35** mounted in favour of offshore law being deemed the proper law of trusts created in offshore jurisdictions. An intriguing question is this: How far are the courts willing to stretch this principle? Would it, for example, apply to persons attempting to 'escape' tax liabilities or mandatory succession regimes, or would other public policy considerations override the claim? There appears to be very little difference on ethical and policy grounds between persons wishing to avoid exchange controls established presumably to protect the state's economy,[44] and those attempting to avoid tax obligations.

Just as important for offshore trust law would be items (1) and (3) outlined in **20.36** *Armenian Patriarch* as relevant factors in ascertaining the law with which the trust was most closely connected.[45] These factors were that the settlor wanted the trust to be controlled in England and that she took the deliberate step of choosing a professional trustee based in England. Indeed, the court in *Armenian Patriach* seemed to place the greatest emphasis on these factors: 'More significant in this case, is the fact that the trustee chosen was a professional trustee based in England . . . This settlor wanted the trust controlled from England. The closest connection is with England.'[46]

The analogy to offshore trusts is obvious. Moreover, given the priority which the **20.37** English courts have given to the above factors when addressing non-offshore cases, factors which are all too common in the circumstances of the offshore trust, it would seem to be inconsistent if those same courts (and by extension, other common law courts) were to use different criteria when assessing the proper law of offshore trusts.

On the authority of *Armenian Patriarch*,[47] therefore, even where no choice of **20.38** the proper law is expressed in the trust instrument, a very strong case is made for a finding of offshore law as the proper law where the settlor expresses a deep desire to have the trust governed by the offshore law. Similarly, the fact that the settlor expressly chooses a professional trustee based in the offshore jurisdiction is a persuasive factor for determining that offshore law is the proper law. The

---

[44] As appeared to be the case in *Armenian Patriarch v Sonsino*, above, n 26, and *Chellaram*, above, n 42.

[45] See above, para 20.32.

[46] *Armenian Patriarch*, above, n 26, 132, *per* Jacob J.

[47] ibid.

case is even stronger where the settlor's actions are motivated by a desire to get money out of his or her country and it is difficult to do so.

20.39 In *Chellaram No 2*,[48] the need for a court to consider these additional factors in the UK was also affirmed. Here, factors such as whether the trust 'ought' to be governed by English law, the fact that the trustees were based in India and only had houses in England, that India was an available forum, and that proceedings were already in train in India, were considered. These factors pointed to the law of India being the proper law.

F. Scope of Proper Law

20.40 Uncertainty may surround the question of which particular aspects of the trust the term 'proper law of the trust' covers. For the purposes of determining the choice of law, several distinct trust issues fall for resolution, namely:

(1) whether the trust instrument is valid according to the appropriately chosen law;
(2) whether the trust itself is valid;
(3) the validity of the transfer of the assets and the capacity to create a trust; and
(4) its administration, construction, variation, and interpretation.[49]

20.41 Case law suggests that at common law, the law governing the trust governs its essential validity, its interpretation or construction, and administration. This includes the question whether creditors can reach beneficiaries' interests.[50] This is now confirmed under the Hague Convention on the Recognition of Trusts, and is also the approach under offshore law.

20.42 While there seems to be acceptance that questions of validity, construction, effect, and so on, may be covered, preliminary questions, such as the capacity to create the trust or its proper establishment, are more suspect. Under the Common Law, these may fall to be resolved by some other law, discussed below.[51] Considerations involving the proper law can be addressed only if such preliminary issues are satisfactorily answered.[52]

---

[48] Above, n 42.

[49] Dicey & Morris, above, n 7, 675.

[50] See *Iveagh v IRC*, above, n 3, and *Trustees Association of Australia v Roberts* [1990] CR 732. But the legality of the transfer under laws relating to creditors or bankruptcy may fall under the law of the settlor, particularly where public policy questions are raised. See *Re Larry Portnoy*, 201 BR 685 (1996) (Bankruptcy Ct, NY) *per* Brozman J, considered below, paras 20.55–20.59.

[51] Chapter 23. But see provisions which specifically include such preliminary matters, below, paras 20.44–20.46. See also n 43.

[52] See also *In the Matter of Commodore Electronics Ltd* (Sup Ct, The Bahamas) No 473/581, decided 24 June 1997.

Offshore legislation may specify particular matters that are to be governed by **20.43** the proper law. For example, in Bermuda, the proper law governs the validity of the trust, its construction, effects, and, in particular:

(a) the appointment, resignation and removal of trustees, the capacity to act as a trustee and the devolution of the office of trustee;

(b) the rights and duties of the trustees among themselves;

(c) the rights of trustees to delegate in whole or in part the discharge of their duties or the exercise of their powers;

(d) the power of trustees to administer or to dispose of trust assets, to create security interests in the trust assets, or to acquire new assets;

(e) the powers of investment of trustees;

(f) restrictions upon the duration of the trust; and upon the power to accumulate the income of the trust;

(g) the relationships between the trustee and the beneficiaries, including the personal liability of the trustees to the beneficiaries;

(h) the variation or termination of the trust;

(i) the distribution of the trust assets;

(j) the duty of trustees to account for their administration.[53]

Offshore law may, in addition to these factors outlined immediately above, also **20.44** include matters such as the capacity to create the trust and its essential validity, as issues to be governed by the proper law.[54]

In Re Larry Portnoy,[55] a US court, in examining an offshore trust whose proper **20.45** law was that of Jersey, made a clear distinction between matters governed by the proper law of the trust and other matters. Only matters associated with the administration of the trust were reserved to the proper law. In its view, the courts of the onshore jurisdiction (the US court in this instance) could properly apply US law to determine questions such as whether the settlor had intended to create a true trust, or whether it was a sham or fraudulent conveyance as these were excluded from the choice of Jersey law as the proper law. Under the Trusts (Jersey) Law 1984, the question of which matters are governed by the proper law is left open, so that the US court did not have to consider the efficacy of any such provision.

The judgment demonstrates the importance of statutory provisions which seek **20.46** to pronounce on this issue. However, there is no evidence that the court would

---

[53] The Trusts (Special Provisions) Act 1989, s 7, of Bermuda. See also s 4 of the Turks and Caicos Trust Ordinance 1990.

[54] See, eg, s 7(1) of the Trusts (Choice of Governing Law) 1989, as amended 1996, of The Bahamas; Part VII, s 90, of the Trusts Law (2001 Revision) of the Cayman Islands; s 13H of the International Trusts Act 1984 of the Cook Islands; s 83A of the Trustee (Amendment) Act 2003 of the BVI; and s 7 of the Trusts (Special Provisions) Act of Bermuda. See chapter 23 for a discussion of the capacity to create a trust.

[55] Above, n 50, considered further below, paras 20.47–20.51 and 20.54– 20.60.

have decided differently on this occasion, as it also found that a settlor had no freedom to make such a choice in the first instance.[56]

G. Distinction Between Choice of Law Rules on the Interpretation of the Trust and the Validity of the Trust

20.47   There may be a distinction between applicable rules on the choice of a proper law as they pertain to:

(1)   the proper law for interpreting the trust, for example, whether there is a breach of trust; and
(2)   the validity of the trust.

It was the second aspect of the conflict of laws rules which was pertinent in the US case of *Re Larry Portnoy*, cited above.[57] Under this category, a settlor did not have a 'free hand' to choose the proper law. The determination was therefore to be made by considering which law had the most significant relationship with the trust. In contrast, with regard to choice of law under category (1), a settlor was unrestricted in his choice of law, and US choice of law principles would generally respect such a designation.[58]

20.48   There is, however, no indication that there is a restriction on such a choice in other jurisdictions; nor, as indicated earlier, does the Hague Convention on the Recognition of Trusts require a settlor to choose the law with which the trust is most closely connected. The freedom to choose the proper law to govern every aspect of the trust properly accords with the Convention and, indeed, the Common Law. Further, the court in *Portnoy* was really making a judgment about preliminary questions in establishing trusts. It is not clear, however, how the court would have considered the effect of offshore provisions which adjudicate on these issues.[59]

20.49   Factors which were deemed important to the US having a more significant relationship with the trust were that there were creditors in the US and beneficiaries domiciled in the US. These are not necessarily conclusive or strong factors, but the settlor maintained his domicile in the US and had substantial

---

[56] Discussed further below, paras 20.47–20.51.
[57] See above, n 50.
[58] *Re Larry Portnoy*, ibid, 697–8. Further, for the purpose of determining the validity of a trust, the settlor was restrained by considerations of public policy. The creation of self-settled, spend-thrift trusts violated public policy concerns in the US. The public policy restriction against choice of law rules is discussed separately, below. See paras 20.54–20.60.
[59] See chapter 23, 'Capacity to Create the Offshore Trust and Initial Transfers of Assets', for a discussion of such preliminary issues.

contact there. The court noted that the 'ramifications of Portnoy's assets being transferred into trust have their most significant impact in the US'.[60]

The court offered another reason for ignoring Jersey law and preferring New York law. It was that under US choice of law rules, a choice of law provision 'will not be regarded where it would operate to the detriment of strangers to the agreement, such as creditors and lienholders'.[61] **20.50**

Notably, the argument that Portnoy, as a beneficiary, had no absolute property rights under a discretionary trust was ignored. In a self-settled trust a creditor is entitled to the maximum amount which the trustee can pay to the beneficiary, even though the trustee in the exercise of his discretion wishes to pay him nothing.[62] **20.51**

H. Challenges to the Parties' Choice of Law

Where shams and the avoidance of creditors are involved, courts have demonstrated a willingness to assume jurisdiction over offshore trusts and treat onshore law as the proper law of the trust. Public policy is frequently used as a collateral justification for such initiatives. The courts seem to justify their assumption of jurisdiction with concerns that certain types of trusts, such as self-settled spendthrift trusts, violate public policy. Other important but more traditional reasons are, as noted earlier, residence on US soil by either the settlor or beneficiaries[63] and the fact that, under domestic law, a choice of law provision will not be regarded where it would operate to the detriment of 'strangers to the agreement' such as creditors and lien holders.[64] In *Re Larry Portnoy*, for example, had Portnoy chosen New York law to govern the trust, creditors would have been able to reach the trust because of the public policy rule against self-settled trusts. Hence, the court felt justified in deeming New York law to be the proper law. **20.52**

The point to be underscored here is that questions on the proper law of the trust may remain even in the face of express choice of law clauses in offshore legislation that seek unilaterally to govern the operation of the trust. Their validity and effectiveness may become contentious. **20.53**

---

[60] *Re Larry Portnoy*, above, n 50, 698.

[61] See *Hong-Kong & Shanghai Banking Corporation Ltd v HFH USA Corporation* 805 F Supp 133, 140 (WDNY) 1992. The only party to the choice of law provision was Portnoy himself. Self-settled spendthrift trusts were also found to be against the principles of equity.

[62] *Vanderbilt Credit Corporation v Chase Manhattan Bank NA* 100 AD 2d 544, 546; 473 NY S 2d 242, 245 (2d Dept 1984).

[63] See *Re Larry Portnoy*, above, n 50, discussed above, paras 20.47–20.51, in the context of choices being upheld for certain trust matters, but not for others.

[64] ibid.

Public policy challenges to choice

20.54   It is open to a court that adheres to the more traditional trust formulation, to hold that the choice of offshore law offends public policy because of its hybrid and more flexible trust law features. The US courts have recently found this approach attractive. In *First National Bank v Daggett*,[65] the court, on public policy grounds, refused to apply a choice of law clause in a trust and instead applied the *situs* rule.

20.55   In *Re Larry Portnoy*,[66] a US citizen established an offshore trust in Jersey in circumstances where it was apparent that he knew that he owed substantial debts. He then sought bankruptcy protection, arguing that his assets were insulated under Jersey law and, further, that he was entitled as a matter of law to a discharge of all debts. The trust was challenged as a conveyance which intended to avoid legitimate creditors. The plaintiff contested the claimed discharge under section 727(a) of the Bankruptcy Code of the US. The plaintiff further alleged that after fraudulently transferring substantially all of his assets to the trust, Portnoy remained the de facto owner by maintaining control over the assets and continued to conceal the trust in violation of the Bankruptcy Code.

20.56   In assessing the claim, the case hinged on two main issues: the question of the jurisdiction of the New York court over the matter;[67] and whether Jersey or New York law applied to the trust. In fact, the latter question involved two separate choice of law questions, the first relating to which law applied to the preliminary question of the validity of the transfer of the assets,[68] and the second relating to which law governed the substantive issue on bankruptcy, in particular, whether the defendant concealed an interest in the property.

20.57   Here, the trust instrument plainly stipulated that Jersey law was to be governing law. Interestingly, although Portnoy was domiciled in New Jersey, this was not put forward as a basis for the proper law, although Brozman J hinted that this may have been a legitimate ground. Rather, it was assumed by both parties that the *lex loci*, New York, and the law chosen by the settlor, Jersey law, were the contenders for the proper law. The court held that, for the purpose of ascertaining whether Portnoy was eligible for the bankruptcy discharge, New York law

---

[65]   242 Neb 734, 497 NW 2d 358 (1993).

[66]   Above, n 50.

[67]   Discussed in chapter 19.

[68]   This aspect is discussed in chapter 23, at paras 23.1–23.12. The court determined that local (onshore) law applied to the preliminary question whether Portnoy retained an interest in the offshore trust, ie, whether he had properly conveyed his assets into the trust or whether it was, in effect, a sham.

and not Jersey law applied to determine the question whether Portnoy retained an interest in the offshore trust.

The trust could not protect the assets against Portnoy's creditors as, under US **20.58** law, it was against public policy to permit a settlor/beneficiary (in a self-settled trust) to tie up the property in such a way that he or she could still enjoy it but prevent creditors from reaching it.[69] This is irrespective of any intent on the part of the settlor to defraud creditors. The fact that intent is not necessary to ground an action for fraudulent conveyancing where self-settled trusts are involved, is a significant difference from offshore laws on fraudulent conveyances, which, in the main, rely on a settlor's intent to defraud in order to ground an action. This means that the more restrictive approach to fraudulent conveyances in offshore jurisdictions is fundamentally opposed to US law, and it is perhaps unsurprising that the issue would be viewed within the context of public policy.

Thus, in *Portnoy*, Jersey trust law offended a fundamental policy of the US, **20.59** which was viewed as the dominant state. In the words of Brozman J:

> . . . it would offend our policies to permit a debtor to shield from creditors all of his assets because ownership is technically held in a self-settled trust, where the settlor/beneficiary nonetheless retains control over the assets and may effectively direct disposition of those assets . . . On the other hand, it is not at all clear what the policy behind the Jersey amendment is except, perhaps to augment business.[70]

The result was that based on 'New York's deep-rooted policies and absent a more compelling countervailing Jersey policy, New York law applies'.[71] As we have noted previously, the existence, in some US states, of provisions which specifically permit self-settled, spendthrift trusts, defeats, or weakens, this public policy rationale.[72]

Since the advent of the Hague Convention on the Recognition of Trusts, **20.60** restrictions on choice are more difficult to justify. As we have seen, under Article 6, the settlor may expressly or impliedly choose the governing law of the trust. Offshore legislation is, therefore, in conformity with the approach of the Hague Convention on the Recognition of Trusts.[73] Yet it is noteworthy that the Convention also recognizes the importance of the public policy limitation. This well-established exception in private international law can still be used to

---

[69] See above, n 50.

[70] *Re Larry Portnoy*, above, n 50, 700.

[71] ibid.

[72] See chapter 5, paras 5.26–5.31.

[73] Under Article 6, the settlor may also choose more flexible provisions to replace rules on validity, so long as such law does not derogate from the original intention of the trust and provided that such law is that of a trust jurisdiction.

thwart choices of governing law.[74] However, this can be a restriction only on narrow grounds, and not against all offshore trusts. Further, as offshore trusts continue to influence onshore trust law, it will be increasingly difficult to justify the resort to public policy arguments.[75]

Choice of law approach should be consistent and given priority

20.61 Interestingly, current US conflict of laws rules allow the settlor to choose the law of more trust-friendly federal states, and one would think that it would be inconsistent to apply a different rule when reviewing an offshore trust.[76] However, in *Re Larry Portnoy*,[77] the traditional approach did not appear to be followed in a case involving an offshore trust. Brozman J seemed to make an assumption that because Jersey law did not assert exclusive jurisdiction over the trust, this somehow impacted negatively on the choice of law clause, although these should have been two separate and distinct questions. Brozman J simply ignored the express choice in favour of conflict of law rules which place a premium on the law of the jurisdiction having the greatest interest in the litigation. On this question, both New York law and Federal conflict of laws rules were the same.[78] Not surprisingly, although conceding that Jersey law had an interest, the greater interest was located under New York law. Jersey's interest was said to be in determining what rights remain in the settlor of a trust.[79] The matter of the proper law was further complicated by consideration of the substantive issue, as Portnoy sought to distribute his non-exempt property to his creditors and in return receive a bankruptcy discharge, a matter which was clearly determinable by domestic law.

---

[74] Under Article 18, where the choice is 'manifestly incompatible'. Articles 15 and 16 also restrict choice where it might thwart the application of mandatory rules (such as forced heirship). This is also relevant to jurisdiction.

[75] Note, eg, the impact of the protector.

[76] W Culp and J Grafting, 'Owning Assets in Trust Results in Tax and Non-Tax Benefits' (1992) 19 Est Plan 284, 285. Choice of law clauses may also be ineffective in fraudulent conveyance suits. In *Ferrari v Barclay's Business Credit Inc* 108 BR 384, 386 (Banker D Mass 1989), modified, 148 BR 97 (Bankr D Mass 1992), the court relied instead on the Restatement's 'most significant relationship' test to find the proper law; Restatement (Second) of Conflict of Laws 6(2) 1971.

[77] See above, n 50.

[78] See, eg, section 403 of the Restatement (Third) of Foreign Relations Law of the US 1987, which suggests an inquiry based on reasonableness, requiring the court to focus on locating the jurisdiction whose laws and policies are the most involved with the controversy. See *Maxwell Communications Corporation plc v Société Générale plc* 186 Bankr 807, 822 (SDNY 1995), aff'd, 93 FF 3d 1036 (2d Cir 1996). For a previous application of New York conflict of laws rules, see *Re Best Products Co* 168 Bankr 35, 51 (Bankr SDNY 1994).

[79] Because of the offshore structure, it was not clear to the court whether the assets were located in the US or in Jersey, so that the determining issue seemed to be the domicile of the settlor and the US beneficiaries and creditors. See above, n 50, 898.

The existence of financial confidentiality laws which apply to trusts may not, in **20.62** itself, be a sufficient variation to oust the application of offshore law as the proper law. In *Green v Jernigan*,[80] a Canadian court upheld the choice of Nevis law as the proper law, finding that there was no good reason not to do so, despite restrictive confidentiality laws. Clear and certain choice of law clauses were to be respected unless there was strong cause to ignore the choice, and this was treated as a high threshold to cross. The judgment offers comfort to those persons fearful that onshore courts will automatically seek to avoid non-traditional offshore law where questions of proper law arise.

Analogy with contracts

There is appropriate judicial authority which considers the question of the **20.63** settlor's freedom to select the law governing the trust by making a judicial analogy with conflict of laws rules on contracts.[81] While the general rule is to give effect to an expressed choice of law based on the premise of the freedom to contract,[82] there are reservations. It is logical to expect that such limitations for trusts will be on similar principles to those on contracts. Under conflict of laws rules governing contracts, limitations are based on the choice:

(1) being bona fide, legal, and not against public policy;
(2) being connected with the contract; and
(3) being meaningful.[83]

Thus, under this route, the emphasis on the autonomy of the settlor may be of little use where the trust or the choice of trust law is viewed as abusive because of a desire to evade a less friendly law.

The meaning of the terms 'bona fide' and 'legal' under category (1), presents **20.64** interesting possibilities about potential challenges to the offshore trust. In the landmark Vita Food case,[84] it was opined that the parties cannot pretend to contract under one law to validate an agreement that clearly has its closest connection with another law. Where one particular provision is void under the proper law and an attempt is made to evade its consequences by claiming that the provision was subject to another legal system, that claim would not be

---

[80] (2003) 6 ITELR 330 (Sup Ct, Br Columbia), *per* Groberman J.

[81] From Australia, in the case of *Augustus v Permanent Trustee Co (Cranberra Ltd)* (1971) 124 CLR 245. Analogies were made to contracts in an attempt to frame relevant and coherent principles for the application of private international law in relation to the trust. In the case of contracts, the validity of the contract is governed by its proper law.

[82] See, eg, *Mackender and Others v Feldia* [1967] 2 QB 590, 602.

[83] Cheshire and North, *Private International Law*, 12th edn (Butterworths, London, 1992) 452.

[84] *Vita Food Products Inc v Unus Shipping Co Ltd* [1939] AC 277. See too *BHP Petroleum Pty Ltd v Oil Basins Ltd* [1985] VR 725.

considered as a bona fide expression of intention. Bad faith may be imputed if there is no real connection between the agreement and the law chosen.

20.65 When one examines the *raison d'être* of the offshore industry, and in particular its use of the offshore trust as a vehicle to achieve its ultimate goal of what may be viewed as commercial expediency, it is at least open to argument that the offshore trust could be a victim of the 'bad faith' test, if challenged. In the typical offshore legal arrangement, little, if any, real connection exists between its underlying business purpose and the choice of the offshore law. Indeed, the classic use of the offshore trust is an attempt to avoid the more restrictive features of the orthodox onshore trust, such as the rule against perpetuities,[85] even though the administration and benefits to be derived from the trust are more closely connected with the onshore law.

20.66 The deliberate manipulation of the international environment of the trust, for example by choosing trustees dissociated with the true controlling environment of the trust, could be viewed as an evasion of the real place of the true 'contract'. Correlation with private international law rules on contracts may give a more realistic interpretation of the proper law.

I. Hague Convention's Influence on Express Choice Tested

20.67 Perhaps the first opportunity to test the efficacy of the provisions of the Hague Convention on the Recognition of Trusts, in particular on the question of expressed choice, came in the case of *Tod v Barton*.[86] Because of an attempt by the beneficiaries to vary the terms of a trust established by an English settlor domiciled in Texas, the court had to consider whether English law or Texas law applied.[87] The trust deed contained a clause expressly choosing English law. In such a case, given the provisions of the Hague Convention on the Recognition of Trusts under Article 6,[88] which allows for expressed choice, the proper law was English law. A collateral point should be noted, that the further step of inquiring into the circumstances of the case can be made only if the choice is implied and not when the choice is expressed.

20.68 Further, where a settlor makes a choice as to the proper law, it is irrelevant if,

---

[85] *Augustus*, above, n 81, is helpful. Here, the contentious issue was whether the trust contravened the rule against perpetuities. It was void for imperpetuity under Australian law.

[86] [2002] EWHC 264 (High Court of Justice, England and Wales).

[87] Had Texas law applied, the variation of the trust would not have been valid.

[88] Article 6(1) reads: 'A trust shall be governed by the law chosen by the settlor. The choice must be expressed or be implied in the terms of the instrument creating or the writing evidencing the trust, interpreted, if necessary, in the light of the circumstances of the case.'

afterward, an unintended effect of that choice occurs. In *Tod v Barton*, it was clear that the settlor did not intend that the beneficiary could vary the trust and give himself an absolute share. In fact, this was what he wished to avoid. Nonetheless, the 'express choice of law cannot be impugned'.[89] Indeed, in 'all systems of law, documents such as contracts and wills may have effects which are unknown to the parties, and which may not fully effectuate their intentions'.[90] A court cannot override the express choice of law on these grounds, and it cannot be taken as evidence that another choice is implied where, once the determination had been made that under the Hague Convention on the Recognition of Trusts rules, the trust was governed by English law and not Texas law, the action of the beneficiaries in varying the trust under the rule in *Saunders v Vautier* (a rule of English law) could stand.

In a rare judgment from a civil law jurisdiction, *Re WKR Trust OD Bank (in liquidation) v Estate of Rey (a Bankrupt)*,[91] the District Court of Zurich had to decide what was the proper law of a trust established in Guernsey and affiliated to underlying Guernsey and Geneva companies. The court first addressed the recognition of a trust issue[92] before finding that Guernsey law, the choice made in the trust instrument, was the applicable law. The entity had been incorporated in Guernsey, and was thus a Guernsey entity under conflict of law rules. **20.69**

J. Choice of Law and Judicial Power to Vary the Terms of the Trust

Where onshore courts have jurisdiction to vary the terms of a trust,[93] it poses important questions about the durability and effectiveness of the offshore trust. The wide discretionary power given to a court to vary a trust may have extraterritorial effect, and may extend to trust assets located in foreign countries and governed by foreign law.[94] In invoking discretionary jurisdiction to vary a trust, the onshore courts may examine the motives behind the trust settlement and the variations requested in the light of public policy.[95] The result may be that they might not view the offshore trust favourably. For example, in *Re Weston's* **20.70**

---

[89] See above, n 86.
[90] ibid.
[91] (1999) 4 ITELR 487.
[92] Giving effect to the trust as a corporation in the form of a holding company under Swiss law. See discussion of the recognition of trusts in chapter 21.
[93] As in the UK under the Variation of Trusts Act 1968.
[94] *Re Kerr's Settlement Trust* [1863] Ch 553.
[95] See *Re Paget's Settlement* [1965] 1 WLR 1046; [1965] 1 All ER 58.

Settlement,[96] the English Court of Appeal refused to approve the appointment of foreign trustees in Jersey for purposes of tax avoidance. The decision clearly hinged on public policy considerations.

20.71 The Hague Convention on the Recognition of Trusts provides that the variation of the trust is a matter governed by the law governing the trust, the proper law.[97] This was effectively demonstrated in *Tod v Barton*.[98] The rule points to the likelihood that a court would disclaim the exercise of such jurisdiction, treating the court of the foreign country as a more appropriate forum. English courts have been cautious in exercising their jurisdiction to vary trusts with substantial foreign elements.[99] Still, although this might be correct in relation to the orthodox trust, no certainty exists that such restraint will be exercised with regard to the offshore trust.

20.72 Since variation of a trust may profoundly affect its validity and not merely its administration, the power of variation has significant implications for the life of the offshore trust. It is questionable whether the choice of offshore law as the governing law can be sustained in the light of such a power. Where English courts have assumed this jurisdiction, no reference has been made to the foreign law to ascertain whether that law would authorize such a variation. Without hesitancy they have proceeded to apply English law.

No variation to enforce rights under foreign law

20.73 In contrast, courts may not appear to have the authority to vary or set aside trusts in order to enforce succession or forced heirship rights under foreign law. In fact, from the perspective of some offshore legislation, such a power may be expressly excluded. Consider, for example, the position in Bermuda:

> Where a trust is validly created under the law of Bermuda the court shall not vary it or set it aside pursuant to the law of another jurisdiction in respect of—
>
> (a) the personal and proprietary effects of marriage;
> (b) succession rights, ... especially the indefeasible shares of spouses and relatives;
> (c) the protection of creditors in matters of insolvency,

unless the law of Bermuda has corresponding laws or public policy rules.[100]

20.74 In other offshore jurisdictions, the power to vary, as expressed under statute, is

---

[96] [1969] 1 Ch 223.
[97] Article 8.
[98] Above, n 86.
[99] See *Re Paget's Settlement*, above, n 95, 1050. See also Dicey & Morris, above, n 7, 1095.
[100] The Trusts (Special Provisions) Act 1989, s 11, of Bermuda. See also s 18 of the International Trusts Act 1995 of Barbados and s 7(6) of the Belize Trusts Act 1992 (rev'd 2000).

the same as under traditional trust law rules.[101] However, it is suggested that a court will need to consider the objectives of related trust provisions which seek to preserve and validate offshore trusts when deciding whether to exercise its discretion to vary. Examples of these conflicting objectives might be the anti-forced heirship, or asset protection, provisions of the legislation. The prohibition on variation where foreign law succession rights were involved, was upheld in *Schindler v Garner and Bermuda Trust Co Ltd*.[102]

K. Change of Proper Law

The issue of a change to the proper law of the trust is particularly relevant in offshore jurisprudence, as it is viewed as a mechanism for protecting the trust assets. This may be by virtue of the 'flight clause'. Under the common law the proper law may be changed by the agreement of all of the beneficiaries.[103] Offshore jurisdictions usually take the route of granting statutory authorization for changes in the proper law. This is subject to an expressed intention in the trust document.[104]   **20.75**

One difficulty with changing the proper law is that it may alter the substantive terms of the trust if the trust laws of the new jurisdiction differ.[105] Offshore legislation may, therefore, authorize a change only if the new law recognizes the change and that law is found to be equal to the existing law. The expectation   **20.76**

---

[101] See, eg, arts 33 and 43 of the Trusts (Jersey) Law 1984, consolidated; and s 72(1) of the Trusts Law (2001 Revision) of the Cayman Islands.

[102] (CA, Bermuda) No 49 of 1992, decided 10 July 1992. See further discussion of this case in chapter 22, paras 22.23–22.26.

[103] *Duke of Marlborough v A-G (No 1)*, above, n 5.

[104] See, eg, art 37 of the Trusts (Jersey) Law 1984; s 4 of the Trusts (Foreign Element) Law 1987 of the Cayman Islands, now incorporated under Part VII of the Trusts Law (2001 Revision) of the Cayman Islands; s 5 of the Trusts (Choice of Governing Law) Act 1996 of The Bahamas; s 4(4) of the Dominica International Trusts Act; s 81 of the Belize Trusts Act; and s 4(4) of the BVI Trust Ordinance. Article 10 of the Hague Convention on the Recognition of Trusts also makes provision for the governing law to be changed. There must be an express power in the trust instrument enabling the change. The Trusts (Jersey) Law 1984, art 37, permits a change in the proper law, but does not provide further for the change to be recognized. A change of proper law will not render the trust void or invalid. See, eg, s 10 of the International Trusts Act 1996 of Grenada; s 29 of the International Trust Law 1996 of Saint Vincent; s 4(5) and (6) of the International Trust Ordinance 1994 of Nevis; s 4(5) and (6) of the Belize Trusts Act 1992 (rev'd 2000); s 46 of The Trusts (Guernsey) Law 1989.

[105] For example, in *Fattorins v Johannesburg Bd of Executors and Trust Co* [1948] (4) SA 806, the settlor could not retain the right to revoke the trust in the changed jurisdiction and the change was consequently invalid.

is that the change will not affect the validity of the trust, or the rights and obligations under the trust.[106]

20.77 This determination is a matter for the jurisdiction where the trust is located. This was confirmed in *Bridge Trust Company and Slatter v A-G*,[107] where a Bahamian trust moved to the Cayman Islands. The court found that the question of validity under the new governing law was a matter for the Cayman courts to decide. It could not be a question for the foreign law, in this case Bahamian law, since that was the very mischief that the provision under the statute, s 4(1) of the Trusts (Foreign Element) Law 1987, was intended to correct.[108]

---

[106] For example, under s 6(2) of the Trusts (Choice of Governing Law) 1996 of The Bahamas; s 8(3) of the International Trusts Act 1995 of Barbados; and s 81(1) and (2) of the Trustee (Amendment) Act 1993 of the BVI. For the change from the BVI to another jurisdiction to be valid, the new proper law must recognize the validity of the trust and the beneficiaries' interests. Section 81 also recognizes trigger clauses where specific events occur.

[107] [1996] CILR 52 (Grand Ct, Cayman Island). The question was whether its charitable purposes were valid.

[108] ibid, 69. Note that the change of law had to be recognized by The Bahamas law in the first instance.

21

RECOGNITION OF THE OFFSHORE TRUST IN CIVIL LAW COUNTRIES

A. Introduction

Even after issues of jurisdiction and proper law have been resolved, the offshore **21.01** trust may be further challenged under a conflict of laws approach. Issues such as whether the onshore country will recognize the trust as a valid trust, or whether trusts are recognizable at all in the onshore jurisdiction at hand, if it is a civil law jurisdiction, will arise. This will lead to further questions, such as the survivability of anti-mandatory succession regimes instituted under offshore trust law, and preliminary questions concerning the capacity to create the trust in the first instance.

Recognition issues in relation to the offshore trust may be viewed from two **21.02** angles. In the first, the issues are discussed within the context of legal systems which are very familiar with the trust but not with the offshore trust, such as the UK. This is, more appropriately, a question of acceptance, and was discussed in chapter 6 above. It is also a topic which permeates many other discussions in this book. This current chapter is concerned with the second aspect, that is, the trans-jurisdictional recognition of the offshore trust in relation to legal systems which are unfamiliar with the trust entity. It is, of course, part of the broader concern regarding the recognition of *any* trust by such legal systems.

B. Civil Law Confrontations with the Trust

21.03 The survivability of the offshore trust as a transnational entity depends, partially, on its ability to transcend Common Law borders and be accepted—if not embraced—by civil law systems. The offshore legal system itself depends on this duality of legal systems existing harmoniously. Yet the trust, as an institution steeped in the Common Law legal tradition, is not easily recognized under civil law legal systems.

21.04 The issue of recognition is even more problematic where the assets of the trust are located in the civil law jurisdiction, the *lex situs* issue. In contrast, where the *lex situs* is a Common Law country, the laws of civil jurisdictions are more sympathetic to the recognition and validity of the trust established by a settlor domiciled in their jurisdiction. This is provided that other controversial questions, such as the establishment of the trust for forced heirship purposes, are not in issue. Yet even this general principle in relation to the *lex situs* assumes more complex dimensions under offshore law, since assets may be intangible, or it may be difficult to identify the *lex situs*.

21.05 Choice of law rules allow the enforcement of a right that is unrecognized, or even repudiated, by the chosen law. Consequently, civil law courts could give effect to the trust by deciding that the matter is one governed by foreign legal rules which recognize the Common Law trust.[1]

21.06 Several offshore jurisdictions have enacted provisions to deem the trust and transfer of assets valid despite the existence of laws which do not recognize the trust.[2] However, where trust assets are in a civil law jurisdiction, the efficacy of the law of the offshore jurisdiction may be challenged, as there may be a presumption of jurisdiction by the civil law country. Further, civil law jurisdictions may have no desire to promote the recognition of the trust, for instance, where the effect will be to override the claims of forced heirs or offend public policy.[3]

21.07 Despite the theoretical challenges to offshore trusts on the issue of recognition, the cases thus far demonstrate a fairly successful outcome to such challenges,

---

[1] L Collins (ed), *Dicey and Morris on the Conflict of Laws*, 13th edn (Sweet & Maxwell, London, 2000).

[2] See, eg, Nevis, under s 29 of the International Exempt Trusts Ordinance 1994; s 91 of the Trusts Law (2001 Revision) of the Cayman Islands; s 7(2) of the Trusts (Choice of Governing Law) Act 1989 (am'd 1996) of The Bahamas; under s 33 of the International Trust Act 1996 of Saint Vincent; s 20 of the International Trusts Act 1996 of Grenada; and s 34 of the International Trusts Act 2002 of Saint Lucia.

[3] This may also apply to Common Law onshore jurisdictions. See, eg, *Re Larry Portnoy*, 201 BR 685 (1996).

whichever route has been taken to recognition. This trend demonstrates a willingness on the part of civil law jurisdictions to treat with trusts, including offshore trusts. Negative outcomes from the perspective of offshore jurisdictions have more to do with failed functions of the offshore trust, for example the tax function, and little to do with difficulties in recognizing the trust itself.

When civil law jurisdictions confront the trust, there are several possibilities for dealing with it. These include: **21.08**

(1) accommodation of the trust;
(2) full recognition of the trust; and
(3) refusal to recognize the trust.

Accommodation of the trust

Civil law jurisdictions may acknowledge and accommodate the trust as a legal entity or arrangement analogous to one familiar in civil law regimes. The older approach is to view the trust as some form of contract. Civil law countries have a broader idea of a contract than do common law jurisdictions, and such a wide view of a contract can encompass the underlying principles of the trust arrangement.[4] However, despite the flexibility of contract law under the civil law tradition, problems may arise in the universal application of the trust, and its use as an offshore vehicle in particular. For example, since contractual rights are merely personal rights, beneficiaries cannot enforce them against the foreign trustees' creditors or transferees unless they knew that the trustees were acting wrongly. **21.09**

More recently, the trust has been deemed to be analogous to a company, or the foundation,[5] the latter being an institution similar to the trust which is found in civil law regimes. **21.10**

The trust does not fit neatly into either of the above analogous concepts, nor is the 'stretch to fit' exercise a simple one. It is not an easy solution to the conflict of laws problem. Indeed, the accommodation of the trust by methods of assimilation, adaptation, or transposition is considered by some to be an attempt 'to torture the trust' to bring it into comparable categories of the civil law forum.[6] **21.11**

---

[4] See, eg, *Courtois v De Ganay*, Rev Cr de dr int pr 518 (1973) (CA Paris) and *Re Harrison* Arrêts du Tribunal Federal Suisse; Recueil Officiel (ATF) 1070 vol 96 11 79. Journal des Tribunaux 1971, 331.

[5] Discussed further below, at paras 21.32–21.39 and 21.21–21.31, respectively.

[6] Alfred E von Overbeck, in his 'Explanatory Report on The Hague Convention on the Law Applicable to Trusts and on their Recognition' (The Hague, 1 July 1985; UKTS 14 (1992); Cm 1823; 23 ILM 1388) 6. See also M Cumyn, 'The Trust in a Civilian Context: The Quebec Case' [1994] 3 JIntP 69, 70.

Full recognition as a trust

21.12   The trust may be recognized fully as a Common Law institution deemed to be recognizable under the Hague Convention on the Law Applicable to Trusts and on their Recognition,[7] or under principles of comity. The recognition process may occur either in conjunction with the choice of the Common Law as the governing law, or with reference to the law of the civil law regime as the governing law, at least in relation to some aspects of the trust.

Refusal to recognize the trust

21.13   Civil law jurisdictions may fail to acknowledge the trust absolutely. This, however, is an unlikely approach.

C. Increasing Use of the Offshore Trust in Civil Law Countries

21.14   It is undeniable that civil law jurisdictions are becoming more familiar with the trust, not least because of the increased use of trusts, in particular offshore trusts, by citizens, nationals, and residents of these jurisdictions.

21.15   In France, for example, French business people have often come into contact with the offshore trust in international markets, mainly because Anglo-Saxon bankers, who naturally have an affinity with the trust, dominate such markets. Trusts promote expediency, and 'French bankers have a tendency to imitate Anglo-Saxon financial structures, including those which incorporate the trust'.[8] The normal route for such arrangements is to ensure that the choice of law for the transaction is common law. This is a necessary, but not always a sufficient, starting point for the enforceability of such transactions by the French courts.

21.16   The result is that, despite potential problems with recognition, the offshore trust is helping to import the trust concept into civil law systems. In addition, the ability of the trust structure to incorporate companies makes it a useful vehicle for international business and is a further testimony to its adaptability, since, although trusts are not recognized in civil law countries, foreign companies are. Experiences with financial unit trusts in 'even the most trust fearing

---

[7] Hereinafter 'The Hague Convention on the Recognition of Trusts' (The Hague, 1 July 1985; UKTS 14 (1992); Cm 1823; 23 ILM 1388).

[8] G Endreo, 'The Use of Trusts in Financial Transactions (France)' in 10th Annual Seminar on International Financial Law, IBA, 1993, 2. A typical example is where a French company issues 'Titres Subordonnés à Durée Indeterminée', (TSDIs), (a type of Instantly Repackaged Perpetuals), to a 'special purpose vehicle' located in an offshore jurisdiction. The vehicle then issues instruments to another country, via a trust. Between 1988 and 1992, FF70 billion-worth of TSDIs were issued.

countries, such as Italy and Spain, [have] led to a general acceptance that a foreign trust may own shares and stock in a local company'.[9] Indeed, because of the continuous interaction with the common law trust, some civil law countries have introduced forms of the trust. A notable example is the French '*la fiducie*'.[10]

The evidence from the emerging case law on offshore trusts established by persons from civil law countries suggests that civil law courts are not, at least, hostile to the concept of the trust. Hayton believes that civil law countries will become   **21.17**

> more familiar and happier with the trust, particularly when it is appreciated how helpful can be the separation between a fiduciary and a private patrimony for commercial purposes and how useful can be the dynastic trust, particularly for looking after the elderly and the young in a family over three or four generations without having to split up valuable family assets due to forced heirship trusts.[11]

D. The Hague Convention and Offshore Provisions on Recognition of the Trust

The advent of the Hague Convention on the Recognition of Trusts has partially alleviated problems of recognition of the trust in civil law countries. In so doing, it has given impetus and legitimacy to offshore law provisions on the recognition of trusts. Although it does not attempt to introduce the trust into non-trust countries, it establishes common private international law rules to decide the particular law or laws applicable to the validity and administration of a trust. This provides an enabling environment for the recognition of the trust.   **21.18**

The limitations of the Hague Convention on the Recognition of Trusts in failing to resolve the controversial issues surrounding forced heirship, public policy, and the capacity to create a trust will be discussed in later chapters.[12] There is a further difficulty, though. While the Hague Convention on the Recognition of Trusts is a step in the right direction, it takes two steps backward   **21.19**

---

[9] T Trumpy, 'Trusts for Closely-held Businesses: the International Perspective' (1994) 84 LS Gaz 2856, 2859.

[10] Introduced in 1992, as part of the Code Civile. See also statutory recognition of the trust in Monaco, under Law 214 of 1936, and by judicial decision in France in the case of *Caron v Ordell* R 1983, 282; R 1986, 66. The trust has also gained considerable acceptance in Italy, both for its role in family succession and in commercial transactions. See J Ingham, 'Recognising the Italian Trust' *Offshore Investment*, June 2002, 13.

[11] D Hayton, 'The Hague Convention on Trusts: A Little is Better Than Nothing But Why So Little?' [1994] 3 JIntP 23, 28.

[12] See chapter 22, 'Rights to Succession, Forced Heirs and the Offshore Trust', and chapter 23, 'Capacity to Create the Offshore Trust and Initial Transfers of Assets'.

under Article 13. This provides that no country is bound to recognize a trust if its 'significant elements' are more closely connected with states where the trust concept is unknown.[13] This provision may seriously undermine the ability of a settlor from a civil law jurisdiction to effect a trust settlement in an offshore jurisdiction, as the domicile of the settlor, the location of assets onshore, and even the existence of heirs or creditors in the civil law country, may point to the onshore state having more significant elements. In fact, similar factors were harnessed in *Re Larry Portnoy*[14] to find that the US had a more 'significant' relationship with the trust in relation to the question of the proper law of the trust.[15]

21.20 Indeed, one could argue that, in civil law countries, the very existence of the institution of the trust is against public policy. However, such an argument would be a negation of the Hague Convention on the Recognition of Trusts itself, when one considers its prime rationale. Countries which have ratified the Hague Convention could not legitimately make such an argument. Interestingly, this argument was rejected by an Italian court in the case of *Casani v Mattei*.[16]

E. The Trust as a Foundation

21.21 The trust has often been likened to a foundation, an institution found in certain European countries which, like a trust, can hold property for another person. Nonetheless, there are important differences between the trust and the foundation. The foundation, for example, is an independent legal person under law. The trust, on the other hand, is not a legal person. Such differences can sometimes lead to distorted or, at best, inconsistent results when attempting to recognize the trust.

21.22 In *Re An Isle of Man Trust*,[17] for example, the Tax Panel of Sweden had to decide the status of a trust established in the Isle of Man by a settlor of Swedish origin who was not resident in Sweden. The settlor sought a preliminary ruling on the application of Swedish wealth and income tax to the trust, since he was contemplating returning to Sweden.

---

[13] This is not expressly identified, but the Explanatory Report reveals that they refer to those mentioned under Article 7, ie, the nationality of the settlor and the habitual residence of the beneficiaries. The place of administration and habitual residence of the trusts are expressly excluded.

[14] Above, n 3.

[15] See chapter 20.

[16] (1998–99) 1 ITELR 925 (Tribunale of Lucca, Italy).

[17] (1998–99) 1 ITELR 103 (Tax Panel, Sweden).

The Tax Panel ruled that the correct approach was to find the nearest **21.23** corresponding Swedish legal body and ascertain whether the rules applicable to that body might apply to the trust. At the time of the judgment, Sweden had not ratified the Hague Convention on the Recognition of Trusts, nor did it have a tax treaty with the Isle of Man. Consequently, there were no international public law obligations which guaranteed the sustainability of a trust established in the Isle of Man.

The Tax Panel found that the nearest Swedish body was the foundation. How- **21.24** ever, it had to stretch the concept of the foundation to cover the trust, as the question of the ownership of the assets between the trust and the foundation was different. It recognized that the assets under the common law did not belong to the trust itself, since the trust was not a legal person. It further accepted that neither the trustee nor the beneficiaries were the legal owners of the trust, as is the case with the foundation. It then solved the dilemma of ownership simply by declaring that, for 'convenience,' the assets would be treated as belonging to the entity, the trust, as is the case with the foundation.[18] The issue of the ownership of the assets was, of course, an important one, as the Panel was assessing tax liability.

The Panel's difficulty was further alleviated by its finding that the entity was **21.25** governed not by Swedish law, but by Isle of Man law, as it had been created by a founder who at that time was resident abroad and under Isle of Man legislation. Consequently, the trust was not liable for wealth taxes. Thus, the founder (or settlor) would have been liable for income tax only where he continued to benefit from the entity.

It is doubtful that the settlor would have achieved a different result had the Tax **21.26** Panel fully recognized the entity as an offshore trust. Ignoring the point that the entity was the creation of Isle of Man law and not of Swedish law for the time being, which factor absolved its tax liability, we find that if the Panel had recognized the trust, tax liabilities would have been placed on the trustee, and not on the settlor. This would have been the case unless the trust was to be declared a sham, or tax countermeasures similar to those found in some countries, which displace tax liabilities from the trustee to the settlor or beneficiaries in non-resident trusts, had been in place.[19]

Yet the different views of the ownership of assets in a foundation do not always **21.27** produce satisfactory results. In *Norway v Olsen*,[20] the Supreme Court of Norway

---

[18] ibid, 113.
[19] Such as in the US or the UK. See chapter 14, 'Overview of Statutory Tax Countermeasures Against the Offshore Trust'.
[20] (2003) 5 ITELR 77 (Sup Ct, Oslo).

considered the tax liability of a trust established in Liechtenstein for the benefit of a Norwegian family. The trustees were not resident in Norway. Focusing on the ownership of the assets in question, the court rejected the notion that the trust should be regarded as a Norwegian family foundation. While it conceded that both trusts and foundations contained a division of ownership rights, trusts could not be regarded as owning themselves. Rather, the legal ownership vested in the trustee. For example, the trust could not be party to a law suit. In contrast, the Norwegian family foundation is a self-owned estate, with an executive board which manages it and is responsible for its legal representation.

21.28   The important point in the case at bar was that, although the beneficiaries had not as yet benefited from the trust, because of their substantial influence over the trust, they, in reality, owned and controlled the trust and its assets. They were thus liable to tax under the relevant tax legislation,[21] which imputed tax liability where the taxpayer owned and controlled the property.

21.29   What the court did, therefore, was to recognize, indirectly, the concept of the trust in principle, but then move on to 'look through' or ignore the particular trust because of the 'sham like' features which it displayed. However, the court, rather adroitly, did not admit to the fundamental principles of the trust. Its indirect approach is thus unsatisfactory as, in the result, it did not explain how it could ignore trust principles that the beneficiaries did not own the trust property. This is particularly in view of the fact that no income had been distributed to them. Had the court found that tax was liable at the point at which the beneficiaries received income, there would have been no difficulty. It did not, for example, explain the circumstances in which a trust arrangement could be ignored. In accepting that, as persons who controlled and influenced the trust, the beneficiaries were to be regarded as the owners of the trust for tax purposes, the court, in effect, disregarded the dual structure of the trust and fundamental trust principles. Yet it did not purport to do so. Had the judgment concerned only beneficiaries who were also settlors, under trust law principles the trust could have been disregarded as a sham trust, or have been viewed as a bare trust. However, only one of the beneficiaries here was the settlor.

21.30   The result is a confusing judgment, in terms both of recognition and tax liability issues. Although not purporting to refuse to recognize trusts, in finding that a 'wider' concept of ownership applied in the instant case, the trust was effectively rejected. Indeed, a more satisfactory theoretical approach might have been to find the trust equivalent to a foundation. The unanswered question lingers: what was the entity? It remained 'neither fish nor fowl'.

---

[21] The Corporation Taxes Act 1992 of Norway, art 7.

The dissenting judgment of Justice Utgard took a more direct approach. **21.31**
He reasoned simply that, as the trust was a legal person without parallels in
Norwegian law, it was unnecessary to consider who owned the trust as the
Norwegian taxpayers, the beneficiaries, did not. He thus accepted absolutely
that the beneficiaries did not own the property. Ironically, it is in the dissenting
judgment that one finds the more positive approach to the recognition of the
trust. This minority judgment was also in accordance with trust law principles.[22]

F. The Trust as a Corporation—Rejecting Contractual Concepts

The treatment of the trust as a type of contract appears to be giving way to the **21.32**
recognition of the trust as a kind of corporation. This route to recognition offers
more useful solutions than does contract law, as it seems to allow greater
opportunity to import trust law principles.

In *Re WKR Trust OD Bank (in liquidation) v Estate of Rey (a Bankrupt)*,[23] the **21.33**
Zurich District Court, faced with a bankruptcy claim, had to assess the place of
the trust under Swiss law. The company in liquidation was held indirectly by a
Guernsey trust under a complex commercial arrangement involving several
companies. Here, the defendant argued that the trust was invalid and, therefore,
the bankrupt indirectly owned the claimant company.

The court found that the applicable law for assessing the validity of the trust **21.34**
was the Swiss Federal Code on Private International Law (CPIL). Under this
law, the trust fell under the conflict of laws rules for corporations.[24] Further,
under article 154 of the CPIL, as the trust was organized according to Guernsey
law under the trust deed, Guernsey law was the governing law. The eventual
result in the instant case was that under Guernsey law, the trust was to be viewed
as a sham.

However, in *G v C Trust Co*,[25] the court acknowledged that not all trusts could **21.35**
be viewed under the rules for corporations. There needed to be organized assets,
or an organized economic unit, as in the form of an express trust. Both the form
and purpose of the entity had to be considered. Here, the entity's purpose was
to administer and manage companies, and no questions regarding family law
or succession were raised. Accordingly, the trust was found to be analogous to a
holding company. As the offshore trust is typically an express trust, it easily
meets the criteria laid down in the instant case.

---

[22] See above, n 20, 116.
[23] (1999) 4 ITELR 487 (Zurich District Court).
[24] Article 150 CPIL.
[25] (2002) 4 ITELR 779 (First Civil Ct, Switzerland).

21.36   The distinction made about family law and succession issues raises the presumption that had the trust had different purposes, such as anti-forced heir-ship purposes, it might not have been considered suitable to fall under the private international rules for corporations. The court in *WKR* said:

> ... the WKR Trust is comparable to a holding company. This main feature justifies the application of the conflict of laws rule for corporations. The holding and administration of subsidiaries is mainly a corporate matter.[26]

21.37   What is significant, however, is that the use of the private international law rules for corporations does not prevent the application of trust law principles to determine the validity of the entity. Hence, the result is that trust law is recognized and given effect to, albeit through a longer, more circular process. The observation made by the court in *WKR* is instructive:

> To assess the validity of the WKR Trust ... one must determine whether the essential and constitutive provisions of the WKR Trust deed are consistent with the principles of trust law.[27]

21.38   The designation of the trust as a type of corporation is a significant and positive departure from the assignment of the trust as a form of contract in earlier civil law litigation. Before *WKR*, the leading decision from the Swiss courts on the recognition of trust was *Harrison v Credit Suisse Bank*,[28] in which a combination of civil law contracts was applied to the trust. This was, however, before the advent of the Swiss Federal Code on Private International Law 1989.

21.39   More important, the recognition of the trust under the laws relating to corporations allows the foreign law—the law designated as the proper law of the trust—to be applied. This is significant for offshore trusts, given the need to ensure that the more adaptable offshore laws are the laws that are applied in offshore trust matters. Where, as is typically the case, the proper law is the law of the offshore jurisdiction, it is that law which will be upheld.

G. Explicit Recognition as a Trust

21.40   The cases examined in this section demonstrate the positive impact of the Hague Convention on the Recognition of Trusts in civil law countries. As such, they provide guidelines for the acceptance of the offshore trust in such countries. In the first, *Casani v Mattei*,[29] the settlor, a person of dual nationality, that

---

[26] *WKR*, above, n 23, 511.
[27] ibid, 512.
[28] ATF 96 (1970) II, 79, Switzerland.
[29] Above, n 16.

is, American and Italian, established a trust under US law by instrument of will. The settlor died in Italy, and thereafter the trust was challenged by the settlor's daughter on the ground that it was void for being contrary to Italian public policy as it ignored the reserved shares under the Italian forced heirship regime.

The Italian court was not willing to grant a declaration that the trust was void. **21.41** Relying on Italy's ratification of the Hague Convention on the Recognition of Trusts, it recognized the trust, despite finding that the substantive law governing the succession was Italian law. The testamentary trust was found to be valid and recognizable in spite of its undermining of the rights of forced heirs. The forced heir remained free to contest his or her property rights in other proceedings, but the mere denial of forced heirship rights did not make the trust invalid. Further, the ratification of the Convention was interpreted to mean that the trust, although a 'peculiar institution' of the Common Law legal tradition, was not fundamentally incompatible with the civil law legal systems which adopted the Hague Convention on the Recognition of Trusts.[30]

The determining factor in finding that Italian law applied to the succession **21.42** aspect of the matter was that the settlor, an Italian citizen, had died in Italy. While the court considered the dual citizenship of the settlor, Italian rules of private international law emphasized the national law of the deceased, in this case, Italian law. The situation of the assets was irrelevant. It was further irrelevant that in other legal systems the *lex loci* principle applied.[31]

It is significant that the decision did not depend on foreign governing laws **21.43** under a conflict of laws approach and that it was Italian law which governed the disposition. The reasoning suggests that the trust concept is fully recognized under the Italian legal system.

Despite finding that the governing law of the succession was Italian law, the **21.44** validity of the trust was assessed in accordance with the law of the *lex loci*, that is, the state of Kentucky in the US. The court accepted that all of the necessary requirements for establishing the trust had been met by the settlor, and this provided sufficient evidence of the validity of the 'will-trust' for the Italian court. Thus, the applicable trust law principles of the *lex loci* were imported into Italy in the recognition process.

Similarly, in *G v C Trust Co*,[32] the trust was recognized as a corporation but the **21.45** Swiss court referred to the Hague Convention on the Recognition of Trusts, although not ratified in Switzerland, thus giving life to the Convention's aim of

---

[30] ibid, 946.
[31] ibid, 943.
[32] Above, n 25.

the recognition of trusts. The matter concerned the involvement of a trust in the contested repayment of loans, thus requiring the status of the trust to be assessed under Swiss law.[33]

21.46 The trust in question was established in St Helier in accordance with the law of Jersey. Under Swiss private international law rules (article 150 of the CPIL), to give effect to the recognition of the trust, the entity must be sufficiently limited, the 'constitutional deed' of the trust specifying who was to administer the property. The court found that express trusts, such as the one before the court, generally fulfilled these conditions.[34] The ratification of the Hague Convention on the Recognition of Trusts by Jersey affirmed this approach that, in accordance with Article 2 of the Convention, the assets 'within a trust constitute a separate and distinct fund held by the trustee who appears as the owner at civil law'.[35]

21.47 Under article 50 of the CPIL 'all organized associations of persons and all organized economic units shall be considered to be companies within the meaning of this Statute'. Article 154 of the CPIL read: '. . . the applicable law for companies is the law according to which the company is recognized'. The trust was thus to be governed by the law of Jersey under article 154 of the CPIL. Under current Swiss law, therefore, it was no longer 'necessary to resort to a contractual designation' of the trust. The trust was to be recognized as a type of company, and the trust law of Jersey, the proper law, was appropriately applied.

Date for recognition

21.48 In *Armenian Patriarch of Jerusalem v Sonsino*,[36] Article 22 of the Hague Convention on the Recognition of Trusts, which provides that the Convention applies to trusts regardless of the date on which they were created, was considered. The case concerned an interpretation of 'charitable objects' of a trust, and whether a trust established for 'advancement in life' was valid as having a charitable object. The court considered the effect of s 1(5) of the Recognition of Trusts Act 1987 of the UK on a settlement created before the Act came into force, but in a situation where the settlement came into *operation* only after the Act's entry into force. The said Act incorporated the Hague Convention on the Recognition of Trusts, and so the court was also determining the impact of the Convention upon the settlement. The court noted that the impact of these instruments was a 'moot point' since, whether the Act or the common law applied, the same result would have been obtained. Thus, the question was not

---

[33] The Swiss Federal Code on Private International Law 1989 (CPIL).
[34] *G v C Trust Co*, above, n 25, 782.
[35] ibid, 783. Note that not all trusts could be so treated.
[36] (2002) 5 ITELR 125.

necessary to decide in the instant case. The court's determination came as a result of its reading of the provisions of the Act, which state that Article 22 of the Convention shall not be construed as affecting the law to be applied in relation to anything done or omitted before the Act came into force.

H. Conclusion

In sum, there has been significant progress in relation to the recognition of offshore trusts in civil law countries. The trend toward recognition has been given impetus by the Hague Convention on the Recognition of Trusts, but exists independently from it, as trusts are recognized as valuable commercial and dispositive entities. This advances the validity of offshore trusts.   **21.49**

However, while the trust itself is today more accepted in civil law countries, where it fulfils certain purposes, it may run counter to important legal principles and policies in civil law jurisdictions. The most notable of these is the forced heirship policy or doctrine. Where a trust is rejected because it conflicts with forced heirship regimes, it is tempting to conclude that this is tantamount to a refusal to recognize the trust. However, we should maintain the distinction between refusing to recognize and accept the trust as a legal entity, and refusing to accept certain trusts which challenge fundamental precepts of onshore law.   **21.50**

The following chapter considers the question of the forced heirship doctrine and its impact on the sustainability of offshore trusts. There again, the developments in the law may be more positive to offshore trusts than might first be imagined.   **21.51**

22

RIGHTS TO SUCCESSION—FORCED HEIRS AND THE OFFSHORE TRUST

A. Introduction—Addressing Mandatory Succession

The offshore trust may be used to avoid onshore laws that grant mandatory **22.01** rights of succession to individuals. Both civil and common law traditions contain provisions which may create such obligations, usually in favour of the settlor's spouse or children. Mandatory succession may take the form of discretionary rights, or 'forced heirship' rights. The former arise, typically, in common law jurisdictions,[1] while the latter are, characteristically, fixed legal rights under civil law and Islamic legal systems. In addition, common law jurisdictions may also have legislative regimes which protect the property interests of divorced spouses and, as such, concern the present discussion.[2]

Offshore trusts have perhaps more typically been used to attempt to overcome **22.02** problems of mandatory rules of the *lex successiones* which involve forced heirship. Under the legal institution of forced heirship, certain members of an

---

[1] See, eg, the UK's Inheritance (Provision for Family and Dependants) Act 1975.
[2] See, eg, *Wagner v Wagner Estate* 85 DLR 4th 699; 1991 DLR LEXIS 455, on alimony.

individual's family, in particular his or her immediate family members, have an indefeasible right to sue for fixed minimum shares in his or her estate.[3]

22.03 At the heart of the problem of the use of offshore trusts to overcome forced heirship, are the opposing philosophies evident between common law regimes on the one hand, which recognize and promote the principle of the individual's disposition of property, and the civil law's acclamation, on the other hand, of mandatory responsibilities in relation to an individual's property with respect to his or her heirs. These two conflicting philosophies are not easily reconciled.

22.04 Further, as the trust is not a legal institution enshrined in civil law systems, the use of the trust to counteract forced heirship regimes is inherently problematic. In such jurisdictions, the theoretical distinction made by Common Law systems between the ownership of the assets by the settlor and the trustee, is not easily accommodated in the civil law regime of forced heirship. Issues are raised concerning the recognition of the trust as a legal entity, the capacity of a person from a civil law jurisdiction to create the trust, and questions of public policy. Trust property may be treated as available to forced heirs on the basis that the settlor owns it. Consequently, no attempt will be made to preserve the essence of the trust, that is, the concept of dual but separate ownership of assets. While this is changing, the extent to which the offshore trust will be recognized is unclear. There is particular uncertainty on the applicable rules of succession for *inter vivos* trusts.[4]

22.05 Mandatory succession laws can, therefore, undermine the survivability of the offshore trust. They may abrogate the freedom of dispositions and override attempts by a settlor to avoid the transfer of assets to his or her heirs or others deemed to be entitled to such assets. As more heirs are challenging offshore trusts, the subject is one of increasing importance.[5]

22.06 The offshore trust can succumb to mandatory rules of *lex successiones*, and in particular the forced heirship doctrine, in three main ways:

(1) where the trust is not a true or valid trust either in form or substance, or is a sham;

(2) where a conflict of laws approach renders the trust susceptible to the

---

[3] The deceased's estate is increased to include gifts made by him or her during his or her lifetime.

[4] L Collins (ed), *Dicey and Morris on The Conflict of Laws*, 13th edn (Sweet & Maxwell, London, 2000). Note that in *Casani v Mattei* (1998–99) 1 ITELR 925 (Tribunale of Lucca, Italy), the question of succession was governed by the onshore law, the civil law of Italy, but this did not affect the validity of the trust nor prevent the anti-forced heirship regime. See further discussion of the case, below, paras 22.29–22.31.

[5] For example, *Lemos v Coutts and Company* [1992–93] CILR 5, where there were corresponding proceedings in Greece which were eventually settled.

jurisdiction of mandatory rules of *lex successiones*, in particular if the capacity to create the trust is judged according to the onshore law. If civil law countries do not recognize the trust, individuals there may be treated as having no capacity to create it;[6] and

(3) in a situation where the offshore trust may be recognizable as an entity in itself, but may be treated as invalid because of the purpose which it serves.

Under the first category, the trust assets have not been properly transferred to another and the settlor is deemed to have de facto control of the assets. Similarly, where the trust violates certain fundamental rules of trust or is not a true trust, such property can still logically be viewed as the settlor's property. These problems of validity and legitimacy have been discussed earlier.[7]   **22.07**

A court, whether onshore or offshore, may also enforce forced heirship laws by regarding arrangements to undermine such laws as against public policy, or as a 'fraudulent' manipulation of conflict of laws rules. In addition, the heirs may claim that the settlor and trustee have conspired to damage their succession rights, a question unrelated to title to property and which may, therefore, be inapplicable to offshore provisions.   **22.08**

Unquestionably, the offshore trust is vulnerable to forced heirship claims. Further, the uncertainty of conflict of laws rules for the trust may increase the opportunities for success by forced heirs who challenge the trust. For the offshore trust to be immune to forced heirship or mandatory succession rules, it must be both a 'safe' trust and subject to a 'safe' jurisdiction, that is, one which is antagonistic to forced heirship laws. Its survivability remains uncertain,[8] although the few cases litigated thus far suggest that such a trust may survive.[9] Still, as a forced heir is entitled only to a fixed share, a civil law court need not destroy the trust. It may merely disturb the trust to the extent of using its assets to fulfil the share expected by the forced heir.[10]   **22.09**

---

[6] Proper law will not be an issue as the proper law of a trust would not be that of a civil law country. However, if the trust is deemed to be something else, such as a corporation, the question of the proper law is relevant. See, eg, *Re Isle of Man Trust* (1998–99) 1 ITELR 103 (Tax Panel, Sweden).

[7] See, eg, chapter 8, 'The Offshore Trust as a Sham'.

[8] A Overbeck, 'The Law Applicable to and Recognition of Trusts in Switzerland: The Possible Future under the Hague Convention' [1996] *Trusts and Trustees* 6, 9, argues against its survivability.

[9] See below, paras 22.16–22.27 and 22.29–22.31, and the earlier discussion in chapter 21.

[10] An heir may not wish to destroy the trust but may, eg, want his or her fixed entitlement instead of trust benefits. See *Lemos v Coutts and Company* [1992–93] CILR 5, where the heirs were also beneficiaries. This may also be the suggestion of *Casani v Mattei*, above, n 4, discussed further at paras 22.29–22.31.

B. Anti-forced Heirship Provisions to Resolve Conflicts

22.10   Not surprisingly, offshore jurisdictions are unwilling to allow onshore legal rules to undermine the viability of trusts set up in their jurisdictions. They have thus created legislation designed to attack mandatory succession rules, in particular the doctrine of forced heirship. These provisions are intended to apply to *inter vivos* trusts.[11]

22.11   Offshore legislatures address potential forced heirship difficulties from several angles. First, statutory provisions against forced heirship may be tied to other provisions purporting to grant capacity to create a trust to a settlor who is presumed not to have such capacity under civil law.[12] These may exist alongside supportive provisions on jurisdiction and the proper law.[13] Thus, the provisions against forced heirship are dependent on the trust being governed by the law of the offshore trusts and on offshore courts assuming jurisdiction over trust matters. The offshore trust is deemed to be valid despite the existence of forced heirship regimes in the settlor's jurisdiction. Legislative efforts offshore also include more aggressive attempts to oust the recognition of forced heirship and mandatory succession regimes altogether by specifically excluding their application. Provisions which provide that foreign judgments that enable forced heirs to defeat the trust and reach the assets will not be recognized, complete the protective regime against mandatory succession and forced heirship regimes. Legislation may be particularly sweeping in breadth and include all such provisions.[14]

22.12   An example of an encompassing statutory provision is found in the Cayman Islands.[15] Here, there is a choice of governing law for the trust. Offshore law applies to the foreign trust, thus bringing it under a jurisdiction which will not recognize any foreign laws on forced heirship or mandatory succession rights and out of a jurisdiction which may not recognize the trust.[16] The settlor is also deemed to have the necessary capacity to create the trust. Lastly, foreign

---

[11]   See, eg, s 90 of the Trusts Law (2001 Revision) of the Cayman Islands.

[12]   See chapter 23, 'Capacity to Create the Offshore Trust and Initial Transfers of Assets'.

[13]   See chapters 19 and 20, 'Jurisdiction Over the Offshore Trust' and 'The Proper Law of the Offshore Trust', respectively.

[14]   Offshore provisions on capacity, proper law, the non-enforcement of judgments, jurisdiction, and the conflict of laws problems which may arise, are discussed separately in this book in chapters 23, 20, 24, and 19 respectively.

[15]   Sections 5 and 6 of the Trust Law (2001 Revision) of the Cayman Islands.

[16]   This is part of a general provision which proclaims the validity of the offshore trust and excludes foreign laws which may affect its validity and deny the settlor the capacity to create the trust. See s 91 of the Trusts Law (2001 Revision) of the Cayman Islands, outlined in the following paragraph.

judgments inconsistent with these provisions will not be recognized. A trust which seeks to avoid forced heirship or mandatory succession foreign laws is expressly declared to be valid. For example, one of the provisions reads:

> . . . it is expressly declared that no trust governed by the laws of the Islands and no disposition of property to he held upon the trusts thereof is void, voidable, liable to be set aside or defective in any fashion, nor is the capacity of any settlor to be questioned, nor is the trustee, any beneficiary or any other person to be subjected to any liability or deprived of any right, by reason that—
>
> (a) the laws of any foreign jurisdiction prohibit or do not recognise the concept of a trust; or
> (b) the trust or disposition avoids or defeats rights, claims or interests conferred by foreign law upon any person by reason of a personal relationship to the settlor or by way of heirship rights, or contravenes any rule of foreign law or any foreign judicial or administrative order or action intended to recognise, protect, enforce or give effect to such rights, claims or interests.[17]

Such a provision may be underscored by other provisions on heirship.[18]

Initially, offshore provisions on forced heirship appear to resolve the conflict **22.13** arising between the rights of persons domiciled or resident in a forced heirship jurisdiction, and the rights and obligations of trustees and beneficiaries. Irrespective of timing, the provisions purport to validate a trust, or any transfer into trust, although the settlor's estate is subject to forced heirship and the trust is not recognized. However, such provisions have not prevented, and cannot prevent, forced heirs from challenging the creation of, or transfer of property

---

[17] The Trusts Law (2001 Revision), s 91, of the Cayman Islands. See also s 20 of the International Trusts Act 1996 of Grenada; s 28 of the International Exempt Trust Act 1997 of Dominica; s 4 of the Nevis International Exempt Trusts Ordinance 1994; s 48 of the International Exempt Trust Ordinance 1994 of Nevis; s 8 of the Trusts (Choice of Governing Law) Act 1989, as amended 1996, of The Bahamas; s 13E of the International Trusts Act 1984 of the Cook Islands; and s 83A (13)of the Trustee (Amendment) Act 2003 of the BVI. The provisions are also identical in Saint Vincent, under s 33 of the International Trust Act 1996, except that there is an additional paragraph, which underscores the ability of the offshore trust to defeat property rights which may accrue onshore. Paragraph (c) speaks of the situations where: 'the international trust creates rights in property that are contrary to other laws relating to the personal or proprietary effects of marriage or the succession rights testate and intestate, of any person, especially the legal right of surviving spouses and the shares of relatives'. See also s 34 of the International Trusts Act 2002 of Saint Lucia; art 8A(1)(b) of the Trusts (Jersey)Law 1984; and s 11A of the Trusts (Guernsey) Law 1989. The provisions in Barbados are differently worded. A trust validly created under Barbados law cannot be varied or set aside pursuant to foreign laws in respect of marriage and succession rights under s 18 of the International Trusts Act 1995. See also s 7(6) of the Belize Trusts Act 1992 (rev'd 2000) and s 11 of the Trusts (Special Provisions) Act 1989 of Bermuda, which are similar to the Barbados provision.

[18] For example, in Dominica, there is an additional provision, s 47, which states: 'An international trust . . . and any disposition of property to be held upon the trusts hereof shall not be declared void, voidable or defective in any manner nor is the capacity of any settlor to be questioned by reason that the trust may avoid or defeat the right, claim or interest of a person held by reason of a personal relationship to the settlor or by way of heirship rights.'

into, an offshore trust. Emerging litigation has yet to give definite answers on the questions associated with such provisions and similar provisions. Thus far, however, the signs from the case law are encouraging. Given the increasing acceptance of trusts in civil law jurisdictions, there is also a view that, in many instances, heirs in such jurisdictions will be prepared to accept the benefits offered to them, and to future generations, under trusts. Consequently, they will be reluctant to challenge such trusts.[19]

Implication of conflict of laws rules on forced heirship—common law presumptions against forced heirship

22.14   As with other aspects of the trust, limited authority exists on conflict of laws rules for forced heirship situations. To govern forced heirship situations, a choice in favour of the proper law of the trust, its *situs*, or place of administration seems suitable. This is compatible with the modern approach. As anti-forced heirship provisions are not exclusive to offshore states, it is useful to examine the survivability of these provisions in onshore jurisdictions. Of particular value are judgments from the US, Canada, and Scotland, since forced heirship rules prevail in certain states in the US, such as Louisiana, and in countries which have hybrid legal systems, that is, a mixture of common law and civil law. These include Canada and Scotland.

22.15   In the main, these decisions treat anti-forced heirship arrangements as legitimate and appropriate mechanisms for facilitating a person's right to dispose of his or her property as he or she wishes. This right is considered to be an important, and even fundamental, policy objective by common law states.

C. US Decisions on Forced Heirship Policies

22.16   In the case of *In the Matter of the Estate of Renard*,[20] a US court rejected choice of law rules which emphasized the domicile of the settlor to address the forced heirship question. This was a claim by the spouse of a settlor, in which the settlor's choice of New York law as the proper law was upheld against the settlor's son's forced heirship rights under the law of France. The decision came despite the fact that the settlor was domiciled in France. The Court of Appeal affirmed the lower court's judgment. The latter court's words are instructive. It said:

---

[19] See J Ingham, 'Recognising the Italian Trust' *Offshore Investment*, June 2002, 13, speaking in the context of trusts established by Italian settlors, which thwart rigid forced heirship regimes.
[20] (1982) 56 NY 2d 973, 439 NE 2d 341, 453 NYS 2d 625.

[T]he Court of Appeal has moved away from mechanical choice of law rules to a balancing approach which requires the identification of the underlying policies in the conflicting laws of the relevant jurisdictions, and the examination of the contacts of those jurisdictions to see which has a superior connection with the occurrence and thus a superior interest in having its policy followed.[21]

Conflicting policies were New York's interest in the freedom of testamentary   **22.17**
disposition and France's policy of narrowly circumscribing testatamentary freedom in favour of descendants. There was no discussion about the possibility that the settlor, who was domiciled in a civil law country, would have lacked the capacity to establish a trust merely because of that domicile. Rather, the question was whether the trust, although validly established in the first instance, should be allowed to stand.

Situation of the assets

A distinguishing feature of the New York statute discussed in *Renard*, is that it   **22.18**
refers specifically to assets physically 'situated' in the US state. In offshore jurisdictions, assets may not be within the offshore state at the time of the initial transfer and the law may not make such specific reference. This might lead to problems in interpretation. A response might be that offshore law does not require assets to be located offshore for offshore law to govern the transaction. Instead, it makes the governing law on capacity dependent on the proper law of the established trust itself, inevitably the offshore law.[22] Thus, offshore legislation aims to be broader than comparable statutes in the US.

Offshore countries, in their continuing quest for foolproof legislation, attempt   **22.19**
to address such potential vagaries in interpretation. One example is that of The Bahamas. The legislation emphasizes that forced heirship rights cannot be recognized as affecting Bahamian trust property 'wherever situate[d]'. The proper law for determining both the validity of the trust and the capacity of the settlor is that of The Bahamas.[23]

The important features of offshore legislation are the priority given to the *choice*   **22.20**
of a settlor and the freedom to dispose of his or her property. These are also viewed as important legal principles under onshore regimes. It may not then matter whether a statute refers specifically to the location of the assets. This underlying public policy is brought out in the lower court's judgment in *Renard,*

---

[21] (1981) 108 Misc 2d 31; 437 NY 2d 860, 866, affirming the decision of *Re Crichton*, (1979) 20 NY 2d 124, and interpreting the Estates Powers and Trusts Law of New York, §3(5).
[22] This is an accepted approach. See the discussion of capacity in chapter 23. See also *Chevron International Oil Co Ltd v AS Sea Tram* [1983] 2 Lloyd's Rep 356.
[23] Under s 9 of the Trusts (Choice of Governing Law) Act 1989 (am'd 1996) of The Bahamas. See also s 92 of the Trusts Law (2001 Revision) of the Cayman Islands.

which the Court of Appeal affirmed. The court referred to the legislative history and purpose of the New York statute, which allowed 'a non-resident testator to escape onerous restrictions on the testamentary laws of his own *domicile*', citing a case involving forced heirship.[24]

22.21   The US courts in *Nahar v Nahar*[25] again considered defensive legislation against forced heirship. In *Nahar*, the settlor was a national of Surinam (a civil law jurisdiction), who established a trust for his wife and minor children. Upon his death, his adult children successfully challenged the trust in Surinam. They then petitioned the Florida courts for ancillary administration of the trust in Florida, seeking to have the trust assets transferred to Surinam for distribution. The courts found that the trust was governed by Florida law, the *situs* of the trust.[26] The Florida statute, similar in intent to typical offshore provisions, could defeat the forced heirship claim although the settlor had been domiciled in Surinam.[27]

22.22   Similarly, in *Sanchez v Sanchez De Davila*,[28] the court decided in favour of the validity of the trust on the basis of its *situs*. Interestingly, at first instance, the court found that the forced heirship regime stood, since the decedent lacked the capacity to create a trust under Venezuelan law: 'By some magic, . . . the children . . . seemed to think that the passage of money from Venezuela to an American bank would cleanse the money of any right . . . under Venezuelan law.'[29] The law in Florida was then changed to grant such capacity and the trust was allowed to survive. The inclusion of capacity provisions in offshore trust legislation would, therefore, point to the survival of such trusts.[30]

D. Other Common Law Decisions on Forced Heirship

22.23   There is a suggestion that UK courts and other common law courts will follow their US counterparts in upholding trusts in the face of mandatory succession regimes. In *Schindler v Garner and Bermuda Trust Co*,[31] the nephew of a settlor who created a trust in Mexico in 1979 in favour of the respondent, challenged the trust on the ground that it was created solely to avoid Mexican inheritance legislation and should not be given effect by the Bermudan courts. The nephew

---

[24]   Above, n 21, 863. See n 20, above, for the Court of Appeal judgment.
[25]   (1995) 656 So 2d 225; 1995 Fla App LEXIS 6086; 20 Fla Law W 1356 respectively.
[26]   It was a 'Totten trust', a type of trust established with banks.
[27]   655.55(1) Florida Statutes, (1991).
[28]   547 So 2d 943 (Fla. 3d DCA), rev denied 554 SO 2d 1168 (Fla 1989).
[29]   ibid, 944.
[30]   See chapter 23.
[31]   (CA, Bermuda) No 4 of 1992, decided 10 July 1992.

was the forced heir in Mexico, and it was clear that the settlor's intention was to disinherit him.

The matter centred around the question whether the Trusts (Special Provisions) **22.24**
Act 1989 of Bermuda, which contained provisions precluding the operation of mandatory succession law, governed the trust. The trust was expressed to be governed by the law of Bermuda, but the matter was more complicated as the Act in question came into force in 1990, after the creation of the trust. The appellant argued that the Act could not be applied retrospectively. However, the Court agreed with the lower court's finding that the provisions of the Act were merely declaratory of existing law in Bermuda. The Court found no evidence that either in Bermuda or in England, under existing law—that is, the common law—had a court ever set aside a trust in such circumstances, simply because it sought to invalidate forced heirship laws. The Court was not persuaded that it had power so to do. Accordingly, it appears that common law courts do not set aside trusts merely because they preclude forced heirs. Intriguingly, a similar finding was made by an Italian court in *Casani v Mattei*.[32]

In relying on the inherent presumptions under the common law, the *Garner* **22.25**
Court was able to sidestep the lower court's preoccupation with interpreting the Act in accordance with its parent Act, the Recognition of Trusts Act 1987 of the UK (the instrument which incorporated the provisions of the Hague Convention on the Recognition of Trusts). Despite the lower court's reliance on the legislative history of the Act,[33] the Court found that the governing law of the trust was Bermuda law, which was also the common law. More important was the fact that the common law was identical in this respect to the Act's provisions.

Interestingly, both the Court and the appellant appeared to accept that, pro- **22.26**
vided the Act applied, it would effectively prevent the forced heir from claiming the assets. Thus, once the contentious issue of retroactivity was resolved, the issue of the survivability of trusts in such circumstances rested, without need for further explanation.[34]

---

[32] Discussed below, paras 22.29–22.31. See also, further discussion of this case at paras 21.20 and 21.40–21.45.

[33] See the decision of the lower court: (Sup Ct, Bermuda) No 318 of 1991, decided 2 March 1992, *per* Sir James Astwood CJ. Noted in [1992] 1 JIntP 51.

[34] Nonetheless, the court placed great store on the purpose of the Act, which was to effect the recognition of trusts in such circumstances.

E. Hague Convention and Forced Heirship

22.27   The Hague Convention on the Recognition of Trusts addresses the forced heir-ship issue under Article 15, which allows mandatory forced heirship rules to be applied under conflict of laws rules. Nevertheless, as the Convention does not resolve the question about which law governs the capacity to create the trust, the effect of the provision is uncertain.[35] If the matter could be determined by the *lex successiones* of the forced heirship jurisdiction, Article 15 would apply favour-ably to the claim made by heirs. This could occur, for example, if the trust money was invested in the forced heirship jurisdiction, or a beneficiary held it there and the claim was brought in that jurisdiction. Hayton suggests that the provision on forced heirship should not affect a safe trust where such a trust relies on the fact that the *lex situs* is grounded in the jurisdiction of the trust.[36] Since the Hague Convention governs the law applicable to the *lex situs*, the trust assets could not be challenged under this route.

22.28   This may not be the only route to safety of the trust. The choice of the offshore law as the proper law may enhance the trust's survival, particularly if the onshore civil law state recognizes trusts in general.

22.29   The Italian case of *Casani v Mattei*,[37] helpfully interprets forced heirship provi-sions in the light of the Hague Convention on the Recognition of Trusts and supports this view. The deceased settlor was born and died in Italy, but had both Italian and American nationality. By his will, he established a trust with the defendant as trustee, for the benefit of his daughter, the plaintiff, and her children. The trust was notarized by a notary public in Kentucky, USA.

22.30   The plaintiff sought a declaration that the will was void as contrary to public policy and because it violated the reserved shares under the forced heirship regime in Italy. She therefore wished to be recognized as the universal heir. Relying on the Hague Convention on the Recognition of Trusts,[38] the court recognized the trust, notwithstanding that it undermined the forced heirship rights of the plaintiff. The court further accepted that the trust was governed by US law, the law with the closest connection to the trust deed. Under that law, the settlor had fulfilled the necessary requirements to establish a trust. The plaintiff correctly emphasized that Article 15 of the Convention did not prevent the application of domestic law rules on mandatory succession. However, her

---

[35] See the discussion in chapter 23.
[36] D Hayton, 'Trusts and Forced Heirship Problems' [1994] 2 JIntP 7.
[37] Above, n 4.
[38] Incorporated into Italian law by Law No 364 of 16 October 1989.

argument that this Article prevented the ouster of mandatory succession laws was rejected, and Article 15 was construed in favour of the settlor. The court, although viewing the Article 15 provision as imprecise, found that it did permit the application of forced heirship laws. However, in such cases, 'the trust does not determine the will', nor does it mean that the trust is automatically void.[39] Nonetheless, the existence of the trust did not prevent the possibility of applying the provisions of domestic law in order to restore the reserved share to the forced heirs. This was the logical implication of Article 15, where it read:

> If recognition of the trust is prevented by application of the previous paragraph, the court shall try to give effect to the objects of the trust by other means.[40]

Thus, a will is not to be voided merely because of the existence of the trust. In other words, the fact that a trust undermines forced heirship rights is not, of itself, sufficient to void the trust, or prelude its recognition. The Hague Convention on the Recognition of Trusts gives validity to the institution of the trust in Italy.   **22.31**

F. Public Policy and Forced Heirship

Civil law legal systems are in natural opposition to the unique common law creature that is the offshore trust. The difference is magnified where the trust challenges directly a characteristic feature of the civil law legal tradition, the forced heirship doctrine. This is not a confrontation limited to aggressive offshore centres and trusts. Rather, it is but another example of fundamentally opposed legal regimes on the question of the ownership, arrangement, and succession of property.   **22.32**

Yet while, in the past, civil law systems have not understood the common law trust, they have not necessarily been hostile to it and have sought to accommodate it. However, the use of the trust to thwart forced heirship introduces more direct and difficult questions of public policy.[41]   **22.33**

The common law's recognition of a person's freedom to dispose of his or her property is opposed in principle to the forced heirship doctrine. Further, the presumption that anti-forced heirship provisions seek only to exclude the needy and deserving is often incorrect. Sometimes, a person wishing to set up a trust to   **22.34**

---

[39] See above, n 4, 947.

[40] ibid.

[41] A unique opportunity to assess these conflicts in an internal environment exists in St Lucia, a hybrid legal system in the Caribbean, which has an offshore legal regime. It is a mixture of the common law and civil legal traditions. See KD Anthony, 'The Viability of the Civilist Legal Tradition in Saint Lucia', in R Landry and E Caparros (eds), *Essays on the Civil Codes of Quebec and St Lucia* (Ottawa University Press, Ottawa, 1984).

prevent forced heirs is acting in the best interest of the family fortune itself. This is the case, for example, where the expectant heir is a spendthrift or wastrel.[42]

22.35 As public policy is a relevant factor under conflict of law rules for trusts, one recognized even by the Hague Convention, it is expected that this may be a significant element in the challenge by civil law regimes to offshore laws against forced heirship. Article 18 of the Hague Convention allows for public policy to preclude the recognition of the trust. The accumulated effect of Articles 13, 16, and 18 of the Hague Convention makes a potential attack on the fundamental activities of the trust even more potent. Yet such an attack seems in conflict with the very purpose of the Convention.[43] To date, however, the case which has directly addressed this question, *Casani v Mattei*, considered above,[44] has not accepted that public policy is an appropriate ground for challenging such trusts, at least where the civil law state is under an obligation to recognize trusts.

Extraterritoriality, public policy, and comity

22.36 One might also question whether anti-forced heirship provisions can have extraterritorial effect. The mere enactment of legislative provisions purporting to undermine the forced heirship doctrine in a particular country may not be able to oust the relevant jurisdiction in another. Certainly, they do not prevent forced heirs from pursuing remedies in their non-domiciliary, national, or residential jurisdictions. There is a danger, therefore, that such provisions may generally be able to protect offshore trustees from action by forced heirs only in the offshore jurisdiction. Ultimately, litigation may be resolved according to the enforcement of foreign judgment rules, discussed below.[45] An offshore court may, however, decide to enforce such a judgment on the grounds of comity.

22.37 Nonetheless, the powerful dissenting judgement in *Nahar v Nahar* found that comity principles were totally inapplicable and 'expressly forbidden' in determining the applicable conflict of laws rule governing trusts. This was purely a choice of law question and not one for comity which would require the

---

[42] Duckworth notes that: 'The two major legal systems of the developed world are in collision, and the offshore trust community finds itself at the point of impact.' A Duckworth, 'An Offshore View of Forced Heirship—Global Conflict and Its Planning Implications' [1995] PCB 270, 272. He believes that forced heirship laws pose a threat to all trusts, onshore as well as offshore.

[43] J Schoenblum, 'The Hague Convention on Trusts: Much Ado About Very Little' [1994] 3 JIntP 5, 17, 18. Those committed to the free flow of wealth ought to oppose the Convention as it is 'an anachronism which fails to address the needs of the vibrant, explosive market of international trusts'. In future, the 1980 Hague Convention on Succession to Deceased Persons' Estates may alleviate some conflicts, thereby protecting trust assets from forced heirs, as it allows testators to expressly choose the *lex successiones* for their estate. See also the discussions in paras 20.60, 21.19, and 21.20.

[44] See above, n 4.

[45] Chapter 24.

balancing of conflicting interests.[46] Jorgenson J linked the issue to public policy, using that concept to enhance, rather than undermine, the survivability of the trust. He held that individuals who established trusts

> in Florida should enjoy the certainty that the disposition of their funds . . . will be governed by the laws of Florida, and not by the vagaries of a distant tribunal. Even under Florida's comity doctrine foreign decrees must bow to this state's legislation and judicial pronouncements of public policy relating to the establishment of survivorship rights.[47]

In *De Wethein v Gothib*,[48] the respect that is given to another country's laws **22.38** under the doctrine of comity was again sidelined. Although the settlor could not derive the benefits of a trust under the laws of his home country, it was held that he had the right, on grounds of public policy, to obtain such benefits. The court thus upheld the *situs* of the trust over the domicile of the settlor. The argument is no less attractive if used by offshore courts.

G. Consideration of Trust Interests in Maintenance and Spousal Awards

Onshore laws on the maintenance of spouses and children will often allow **22.39** consideration of a defendant's interests in trusts, whether domestic or offshore trusts. Where there is evidence that the person from whom maintenance and support is claimed enjoys, or can enjoy, benefits from trusts, such benefits may be taken into account in making maintenance awards. In the case of an offshore trust where the settlor or other person is viewed as having influence and control over the trust, this will increase the chances of the trust being successfully challenged.

An example of this is seen in *Alvares-Correa v Alvares-Correa*.[49] Here, the appel- **22.40** lant, the wife of the defendant, sued for child support and maintenance for herself from the defendant in a divorce action. The husband was found to have substantial interests in four trust funds established in the BVI by the defendant's grandmother. The trust assets were worth more than US $37 million, and the defendant was a vested beneficiary of the trusts and had the sole power of appointment for three of the trusts. More important, the court found that the defendant and his brothers had control and management of the trusts and unfettered access to the trust funds. In such circumstances, it was well established

---

[46] See above, n 25, 231. See also *Renard*, above, n 20.
[47] *Nahar*, above, n 25, 239.
[48] 594 N Y S 2d 230 9AD 1 Dept (1993).
[49] 285 AD 2d 123; 727 NYS 2d 668 (2001) Sup Ct, NY.

that the defendant's interests in the trusts could be taken into account when making maintenance and child support awards.[50]

22.41 Similarly, the Royal Court of Jersey, in *Compass v McBurnett*,[51] found that a discretionary Jersey trust was capable of being varied for the benefit of the parties and children.[52]

H. Forced Heirship Provisions do not Override Trustees' Discretion

22.42 The line of cases in which excluded heirs attempt to invalidate offshore trusts should be distinguished from instances where trustees are called upon to exercise their discretion to benefit such heirs indirectly. The best case scenario would be where a beneficiary requests the trustees to make a distribution to enable him to fulfil obligations to a spouse or child under, for example, legislation securing rights to matrimonial property. Such cases may not be hostile trust litigation as was the case in *Compass*.[53]

22.43 It is suggested that the forced heirship provisions do not extinguish a trustee's discretion to make a distribution as he or she sees fit. Rather, the provisions contemplate only the situation where there is hostile litigation which seeks to invalidate the trust in order to secure forced third party rights under foreign law. Accordingly, trustees may exercise their discretion in favour of beneficiaries where a consensual approach is evident. The trustee may decide to do so for a number of reasons, including the need to comply with moral obligations of a beneficiary, or in instances where the beneficiaries consent, as was seen in *Re Esteem Settlement*.[54]

22.44 A similar situation to that in *Re Esteem Settlement* arose in *In re X Trust*,[55] albeit in a domestic context and not in relation to an offshore trust. The husband, a beneficiary of a Jersey trust, had been ordered to pay a substantial sum to his wife to satisfy a matrimonial claim. He was unable to do so out of his personal funds, and therefore applied to the trustee for a distribution from the trust to make the payment. The trustee sought permission from the court for the distribution to be made. Since the benefit would go to the beneficiary's wife,

---

[50] Relying on *Rothberg v Rothberg* 174 AD 2d 359.
[51] [2002] JLR 321 (Royal Ct, Jersey), *per* Le Cras, Commr.
[52] Following the dicta in *Brooks v Brooks* [1995] 2 FLR 13.
[53] Above, n 51.
[54] [2001] JLR 7.
[55] [2002] JLR 377.

who herself was not a beneficiary, the Royal Court considered whether the distribution would constitute a fraud on a power.

The court approved the distribution, finding that it would be in the interests of **22.45** the beneficiary, albeit a non-pecuniary interest. It would be in the beneficiary's interest to put an end to the bitterly contested litigation with his wife about money. Likewise, the court considered that it would also be in the interest of the beneficiary's children to have such adversarial litigation ended and further litigation avoided. Consequently, this would also be in his interest. Further, the distribution would be proper as it complied with a moral obligation of a beneficiary. Where he consented, this also constituted a benefit and was in his interest.[56]

In an offshore trust where the beneficiary's obligations originate in a foreign **22.46** judgment, the power to distribute, as applied in *Re X*, should apply no less equally. Certain key points should be emphasized with respect to the effect of the forced heirship provisions, including the non-enforcement of foreign judgments. First, as described in *Re X*,[57] the decision to distribute is to be made in the interest of the beneficiaries, not with a view to satisfying a foreign judgment. Secondly, the trust will remain valid, as offshore provisions on anti-forced heirship envisage. Lastly, the distribution is consensual, further underscoring the beneficiaries' interests in the trustee's action.

It is suggested, however, that while the provisions of the trust deed may allow **22.47** partial distributions from the trust in such circumstances, they may not allow all of the trust's assets to be utilized for such a purpose. To do otherwise would be to cause the termination of the trust, which would, it is suggested, violate the presumption of validity of anti-forced heirship legislation.

I. Validity of Hostile Beneficiaries Clauses

A settlor may institute a clause in a trust deed which seeks to preclude entirely **22.48** beneficiaries who contest the settlement. Such clauses are called 'hostile beneficiaries clauses', and are often inserted where a settlor ignores a forced share of an heir or a spouse and makes some other arrangement under the trust.

The validity of such clauses was recently upheld by the UK courts in the case of **22.49** *Nathan v Leonard*.[58] The testator executed a will which included gifts to her family, as well as to friends and charity. She inserted a hostile beneficiary clause

---

[56] On this last point, the court affirmed the judgment of *In re Esteem Settlement*, above, n 54.
[57] See above, n 55.
[58] [2003] 4 All ER 198; [2003] 1 WLR 827 (Ch D).

to the effect that if any of the family members challenged the will, the entire estate would pass to the friends, thereby excluding the family entirely. The settlor's son sued under the provisions of the Inheritance (Provision for Family and Dependants) Act 1975 of the UK.

22.50   On the question of the validity of the hostile beneficiary clause, the court found that such clauses were valid on the basis that, under English law, a testator could dispose of his or her estate as he or she wished. Further, such clauses were not void on public policy grounds as they did not preclude beneficiaries from bringing actions for relief under the Inheritance (Provision for Family and Dependants) Act 1975. Both rationales given by the court support the findings and presumptions made in relation to more general anti-forced heirship laws.

22.51   In the particular case, the clause was held to be void for uncertainty. Nonetheless, the court stated, *per curiam*, that had this not been the case, it would have had jurisdiction to relieve any beneficiaries who had forfeited their interests as a result of a challenge. Such jurisdiction would be exercised, however, only where it did not do serious damage to the settlor's intentions. In the instant case, no such relief would have been available.

J. Forced Heirship and Disclosure

22.52   It appears that offshore courts will not otherwise facilitate parties challenging the trust, even in procedural matters, such as requests for disclosure of information on the trust. Forced heirs are inevitably engaged in such hostile actions.[59]

K. Conclusion

22.53   Despite the attempts by offshore jurisdictions to give immunity from the applicability of forced heirship provisions, the matter remains a contentious one with continuing potential for litigation. Yet the emerging principle on anti-forced heirship laws, such as those found in offshore jurisdictions, is that they may be sustained against mandatary succession regimes and policies. The conflict of laws approach is to treat the proper law of the trust as the grounding principle for assessing such laws, at minimum, where the proper law is one that recognizes trusts.

---

[59] See, eg, *In re CA Settlement* [2002] JLR 312 and *In Re Lemos Trust Settlement* [1992–93] CILR 26.

23

CAPACITY TO CREATE THE OFFSHORE TRUST AND INITIAL TRANSFERS OF ASSETS

A. Introduction—The Importance of Preliminary Questions

With *inter vivos* trusts, there is a distinction to be made between the validity of   **23.01**
the instrument, or the process creating the trust, and the validity of the trusts
thereby created. The first concern preliminary questions relating to the transfer
or conveyance of property, or whether there is capacity to create the trust.
These are not questions about the validity of the trust itself. For example, the
trust may violate mandatory succession rules, and the alienation of the property
may be questioned on this basis. These are questions which are entirely
divorced from the question whether a person can validly transfer property into
a trust.[1]

These preliminary questions are, therefore, discussed separately in this chapter,   **23.02**
as they conjure up different problems for the viability of the trust. The
appropriate conflict of law rules governing such preliminary issues must be
identified. However, the legal rules on these issues are, in some cases, uncertain,
particularly in relation to the transfer of movables. The uncertainty prevailing

---

[1] The analogy of a rocket, as distinct from the rocket-launching process, has been used to describe this distinction by Alfred E von Overbeck, in his 'Explanatory Report on the Hague Convention on the Law Applicable to Trusts and on their Recognition' (The Hague, 1 July 1985; UKTS 14 (1992); CM 1823; 23 ILM 1388).

over preliminary questions may compromise the validity of the offshore trust and its attempts to protect against onshore laws.

23.03   In addition, different preliminary questions may require separate conflict of laws approaches. Consequently, the discussion in this chapter is divided into:

(1)   the validity of the actual transfer of the assets; and

(2)   the capacity to create the trust.

It should be noted that the second question on capacity is appropriately a question of trust law, while the first goes beyond matters of trust and will apply to any transfer of property.

23.04   In the context of offshore trusts, these preliminary issues, and in particular the question of capacity, arise most frequently in the context of potential settlors from civil law jurisdictions where the law of trusts is not part of the legal system. As such, it is suggested that these issues are intimately linked with the question of the recognition of trusts in civil law jurisdictions.[2]

B. Offshore Aims in Relation to Preliminary Issues

23.05   It is important to have satisfactory resolutions of these preliminary questions to ensure the validity of the trust. Thus, offshore legislation seeks to create solutions to the problems raised. As the focus of the problems on these preliminary issues is on persons from civil law jurisdictions desirous of establishing trusts, they are the prime targets of the legislation. In general, offshore jurisdictions attempt to engage the would-be settlor at the initial stages of trust planning. They aim to prevent potential problems, such as a perceived lack of capacity to create a trust and problems relating to the actual transfer of the assets into the trust. While there are doubts as to whether any jurisdiction may unilaterally prescribe conflict of laws rules which will be adhered to, it will be seen that these offshore provisions do not contradict what may be described as appropriate conflict of laws rules for these preliminary questions, as discussed below. For instance, the offshore conflict of laws provisions do not presume to oust the application of the law of the settlor's domicile relating to questions on the general disposition of property, only the actual disposition of property into a trust.[3] As noted earlier, these are provisions which are primarily concerned with recognition and anti-forced heirship issues.

23.06   Given that the aim of these statutory provisions is to correct perceived deficiencies

---

[2] See chapter 21.
[3] See paras 23.35–23.38.

and gaps in conflict of laws issues, it is also important to discuss what the appropriate conflict of laws rules are in fora outside of such legislation. This will enable us more accurately to assess these statutory provisions. The relevant statutory provisions relating to the transfer of assets and the capacity to create a trust, are discussed in greater depth below.[4]

C. Validity of the Transfer—Alienation of the Property

Before we can assess whether the settlor had the capacity to create the trust, it is necessary to determine whether the settlor had authority to alienate the property that he or she wished to transfer into the trust in the first instance. This is not, in reality, a question of trust law. A person may have the capacity to create a trust and still go wrong on the transfer question. For example, he or she may attempt to transfer property which legally does not belong to him or her. Any such transfer will render the transfer and the trust invalid. Yet were he or she to own the property lawfully, there would be no doubt that he or she would have the capacity to create the trust in question. Since preliminary matters such as the title of the property may need to be determined before the transfer, and these are issues not of trust law, but of property and other law, the question of the law which governs this matter should be left to the *lex situs*. This is, in fact, the approach embodied in several legislative provisions.[5]

23.07

Alienation of property not invalidated because of existence of a trust

In assessing the validity of the transfer of the assets where potential settlors from civil law jurisdictions are involved, there often appears to an erroneous assumption that the mere alienation of one's assets, where trusts are involved, is invalid. However, such an alienation of property should be treated like any other disposition. If, for example, there was nothing to preclude the would-be settlor from alienating his or her property, all things considered, the disposing of it by way of a trust is valid. In the case of mandatory heirs, which gives rise to the most difficulties, if there appears to be nothing which precludes the settlor from disposing of his or her property before death by, for example, giving it away, or selling it and giving the money to charity, he or she is free to place it on trust. Were he or she to do so, his or her heirs would have no recourse. If the mandatory succession law takes effect only upon death, it being a law about succession and inheritance, and not a law on investment or conveyance of property itself, it should not selectively affect trusts which are *inter vivos*. Conversely, if the

23.08

---

[4] See paras 23.26–23.38.
[5] See below, paras 23.34–23.38.

onshore law precludes a person, while living, from disposing of assets in certain situations, such prohibitions will apply to the potential settlor and may render the transfer invalid.

23.09 The validity of the transfer of the assets into trusts is not an issue peculiar to jurisdictions which do not have trusts in their law. There is no reason for that issue to be elevated to an extraordinary position in relation to trusts or offshore trusts. Indeed, the transfer question is not even peculiar to trusts. A transfer of assets into a company can also be challenged in certain circumstances, for example if the assets are the proceeds of money laundering.

Capacity question confused with transfer question

23.10 The phrase 'capacity to create a trust' has often been misappropriated and applied to areas which are, in truth, wider than the capacity issue. Where civil law is involved, for example, the issue of the capacity to create a trust is often confused with the other preliminary question of the validity of the transfer of the assets. This is particularly the case where trusts established to prevent mandatory succession laws are involved. The suggestion is that because a person is expected to leave assets to his or her heirs, and he or she declines to do so by placing them into a trust, the settlor lacked the capacity to establish the trust in the first instance. The argument appears to be a circular one. As has been seen, an unlawful transfer of property into a trust may have nothing to do with capacity but with the validity of the transfer. Although the outcome of such a trust might be the surrender of the trust property to a competing legal principle, the settlor's capacity remains intact. He or she may, for example, establish another trust for different reasons without fear of challenge.

Transfers outside of the jurisdiction

23.11 We should also consider the question whether any restrictions on the alienation of the property will extend to transactions which are effected, or which will impact, outside of the civil law jurisdiction. Once the assets leave the country, the disposition may be valid. Is there a law, for example, which says that X cannot transfer money out of country A and invest it in country B? Unless that is so, there may be no issue to resolve, as the creation of the trust actually takes place in country B. The validity of the transfer of the property out of a company in country A, for example, into a trust entity B in another country, or alternatively, the transfers of the assets into an international company in another country, are not trust questions but rightly questions about the transfers. This is a question for the *lex fori*. It may or may not be a legitimate transfer. For example, if X is carrying out the transaction for tax avoidance purposes, such a transaction might be treated as constituting composite steps in a single transaction and violate country A's tax laws. Similarly, X might offend the rules of the *lex fori* if he or she transferred money which was the proceeds of money laundering. However, these are questions which have nothing to do with the trust itself. They are not, for instance, questions about the capacity to create the trust or on the recognition of a trust.[6] Further, if the true rationale of contesting the transfer into the trust is on grounds of public policy, such as the need to protect mandatory succession regimes, we can see that X's rationale had nothing to do with these public policy issues. Thus, the disposition into trust should not be negatively affected.

It is self-evident that the transfer of the assets and the validity of the trust itself are two separate questions. Even if, for example, the transfer is valid, it is not necessarily the case that the trust is valid. But the reverse is not true. The trust cannot be valid if the transfer is invalid. **23.12**

D. Capacity to Create the Trust

Once it is determined that the potential settlor can dispose of the assets, the second question, whether he can create a trust with the said property, arises. This is an appropriate question of trust law and should, it is suggested, logically fall to the law governing the trust. This is particularly the case where civil law jurisdictions which do not have the trust concept of the common law tradition as part of their law, are involved. An interpretation giving priority to the settlor's domicile would create an absurdity. The former is, in fact, the approach followed in offshore jurisdictions and validated in the case of *Casani v Mattei*.[7] **23.13**

The beneficial transfer

The point can be raised that the trust may fail if its governing law does not permit a beneficial transfer and that governing law is determined by the settlor's domicile. Arguably, this may be the case under civil law, which may only recognize absolute ownership, although, as suggested previously, the argument that civil law settlors lack inherent capacity is suspect. It will therefore be imperative that the governing law is a trust-friendly law, such as the offshore law, thereby enabling the equitable rights in the trust transaction to be obtained. **23.14**

---

[6] Note that, for recognition purposes, the Convention on the Law Applicable to Trusts and on their Recognition (The Hague, 1 July 1985; UKTS 14 (1992); Cm 1823; 23 ILM 1388), hereinafter 'The Hague Convention on the Recognition of Trusts', does not affect fiscal matters.

[7] (1998–99) 1 ITELR 925 (Tribunale of Lucca, Italy), discussed further below, paras 23.49–23.57. See also, the legislative provisions outlined below, paras 23.26–23.38.

The problem was demonstrated in the case of *Re Pearse's Settlement*.[8] Here, the issue was whether property in Jersey would be caught by a covenant to settle property which was originally subject to an English settlement. The settlor, under the law of Jersey, was not able to transfer the assets in Jersey to trustees. The case is, however, not typical of offshore trust structures, not least because the transfer was to be effected in the problem jurisdiction, which denied capacity.

23.15 There would seem to be no logical reason why the aspect of the transfer in which the beneficial ownership is transferred to the trust, should be governed by the civil law, which does not contain trusts as part of its legal tradition, and not by trust law. This is clearly a trust law question and should, therefore, be resolved by the proper law of the trust.

23.16 Even if it is the case that the settlor from a civil law jurisdiction cannot, while residing in the civil law jurisdiction, transfer his or her assets beneficially into a trust, such a settlor always has the option of transferring his or her assets into another entity, for example a company, as a first step. As there is no difficulty of lack of capacity or invalidity in relation to companies, once the assets are safely lodged, a trust can thereafter be created.

23.17 Yet two decided views are expressed about the governing law of this initial transaction and the question of capacity. One emerging principle is in favour of the law that applies to the actual trust, that is, the proper law of the trust.[9] In contrast, Matthews and others suggest that the law of the domicile of the settlor should govern.[10] The difference is crucial to the offshore sector. The courts will also look at the *lex situs*, and the law of the 'place of acting'.

Capacity and forced heirship under the Hague Convention

23.18 The Hague Convention on the Recognition of Trusts[11] is not as helpful on the capacity question as in other areas concerning trusts law. Article 4 specifically excludes the question of capacity from its scope. The omission of capacity can sometimes produce confusing results. In *Garner v Bermuda Trust Co Ltd*

---

[8] [1909] 1 Ch 304.
[9] See L Collins (ed), *Dicey and Morris on The Conflict of Laws*, 11th edn (Stevens, London, 1987) 1075, for one of the earlier views, although inconsistent, as surprisingly the later edition, the 12th edition, did not address the issue. *Trendtex Trading Corporation v Crédit Suisse* [1980] QB 629. Different rules may apply depending on whether these are tangible or intangible movables.
[10] P Matthews and T Sowden, *The Jersey Law of Trusts* (Key Haven Publications, London, 1993) 45. This view is in keeping with older authorities such as *A-G v Bellios* [1928] 1 KB 798 and *Cooper v Cooper* (1888) 12 App Cas 88.
[11] Above, n 6.

and Schindler,[12] the Chief Justice of Bermuda indirectly relied on the Hague Convention on the Recognition of Trusts to uphold a Bermudan trust created in Mexico, which sought to exclude Mexican forced heirship rules. The case has been much criticized as erroneously relying on the Convention to, in effect, grant capacity to a settlor in a civil law country, notwithstanding that preliminary issues such as capacity are not addressed by the Convention. The criticism is perhaps grounded in the Chief Justice's statement that the Act[13] was 'passed to give effect to the Hague Convention'.[14]

Yet the Chief Justice did not specifically rely on the question of capacity. Rather, he based his reasoning substantially on the origin and intent of the legislation in question, which has as its parent Act the Recognition of Trusts Act 1987 of the UK. That legislation incorporated the Hague Convention on the Recognition of Trusts. He then made the assumption that once the trust could be recognized, it could survive, as the settlor would have been deemed to have the capacity to create a trust.   **23.19**

This is not actually a far-fetched approach, as the Italian court in *Casani v Mattei*[15] made a similar link. The decision could perhaps more satisfactorily be criticized for its failure, in relying on the Convention's intent, to ask whether Mexico had ratified the Convention, and thus whether it permitted the recognition of trusts. An alternative rationale, perhaps underlying the ideology behind the recognition of trusts which challenged mandatory succession, would have sufficed. This rationale may point to the acceptance of such trusts even in the face of perceived difficulties in form which relate to capacity. It may be that on grounds of policy, common law courts should always uphold such trusts, in their support of the freedom of the disposition of property. Perhaps this is what the Chief Justice had in mind when he quoted extensively from the speech of the Lord Chancellor in the House of Lords at the reading of the Bill on the Recognition of Trusts of the UK: **23.20**

> The purpose of the Convention is to establish common principles between states on the law of trusts . . . [The] Convention . . . in effect, allows us to export to civil law countries, first the concept of the trust;[16] secondly, our rules laying down the law which governs such a trust, and thirdly, the circumstances in which it should be recognised. The Convention will thus principally be of benefit to common law countries . . .

---

[12] (Sup Ct, Bermuda) No 318 of 1991, decided 2 March 1992, *per* Sir James Astwood CJ. Noted in [1992] 1 JIntP 51. See the Court of Appeal judgment which upheld the decision, (CA, Bermuda) No 4 of 1992, decided 10 July 1992.

[13] The Trusts (Special Provisions) Act 1989.

[14] Above, n 6.

[15] Above, n 7.

[16] It is debatable whether this is a purpose of the Convention.

23.21   Were the Convention to apply legitimately to Mexico, an alternative response to the question of retroactivity is found under Article 22, which states that the Convention applies to trusts regardless of the date on which they were created. It was perhaps in this sense that the Chief Justice meant that the Bermudan Act was not applying law retroactively but declaring what the law is, in that the law, being based on the Convention, was inherently retroactive, and the law as it currently stood applied to all trusts whenever created.

Argument against *lex fori* and domicile

23.22   Neither the *lex fori*, nor the law of the settlor's domicile is satisfactory to govern the question of capacity. To allow the *lex fori* to determine the question of capacity is to allow extraterritorial jurisdiction to regulate an entity which is not a civil law entity. The best connection to the civil law jurisdiction could not be based on the fact that the 'assets came from a civil law jurisdiction', otherwise that rule would prejudice many trusts, even those created in the UK by UK domiciliaries. For example, if a UK settlor used assets from his or her company which is incorporated in France, and created a trust in the UK, would that mean that (i) he or she lacked capacity; and (ii) the transfer was invalid? Clearly not! Similarly, would a UK settlor lack the capacity to create, for example, a purpose trust outside of the UK, simply because such trusts may not be recognized as valid in the UK? Again, the answer would appear to be in the negative.

23.23   It is further suggested that if the trust itself is to have operation in another country, then it is that country that should determine the question of capacity. This is because, as discussed below,[17] the questions of recognition and validity are actually the most fundamental questions of the trust. Indeed, a rule that X in country A could not enter into a legal relationship, or treat with a legal entity or enterprise, in country B simply because X is domiciled or resident in country A, in a situation where such entity or relationship does not exist in country A, would turn the law of international commerce on its head. It would be not very different if the enterprise in country B was illegal in country A, for example casino gambling, since country A would still not be able to prosecute unless its law specifically had extraterritorial effect. There would seem to be no reason why X could not use his or her assets from country A to set up his or her casino business in country B. The business would be regulated entirely in country B. Country B would look retroactively to determine whether X met whatever criteria were laid down by its laws on casino gambling. Unless country B's laws specifically excluded persons or assets from country A, there would be no reason

---

[17] See *Casani*, above, n 7.

why X could not sustain a valid casino enterprise. The question of capacity would rest entirely with country B and its laws.

It would, of course, be an entirely different question as to whether country A's **23.24** laws prohibited X from removing his or her money from the jurisdiction—for example, if foreign exchange laws precluded this. Were X to breach those laws, whatever transactions he or she might have entered into would be void. However, that would have nothing to do with X's capacity to establish a casino.

The question of capacity remains a question of trust law, regardless of the origin **23.25** of the settlor. It is untenable that a non-trust jurisdiction can assess this question from the perspective of its own law. Once the transfer of assets into the trust is valid, the capacity to create the trust becomes a question for the proper law of the trust, which, in offshore jurisdictions, will likely be the offshore law.

Offshore legislative approach to potential defects of capacity

As we have noted, many offshore jurisdictions have attempted to clarify the **23.26** uncertainties in the laws on the capacity to create trusts and other preliminary issues in their favour. The method chosen is to make a unilateral assumption that the capacity question is to be resolved by the law of the offshore jurisdiction, and thereafter to gift to any settlor establishing an offshore trust the necessary capacity.

As an initial step, offshore trusts are to be adjudged according to the offshore **23.27** law as the proper law. This proper law thereafter grants settlors the necessary powers to overcome any difficulties, such as any incapacity to create a trust. Requirements for capacity are, therefore, to be adjudged according to the laws of the offshore jurisdiction, and these will not seek to obstruct settlors from civil law jurisdictions or other onshore jurisdictions from easily establishing trusts in the offshore country.[18] For example, in the Turks and Caicos, where the law of Turks and Caicos is the proper law, questions arising in regard to the validity of the trust or disposition, or of capacity, 'are to be determined according to the laws of the Turks and Caicos without reference to any other jurisdiction with which the trust or disposition may be connected'.[19] Thus, the question-mark concerning whether capacity is to be determined by the law of the settlor's domicile, the place of the trust or assets, or the proper law of the trust, is

---

[18] See, eg, s 15 of the International Trusts Act 1995 of Barbados, which perhaps states the obvious: 'A person may create (a) an *inter vivos* trust if the trust property is movable and the person has the capacity to create a trust of movable property under the law of Barbados.'

[19] The Trusts Ordinance 1990, s 13, as amended 1998, of the Turks and Caicos. See also s 13H of the International Trusts Act 1984 of the Cook Islands; s 7(1) of the Trusts (Choice of Governing Law) 1989, as amended 1996, of The Bahamas; Part VII, s 90 of the Trusts Law (2001 Revision) of the Cayman Islands. Such provisions appear to be absent in Belize.

avoided. The legislation thereby purports to grant capacity to the settlor, targeting potential settlors from civil law jurisdictions.

23.28   An alternative approach is that offshore trusts which are defined under special legislative provisions, are simply declared to be incapable of being void or voidable due to a lack of capacity, or other conflicts which may potentially be raised by civil law regimes. Both approaches may be utilized together.

23.29   In addition, consistent with the holistic legal regime which seeks to protect offshore trusts from onshore challenges, the provisions on capacity are to be read in conjunction with provisions on the non-enforcement of judgments,[20] the reservation of jurisdiction by offshore courts,[21] and, as noted earlier, the presumptions embodied in the law concerning the proper law of the trust.[22]

23.30   For example, in Dominica, offshore trusts, called 'international trusts', are specially defined trusts which fall under, and are registered under, the International Exempt Trusts Act 1997. There is a presumption that an international trust, so defined, will have as its proper law, the law of Dominica if no choice of proper law is made.[23] More important, for our present discussion, is s 28, which precludes the effect of foreign laws which may prejudice the validity of the trust. This includes preliminary issues. It reads:

> Neither an international trust governed by the Act and any disposition of property to be held upon the trust shall be declared void, voidable, liable to be set aside or defective in any fashion, nor is the capacity of any settlor to be questioned by reason that the—
>
> (a) laws of any foreign jurisdiction prohibit or do not recognise the concept of a trust, either in part or in whole;
> (b) international trust or disposition avoids or defeats rights, claims or interests conferred by the law of a foreign jurisdiction upon any person, or contravenes any rule, law, judicial or administrative order or action intended to recognise, protect, enforce or give effect to any such rights, claims or interests; or
> (c) laws of Dominica or the provisions of this Act are inconsistent with any foreign law.

---

[20] See chapter 24.
[21] See chapter 19.
[22] See chapter 20.
[23] International Exempt Trust Act 1997, s 4, particularly s 4(1)(c), which, although providing that the governing law in the absence of the settlor's choice is to be the law with which the trust is most closely connected, goes on to ensure that such a law cannot defeat the offshore trust. This is because the law of Dominica is to be the proper law if the law of the closest connection does not provide for the kind of international trust established, as permitted under Dominica's laws. Such a provision aims to defeat all onshore law which may be hostile to the offshore trust, not merely the onshore law of civil law jurisdictions. See also s 4 of the Nevis International Exempt Trusts Ordinance 1994.

In this construct, since the proper law will almost certainly be the law of **23.31** Dominica, it will be this provision which would obtain.[24] The provision is given added support by a section which validates offshore trusts even if invalid according to the law of the settlor's domicile, or its residence, or place of current incorporation.[25]

The substance of the capacity provision is then repeated, specifically with **23.32** respect to trusts established to defeat forced heirship rights and other forced interests.[26]

In Grenada, the provisions on capacity go further than merely seeking to oust **23.33** foreign law which may defeat the trust. Section 21 of the International trusts Act 1996 virtually deems capacity to settlors:

(1) . . . any person who, under the law of Grenada, has the capacity to own or transfer property may be a settlor of an international trust.
(2) A settlor who transfers property or disposes of assets to an international trust shall be deemed to have the capacity to do so if at the time of the transfer or disposition the settlor is of full age and sound mind under the law of the country in which he is resident.

Similarly, in Jersey, a person domiciled outside of Jersey who transfers property **23.34** to an *inter vivos* Jersey trust, 'shall be deemed to have had capacity to do so if at the time of such transfer or disposition' he was of 'full age and sound mind

---

[24] The same provisions are found in Nevis, under the International Exempt Trusts Ordinance 1994, s 29, and, under s 91 of the Trusts Law (2001 Revision) of the Cayman Islands. However, in the Cayman Islands, certain dispositions are excluded. See below, paras 23.35–23.38. A similar provision to that of the Cayman Islands is found under s 7(2) of the Trusts (Choice of Governing Law) Act 1989, as amended 1996, of The Bahamas. The provisions are also identical in Saint Vincent, under s 33 of the International Trust Act 1996, except that there is an additional paragraph, which underscores the ability of the offshore trust to defeat property rights which may accrue onshore. Section 33(c) reads: 'the international trust creates rights in property that are contrary to other laws relating to the personal or proprietary effects of marriage or the succession rights testate and intestate, of any person, especially the legal right of surviving spouses and the shares of relatives'. See also s 20 of the International Trusts Act 1996 of Grenada, which is to be read in conjunction with its ss 21 and 26, discussed below, paras 23.33–23.35. The provision in Saint Lucia is similar to that of Grenada, but does not go on to deem capacity. See s 34 of the International Trusts Act 2002 of Saint Lucia.

[25] International Exempt Trusts Act 1007, s 3. See also s 3 of the International Exempt Trusts Ordinance 1994 of Nevis; s 6 of the International Trust Act 1996 of Saint Vincent; and s 15 of the International Trusts Act 2002 of Saint Lucia,

[26] Under s 47 of the International Exempt Trust Act 1997 of Dominica. The provision reads: 'An international trust or any aspect of such trust governed by this Act and any disposition of property to be held upon the trusts thereof shall not be declared void, voidable or defective in any manner nor is the capacity of any settlor to be questioned by reason that the trust may avoid or defeat the right, claim or interest of a person held by reason of a personal relationship to the settlor or by way of heirship rights.' See also s 48 of the International Exempt Trusts Act 1994 of Nevis and s 51 of the International Trust Act 1996 of Saint Vincent.

under the law of his domicile'.[27] Forced heirship and other foreign laws on inheritance and succession do not affect the validity of such a trust.[28]

23.35 As in the Cook Islands, the law in Grenada precludes from its purview preliminary questions which do not concern specifically dispositions of property into a trust but speak generally to alienations of property. These are reserved to the foreign law, the law of the settlor's domicile or other appropriate law. Thus, in Grenada, dispositions of property which are not owned by the settlor are not validated. In addition, Grenada law does not presume to determine the ownership of such property.[29]

23.36 The new provisions in the British Virgin Islands (BVI) are noteworthy. They refer specifically to the preliminary matters alluded to in Article 4 of the Hague Convention on the Recognition of Trusts.[30] These preliminary matters, that is, questions on capacity and dispositions into the trust, are to be determined in accordance with the provisions of BVI law.[31] Consequently, the formal and essential validity of *inter vivos* dispositions of immovable property, and the capacity to make such dispositions, are to be determined according to the law of the state in which the property is situated at the time of the dispositions.

23.37 However, the formal and essential validity of *inter vivos* dispositions of

---

[27] The Trusts (Jersey) Law 1984, art 8A.

[28] ibid, art 8A(2)(b). See also a similar provision under s 11A of the Trusts (Guernsey) Law 1989. *Inter vivos* Guernsey trusts and dispositions of property, or any interests made to a Guernsey trust cannot be '(a) . . . invalidated by any foreign rule of forced heirship or by reason of the fact that the concept of trusts is unknown to or not admitted by the law of a jurisdiction other than Guernsey; (b) the settlor shall be deemed to have had capacity to create the trust or to make the transfer or disposition if he had capacity to do so under—(i) Guernsey law; (ii) the law of his domicile or nationality; (iii) the proper law of the transfer or disposition.'

[29] The International Trusts Act 1996, s 26, of Grenada and s 13H of the International Trusts Act 1984 of the Cook Islands. A similar provision appears in Barbados under s 17 of the International Trusts Act 1995. However, the provisions on capacity in Barbados do not appear to be as strong as in other jurisdictions. The Act does not specifically oust the application of foreign laws which may threaten the trust, and does not specifically address the question whether a person from a civil law jurisdiction can establish a trust. It merely declares that capacity is to be adjudged according to the laws of Barbados, but one is unsure how even the courts of Barbados will assess settlors from civil law jurisdictions. The Barbados provisions are similar to those found under s 10 of the Trusts (Special Provisions) Act 1989 of Bermuda. Under Part VII, s 90(i) to (vi) of the Trusts Law (2001 Revision) of the Cayman Islands, a similar proviso appears. These capacity provisions do not apply to property ownership questions, to dispositions of property where the property is not owned by the settlor, to other formalities for property disposition, immovable property, or to testamentary trusts or dispositions which are invalid according to the laws of the testator's domicile. It should also be noted that under s 88 of the Cayman Islands Act, the provisions apply to all such trusts, regardless of where the property is situated. See also s 7(2) of the Trusts (Choice of Governing Law) Act 1989, as amended 1996, of The Bahamas.

[30] Which applies to the BVI by virtue of the Recognition of Trusts Act 1987 (Overseas Territories). Order 1989, SI 1989 No 673.

[31] Under s 83A of the Trustee (Amendment) Act 2003, in particular, subsections (7) to (11).

intangible property, and the capacity to make such dispositions, shall be determined according to the proper law of the trust. But this law does not govern the actual disposition of property. That question is reserved to the law of the state in which the interest is situated.[32]

23.38 The BVI Act provides further that the 'capacity to subject property to a trust, not being a testamentary trust, as distinct from the capacity to dispose of that property, shall be determined in accordance with the law governing the essential validity of the trust'.[33] Where the person declares a trust of his or her own property, 'there shall be no requirement for compliance with the rules on formal or essential validity or capacity applicable to a disposition of that property or of any interest in it'.[34]

Capacity of persons from civil law countries

23.39 It is apparent that the legislation on capacity also assumes, as a 'fail safe' measure, that certain persons, in particular those resident or domiciled in civil law countries, to whom the legislation is targeted, lack the capacity to establish trusts in the first instance. This is so even where the trust is to be established elsewhere, in trust law countries. This is presumably because civil law countries do not have the trust as part of their laws. However, this is a presumption which is by no means certain, and the provisions which embody it are perhaps misleading. Rather, it is suggested that there is no innate inability of persons from civil law countries to establish trusts in trust law countries, although they may, or may not, be able to do so in their own countries. Indeed, today, when onshore civil law jurisdictions are confronted with questions of trusts established by their own nationals or citizens, they are more likely to treat them as questions of recognition, and not questions of capacity. This is borne out by the cases discussed below.[35]

23.40 The fundamental flaw in the premise that civil law settlors inherently lack capacity to create trusts, is perhaps exposed if we return to basic principles. What determines capacity? Is it the personal characteristics of a settlor, the situation of residence, the fact of nationality or citizenship, or whether the resident law recognizes a trust?

---

[32] ibid, First Sch, para (4): '(A) As regards disposability, the law governing the essential validity of the trust or interest. (B) As regards the disposition itself, the law of the State in which the equitable interest is situated.'

[33] ibid, s 83A(9).

[34] ibid, s 83A(10). The provision also clarifies the question on *renvoi* in relation to preliminary questions: 'the choice of law rules of the Territory shall designate the internal law of the Territory to determine the issue' (ibid, s 83A(11)).

[35] Paras 23.49–23.57. See also chapter 21, 'Recognition of the Offshore Trust in Civil Law Countries'.

23.41 Generally, in traditional trust law cases, capacity is assessed by factors relating to personal characteristics, such as insanity and so on. This undermines the view that the mere fact that a settlor is a citizen of, or is domiciled in, a civil jurisdiction denies him or her the capacity to create a trust. It is suggested that, were that the case, it would mean that if the settlor migrated to another country without changing his or her domicile, he or she would still be unable to create a trust. Alternatively, is the alleged lack of capacity due to the fact that the assets are situated in a civil country and its laws control them? Consider the situation where a settlor from a civil law jurisdiction inherits money from England. Could he or she use such monies to establish a trust in England; or does the rule come into effect only when the assets are located in the civil law country? If so, what we are really speaking about is the validity of the transfer of the assets. As established earlier, the question whether a settlor from a civil law jurisdiction is able successfully to establish a trust is different to that of whether he or she has the capacity to do so.[36] This is true even for onshore trusts. An alternative scenario is also problematic, as it would mean that if an English citizen became resident in France, he or she could not, similarly, create a trust. Both suggestions, that the lack of capacity is derived from being a national, or being physically resident in the civil law country, are therefore laced with conceptual difficulties.

23.42 It is reiterated that the more important issue for offshore trusts has to do with the recognition of the trust and not the capacity to create the trust. Even if it were true that, before, as a general rule, trusts were not recognized in civil law countries, it is no longer the case. This is particularly so since the advent of the Hague Convention on the Recognition of Trusts, which enables trusts to be recognized in principle, despite the existence of certain exceptions.

23.43 However, the recognition of a trust and the capacity to create a trust are issues which must be kept separate. Even the UK courts may refuse to enforce or recognize certain trusts. This does not mean that they do not recognize (in the sense of affirming the existence of) trusts in general. Certainly, it does not mean that the settlor does not have capacity.

23.44 It is further suggested that capacity should remain as an issue associated with the innate characteristics of the settlor, such as the state of his or her mind, and so on. The civil law country may, in fact, have no problems with trusts designed for certain purposes. Problematic purposes, such as anti-forced heirship, have more to do with what the settlor wants to do with his or her assets rather than how he or she does it. As we have seen, the law could similarly object, for example, if the civil law owner of the assets were to place all of them in a company which had

---

[36] We can make an analogy with a person who votes. When X votes, the question is whether it was a valid or proper vote, or a 'hanging' vote, not whether he or she had the capacity to vote.

sufficient flexibility to defeat his or her heirs. Surely, that could not mean that the owner of the assets had no capacity to create a company, if the conveyance was challenged? Similarly, if the settlor from a civil law jurisdiction took assets reserved for his or her heirs and bought a house for his or her lover, this might be just as unlawful in the eyes of the civil law. This does not mean that he or she did not have the capacity to purchase a house. Once again, the problem here does not appear to concern capacity but the transfer of the assets itself. The offshore approach, and that of those who are fearful about the capacity question, may, consequently, be misplaced.

There is, therefore, a conceptual difficulty with the offshore legislative provi-   **23.45**
sions. While they speak to the capacity to create a trust, the question of capacity is treated as if it were the same as the actual transfer of the assets. This also seems to be the view of some commentators on the subject. Yet in reality, the capacity question is more a theoretical question which goes to the issue of whether one has the ability to create a thing.

Notwithstanding the view expressed below that persons from civil law jurisdic-   **23.46**
tions do not lack the capacity to create trusts in trust law countries, the potential efficacy of offshore provisions which make the opposite assumption is welcomed. At minimum, they may undermine attempts by those who share the view that civil law settlors lack capacity, to discredit offshore trusts. In such attempts, it is unlikely that challengers to the trust can point to any clear legal rule to support their position. Offshore provisions present an opportunity for those seeking to uphold the trust to provide a clear rule on the issue, one that may gain support in the courts. Indeed, this is an ineluctable conclusion from the emerging case law, discussed in the following section.

Offshore trust law efficient in precluding foreign onshore law

Not surprisingly, given their relative infancy, there have been few decisions   **23.47**
examining the offshore provisions on capacity, and even fewer examining the issue without the context of specific legislation. These rare judgments suggest, however, that settlors from civil law jurisdictions may not be unduly restricted because of defects in capacity.

In *Bridge Trust Company and Slatter v A-G*,[37] for example, the Grand Court of   **23.48**
the Cayman Islands interpreted the capacity provisions under the Trusts (Foreign Element) Law 1987 of the Cayman Islands, in a question involving the validity of a trust transferred from The Bahamas to the Cayman Islands. The

---

[37] [1996] CILR 52 (Grand Ct, Cayman Islands). The question was whether its charitable purposes were valid.

court found that the 'proposition that, in determining the terms of the trust, its validity under another foreign law has to be ascertained, . . . [was] the very mischief which these subsections were intended to address'. As such, the only relevant question was whether the trust was valid under the law of the Cayman Islands. Once the proper law considered the trust to be valid, capacity was assumed.

23.49 This also seems to be the approach of the Italian court in *Casani v Mattei*,[38] a more authoritative judgment since it came from a civil law jurisdiction, the very target of offshore legislative provisions on capacity. Whilst not a case involving an offshore jurisdiction, it pronounces on the broader point of the capacity of settlors from civil law jurisdictions validly to establish trusts in trust law states.

23.50 The *Casani* judgment suggests that the question of capacity is properly to be assessed under the proper law of the trust, which law determined, generally, its validity.[39] In this case, which involved a challenge to a trust established to undermine forced heirship rights in Italy, the court rejected the plaintiff's argument that the will trust was void and that the testator lacked the capacity to create such a trust. It referred dismissively to the plaintiff's argument, speaking of the 'alleged (but unproved) lack of capacity to make a will'.[40] It was the proper law of the trust and the *lex loci*, in this instance US law, that determined both the validity and effectiveness in relation to the form and capacity of the testator, and indeed, the trust itself. The proper law was determined on the basis that the trust was more closely connected with US law, since the place of the assets, the place of administration designated by the settlor, the trustee's place of business, and the jurisdiction under which the trust was established, all pointed in the direction of US law.[41]

23.51 Offshore provisions on capacity were also considered in the Bermudian case of *Garner v Bermuda Trust Co*[42] and in *Re Lemos Trust Settlement*,[43] and found to be effective. In *Re Lemos*, the court made *obiter* remarks to the effect that the trust would be valid even against forced heirship claims where the Greek settlor initially had no capacity to create a trust.

---

[38] Above, n 7, considered further below, paras 23.52–23.62.
[39] So that, if one were assessing more detailed questions of capacity, such as whether the settlor lacked capacity because of insanity, this would be examined according to the trust law principles of the trust jurisdiction, the proper law.
[40] See above, n 7, 944.
[41] ibid, 945.
[42] Above, n 12.
[43] [1992–93] CILR 26.

Recognition grants capacity

In *Casani v Mattei*,[44] the Italian court treated the issue of capacity as a 'given'   **23.52**
once it was established that the trust could be recognized by the civil law
jurisdiction, in this case Italy. As noted previously, the court proceeded on the
basis that the question of validity was to be determined according to the proper
law of the trust, the foreign law; and once this law acknowledged the trust as
valid, the general question of capacity under Italian law was irrelevant, since the
trust was recognizable.

Casani clearly dispels the notion that there is some innate element to be attri-   **23.53**
buted to nationals and domiciliaries of civil law jurisdictions which prevents
them from becoming settlors of trusts, including offshore trusts. Rather, the
essential question is not the place of the settlor, but that of the trust. Once the
proper law is identified as that of the trust law jurisdiction, and the features of
the trust are valid according to that law, the trust may be imported into the civil
law jurisdiction where there is a requirement or willingness that trusts should be
recognized.

The analysis is helped by the provisions of the Hague Convention on the   **23.54**
Recognition of Trusts,[45] which allow trusts to be recognized regardless of where
they were created. To defeat the recognition of such trusts because of an alleged
lack of capacity is to defeat the true purpose of the Convention.

In other cases where the recognition of the trust was the main issue, the courts,   **23.55**
in similar fashion to the court in *Casani*, were not preoccupied with the question of any perceived lack of capacity by civil law persons to create trusts in trust
law jurisdictions.[46]

The question of capacity, therefore, is not to be determined by the law of the   **23.56**
civil law or onshore country. Rather, it is but one element of the validity of the
trust, and is properly considered under the proper law of the trust. As the proper
law of the trust is, in most cases, the offshore law, the issue of capacity is unlikely
to derail offshore trusts.[47] Further, *Casani* underscores the distinctions to be

---

[44] Above, n 7.
[45] Above, n 6, Art 22.
[46] See the discussion in chapter 21 and cases such as *Re Isle of Man Trust* (1998–99) 1 ITELR
103 (Tax Panel, Sweden) and *Re WKR Trust OD Bank (in liquidation) v Estate of Rey (a Bankrupt)*
(1999) 4 ITELR 487 (Zurich District Court). Both of these cases concerned trusts established by
settlors of civil law jurisdictions which were recognized by civil law courts without difficulties
relating to capacity. Cf *Sanchez v Sanchez De Davila* 547 SO 2d 943 (Fla 3d DCA) rev denied 554
SO 2d 1168 (Fla 1989). However, statutory provisions on capacity ensured the survival of the
trust afterward.
[47] See chapter 20, 'The Proper Law of the Offshore Trust'.

made between the question of capacity to create the trust, other preliminary issues, such as the validity of the actual transfer of the assets into trust, and general questions of succession. Indeed, in *Casani*, the question of succession was properly acknowledged as belonging to Italian law, but this did not invalidate the trust, nor prejudice the capacity question.

23.57 Cases such as *WKR*[48] and *Casani*[49] demonstrate that the issue of capacity need not be an obstacle to settlors from civil law jurisdictions at all. The trust is recognizable as a familiar entity, and the relevant rule of private international law identifying the proper law or governing law, found and applied. It will then be that identified governing law which decides the question of the validity of the trust.

Retroactive effect of capacity provisions

23.58 One objection to offshore legislative provisions on capacity is that they purport to give legality or validity to something which has already occurred and are, therefore, of retroactive effect. They therefore seem to contradict established principles of statutory interpretation that legislation is to operate prospectively unless specifically expressed to be retroactive. A possible view of any court is that offshore provisions deeming capacity to exist should be allowed to stand only if they are expressly retrospective. It is reiterated that only some offshore jurisdictions have taken this further step.[50] Nevertheless, the question may be asked whether such provisions are truly retroactive and, if so, whether retroactivity is at all necessary to protect the trust. More important, the courts thus far have failed to make this distinction, or to find that this would defeat the provision in any way. Indeed, the question of capacity is to be considered solely at the time when the question of the validity of the trust itself is being considered. It is always, therefore, a 'hindsight question'.

Jurisdiction and capacity

23.59 Preliminary questions such as capacity may turn, ultimately, on jurisdiction. Consequently, the most reliable protection for the offshore trust may be its ability, at the outset, to prevent the onshore court from assuming jurisdiction. In sum, if the onshore state assumes jurisdiction, the possibility is increased that the proper law will be chosen with reference to the settlor, basing this on his or her domicile, residence, etc. Conversely, if the offshore court assumes jurisdiction, it will almost certainly hold that the law governing the question of capacity

---

[48] See above, n 46.
[49] See above, n 7.
[50] Such as the Cayman Islands.

is the offshore law. Under such law the settlor will be deemed to have capacity to create the trust.

Responding to approaches which confuse capacity with other questions

The question of capacity should be divorced from other questions, such as **23.60** whether anti-forced heirship trust provisions will survive. A settlor may have the capacity to create a perfectly valid trust, but may fail, for example, for reasons of public policy. Alternatively, the trust itself may stand, at least in form, but some other way may be found to reach the assets. For example, in *Casani*,[51] the forced heir could have applied to the courts by another route to get a share of the assets, but the trust itself was recognized as valid.

We can compare this situation to that of, a settlor who establishes a trust which **23.61** is deemed to be a fraudulent conveyance. If, for example, the settlor's debt was only $10,000, but the trust is worth more than US $1 million, it is possible for the trust itself to stand and for some of the assets to be used to honour the debt. There is no clear precedent that the trust should be treated as automatically voided in such situations. Indeed, offshore law actively encourages such partial distributions of the trust property.[52] These extraneous challenges to the trust have nothing to do with the capacity question, nor with the essential validity of the trust.

Characterization of the Initial Transfer

In resolving the choice of law question, a court may have to determine the **23.62** nature of the matter before it. This is a difficult exercise. In such cases, different conflict of laws principles to those of the trust may apply. These may defeat the trust. The onshore court could, for example, characterize the transaction as a matter of succession, administration of estates, or even as a 'fraud on the law'.[53] In *Casani*,[54] for example, the transfer of assets into a will trust was viewed as a succession matter, yet this did prove detrimental to the trust. Here, the difficulty is not with lack of capacity but illegality. The type of offshore capacity provision enacted would, therefore, be relevant. If it refers specifically to the trust, or is

---

[51] See above, n 7.
[52] See, eg, chapter 9, 'The Law on Fraudulent Conveyances and the Offshore Trust'.
[53] The last is a civilian notion similar to an illegal contract in common law systems, where a transaction which is motivated by an intention to avoid the effect of a mandatory rule of law is void. See I Cricenti, 'Contratti in Frode alla legge', noted in P Matthews, 'No-Trust Judgments in Trust States' [1996] *Trusts and Trustees* 6.
[54] See above, n 7.

expressed specifically in relation to a rule relating to inheritance or succession, it could fail to effect its purpose.[55] Only where the legislation is broad in its scope, as in the Cayman Islands for example, where it could even cover fraud on the law, might the provision succeed.[56]

---

[55] See, eg, art 8A of the Trusts (Jersey) Law 1984: 'no rule relating to inheritance or succession'. In the context of forced heirship, a claim of a conspiracy to damage the heirs' succession rights might also arise. This might be characterized either as an action concerning succession rights, or as one in tort (delict) and not, prima facie, one relating to title to property or capacity to transfer such title. Matthews, above, n 53, 8.

[56] See, eg, s 90 of the Trusts Law (2001 Revision) of the Cayman Islands, which reads: 'All questions arising in regard to a trust which is for the time being governed by the laws of the Islands or in regard to any disposition of property upon the trusts thereof.' See paras 23.26–23.38 for a discussion of similar provisions in other offshore jurisdictions.

24

THE NON-ENFORCEMENT OF
FOREIGN JUDGMENTS UNDER
OFFSHORE TRUST LAW

A. Introduction

24.01 In the event that all of the other conflict of laws questions have been resolved and a judgment obtained in the onshore jurisdiction, the matter of the enforcement of the judgment in the offshore jurisdiction will surface. Whether offshore trusts can be preserved against judgments emanating from onshore jurisdictions is a question crucial to the effectiveness, and indeed the validity, of such trusts. It is not in the interest of offshore jurisdictions that onshore judgments are allowed to undermine the carefully orchestrated legal protections offered by such jurisdictions. Often, such foreign judgments will directly challenge not just the assets placed into the offshore trust, but the very trust principles which offshore legislatures have created.

24.02 Securing preliminary remedies, such as injunctions and other restraint orders, is also an important goal of onshore challengers to the trust and its assets. In this regard, however, we may note a more flexible attitude on the part of offshore jurisdictions.

Special laws against enforcement

24.03 The most significant development in offshore law jurisprudence on the enforcement of judgments is the enactment of specific legislation which expressly precludes the enforcement of foreign judgments, that is, onshore judgments.

24.04 Thus, the attempt to circumvent onshore law which challenges the offshore trust extends to these special laws on the non-enforcement of foreign judgments. Such laws may apply to all judgments, or to selected judgments. For example, the offshore law might state that a foreign judgment which gives effect to forced heirship rights, thereby threatening trusts established to defeat such rights, may not be enforced. Similarly, judgments obtained onshore seeking to give effect to rights under matrimonial property legislation, may be specifically excluded.[1] Some legislatures go further and seek to preclude onshore creditor judgments, whether directly or indirectly.[2] Typically, such legislation will be found in offshore jurisdictions which have special legislation on fraudulent conveyances.[3] Even if it is established onshore that the judgment debtors are legally entitled to the assets in the offshore trust, those assets may still be out of their reach.

24.05 The International Exempt Trust Act 1997 of Dominica provides a good example of offshore trust legislation which seeks to preclude totally the enforcement of onshore judgments which may impact negatively on the trust. It provides:

> Notwithstanding the provisions of any treaty . . . statute, rule of law or equity, to the contrary, any proceedings for or in relation to the enforcement or recognition of a judgment obtained in a jurisdiction other than Dominica . . . shall not be entertained by any Court in Dominica where that judgment—
>
> (a) is based on the application of any law inconsistent with the provisions of this Act; or

---

[1] See, eg, s 6 of the Trust (Foreign Elements) Law 1987, now incorporated into Part VII of the Trusts Law (2001 Revision), s 91 of the Cayman Islands. The rule on non-enforcement may affect all offshore business, not just the trust. See also s 8 of the Trusts (Choice of Governing Law) Act 1989 of The Bahamas and s 91 of the Trusts Law (2001 Revision) of the Cayman Islands, which preclude rights arising 'by reason of a personal relationship with the settlor', which includes former and current marriage relationships. Such provisions are to be read together with provisions which specifically preclude related foreign judgments. See, eg, s 92 of the Cayman Act, which states: 'A foreign judgment shall not be recognized, enforced or give rise to any estoppel insofar as it is inconsistent with s 91 or 92' and a similar provision under s 10 of The Bahamas Act. The Trustee Amendment Act 2003, s 83A, of the British Virgin Islands has a different formulation. It reads: 'To the extent that it is inconsistent with subsections (13) and (18), a foreign judgment shall not be recognized or enforced or give rise to any estoppel, and both its recognition and its enforcement shall be regarded as contrary to the public policy of the Territory.' The subsections referred to concern forced heirship rights and rights granting capacity to settlors from civil law jurisdictions. See generally, too, provisions which preclude foreign laws where they undermine forced heirship or deny capacity to settlors, discussed at paras 22.10–22.13 and 23.26–23.38.

[2] See the discussion of the likely effect of such provisions in chapter 9, especially paras 9.94–9.114.

[3] See, eg, s 7(6)(c) of the Trusts Act 1992 (rev'd 2000) of Belize. See chapter 9.

(b) relates to a matter or particular aspect that is governed by the laws of Dominica.[4]

Since Dominica has special laws enabling the creation of offshore trusts which also apply to settlors from civil law jurisdictions, including those attempting to avoid forced heirship laws, and, in addition, special laws which make onshore fraudulent conveyance claims more difficult, any judgment threatening to undermine such laws will not be enforced.

These special laws against the enforcement of foreign judgments make a signifi-   **24.06**
cant contribution to the sustainability of the offshore trust, seeking to preserve assets placed into trusts against challenges from onshore jurisdictions. We should note, too, that even if an onshore plaintiff obtains an order against a trustee requiring him or her to pay funds from the trust, the typical offshore trustee would be outside of the jurisdiction of the onshore court and well advised to remain that way. If the trustee declines to enforce the order, as would be the case, the order would be incapable of enforcement. Often, the onshore party's only recourse would be to levy some form of a penalty on the debtor-settlor or beneficiary who, typically, will be within the jurisdiction of the onshore courts. Thus, in *Affordable Media*[5] and *Re Stephen Lawrence*,[6] for example, the remedy sought and obtained was an order for contempt of court because of the settlor-beneficiary's disobedience of the court's orders to return the assets to satisfy debts owed.

In *T v T and Others*,[7] an English court ordered that the trustees of a Jersey trust   **24.07**
be joined to proceedings to recover assets allegedly placed into the trust by a husband in order to hide them from his wife. The trustees had refused to hold the money to the order of the Royal Court.

B. Traditional Rules on Enforcement

Where special offshore legislation against the enforcement of foreign judgments   **24.08**
does not apply, orthodox rules on enforcement encapsulated under the common law and domestic policy need to be considered.

There is no presumption in private international law that the judgments of one   **24.09**

---

[4] Section 27. See also s 7 of the Trusts Act 1992 (rev'd 2000) of Belize; s 39 of the International Trusts Act 2002 of Saint Lucia; s 131 of the International Trusts Act 1984 of the Cook Islands; and s 28 of the International Exempt Trust Ordinance 1994 of Nevis.
[5] *Federal Trade Commission v Affordable Media* (1999) 2 ITELR 73; LLC 179 F 3d 1228 (CA-9, 1999).
[6] (2002) 5 ITELR 1.
[7] [1996] 2 FLR 356.

country must be enforced by another as of right. In this regard, therefore, offshore provisions which preclude the enforcement of foreign judgments are not as radical as they first appear. However, this basic presumption is considerably weakened by the competing principle of the comity between nations. In practice, countries have developed a range of principles and laws which will enable them to enforce foreign judgments, leaving aside certain particularly sensitive areas, such as fiscal law and penal law.[8] In the Cayman Islands, for example, the common law will still apply and, in general, the courts will enforce the final and conclusive money judgments of competent foreign courts, in the absence of statutory provisions governing a specific matter. To be treated as final and conclusive, the foreign judgment must be regarded as *res iudicata* by the foreign court.[9]

24.10   Further, countries will usually enact general legislation permitting the enforcement of foreign judgments with selected jurisdictions on a reciprocal basis.[10] Nonetheless, offshore jurisdictions which have promoted aggressive trust legislation will be less likely to negotiate treaties on reciprocal enforcement of judgments on matters which relate to the offshore sector, as this would run counter to the inherent purposes of offshore law and legal policy. Yet such cooperation cannot be ruled out. Existing reciprocal arrangements, will though, be overridden by the specialist laws on non-enforcement which apply to offshore trusts.[11]

Jurisdiction issues

24.11   The issue of jurisdiction may nevertheless determine the question of enforcement. Under rules of private international law, such rules may require the foreign court to have competent jurisdiction over the proceedings in the first instance, for its judgment to be enforced elsewhere. Thus, if neither the trustee nor the assets were present in the onshore country, offshore courts may legitimately refuse to enforce the judgment because of an absence of territorial jurisdiction.

24.12   This means that it is important for the trust to remain isolated from the onshore jurisdiction. As we saw in our discussion of jurisdiction in chapter 19, this is a contentious issue and may be assumed on a number of grounds. For example, if the assets are located in the onshore jurisdiction, or if the assets are invested

---

[8] Discussed below, paras 24.24–24.34.

[9] *Peterdey v Dennis* [1998] CILR N9 (Grand Ct, Cayman Islands), *per* Smellie CJ.

[10] See L Collins (ed), *Dicey and Morris on The Conflict of Laws*, 13th ed (Sweet & Maxwell, London, 2000). Several offshore countries have signed Reciprocity Agreements on the enforcement of judgments with onshore countries, particularly the UK, because of the ex-colonial relationship. The US is not a party to any such treaty.

[11] See, eg, s 7(7) of the Belize Trusts Act 1992 (rev'd 2000), which expressly overrides the Reciprocal Enforcement of Judgments Act 1980 (rev'd), as it relates to offshore trusts.

there, or transferred to a beneficiary there, these may be bases for assuming jurisdiction. Such actions broaden the possibility of judgments being pursued and enforced in the onshore jurisdiction itself, even if it is not possible in the offshore trust jurisdiction.[12] Such potential dangers should, therefore, be avoided if the integrity of the trust is to be maintained.[13]

Other routes to non-enforcement

Apart from statutory ousters of onshore judgments, offshore trusts may also be protected by well-established rules on the non-enforcement of foreign judgments. These may be divided into two categories:

24.13

(1) well-recognized exceptions to a category of judgments which will normally be enforced; and
(2) judgments which will not be enforced because of the well-established rule of private international law that one state will not enforce the penal or fiscal laws of another.

Even where foreign judgments are enforceable in general, exceptions are recognized. These include judgments obtained by fraud,[14] breaches of natural justice, judgments that offend public policy, or comity, or those which infringe human rights.[15] Offshore courts have applied all of these exceptions.

24.14

Public policy

Offshore jurisdictions may easily refuse to enforce foreign judgments on the grounds of public policy, or comity.[16] From the perspective of offshore jurisdictions, the enforcement of judgments which threaten offshore entities, such as trusts, may be against public policy, because such judgments seek to undermine the very purposes for which offshore legislation has been created. These include laws protecting against forced heirship, granting capacity to the trust, and so on. The focus of such legislation is the sustainability of offshore entities. The important role of this special legislation in protecting against onshore threats, was recognized in *Bridge Trust Company v AG*.[17] Similarly, in *Douglas v Pindling*,[18]

24.15

---

[12] As demonstrated in cases such as *Duttle v Bander and Kass* (1992) 82 Cir 5084 (KMW) and *Re Larry Portnoy* 201 BR 685 (1996).
[13] ibid.
[14] See, eg, *Owens Bank v Bracco* [1992] 2 AC 443.
[15] *Williams & Lambert Ltd v W&H Trade Marks (Jersey) Ltd* [1986] AC 368, 428.
[16] *Vervacke v Smith* [1983] 1 AC 145. See also *Muhl Insurance Co v Ardra Insurance Co Ltd* [1997–98] 1 OFLR 19, where a Bermuda court refused to enforce a judgment from an US court. In view of the security procedures in the US, the court found that the judgment had been obtained in breach of accepted principles of natural justice and was, therefore, against public policy.
[17] [1996] CILR 52.
[18] [1996] 3 WLR 242.

the Privy Council also acknowledged that the protection of laws and offshore financial products in offshore jurisdictions was in the public's interest.

Enforcement on the grounds of comity

24.16   Despite the provisions against the enforcement of foreign judgments, in a proper case, offshore courts will also be willing to enforce judgments on grounds of comity, which is the respect given by one court to a foreign court. For example, an offshore court may enforce a foreign judgment for the support and maintenance of children in a marriage, or of a spouse. This exception was considered in *Compass v McBarnett*,[19] a case which examined the power of the Jersey courts to give effect to an English judgment to vary a discretionary trust established in Jersey, so that the wife and children of the settlor could be maintained.

24.17   In *Compass*, the Royal Court considered that although article 8A of the Trusts (Jersey) Law 1984 (as amended) precluded the automatic enforcement of foreign judgments,[20] there remained a residual discretion originating from the common law on the part of the courts, to enforce a judgment in an appropriate case. In deciding whether to exercise its discretion to enforce a foreign judgment by varying the trust, the court had to consider whether the foreign court had exercised its discretion, in deciding to provide capital to the wife, excessively or unfairly. In this case it had not, and comity dictated that the judgment be enforced. On this point the court relied on the earlier case of *Lane v Lane*:[21]

> Where on the matter before the Royal Court, there was a declaration of a competent English court, properly made, submitted to by the same parties and not appealed, the doctrine of comity required that the declaration be given effect to, provided that it was clear that the defendant had had every opportunity to raise all relevant defences at that hearing.[22]

24.18   The Jersey Royal Court also put forward comity as the reason for enforcing the foreign judgment in the case of *Re Rabaiotti 1989 Settlement*.[23] The judgment in question was an order from an English court for the disclosure of trust documents for the benefit of a beneficiary. The Deputy Bailiff noted that, as a matter of comity, the Royal Court of Jersey should not impede the English courts in the exercise of their proper roles. Remarkably, the order was enforced despite the fact that two of the trusts in question were British Virgin Islands trusts and not Jersey trusts, although they were administered in Jersey.

---

[19] [2002] JLR 321 (Royal Ct), *per* Le Cras, Commr.
[20] Relying on *T v T* [1996] 2 FLR 366.
[21] [1985–86] JLR 48 (Royal Ct), 49–50.
[22] *Lane*, ibid, quoted in *Compass*, above, n 19, 327.
[23] [2000] JLR 173 (Royal Ct).

Enforcement of judgments where the trust is discredited

Where the trust is discredited, by being deemed either a sham or a fraud, it is **24.19** clear that any judgments for debt entered against the settlor are enforceable, as the trust is voided and the assets are treated as belonging to the settlor. The situations where the trust may be deemed a sham or fraudulent conveyance have been discussed in previous chapters.[24]

Enforcement where the settlor or beneficiary owes a debt

We have already discussed the difficulties in situations where the settlor or **24.20** beneficiary is called upon by the onshore tax authorities to pay taxes. With respect to the trust, the trustee is called upon to honour this tax debt, through payment from the trust fund, either directly or indirectly, by reimbursing the settlor or beneficiary. The settlor or beneficiary may, in fact, have any kind of debt, including creditors' debts. If a judgment is obtained against a settlor or beneficiary, should the trustee enforce that judgment, albeit indirectly, by distributing funds from the trust, in order to satisfy that debt? Once again, our discussion of the general principle in favour of trustee actions in the interest of the beneficiaries is pertinent.[25] There would be situations where the settlor, who is often a beneficiary, would be compelled to repatriate trust assets and face harsh penalties for failing to do so.[26]

A Jersey case, *Re Abacus (CI) Ltd ('Trustee of the Esteem Settlement) Grupo Torras* **24.21** *SA v Al Sabah,*[27] raises a novel point. This concerns the question to the court whether the trustee could distribute trust assets against the wishes of a beneficiary to satisfy a judgment. Here the settlor/beneficiary had specifically requested that no distributions be made to him, so as to prevent a debtor from reaching the trust assets. This was in a situation where a UK court had given judgment against the settlor for fraud to the amount of more than $400 million. The settlor had placed all of his assets into several trusts, and argued that he was unable to pay the debt as he no longer had control over the assets.

The litigation surrounding the fraud involved several components. The Royal **24.22** Court of Jersey found that a distribution from the trust could be made to the

---

[24] See chapters 8 and 9.

[25] See chapter 17.

[26] Recall *Federal Trade Commission v Affordable Media*, above, n 5, where the settlor was held in contempt of court.

[27] Hereinafter *In Re Abacus (CI) Ltd* (2003) 6 ITELR 368 (Royal Ct, Jersey); [2003] JRC 92. This was another arm of the complex litigation by Grupo Torras against the settlor Sheik Fahad, who established trusts in several offshore jurisdictions.

settlor, Sheik Fahad, even against his wishes, (that is, a trustee could grant a benefit to an unwilling beneficiary). However, in the particular circumstances of this case, a distribution by way of payment to Grupo Torras, the settlor's creditors, would not be for his 'benefit' and could not be made. Further, the court found that the trustee could not impose his own moral view on a distribution. The fact that the debt originated in fraud was irrelevant. Any distributions had to be considered within the context of the beneficiary's interest. The judgment could not, therefore, be enforced through this indirect route.[28]

24.23   An intriguing element of the case also is whether the major part of the trust fund should be distributed to the settlor-beneficiary's creditors ahead of all of the other beneficiaries. This was particularly in view of the fact that the request for payment seemed to be premature. It was made before a decision had been reached with respect to litigation concerning whether the trust was invalid, or intended to defraud creditors. This, however, did not dissuade the court from its determination.

C. The Rule on Non-enforcement of Foreign Revenue, Penal, and Public Penal Law

24.24   The established rule of private international law, that foreign penal, public, or revenue laws will not be enforced, is also of importance to offshore trusts. In fact, the enforcement of such laws may be an infringement of sovereignty.[29] On the same principles, offshore courts may correctly refuse to enforce revenue laws which seek to expand the territorial jurisdiction of a country to tax its residents and citizens where the relevant assets are located offshore.[30]

24.25   For convenience, we have discussed the rule against the enforcement of foreign revenue law in another chapter in Part III on taxation.[31] We recall the principles and new developments here, and note that the rule is to be considered as only one aspect of the wider rule, that a state does not enforce the penal, public law, or revenue laws of another.

---

[28] The court also appeared to be influenced by the fact that the assets in the trust represented only a fraction of the debt owed and that the honouring of the debt would have resulted in considerable disadvantage to the other beneficiaries.

[29] *In re the Matter of H* [1996] CILR 237, 243 (Grand Ct), *per* Smellie J.

[30] Such as those from the USA.

[31] See chapter 16, paras 16.1–16.32.

Non-enforcement of penal law and public law

The aspect of the rule which relates to the non-enforcement of foreign public **24.26**
law was considered in the case of *United States of America v A Ltd.*[32] This is
actually a sub-rule of the more general rule against the enforcement of foreign
penal law, considered as such in *Huntingon v Attril,*[33] where the term 'penal' was
defined to include not only crimes in a strict sense, but 'all breaches of public
law punishable by pecuniary mulct or otherwise, at the instance of the state
government, or someone representing the public'.[34] The court noted that this
part of the rule is contentious, but had been accepted in a number of cases,
including that of *AG for the UK v Wellington Newspapers Ltd.*[35]

In *United States of America v A Ltd*, the Federal Trade Commission (FTC) of **24.27**
the US, after obtaining judgment in the US against a business for fraud, sued in
the Cook Islands for the recovery of some US $2.25 million held in a trust
fund set up by the business, on the ground that the money had been acquired
fraudulently and disposed of through the trust.

The trustee argued that the suit amounted to the enforcement of a public law of **24.28**
a foreign state. The court first examined the nature of the powers given to the
FTC. It found that the FTC had wide powers to enforce regulations under its
parent Act, the Federal Trade Commission Act 1914 of the US, to prevent and
control trading that was fraudulent or otherwise illegal. The court then
emphasized that it was the substance, rather than the form of the action of
the interest sought to be enforced, which determined whether the matter was
one of public law.

The action by the FTC was taken to enforce the law and was, at least in part, **24.29**
penal. It was also a public law sought to be enforced by a foreign state for
regulatory purposes, and therefore could not be enforced in the Cook Islands.

The expression 'public law' refers to 'all those rules (other than penal and **24.30**
revenue laws) which are enforced as an assertion of the authority of the central
or legal government'.[36] In the instant case, the action related to rights and
powers which had a 'flavour of punishment' and rightly fell under the rule
against penal law and the sub-rule. The court should not concentrate on the
private law character of a cause of action, where its substance and central interest
were really of public law and would, therefore, be inappropriate.

---

[32] (2002) 4 ITELR 797 (High Ct, Cook Islands).
[33] [1893] AC 150, 156 (PC).
[34] Reproduced in *United States of America v A Ltd*, above, n 32, 801.
[35] [1981] 1 NZLR 129.
[36] *USA v A Ltd*, above, n 32, 801, relying on *AG of New Zealand v Ortiz* [1984] AC 1, 34–35.

24.31 The question of the non-enforcement of foreign penal law was further considered in *In the Matter of H.*[37] Here, a subpoena was issued by the US grand jury on an US citizen, to give evidence in relation to assets in a Cayman Islands trust. The matter fell squarely under the rule on the non-enforcement of penal law. The court also considered whether the fact that the person affected by the request was a US citizen subject to the jurisdiction of the US courts, made any difference to the application of the rule. It found that this was irrelevant since the request was intended to have extraterritorial effect, which was in breach of Cayman Island law. Moreover, the attempt to enforce US law through the use of the subpoena was an infringement of Cayman Islands sovereignty.[38] In addition, as a matter of comity, the court was not obliged to facilitate the operations of the grand jury.[39]

Enforcement and variation powers

24.32 In the *Compass* case,[40] the route to enforcement was through the variation of the trust and the general powers of variation under article 47 of the Trusts (Jersey) Law 1984 and the common law. In purporting to vary a trust, a court is acting in place of the trustee. Accordingly, its primary duty is to the beneficiaries. This suggests that if enforcement of the foreign judgment will be in the interest of the beneficiaries, a court may be persuaded to vary the trust. In the instant case, the wife was a former beneficiary under the trust, but the trust instrument clearly excluded any former wives of the settlor from the discretionary class of beneficiaries. As the wife had already obtained a *decree nisi* of divorce at the time of the application for enforcement, she was no longer a beneficiary. However, the court was able to overcome this obstacle by holding that for the purposes of deciding whether the wife was a beneficiary, and thus entitled to the benefit of a variation of the trust, the appropriate time was the time when the actual judgment was obtained. Here, the wife had not yet obtained the *decree nisi* when the initial judgment was obtained in England. She was, therefore, a legitimate beneficiary.

24.33 The mere fact that the wife obtained a decree absolute after the English judgment was not sufficient to exclude her from benefiting from the variation. Accordingly,

---

[37] Above, n 29, *per* Smellie, J.

[38] ibid, 243–4. See R-M B Antoine, *Confidentiality in Offshore Financial Law* (Oxford University Press, Oxford, 2002), chapter 10.

[39] This is due to the general principle that in requests for assistance from foreign courts, courts will not heed requests from bodies which have merely investigative powers, particularly broad investigative powers, as opposed to judicial powers: ibid. Common Law courts are particularly reluctant to assist grand juries. Here, the court was following *Rio Tinto Zinc Corporation v Westinghouse Electric Corporation* [1978] 1 All ER 435, 481.

[40] Above, n 19; and see paras 24.17–24.18.

the court was able to vary the trust to give effect to the foreign judgment. Nonetheless, the importance of the appropriate drafting of the trust instrument where a different result is desired, should be noted here.

Trend in changes of the rule

We have seen that, despite the general thrust toward the non-enforcement of judgments in offshore financial centres, there are several situations in which the courts will relax their restrictive stance in favour of enforcement. However, it should be noted that the changing character of the rule against non-enforcement has been limited mainly to its application to foreign revenue matters, a clear indication of the public policy dimensions of the change.   **24.34**

D. Obtaining Restraint Orders against Offshore Trusts

Trust characteristics favourable to restraint orders

While there are significant hurdles to enforcing foreign judgments in offshore jurisdictions, there is no real impediment to obtaining preliminary remedies, such as restraint orders. Indeed, recent jurisprudence suggests that, in some respects, restraint orders may be more easily obtained in offshore jurisdictions than in onshore jurisdictions.   **24.35**

In offshore jurisdictions, the legal principles pertaining to the award of restraint orders, such as *Mareva* injunctions[41] and *Anton Piller* orders,[42] are no different to those onshore. Thus, principles identified under the common law apply. However, the situation in relation to the subjects of actions for restraint orders in offshore jurisdictions, may vary considerably from those in onshore jurisdictions. Courts, both offshore and onshore, have recognized these contrasting situations when considering whether to award restraint orders. The relevant principles appear to be applied more favourably toward onshore applicants than offshore trusts.   **24.36**

The most important difference, in the view of courts, is the existence of special features in offshore trusts which are conducive to the fast removal of assets. These features are flight and duress clauses, which allow the trust to be relocated quickly, or certain interests severed, in the event of any potential threats to   **24.37**

---

[41] Now termed 'freezing injunctions' in the UK, originally named from the case of *Mareva Cia Naviera SA v International Bulkcarriers SA* [1975] 2 Lloyd's Rep 509 (CA).

[42] Now termed 'search orders' in the UK, originally named from the case *Anton Piller KG v Manufacturing Processes Ltd* [1976] Ch 55, empowering the search for, inspection of, and removal of relevant evidential material to prevent its destruction or concealment.

the trust and its assets. Such features permit the removal of trust assets before attachment is secured by the enforcement of a foreign judgment. Also important, in the view of the courts, is the fact that, typically, offshore settlors are not attached to the offshore jurisdiction. Further, settlors who are 'foreigners' to the offshore jurisdiction have no real ties to that jurisdiction.[43] Offshore trusts are inherently transnational, operating easily across borders. These factors, according to the courts, create a greater risk that law enforcement efforts will be hindered, thus pointing in the direction of restraint orders.

24.38   This more aggressive assertion of jurisdiction by the courts in relation to off-shore trusts, appears to be based on the view that such entities, and indeed offshore finance, are susceptible to abuse and should, therefore, be restrained in the public interest. Judicial enthusiasm for curtailing perceived potential abuses of offshore trusts by easily granting restraint orders, has not been confined to onshore courts. For a variety of reasons, offshore courts have been just as pro-active, sometimes leading the way in the endeavour.[44] Indeed, courts deliberating on applications for restraint orders in relation to offshore trusts, can be accused of being too zealous in their approach.

24.39   The analogy may be made in relation to offshore companies, as seen in *Kilderkin Investments Ltd v Player*.[45] This case concerned an application for a *Mareva* injunction brought by a Canadian receiver to identify, preserve, and recover assets of the defendants located within the Cayman Islands. The substantive action was for alleged fraud. The court noted the greater risk of the removal of assets by defendants in offshore jurisdictions than elsewhere:

> Where . . . the persons concerned have no strong ties to the Islands, or a company is involved which can easily fold or be stripped of its assets, the temptation to remove assets from the jurisdiction to escape the effects of a judgment of this court must be great . . . [giving] rise to a risk. Risk may be inferred from circumstances here which might not give rise to the same inference in England.[46]

Such considerations, in the view of the court, led to a presumption in favour of granting a *Mareva* injunction.

---

[43] But this is not conclusive. Contrast, eg, the case of *Bank of Nova Scotia v Emerald Seas Ltd* [1984–85] CILR 180, where the Grand Court held that the fact that the first and second defendants were foreigners within the jurisdiction (and therefore not bound to remain for a trial, or to maintain their assets within the jurisdiction) did not of itself warrant the injunction.

[44] For example, they do not wish to appear to be facilitating fraud, or they may do so in the interest of comity.

[45] [1980–83] CILR 403.

[46] ibid, 408.

Increased availability of restraint orders due to flight and duress clauses

While flight clauses and similar features are not confined to offshore trusts, **24.40**
their prevalence in offshore structures makes the offshore trust a more likely
target of restraint orders. Indeed, the very notion of asset protection trusts raises
the suspicion of courts, tempting them to secure the safety of assets.

The existence of flight and duress clauses encouraged the courts to grant *Mareva* **24.41**
injunctions in several cases.[47] The ease with which such trusts could be
relocated, given the wide discretionary powers of the trustees to do so, was
expressly noted in *Lemos,* and the court viewed this as creating 'very real risk'
that the Cayman proceedings could be aborted by relocating the trust. In *Private
Trust Corporation,* the Court of Appeal of The Bahamas noted that provisions
such as duress clauses, and those which allow the transfer of the trust to the
exclusive jurisdiction of another state, were provisions which create the 'very
kind of situation which the *Mareva* injunction was developed to counteract'
flight of funds or dissipation of assets which could frustrate the execution of a
possible judgment'.[48]

However, we should note the caution sounded in *Private Trust Corporation,* **24.42**
insisting, despite the award of the injunction, that future plaintiffs should not
believe that 'injunctions and discovery against trustees in The Bahamas are to be
had for the asking . . . at the whim of a litigant who comes up against the
prohibitory provisions of the Banks and Trust Companies Regulation Act'.[49] In
many instances, therefore, the existence of a flight or duress clause, of itself,
might not be sufficient to ground a restraint order. Another risk factor may be
necessary, such as whether the trust is prima facie a sham or fraud, elements
which are considered in the following section.

Greater availability of restraint orders for shams and frauds

The courts have demonstrated that they will be easily persuaded to grant **24.43**
restraint orders against offshore trusts which are, prima facie, shams or frauds.[50]
This was demonstrated in *Banco Ambrosiano Holdings v Clara Canetti Calvi,*[51]
in which an insolvent settlor established a network of foreign and English trusts

---

[47] See, eg, *Private Trust Corporation & Others v Grupo Torras SA & Another,* [1997–98] 1
OFLR 443; *Banco Ambrosiano Holdings v Clara Canetti Calvi* (Sup Ct, The Bahamas) No 237 of
1987; and *Lemos v Coutts & Company (Cayman) Ltd & Others* [1992–93] CILR 5, 13.

[48] *Private Trust Corporation,* above, n 47, 452.

[49] ibid, 453.

[50] See chapters 8 and 9, 'The Offshore Trust as a Sham' and 'Fraudulent Conveyances and the
Offshore Trust' respectively, for discussions of the offshore trust as a sham or fraud. Where these
situations arise, strict confidentiality laws in the offshore jurisdiction will not be obstacles to the
award of restraint orders. See the discussion below, paras 24.75–24.78.

[51] (Sup Ct, The Bahamas) No 237 of 1987.

so that his true beneficial interests were concealed and could not be reached. A *prima facie* case of a 'sham' trust was identified, and this was sufficient to award the injunction. The court noted that, in such a situation, 'judicial timidity' should not be permitted to prevent the award of an injunction, as there is a real risk of assets being withdrawn from the jurisdiction.[52] It would be 'judicial irresponsibility' to turn a blind eye to the evidence of fraud.

24.44 Other elements commonly found in offshore trusts which would ring 'alarm bells' for the courts and persuade them to award *Mareva* injunctions, are provisions for the cessation of the tenure of trustees by the settlor, either directly or indirectly, the divestment of the property and title thereto, and provisions for the ouster of the jurisdiction of the courts hearing the matter. In the last scenario, an attempt is made to transfer jurisdiction to another forum, which will have exclusive jurisdiction. This last is an unusual feature remarked upon by Gonsalves-Sabola P, of the Court of Appeal of The Bahamas.[53]

Permitting worldwide restraint orders and aiding foreign proceedings

24.45 Restraint orders are also now available against defendants in relation to their worldwide assets.[54] These extended powers have significant implications for offshore trusts, which are often transnational in nature. They also undermine the capacity of offshore trusts to transfer assets from one offshore jurisdiction to another via 'flight clauses', when assets are in danger.[55] This assumption of jurisdiction will also impact on third parties who are in possession of assets being challenged.

24.46 Not surprisingly, given the inherent transnational nature and flexibility of offshore trusts, courts have been somewhat eager to award worldwide *Mareva* injunctions against them. Straughton LJ put it this way in the case of *Republic of Haiti v Duvalier*:[56]

> If it happens that there is a bank account in the Channel Islands . . . which can be operated on the signature of an English resident . . . I would find it offensive that he should be free to cross the Channel and sign away the money.

24.47 In *Walsh v Deloitte & Touche Inc*,[57] the Judicial Committee of the Privy Council confirmed that the courts of The Bahamas had the power to award worldwide

---

[52] ibid, 11.

[53] In the case of *Private Trust Corporation v Grupo Torras*, above, n 47, 452.

[54] See, eg, *Babanaft International Co SA v Bassatne* [1989] 2 WLR 232; *Republic of Haiti v Duvalier* [1989] 2 WLR 261 (CA); *Derby & Co v Weldon (No 6)* [1990] 1 WLR 1139 (CA).

[55] In *Derby & Co*, above, n 54, where the Court of Appeal asserted its right to order assets that were situated abroad to be transferred from the foreign territory prior to trial and judgment.

[56] Above, n 54, 275.

[57] [2001] UKPC 58 (PC, The Bahamas).

Mareva injunctions. The case involved a Canadian company which made a voluntary assignment in bankruptcy. Proceedings were on foot in Canada. However, the defendant, who was the company's chief executive, moved to The Bahamas. Thereafter, the trustee in bankruptcy instituted proceedings in The Bahamas for breach of fiduciary duty. However, it was accepted that the main purpose of the proceedings was to obtain interlocutory relief in the form of a *Mareva* injunction restraining the defendants from dealing with their assets worldwide and an order for disclosure of the value, location, and other particulars of such assets.

The authority of the courts in The Bahamas to grant *Mareva* injunctions springs from s 21(1) of the Supreme Court Act 1996 of The Bahamas. Under this instrument, the court may award such injunctions 'where it appears to the court to be just and convenient to do so'. Lord Hoffman noted that The Bahamas statute was based on an earlier English statute which had been extended by an additional section.[58] This latter section amplified considerably the jurisdiction of the English courts to award *Mareva* injunctions which have extraterritorial effect. The Bahamas had not subsequently modified its own legislation to reflect the UK provisions. Nonetheless, the Privy Council found that the authority to grant *Mareva* relief in respect of assets within or without the jurisdiction, and against residents or foreigners, was well established in England before the passing of the 1981 Act.[59] This authority therefore subsisted under the common law. Accordingly, the courts of The Bahamas had a similar jurisdiction and could award the *Mareva* injunction sought.   **24.48**

The debate on the need for substantive causes of action for *Mareva* injunctions

Perhaps the more contentious issue with respect to the assertion of extraterritorial jurisdiction as it relates to *Mareva* injunctions, is the issue surrounding the requirement that interlocutory orders be ancillary to substantive jurisdiction. On this question, where offshore matters are involved, some courts, even offshore courts, have not contented themselves with merely applying traditional principles on restraint orders, including generous application of such principles. Rather, they have been more innovative in their approach and redefined the rule on jurisdiction requirements in relation to the award of *Mareva* injunctions.   **24.49**

The traditional rule requires that applications for interlocutory orders must originate from a substantive action over which the court has jurisdiction in the   **24.50**

---

[58] The Supreme Court 1981 Act, s 37, of the UK. For example, the provision gives the UK courts express power to grant interlocutory relief in respect of assets within the jurisdiction, whether or not the defendant is domiciled, resident, or present within that jurisdiction.

[59] Relying on *Derby & Co Ltd*, above, n 52, for example.

first instance.[60] Currently, two distinct schools of thought have emerged in offshore jurisdictions seized of the issue: one school adheres strictly to the traditional rule and the other rejects it entirely. The disparity is fuelled by the continuing debate about the merits or demerits of the *Siskina*[61] case, the authority for the traditional rule, as opposed to those of the *Mercedes-Benz*[62] approach.

24.51   In *Mercedes-Benz*, Lord Nicholls expressed a minority opinion that the established rule, as promulgated in *The Siskina*, was 'bad law' and lagged behind the realities of modern commercial life, thereby failing to meet the needs of society. Indeed, the law, as expressed in *The Siskina*, was subsequently changed by statute in the UK.[63] Since equivalent statutes have not been forthcoming in other common law jurisdictions, in particular in offshore jurisdictions, the courts have been forced to resolve the issue. Thus, this is an important issue which remains alive in many Common Law jurisdictions, including offshore jurisdictions.

Cases supporting extraterritorial jurisdiction and the Mercedes Benz approach

24.52   Several offshore courts have preferred to adopt the view expressed in *Mercedes-Benz*, thereby rejecting the *Siskina* rule and awarding worldwide *Mareva* injunctions where they have no jurisdiction over the substantive action.[64] These courts have been willing to do so for reasons of public policy, comity, and 'moral principle'. In such cases, the courts have identified the increased sophistication of the international banking and financial system, which enables wrongdoers to move money speedily across borders, as a key reason for such assistance.[65] For example, in *Canada Trust Company v Stolzenberg*,[66] the court was of the opinion that without an extended territorial jurisdiction, in the face of 'rampant transnational fraud' the worldwide *Mareva* injunction would be 'a relatively toothless procedure', since:

> [i]n many cases . . . the connection and transactions with different countries will enable the defendant to raise jurisdictional challenges which may [cause] . . .

---

[60]   *The Siskina, In Re* [1979] AC 210.
[61]   ibid.
[62]   From the case *Mercedes-Benz v Leiduck* [1996] AC 284 (PC).
[63]   By s 37 of the Supreme Court Act 1981 of the UK and the Civil Jurisdiction and Judgments Act 1982 (Interim Relief) Order 1997 (SI 1997 No 302) of the UK, which entered into force on 1 April 1997. The latter instrument incorporates Art 24 of the EEC Convention on Jurisdiction and Enforcement of Judgments in Civil and Commercial Matters (The Brussels Convention on Civil Jurisdiction and Enforcement of Judgments 1968) (Brussels, 27 September 1968, EC 46 (1978); Cmnd 7395; [1978] OJ L304/1, 8 ILM 229), hereinafter 'the Brussels Convention 1968', which confers a statutory jurisdiction on contracting states to grant interim relief in aid of proceedings brought or to be brought in another contracting state.
[64]   See, eg, *Krohn GmbH v Varna Shipyard (No 2)* [1997–98] 1 OFLR 482 (Royal Ct, Jersey); and *Solvalub Ltd v Match Investments Ltd* [1997–98] 1 OFLR 152 (CA, Jersey).
[65]   See *Krohn GmbH*, above, n 64, 486.
[66]   [1997/98] 1 CILR 606, 625–6.

such a lengthy delay it would be impossible to 'police' the *Mareva* . . . any delay in enforcing the disclosure order will give [the defendant] ample opportunity to protect himself against a possible judgment . . . by moving his assets to financial safe havens. The balance tilts in favour of disclosure now.[67]

In *Solvalub Ltd v Match Investments Ltd*,[68] the Court of Appeal of Jersey adopted Lord Nicholls's dissenting view in *Mercedes-Benz* and held that the Jersey courts had jurisdiction to award *Mareva* injunctions even in the absence of a substantive action before them. It based its finding on public policy grounds, specifically, the need to protect the reputation of Jersey as a reputable financial centre willing to suppress international crime, and the desire to act in accordance with comity. The judgment was followed in another Jersey case, *Krohn GmbH v Varna Shipyards (No 2)*.[69]   **24.53**

The issue of jurisdiction in the absence of a substantive action was also addressed by the High Court of the Isle of Man, in the case of *Securities and Investments Board v Michael Ivor Braff*.[70] This court also followed the *Mercedes-Benz* approach, in a judgment with reasoning which resembled that in *Solvalub*.   **24.54**

The courts may also be able to justify circumvention of the rule which requires jurisdiction over the substantive matter, by relying on the fact that the proper law of the trust is the law of the jurisdiction in which the court presides. This was the approach of the Supreme Court of The Bahamas in the case of *Grupo Torras SA v Meespierson (Bahamas) Ltd*,[71] albeit a lower court judgment which was subsequently overturned.[72] The principle, however, may be useful before other courts.   **24.55**

In a more recent case, *The State of Qatar v Sheikh Khalifa*,[73] the Royal Court of Jersey was asked specifically to decide whether *The Siskina* judgment was binding in Jersey, thereby pronouncing cases like *Krohn* and *Solvalub*, which had refused to follow *The Siskina*, wrongly decided. The court emphatically rejected the view that *The Siskina* was binding in the Jersey courts. Intriguingly, it held that the doctrine of binding precedent was not part of the law of Jersey because of its legal history, which is based heavily on French law.[74] Consequently, the   **24.56**

---

[67] ibid.

[68] Above, n 64, 161 et seq.

[69] Above, n 64.

[70] (1997–98) 1 OFLR 553 (High Ct).

[71] [1998–99] 2 OFLR 553 (SC, The Bahamas).

[72] *Meespierson (Bahamas) Ltd v Grupo Torras SA* (1999) 2 ITELR 29 (CA).

[73] (1999) 2 ITELR 143 (Royal Ct, Jersey), *per* Sir Philip Bailhache (Bailiff).

[74] It affirmed, too, that the Jersey courts are not bound to Privy Council judgments from other jurisdictions: ibid, 151. In contrast, the Bahamian Court of Appeal in *Meespierson (Bahamas) Ltd v Grupo Torras SA*, above, n 72, considered further below, paras 24.58–24.63, had a restrictive approach to precedent and felt unable to deviate from *The Siskina* precedent.

Jersey courts had the leeway to decide the issue of jurisdiction with respect to *Mareva* injunctions afresh. The court found that there were important policy reasons[75] to permit the grant of *Mareva* injunctions in the absence of substantive proceedings before the court hearing the application. It therefore adopted the approach in *Mercedes-Benz* as the law in Jersey. The court thereby confirmed the dicta in earlier cases such as *Krohn.*[76]

Decisions supporting The Siskina

24.57　In contrast to the decisions from the Channel Islands, discussed in the preceding section, offshore courts elsewhere have taken a conservative approach to the issue of jurisdiction to grant *Mareva* injunctions where unrelated to substantive actions. These other jurisdictions have not, however, always been consistent in the rationales for their decisions.

24.58　In The Bahamas, the matter has been quite litigious, but the approach to the issue has been somewhat convoluted. In the Court of Appeal judgment in *Meespierson (Bahamas) Ltd v Grupo Torras SA,*[77] the Court was preoccupied with the same question, whether to follow *The Siskina,* or the more liberal approach found in *Mercedes-Benz.* Carey JA and Gonsalves-Sabola P rejected Lord Nicholls's dissenting opinion in *Mercedes-Benz* outright, preferring to rely on 'long standing orthodoxy'.[78] However, while Hall JA came to the same conclusion as the other judges, his reason for the finding appeared to differ. He seemed to have no objection to following *Mercedes-Benz* in a case where there was a substantive cause of action in *some* forum—in a foreign country or *somewhere.* However, he declined to assume jurisdiction where there were not as yet any substantive actions in any jurisdiction, as was the case in *Meespierson.* Indeed, the fact that there was no cause of action *anywhere,* is an important distinction in the case. The Court agreed that there was 'no decision to be found where *Mareva* relief has been granted against a sole defendant or defendants in circumstances where no substantive claim exists or has been made or asserted against that defendant or defendants anywhere in the world'.[79]

24.59　In *Meespierson,* Gonsalves-Sabola P reasoned that *Mercedes-Benz* was not a credible precedent. This was because the majority in *Mercedes-Benz* had found that the question of whether the court had power to grant a *Mareva* injunction

---

[75]　*The State of Qatar,* above, n 73, 152. These were the social and policy considerations alluded to in the earlier cases of *Solvalub Ltd v Match Investments,* above, n 64, and *Krohn GmbH v Varna Shipyards (No 2),* above, n 64, which the court adopted, ibid, 152.

[76]　*The State of Qatar,* above, n 73, 152.

[77]　Above, n 72.

[78]　ibid, 38.

[79]　ibid, 40.

in the absence of a substantive cause of action within the jurisdiction, which Lord Nicholls had answered affirmatively in his dissent, did not arise for decision. Further, Lord Nicholls's reasoning was based on the possibility of the enforcement of a foreign judgment in the court being petitioned for the *Mareva*, and this was not possible in the instant case. More important, the Court in *Meespierson* could find no plausible reason to disturb the status quo, as expressed in *The Siskina* precedent. The precedent had been disturbed in the UK courts only by statute, and since there was no statutory equivalent in The Bahamas, the precedent should stand until such time that Parliament sought to reverse the rule by legislation. To do otherwise would be unwarranted judicial activism.[80]

The Court in *Meespierson* also responded to initiatives which reversed the rule in **24.60** *The Siskina* on grounds of comity and justice, finding that these bases were insufficient to overrule the established precedent. Gonsalves-Sabola P quoted Lord Diplock's gentle rebuke of Lord Denning's call for judicial activism on this ground, where he had said:

> . . . there may be merits in Lord Denning MR's alternative proposals for extending the jurisdiction of the High Court over foreign defendants but they cannot, in my view, be supported by considerations of comity or by the Common Market treaties. They would require at least subordinate legislation . . . It is not for the Court of Appeal to exercise these legislative functions, however tempting this may be.[81]

The Court was, therefore, not persuaded to follow the approach seen in the **24.61** Channel Islands which had relied on public policy, such as considerations of comity, although the situations in those countries were similar to The Bahamas.[82] Gonsalves-Sabola P said:

> I do not regards these Channel Island decisions, for all the reasons given earlier, as persuasive authority. I do not perceive a public policy in The Bahamas, standing as a sovereign state, which drives the Bahamian judge to be creative to the extent of making a serendipitous discovery of a common law principle equivalent to the provisions of s 25 of the Civil Jurisdiction and Judgments Act 1982 which the English Parliament saw fit to enact to empower free-standing interim relief to be given in aid of proceedings brought or to be brought in a Contracting State to the Brussels or Lugano Convention.[83]

The Court also underscored and explained the ancillary nature of the *Mareva* **24.62** injunction, in what it considered to be 'commonsense observations':

---

[80] ibid, 38–9.

[81] ibid, 39, quoting from *The Siskina*, above, n 60, 260. The court thus expressly disagreed with its lower court's reliance, by Sawyer CJ, on these Channel Islands cases. The lower court's judgment is found at [1998–99] 2 OFLR 163.

[82] See above, *Krohn* and *Solvalub*, 64. Like The Bahamas, there were no statutory bases for the change in jurisdiction.

[83] See above, n 72, 38.

The essential nature of the *Mareva* is that it is interlocutory. It essentially derives from substantive proceedings as ancillary relief. If it did not so derive there would be a lack of logic, in the legal sense, of its grant. The court which is applied to for *Mareva* relief would not be able to have in view a prospective judgment whose probability . . . could be used as a touchstone to determine whether it was 'just and convenient' to grant the relief. The court would perforce make but a strained effort to discharge its duty to make that determination . . .[84]

24.63 Thus, *Meespierson* clearly puts the case in favour of a restrictive approach to jurisdiction in relation to *Mareva* relief.

Placing Walsh v Deloitte & Touche *in context*

24.64 The issue as it relates to The Bahamas was revisited in the case of *Walsh v Deloitte & Touche Inc*,[85] this time by the Privy Council. As noted above, it was accepted that the primary purpose of The Bahamas proceedings for breach of fiduciary duty, was to obtain interlocutory relief in the form of a *Mareva* injunction.[86] In this case, the *Mareva* was awarded. The judgment has been heralded as supporting the *Mercedes-Benz* line of cases that a court can order a *Mareva* in support of foreign proceedings in the absence of a substantive cause of action before it. It is suggested, however, that the facts of the case do not lend themselves to claiming such a victory. While Lord Hoffman felt that there 'was no objection in principle' to awarding a *Mareva* solely in aid of foreign proceedings, his words must be viewed in context. Most important is the fact that the Privy Council did not need to consider the issue, as there was, in fact, a substantive cause of action before The Bahamas court. The confusion arises because it was acknowledged that The Bahamas proceedings were simply being used as a 'stepping stone', merely to give efficacy to the 'real' proceedings, that is, the foreign proceedings in Canada. The intention of the trustee was that, after obtaining *Mareva* relief, it would stay The Bahamas action and proceed with the action in Ontario. Lord Hoffman's remark that there was no objection to award the *Mareva* solely in aid of foreign proceedings may be taken to mean that he saw nothing wrong with this 'roundabout' route to obtaining the *Mareva*, even understanding that the real objective was to aid foreign proceedings. The fact remained, however, that The Bahamas court had a substantive action before it.

24.65 Further, Lord Hoffman's other remarks need to be reconciled. Earlier in the judgment he specifically cited *The Siskina* as the appropriate authority, and in fact made no mention of *Mercedes-Benz* or its progeny. He said:

---

[84] ibid, 39.

[85] Above, n 57.

[86] See above, paras 24.47–24.48. The *Mareva* sought was to restrain the defendants from dealing with their assets worldwide, and an order for disclosure of the value, location, and other particulars of such assets.

Interlocutory jurisdiction is ordinarily ancillary to substantive jurisdiction and in *Siskina* . . . the House of Lords decided that a court could not (in the absence of statutory authority) grant *Mareva* interlocutory relief unless the defendant was 'amenable to the jurisdiction of the court' in respect of a substantive cause of action.[87]

Indeed, if one were to consider that Lord Hoffman was arguing in favour of an outright rejection of *The Siskina* principle, his use of the case of *Crédit Suisse Fides Trust SA v Cuoghi*[88] as an example, would place his judgment dangerously close to being *per incuriam*. This is because *Crédit Suisse* was argued on the basis that, unlike in The Bahamas, there was in place a statute which permitted such an exercise of jurisdiction in England. The courts merely had to decide whether it was appropriate, that is, just and expedient, for then to exercise this jurisdiction. The better view, therefore, was that Lord Hoffman's affirmation of principle was more general in nature, confined to wider extensions of territorial jurisdiction of the kind which permit worldwide *Mareva* injunctions in general, the main tenet of his judgment. Clearly, he was concerned that courts should be aware of the ramifications of the exercise of, or failure to exercise, their jurisdiction on international crime.[89]

24.66

It is clear, therefore, that the debate on whether a *Mareva* can be granted in aid of foreign proceedings where there is no substantive action before the local court, was not fully explored in the *Walsh* case. While *Walsh v Deloitte & Touche* did not appear to rule out the more modern approach (as reflected in *Mercedes-Benz*) entirely, it was more concerned with the award of a worldwide *Mareva* where there were, in fact, proceedings before the local court. Consequently, it cannot be viewed as an authoritative or determinative decision on this particular issue. At best, with respect to this matter, the *Walsh* case is ambiguous, and its contribution to the debate is slight.

24.67

In *Securities and Exchange Commission v Banner Fund International*,[90] the Supreme Court of Belize refused to expand its jurisdiction in this manner and reverted to the traditional rule that it must have jurisdiction to hear the substantive proceedings before it could award such injunctions. In the British Virgin Islands, the position also appears to be in accord with the traditional

24.68

---

[87] See above, n 57, 61–62.

[88] [1998] QB 818.

[89] For example, he stated that 'international judicial cooperation should be encouraged'. He further pointed out that it was 'commonplace that the most convenient forum may not be the place where it is desirable to obtain *Mareva* relief, either because the defendant resides there and is amenable to the enforcement jurisdiction of the local court, or because the assets are there and notice can be served upon persons . . . who have them under control'. See n 57, above, 64–5.

[90] (1996) WIR 123 (SC, Belize), *per* Gonsalez J.

approach and the view that the granting of a *Mareva* should be treated with caution.[91]

Is potential enforcement the underlying rationale for Mareva awards?

24.69 One aspect of the discussion which has not, perhaps, been fully aired, is the underlying premise of Lord Nicholls's dissent in *Mercedes-Benz*.[92] This is the point on the potential enforcement of any resulting judgment by the court being asked to award the *Mareva*. In Lord Nicholls's view, this was a prime rationale for awarding it. Thus, the issue should turn not on the underlying cause of action, but on the enforcement of a prospective judgment. Lord Nicholls stated:

> So long as the foreign judgment when obtained will be recognised and enforceable in Hong Kong, the Hong Kong court should be as able to exercise its wide powers to grant an injunction in such a case as in a case where the judgment is being sought from the Hong Kong court itself.[93]

24.70 In the context of offshore cases this element assumes greater importance, and could lead perhaps to results radically different from what Lord Nicholls envisaged. The point of departure is the general thrust against the enforcement of certain foreign judgments in offshore jurisdictions.[94] If the rationale for the change from the *Siskina* principle is to rest on the capacity of the foreign judgment to be enforced, it would appear to be inapplicable in the offshore context. We are left only with policy rationales such as comity, identified in cases like *Krohn* and *Solvalub*.[95]

24.71 Further, despite declarations of public policy in favour of such *Mareva* injunctions in some offshore courts, there is at least an equally weighted public policy rationale against the grant of such restraint orders, in view of the legislative focus on non-enforcement. In addition, the cautions sounded in other cases about the need to be circumspect regarding the granting of *Mareva* injunctions, need to be heeded.[96]

Assistance for orders unavailable in the foreign court

24.72 Another point of note would be the question whether the local court has power to aid foreign proceedings to give effect to an order which is unavailable in the foreign court that is hearing the substantive proceedings and which it is

---

[91] See, eg, *Lisa SA v Lomax Trading Company Ltd* (High Ct, BVI) No 21 of 1999, decided 13 April 2000, where the request for a *Mareva* injunction was denied.
[92] See above, n 62.
[93] ibid, 305.
[94] See the discussion above, paras 24.3–24.10.
[95] See above, n 64.
[96] See below, paras 24.79–24.84.

assisting. This was considered in the case of *Crédit Suisse Fides Trust SA v Cuoghi*.[97] In that case, the Swiss courts, before which the substantive proceedings were being held, could not make orders to force non-residents to disclose assets not located in Switzerland. The English court had jurisdiction to award *Mareva* injunctions to aid Swiss proceedings generally, and was in a position to make such orders. The question was whether the English courts could act, in aid of the foreign proceedings, and order that those assets be disclosed and frozen where such an order was unavailable in Switzerland. The defendant argued that it could not, as such an act would be seeking to remedy a defect in the foreign law, which was not a permissible exercise of jurisdiction. The court disagreed, finding that it had jurisdiction to aid foreign proceedings in this way and that its action was not remedying a defect in the foreign law. The court's reasoning was based on the underlying principles of Article 24 of the Brussels Convention.[98] This articulated that each contracting state should be willing to assist the courts of another contracting state 'by providing such interim relief as would be available if its own courts were seized of the substantive proceedings'.[99]

24.73 For those offshore courts which have asserted jurisdiction to aid in foreign proceedings, and thereby adopted the general principles under the Brussels Convention, as reflected in more modern English legislation, it would appear that this broader extension of jurisdiction is plausible.

No uniform approach

24.74 In conclusion, it may be said that, on this issue, there is no uniform approach amongst offshore courts. The respective courts are caught between the dilemma of being faithful to the inherent logic of the interlocutory relief that is the *Mareva*, and the need to be part of the growing international trend toward cooperation and comity where international crime is concerned. Against this backdrop there lies the clear contradiction between expanded territorial jurisdiction, and the policies of offshore courts against the enforcement of foreign judgments and foreign laws where such judgments can prejudice the continued existence of offshore entities, such as offshore trusts. Nonetheless, the general rule remains that as expressed in *The Siskina*.

Confidentiality obstacles to restraint orders

24.75 Offshore confidentiality laws may prove to be significant obstacles to attempts both to obtain restraint orders and to enforce onshore judgments. However,

---

[97] Above, n 88.
[98] To which it was a party. See above, n 63.
[99] *Crédit Suisse*, above, n 88, 823–4.

where there is *prima facie* evidence of a crime, courts will usually override confidentiality obligations.[100]

Concerns about comity and sovereignty in restraint order applications

24.76 Regard for comity or sovereignty might influence the courts in their deliberations about whether to award *Mareva* injunctions. Notwithstanding, onshore courts have not always respected the laws of offshore jurisdictions, in particular their confidentiality laws. For example, in *Canada Trust Co v Stolzenberg*,[101] the English High Court held that a *Mareva* injunction and an award for the disclosure of trust assets in Liechtenstein should be granted despite the fact that the disclosure requirements of the *Mareva* would have required the defendant to breach the law of another country. While this was viewed as a relevant factor in the decision, it was not a conclusive factor.[102]

24.77 Even offshore courts have been willing to sacrifice their interest in upholding their own laws in favour of comity, through rendering assistance to onshore litigants. One reason given was that such an approach helps to protect the reputation of the offshore financial jurisdiction as a responsible financial centre.[103] Yet, in the case of offshore courts, concerns about sovereignty and the need to preserve their right to enact laws, may assist in tempering their apparent zeal in awarding restraint orders.

Recent developments restricting the application of restraint orders

24.78 As we have demonstrated, in recent times the courts, both offshore and onshore, have been generous, in the interest of law enforcement, in awarding restraint orders. They have been particularly facilitative with regard to *Mareva* injunctions:

---

[100] See, eg, *Kilderkin* above, n 45, 406, (Grand Ct, Cayman Islands). This concerned a *prima facie* case of fraud. Awarding the restraint order, the court said that 'it was the duty of the court to assist the plaintiff ... to trace, recover or preserve the assets. The *Confidential Relationships (Preservation) Law* did not inhibit the making of such an order', Such orders may be obtained provided that the required procedural steps under the statute are carried out. See also *Stewart v Stewart ASK Securities Ltd* [1986–87] CILR 28 (Grand Ct, CI). The plaintiff alleged that her husband had misrepresented the value of his offshore shares to which she was entitled under Californian law. Confidentiality obligations did not, as a matter of public policy, preclude the order. *Re Tucker, A Bankrupt* [1987–88] Manx LR 8, also found that confidentiality should not 'cloak irregular financial dealings'. For a more thorough analysis of the implications of confidentiality for restraint orders, R-M B Antoine, *Confidentiality in Offshore Financial Law* (Oxford University Press, Oxford, 2002), chapter 7. See too, in this book, chapter 7, 'Disclosure and Confidentiality Obligations'.

[101] Above, n 66.

[102] See also *Crédit Suisse Fides Trust SA v Cuoghi*, above, n 88, which concerned a request for the restraint of assets connected to offshore fraud. The English court held that concerns for comity did not prevent the courts from providing assistance to each other.

[103] As proclaimed by the Jersey court in *Solvalub Ltd v Match Investments*, above, n 64.

they have been generous with the jurisdiction to award worldwide *Mareva* injunctions generally, and have gone as far as rewriting traditional legal rules which preclude the award of worldwide *Mareva* injunctions where the court does not have jurisdiction to hear the substantive matter. Both of these recent developments are far-reaching jurisdictions which have significant international aspects and impact considerably on offshore investments. The courts have justified this expansion of the law by the purported increased vulnerability of offshore structures to criminal abuse, for example, the prevalence of 'flight clauses' which allow offshore assets to be moved easily.

However, some recent developments suggest that the legal landscape in relation to the award of restraint orders might be changing. First, a dramatic decision from the US courts may stem the tide of *Mareva* injunctions being granted in relation to offshore assets. In *Grupos Mexicano de Desorollo SA v Allison Bond Fund Inc*,[104] the US Supreme Court decided that the US Federal courts have no power to grant interlocutory injunctions to restrain defendants from disposing of their assets pending the determination of an action. The decision was based on a finding that such a jurisdiction had not been received in US law since, in 1789, the date of reception in the USA, there had been in existence a well-established general rule that a judgment establishing a debt was necessary before a court would interfere with a debtor's use of his property. **24.79**

The judgment significantly weakens the reach of US courts over offshore assets, and could be considered a victory for those prioritizing confidentiality and the physical integrity of offshore trusts. Nonetheless, it should be noted that trust assets may be reached in the USA by other means. For example, under state law, a plaintiff may obtain an attachment of assets within the state pending trial. **24.80**

Secondly, certain courts, in particular certain Canadian courts, have also expressed reservations about the unrestrained use of *Mareva* injunctions when dealing with offshore trusts. In *Green v Jernigan*,[105] Groberman J, of the Supreme Court of Vancouver, cautioned that *Mareva* injunctions were draconian remedies and required that a strong *prima facie* case be demonstrated before they should be awarded. According to him: **24.81**

> In recent years . . . many litigants have forgotten that *Mareva* injunctions are extraordinary and invasive remedies. The courts have gradually made such injunctions more commonplace . . . it is important that the courts not be complacent in issuing *Mareva* relief . . . the balance of convenience [must] justify the very restrictive nature of the injunction.[106]

---

[104] 119 Sup SL 1961 (1999).
[105] (2003) 6 ITELR 330 (Sup Ct, Vancouver).
[106] ibid, 334.

Here, the defendant, the trustee, was accused of a breach of trust, which resulted in the unlawful acquisition of property from the trust funds. Normally, in such cases, the test would require a plaintiff to do more than simply allege that the property was acquired through the proceeds of a breach of trust. At minimum, the plaintiff must show that the property was acquired in suspicious circumstances. In the instant case, the plaintiffs had not met the test and the injunction was not to be granted.

24.82 Concern about the use of worldwide *Mareva* injunctions and extraterritorial jurisdiction, in particular their effect on third parties, has also been raised in *Crédit Suisse Fides Trust SA v Cuoghi*.[107] The reluctance of The Bahamas Court of Appeal to extend its jurisdiction in favour of *Mareva* awards in the absence of a substantive cause of action before it, also underlines the more conservative approach taken by some courts.[108] In *Lisa SA v Lomax Trading Company Ltd*,[109] Moore J put it this way:

> The principles governing the grant of *Mareva* injunctions or freezing orders are well settled and established throughout the common law world. The British Virgin Islands is not about to stray into the uncultivated pastures of jurisprudential heterodoxy in this field of law. The purpose of the *Mareva* is limited in nature. All the more because of the awesome impact which it is capable of having upon an unsuspecting and *a fortiori* an unheard defendant.

He further agreed with counsel's description of the *Mareva* injunction as 'draconian' and one of the court's 'nuclear weapons'.[110]

24.83 The judgment suggests that a judicial attitude which views as sufficient the mere fact that the trust is an offshore trust and exhibits characteristics typical of offshore trusts, may not be appropriate. This is particularly in view of the fact that offshore trusts are created with legislative approval.

---

[107] Above, n 88, 821–2.

[108] See the discussion above, paras 24.57–24.64.

[109] (High Ct, British Virgin Islands) No 21 of 1999, decided 13 April 2000, where the request for a *Mareva* injunction was denied.

[110] ibid, 10.

BIBLIOGRAPHY

A Lord Chancellor's Department Consultation Paper: The Rule against Excessive Accumulations—Consultation Paper on the partial implementation of the Law Commission's Report, 'The Rules against perpetuities and Excessive Accumulations' by way of a Regulatory Reform Order, September 2002. *www.lcd.gov.uk/consult/rro.exacc.htm.*

Amari, Richard 'Asset Protection Trusts—Nuclear Bomb Shelter' [1992] Flor B J, 1.

Anthony, K D 'The Viability of the Civilist Legal Tradition in St. Lucia,' in Landry, R and Caparros, E (eds) *Essays on the Civil Codes of Quebec and St. Lucia* (Ottawa University Press, Ottawa, 1984).

Antoine, R-M B *Confidentiality in Offshore Financial Law* (Oxford University Press, London, NY, 2002) Ch 10.

Antoine, R-M B 'Obtaining' Mareva Injunctions and Related Orders Against Offshore Assets'(1998) Carib LR 212.

Baxendale-Walker, P *Purpose Trusts for Commercial and Private Use* (Butterworths Tolley, UK, 1999).

Bennet, Tim 'Asset Protection and Offshore Creditor Trusts', in *Tolley's International Tax Planning* (Tolley, UK, 1994).

Brownbill, D 'The Proper Constitution of a Trust' in Antoine R-M B (ed) *Legal Issues in Offshore Financial Law* (Caribbean Law Publishing Company, Jamaica, 2004).

Cabinet Office Report, Private Action.

Cash, E and 'The Bahamas: An Overview of the Perpetuities Act 1995,' [1995] 4 JIntP, 104.

Cheshire & North, Private International Law (12th edn, Butterworths, UK, 1992) 879.

Chown, J and Edwardes-Kerr, M 'Tax Havens and Offshore Investment Centres' (1974) The Banker Annual Review, 479.

Collins, Lawrence (ed.) *Dicey and Morris on The Conflict of Laws,* (13th edn, Sweet and Maxwell, London, 2000).

Culp, W And Grafting, J 'Owning Assets in Trust Results in Tax and Non-Tax Benefits' (1992) 19 EST PLAN 284.

Cumyn, M. 'The Trust in a Civilian Context: The Quebec Case' [1994] 3 JIntP 69.

Dessain, Anthony 'The Duties and Liabilities of Protectors' [1999] November, *Trusts and Trustees,* 34.

Dicey, A V *The Law of the Constitution* (10th edn, Publisher, Place, 1960).

Duckworth, A 'A View of Forced Heirship' [1995] PCB 270, 272.

Duckworth, A 'An Offshore View of Forced Heirship—Global Conflict and Its Planning Implications,' [1995] PCB 270 at 272.

Duke, Richard 'Tax Compliance and Reporting for Offshore Trusts and Uses of Foreign Life Insurance' in *International Estate Planning, Asset Protection Strategies: Planning with Domestic and Offshore Entities* (American Bar Association, USA, 2002).

Endreo, G 'The Use of Trusts in Financial Transactions (France)' in 10th Annual Seminar on International Financial Law, IBA, 1993.

Engel, B 'When Is A Subsequent Creditor Not A Subsequent Creditor?' [1994] 3 JIntP, 105.

Geer, John 'In Foreign Countries We Trust' [1994] 1 Financial Planning, 6.

Goode, R 'The Nature and Transfer of Rights in Dematerialized and Immobilized Securities', [1996] JIBFL 16.

Grundy, M *Grundy's Tax Havens: A World Survey*, (Sweet and Maxwell, London, 1993).

Hanbury and Martin, *Modern Equity* (15th edn, Sweet and Maxwell, London, 1997).

Harmful Tax Competition—An Emerging Global Issue, (OECD, Paris 1998) and *Toward Global Tax Cooperation—Progress in Identifying Harmful Tax Practices* (OECD, Paris, 2000).

Hayton, D 'Time to Overhaul Trust Laws,' [1991] 141 NLJ 210.

Hayton, D 'Trusts and Forced Heirship Problems' [1994] 2 JIntP 7.

Hayton, D 'The Irreducible Core Content of Trusteeship', in AJ Oakley (ed.) *Trends in Contemporary Trust Law* (Clarendon Press, Oxford, 1996).

Hayton, D 'The Hague Convention on Trusts: A Little is Better Than Nothing But Why So Little?' [1994]3 JIntP 23.

Ingham, Judith 'Recognising the Italian Trust', June [2002] *Offshore Investment*, 13.

Interpretation Bulletin IT-447 *Residence of a Trust or Estate*, 30 May 1980, Government of Canada.

Kodilyne, G and T Carmichael, *Commonwealth Caribbean Trusts Law*, (2nd edn, Cavendish Publishing Ltd, 2002).

Langbein, J 'The Contractarian Basis of the Law of Trusts' (1995) 105 Yale L J 625.

Langbein, J 'The Secret Life of the Trust: The Trust as an Instrument of Commerce', 107 Yale L J 163, 165 (1977).

Langer, M *Practical International Tax Planning* (Practising Law Institute, NY, 1988).

Lawrence, Robert C 'The Role of the Protector—An Insulator for Corporate Fiduciaries?' [1993] (2) JInTCP, 89.

Legal Remedies of the Unsecured Creditor after Judgment, Third Report of the Consumer Protection Project, Vol. 11, New Brunswick,(1976).

Lord Walker 'The Limits of the Principle in *Hastings-Bass*' [2002] PCB 226.

Maitland, FW 'The Origin of Uses' 8 Harv L Rev 127, 130 (1894).

Manitoba Law Reform Commission, Non-Charitable Purpose Trusts September 1992, Report No 77 and *Law Reform Commission of British Columbia, Non-Charitable Purpose Trusts*, November 1992, LRC 128.

Matthews & Sowden, *The Jersey Law of Trusts* (Key Haven Publications, London, 1993).

Matthews, P 'The New Trust: Obligations Without Rights,' International Trusts Association Seminar, UK.

Matthews, P 'No-Trust Judgments in Trust States,' [1996] *Trusts and Trustees*, 6.

McDowell & Monroe, *Kerr on the Law of Fraud and Mistake* (7th edn, Sweet & Maxwell, London, 1952).

McKenzie, C 'Maintaining the Integrity of Trusts', unpublished mimeo, BVI 2002.

Moshinsky, M 'Securities Held Through a Securities Custodian—Conflict of Laws Issues', Paper prepared for a Colloquium at Oxford, May 1998, 7.

Newhof and Pavell (eds) *Trusts and Foundations in Europe* (Publisher, Place, 1971).

Osborne, *Asset Protection, Domestic and International Law Tactics* (Clark, Boardman, Callaghan, USA, 1995).

Palmer, Martin 'MacNiven (Inspector of Taxes) v Westmoreand Investments Ltd: An Unexpected Boon for UK Taxpayers?' [2002] JTCP 1.

Palmer, Robert L 'Toward a Unilateral Coherence in Determining Jurisdiction to Tax Income' (1989) 30 Harv Int LJ 1.

Peters, R 'The New Trust Law,' *Offshore Trust Yearbook* (International Money Marketing, UK, 1993).

Picciotto, Sol *International Business Taxation—A Study of the Internationalization of Business Regulation* (Weidenfeld & Nicolson, London, 1992).

Public Benefit, *www.cabinet-office.gov.uk/innovation/2002/charity/inded.shtml*

Report on Fraudulent Conveyances and Preference, Law Reform Commission of British Columbia, 1988, 93.

Schoenblum, J 'The Hague Convention on Trusts: Much Ado About Very Little' [1994] 3 JINTP 5.

Toward Global Tax Competition—Progress in Identifying Harmful Tax Practices (the OECD Report 2000) (Paris, OECD, 26 June 2000).

Trumpy, Thomas 'Trusts for Closely-held Businesses: The International Perspective' (1994) 84 *Law Society Gazette*, 2856.

von Overbeck, Alfred E, 'Explanatory Report on The Hague Convention on the Law Applicable to Trusts and on their Recognition', The Hague, 1 July 1985; UKTS 14 (1992); CM 1823; 23 ILM 1388.

'The Law Applicable to and Recognition of Trusts in Switzerland: The Possible Future under the Hague Convention' [1996] *Trusts and Trustees*, 6.

Ward, D and Brownbill, D 'The International Company Act, 1997' [1997] JIntP 15.

Waters, D 'Protectors and Enforcers: Drafting the Trust Instrument' Vol 8(4) 2000 JInTCP 237.

Wheatcroft, GA 'The Attitude of the Legislative and the Courts to Tax Avoidance' [1955] MLR 209.

Wiggin, H 'Asset Protection for MNCs' in McKendrick, P (ed.) *Communal Aspects of Trusts and Fiduciary Obligations* (Publisher, Place, 1995) 195.

Willoughby, P 'International Trusts Under Fire: The Increasing Scope for Litigation' [1996] PCB 226.

INDEX